FATEFUL LIGHTNING

FATEFUL LIGHTNING

A NEW HISTORY
OF THE CIVIL WAR &
RECONSTRUCTION

ALLEN C. GUELZO

OXFORD
UNIVERSITY PRESS

OXFORD
UNIVERSITY PRESS

Oxford University Press, Inc., publishes works that further
Oxford University's objective of excellence
in research, scholarship, and education.

Oxford   New York
Auckland   Cape Town   Dar es Salaam   Hong Kong   Karachi
Kuala Lumpur   Madrid   Melbourne   Mexico City   Nairobi
New Delhi   Shanghai   Taipei   Toronto

With offices in
Argentina   Austria   Brazil   Chile   Czech Republic   France   Greece
Guatemala   Hungary   Italy   Japan   Poland   Portugal   Singapore
South Korea   Switzerland   Thailand   Turkey   Ukraine   Vietnam

Published by Oxford University Press, Inc.
198 Madison Avenue, New York, NY 10016

www.oup.com

Oxford is a registered trademark of Oxford University Press

The first edition of this book was published as *The Crisis of the American Republic: A History of the Civil War and Reconstruction Era* (St. Martin's Press, 1994).

Library of Congress Cataloging-in-Publication Data
Guelzo, Allen C.
Fateful lightning : a new history of the Civil War and Reconstruction / Allen C. Guelzo.
   p.   cm.
"First edition . . . was published as The crisis of the American Republic : a history of the Civil War
and Reconstruction Era, St. Martin's Press, 1994"—T.p. verso.
Includes bibliographical references and index.
ISBN 978-0-19-984328-2 (pbk.)
1. United States—History—Civil War, 1861–1865.
2. Reconstruction (U.S. history, 1865–1877)
I. Guelzo, Allen C. Crisis of the American republic. II. Title.
E468.G85   2012
973.7—dc23   2011041918

9 8 7 6 5 4 3 2 1

Printed in the United States of America
on acid-free paper

FOR DEBRA

CONTENTS

ACKNOWLEDGMENTS

In acknowledging the help, encouragement, and support of so many others in the creation of this book, the mere extension of thanks seems but a poor reward for the value of those contributions. Nevertheless, the well of personal gratitude for the time, labor, and sympathy which was given by those whom I salute here is real and profound. I begin with two of my former students in the Civil War Era Studies program at Gettysburg College, Brian M. Jordan (Yale University) and Brandon R. Roos (King's College, London), who devoted long nights and caffeine-fueled energies to fact-checking, and on a purely volunteer basis. Various other debts have been accumulated in the name of Thomas Legg (West Chester University), Stephen Fratt (Trinity College), Steven E. Woodworth (Texas Christian University), Thomas Askew (Gordon College), and James Geary (Kent State University). Steven J. Wright, former curator of the old Civil War Library & Museum, Roland Baumann of the Oberlin College Archives, and James Mundy of the Union League of Philadelphia cheerfully provided access to rare Civil War materials in their collections.

The images in this book are the result of a long process of collection and selection, which included generous cooperation by David Charles (1926–2004), Blake Magner (1950-2011), Henry Deeks, and the Library Company of Philadelphia. Cathy Bain, Lauren Roedner and Tim Koenig of Gettysburg College provided invaluable assistance in acting as liaison between myself and Oxford University Press, where Nancy Toff and Sonia Tycko played the key roles as readers, managers, schedule-keepers, and editors of the manuscript. Michele Rubin and Brianne Johnson of Writer's House, Inc., provided a helping hand at a key point in the evolution of this project. Dorothy Bruton (1925–2009) of Dallas, Texas, knew what the rebel yell really sounded like, and generously granted me permission to use the letters of her grandfather, George Asbury Bruton of the 19th Louisiana. My wife, Debra, has been a loving and faithful reader and exhorter all through the writing of this book, and I have at times had the peculiar pleasure of being outrun by her in a mutual enthusiasm for it. She has hallowed it far above my poor power to add or detract.

FATEFUL LIGHTNING

CHAPTER ONE

A NATION ANNOUNCING ITSELF

Inauguration Day, March 4, 1865, dawned over the city of Washington with a blustery, overcast chill. It rained early in the morning, cleared, then rained again. But even without the cooperation of the weather, thousands upon thousands—"a crowd almost numberless," wrote a visitor—braved the drizzle and cold to watch a giant parade, with now sodden floats, wheel up Pennsylvania Avenue toward the newly completed dome of the Capitol building. There, in the Capitol, the principal actor in this inauguration pageant, Abraham Lincoln, the president of the United States, was already at work, signing the last pieces of legislation passed by the outgoing Congress and witnessing a new Senate being sworn into office.

The ceremonies held few surprises for Lincoln, since this day would mark Lincoln's second presidential inauguration. He had come to the Capitol on March 4, 1861, as a newly elected president, untried and unprepared, and now, four years later, the country had chosen him a second time as its chief executive. When the congressional ceremonies within the Capitol were over, a great file of legislators, cabinet secretaries, ambassadors, and judges streamed out onto the Capitol steps, where a broad platform had been constructed for the president to take his oath of office in public view. Last of all onto the platform came Lincoln, holding in his hand a single large sheet of paper. A band struck up "Hail to the Chief" as "cheer upon cheer arose."[1]

---

1. Ronald C. White, *Lincoln's Greatest Speech: The Second Inaugural* (New York: Simon and Schuster, 2002), 30–31, 33; Noah Brooks, "Inauguration Day," in *Lincoln Observed: Civil War Dispatches of Noah Brooks*, ed. Michael Burlingame (Baltimore, MD: Johns Hopkins University Press, 1998), 167–68.

Four years before, when he first stood on a platform like this to take his presidential oath, the weather had still been thick with early spring chilliness and damp, but the sun shone with a hard and resolute cheerfulness. And in 1861 the sunshine was almost the only thing smiling upon Abraham Lincoln. Even as he took his first oath of office, swearing to "preserve, protect and defend the Constitution of the United States," seven of those supposedly united states had renounced their attachment to the Constitution. They had already organized a rival government, elected a rival president, and demanded that any of the property of the United States government sitting at that moment within their boundaries be turned over to them at once. Lincoln refused, and in short order it all came to war, the rebel states insisting that they were now an independent country with a right to determine their own future, and Lincoln insisting that they were only insurgents who had to be suppressed like any other treasonous coup d'état. It was war such as few Americans had ever imagined: four years of it, with horrendous costs in life and property, and the ghoulish echo of homespun place-names made hideous in blood—Gettysburg, Chancellorsville, Shiloh.

And now the spring of 1865 was coming. Lincoln's armies had finally turned the tide and the war was stumbling toward what looked like the end. In November the country had given Lincoln its vote of confidence by electing him to a second term as president. Now, on this raw March afternoon, as he stepped up to the low dais where he would deliver his inaugural address and take his second oath of office, he was ready to begin asking why the great horror of civil war had spread across his country. At that moment, the clouds parted and the long-hidden sun shone a golden aura down on Lincoln, the Capitol, and the hushed citizens below him.

There were, Lincoln said, three fundamental causes that had pushed the United States into the war. One of them was political, and that was the fact that the United States had been organized since its birth as a *union*. It was the creation of thirteen former English colonies, huddled along the eastern seaboard of North America, that had declared themselves independent states in 1776 but also linked themselves together under a joint congress as a confederation. Ever since, there had been voices within those states arguing irritably that this Union was a bad bargain that ought to be terminated. The voices had come to a crescendo in the Southern states of the Union in 1861, and Lincoln had found himself as president "devoted altogether to *saving* the Union without war" while at the same time having to deal with people who thought it right and proper "to *destroy* it without war—seeking to dissolve the Union, and divide effects, by negotiation."[2]

But simply because the Southern states thought the Union should be dissolved did not necessarily mean that it had to be, ought to be, or even could be, and that led Lincoln to the next fundamental reason for civil war. "One eighth of the

2. Abraham Lincoln, "Second Inaugural Address," in *Collected Works of Abraham Lincoln*, ed. Roy F. Basler (New Brunswick, NJ: Rutgers University Press, 1953), 8:332–33.

whole population were colored slaves, not distributed generally over the Union, but localized in the Southern part of it." Protecting slavery, Lincoln declared, had become the chief irritant that provoked the Southern states to reach for the solution of disunion. "These slaves constituted a peculiar and powerful interest," one that Lincoln and the northern states of the Union had declared a moral abomination that needed to be contained and suffocated. Though the Southern states hotly denied that they wanted to withdraw from the Union merely for the pleasure of enslaving people, Lincoln insisted that "all knew that this interest was, somehow, the cause of the war." Waving aside all the other supposed reasons for secession and war, Lincoln insisted that "to strengthen, perpetuate, and extend this interest was the object for which the insurgents would rend the Union, even by war."

Even that much did not explain matters fully. Lincoln had come into office in 1861 swearing to uphold the Constitution, which gave a number of vague guarantees to slaveholding in the fifteen Southern states where it was legal, and which gave presidents no power to meddle in state affairs such as slavery. In his first inaugural address, he had taken pains to acknowledge that, as president, he had no "right" and no "inclination" to attack slavery in those states. But across the Mississippi River, out over the broad prairies of the western half of the North American continent, were the immense miles of U.S.-owned territory that had not yet been peopled and organized by white Americans, and which one day would want to be recognized and admitted to the Union as states equal to all the other states. Should slavery be permitted to plant itself in those territories?

There, Lincoln and his party had drawn the line: they would not crush slavery where it was, but they would not allow it to spread, either. The Southern states were outraged at this denial, fearful that if slavery could not grow and extend itself, it was doomed to a slow death. "The government claimed no right to do more than to restrict the territorial enlargement of it," but that was more than sufficient to make the slaveholding South begin thinking of cancelling its membership in the Union. "Both parties deprecated war," Lincoln said, "but one of them would *make* war rather than let the nation survive; and the other would *accept* war rather than let it perish." Lincoln paused for a long moment, looking out over the upturned faces crowding the Capitol steps. "And the war came."

Since Lincoln uttered those words—and they amount to no more than two paragraphs in an inaugural address only four paragraphs long—something close to 50,000 books and articles on the American Civil War have been published. Still, we would be hard-pressed to find a more concise statement of just what it was that caused the American Civil War. If we want to understand what plunged the American republic into its greatest crisis, and map out the paths and highways that led Americans to four years of unplanned-for and unlooked-for carnage, we can hardly do better than to take our bearings from the three signposts that Abraham Lincoln left us.

THE AMERICAN UNION

Underlying everything else that pushed or pulled nineteenth-century Americans toward the abyss of civil war was one very plain fact about the United States of America: its political structure—that of a union of states—was a standing invitation to chaos.

The origins of this situation extend far into the American past, all the way to the founding of the first English-speaking colonies in North America. Beginning in 1607 with Jamestown, Virginia, these settlements had been individually laid out, funded, settled, and organized, with next to nothing in the way of supervision from the English government. Right down to the outbreak of the American Revolution, the British North American colonies operated on different currencies, commissioned separate defense forces, and maintained separate agencies in London to represent their interests to the English Parliament. A dozen years of spectacular political bungling by Parliament provoked thirteen of those colonies to declare themselves independent of British rule in 1776. But even in the face of British armies sent to suppress their revolt, the American colonies were unwilling to cooperate with each other on more than a hit-or-miss basis. The Continental army that the colonies raised as a joint defense force to fight the British was continually starved for men and supplies, while the local colonial militias played politics at home. The Continental Congress that they formed to act as their parliament looked more like a steering committee than a government, and even then its deliberations were racked with dissension and bickering. Frequently on the run from the British, the Continental Congress had no power to levy taxes and only the slimmest public credibility. Even the Congress's Declaration of Independence, which was supposed to be the joint announcement that the colonies were now "Free and Independent States," had been co-opted by several over-eager colonial legislatures that bolted ahead to declare their own separate independence from British rule.[3]

It took five years after the Declaration of Independence for the Continental Congress to persuade the new states to adopt some form of unified national government, and the states agreed only because they could not obtain an alliance with France (which they needed for survival) without forming themselves into something that the French could recognize as a government. What they finally created in 1781 was based on a flimsy document known as the Articles of Confederation. Under the Articles, each of the thirteen new states would receive equal representation in a new Confederation Congress, regardless of each state's size or population—a formula that amounted to allowing the states to come to the Confederation Congress as separate but equal powers, rather than participants in a national assembly.[4]

3. Pauline Maier, *American Scripture: Making the Declaration of Independence* (New York: Knopf, 1997), 69–90.

4. Kenneth Stampp, "Unam Aut Plures? The Concept of a Perpetual Union," in *The Imperiled Union: Essays on the Background of the Civil War* (New York: Oxford University Press, 1980), 21–29.

There could have been only one end to this. Soon enough, individual states would find themselves quarreling with each other while the Confederation Congress stood on the sidelines, wringing its hands. Then the quarrels would explode into civil war, and the war would so weaken the United States that some powerful European monarchy (perhaps the British again) would intervene and force the Americans under European control all over again. In the 1780s almost all the rest of the world was still governed by kings who looked upon the kingless American republic as a bad example to their own restless subjects. Those kings had armies and navies that were too close to the American borders for comfort. Britain still occupied Canada to the north, and Spain still ruled the western half of North America and all of Central and South America, and neither of them liked what they saw in the new republic. If the American states divided, the European powers might take the opportunity to conquer.

So it was fear more than unity of purpose that finally drove the Americans to scrap the Articles of Confederation and write a new constitution in 1787. The Constitution equipped the national government with the power to raise its own income by imposing taxes on the states, and created an executive president who had the authority and the means to enforce the decisions of Congress. Even so, there were ambiguities and compromises in the Constitution that allowed the individual states to retain a large measure of their jealously guarded autonomy. The most obvious example of compromise concerned the Congress. The Constitution divided the old Confederation Congress into two houses, the Senate and the House of Representatives. Members of the House were elected directly by the voters of each state, with the population of each state determining how many representatives each state could elect. By contrast, the members of the Senate were elected by the state legislatures, and each state had two senators regardless of size, giving each state equal voice in the Senate, just like in the Confederation Congress. What this meant, in effect, was that in the House, the representatives would speak for the people of the United States as a whole, but in the Senate, the senators were clearly understood to be representing the interests of the states.

There were other telltale problems, too. The Constitution created a confusing and cumbersome system for electing the national president. As it was, the Constitution did not specify who was permitted to vote for the president (the eligibility of voters was a question left to the individual states). For those who could vote, the Constitution specified that they would cast their ballots not for a particular presidential candidate but for a handful of state electors, who would then assemble in an electoral college and vote as state delegations for the next president. So it was not the people of the United States who elected a president, but committees of state electors. Ominously, the states made no pledge in the text of the Constitution to treat the arrangement as a perpetual one. Three of the state conventions that eventually ratified the Constitution—those of New York, Virginia, and Rhode Island—agreed to ratification only after adding resolutions that declared that they still retained the right to retrieve the powers they had surrendered "whensoever it shall become necessary to their happiness."[5] And some of them quickly came close to doing just that. In 1798, the second president, John Adams, attempted to quell political opposition to his administration through the so-called Alien and Sedition Acts. In reply, two of the foremost American political thinkers, Thomas Jefferson (the author of the Declaration of Independence) and James Madison (the architect of the Constitution), drafted the Virginia and Kentucky Resolutions, which announced to President Adams that the individual states still reserved the privilege of declaring acts of the national Congress unconstitutional and non-operative.

As late as the 1830s, the United States of America looked and behaved more like a league or a compact of states than a single country, and its Constitution was still regarded as something of an experiment, embraced mostly for its practicality. "Asking a State to surrender a part of her sovereignty is like asking a lady to surrender part of her chastity," declared the eccentric Virginia politician John Randolph of Roanoke, who even on the floor of Congress made his loyalties clear by insisting that "when I speak of my country, I mean the Commonwealth of Virginia." The English travel writer George Featherstonhaugh was confounded to hear a South Carolinian declare: "If you ask *me* if I am an American, my answer is, No, sir, I am a South Carolinian." The framers of the Constitution, fearing the possibility that state antagonisms, economic competition, and political corruption would easily derail the national system, appealed to the spirit of union or the virtue of political compromise to defuse the threat of divisive issues, but did not appeal to some elusive national authority.[6]

This is not to say, though, that Americans were not becoming a nation in other ways. No matter how jealously the states regarded and defended their individual political privileges and identities, it would have been hard for a people who spoke the same language, read the same books, heard the same music, and voted in the same elections not to develop some sort of fellow-feeling, irrespective of state boundaries. This was especially true for those Americans who had actually borne the brunt of the fighting in the Revolutionary War, and who carried out of the Revolution a highly different perspective on the unity of the American republic. In the snows of Valley Forge and in the heat of the Carolinas, in victory and in defeat, soldiers from Virginia, Massachusetts, Pennsylvania, and all the other states had undergone so many hardships together that their different backgrounds faded to unimportance.

One of these soldiers, John Marshall, began the Revolution as a Virginia militiaman, then enlisted in the Continental army, and endured the army's winter at Valley Forge. He remembered later, "I was confirmed in the habit of considering America as my

5. Ralph Ketcham, *The Anti-Federalist Papers and the Constitutional Convention Debates* (New York: Signet Classic, 2003), 225.

6. Robert Dawidoff, *The Education of John Randolph* (New York: W. W. Norton, 1979), 34, 154; Peter B. Knupfer, *The Union as It Is: Constitutional Unionism and Sectional Compromise, 1787–1861* (Chapel Hill: University of North Carolina Press, 1991), 115–17; George Featherstonhaugh, *Excursion Through the Slave States, from Washington on the Potomac to the Frontier of Mexico* (London: John Murray, 1844), 2:341.

country and Congress as my government," not Virginia.[7] And Marshall would later rise, as chief justice of the Supreme Court, to shape a system of national jurisprudence that transcended state boundaries and loyalties. A South Carolinian (turned Tennessean) named Andrew Jackson lost two brothers and his mother to the Revolution. Captured by the British, he refused a British officer's order to clean the officer's boots and was rewarded with a blow from the officer's sword. It left a scar Jackson carried with him for the rest of his life, and it also left a burning hatred of all enemies of his country, whether they were British invaders or (as it turned out later) fellow Southerners trying to nullify congressional legislation.[8]

By the end of the 1830s, the Union, crisscrossed by "mystic chords of memory," had ascended to the level of a national faith. The belligerent Tennessee parson and newspaper editor William G. Brownlow attacked the notion that the Constitution was merely a temporary political umbrella put up by the individual states to protect their state interests. "The Constitution," insisted Brownlow, was the political creation of the American people as a single nation, and it "was formed by the *people* to govern the *people*, and no single individual State was called upon as a separate 'sovereignty' to sign or ratify that Constitution." Alexander Stephens, who one day would serve as the vice president of the Confederate States, said that for Abraham Lincoln the Union "rose to the sublimity of a religious mysticism," and even a perfectly straightforward politician such as William H. Bissell of Illinois felt no embarrassment in claiming that whenever anyone in the West carelessly broached the idea of "destroying this Union," there would not be "a man throughout that vast region who will not raise his hand and swear by the Eternal God, as I do now, that it shall never be done, if our arms can save it." When, as it turned out, other members of the Union did just that and asked the Lincolns and Bissells to choose between state or local interests and the Union, the answer would more and more be the Union.[9]

The experience of the Revolution and the development of political maturity were only the first steps away from disunity and suspicion. The new political generation of Americans in the 1830s found two other important cultural paths by which to rise above their divisions. One of these was the embrace of a common religion. Although the Constitution forbade Congress from singling out any particular religion or religious denomination as a national "established" church, it was nevertheless clear that Americans in all parts of the country overwhelmingly favored Protestant, evangelical Christianity. The overall number of Christian congregations rose from 2,500 in 1780 to 52,000 in

7. Joseph Story, *A Discourse upon the Life, Character, and Services of the Honorable John Marshall* (Boston: J. Munroe, 1835), 20.

8. Samuel Putnam Waldo, *Memoirs of Andrew Jackson: Major-General in the Army of the United States* (Hartford, CT: Silas Andrus, 1818), 30.

9. William G. Brownlow, *Sketches of the Rise, Progress, and Decline of Secession* (Philadelphia: Applegate, 1862), 227; Alexander H. Stephens, *A Constitutional View of the Late War Between the States* (Philadelphia: National Publishing, 1870), 2:448; Eric Foner, *Free Soil, Free Labor, Free Men: The Ideology of the Republican Party Before the Civil War* (New York: Oxford University Press, 1970), 179.

1860. Along with the new congregations came new publication agencies, such as the American Bible Society and American Tract Society, which spun off a million Bibles and 6 million religious books and pamphlets each year, and a constellation of inter-locked social reform and missionary agencies. Evangelical Protestant churches claimed approximately 15 percent of the American population as full members, and as much as 40 percent of all Americans as "attenders" or "hearers."[10] There were many differ-ences between various groups of evangelical Protestants, and they organized themselves into more separate and subdivided denominations—Presbyterians, Baptists, Method-ists, Congregationalists, and so on—than there were states. But one thing they had in common was a commitment to the basic outlines of evangelical piety—a direct appeal to the person of Jesus Christ as God, the experience of conversion from unbelief or half belief to fervent piety, reverence for the authority of the Bible, and an ambition to promote the conversion of others for their own good and the good of the larger society.

This broadly embraced Protestant evangelicalism was heightened by the control these denominations exercised over American higher education. Almost all of the seventy-eight American colleges founded by 1840 were church-related, with clergy-men serving on the boards and the faculties. Most possessed as president a prominent clergyman, who capped off the senior year of his students with a major course in moral philosophy, based on a handful of Protestant ethics textbooks (the runaway favorite being Francis Wayland's *Elements of Moral Science*) that were used across the country. In this way, not only American religion but also the development of Ameri-can ethics and philosophy were shaped by a common Protestant evangelicalism.[11]

Just as powerful a common bond as evangelical Christianity was the political ideology that Americans embraced in the Revolution. However much the struc-ture of American politics was compromised and frustrated by state demands and state loyalties, Americans in all the states agreed that the states and the federal government alike were to be a republic and follow a republican form of govern-ment. Republicanism in the eighteenth century was the political fruit of the Enlightenment, that sea-change intellectual movement whose principal mission was to overthrow authority's chokehold on European intellectual life and replace it with what was natural, as discovered by reason and experiment. The Enlighten-ment began in the 1600s when Newton and Galileo overturned the principles of physical science that had been based on Aristotle's writings and replaced them with a new mechanical physics based on observable patterns of motion. By the 1700s, the *philosophes* of the Enlightenment had extended the reach of nature, reason, and experiment to the realms of politics and society, and proposed to overturn any form

10. Jon Butler, *Awash in a Sea of Faith: Christianizing the American People* (Cambridge, MA: Harvard University Press, 1990), 270, 278; Richard J. Carwardine, *Evangelicals and Politics in Antebellum America* (New Haven, CT: Yale University Press, 1993), 3–18.

11. Donald H. Meyer, *The Instructed Conscience: The Shaping of the American National Ethic* (Philadelphia: University of Pennsylvania Press, 1972), 13; Daniel Walker Howe, *What Hath God Wrought: The Transfor-mation of America, 1815–1848* (New York: Oxford University Press, 2007), 288.

of political organization built on such nonrational factors as monarchy or aristocracy. Enlightenment thought was the principal impulse behind the American Declaration of Independence in 1776, and it had its gospel in the writings of Montesquieu, Cesare Beccaria, James Harrington, Algernon Sidney, and above all John Locke, as well as in the classical examples of ancient Greece and Rome.[12]

But a more practical source of republicanism in America came simply from the governments the Americans had been compelled to improvise in their infancy as British colonies. The British government had taken a hands-off (and no-investment) stance toward the colonies founded in its name on the North American eastern seaboard, allowing the tasks of creation and maintenance to be left to corporate entrepreneurs (such as the Virginia Company) or to religious dissidents (such as the Quakers, Puritans, and Catholics) whom the British crown was only too happy to see disappear westward across the ocean. Not until much later did the British government awaken to (and begin demanding oversight of) the extraordinarily productive successes that three or four generations of this onetime riffraff had created for themselves in America. By 1750, the American colonies had developed in practice what looked for all the world like what Locke and his coadjutors had described on paper—little self-governing commonwealths. The Revolution was in large measure the response of the Americans to a British ultimatum to surrender that self-government.

Self-government meant that political sovereignty originated in the people, who possessed all the competence required for governing, and who should be free from having to cringe before aristocrats or beg their bread from wealthy landowners. Not that Americans ever felt that they needed to, since America possessed no domestic aristocracy to start with and, apart from the great manors of the Hudson River Valley and the plantations of the Virginia tidewater, no vast château-bred landlords. During the Revolution the Whigs proceeded to expel the Tory loyalists who had represented the wealthiest segment of the old colonial society. The new republic was able to begin its life with more than 90 percent of its citizens owning their own property and producing their own sustenance. In the Treaty of Paris the United States also acquired the wilderness beyond the Appalachians, where landowning could be thrown open to new generations; these lands would be organized as federal territories and eventually admitted to the Union as states.[13]

Every new territory wanted to move as swiftly as possible toward statehood, and to do that, they had to meet requirements for minimum numbers of voters. That, in turn, created pressure in the West to lower the eligibility requirements for voting because the more voters who could be counted, the faster a territory could advance to the privileges of statehood. For that reason, the United States would be a republic, but it would be

12. Bernard Bailyn, *The Ideological Origins of the American Revolution* (Cambridge, MA: Harvard University Press, 1967), 45.

13. Edward J. Renehan, *The Treaty of Paris: The Precursor to a New Nation* (New York: Chelsea House, 2009), 84–85.

driven to become a more and more *democratic* republic. Republics, after all, are simply governments that dispense with kings and aristocrats; the definition of who can be a citizen is what makes a republic more or less democratic. The classical republics of the ancient world were actually very narrow in their definitions of who could be a citizen. The American republic, by contrast, started off on a much more democratic footing than almost any other republic in history, and in its first half century of existence it became increasingly more so, to the point where Americans would use the terms *democracy*, *republic*, *republican*, and *democratic* almost as synonyms.

A common religion and a highly democratic republicanism were cultural tools that helped Americans transcend narrow state loyalties. But there were also forces at work that were just as likely to push in the other direction and increase rather than diminish the instability of the American union.

The most serious of these forces was economic. Enlightenment philosophes struggled to bring economics as much into conformity to the rule of nature and reason as physics and politics were, and the chief among these economists was the Scot Adam Smith. In *An Inquiry into the Nature and Causes of the Wealth of Nations* (published, in a significant coincidence, in the same year as the American Declaration of Independence), Smith cast down the restraints on commerce and trade imposed by contemptuous aristocrats all across Europe in favor of allowing the instinctive human passion for competitiveness a free hand in determining economic outcomes. "Every individual," wrote Smith, "intends only his own security; and . . . intends only his own gain, and he is in this . . . led by an invisible hand to promote an end which was no part of his intention," in just the same way that Newton's apple obeyed a law of gravity. Just as it would be absurd to ask governments to intervene in the laws of physics, it should be considered just as absurd for governments to intervene in the laws of the markets. "The obvious and simple system of natural liberty establishes itself of its own accord. Every man, as long as he does not violate the laws of justice, is left perfectly free to pursue his own interest his own way, and to bring both his industry and capital into competition with those of any other man, or order of men." The irony of this, however, is that "by pursuing his own interest he frequently promotes that of the society more effectually. . . ."[14]

Speaking of Adam Smith and *The Wealth of Nations* means that it is also necessary to speak about capitalism, if only because capitalism has become synonymous with Smith's description of a "natural liberty" in economics. Actually, capitalism represents at least four different ways of organizing a nation's production and consumption of goods. Capitalism can be understood as shorthand for the pursuit of profits from the sale of goods or services, and in that sense, capitalism has been around since the dawn of history itself—hence Smith's claim

14. Smith, *An Inquiry into the Nature and Causes of the Wealth of Nations*, ed. C. J. Bullock (New York: P. F. Collier, 1909 [1776]), 351, 466.

that it was "obvious and simple." Capitalism might also be regarded as a system of economic organization where governments, eager to promote the prosperity of their nations, open a "level playing field" and do no more than wish that the best economic man win. However, it still remains government's task to define the rules and police the boundaries of the playing field, since the great temptation of every competitor is to bribe the referees and kill the competition, literally or otherwise. Capitalists, in that respect, were the last people whom government should wish to entrust with the keys to the playing field's maintenance locker, and Smith was certainly no exponent of removing government's referee role. In the most complicated sense of the word, *capitalism* refers to a system by which the owners of productive mechanisms—whether the "mechanism" is a farm or a factory—employ laborers to whom they pay wages. The wages are never equivalent to the value the laborers put into the goods and services they produce. Because they do not own these mechanisms, laborers have no say in what price the real owners obtain for those goods and services. Hence, the owners sell the goods and services but only pay the producers a wage; the difference between the selling price and the wages (the "surplus value") becomes the owners' capital and is plowed back into the farm or factory to hire more wage laborers and produce more goods. This version— which is how Karl Marx defined capitalism—is also the most negative, as though capitalism were little more than systematic theft of the real value that exploited laborers imparted to goods. On the other hand, at its simplest the term *capitalism* can be used to describe any system in which an attitude of entrepreneurship and self-improvement is the key.

Monarchies were never friendly to capitalism, any more than they were to re- publicanism. They preferred stability in their nations' economic as well as politi- cal lives, and the more rigid the structure of a nation's monarchy, the less favor with which it was likely to look upon the brash self-promotion of shopkeepers, shoemakers, and town burgesses (*burgess* being the term from which *bourgeoisie* developed to describe the class of people most friendly to capitalism). But this self-promotion, based on cleverness, talent, and a strict eye to the main chance rather than noble birth, is also why the Enlightenment, which was in the business of overthrowing irrational appeals to mere authority, found in capitalist entrepre- neurs and an independent-minded bourgeoisie its favorite heroes. "I don't know which is the more useful to the state," Voltaire (the pen name of the French satirist François-Marie Arouet) speculated wickedly, "a well-powdered lord who knows precisely what time the king gets up in the morning and what time he goes to bed, and who gives himself airs of grandeur while playing the role of slave in a minis- ter's antechamber, or a great merchant who enriches his country, sends orders from his office to Surat and to Cairo, and contributes to the well-being of the world." Joseph Addison was "wonderfully delighted" to see "the grand scene of business" among London's merchants, "thriving in their own private fortunes, and at the same time promoting the public stock . . . by bringing into the country whatever is wanting, and carrying out of it whatever is superfluous."¹⁵ The Enlightenment's ideal social order would thus be a mix of mildly democratic republicanism in the political realm and a free-market regime in the economic realm, a combination that became known through the early decades of the nineteenth century simply as liberalism.

France liked to think of itself as the intellectual home of the Enlightenment, but (ironically, for American observers) enlightened French thinkers looked to Britain as their favorite model of a liberal society because there the monarchy's reach was at its weakest in all of Europe, and its shopkeepers and entrepreneurs were at their most vigorous and unrestrained. "Commerce," added Voltaire, "which has brought wealth to the citizenry of England, has helped to make them free, and freedom has developed commerce in its turn."¹⁶ British capitalists were also the most scientific, for it was the British who invented the technology (beginning with the steam engine) that turned the small-scale production of handmade goods and harvest-time services into industrial manufacturing.

To supply the labor for steam-powered production, the British economy moved large segments of its population out of agriculture and into factory production. Since the factory worker did nothing but work in the factory, British capitalists needed new sources for feeding and clothing that new workforce, and they found those sources in American agriculture. Only a few Americans were prepared for this. Before 1800 in the United States, only farmers in the hinterlands of the major ports, such as Philadelphia, Charleston, and Chesapeake Bay, were seriously committed to raising crops to sell for cash on foreign markets, if only because for others the costs of getting those products to markets for sale was greater than any profit that could be reaped from the selling. An ordinary stagecoach ride from Boston to New York cost between $10 and $11 in 1820—two weeks' wages—and that said nothing about the cost of shipping produce or driving cattle to market; five weeks were needed to move that stagecoach from Nashville to Washington. Most American farmers were still organized around a household economy that sold little except small surpluses off the farm and which relied on barter and extended loans for the few manufactured goods it needed.¹⁷

But by the 1830s, the allurements of selling agricultural produce to British and foreign markets had become too great to resist, largely because access to those markets had become too easy to ignore. The steam engine, which had made large-scale manufacturing possible among England's "dark, satanic mills," produced an unlooked-for by-product when inventors such as John Fitch and Robert Fulton bolted steam

15. Voltaire, *Philosophical Letters: Letters Concerning the English Nation*, ed. Ernest Dilworth (Indianapolis, IN: Bobbs-Merrill, 1961 [1734]), 40; Addison, "The Spectator No. LXIX" (May 19, 1711), in *The Spectator in Eight Volumes* (Philadelphia: Samuel Bradford, 1803), 1:316.

16. Voltaire, *Philosophical Letters*, 39.

17. Paul A. Gilje, "The Rise of Capitalism in the Early Republic," in *Wages of Independence: Capitalism in the Early American Republic*, ed. Paul A. Gilje (Lanham, MD: Rowman and Littlefield, 2006), 12.

engines onto riverboats to push them up and down rivers; and then bolted steam engines onto platforms that rolled on iron tram rails. The steamboats and the railroads became the chief force in driving down the costs of access to markets, and slowly, American farmers moved away from multicrop farming and livestock raising for their own subsistence and toward single-crop agriculture, where their produce could be sold for cash, and the cash used to buy manufactured clothing or tools made in other people's factories.[18]

It was at this point that the hinge between democratic republicanism and liberal capitalism began to squeak. Republicanism was based upon liberty, and liberty was based upon independence, but who could consider American farmers independent if their well-being now hung on the price their crops or meat or poultry might get on a faraway exchange market? And how independent could a shoemaker be when he was forced to close up his shop because cheaply manufactured British shoes cost less than his handmade ones, and take a wage-based job in a factory or mill built on the British model? On the other hand, how independent would America remain if it stuck its economic head in the sand, persisted in the old patterns of household agriculture, and became a relative weakling among the emerging capitalist economies of Europe?

These questions were posed, in the name of protecting the Republic, by republicans who now found themselves differing seriously from one another. Beginning with Alexander Hamilton and the Federalist Party, liberal republicans argued that American independence depended on the strength and competitiveness of its economy on the world capitalist markets. Hamilton, in particular, favored direct federal government intervention in the American economy to encourage manufacturing development, trade (through publicly financed roads, bridges, and canals), and finance (by chartering a national bank, which could lend money to entrepreneurs). Power, if used judiciously, could actually protect and promote liberty. Classical republicans, championed by Thomas Jefferson and represented in the Democratic Party, argued that the Constitution gave the federal government no such powers of economic intervention. Even if it did, encouraging Americans to join the system of world markets would only mortgage the American republic to foreign interests and encourage Americans to thirst for money and power over their fellow citizens. Classical republicans wrapped themselves in the toga of the Roman republic and reminded modern Americans that in ancient Rome, materialism and self-interest on Adam Smith's scale were unknown:

> Then none was for a party;
> Then all were for the state;
> Then the great man helped the poor,

18. Charles G. Sellers, *The Market Revolution: Jacksonian America, 1815–1846* (New York: Oxford University Press, 1991), 8–23, 27–28.

And the poor man loved the great:
Then lands were fairly portioned;
Then spoils were fairly sold:
The Romans were like brothers
In the brave days of old.[19]

Jeffersonian Democrats especially opposed calls for government-financed public works, or "internal improvements," since it was obvious that the new roads, bridges, and canals could serve only one purpose—to make it easier for farmers to reach distant markets, and for the markets to tempt American farmers into their grasp. It also went without saying that "internal improvements" could be financed only through federal taxation, and farmers who grew or manufactured only for their own households would never be able to find the money to pay those taxes without surrendering their cherished independence and growing what the market would pay them for in cash. Power was toxic, and no amount of it was safe for liberty. "The market is a canker," warned a contributor to the *New England Farmer* in 1829, "that will, by degrees, eat you out, while you are eating upon it."[20]

The Democrats reserved their greatest venom for the two newest instruments of capitalist finance, the bank and the chartered corporation. America had known no banks until the very end of the American Revolution and had only eighty banks by 1810. By 1840, however, there were nearly a thousand of them, including a congressionally chartered "monster" Bank of the United States in Philadelphia, organized in 1816 with an initial capitalization of $35 million. Democrats hated the banks because the banks were the chief processing agents of the markets: they extended credit for investment (which Democrats attacked as "phony" wealth) and either made windfall profits from manufacturers and farmers when those investments succeeded or else seized the property of those whose enterprises failed. Liberty and virtue dwelt in the hearts of independent farmers sitting under their own vines and fig trees, unmolested by tax agents and bill collectors. "Corruption or morals in the mass of cultivators," Jefferson wrote in his celebrated *Notes on the State of Virginia*, "is a phenomenon which no age nor nation has furnished an example." No one seemed to personify that ideal more than Jefferson's fellow Virginian and virtuous senator, John Taylor of Caroline, who impressed a colleague as "plain and solid, a wise counsellor, a ready and vigorous debater, acute and comprehensive, ripe in all historical and political knowledge, innately republican—modest, courteous, benevolent, hospitable—a skilful, practical farmer, giving his time to his farm and his books, when not called by

19. Thomas Babington Macaulay, "Horatius," in *Lays of Ancient Rome* (London: Longman, Brown, Green and Longmans, 1844), 60.

20. Christopher Clark, *The Roots of Rural Capitalism: Western Massachusetts, 1780–1860* (Ithaca, NY: Cornell University Press, 1990), 154.

an emergency to the public service—and returning to his books and his farm when the emergency was over."[21]

Banks, on the other hand, looked like precisely the enormous concentrations of power and self-interest that were the source of corruption, and those fears of corruption were not eased when large-scale banks such as the Bank of the United States began paying handsome retainers to members of Congress to sit on its board of directors. Democrats were equally fearful of chartered corporations, since large-scale corporations could just as easily acquire the same enormous wealth as banks and, with it, the same power for corrupting state and local legislatures. It was a point of pride to John Randolph of Roanoke, one of the sharpest-tongued Jeffersonians in the House of Representatives, that "I am the holder of no stock whatever, except livestock, and had determined never to own any . . . because it is the creation of a great privileged order of the most hateful kind to my feelings, and because I would rather be the master than the slave. If I must have a master let him be one with epaulettes, something that I could fear and respect, something I could look up to—but not a master with a quill behind his ear."[22]

For the first three decades of the American republic, it was clearly the fears of the Democrats that had the upper hand. Of the 4 million people living in the United States in 1790, 3.7 million of them lived in the countryside and only about 200,000 in towns or ports larger than 2,500 people. Although the first two presidents, Washington and Adams, favored development and competition on the world markets as the best method for toughening the independence of the American economy, the costs of that encouragement were federal taxes. A country that had formed in a revolt against British taxes was in no mood to pay them to the federal government. Thomas Jefferson, promising an "empire for liberty," was swept into the presidency in 1800 in a tremendous landslide, which secured Democratic control of the federal government for the next quarter century. Accordingly, the Democrats allowed banks and corporate charters to wither, and in 1807 Jefferson briefly imposed an absolute embargo on all foreign trade. If the surrounding economic world required that Americans dabble in economic power in order to safeguard political liberty, then better to quarantine the Republic economically rather than surrender it to world markets.[23]

What Jefferson had not entirely counted upon was the degree to which isolation really did translate into weakness. Britain, then at the height of its titanic grapple with Napoleon Bonaparte, discovered that an American government without a bank for borrowing or taxes for spending had no way to fund a navy for protection, and

21. Thomas Jefferson, *Notes on the State of Virginia* (London: John Stockdale, 1787), 274; Thomas Hart Benton, *Thirty Years' View; or, A History of the Working of the American Government, from 1820 to 1850* (New York: D. Appleton, 1854), 1:45.

22. Hugh A. Garland, *The Life of John Randolph of Roanoke* (New York: D. Appleton, 1850), 2:83.

23. Gordon S. Wood, *Empire of Liberty: A History of the Early Republic, 1789–1815* (New York: Oxford University Press, 2009), 315–16, 376.

so British warships shamelessly boarded American ships and impressed American sailors to fill up depleted British crews. In 1812, Jefferson's handpicked successor as president, James Madison, responded by leading the country into war against the British. It was a catastrophe. "Our commerce [had been] put in fetters by non-importation acts and embargoes; and the crisis that succeeded found us without the most ordinary resources of an independent people," complained John Pendleton Kennedy, a Whig congressman from Maryland. "Our armies went to the frontier clothed in the fabrics of the enemy; our munitions of war was gathered as chance supplied them from the four quarters of the earth; and the whole struggle was marked by the prodigality, waste and privation of a thriftless nation, taken at unawares and challenged to a contest without the necessary armor of a combatant."[24] The unprepared American armies were routed by a British empire that was already fighting with one arm tied behind its back by Napoleon, and the household-based American economy fell apart. By the end of the war, only major loans from private bankers kept the United States Treasury from collapse. And only British exhaustion from its European wars kept Britain from turning the American republic back into British colonies.[25]

The disaster of the War of 1812 frightened many republicans away from Jefferson's fond dream of a nation of liberty-loving but economically powerless farmers. "These disasters opened our eyes to some important facts," Kennedy recalled in 1831. "They demonstrated to us the necessity of extending more efficient protection, at least, to those manufactures which were essential to the defence of the nation" as well as the establishment of "the value of a national currency, and the duty of protecting it from the influence of foreign disturbance" through the shield of a national banking system. Led by Henry Clay of Kentucky, a new party of National Republicans, or Whigs (as Clay renamed them in the 1830s), resurrected the program of government support for internal improvements, government-sponsored banking, and a new program of protective tariffs to keep out cheap imported British manufactured goods and stimulate manufacturing at home. "National independence was only to be maintained by national resistance against foreign encroachments," declared Clay in 1816, "by cherishing the interest of the people, and giving to the whole physical power of the country an interest in the preservation of the nation." Clay went on to endorse the new military program, "a chain of turnpikes, roads and canals from Passamaquoddy to New Orleans," and tariffs to "effectually protect our manufacturers."[26]

Although the presidency remained firmly in the hands of the Democrats (except for a brief interlude under John Quincy Adams from 1824 to 1828), Clay's influence in Congress pushed large elements of this "American System" into being anyway.

24. John Pendleton Kennedy, "Address of the Friends of Domestic Industry" (October 26, 1831), in *Political and Official Papers* (New York: Putnam, 1872), 119–20, 122–23.

25. Alan Taylor, *The Civil War of 1812: American Citizens, British Subjects, Irish Rebels* (New York: Knopf, 2010), 46.

26. Robert V. Remini, *Henry Clay: Statesman for the Union* (New York: W. W. Norton, 1991), 136–37.

It was not until the election of Andrew Jackson, an unreconstructed Jeffersonian radical, as president in 1828 that the Democrats struck back. Jackson vetoed congressional appropriations for public roads, effectively destroyed the Bank of the United States by refusing to deposit federal money there, and paid off the national debt so that there would no need for federal taxes and (above all) no need for federal tariffs to protect American industries and corporations.[27]

Jackson's war against liberal market-based power was, in the long run, far from successful. Clay, in the role of Jackson's nemesis, remained a powerful figure in American politics, and many banks protected themselves from Jackson's wrath by obtaining charters from cooperative state legislatures. Still, that lack of success cannot obscure the anger and violence with which Whigs and Democrats—both supposedly dedicated to republicanism—had come to regard each other. By the 1840s, the Whigs had defined themselves as the party of liberal democracy, of an upwardly mobile middle class, willing to embrace the fluidity of the market and eager to promote national unity and government support for railroad construction, canals, and even steamship lines. They spoke for the small-scale manufacturer who worked beside his employees in making boots and shoes, forging iron, tanning leather; for the banker who lent him the money to start up his business and the lawyer who collected his debts; and for the commercial farmer who grew crops for cash sale on distant markets. In an economy where the average number of employees per manufacturing establishment was only fourteen, it was not unreasonable for the Whigs to see themselves as the friends of "the enterprising mechanic, who raises himself by his ingenious labors from the dust and turmoil of his workshop, to an abode of ease and elegance; the industrious tradesman, whose patient frugality enables him at last to accumulate enough to forego the duties of the counter and indulge a well-earned leisure." Perhaps most important, the Whigs had enlisted the support of a vast majority of Protestant evangelicals, and they wedded their economic gospel of hard work and thrift to the evangelical gospel of moral self-control.[28] They were the party of the bourgeoisie, the "middling sort," who bridled at slavery and aristocracy in equal portions, and who wanted nothing but the liberty to "improve" themselves without molestation.

The Democrats remained dedicated to resisting "consolidated" national government with its tariffs and "improvements." They appealed most strongly to the old elite families of the Republic, who feared and resented the ambitious rise of Whig entrepreneurs, and to the poorest farmers and urban workers, who suspected that the Whigs were merely the agents of a "money power" out to rob them, through taxes or

---

27. Harry Watson, *Liberty and Power: The Politics of Jacksonian America* ((New York: Hill and Wang, 1990), 132–55.

28. Jeremy Atack and Peter Passell, *A New Economic View of American History, from Colonial Times to 1940*, 2nd ed. (New York: W. W. Norton, 1994), 192; *New York American*, June 20, 1834, in Remini, *Henry Clay*, 463; Carwardine, *Evangelicals and Politics in Antebellum America*, 103–10; Daniel Walker Howe, *The Political Culture of the American Whigs* (Chicago: University of Chicago Press, 1979), 152–78.

through financial chicanery, of the little they had. "An organized, concentrated, and privileged money power is one of deadly hostility to liberty," warned a Democratic convention in Ohio in 1845. That included "any form or reform of banking" and any encouragement to manufacturing. "Manufactures are not of themselves objects of desire to a free people, or of favor for a free government," since they "involve the necessity of a crowded population, subject to a very arbitrary control over their comfort by a few wealthy persons, and devoted to unwholesome employment." Both parties spoke the language of democratic republicanism, but both were also convinced that their brand of democratic republicanism was the best guarantee of liberty. As one historian has summed up, the Whigs were the party of America's hopes, the Democrats the party of its fears.[29]

The great danger posed by these arguments over power, liberalism, and republics was the possibility that they might find an outlet in the ramshackle structure of the federal Union. During the War of 1812, New Englanders were hard hit by the naval blockade that British warships imposed on them, and the more they suffered from this blockade, the more the suffering seemed to be the fault of people from other parts of the country, such as President Madison (a Virginian), whose section presumably had something to gain from the war that New England did not. In December 1814 delegates from Massachusetts, Connecticut, and Rhode Island met at Hartford, Connecticut, to express their opposition to the war and make ugly suggestions about seceding from the Union and making a separate peace with Great Britain. The delegations' threats all blew over because the war ended a month later, but the event was a dangerous indication that states or sections of the country who suspected that their liberties were being leeched by someone else's thirst for power might take advantage of the autonomy provided them by the federal Union, and leave the Union for good.

A more dramatic example of the intersection of ideology and self-interest occurred in 1832 over the federal tariff. For more than a decade, South Carolina and the other Southern states had been vigorously protesting the use of tariffs to protect American industry. Tariffs such as the one imposed in 1816 boosted the price of imported manufactured goods by 25 percent over their original valuation, and forced consumers to buy American-made goods, which were considerably more costly than the imports had originally been. South Carolina's John Caldwell Calhoun observed that this was fine for New England, which was home to many of America's infant industries, but it was very hard on South Carolina, which specialized in cotton

---

29. "Letter to the Secretary of the Treasury, on the Effect of the Tariff of 1842, on the Agricultural and Other Interests of the West, by a Committee of the Democratic Convention of Hamilton County, Ohio," August 30, 1845, in *Public Documents Ordered Printed by the Senate of the United States, First Session of the 29th Congress* (Washington, DC: Ritchie and Heiss, 1846), 2:852, 855; Marvin Meyers, *The Jacksonian Persuasion: Politics and Belief* (Stanford, CA: Stanford University Press, 1957), 13; Marc W. Kruman, "The Second American Party System and the Transformation of Revolutionary Republicanism," *Journal of the Early Republic* 12 (Winter 1992): 509–37.

growing and needed to buy manufactured goods from elsewhere. Congress was not inclined to give the South Carolinians relief, and in 1828, Congress passed a tariff so stiff (it imposed import duties up to 50 percent on the value of some imports) that South Carolina dubbed it "the Tariff of Abominations."

Calhoun saw the tariff not just as an economic issue but also as a challenge by the federal government to South Carolina's liberty as a state. For two years, while he was serving as Andrew Jackson's vice president, Calhoun fought the tariff through his political lieutenants in Congress, insisting that South Carolina had the authority to nullify any federal law it deemed unsatisfactory (including tariffs) unless three-quarters of the other states had the opportunity to review the law and approve it. Early in 1830, Robert Hayne of South Carolina, acting as Calhoun's mouthpiece, delivered a long and powerful polemic on the floor of the Senate, defending the state sovereignty of South Carolina against a "consolidated" Union. Hayne was argued down by Massachusetts senator Daniel Webster, who proclaimed (in words that subsequent generations of American schoolchildren were required to memorize) that the federal government was "the people's constitution; the people's government" and the power of the Union should not be splintered by one state under the specious plea of liberty. "Liberty *and* Union," Webster concluded, must be "now and forever, one and inseparable."[30]

Undeterred by Webster's eloquence, Calhoun hoped to play on the anti-tariff sympathies of President Jackson, calculating that Jackson would not use force to impose a tariff he did not welcome, and certainly not in the state in which he had been born. Jackson was invited by Calhoun and his friends to a Jefferson's birthday dinner on April 13, 1830, in the hope that Calhoun might prod an anti-tariff statement out of Jackson. After dinner, the toasts went round the table, beginning with Calhoun and building one by one to a carefully orchestrated anthem of praise for state sovereignty. But when Jackson rose to present his toast, he stared point-blank at Calhoun and proposed, "Our Federal Union: it must be preserved!" then held his glass aloft as a sign that the toast was to be drunk standing. Calhoun and the others struggled weakly to their feet, Calhoun spilling a trickle of wine as he trembled in shock. "The Union," Calhoun gasped in response, "next to our liberty the most dear."[31]

Calhoun had greatly misjudged Jackson's loyalty to the Union. Realizing that he had lost all hope of influencing Jackson, he resigned his vice presidency and returned to South Carolina. On November 24, 1832, the Calhounites led a specially called convention in South Carolina to nullify the collection of the tariff within South Carolina, threatening secession from the Union if the federal government interfered. Jackson replied on December 10, 1832, with a proclamation announcing

30. "Speech of Mr. Webster, of Massachusetts," January 26 and 27, 1830, in *The Webster-Hayne Debate on the Nature of the Union: Selected Documents*, ed. Herman Belz (Indianapolis, IN: Liberty Fund, 2000), 144.

31. "The Autobiography of Martin van Buren," ed. John C. Fitzpatrick, in *Annual Report of the American Historical Association for the Year 1918* (Washington, DC: Government Printing Office, 1920), 2:416; Ted Widmer, *Martin Van Buren* (New York: Times Books, 2005), 82.

that nullification was "incompatible with the existence of the Union. . . . The Constitution forms a government, not a league." On that note, nullification was dealt a staggering blow, and Jackson went on to take a further swipe at secession by adding, "To say that any state may at pleasure secede from the Union is to say that the United States is not a nation."

Jackson had no more love than Calhoun for banks, tariffs, and federally funded "improvements" projects, but he was also the president of the United States, and he was not used to challenges from what he called a "coward, hypocrite, conspirator, traitor and fool" such as Calhoun. Jackson obtained from Congress a Force Bill, which authorized him to use the army and navy to suppress South Carolina resistance. Before force became necessary, however, the more conciliatory Henry Clay had produced a compromise measure that provided for the graduated reduction of the tariff. On March 15, 1833, Calhoun and the South Carolinians rescinded their nullification ordinance.[32]

They did not, however, renounce the principle of secession. That meant that whatever else Americans might hold in common, their political structure—a Union of sometimes grudging and suspicious states—remained vulnerable in any crisis in which any state with a grievance might try to end its cooperation with the others and stalk out of the Union. "Altho I am for the *Union* & no *Nullifier*," wrote one uneasy Virginian in January 1833, "yet my southern feelings & prejudice are so strong, that I know I should hate to see a Southern man vanquished by a northern one. . . ."[33] Jackson might have prevented disunion over the tariff, and Clay might have demonstrated how compromise was the best method for disarming confrontation, but as far as Calhoun was concerned, that did not mean that the remedy of secession would not be available for future use if a more demanding set of circumstances called for it. And, as many Americans could already see, such a set of circumstances was very likely to appear in the form of the issue of slavery, as it was practiced in the Southern states. No one less than Andrew Jackson had already glumly predicted, after the nullification crisis had passed, that "the nullifiers in the South intend to blow up a storm on the slave question. . . ." Nullification might be defeated, he told his aide John Coffee, but "they will try to arouse the Southern people on this false tale. This ought to be met, for be assured these men will do any act to destroy the union, & form a southern Confederacy, bounded north, by the Potomac river."[34]

But even with all the forces that appeared to be pulling Americans apart—from the fissiparous nature of the federal Union to the clashing economic visions of Whig and Democrat—none of them had the weight to outbalance the forces making the

32. James Parton, *Life of Andrew Jackson* (New York: Mason Bros., 1860), 3:447, 460, 468, 474.

33. Richard E. Ellis, *The Union at Risk: Jacksonian Democracy, States Rights, and the Nullification Crisis* (New York: Oxford University Press, 1987), 191.

34. Robert V. Remini, *Andrew Jackson and the Course of American Democracy, 1833–1845* (New York: Harper and Row, 1984), 42.

American Union stronger with every decade, nor did they have the power by themselves to fracture the Union. That sort of disruption would require the introduction of a catalyst, which would act on all the divisions of Americans to worsen them.

That catalyst would be slavery.

SOCIOLOGY FOR THE SOUTH

Jefferson Davis did not like Yankees.

Born in Kentucky and raised in Mississippi, Davis found it something of a novelty to meet Northerners when he arrived at the United States Military Academy at West Point as a cadet in 1824. But it was not a novelty he enjoyed. He found Yankees tight-fisted, chilly, and unsociable. "The Yankee part of the corps [of cadets] . . . are not . . . such associates as I would at present select." Northerners were dedicated to making money, pinching pennies, and building factories; they were all "vulgar parvenus . . . vulgar landlords, capitalists, and employers." Henry Rootes Jackson, a Georgian who, like Davis, had gone north for his collegiate education, experienced the same revulsion. "Yankees, and Yankee gold" brought in their penny-pinching wake everything "impure, inhuman, uncharitable, unchristian and uncivilized." A Virginian on tour in New England in 1834 was reminded that "*Yankee tricks*, and *Yankee knavery*, are ideas inseparable from the word *Yankee*." Southerners were another quantity altogether. Southerners preferred the relaxed pace of agricultural life close to the rhythms of nature; they were aristocratic, noble-minded, generous, traditional. In fact, Southerners even *looked* different from Northerners. "Foreigners have all remarked on the care-worn, thoughtful, unhappy countenances of our people," George Fitzhugh, a Virginian, wrote in 1854, but that description "only applies to the North, for travellers see little of us at the South, who live far from highways and cities, in contentment on our farms." By 1861, claimed Albert Pike, it had become manifest that "the people of the South and those of the North are essentially two races of men, with habits of thought and action very unalike."[35]

Fitzhugh and Pike were at least partly right. After the Revolution, European tourists and journalists flocked to America to gawk at the operation of the new republic, and they did agree that the Southern states of the American democracy seemed like a country unto itself, although the watchers did not always mean that observation

35. Davis to Joseph Davis (January 12, 1825), in *The Papers of Jefferson Davis*, ed. H. M. Monroe and J. T. McIntosh (Baton Rouge: Louisiana State University Press, 1971), 1:18; Shearer Davis Bowman, *At the Precipice: Americans North and South During the Secession Crisis* (Chapel Hill: University of North Carolina Press, 2010), 74; "Letters from New England No. 2, by a Virginian," July 26, 1834, in *Southern Literary Messenger* 1 (January 1835), 219; George M. Fitzhugh, *Sociology for the South, or the Failure of Free Society* (Richmond, VA: A. Morris, 1854), 258; Albert Pike, "State or Province? Slave or Free?" in *Southern Pamphlets on Secession, November 1860–April 1861* (Chapel Hill: University of North Carolina Press, 1996), 341; Elizabeth Fox-Genovese and Eugene D. Genovese, *The Mind of the Master Class: History and Faith in the Southern Slaveholders' Worldview* (New York: Cambridge University Press, 2005), 97.

to be a compliment. The statistics the travelers amassed, or culled from the United States census reports, put a decidedly different spin on Fitzhugh's praise of Southern agriculture. In 1850, the South possessed only one-quarter of the railroad mileage of the Republic, and less than one-fifth of the country's manufacturing capacity. Three times as many Northerners lived in cities, while value of northern farmland was reckoned, acre for acre, at more than twice that in the South. In the North, less than 5 percent of the population was illiterate; in the South, illiteracy ran as high as 40 percent in some areas. For "the first time in the States," wrote English correspondent William Howard Russell as his train crossed through into North Carolina in 1861, "I noticed barefooted people" and "poor broken-down shanties or loghuts" filled with "paleface . . . tawdry and ragged" women and "yellow, seedy-looking" men.[36]

And yet the impressions of difference that foreign travelers gained from their tours of the South were also likely to miss many of the subtleties of Southern money and manners. The political and social economy of the Southern states was an exceedingly complex affair, compounded by deceptively stable appearances and highly aggressive commercial enterprise. It was a rash traveler indeed who rushed in to announce that the enigma of the South was now solved.

The first appearance that shaped the initial impressions of onlookers was the dominance of cotton agriculture in the South. Single-crop agriculture was actually a habit with a long history in the Southern states, stretching back into colonial times when the South's prosperity had relied almost entirely on tobacco grown around Chesapeake Bay and rice or indigo in the South Carolina lowlands. The soils of the South faded fast, though. Lands farmed for five years had to be left fallow for five or even ten years to regain their fertility. By the time of the Revolution, tobacco and indigo production had gone into decline, and the South faced an agricultural crisis of alarming proportions. Then, in 1793, a New England–born inventor, Eli Whitney, constructed a simple device known as the cotton gin, which was able to take raw cotton, separate the fiber of the cotton from the seeds, and produce a usable product with no more than the effort needed to turn a handle. At one stroke, cotton production became mechanically simple and economically viable.

At virtually the same moment that Whitney's gin simplified the production process, Great Britain's factory-based textile industry began its clamor for new, cheap sources of cotton. Demand met supply, and between the 1790s and 1850, British cotton imports from the South leapt from 12 million pounds a year to 588 million pounds; in the same period, British exports of finished cotton products rocketed from 40 million square yards to 2 billion square yards, while the costs of cotton goods fell by 1850 to 1 percent of what they had been in the 1780s. Cotton brought Britain power and prosperity, employing 1.5 million workers in the textile factories alone. Cotton, in return, brought the South economic and political power in the American republic. By 1860, Southern cotton constituted 57 percent of all American exports;

36. W. H. Russell, *My Diary North and South*, ed. Fletcher Pratt (New York: Harper, 1954), 52.

compared to Northern grain farms, which exported only 5 percent of their total crop, Southern cotton plantations shipped 75 percent of their cotton abroad.[37]

But cotton brought the South bane as well as blessing. The rage for cotton profits meant that the South was forever having to import manufactured goods, either from the North or else from abroad over the intolerable hurdle of federal tariffs. To buy these goods, Southern planters were compelled to mortgage their next crop to Northern manufacturers and bankers in order to buy the cotton gins and other tools they needed to plant and harvest the crop in the first place. The money that flowed from English cotton buyers back to the South generally came in the form of bills and drafts that were then forwarded to New York banks to pay Southerners' bills to Northern merchants. This created cycles of debt for cotton growers, especially in the oldest parts of the South, and most of the debt was owed to northern bankers. "We have been good milk cows," South Carolinian Mary Boykin Chesnut complained in 1862, "milked by the tariff, or skimmed . . . Cotton pays everyone who handles it, sells it, manufactures it, &c &c—rarely pays the men who make it."[38] The faster planters in the old cotton states ran to produce more cotton, the faster they piled up debts for the costs of production. By 1850, some of them were surviving on profit margins as low as 2 or 3 percent.

As a result, some Southerners came to resent the burden that the cotton system placed upon them. As early as 1818, John Taylor of Caroline warned that in the upper South, cotton was accelerating soil exhaustion: "The fertility of our country has been long declining, and . . . our agriculture is in a miserable state," and only a vigorous and intelligent program of manuring, drainage, and crop rotation could save it. Thirty years later, the Virginia planter and amateur agricultural scientist Edmund Ruffin pleaded for more intelligent use of fertilizers and crop rotation, and called for state aid to agricultural societies. Governor James Henry Hammond of South Carolina plowed up strips of ground beside public roads and advertised the use of new fertilizers on them so that passersby could have an example to follow with their own lands. In 1849, Hammond harangued the South Carolina State Agricultural Society on how "a combined system of Agriculture, Manufactures, and Commerce, are essential in promoting the prosperity and happiness of a community." And in 1852, Southerners reorganized the Southern Commercial Convention so that the convention could become an agency for promoting railroads, steamship lines, port facilities, banks, factories, and other market enterprises. Unfortunately, few of these proposals seemed to produce results. J. B. D. DeBow, the publisher of the Southern commercial magazine *DeBow's Review*, was chagrined to discover that Northern purchasers of his *Industrial Resources of the Southern and Western*

---

37. Allan Nevins, *Ordeal of the Union: Fruits of Manifest Destiny, 1847–1852* (New York: Scribner's, 1947), 466; Eric Hobsbawm, *The Age of Revolution, 1789–1848* (New York: World, 1962), 51–55.

38. Diary entry for July 8–9, 1862, *Mary Chesnut's Civil War*, ed. C. Vann Woodward (New Haven, CT: Yale University Press, 1981), 410.

States (1853) outnumbered Southern ones six to one; he was even more chagrined by the fact that two-thirds of his meager 825 *Review* subscribers were in arrears for their subscriptions.[39]

In their effort to understand why Southerners would set aside the opportunity to diversify their economy, journalists and travelers could only guess that Southerners were in some peculiar way willing to exchange solid modern profits for the social values that came attached to traditional agriculture. They were helped to this conclusion by the unceasing Southern voices that proclaimed their preference for a way of living that (whether it was profitable or not) provided more graciousness of style, more leisure, and more sense of the past than the frantic, money-grubbing lives of modern Northern manufacturers and their armies of faceless wage-paid factory hands. Edward Pollard, the editor of the *Richmond Examiner*, liked to think of the Southern cotton planters as the last survival of a noble and knightly virtue where "the affections were not entirely the product of money," a sort of American aristocracy holding its own against the onslaught of Yankee capitalism.[40]

They derived encouragement for this sort of thinking from new winds blowing out of Europe. The American republic had been the eldest child of the Enlightenment; when a revolution overthrew the king of France in 1789, it seemed that family of reason, liberalism, and republics was on the increase. But then the French Revolution collapsed into the Reign of Terror, which in turn was replaced by the tyranny of Bonaparte, and by 1815 the rule of reason and the viability of republics had become seriously tarnished. A backlash against the Enlightenment emerged out of the shambles of post-Napoleonic Europe, which snarled at the failures of reason and glorified the romance of authority, especially when it was rooted in knightly myth, chivalrous orders, and medieval faith. Its cultural paladins were Edmund Burke and Sir Walter Scott, Hector Berlioz and Georg Friedrich Hegel, Johann Wolfgang von Goethe, Johann Gottlieb Fichte, and Victor Hugo, and its name was Romanticism.[41]

The political theorists of the Enlightenment—not just Locke but Montesquieu, Beccaria, Mandeville, Harrington, and Hume—based their politics on the possession by all humanity of "certain inalienable rights," which could be encoded in

39. John Taylor, *Arator; Being a Series of Agricultural Essays Practical and Political*, ed. M. E. Bradford (Indianapolis: Liberty Fund, 1977), 70; Drew Gilpin Faust, "The Rhetoric and Ritual of Agriculture in Antebellum South Carolina," in *Southern Stories: Slaveholders in Peace and War* (Columbia: University of South Carolina Press, 1992), 32–34; James M. McPherson, *Ordeal by Fire: The Civil War and Reconstruction* (New York: Knopf, 1982), 27; Michael O'Brien, *Conjectures of Order: Intellectual Life and the American South, 1810–1860* (Chapel Hill: University of North Carolina Press, 2004), 1:542.

40. Fox-Genovese and Genovese, *Mind of the Master Class*, 313.

41. Tim Blanning, *The Romantic Revolution: A History* (New York: Random House, 2011), 67, 95, 121. H. J. Eckenrode, Virginia's longtime state archivist, once complained that "beyond doubt Scott gave the South its social ideal, and the South of 1860 might be not inaptly nicknamed Sir Walter Scottland." See Eckenrode, "Sir Walter Scott and the South," *North American Review* 206 (October 1917): 601.

written (and reasonable) constitutions. Looking out over the wreckage of Napoleon's empire, observers found that this seemed like drivel. Not rights but the ineffable experience of nationhood was what governed politics. "Those who speak the same language are joined to each other by a multitude of invisible bonds by nature herself, long before any human art begins," Fichte proclaimed in 1806; "they understand each other and have the power of continuing to make themselves understood more and more clearly; they belong together and are by nature one and an inseparable whole."[42] And Hoffman von Fallersleben sang of Germany:

Union, right and freedom ever
For the German fatherland!
So with brotherly endeavour
Let us strive with heart and hand!
For a bliss that wavers never
Union, right and freedom stand—
In this glory bloom forever,
Bloom, my German fatherland![43]

"There is no such thing as man in the world," the revolutionary exile Joseph de Maistre sneered. "During my life, I have seen Frenchmen, Italians, Russians, and so on . . . but I must say, as for man, I have never come across him anywhere. . . ." It was each nation's collective and organic experience that made its people what they were, not some inherent human qualities shared equally by everyone. Albert Taylor Bledsoe, who would serve in the Confederate government, agreed that civil society "is not a thing of compacts, bound together by promises and paper . . . It is a decree of God; the spontaneous and irresistible working of that nature, which, in all climates, through all ages, and under all circumstances, manifests itself in social organizations."[44]

Southerners found Romanticism irresistibly convenient for justifying the plantation culture—even in the older South, where plantation agriculture faced bankruptcy—because the plantation embodied the mystery of Southernness. "The South had an element in its society—a landed gentry—which the North envied, and for which its substitute was a coarse ostentatious aristocracy which smelt of the trade," Pollard explained. He acknowledged that "the South was a vast agricultural country," and its "waste lands, forest and swamps" featured "no thick and intricate nets of internal improvements to astonish and bewilder the traveller." All the same, "however it [the South] might decline in the scale of gross prosperity, its people

---

42. Johann Gottlieb Fichte, *Addresses to the German Nation*, trans. R. F. Jones and G. H. Turnbull (Chicago: Open Court, 1922), 223–24.

43. Heinrich Hoffmann von Fallersleben, "German Land Above All Others," in *A Harvest of German Verse*, ed. and trans. Margarete Münsterberg (New York: D. Appleton, 1916), 121–22.

44. De Maistre, "Considerations on France," in *The Works of Joseph de Maistre*, ed. J. Lively (New York: Schocken, 1971), 80; Bledsoe, *An Essay on Liberty and Slavery* (Philadelphia: J. B. Lippincott, 1856), 34.

were trained in the highest civilization." Southerners began to speak of themselves as though they were American Tories, basking in a regenerated feudalism. "All admit that a good and wise despotism is the wisest of earthly governments," wrote a Louisiana sugar planter in his diary in 1856. In 1861, numbers of them astounded William Howard Russell by insisting that they were descended "from a race of English gentlemen," full of "admiration for monarchical institutions on the English model, for privileged classes, and for a landed aristocracy," and happy to persuade him that "if we could only get one of the royal race of England to rule over us, we should be content."

They were, of course, fooling themselves, and Russell knew it. No people who wanted to be ruled by aristocrats ever defended states' rights with the doggedness that Southerners demonstrated: "Nothing like it has been heard before, and no such Confederation of sovereign states has ever existed in any country in the world." The Prussian-born Francis Lieber, who taught at South Carolina College in the 1840s and 1850s and who knew an aristocrat when he saw one, thought that the great planters "are arrogant indeed but not aristocrats." They were, in truth, something even more peculiar.[45]

It was not only the South's mysterious preoccupation with cotton agriculture that seemed to foreign observers to have shaped a culture of Romantic conservatism. It was the particular form of labor that the South used in cotton agriculture—slaves—that seemed to set the region off, not only from the North but also from the rest of the nineteenth century. Western Europeans had kept slaves ever since the end of the Roman Empire, and even in the heyday of classical Greece and Rome, slavery had been an everyday feature of urban and rural life. The reason for this was simple: in ages that knew only the most basic forms of labor-saving machinery, slaves provided a docile workforce that did not require an equal share of one's wealth or success. Yet slavery was not always successful and slaves were not always docile, and over the course of the Middle Ages the institution of slavery was gradually narrowed to serfdom, which slowly yielded to simple renter, or tenant, status.[46]

Still, slavery did not disappear entirely. Western Christianity, although it gave little reason to encourage slavery, did not forbid it, either. The rediscovery of ancient Greek and Roman literature in the Renaissance further reminded western Europeans that slavery had once been an important part of great societies that European

45. Edward Pollard, *The Lost Cause: A New Southern History of the War of the Confederates* (New York: E. B. Treat, 1867), 51; Lord John Manners, *England's Trust, and Other Poems* (London: J. Rivington, 1841), 16–17; Russell, *Pictures of Southern Life, Social, Political and Military* (New York: James G. Gregory, 1861), 3, 7, 63; Fox-Genovese and Genovese, *Mind of the Master Class*, 29, 121; Lieber, in O'Brien, *Conjectures of Order*, 1:368.

46. Hugh Thomas, *The Slave Trade: The Story of the Atlantic Slave Trade, 1440–1870* (New York: Simon and Schuster, 1997), 28–31.

humanists admired. Above all, the decimation of European society that resulted from the waves of lethal epidemics and national warfare in the fourteenth century created a revived need for cheap labor, and slave labor was the easiest way to fill that bill. By the end of the 1400s, one-tenth of the population in the Portuguese seafaring capital, Lisbon, was in some form of slavery. Over the next 400 years, as Europeans began pushing outward to the Indies and the New World, the demand for enslaved labor kept pace. More than 10 million Africans were snatched from the West African coastal regions, from Senegal to Angola, and shipped as slave labor to the New World; close to half a million of these victims were shipped to North America, with more than half of those sucked directly to the Southern ports of Charleston and Savannah.[47]

Slavery in the American South appeared, at first glance, to be simply a continuation of the slavery people knew from the Bible or from Caesar, Livy, or Suetonius. But in many respects, Southern slavery, like the other forms of New World slavery from Columbus onward, was a very different affair from what Europeans had known in ancient times. Like ancient slavery, Southern slavery had been called into being by economic circumstances—in colonial Virginia, by the need for a cheap labor force to harvest tobacco, a crop that became profitable only when harvested in greater volume than one tobacco farmer could undertake. In the New World case, however, there was a significant difference from all the other forms of slavery that Western civilization had known. This time, slavery was based on race.

Although colonial Southerners searched for cheap sources of labor in white indentured servants, redemptioners, Indians, and prisoners of war, almost all of these forms of forced labor had time limits and legal obligations attached to them, and fugitives could easily blend into the white or Indian population without much fear of being identified and tracked down. While those limitations eventually forced these practices out of existence, before the end of the 1600s Southern white colonists had found a permanent solution to their labor problems by opening their ports and plantations to the thriving transatlantic African slave trade. African slave labor turned out to be easily transferable to Chesapeake tobacco growing. Using captured Africans as slaves paid additional dividends to colonial slaveholders: their complexion marked them off as a different race of beings to European eyes, so fugitives could be more easily identified and recaptured. Because their owners saw all people of African descent as a coherent group—black—their labor could be bounded with an entirely different set of assumptions than would prevail for white labor. This lent the twist of race to Southern slavery, making what had ordinarily been a matter of economic exploitation into a system of racial exploitation as well.[48]

47. J. J. Sharp, *Discovery in the North Atlantic, from the 6th to the 17th Century* (Halifax, NS: Nimbus, 1991), viii–ix; David Eltis, "The U.S. Transatlantic Slave Trade, 1644–1867: An Assessment," *Civil War History* 54 (December 2008), 354–56.

48. Peter Kolchin, *American Slavery, 1619–1877* (New York: Hill and Wang, 1993), 12–13.

Colonial slavery was also a far more brutal and ruthless system of labor organization than the slaveries of the dim past. American slavery involved from the start the kidnapping of other human beings from their homes, subjecting them to the horrors of transportation across the Atlantic Ocean in fetid and disease-ridden slave ships, where as many as half died en route, and then selling them like cattle; slaves had no real hope of ever obtaining their freedom again. This kind of brutality toward other human beings, which departed dramatically from anything Protestant Americans could read concerning slavery in their Bibles, could not be justified in an avowedly Christian society—unless, of course, it could be shown that the slaves were not really human beings at all.[49]

It was here that the Romantics served yet another purpose. Taking de Maistre one step further, Arthur de Gobineau, in his *Essay on the Inequality of the Human Races* (published in four volumes from 1853 to 1855), located the unbridgeable differences of human nations in the biology of races. "I was gradually penetrated by the conviction," wrote Gobineau, "that the racial question overshadows all other problems of history, that it holds the key to them all, and that the inequality of the races from whose fusion a people is formed is enough to explain the whole course of its destiny." Americans seized on Romantic racism to protect themselves from the charge of kidnapping and murder by declaring that black Africans were members of a race that was irreversibly underdeveloped or perhaps even subhuman. "He is by nature a dependent," argued a contributor to *DeBow's Review* in 1861 of blacks, "his normal state is that of subordination to the white man," and "his nature is eminently parasitical and imitative." It was impossible, added Mississippi physician William Holcombe, that either "circumstances or culture could ever raise the negro race to any genuine equality with the white." Even in a northern state such as Illinois, a farmer-politician from DeWitt County, George Lemon, "did not believe they were altogether human beings. . . . If any gentleman thought they were, he would ask them to . . . go and examine their nose; (roars of laughter) then look at their lips. Why, their sculls were three inches thicker than white people's."[50]

But slavery contained more deadly poisons than racism. A slave, by simple definition, has no legal or social existence: a slave could have no right to hold property, could enjoy no recognition of marriage or family, and could not give testimony (even in self-defense) before the law. Slaves could be beaten and whipped: Josiah Henson, born a slave in 1789 in Charles County, Maryland, remembered that his

49. Ibid., 57–62; Wilma A. Dunaway, *Slavery in the American Mountain South* (New York: Cambridge University Press, 2003), 166; Philip D. Morgan, *Slave Counterpoint: Black Culture in the Eighteenth-century Chesapeake and Lowcountry* (Chapel Hill: University of North Carolina Press, 1998), 264–65.

50. Arthur de Gobineau, "From the Author's Dedication," in *The Inequality of Human Races*, trans. Adrian Collins (New York: G. P. Putnam's Sons, 1915), xiv; "The Black and White Races of Men," *DeBow's Review* 30 (April 1861): 448–49; William Holcombe, "The Alternative: A Separate Nationality or the Africanization of the South," *Southern Literary Messenger* (February 1861), 83; Charles Robert McKirdy, *Lincoln Apostate: The Matson Slave Case* (Jackson: University Press of Mississippi, 2011), 14.

father had "received a hundred lashes on his back" and had "his right ear . . . cut off close to his head" for stopping a white overseer from beating Josiah's mother. Slaves could be bullied and brutalized: Frederick Bailey, also born a slave in Maryland in 1818, was turned over by a fearful owner to a professional "slave-breaker," Edward Covey, who whipped and beat Bailey without mercy for six months to bring him into "submission." Slaves could be raped: in 1855, Celia, the slave of Robert Newsom, killed Newsom in self-defense when Newsom attempted to rape her. The Missouri court she appealed to in *State of Missouri v. Celia* would not admit her testimony, but it did execute her.[51] Above all, slaves could be bought and sold, and slave families broken up for auction, without any regard for ties of kinship or marriage. Francis Lieber was appalled to happen upon "a group of well-dressed negros" in Washington, "loudly talking while one them screemed and groaned and beat himself."

> I hurried toward them asking what was the matter, supposing at the time the man had been seized with the cholera. Only think said a woman, he just came home and found his house empty—wife, children—all gone. . . . Her master sold them all, and he did not know a word of it. My God, my God! And this is suffered? And slavery yet defended! Oh, God, what a black thing is man![52]

And yet slaveholders could not have everything their own way, no matter what the law or race had to say. A black slave *was* a human being, and any master who aspired to civilized refinement had to recognize that fact just to get any work out of a slave at all. What was more, no master could easily deny that slaves spoke the same language, worshipped the same God, and obstinately behaved like people. It also went without saying that a beaten or dead slave was one less production unit, and in a system where the labor force represented the owner's capital investment, it did not do to live too much by the whip alone. Many slave owners felt paralyzed by guilt, not necessarily because of slavery but because of the abuses endemic to Southern slaveholding. Nor did African American slaves wait upon the indulgence of whites to work out their own degrees of independence. They formed their own black Christian congregations, which became (and have remained) the center of African American community life; they sang their own songs; and to a degree that ordinarily would seem unimaginable, they kept their fragile families together. For their part, white masters frequently had little choice but to accept these manifestations of extremely human behavior and quietly tolerate them. All arrangements of

51. Melton A. McLaurin, *Celia: A Slave* (Athens: University of Georgia Press, 1991), 134–35.

52. Orlando Patterson, *Slavery and Social Death: A Comparative Study* (Cambridge, MA: Harvard University Press, 1982), 7–10; James Oakes, *Slavery and Freedom: An Interpretation of the Old South* (New York: Knopf, 1990), 3–14; Samuel Atkins Eliot, *The Life of Josiah Henson: Formerly a Slave, Now an Inhabitant of Canada* (Boston: A. D. Phelps, 1849), 1–2; Frederick Douglass, *My Bondage and My Freedom* (New York, 1855), 214, 242–46; Lieber, in O'Brien, *Conjectures of Order*, 1:76–77.

employers and labors are negotiations, and the practical realization that real human beings were providing free goods and services induced among whites a sense of obligation that sometimes cushioned the slaves from the excesses of white behavior that the law otherwise permitted.[53]

And as whites made the grudging concession that their slaves were human beings after all, this produced a clamorous urge on the part of white Southerners to justify the continuation of slavery on the grounds that slavery was actually a benefit of sorts to African Americans. The captain of the steamboat that carried William Howard Russell down the Alabama River in 1861 insisted on arranging a "dance of Negroes . . . on the lower deck" to demonstrate "how 'happy they were.'" "Yes sir," Russell's host intoned, "they're the happiest people on the face of the earth." At almost the same moment, in Georgia, Susan Cornwall Shewmake was writing, "It is certain there is not so much want among them. They are the happiest laboring people on the globe." Georgia senator T. R. R. Cobb repeated, "Our slaves are the most happy and contented, best fed and best clothed and best paid laboring population in the world, and I would add, also, the *most faithful* and least feared." Concurrently in Virginia, Governor Henry Wise was claiming that "the descendants of Africa in bondage" find themselves in "bodily comfort, morality, enlightenment, Christianity. . . . universally fed and clothed well, and they are happy and contented."[54]

This was, said Russell, the "universal hymn of the South." At the same time, though, the guilt that provoked white people to justify slavery on the grounds of its good works also provoked revealing displays of disgust and helplessness over slaveholding. Senator James Chesnut of South Carolina told his wife, Mary Boykin Chesnut, that his slaves owed him $50,000 for the food and clothing he had given them; when asked if his slaves had ever attempted to run away, he exclaimed, "Never—pretty hard work to keep me from running away from them." In her diary, Mary Chesnut suggested:

> Take this estate. John C. says he could rent it from his grandfather and give him fifty thousand a year—then make twice as much more for himself. What does it do, actually? It all goes back in some shape to what are called slaves here—operatives, tenants, &c elsewhere. . . . This old man's [money] goes to support a horde of idle dirty Africans—while he is abused and vilifed as a cruel slave owner. . . . I hate slavery.[55]

53. Eugene D. Genovese, *A Consuming Fire: The Fall of the Confederacy in the Mind of the White Christian South* (Athens: University of Georgia Press, 1998), 51, and Eugene D. Genovese, *Roll, Jordan, Roll: The World the Slaves Made* (New York: Pantheon, 1974), 89–91.

54. Russell, *My Diary North and South*, 106; Randall Jimerson, *The Private Civil War: Popular Thought During the Sectional Conflict* (Baton Rouge: Louisiana State University Press, 1988), 54; T. R. R. Cobb, "T. R. R. Cobb's Secessionist Speech," in *Secession Debated: Georgia's Showdown in 1860*, ed. William H. Freehling and Craig M. Simpson (New York: Oxford University Press, 1992), 11; Craig M. Simpson, *A Good Southerner: The Life of Henry A. Wise of Virginia* (Chapel Hill: University of North Carolina Press, 1985), 103.

55. *Mary Chesnut's Civil War*, 246, 283.

Richard Taylor, a Louisianan and the son of a president, commented bitterly long after slavery had disappeared that "extinction of slavery was expected by all and regretted by none." Even in the throes of slavery, enslaved African Americans imposed a strong psychological tension on their masters that robbed the whites of whatever joys there were to be had in owning another human being.[56]

And so, once again, the question emerged: *why*, if slavery held so much woe, not only for black slaves but for white masters as well, did Southerners cling to slavery as they clung to cotton agriculture? The easiest answer available was a Romantic one: because slavery promoted a peculiar culture, a certain way of living, for which white Southerners were willing to pay the price. "It was a medieval civilization, out of accord with the modern tenor of our time," Fanny Andrews, a Georgian, recalled, as though she had been living rather than merely reading a Walter Scott novel. "It stood for gentle courtesy, for knightly honor, for generous hospitality; it stood for fair and honest dealing of man with man in the common business of life, for lofty scorn of cunning greed and ill-gotten gain through fraud and deception of our fellowmen. . . ." James Walker, a Charleston lawyer, went so far as to insist that "ours is in truth not so much slavery as feudality."[57] This was an ingenious rationalization. The problem is that it is too simple.

The slave-based cotton agriculture of the Southern states was an intricate and complicated system in which appearances were not always uniform and not always the safest guide. Alongside the Romantic image of magnolias at midnight lay a relentless economic rationality; alongside the facade of racial reciprocity lay resistance and revolt; and alongside the casual tolerance of slave labor in producing their most lucrative commodity, Southerners displayed a fierce personal independence and a resentment at condescension and control. Southerners veered between assertions that theirs was a thoroughgoing slave society, in which "every fibre . . . is so interwoven with it, that it cannot be abolished without the destruction of the other," and realizations that Southerners were as much participants in a liberal democratic order as any other Americans, though one inexplicably incorporating the quirk of slave labor. This uncertain swinging between two poles would come back to cripple them in the 1860s when Southerners had to decide whether the survival of slavery or the survival of Confederate nationalism was more important to them.[58]

The South was divided in other ways as well. Geographically and socially, there were actually *three* slaveholding Souths, embracing masters, slaves, and nonslaveholding

56. T. Michael Parrish, *Richard Taylor: Soldier Prince of Dixie* (Chapel Hill: University of North Carolina Press, 1992), 446.

57. Fox-Genovese and Genovese, *Mind of the Master Class*, 143; Jimerson, *The Private Civil War*, 249.

58. "American Slavery in 1857," *Southern Literary Messenger* 25 (August 1857): 81; O'Brien, *Conjectures of Order*, 1:17.

whites, and spread across an uneven and uncooperative geography. The first South anyone who crossed the Ohio River or the Mason-Dixon Line found was the Border South (Kentucky, Maryland, northern Virginia); below this lay the Middle South (Arkansas, northern Louisiana, Tennessee, southern Virginia, and the upcountry of Alabama, Mississippi, South Carolina, Georgia, and North Carolina); and bordering the Gulf and south Atlantic coastlines was the Deep South (New Orleans to Charleston).

In the Border South, cotton had long since ceased to be the dominant crop and slavery the primary labor system. There, soil exhaustion drove fortune-hunting planters southward, slaves in tow; or, for those who did not plan on moving themselves, the proximity of the border states to the free states of the North, making slave flight as easy as it would be anywhere in the South, would persuade planters who stayed to sell off their slaves to the Deep South at a tidy profit. Either way, slavery was an institution in motion, mostly southward. One North Carolinian who lived "on one of the great thoroughfares of travel . . . on the Yadkin River" recalled seeing "as many as 2,000 slaves in a single day going South" during the prewar years, "mostly in the hands of speculators." By 1860, Virginia and Maryland had only 18 percent of all Southern slaves within their borders, and only a quarter of the South's cotton output; less than a third of the populations of Delaware, Missouri, Kentucky, Maryland, Tennessee, and Virginia were slaves (compared to 57 percent in South Carolina, 45 percent in Alabama, 55 percent in Mississippi, and 47 percent in Louisiana). In eastern Tennessee, only 10 percent of the population were slaves, and most of Tennessee grew not cotton but wheat.[59] In this environment, it was easier to find the remaining slave owners imbued with the Romantic conviction that they were upholding, to their own financial loss, an economic system that preserved the ancient atmosphere of the castle, moat, and manor.

But move into Alabama, Mississippi, and Louisiana, and there the plantations not only were newer but also constituted some of the richest cotton- and sugarcane-growing soil on the face of the earth. Between 1790 and 1860, nearly a quarter of the slave population was moved into the new cotton states; the slave population of the Border States, meanwhile, fell by almost half. By the 1850s, large-scale cotton plantations and large-scale slave labor were concentrated mainly along the lower Mississippi River valley (where slaves constituted as much as 70 percent of the

59. James L. Huston, *Calculating the Value of the Union: Slavery, Property Rights, and the Economic Origins of the Civil War* (Chapel Hill: University of North Carolina Press, 2003), 28; William W. Freehling, *The Road to Disunion: Secessionists Triumphant, 1854–1861* (New York: Oxford University Press, 2007), 14; James Oakes, *The Ruling Race: A History of American Slaveholders* (New York: Knopf, 1982), 121, 203, 209–17; B. S. Hedrick, in Rosser H. Taylor, "Slaveholding in North Carolina: An Economic View," *James Sprunt Historical Publications* (Chapel Hill: University of North Carolina Press, 1926), 18:43; Thomas V. Ash, *Middle Tennessee Society Transformed, 1860–1870: War and Peace in the Upper South* (Baton Rouge: Louisiana State University Press, 1988), 10, 18.

population of the fertile cotton-growing districts) and the Carolina and Georgia coastlines; a lesser concentration of slavery and cotton growing stretched in a broad belt from southern Arkansas through central Mississippi and Alabama and up through the Carolinas to the shores of Chesapeake Bay.[60]

On good, new Mississippi valley soils, there were immense profits to be made, and Romantic paternalism be damned. Harriet Martineau toured cotton plantations in Alabama in the mid-1830s where the profit margin was 35 percent. "One planter whom I knew had bought fifteen thousand dollars' worth of land within two years. . . . He expected to make, that season, fifty or sixty thousand dollars of his growing crop." Joseph H. Ingraham in 1835 had met raw new cotton planters in southwestern Mississippi with net annual incomes between $20,000 and $40,000. Making the adroit move to the most advantageous location could generate immense and quick wealth in cotton. The cotton crop could gross $74 million per annum in the 1840s; a decade later, it would sell for $169 million, and between 1856 and 1860, it topped $207 million a year. In 1860, half of the ten wealthiest states in the Union were slave states, and six of the top ten in terms of per capita wealth were slave states; calculated solely on the basis of the wealth of white inhabitants, eight of the top ten wealthiest states in the Union were slave states. The single wealthiest county in the United States, in terms of per capita wealth, was Adams County, Mississippi. It was ambitious Alabama and Mississippi planters, and not avaricious Northern factory owners, that Martineau described as being, "from whatever motive, money-getters; and few but money-getting qualifications are to be looked for in them." Slave owners might preen themselves upon their gentry manners, but they had no objection at all to making handsome profits.[61]

In this environment, slave owners proved to be quite as grasping as their despised Yankee counterparts. "Us was same as brutes en cows back dere," remembered a South Carolina slave years later. "Dey would beat de colored people so worser till dey would run away en stay in de swamp to save dey hide." Because "I was black it was believed I had no soul," wrote William Henry Singleton; "in the eyes of the law I was but a thing." The signposts of the slave's life were "the steel shackles of slavery, the slave block of the market place where husbands and wives, parents and children, were ruthlessly torn apart and scattered asunder, the whipping post, the slave quarters, the inhuman restrictions, such as denial of our own religious privileges, no ministers or churches of our race, no educational advantages to speak

60. Robert Fogel, *Without Consent or Contract: The Rise and Fall of American Slavery* (New York: W. W. Norton, 1989), 65; William W. Freehling, *The Road to Disunion: Secessionists at Bay, 1776–1854* (New York: Oxford University Press, 1990), 18, 24, 35, 201–7.

61. Harriet Martineau, *Society in America* (New York: Saunders and Otley, 1837), 2:228; Joseph H. Ingraham, *The South-West, by a Yankee* (New York: Harper, 1835), 2:90–91; Lee Soltow, *Men and Wealth in the United States* (New Haven, CT: Yale University Press, 1972), 105; Huston, *Calculating the Value of the Union*, 30.

of, no social freedom among ourselves. . . ." Slavery was nothing but "jest a murdering of de people."[62]

So slaves rebelled when they could, as Denmark Vesey and his conspirators tried to do in Charleston in 1822, and as Nat Turner and his band of slaves actually did in Virginia in 1831. When outright rebellion was impossible, slaves found other ways to isolate and terrify their tormentors, including work slowdowns, breakage of tools, and abuse of work animals. Frederick Law Olmsted was told by one slave mistress, "There is hardly one of our servants that can be trusted to do the simplest work without being stood over. If I order a room to be cleaned, or a fire to be made in a distant chamber, I never can be sure I am obeyed unless I go there and see for myself. . . . They never will do any work if you don't compel them." Some slaves fought back: when James Knox Polk's overseer, John L. Garner, tried to make "Henry, Gilbert, and charls" less "indifferent" about their "duty," one of them "resisted and fought mee."[63]

And they ran away. Sometimes for short periods of time to evade punishments, sometimes to escape from slavery entirely, the slaves ran whenever the threats or the opportunities became too great to resist. When Josiah Henson's master moved him from Maryland to a new plantation down the Ohio River in 1830 and then began toying with the idea of selling Henson away from his wife and children, Henson "determined to make my escape to Canada, about which I had heard something, as beyond the limits of the United States." In mid-September 1830 he arranged to collect his wife and children, persuaded a fellow slave to ferry them over the Ohio River by night, and trudged all the way to Canada on foot.[64]

Frederick Bailey returned to his master, scheming all the while how to buy his freedom with the money he earned on odd jobs performed for other whites. But when his master suspended his outside work privileges, Bailey decided that he had paid his master all he deserved, and in 1838 he boarded a train headed for Philadelphia, dressed as a sailor and carrying false identification papers. He found his way to New Bedford, Massachusetts, where he changed his name to Frederick Douglass. In 1841, Douglass was recruited as an agent for the Massachusetts Anti-Slavery Society; four years later he published his *Narrative of the Life of Frederick Douglass, an*

62. Ryer Emmanuel (Claussens, SC), and Sam Mitchell (Beaufort, SC), in *The American Slave, A Composite Autobiography*, vol. 2, part 2: *South Carolina Narratives*, and vol. 3, part 3: *South Carolina Narratives*, ed. George P. Rawick (Westport, CT: Greenwood Press, 1972), 24–25, 203; William Henry Singleton, *Recollections of My Slavery Days*, ed. K. M. Charron and D. S. Cecelski (Raleigh: Division of Archives and History, North Carolina Dept. of Cultural Resources, 1999), 31–32; Louis Hughes, *Thirty Years a Slave: From Bondage to Freedom* (Detroit: Negro History Press, 1969 [1897]), 78–79; Newton, *Out of the Briars: An Autobiography and Sketch of the Twenty-ninth Regiment Connecticut Volunteers* (Miami: Mnemosyne, 1969 [1910]), 19–20.

63. Frederick Law Olmsted, *A Journey in the Seaboard Slave States: With Remarks on Their Economy* (New York: Dix and Edwards, 1856), 196; John Spencer Bassett, *The Southern Plantation Overseer as Revealed in His Letters* (Northampton, MA: Smith College, 1925), 146–47.

64. Eliot, *Life of Henson*, 48.

American Slave. Within a decade he had become the most famous African American on the continent, and one of slavery's deadliest enemies.[65]

If slave owners worried about the misbehavior of their slaves, they experienced just as much anxiety over non-slaveholding whites. Although slaves were held by a remarkably broad section of Southern society—overall, one out of every four white families in the South in 1860 owned slaves, an extraordinary figure when it is remembered that by 1860 the cost of a strong, healthy field hand had reached $1,500—the distribution of that ownership varied considerably. Less than 1 percent of Southern white families (comprising a group of less than 12,000 people across the South) owned more than a hundred slaves, and only 46,000 (3 percent of all Southern families) owned more than twenty. The overall median for cotton plantations was thirty-five slaves.[66]

The largest group of slave-owning families held between one and four slaves, and those families accounted for almost half the slaveholding in the entire South. This meant, for one thing, that Southern slavery was, in most cases, an affair of small-scale farming, in which white farmers extracted the help of a slave or two to plow up and harvest holdings of less than a hundred acres. It also meant that, beyond the actual slaveholders themselves, there existed a large population of nonslaveholding whites, and without their cooperation, slavery could never have survived. Apart from a tiny population of urban professionals, the nonslaveholding white population of the South was the very model of the yeoman republican farmer that the Jeffersonians had assumed to be the salt of the earth in the early years of the Republic. At the same time, they had been shunted into the least desirable lands by the greater purchasing power of cotton, and there they clung to the old model of self-sufficient corn-and-livestock agriculture. These white yeoman farmers had every reason to resent the economic success of the planters, the loss of yeoman independence, and the way the planters turned their cotton profits into political dominance throughout the South. "In what else besides Negroes were these rich men better off then when they called themselves poor?" asked Frederick Law Olmsted, the noted American journalist and architect, and that was precisely the question surly slaveless farmers wanted to ask.[67]

At some point, an economically and politically alienated population of white yeomen with a curiosity on such subjects might easily decide that its mutual interests lay in directions other than those of the great planters, and thus become an engine for abolition or (in the most hideous scenario) a refuge for slave runaways and rebellion. Southern planters fantasized about Northern plots "to array one class of our citizens

65. *Narrative of the Life of Frederick Douglass, an American Slave, Written by Himself* (London: H. G. Collins, 1851), 99–100.

66. Fogel, *Without Consent or Contract*, 31; Huston, *Calculating the Value of the Union*, 28.

67. Frederick Law Olmsted, *The Cotton Kingdom: A Traveler's Observations on Cotton and Slavery in the American Slave States*, ed. A. M. Schlesinger (New York: Da Capo Press, 1996), 534.

38   FATEFUL LIGHTNING

against the other, limit the defense of slavery to those pecuniarily interested, and thereby eradicate it." It thus became vital to the peace of the planters' minds that the frustrations of the "crackers," "sandhillers," or "poor white trash" be diminished or placated at all costs. This involved, first and foremost, keeping the bogeyman of race ever before the nonslaveholders' eyes, for whatever hatreds the poor whites nursed against the planters, they nursed still greater ones against blacks.

Even if slavery was wrong, its wrongs were cancelled out for nonslaveholders by the more monstrous specter of racial equality. Abolish slavery, and white farmers would find that blacks were now their legal equals and economic and social competitors. "You very soon make them all tenants and reduce their wages for daily labor to the smallest pittance that will sustain life," prophesied Georgia governor Joseph E. Brown, and that would eventually force poor whites and blacks "to go to church as equals; enter the Courts of Justice as equals, sue and be sued as equals, sit on juries together as equals, have the right to give evidence in court as equals, stand side by side in our military corps as equals, enter each others' houses in social intercourse as equals; and very soon their children must marry together as equals. . . ." Southern elites such as Brown felt certain that when nonslaveholding whites realized the full racial consequences of abolition, they would become slavery's strongest supporters. "The strongest pro-slavery men in these States are those who do not own one dollar of slave property," insisted a Louisville newspaper, "They are sturdy yeomen who cultivate the soil, tend their own crops; but if need be, would stand to their section till the last one of them fell."[68]

Ensuring the loyalty of nonslaveholding whites involved a measure of social humiliation on the part of the "intelligent proud, courteous slave barons" who found themselves forced at every election to solicit the votes of "ignorant, slovenly, poor white trash in the country" with "frequent treats that disgrace our elections" and to advocate as a social ideal not aristocracy but white man's democracy—a kind of equality in which all the members of a superior race are more equal, socially and politically, to each other than to any members of an inferior race. By arguing that slavery was a benefit to slaveholders and nonslaveholders alike, the slave owners could weld the loyalty of the nonslaveholding white to their standard forever. "The existence of a race among us—inferior by nature to ourselves, in a state of servitude—necessarily adds to the tone of manliness and character of the superior race," argued Alabama governor John A. Winston.[69]

68. "An Appeal to Non-Slaveholders," Louisville, KY, *Statesman*, October 5, 1860, in *Southern Editorials on Secession*, ed. Dwight Lowell Dumond (New York: Century, 1931), 174–75; Brown, in *Secession Debated*, eds. Freehling and Simpson, 153.

69. John William Burgess, *Reminiscences of an American Scholar: The Beginnings of Columbia University* (New York: Columbia University Press, 1934), 3; Charles C. Bolton, *Poor Whites of the Antebellum South: Tenants and Laborers in Central North Carolina and Northeast Mississippi* (Durham, NC: Duke University Press, 1994), 123; Shearer Davis Bowman, *Masters and Lords: Mid-19th-Century U.S. Planters and Prussian Junkers* (New York: Oxford University Press, 1993), 161.

What was more, assigning menial work to black slaves assured poor whites that they would never have to worry about being reduced to the same level of drudgery. Explained James Henry Hammond in 1858, "In all social systems there must be a class to do the menial duties, to perform the drudgery of life," a class that "constitutes the very mud-sill of society and political government." White Southerners had found that "mud-sill" in black slaves, who performed the "duties" no white man would stoop to. With that class beneath them, all Southern whites could feel that they were members of a ruling class. "African slavery," announced another slaveholder, James P. Holcombe, "reconciles the antagonism of classes that has elsewhere reduced the highest statesmanship to the verge of despair, and becomes the great Peace-maker of our society." Compared to the black slave, every white was an "aristocrat," and not just the thousand-bale planters. Of course, arguing thusly forced slavery's apologists to sing a different tune than the one that assured the world that slavery existed to bestow happiness on the slave. Alongside the happiest-people-on-the-face-of-the-earth argument, planters had to offer a parallel argument for slavery based on the vilest form of racism and calculated to enlist the racist sympathies and fears of nonslaveholders. "The privilege of belonging to the superior race and of being free was a bond that tied all Southern whites together," wrote the Alabama lawyer Hilary Abner Herbert, "and it was infinitely strengthened by a crusade that seemed from a Southern stand-point, to have for its purpose the levelling of all distinctions between the white man and the slave hard by."[70]

This appeal to white racial solidarity disguised the fact that Southern yeomen may have had a great deal more to fear from slavery, so far as their economic futures were concerned, than they suspected. Slavery has become so fixed in the historical memory as a form of agricultural labor that it has been easy to miss how steadily, in the 1850s, black slaves were being slipped out of the "mud-sill" and into the South's small industrial workforce. More than half of the workers in the new iron furnaces along the Cumberland river in Tennessee were slaves, and after 1845 most of the ironworkers in the Richmond iron furnaces in Virginia were slaves as well. The hemp factories of Kentucky, which had actually begun using slave labor as early as the 1820s, defended the decision to use slave operatives on the grounds that they were so much easier to exploit than free white workers: "They are more *docile*, more constant, and cheaper than freemen, who are often refractory and dissipated; who waste much time by frequenting public places, attending musters, elections, etc., which the operative slave is not permitted to frequent." And, added Tennessee iron producer Samuel Morgan in 1852, they did not strike.[71]

70. Hammond, "Mud-Sill Speech," in *Slavery Defended: The Views of the Old South*, ed. Eric L. McKitrick (Englewood Cliffs, NJ: Prentice-Hall, 1963), 122–23; Holcombe, "Is Slavery Consistent with Natural Law?" *Southern Literary Messenger* 27 (December 1858): 417; Hugh B. Hammett, *Hilary Abner Herbert: A Southerner Returns to the Union* (Philadelphia: American Philosophical Society, 1976), 37.

71. Robert S. Starobin, *Industrial Slavery in the Old South* (New York, 1970), 214–22; Eugene D. Genovese, *The Political Economy of Slavery* (New York: Pantheon, 1965), 222–23.

Furthermore, when the great California gold rush of the late 1840s opened up for Americans the prospect of large-scale mining in the West, it was not forgotten by Southerners how successful slave-based gold mining had been in South America. By 1861, nonslaveholding whites in Texas were petitioning the state legislature to protest "being put in Competition With Negro Mechanicks who are rival to us in the obtaining of Contracts for the Construction of Houses Churches and other Buildings. . . . We say Negroes forever but Negroes in their Places (Viz: in Corn & Cotton Fields)."[72] With the right circumstances and a sufficient amount of time, slave labor could have easily become an industrial serfdom, made permanent by its identification through race, and nudging expensive white laborers out of the trades they had been assured were secure forever.

For slavery was neither a backward nor a dying system in the 1850s. It was aggressive, dynamic, and mobile, and by pandering to the racial prejudices of a white republic starved for labor, it was perfectly capable of expansion. In 1810, the Southern states had a slave population of just over 1 million; by 1860, in defiance of every expectation for what a system of organized violence could do to the survival of a people, the slave population stood at just under 4 million. No matter that to outside observers the South looked like anything but a market society, and no matter that slavery was based on the absurd and irrational prejudice of race; slavery's greatest attractions were its cheapness, its capacity for violent exploitation, and its mobility. Southerners understood that slavery was precisely the element that would help them transcend the limitations of poor soils and single-crop dependency and emerge into the dazzling light of a modern economy. As it was, considered as a separate nation from the northern states, the South would rank as the fourth most prosperous nation in the world in 1860, surpassing France and Germany, and outdistanced in Europe only by Great Britain.[73]

In the North, predicted South Carolina's Leonidas Spratt, free laborers and employers must inevitably come to a confrontation, for the goal of the employer is always to screw down the wages, and the goal of the laborer is always to increase them. "We look with perfect certainty to see the breaking up of free society into its elements" in the North, announced Spratt, while in the South, compliant and docile slaves would take up the levers of industry and make them a perfect success. Slaves might not have the skill, intelligence, or incentives that free white laborers had, but technology made all of that irrelevant. "Improvements in machinery have superseded the necessity of more than mere manipulation upon the part of operatives,"

---

72. T. Stephen Whitman, "Industrial Slavery at the Margin: The Maryland Chemical Works," *Journal of Southern History* 51 (February 1993): 31–62; "W. T. Smith et al., Marshall, to Texas Assembly, 1861," January 17, 1861, in *The Southern Debate over Slavery*, vol. 1: *Petitions to Southern Legislatures, 1776–1864*, ed. Loren Schweninger (Urbana: University of Illinois Press, 2001), 249.

73. Robert William Fogel, *The Slavery Debates, 1952–1990: A Retrospective* (Baton Rouge: Louisiana State University Press, 2003), 63.

and "of manipulation the negro is singularly capable." Because the available supply of slaves was so much needed in agriculture, no one had realized what a resource slave labor could be in manufacturing; it was "only for reason of the exceeding profit of agriculture at the South that the negro has not been yoked to the harness of other pursuits and that he has not given still more astonishing evidences of efficiency in that institution which evokes his powers than even that afforded by the products of the South." And when that happened, slavery "will evolve an energy of light and life that will enable it to advance over existing forms of society with a desolating and resistless power, and . . . stand from age to age impregnable."[74]

"African slavery is no retrograde movement," warned William Holcombe on the pages of the *Southern Literary Messenger* in 1861, "but an integral link in the grand, progressive evolution of human society." If California had been turned over to Southerners, speculated Virginia governor Henry Wise, "every cornfield in Virginia and North Carolina, in Maryland, Missouri, Tennessee and Kentucky, would have been emptied of black laborers, and I doubt whether many slaves would have been left to work the cotton and sugar estates of the other Southern plantation."[75]

But to expand, slavery would need protection and reassurance. Southerners would tolerate the annoyance of tariffs and the like, but they would not permit interference with or restriction upon slavery or its growth. And the federal Union in which the Southern states participated was a sufficiently rickety structure that any serious attack on slavery would be an excuse for Southerners to tear the whole structure of the Union down.

"AND I WILL BE HEARD"

The cultural differences and economic aggressiveness of the slave system and the political weakness of the Union were an unhappy combination within the American republic, but there was nothing in either of them that necessarily threw one into collision with the other. South and North still shared large areas of cultural continuity, and Northern merchants happily made fortunes feeding slavery's economic drives. There was no clash of civilizations between North and South, except in the imaginations of Virginian George Fitzhugh and the slave system's most ardent Romantic admirers. In fact, there might never have been a civil war at all in 1861 had it not been for two facts of geography that forced the sections onto a collision course. The first of these facts was that by 1860 there were virtually no slaves in the Northern

---

74. Leonidas W. Spratt, *A Series of Articles on the Value of the Union to the South: Lately Published by the Charleston Standard* (Charleston: James, Williams and Gitsinger, 1855), 22.

75. William Holcombe, "The Alternative: A Separate Nationality of the Africanization of the South," *Southern Literary Messenger* (February 1861), 84; Simpson, *A Good Southerner*, 104; Leonard L. Richards, *The California Gold Rush and the Coming of the Civil War* (New York: Knopf, 2007), 37.

states, and the second was that there was an enormous amount of land in the American West that no one quite knew what to do with.

Under British rule, nearly all white American colonists who owned their own farm or merchandise had servants of various sorts, although *servant* was a term that included everything from wage laborers to outright slaves. Slavery was part of this overall use of servant labor, and it persisted in all parts of the American colonies up until the American Revolution and beyond. As late as 1800, two-thirds of New York's black population was enslaved, and the legislation that eventually freed them was linked to a timetable that kept some black people in bondage until the beginning of the 1850s. There were still 1,488 slaves in New England in 1800, and Rhode Island and Connecticut possessed a smattering of slaves as late as 1810; Pennsylvania had some slaves living within its borders in 1830; in New Jersey, there were still eighteen lifetime black "apprentices" when the Civil War broke out.[76]

Had slavery remained a legal and economic force in every northern state and survived in significant numbers, then slavery would still have posed a moral problem to the Republic. It would have been a problem that every state shared, though, and it never would have developed into a strictly sectional issue, fanning animosities between states in which slavery was legal and those in which it was not. It might have been dealt with as an object of social reform, not civil war, and (as Abraham Lincoln once speculated) might have been gradually phased out of American life, with assistance and compensation to owners, by about 1910.[77]

But slavery did not remain a national institution. Instead, it became a sectional one. Apart from the small pockets of slaves that survived in the North in the early nineteenth century, slavery gradually became a dead letter north of the famous Mason-Dixon Line and the Ohio River. This disappearance has often been explained as a result of climate and soil: the North's climate was too cold to grow cotton, and Northerners felt none of the enthusiasm Southerners felt for the explosive growth of cotton agriculture in the nineteenth century—and therefore the North had no need of slaves. "Because the climate of New England was healthful, and the white man could labour beneath its sun, and no pestilence drove him from its marshes," black slavery disappeared, wrote Jonathan Wainwright, an Episcopal clergyman in New York City. (He did not intend this as a compliment to New England, though: "Had the banks of the Connecticut been rice meadows, its uplands the soil for cotton, and its summer climate fatal to all but the African race, the African race would, in all human probability, still be in bondage among us.")[78]

76. Bowman, *At the Precipice*, 250–51; C. Duncan Rice, *The Rise and Fall of Black Slavery* (New York: Macmillan, 1975), 210–11; Freehling, *The Road to Disunion*, 132–35; Joanne Pope Melish, *Disowning Slavery: Gradual Emancipation and Race in New England, 1780–1860* (Ithaca: Cornell University Press, 1998), 7.

77. Lincoln, "Remarks and Resolution Introduced in United States House of Representatives Concerning Abolition of Slavery in the District of Columbia," January 10, 1849, in *Collected Works*, 2:20–22.

78. Wainwright, in *Episcopal Watchman* 2 (September 13, 1828): 204.

Instead, the North turned to factory-based manufacturing, which could afford to dispense with a large permanent labor force and get along with a smaller, wage-paid labor supply. Beginning in 1813, when Francis Cabot Lowell built the first cotton textile factory (from plans stolen from British textile manufacturers), the old Northeast sprouted textile mills and manufacturing operations, employing 1.3 million workers. As early as 1826, Pennsylvania's Chester County already had fourteen woolen factories and thirteen cotton mills, and by 1860 there were forty-nine mills and workshops along just one five-mile stretch of the Connecticut River in western Massachusetts. The coming of the mills to the cold and stony Northern states left only the cotton fields of the South as a viable home for slavery. By the time slavery began to be seen as a moral problem in the United States, it had become a Southern problem as well.

Yet the climate-and-soil argument cannot carry all the weight of explaining why the North lost slaves while the South multiplied them. After all, neither the climate nor the soil of much of the Northern states differed all that much from the climate and soil in a good deal of the slaveholding South. Even if cotton could not be easily grown in Connecticut, wheat could, and wheat was being harvested by slave labor in both Kentucky and Tennessee. Wheat, in fact, had been planted and harvested by slave labor in Pennsylvania as early as the 1680s, and 20 percent of all the manual labor in Quaker Philadelphia in the 1750s was being performed by black slaves. As Southerners themselves had begun to realize, there was no reason why slave labor could not run the mills as easily as hired white labor.[79]

The reasons for slavery's disappearance in the North also have to be looked for in a number of more or less intangible sources. One of the least intangible of these causes was the American Revolution. In an effort to weaken American resistance, British occupation forces frequently lured "all indented Servants, Negroes, or others . . . willing to bear arms" to desert their masters and enter British lines, where freedom was promised as a reward. More often than not, that promise was honored in the breach. Slaves who ran away in Pennsylvania to join Sir William Howe's occupation of Philadelphia or who ran away in Virginia to join Lord Dunmore's "Ethiopian regiment" found themselves dumped by their erstwhile allies in Nova Scotia or sold back into slavery in the Bahamas. In May 1787, the abolitionist Granville Sharp employed 1,200 of them as the core of a black colonization experiment in Sierra Leone, on the west coast of Africa.

But the effect on the structures of slavery was significant: more than 5,000 Georgia slaves fled to the protection of King George when the British invaded Georgia in 1779, another 20,000 South Carolina slaves found refuge under British guns in Charleston, and 5,000 more (including thirty slaves belonging to Thomas Jefferson)

79. Edward Raymond Turner, *Slavery in Pennsylvania* (Baltimore: Lord Baltimore Press, 1911), 11–12, 67; Billy G. Smith, *The "Lower Sort": Philadelphia's Laboring People, 1750–1800* (Ithaca: Cornell University Press, 1990), 18–19; Gary B. Nash, *The Urban Crucible: Social Change, Political Consciousness, and the Origins of the American Revolution* (Cambridge, MA: Harvard University Press, 1979), 108–10.

followed Lord Cornwallis's ill-fated army to Yorktown. In New York City, which the British had occupied for most of the Revolution, runaway slaves swelled the free black population, while in Philadelphia the slave population had fallen from 1,400 to 400 by the close of the Revolution. Over the course of the war, upward of 80,000 American slaves (a fifth of the entire American slave population) ran away, joined the British, or found some other way of beating a path to freedom.[80]

The political idealism of the Revolution also encouraged, and sometimes forced, white slave owners to liberate their slaves. There were, as Samuel Johnson remarked, few things more incongruous than listening to yelps for liberty from the mouths of slave drivers. It remained the great and abiding paradox of the American argument over liberty and power that Jeffersonian and Jacksonian Democrats, who wailed so persistently against the encroachments of power, rested their fortunes so routinely on depriving black slaves of liberty; and that Federalists and Whigs, who saw much more need for the exercise of power in government and commerce, were the least enthusiastic about slavery.

A number of Americans felt the pain of that paradox enough to manumit their slaves (as George Washington did in his will) or pass laws that at least ended the slave trade in their states. As early as 1774, the Massachusetts Provincial Convention suggested "that while we are attempting to free ourselves from our present embarrassments, and preserve ourselves from slavery, that we also take into consideration the state and circumstances of the negro slaves in this province." By the time the Constitution was written, laws prohibiting the slave trade had been passed in Pennsylvania, Rhode Island, and Connecticut, and slave owners such as Abijah Holbrook, a Connecticut miller, were "influenced by motives of humanity and benevolence" to free their slaves, "believing that all mankind are entitled to equal liberty and freedom." Joseph Story, the brightest luminary among American lawyers, insisted in 1819 that "our constitutions of government have declared, that all men are born free and equal, and have certain inalienable rights, among which are the right of enjoying their lives, liberties, and property, and of seeking and obtaining their own safety and happiness. May not the miserable African ask, 'Am I not a man and a brother?'"[81]

Free blacks also took the future of their own people in hand. "Freedom suits" were filed by black Americans in northern courts, and litigious slaves in Massachusetts such as Quok Walker in *Walker v. Jennison* in 1781 (and its companion case, *Jennison v. Caldwell*) and Elizabeth Freeman in *Brom and Bett vs. Ashley*, also in 1781, claimed freedom on the grounds that the new Massachusetts constitution had declared that

80. Gary B. Nash, *Forging Freedom: The Formation of Philadelphia's Black Community, 1720–1840* (Cambridge, MA: Harvard University Press, 1988), 65; David Brion Davis, *Inhuman Bondage: The Rise and Fall of Slavery in the New World* (New York: Oxford University Press, 2006), 150–51; Cassandra Pybus, *Epic Journeys of Freedom: Runaway Slaves of the American Revolution and Their Global Quest for Liberty* (Boston: Beacon Press, 2006), 8–9.

81. William W. Story, *Life and Letters of Joseph Story* (Boston: Little, Brown, 1851), 1:340–41.

all individuals were "born free and equal." Others organized manumission societies to assist in purchasing the freedom of other blacks still in bondage, or prosecute slave owners guilty of abuse.[82]

More than secular political ideas, however, religious commitment formed the backbone of much of the North's hostility to slavery. Protestant evangelicalism was as fully devoted to the importance of individual spiritual freedom as republicanism was devoted to political freedom, and the two ideologies found a common cause in opposing slavery just as evangelicals and Whigs had found common cause in promoting personal self-transformation. The most famous evangelical preacher in the North before the Civil War, Charles Grandison Finney, denounced "the abominable institution of slavery" and openly declared that "no slave holder could come to our communion." The evangelicals were joined by other streams of religious dissent. The Quakers, awakened by the writing and preaching of Anthony Benezet and John Woolman, moved to admonish and then discipline slaveholders in 1750s, and by the time of the Revolution, slavery had disappeared almost entirely from American Quaker communities.[83]

Not all of the rising agitation against slavery was limited to the North. Prior to the 1830s, many Southerners expressed a sense of shame over slavery for both political and religious reasons. Thomas Jefferson offers one of the best-known and most ambivalent cases of Southern anti-slavery feeling, for Jefferson fully understood that slavery was a vicious and unjust system that mocked the liberty and equality he had made his political gospel. "Nothing is more certainly written in the book of fate than that these people are to be free," Jefferson declared; if there was no initiative to free the slaves, he could only "tremble for my country," for he knew "that God is just; that his justice cannot sleep forever; that considering numbers, nature and natural means only," a slave uprising "is among possible events." In that case, "the Almighty has no attribute which can takes side with us in such a contest."[84]

And so Jefferson wrote the Northwest Ordinance of 1787, which organized the new territories of Ohio, Indiana, Illinois, Michigan, and Wisconsin so that slavery

82. William Lincoln, ed., *The Journals of Each Provincial Congress of Massachusetts in 1774 and 1775* (Boston: Dutton and Wentworth, 1838), 29; Arthur Zilversmit, *The First Emancipation: The Abolition of Slavery in the North* (Chicago: University of Chicago Press, 1967), 190–91; Duncan J. McLeod, *Slavery, Race, and the American Revolution* (Cambridge, MA: Harvard University Press, 1974), 121–22; Benjamin Quarles, "The Revolutionary War as a Black Declaration of Independence," in *Slavery and Freedom: The Age of the American Revolution*, ed. Ira Berlin and Ronald Hoffman (Urbana: University of Illinois Press, 1986), 283–301; Arthur Zilversmit, "Quok Walker, Mumbet, and the Abolition of Slavery in Massachusetts," *William and Mary Quarterly* 25 (October 1968): 614–16.

83. Charles E. Hambrick-Stowe, *Charles G. Finney and the Spirit of American Evangelicalism* (Grand Rapids, MI: Eerdmans, 1996), 142–43; *The Memoirs of Charles G. Finney: The Complete Restored Text*, ed. Garth A. Rosell and R. A. G. Dupuis (Grand Rapids, MI: Zondervan, 1989), 362, 366.

84. Jefferson, *Notes on the State of Virginia*, 272; Willard Sterne Randall, *Thomas Jefferson: A Life* (New York: Henry Holt, 1993), 591.

would be permanently illegal there. As late as 1827, there were 106 anti-slavery societies in the Southern states as opposed to 24 in the North, and with nearly five times
as many members. In 1829, a convention called to rewrite Virginia's state constitution heatedly debated the wisdom of perpetuating slavery in the Old Dominion.
"I wish, indeed, that I had been born in a land where domestic and negro slavery is
unknown," announced one delegate to the convention. "I shall never wish that I had
been born out of Virginia—but I wish, that Providence had spared my country this
moral and political evil."[85]

But anti-slavery opinion in the South remained weak, and palsied by racism.
For all of Jefferson's guilt over slaveholding, the right time and the right conditions
for emancipation never quite seemed to come. As president, he deliberately turned
a deaf ear to cooperation with a new black revolutionary republic in Haiti, which
was at that moment struggling to throw back an invasion by the soldiers of a man
Jefferson had declared to be a tyrant, Napoleon Bonaparte. In 1824, Georgia senator
John Berrien, appearing before the Supreme Court as counsel for the owners of an
illegal cargo of slaves seized on the high seas, actually asserted that slavery "lay at
the foundation" of the Constitution, and that slaves "constitute the very bond of your
union," irrespective of any "speculative notions" of morality.[86] The Virginians in the
state constitutional convention who called for an end to slavery also wanted an end
to African Americans in Virginia, and wished them to be bundled out of the sight
of white people entirely. Farther South, as cotton grew more and more profitable,
republican enthusiasm for abolition waned past the vanishing point.

The death blow to any form of Southern abolition movement came in August 1831
when a religious visionary named Nat Turner led seventy of his fellow-slaves in a
short-lived but bloody insurrection in southeastern Virginia. The revolt was quickly
and brutally put down, with Turner and his followers captured or butchered, but not
before fifty-seven whites had also died. At Turner's trial, it became apparent that he
had cheerfully ordered the execution of every white man, woman, and child he had
encountered, whether they were slave owners or not, and had hoped to spread his
revolt throughout Virginia. Turner's confessions served notice on Southern whites
that it mattered nothing what their personal opinions on slavery were; Nat Turner
would have massacred them all if given the chance.[87]

This realization served to drive nonslaveholding yeomen straight into the arms
of planters, simply in the interest of self-protection. When the Virginia House of

85. Fox-Genovese and Genovese, *Mind of the Master Class*, 231; Benjamin Watkins Leigh, November 4,
1829, in *Proceedings and Debates of the Virginia State Convention of 1829–30* (Richmond, VA: S. Shepherd,
1830), 173; Erik S. Root, *All Honor to Jefferson? The Virginia Slavery Debates and the Positive Good Thesis*
(Lanham, MD: Rowman and Littlefield, 2008), 90–91, 120.

86. Berrien, in R. Kent Newmyer, *John Marshall and the Heroic Age of the Supreme Court* (Baton Rouge:
Louisiana State University Press, 2001), 431–32.

87. Stephen B. Oates, *The Fires of Jubilee: Nat Turner's Fierce Rebellion* (New York: Harper and Row, 1975), 105.

Delegates resumed debate over the future of slavery in 1832, the question was put purely in terms of white survival: either expel the blacks completely from Virginia or institute measures that were even more repressive and ban all discussion of abolition as dangerous incitement. By a margin of 73 to 58, the decision came down, in effect, on the side of repression. After 1832, Virginians' calls for abolition and transportation faded, and elsewhere in the South, any further attempts by whites to advocate freeing the slaves were denounced as treason and punished accordingly.[88]

This steady swing back in favor of the continuation of slavery in the 1820s produced, in the North, an equal but opposite reaction. With all the energies of religious and secular idealism flowing, free African Americans raised their voices in a chorus of eloquent protest. "I speak, Americans, for your good," wrote David Walker, a free black shop owner in Boston in 1829. "We must and shall be free, I say, in spite of you. . . . God will deliver us from under you. And wo, wo, will be to you if we have to obtain our freedom by fighting."[89] Northern anti-slavery societies denounced the slide backward with new militancy, and on January 1, 1831, William Lloyd Garrison published the first issue of the anti-slavery newspaper the *Liberator* from an office in Boston within sight of the Bunker Hill monument. With one sweep of defiant rhetoric, Garrison demanded an unconditional and immediate end to slavery. "I *will be* as harsh as truth, and as uncompromising as justice," Garrison promised on the first page of the *Liberator*. "I will not equivocate—I will not excuse—I will not retreat a single inch—AND I WILL BE HEARD." Garrison gave up any hope of converting the South to anti-slavery opinions. He was bent upon radicalizing the North, and his weapons were provocation and shock: "Be not afraid to look the monster SLAVERY boldly in the face," Garrison cried in 1832. "He is your implacable foe—the vampyre who is sucking your life-blood—the ravager of a large portion of your country, and the enemy of God and man."[90]

If necessary, Garrison was willing to have the free states secede from the Union rather than continue in an unholy federation with slave states. "It is said if you agitate this question, you will divide the Union," Garrison editorialized, "but should disunion follow, the fault will not be yours. . . . Let the pillars thereof fall—let the superstructure crumble into dust—if it must be upheld by robbery and oppression." In 1833, Garrison joined with the wealthy evangelical brothers Arthur and Lewis Tappan (who were also bankrolling Charles Grandison Finney) and founded the American Anti-Slavery Society in Philadelphia, which demanded the "immediate abandonment" and "entire abolition of slavery in the United States." Slavery was "an

88. Lacy K. Ford, *Deliver Us from Evil: The Slavery Question in the Old South* (New York: Oxford University Press, 2009), 363–84.

89. *David Walker's Appeal, in Four Articles*, ed. Charles M. Wiltse (New York: Hill and Wang, 1965), 70.

90. Garrison, "Introduction" and "The Great Crisis," December 29, 1832, in *Documents of Upheaval: Selections from William Lloyd Garrison's* The Liberator, *1831–1865*, ed. Truman Nelson (New York: Hill and Wang, 1966), xiii–xiv, 57.

audacious usurpation of the Divine Prerogative, a daring infringement on the law of nature, a base overthrow of the very foundations of the social compact."[91]

These demands were infinitely more than Southerners could take. They were also more than many Northerners could take. Just as the South's cotton agriculture bound Southern whites to the defense of slavery, it also bound the Northern bankers and merchants who lent the planters money to the toleration of slavery. Immediate abolition meant the disappearance of the immense fortunes that had been invested in the purchase of slaves; this would bankrupt not only the planters but also every Northerner who had invested in Southern cotton.[92] Even the ordinary Northern mill owner, who depended on shipments of Southern cotton for the manufacture of finished textile products, stood to lose by Garrison's frank willingness to break up the Union over slavery. There was, as it turned out, a very significant gap between being anti-slavery and being an abolitionist. A Northerner could oppose, criticize, and even denounce slavery without being at all inclined to take the risks of abolition.

It was for just this reason that Northern factory workers could be thoroughly hostile to slavery and yet also be suspicious of the abolitionists. The Northern labor movement was, like the anti-slavery movement, making its first attempts at large-scale organization in the late 1820s, and Northern workers were hostile to an abolitionism that concerned itself only with the plight of slave laborers and not northern "wage slaves." Garrison did not help matters when he discounted any comparisons between slavery and the working conditions in many Northern mills: "It is an abuse of language to talk of the slavery of wages. . . . We cannot see that it is wrong to give or receive wages." The close identification of evangelical Protestantism with the American Anti-Slavery Society did not improve the workers' opinion of the abolitionists. Many Northern workers were new immigrants from Roman Catholic Ireland or southern Germany, and they spurned the anti-slavery zealots as part of an overall stratagem of evangelical Protestants to Americanize the immigrant. It could not have been far from the mind of Northern workers that a sudden flood of free black labor onto the country's labor markets would depress white wages and jeopardize white jobs.[93]

Farmers in the free states also pulled shy of the abolitionists in the 1830s. Although Illinois was technically a free state (under the original mandate of the Northwest

91. Russel B. Nye, *William Lloyd Garrison and the Humanitarian Reformers* (Boston: Little, Brown, 1955), 72; Henry Mayer, *All on Fire: William Lloyd Garrison and the Abolition of Slavery* (New York: St. Martin's, 1998), 112–13, 313.

92. Harold D. Woodman, *King Cotton and His Retainers: Financing and Marketing the Cotton Crop of the South* (Columbia: University of South Carolina Press, 1990), 28–29.

93. Eric Foner, *Politics and Ideology in the Age of the Civil War* (New York: Oxford University Press, 1980), 64–76; John Ashworth, *Slavery, Capitalism, and Politics in the Antebellum Republic*, vol. 1: *Commerce and Compromise, 1820–1850* (New York: Cambridge University Press, 1995), 160–68; Michael Sandel, *Democracy's Discontent: America in Search of a Public Philosophy* (Cambridge, MA: Harvard University Press, 1996), 172–77.

Ordinance), the ordinance had exempted French-speaking slave owners whose settlement predated the Revolution, and the Illinois legislature adopted highly flexible "transit laws," which permitted slave laborers to be brought into Illinois for up to a year at a time. Illinoisans opposed legalizing slavery, but that was because they banned not only slaves but any African Americans at all, free or slave, from their state; in 1848, the new state constitution required the legislature to "pass such laws as will effectually prohibit free person of color from immigrating to and settling in this state, and to effectually prevent the owners of slaves from bringing them into this state." So when the militant evangelical abolitionist Elijah Lovejoy set up an anti-slavery newspaper in Alton, Illinois, mobs threw his press into the Mississippi River, and when he persisted in setting up a new one, they attacked his office on November 7, 1837, and murdered him. It had not helped that Lovejoy was a rabid anti-Catholic who described Roman Catholicism as "an unmixed evil," thereby uniting immigrants and Southern migrants in seeing him as a threat to their community identities. So long as the abolition movement chose men such as Lovejoy as its martyrs and examples, large segments of Northern society would balk at abolition.[94]

As it was, Garrison could scarcely hold his own followers together. The American Anti-Slavery Society was supposed to draw its support from a network of local and state auxiliary societies, but few of those auxiliaries kept their donations up to the necessary level. Although the anti-slavery societies claimed as many as 250,000 members, the *Liberator* had only 1,400 subscribers, and the Tappan brothers had to continually bail out Garrison's newspaper. Garrison himself only made matters more difficult. When evangelical ministers questioned Garrison's "harsh, unchristian vocabulary," Garrison lashed out at them as "a cage of unclean birds and a synagogue of Satan." When the Tappan brothers and other evangelical supporters of the American Anti-Slavery Society began to balk at Garrison's criticism of the ministers, Garrison immediately accused them of plotting "to see me cashiered, or voluntarily leave the ranks."[95]

Instead, Garrison cashiered the evangelicals. Garrison had been deeply impressed in the 1830s with the fervency and eloquence of two former South Carolina cotton heiresses, Sarah and Angelina Grimké, who had been converted to abolition. Garrison promoted them as lecturers on the circuit of the local anti-slavery societies, and they brought Garrison into close contact with the new women's rights movement and its leaders, Elizabeth Cady Stanton, Abby Kelley, and Lydia Maria Child. These early feminists argued that a campaign to emancipate slaves could not avert its eyes

94. Merton L. Dillon, *Elijah P. Lovejoy, Abolitionist Editor* (Urbana: University of Illinois Press, 1961), 38–43; Paul Finkelman, "Slavery, the 'More Perfect Union,' and the Prairie State," *Illinois Historical Journal* 80 (Winter 1987), 248–69.

95. Bertram Wyatt-Brown, *Lewis Tappan and the Evangelical War Against Slavery* (Cleveland, OH: Press of Case Western Reserve University, 1969), 190.

from the need to emancipate American women from social conventions and legal restraints that prevented them, like the slave, from owning property and voting, and kept them altogether subservient to the interests of white males. "Woman," declared Stanton, is "more fully identified with the slave than man can possibly be . . . for while the man is born to do whatever he can, for the woman and the negro there is no such privilege." And even if women's rights did not fall precisely within the goals of an anti-slavery society, at least that society could admit women to its membership and leadership, and allow them to bear their "subjective" testimony against slavery. But when Garrison attempted to place Abby Kelley on the business committee of the American Anti-Slavery Society at its annual meeting in May 1840, the Tappan brothers and fully half of the society's delegates rose and withdrew.[96]

Garrison was left with a rump society, and although he now had a free hand to place three feminists—Lucretia Mott, Lydia Child, and Maria Chapman—on the society's executive committee, the American Anti-Slavery Society was never more than a shadow of what it had been in the 1830s. The Tappans, meanwhile, organized a rival anti-slavery society, the American and Foreign Anti-Slavery Society, whose constitution expressly barred women from voting in its deliberations. Many of the other leaders and followers of the abolitionists wandered off to support various schemes of "gradual emancipation" or colonization for freed blacks in Africa or the Caribbean. Colonization turned out to be a particularly popular solution to the slavery problem, since it promised to eliminate both slavery and blacks from white view. The colonizationists did not much worry about the injustice of colonizing African Americans back to a continent from which many of them were six to eight generations removed.

But the South increasingly failed to see this evidence of fragmentation, poverty, and outright resistance to abolition in the North, and ignored how easily Northerners might oppose slavery on a variety of grounds without necessarily wishing for its abolition in the South. Instead, South Carolina governor James Hamilton thrust copies of the *Liberator* under the noses of state legislators, claiming that Nat Turner's revolt had been "excited by incendiary newspapers and other publications, put forth in the non-slaveholding states," and in 1836 the legislatures of South Carolina, Virginia, Georgia, and Alabama formally sent to the legislatures of ten northern states requests that the publication and distribution of "newspapers, tracts, and pictorial representations, calculated and having an obvious tendency to excite the slaves of the slave states to insurrection and revolt," be made a criminal offense, and John C. Calhoun tried to persuade Congress to prosecute any postmaster who would "knowingly receive or put into mail any pamphlet, newspaper, handbill, or any printed, written, or pictorial

96. Dorothy Sterling, *Ahead of Her Time: Abby Kelley and the Politics of Antislavery* (New York: W. W. Norton, 1991), 104–5; Keith Melder, "Abby Kelley and the Process of Liberation," in *The Abolitionist Sisterhood: Women's Political Culture in Antebellum America*, ed. Jean Fagin Yellin and John C. Van Horne (Ithaca, NY: Cornell University Press, 1994), 243–44.

representation touching the subject of slavery."[97] Never mind that no connection between Turner and Garrison was ever demonstrated—Southern pressure forced Postmaster General Amos Kendall to turn a blind eye when Southern postmasters began censoring suspicious mail and newspapers from the North.[98]

Because Northern state and local governments did not likewise act at once to silence the abolitionists, Southerners concluded that Northerners were actually in quiet collusion with the abolitionists to produce more Nat Turners. Throughout the 1840s and early 1850s, Southerners turned away from the Whig Party to the Democrats, convinced that the Whig programs for federal intervention in the economy were only laying the groundwork for federal tampering with slavery. The tide of Southern suspicion and Southern temper rose higher and higher, and Southerners forgot that they had ever discussed emancipating their slaves. The happiest-people-on-the-face-of-the-earth argument silenced Jefferson's warning that the South had by the ears a wolf that it could neither master nor release. Southerners who coveted independence and liberty also found themselves extolling white men's democracy and passing solemn resolutions that warned that "freedom of speech and press do not imply a moral right to freely discuss the subject of slavery. . . ."[99]

Eventually, by the mid-1850s, they came to the point of claiming that the political liberties enjoyed by Northern workers were useless frauds compared to the cradle-to-grave care given by the slaveholder to the slave. "The negro slaves of the South are the happiest, and, in some sense, the freest people in the world," George Fitzhugh intoned yet again in 1857. "We do not know whether free laborers ever sleep," Fitzhugh snickered; "the free laborer must work or starve," while the slaves "enjoy liberty, because they are oppressed neither by care not labor." The Northern worker is actually "more of a slave than the negro, because he works longer and harder for less allowance than the slave, and has no holiday, because the cares of life with him begin when its labors end. He has no liberty, and not a single right." At that moment, the slaveholders ceased to be an accident within a liberal democracy and became its enemies.[100]

But it was not enough for Southerners merely to justify the "positive good" of slavery in books, learned treatises, and sermons. Nat Turner had been no respecter of arguments, and so the pro-slavery defenses began to sprout demands that the federal government and the Northern states issue assurances that the abolitionists would never be allowed to tamper with what John Calhoun delicately described as

97. John L. Thomas, *The Liberator: William Lloyd Garrison* (Boston: Little, Brown, 1963), 137; Nye, *William Lloyd Garrison*, 54, 98–100; Calhoun, "Incendiary Publications," February 4, 1836, *Congressional Globe*, 24th Congress, 1st Session, 165.

98. Donald B. Cole, *A Jackson Man: Amos Kendall and the Rise of American Democracy* (Baton Rouge: Louisiana State University Press, 2004), 200–201.

99. Stephen M. Feldman, *Free Expression and Democracy in America: A History* (Chicago: University of Chicago Press, 2008), 126.

100. Fitzhugh, *Cannibals All! or, Slaves Without Masters* (Richmond, VA: A. Morris, 1857), 29–30.

the South's "peculiar domestic institution." Slavery became the lens through which Southerners looked at every question, the red dye that tainted every American conflict. Opposition to Henry Clay's "American System" was not merely a matter of agrarian economic theory; it sprang from the fear that a national government capable of interfering that deeply in the structure of the economy might prove capable of interfering with slavery, too. North Carolina senator Nathaniel Macon suspected, as early as 1818, that "the passage of a bill granting money for internal improvements" would also make "possible a bill for the emancipation of the negroes," and he "desired to put North Carolinians on their guard, and not simply North Carolinians, but all Southerners." And one no less than John Calhoun admitted that nullification of the tariff was really only a mechanism for ensuring that the federal government would never be able to tamper with slavery.[101]

> I consider the tariff but as the occasion, rather than the real cause of the present unhappy state of things. The truth can no longer be disguised, that the peculiar domestick institution of the Southern states, and the consequent direction, which that and her soil and climate have given to her industry, has placed them in regard to taxation and appropriation in opposite relation to the majority of the Union; against the danger of which . . . they must in the end be forced to rebel or submit to have their permanent interests sacrificed, their domestick institutions subverted . . . and themselves and children reduced to wretchedness.[102]

Still, Southern slaveholders need not have worried overmuch, since the Constitution had sanctioned the existence of slavery by allowing the slave states to count three-fifths of their slave populations toward the creation of federal congressional districts. (This arrangement, to the disgruntlement of the free states, effectively granted the South something like two dozen extra members of Congress, though their constituents could not vote.) "Slavery existed in the South when the constitution was framed," declared Calhoun on the floor of the Senate in 1848, and "it is the only property recognized by it; the only one that entered into its formation as a political element, both in the adjustment of the relative weight of the States in the Government, and the apportionment of direct taxes; and the only one that is put under the express guaranty of the constitution." William Lloyd Garrison found himself powerless to disagree: "It is absurd, it is false, it is an insult to the common sense of mankind, to pretend that the Constitution . . . or that the parties to it were actuated by a sense of justice and the spirit of impartial liberty. . . ."[103] And when it

101. William Edward Dodd, *The Life of Nathaniel Macon* (Raleigh, NC: Edwards and Broughton, 1903), 313.

102. Calhoun to Virgil Maxcy, September 11, 1830, in William Montgomery Meigs, *The Life of John Caldwell Calhoun* (New York: G. E. Stechert, 1917), 1:419.

103. Calhoun, "Speech on the Oregon Bill," June 27, 1848, in *Union and Liberty*, 543; Garrison, "Massachusetts Resolutions," May 3, 1844, in *Documents of Upheaval*, 201.

came to choosing between abolition and the Union, Northerners were content to choose the Union.

Content, that is, until the time came for Americans to deal with the West.

At the end of the Revolution, the outward fringe of the thirteen newly independent United States stopped pretty much at the foothills of the Appalachians. But the British surrendered to the American republic complete title to all their remaining colonial lands below Canada, stretching west beyond the Appalachians to the Mississippi River. Then, in 1803, President Jefferson bought up 830,000 square miles of old Spanish land beyond the Mississippi River for the United States for $15 million in spot cash from Napoleon Bonaparte, who had finally despaired of his project to re-create a French colonial empire in America. Both the midwestern land won from the British and the western lands bought by Jefferson originally had next to nothing in the way of American settlers in them, but there was no reason any of them could not soon fill up with settlers, organize themselves as federal territories, and then petition Congress for admission to the Union as states on an equal footing with the original states.

Because the Northwest Ordinance had already barred slavery from the upper midwestern land, the territories of Ohio, Indiana, Illinois, and Michigan all entered the Union as free states; slaveholders, skirting southward below the Ohio River, were content to organize Alabama, Mississippi, Tennessee, Kentucky, and Louisiana as states where slavery would remain legal. The trouble began when people started to look westward, beyond the Mississippi, where no Northwest Ordinance mandated the slave or free status of the land. Southerners anxious to keep open the way to new cotton land reasoned fearfully that if nonslaveholding Northerners squatted in the Louisiana Purchase lands and settled them as free states, the South could easily find itself barricaded in behind the Mississippi and Ohio Rivers. Surrounded by free states on the Mississippi and Ohio lines, and by Louisiana's border with Spanish-held Mexico, cotton and slavery would suffocate, no matter what the Constitution said.

And so came the first of the great angry Southern demands for assurances about the future of slavery, in the form of the Missouri controversy of 1819, and with that controversy, the first in a series of threats that the slave states would leave the Union if sufficient assurances were not forthcoming. Then, and again in 1850, slaveholders would turn the Garrisonian gospel on its head and ask the rest of the United States to choose between slavery and the Union. Both times, desperate politicians would find a way to avert the choice, until finally, in 1861, the choice had to be made.

And the war came.

CHAPTER TWO

THE GAME OF BALANCES

The fatal sequence of public events in the United States that stretched from 1820 until 1861 and the outbreak of the American Civil War can be visualized as a game of balances, with the Union as the balance point along the beam, and the two trays representing the interests of North and South, slave and free. During those years, the federal Union became increasingly threatened and unstable as states or sections or interests laid the weight of their demands on one or the other of the trays and waited to see if the other states or sections or interests would produce reassurances and compromises weighty enough to right the balances.

Of all the issues that divided Americans and provoked them to threaten that equilibrium—tariffs, trade, banks, reform—nothing proved so heavy or so liable to plunge the balance off the table entirely as slavery. Slavery pitted cultures, economic interests, and moral antagonisms against each other; worse, it pitted states against other states; worst of all, it pitted whole associations of states (in this case, the South), which could plausibly regard themselves as a nation, against other whole associations of states (namely, the free North of the old colonies and the free West of the Northwest Ordinance). It was bad enough that in 1832 one single state had been willing to defy and disrupt the Union over the tariff question. It was almost unimaginable what might happen if several states, sharing common borders in a common section of the country, with a common culture and common economy, came to believe that their very way of life was at stake, and decided that self-preservation required disunion. Had slavery been legal only in far-removed places such as Minnesota and Florida, or Maine and Alabama, it is hard to see anyone there arguing that they could stand independently on their own among the nations of the world. There would be no such difficulty, however, if the fifteen slave states were grouped together in a single landmass, comprising 750,000 contiguous miles, and thus able to cooperate, communicate, and support one another. They would look like a nation, rather than just islands of complaint.

So long as some Americans still believed that the Union was *only* a federal union—only a league or federation of quasi-independent states that could be terminated at will—and so long as Southerners continued to believe that northern anti-slavery attacks on slavery constituted a real and present danger to Southern life and property, then disunion could not be ruled out as an ugly resort. And if the Northern states, and the federal government in Washington, failed to place on their balance pan a weight of assurances equal to Southern demands for reassurance about slavery, then the South would drop onto its pan the immense and destructive weight of disunion and the balance would be wrecked, perhaps forever.

That made the threat of secession useful.

The key word in understanding the South's behavior throughout the four critical decades before the Civil War is *threat*. The Union had increasingly taken on the lineaments of a nation ever since the ratification of the Constitution, no matter what the secession-mongers liked to say, and the American Constitution had become increasingly intertwined with the idea of an American nation. It would always be easier to challenge both the Union and the Constitution in fustian rhetoric, but in practice, compromise within the Constitution would always get the greatest applause. Of course, in any compromise situation, threats are the weightiest chips to bargain with. So from the 1820s onward Southerners would begin talking a great deal about seceding from the Union, but frequently it was little more than intimidating talk, meant to squeeze out concessions during the compromise process rather than to announce action. There were few Southerners in 1820 who seriously wanted to leave the Union, and most of them lived in South Carolina. But Southerners were willing to *talk* secession because of the leverage such talk easily acquired within a federal union. If it was believed that disunion was a possible political outcome of the balancing game, then using secession as a threat could be highly useful in cajoling favorable responses out of the rest of the Union. "It has come to this," complained one Northern senator, "that whenever a question comes up between the free States and the slave States of this Union, we are to be threatened with disunion, unless we yield."[1] It mattered little enough whether secession was likely or even desirable, or whether in fact the balance itself was far more indestructible than any of the players realized. So long as the threat of secession and disunion continued to pry assurances out of the rest of the country that slavery would never be imperiled, then the South would stay in the Union.

1. William Pitt Fessenden, "The Kansas and Nebraska Bill—Debate," March 3, 1854, *Congressional Globe*, 33rd Congress, 1st session, Appendix, 323.

"YOU HAVE KINDLED A FIRE"

The first round of threats and assurances played out in February 1819, when Missouri applied for admission to the Union with a state constitution that legally recognized slavery. Missouri's application was a moment for celebration, since it was the first territory that lay entirely west of the Mississippi, in the Louisiana Purchase lands, to apply to Congress for statehood. What was less obvious was that Missouri's petition also represented a challenge to the free states, since the Union in 1819 was perfectly balanced between eleven free states and eleven slave states. Allow Missouri to enter the Union as a slave state, and it would add two "slave" senators to the Senate and an indeterminate number of representatives to the House (artificially swollen, as Northerners saw it, by the three-fifths rule). That, in turn, might give the South enough of an edge in Congress to disrupt the Northern campaign to protect American manufacturing and weaken the demands of Henry Clay and the National Republicans for an "American System" of federally tax-supported roads, turnpikes, canals and other "internal improvements." So on February 13, 1819, New York congressman James Tallmadge rose in the House to add an amendment to the Missouri statehood bill that would bar the further importation of slaves into Missouri and emancipate any slave living in Missouri who reached the age of twenty-five.[2]

Southern congressional delegations erupted in rage and panic. Not only was Missouri the first of the Louisiana Purchase territories to be added to the Union, but it also represented the only direct highway that the South possessed to lands further west. The land President Jefferson had purchased lay within a rough triangle, with the long side running from a point on the north Pacific coast in Oregon to Louisiana's border with the old Spanish empire, and the great bulk of the area lying along the United States' northern boundary with British Canada. Northern settlers could expand straight westward, across the Mississippi River, without being crammed together, but Southern settlers moving west were forced into the narrow lower corner of the triangle, against the border of Spanish Texas. Unless Southerners and slavery were allowed to expand equally into the Louisiana Purchase territories with Northerners, then the South could hope to develop only one or two future slave states. In short order, their alarm turned into threats of disunion and demands for assurance.

Tallmadge's amendment, warned Thomas W. Cobb of Georgia, was full of "effects destructive of the peace and harmony of the Union . . . They were kindling a fire which all the waters of the ocean could extinguish. It could be extinguished only in oceans of blood."[3] Nevertheless, the Tallmadge restrictions passed the House, 78 to 66, with representatives voting along virtually exclusively sectional North-South lines, and only the phalanx of Southern senators in the Senate (and five free-state allies) killed the

2. Leonard L. Richards, *The Slave Power: The Free North and Southern Domination, 1780–1860* (Baton Rouge: Louisiana State University Press, 2000), 74–75.

3. Thomas W. Cobb, "Missouri State," March 2, 1819, *Annals of Congress*, 24th Congress, 2nd session, 143.

amended Missouri bill there. The House sent the amendments back to the Senate again, and at that point, in March 1819, Congress adjourned and left matters hanging.

The brief pause the intersession brought did nothing to allay the fears of onlookers. For the first time, slavery and sectionalism had reared their heads in Congress as a matter of national debate, and almost immediately Congress had divided along sectional lines. "This momentous question, like a fire-bell in the night, awakened and filled me with terror," wrote an aging Thomas Jefferson. "I considered it at once the knell of the Union."[4] To Jefferson's relief, a solution quickly appeared in the form of Maine and Henry Clay. By the time Congress had settled back into Washington, another petition for admission to the Union had been received from Maine, which had been governed since colonial times as a province of Massachusetts. Henry Clay, then the Speaker of the House of Representatives, proposed to damp down the anxieties about upsetting the sectional balance in Congress by simultaneously admitting Missouri (as a slave state) and Maine (as a free state) to the Union. For the future, Clay called for the division of the Louisiana Purchase into two zones along the latitude line of 36°30' (the southern boundary line of Missouri), with the northern zone forever reserved for "free" settlement only and the southern zone left open to the extension of slavery. Adroitly sidestepping the partisans of both sections, Clay maneuvered the legislation through the House and greased its way through a joint House-Senate reconciliation committee to the desk of President James Monroe, who signed it on March 6, 1820.[5]

The Missouri Compromise made the reputation of Henry Clay as a national reconciler and champion of the Union, and the 36°30' line became the mutually agreed line of settlement that was supposed to squelch the need for any further antagonistic debates over the extension of slavery. It is difficult, looking back on the Missouri Compromise, to see just what advantages slaveholders believed they had won, since the available Louisiana Purchase territory lying south of the 36°30' line was actually fairly minimal (only one other slave state, Arkansas, would ever be organized from it). Most of the recently acquired territory lay north of 36°30', and even then it was by no means certain in the 1820s that the Canadian border was so permanently fixed that the United States could not expand further north. Great Britain and the United States had agreed to mutually govern the Oregon territory after 1812, and the Oregon boundaries then ran as far north as Russian-owned Alaska. With the right use of bluster and bluff on the British, the limits on free settlement above 36°30' could be made almost unlimited. The South's acquiescence in the 36°30' agreement makes sense only if it had become fairly widely assumed by 1820 that the United States would also apply some bluff, bluster, and expansion to the Spanish territory that lay south of the Louisiana Purchase boundary, in Texas.

---

4. Jefferson to John Holmes, April 22, 1820, in *The Works of Thomas Jefferson: Correspondence and Papers, 1816–1826*, ed. Paul Leicester Ford (New York: G. P. Putnam, 1905), 12:158.

5. Robert V. Remini, *Henry Clay: Statesman for the Union* (New York: W. W. Norton, 1991), 184.

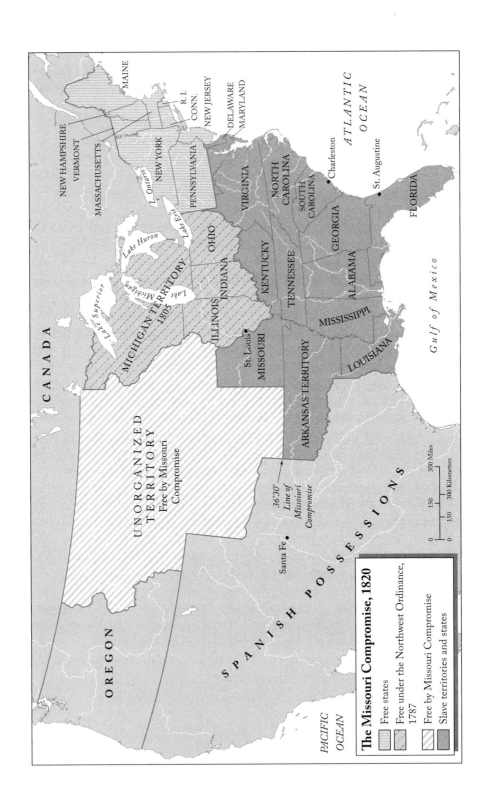

The Missouri Compromise, 1820

Free states

Free under the Northwest Ordinance, 1787

Free by Missouri Compromise

Slave territories and states

CANADA

ATLANTIC OCEAN

PACIFIC OCEAN

Gulf of Mexico

OREGON

SPANISH POSSESSIONS

UNORGANIZED TERRITORY
Free by Missouri Compromise

MICHIGAN TERRITORY 1805

MAINE

NEW HAMPSHIRE

VERMONT

MASSACHUSETTS

R.I.

CONN.

NEW YORK

NEW JERSEY

DELAWARE

MARYLAND

PENNSYLVANIA

OHIO

INDIANA

ILLINOIS

VIRGINIA

NORTH CAROLINA

SOUTH CAROLINA

GEORGIA

FLORIDA

KENTUCKY

TENNESSEE

ALABAMA

MISSISSIPPI

MISSOURI

ARKANSAS TERRITORY

LOUISIANA

St. Louis

Charleston

St. Augustine

Santa Fe

36°30′ Line of Missouri Compromise

Lake Superior

Lake Huron

Lake Michigan

Lake Erie

L. Ontario

0   150   300 Miles

0   150   300 Kilometers

THE GAME OF BALANCES

That some Americans were prepared to act on that assumption was clear from what was already beginning to happen in Texas. In 1820 Spain still clung tenaciously to large parts of the New World empire it had won under the conquistadors of the 1500s. But Spain's political strength had been ebbing for 200 years, and by 1800 it was proving more and more difficult for the Spaniards to control an American dominion that still stretched from the southern cone of South America up to the Missouri and Mississippi Rivers. One by one, pieces of that dominion in South America had thrown off Spanish rule and established republics based on the liberties and slogans of the American revolution of 1776. Then in 1820 the Spanish king, Ferdinand VII, was challenged by an uprising among his own officers, who demanded reform and a republic. While Spanish attention was preoccupied with its own revolution, the Spanish province of Mexico took its future in its own hands and established a revolutionary monarchy under Agustín de Iturbide in 1821. Iturbide's monarchy proved only marginally more popular than Spain's. In 1823 Iturbide was overthrown, and the following year a republic was established.[6]

The Mexican republic had a rocky history, especially since the individual Mexican states had notions of independence and autonomy not unlike some of those held by their North American neighbors. At length, in 1833, an ambitious general, Antonio Lopez de Santa Anna, solved the republic's problems by overthrowing it and setting up a personal dictatorship. In the meantime, the Mexican states dealt with their internal problems pretty much by their own lights. For the state of Coahuila, which included the province of Texas, the principal problem was the sparsity of the population. From the 1820s onward, Coahuila proposed to cure that barrenness by franchising out large, vacant stretches of eastern Texas prairie to land-hungry Americans. Guided by *empresarios* and land brokers such as Moses and Stephen Austin, who acted as middlemen between Coahuila and potential American settlers, large colonies of Americans migrated to Texas, some 20,000 of them by the end of the decade and 30,000 by 1835. They found under the Mexican flag a land perfectly formed for raising livestock and farming—especially cotton. And cotton meant slaves. By 1830 the Anglo-Americans in Texas already had 1,000 slaves working in the rich new cotton fields of east Texas.[7]

What had at first seemed like the ideal solution to the emptiness of their land soon turned sour for the Mexicans. Not only did the American colonists blithely disregard agreements that bound the colonists to convert to Roman Catholicism and adopt Spanish as the civil language, but their numbers eventually dwarfed the tiny Mexican population of Texas. Anxious that the Americans would soon attempt to set up an independent Texan government, Santa Anna attempted to seal off the

6. Frederic Logan Paxson, *The Independence of the South American Republics: A Study in Recognition and Foreign Policy* (Philadelphia: Ferris and Leach, 1916), 105–27; Teresa A. Meade, *A History of Modern Latin America: 1800 to the Present* (New York: Wiley-Blackwell, 2010), 70.

7. Randolph B. Campbell, *An Empire for Slavery: The Peculiar Institution in Texas, 1821–1865* (Baton Rouge: Louisiana State University Press, 1989), 20–32.

Texas border with Louisiana to control further immigration. Instead, the Mexican troops, under the clumsy command of Santa Anna's brother-in-law, provoked an uprising in Texas, and in December 1835 the enraged Texans drove Santa Anna's men back across the Rio Grande into Coahuila.

The resulting Texan war of independence was short but spectacular. Many of the Mexican grandees of Texas had no more love for Santa Anna's dictatorship than the American colonists did, and the Tejanos and their Anglo neighbors declared Texas an independent republic in March 1836. The odds for the Texan republic's survival were at first not very good. Santa Anna gathered an army of 4,000 and staged a midwinter march into Texas that threw the Texans into a panic. The small Anglo-Tejano garrison in San Antonio barricaded itself into a crumbling Catholic mission known as the Alamo and held up Santa Anna's advance for thirteen days until a predawn Mexican attack overwhelmed the Alamo's 183 defenders. The Alamo was not particularly significant from a military point of view (the Alamo garrison had originally been instructed to blow the place up and retreat), although Santa Anna did waste the lives of a few hundred of his men in the effort to capture the Alamo. What turned the Alamo from a military annoyance into a catastrophic misjudgment was Santa Anna's temperamental decision to put every survivor of the Alamo garrison to death. Across east Texas, the American colonists were both terrified and outraged, and "Remember the Alamo" became an electrifying war cry. A ragtag Texan army, under an old protégé of Andrew Jackson named Sam Houston, fell back before Santa Anna's advance, lulling the Mexicans into a false sense of certain conquest. Santa Anna unwisely divided his forces in pursuit, and on April 21, 1836, Houston and the Texan army turned and struck Santa Anna's troops at San Jacinto, routing the Mexicans and capturing Santa Anna himself. As a condition of his release, Santa Anna signed an agreement recognizing Texan independence (an agreement he promptly repudiated when Santa Anna reached Mexico City again).

The aim of the Texans, however, was not to remain independent but to join the United States as a new state as soon as possible. Here the trouble began anew. President Martin Van Buren, a Democrat, was Andrew Jackson's anointed successor in the presidency, and he owed a great deal to the Democratic constituencies of the Southern states. Van Buren was also a New Yorker who was less than eager to promote the expansion of slavery, much less involve the United States in a dispute over an insurgent province that was still technically the property of Mexico. It did not help that Van Buren found himself embroiled at that moment in a major economic depression, and he was not eager to annex Texas and assume responsibility for the debts the Texans had run up in financing their revolution. In fact, the depression cost Van Buren the White House in the election of 1840 and brought a Whig to the presidency for the first time in the person of William Henry Harrison. The Whigs preferred to pour the nation's resources into developing the internal American economy rather than pick up the bills for expansionist adventures, and so Texas unwillingly remained an independent republic.

Poor William Henry Harrison died in 1841, only one month after his inauguration as president, and the Whig Party suddenly found itself saddled with John Tyler, Harrison's vice president, as the country's chief executive. Although Tyler was nominally a Whig, he soon found himself at odds with Henry Clay and Daniel Webster, the real chiefs of the Whig Party, and two men who were sure that they deserved the presidency more than the man people sneered at with the sobriquet "His Accidency." Every bill that Clay and a Whig Congress wrote for the pet projects of the Whigs—internal improvements, protectionist tariffs, a new Bank of the United States—was vetoed by Tyler, and eventually all the Whigs in the Cabinet resigned. Shunned by the Whigs, Tyler tried to assemble his own independent political power base, and as a Virginian and a slaveholder, he was not shy about bidding for Southern support. As bait to his fellow Southerners, Tyler and his new secretary of state, Abel Upshur, negotiated an annexation treaty for Texas and tried to turn Texas annexation into a campaign issue that Tyler could ride back into the White House in 1844 as a "Southern candidate." Texas, as Upshur told one of John Calhoun's political allies, is "the only matter, that will take sufficient hold of the South and rally it on a Southern candidate and weaken Clay and Van Buren."[8]

Tyler succeeded in making Texas an issue, but not himself president. The Democrats snubbed the unhappy Tyler and ran one of Andrew Jackson's old lieutenants, James Knox Polk of Tennessee, for the presidency in 1844. The Whigs had no time at all for Tyler and put up Henry Clay instead, hoping to feed on fears that an annexation of Texas would provoke war with Mexico. Clay undercut his own candidacy by conceding to Southern Whigs that he might be willing to accept the annexation of Texas if could be done "without dishonor, without war, with the common consent of the Union." What Clay gained among the Southern Whigs he promptly lost among the Northern ones, and Polk squeezed into the White House after winning Pennsylvania and New York with majorities of only 7,000 votes.[9]

There was no question about James Knox Polk's plans for Texas—Polk was an outright annexationist, and even hoped to edge the British out of Oregon—and so before his inauguration the disheartened Whigs gave up the fight and allowed a joint congressional resolution to adopt the Texas annexation treaty in December 1844. The Mexican government did not back down in the face of Polk's determination to have Texas, withdrawing its ambassador from Washington in protest. Sensing trouble (and not finding trouble with Mexico all that unwelcome), President Polk sent Brigadier General Zachary Taylor to the Texas border with 1,500 United States soldiers in July 1845. Ten months later, there was a bloody clash between Mexican

8. Virgil Maxcy to Calhoun, December 10, 1843, *Correspondence of John C. Calhoun, Volume 2, Part 2*, ed. J. Franklin Jameson (Washington, DC: Government Printing Office, 1900), 903.

9. Clay to Thomas M. Peters and John M. Jackson, July 27, 1844, in *The Papers of Henry Clay: Candidate, Compromiser, Elder Statesman, January 1, 1844–June 29, 1852*, ed. M. P. Hay and Carol Reardon (Lexington: University of Kentucky Press, 1991), 10:91.

and American troops over a disputed border area, and Polk used the clash as an excuse for rallying Congress to declare war on Mexico on May 13, 1846.

The Mexican War was, compared to the Alamo and San Jacinto battles, a relatively unglamorous affair. The American forces were divided into four small field armies under John Ellis Wool, Zachary Taylor, Stephen Kearny, and Alexander Doniphan for the invasion of Mexican territory. Taylor (alongside Wool) won a major victory over Santa Anna at Buena Vista and occupied most of northern Mexico. Kearny plunged into New Mexico and chased Mexican forces from Santa Fe, then moved on into southern California, where scattered colonies of American settlers helped him overthrow the Mexican provincial government. The greatest laurels were won by Major General Winfield Scott, who led a daring invasion column from Mexico's Gulf coast inland to Mexico City, which fell to Scott on September 13, 1847. No less a military authority than the victor of Waterloo, the Duke of Wellington, had predicted at the outset that "Scott is lost. He has been carried away by his successes! He can't take the city, and he can't fall back upon his base!" But when Scott indeed captured Mexico City, the Iron Duke generously reversed himself: "His campaign was unsurpassed in military annals. He is the greatest living soldier."[10]

The following February, the Treaty of Guadalupe Hidalgo was signed, with Mexico grudgingly surrendering to the United States the territory that is now New Mexico, California, and parts of Arizona, Colorado, Utah, and Nevada. As if to illustrate that fortune favors the bold (or at least the unscrupulous), no sooner was California an American possession than one James Marshall discovered gold in a streambed near Sacramento, thus setting off the mighty California gold rush and stampeding thousands of American settlers into the newly acquired territories.

It was at this point that the old balancing game of threats and assurances began again.

The Missouri Compromise had settled what to do with the half of the far West that the United States had owned in 1820; the South had been anxious to resolve the question then, because in 1820 most of the old Louisiana Purchase looked like it was going to fall into the hands of free-state settlers. Now, in 1848, the Mexican War had brought the United States the other half of the far West—the southern half, running in a clear straight line from Louisiana to the southern California coast—and this time it appeared that these new territories would surely develop into slave states. In fact, there was no reason to assume that the United States might not want to keep pecking away at Mexico, or at the Spanish-held island of Cuba or even Central America, and obtain still more territory, which would obviously come under the wing of the old slave states. Robert Toombs of Georgia boldly warned Congress, "in the presence of the living God, that if by your legislation you seek to drive us from the territories of California and New Mexico, purchased by the common blood and

10. Allan Peskin, *Winfield Scott and the Profession of Arms* (Kent, OH: Kent State University Press, 2003), 175, 191.

treasure of the whole people . . . thereby attempting to fix a national degradation upon half the states of this Confederacy, *I am for disunion.*"[11]

What Toombs did not reckon with was the feeling of many Americans that the Mexican War had been something less than a source of national pride. In Congress, Southern Whigs such as Alexander Stephens of Georgia repeatedly assailed Polk's war as "an aspersion and reproach."

> The principle of waging war against a neighboring people to compel them to sell their country, is not only dishonorable, but disgraceful and infamous. What, shall it be said that American honor aims at nothing higher than land—than the ground on which we tread? . . . I have heard of nations whose honor could be satisfied with gold—that glittering dust, which is so precious in the eyes, of some—but never did I expect to live to see the day when the Executive of this country should announce that our honor was such a loathsome, beastly thing, that it could not be satisfied with any achievements in arms, however brilliant and glorious, but must feed on earth—gross, vile, dirt!—and require even a prostrate foe to be robbed of mountain rocks and desert plains![12]

Even in the army, young lieutenants out of West Point such as Ulysses Simpson Grant acknowledged that "the Mexican War was a political war," and nearly 7,000 American soldiers (of the 115,000 mustered into service) actually deserted.[13]

The most unpopular aspect of the war was the realization that slavery stood to gain a political windfall from it. To the disappointment of Northerners, Polk had negotiated a fairly timid treaty with Great Britain, which surrendered most of the bolder American claims to northern territory and put what amounted to a geographical cap on northern expansion; but Polk had grabbed nearly 1.5 million square miles of Mexican territory to the south, with no certainty that slaveholders might not go on from there to destabilize other Latin American republics, transplant slavery there, and claim them for admission to the Union. As it was, the size of just the newly acquired western lands offered enough material to create so many new states below the 36°30′ line that slaveholders might at last acquire a decisive numerical advantage in the Senate, if not the House as well. With that prospect before him, Frederick Douglass denounced the war as "this slaveholding crusade" from which "no one expects any thing honorable or decent . . . touching human rights." Lieutenant Grant could hardly avoid the conclusion that everything from the Texas annexation onward had been "a conspiracy to acquire territory out of which slave states might be formed for the American Union." John Pendleton Kennedy, an angry Whig who had

11. Ulrich Bonnell Phillips, *The Life of Robert Toombs* (New York: Macmillan, 1913), 68.

12. *Speech of Mr. Stephens, of Georgia, On the War and Taxation*, February 2, 1848 (Washington, DC: J. and G. S. Gideon, 1848), 14.

13. Ulysses S. Grant, "Personal Memoirs," in *Memoirs and Selected Letters*, ed. M. D. McFeely and W. S. McFeely (New York: Library of America, 1990), 41, 83.

lost his congressional seat over the Texas annexation, was convinced that "at the bottom of this scheme" was "an ultimate purpose to form a new Confederacy, of which it shall be a prominent feature that no free State shall come into the League."[14]

As early as August 1846, four basic political agendas took shape for dealing with the Mexican Cession (the territory in the far West surrendered by Mexico). The first of these was proposed on August 8, 1846, when President Polk, admitting publicly for the first time that "a cession of territory" by Mexico was a possible result of the war, asked the House to approve $2 million in negotiating funds. A first-term Democratic representative from Pennsylvania named David Wilmot rose to move an amendment to the appropriations bill that added a deadly proviso: "As an express and fundamental condition to the acquisition of any territory from the Republic of Mexico . . . neither slavery not involuntary servitude shall ever exist in any part of said territory, except for crime."[15]

The Wilmot Proviso was, like the Tallmadge Amendment in 1819, a paraphrase of the Northwest Ordinance of 1787, whose sweeping ban against slavery Wilmot now wanted applied to the southwestern territories of the Mexican Cession. More than just a frank declaration against slavery, it was an even franker assertion that Congress (based on Article 3, Section 3 of the Constitution) had the authority to make judgments about the future of the territories. Just as in 1820 with the Tallmadge Amendment, Congress quickly fractured along sectional rather than party lines. The Northern Whigs and all but four Northern Democrats in the House overrode Southern votes in the House and sent the appropriations bill with its lethal proviso to the Senate, where Polk and the Southern Democrats killed it.

Polk was particularly mortified by the Wilmot Proviso, since the blow had come from a member of his own party. "If the Wilmot Proviso was engrafted on the appropriation or any other Bill and was made to apply to any portion of the acquired territory lying South of 36°30', the Missouri compromise line," Polk promised, "I would certainly veto it, be the consequences what they might."[16] As it was, the administration had its own plan ready to launch: extend the Missouri Compromise line all the way through the Mexican Cession. This does not seem like a particularly imaginative proposition, but the idea had behind it the indisputable fact that the Missouri Compromise had worked for twenty-six years in keeping the slavery issue from polarizing Congress, and it offered what looked like a solution that everyone

14. Douglass, "The War with Mexico," January 21, 1848, in *The Life and Writings of Frederick Douglass*, ed. Philip S. Foner (New York: International, 1950), 1:293; John Pendleton Kennedy, "The Annexation of Texas," in *Political and Official Papers* (New York: Putnam, 1872), 608.

15. Chaplain W. Morrison, *Democratic Politics and Sectionalism: The Wilmot Proviso Controversy* (Chapel Hill: University of North Carolina Press, 1967), 18.

16. Polk, diary entry for February 22, 1849, in *The Diary of James K. Polk During His Presidency, 1845 to 1849*, ed. Milo M. Quaife (Chicago: A. C. McClurg, 1910), 4:347.

had already agreed to earlier; most important of all, President Polk was prepared to swing all the weight of his office behind it. "The Missouri question had excited intense agitation of the public mind, and threatened to divide the country into geographical parties," Polk reasoned. "The compromise allayed the excitement, tranquilized the popular mind, and restored confidence and fraternal feelings," and he was confident that "a similar adjustment of the questions which now agitate the public mind would produce the same happy results."[17]

The trouble with merely tinkering with the Missouri Compromise, however, was that a good deal of angry water had flowed under the bridge since 1820, and a quarter century later, Southerners were no longer satisfied with the spoils they had been awarded then. The new Mississippi senator, Jefferson Davis, warned that "as a property recognized by the Constitution, and held in a portion of the States, the Federal government is bound to admit [slavery] into all the Territories, and to give it such protection as other private property receives." On February 19, 1847, the white-haired and hollow-cheeked John Calhoun rose to offer a set of resolutions arguing that "the territories of the United States belong to the several States composing this Union, and are held by them as their joint and common property." This meant—and Calhoun explained himself with frightening lucidity—that "Congress, as the joint agent and representative of the States of this Union, has no right to make any law . . . that shall . . . deprive the citizens of any of the States of this Union from emigrating, with their property, into any of the territories of the United States."[18]

By Calhoun's logic, the territories were the common property of all of the states, not the federal government. Congress, in organizing and readying federal territories for statehood, was merely acting as a trustee on behalf of the entire people of the United States. Citizens of any one of the states had equal title to the territories, and therefore ought to be able to take any of their property, including slaves, into any of the territories. Hence, not only did Congress have no authority to enact the Wilmot Proviso, which banned the transportation of slave "property" to the territories, but it had had no authority in 1820 to enact the Missouri Compromise, which banned the transportation of slaves to some of the territories. With this one gesture, Calhoun swung the door of every federal territory open to slavery, and delighted Southern Whigs and Democrats fell in behind him, turning him into the South's great political figurehead.

17. William Dusinberre, *Slavemaster President: The Double Career of James Polk* (New York: Oxford University Press, 2003), 141–48; Robert W. Merry, *A Country of Vast Designs: James K. Polk, the Mexican War, and the Conquest of the American Continent* (New York: Simon and Schuster, 2009), 453–60; Polk, Special Message to Congress, August 14, 1848, in *A Compilation of the Messages and Papers of the Presidents, 1789–1908*, ed. J. D. Richardson (Washington, DC: Government Printing Office, 1908), 4:608.

18. Jefferson Davis, "Slavery in the Territories," February 13, 1850, *Congressional Globe*, 31st Congress, 1st session, Appendix, 149; John Calhoun, "The Slavery Question," February 19, 1847, *Congressional Globe*, 29th Congress, 2nd Session, 455.

The Northern Democrats, however, were less than enthralled with Calhoun's logic. In December 1847 one of Polk's chief rivals within the Democratic Party, Michigan senator Lewis Cass, brought forward yet another solution to the problem of
the Mexican Cession territories. In a letter published in the *Washington Union*, Cass
gingerly agreed with Calhoun that Congress had no authority to impose a settlement of the slavery issue on any of the territories. Surely, observed Cass, the people
who were actually living in each of the territories had the right to adopt a "slave" or
"free" settlement for themselves. Let the slavery question in the Cession be "left to
the people . . . in their respective local governments," he argued, and let the sovereignty of the people defuse the confrontations in Washington over slavery and free
Congress from the responsibility of solving the problem. Congressional mandates of
the sort Wilmot and Calhoun were seeking

> should be limited to the creation of proper governments for new countries, acquired
> or settled, and to the necessary provision for their eventual admission into the Union;
> leaving, in the meantime, to the people inhabiting them, to regulate their internal con-
> cerns in their own way. They are just as capable of doing so as the people of the States;
> and they can do so, at any rate, as soon as their political independence is recognized by
> admission into the Union.[19]

Cass's "popular sovereignty" proposal appealed to the fundamental American ideological instinct that a democratic people had the right to make their own political
decisions. Cass's letter might have taken him further along the road to the presidency if he had not already managed to make a host of enemies within the Democratic
Party. As it was, an unpersuaded President Polk attempted to ram the Missouri
Compromise solution through Congress during the summer of 1848, and came out
at the end of the session with nothing more to show for his efforts than a single bill
authorizing the organization of the Oregon territory without slavery. Chronically ill
and disappointed at the defections from Democratic unity by Calhoun, Wilmot, and
Cass, Polk announced that he would not seek a second term as president in 1848. The
Missouri Compromise extension proposal fizzled.

Worse for the Democrats was yet to come. The party's presidential nominating convention, as might have been expected, picked Lewis Cass as its nominee.
Agitated Northern Democrats wanted the Wilmot Proviso or nothing, and they
suspected that if Cass and popular sovereignty were allowed to rule the future of
the territories, the popular will could just as easily announce itself in favor of slavery
as not. "I am jealous of the *power* of the South," wrote David Wilmot. "The South
holds no prerogative under the Constitution, which entitles her to wield forever
the Scepter of Power in this Republic." Wilmot added that if he could "strike an

19. Cass to A. O. P. Nicholson, December 24, 1847, in William T. Young, *Sketch of the Life and Public
Services of General Lewis Cass* (Detroit: Markham and Elwood, 1852), 321, 323.

effectual & decisive blow against its dominion at this time, I would do so even at the temporary loss of other principles."[20]

Wilmot got his chance in June 1848, when a group of anti-slavery Northern Democrats met in Utica, New York, to organize a splinter movement based on the principle that Congress had full authority to ban slavery from the territories. Two months later, in Buffalo, a national "Free-Soil" convention assembled under a great tent, with luminaries as varied as Wilmot and Frederick Douglass among the delegates. In a decisive repudiation of the Democratic Party's leadership, they nominated Martin Van Buren as the presidential candidate for the Free-Soil Party under the banner, "Free soil, free speech, free labor, and free men."[21] Even more ominous, the split-off of the Free-Soilers marked the movement of the slavery issue from a moral question to a sectional political issue capable of wrecking even the sturdiest of national institutions.

The Whigs might have suffered the same splintering had it not been clear that the divisions among the Democratic Party were the Whigs' golden opportunity. Rather than risk North-South bickerings within the party, the Whigs nominated Zachary Taylor for the presidency. Taylor's victory at Buena Vista gave him instant name recognition; on the other hand, to the dismay of many anti-slavery Whigs, he was also a Louisiana slaveholder. Still, at least Taylor had taken no known stand on the territorial question. After reflecting upon the wisdom of nominating candidates with no inconvenient political views to disturb the voters, the Whig Party decided to do likewise, and adopted no party platform. By the end of the summer, it was plain that Taylor was going to beat Cass handily.[22]

To nearly everyone's surprise, Zachary Taylor turned out to be no blank slate on the issue of the territories. "No man of ordinary capacity can believe," Taylor wrote, that Congress would allow slavery into the Mexican Cession or "will ever permit a state made from it to enter our Union with the features of slavery connected with it." By the time he was inaugurated in March 1849, the California gold rush was in full swing, and Sacramento, the site of the original gold strike, had exploded from a village of four houses into a boom city with a population of 10,000. In order to provide California and the New Mexico territory with some sense of public order, a bill for territorial organization had to be offered at once, and Taylor dispatched his own personal emissaries to prod the California, Utah, and New Mexico settlers into writing state constitutions that would bypass the need for (and the inevitable wrangling over) territorial organization.

20. Michael F. Holt, *Political Parties and American Political Development from the Age of Jackson to the Age of Lincoln* (Baton Rouge: Louisiana State University Press, 1992), 69.

21. Frederick J. Blue, *The Free Soilers: Third Party Politics, 1848–54* (Urbana: University of Illinois Press, 1973), 296.

22. Michael F. Holt, *The Rise and Fall of the American Whig Party: Jacksonian Politics and the Onset of the Civil War* (New York: Oxford University Press, 1999), 368–70.

Taylor was responding to more than just the practical demands of the California situation. A political novice, Taylor had fallen under the sway of some of the most radical anti-slavery Whigs, especially William Henry Seward of New York, and under their influence Taylor was determined that the California and New Mexico applications would be "free and Whig," even at the risk of more Southern threats of disunion. By December 1849 Taylor had pushed the Californians to the point where they were ready to make an application to Congress for immediate statehood and thus "remove all causes of uneasiness . . . and confidence and kind feeling be preserved." The application would be as a free state.[23]

Southerners read President Taylor's proposal as nothing less than the Wilmot Proviso in disguise, and in June 1850 a convention of representatives from the slave-holding states met in Nashville to discuss what their future could be in the Union. At the same time, Taylor faced a challenge from within his own party in the person of Henry Clay, who still believed, even at age seventy-three and after three unsuccessful nominations, that he would have made a better Whig president than Taylor, the "Military Chieftain."[24]

On January 29, 1850, Clay laid before the Senate a "comprehensive scheme" of eight resolutions that offered to settle the territorial dispute in practical little pieces rather than by sweeping formulas such as "common property" or "popular sovereignty." Clay proposed to admit California as a free state (the California constitutional convention had already adopted free-state provisions and there was nothing gained by trying to force them to change their minds), but in order to show that this established no principle for the other territories, New Mexico and a separate Mexican Cession territory of Deseret (or Utah) would be allowed to organize themselves as territories on the basis of popular sovereignty (which left open the possibility that these territories might become slave states). To sweeten the loss of the "common property" principle for Southerners, Clay added a provision for a new Fugitive Slave Law, which would give slaveholders broader powers to stop the flow of runaway slaves northward to the free states, and he offered a final resolution denying that Congress had any authority to regulate the interstate slave trade.[25]

Clay's two-day presentation of his compromise was a rhetorical masterpiece, but he fell considerably short of winning the votes he needed for it. The partisans of slavery in the Senate regarded the concession of California as tantamount to accepting the principle, if not the fact, of the Wilmot Proviso, while Northern Free-Soilers

23. Holman Hamilton, *Zachary Taylor: Soldier in the White House* (Indianapolis, IN: Bobbs-Merrill, 1951), 45, 142–43, 168–70; K. Jack Bauer, *Zachary Taylor: Soldier, Planter, Statesman of the Old Southwest* (Baton Rouge: Louisiana State University Press, 1985), 291; Michael F. Holt, *The Fate of Their Country: Politicians, Slavery Extension, and the Coming of the Civil War* (New York: Hill and Wang, 2004), 58–61.

24. Remini, *Henry Clay*, 688–90.

25. Holman Hamilton, *Prologue to Conflict: The Crisis and Compromise of 1850* (1964; Lexington: University Press of Kentucky, 2005), 95.

regarded the popular sovereignty allowance for New Mexico and Utah as little more than surrendering the territories outright to slavery. Clay also committed a major tactical error by insisting that all the resolutions be voted upon together as one "omnibus," without recognizing that while all of the senators would like some of the resolutions, only some of the senators would like all of the resolutions, and the senators in that group were not numerous enough to carry the day.

' In particular, Clay's "comprehensive scheme" did not satisfy the mortally ailing John Calhoun. On March 4, 1850, Calhoun had another senator, James M. Mason of Virginia, read a lengthy and shrewd attack on Clay's plan, calling again for "an equal right in the acquired territory . . . to cease the agitation of the slave question, and to provide for the insertion of a provision in the constitution, by an amendment, which will restore to the South, in substance, the power she possessed of protecting herself, before the equilibrium between the section was destroyed by the action of this government." Otherwise, threatened Calhoun, "the Southern States . . . cannot remain, as things now are, consistently with safety and honor, in the Union."[26]

Three days later, Daniel Webster of Massachusetts took the floor of the Senate to deliver what many anticipated would be an equally scathing critique of Clay's omnibus, this time from an anti-slavery position. To the amazement of the packed Senate galleries (and howls of indignation from anti-slavery Northerners), Webster rose "to speak today not as a Massachusetts man, nor as a Northern man, but an American. . . . I speak today for the preservation of the Union. 'Hear me for my cause.'"[27] From there, Webster's great oratory rolled on for three hours, denouncing disunion and calling for the adoption of Clay's omnibus. Webster paid dearly in Massachusetts for befriending Clay, with mutterings about treason and derangement.

Clay and Webster were acting to save a Union that they could easily see was headed for the breakers, and a Union that Calhoun was only too ready to see hit them. Day after exhausting day, Clay dragged himself to the Senate floor to defend his resolutions on the wings of words that soared far above his own personal political ambitions for the presidency. "I conjure gentlemen"—Americans North and South—to stop and "by all they hold dear in this world—by all their love of liberty—by all their veneration for their ancestors—by all their regard for posterity—by all their gratitude to Him who has bestowed upon them such unnumbered blessings . . . to pause—solemnly to pause—at the edge of the precipice, before the fearful and disastrous leap is taken into the yawning abyss below, which will inevitably lead to certain and irretrievable destruction." And if the grappling sections did hurl themselves over the cliff into civil war, Clay's prayer was, "as the best blessing which heaven can bestow upon me upon earth, that if the direful and sad event of the

26. John Calhoun, "The Compromise," March 4, 1850, *Congressional Globe*, 31st Congress, 1st Session, 451, 455.

27. Daniel Webster, "The Compromise," March 7, 1850, *Congressional Globe*, 31st Congress, 1st Session, 476; Irving Bartlett, *Daniel Webster* (New York: W. W. Norton, 1978), 116–21.

dissolution of the Union should happen, I may not survive to behold the sad and heart-rending spectacle."[28]

One person, at least, who was moved by none of this rhetorical display in the Senate was President Taylor, and between the upper and nether millstones of Taylor and the Calhounites, the omnibus was ground to bits. When the Senate Committee on Territories finally reported out Clay's resolutions as a single bill, its component pieces were hacked out by amendments and counterproposals, and on July 31, 1850, all but the provisions for the territorial organization of Utah had crashed to defeat. An enfeebled Henry Clay left the Senate, his political career effectively over, and sick with the tuberculosis that would kill him in less than two years; Webster returned to Massachusetts to be vilified by the anti-slavery press as a "fallen angel," and he followed Clay to the grave four months later; John Calhoun was dead on March 31, 1850, less than three weeks after his last defiant speech in the Senate.

At this last point before the abyss, the enemies of compromise obligingly removed themselves from the scene. The death of Calhoun in March was followed by the unexpected death of President Taylor in July, and his successor, a self-made and surprisingly capable anti-slavery New Yorker named Millard Fillmore, quickly proclaimed his support for Clay's compromise. Clay himself withdrew from the Senate after the July 31 debacle, but into his shoes stepped the junior senator from Illinois, a short, scrappy Democrat named Stephen A. Douglas.

Douglas had been born in Vermont in 1813 and half orphaned by the premature death of his lawyer father two years later. He was apprenticed to a cabinetmaker in upstate New York. At age twenty, looking for opportunities whose traces he could see only as they led westward, Douglas moved to Ohio, then to St. Louis, then to Winchester, Illinois. He set up a school, earned enough money to support a year's law study, and in 1834 was licensed to practice law in Illinois. At a stumpy five feet four inches, Douglas was anything but imposing-looking. But he had energy in overbrimming quantities, and a chip-on-the-shoulder attitude earned him the nickname "the Little Giant." He was a "perfect 'steam engine in breeches,'" and starting in 1840 he was appointed to the Illinois state supreme court, elected to Congress, then elected to the U.S. Senate. He was, from the start, a partisan Democrat. Whigs were nothing but the toadies of "consolidation, monopoly, and property privilege." Douglas was also a man with an eye for the main chance, and he saw in an alliance with Henry Clay a straight path to political stardom.[29]

---

28. "Compromise Resolutions—Speech of Mr. Clay," February 5–6, 1850, in *Congressional Globe*, 31st Congress, 1st Session, Appendix, 127; Remini, *Henry Clay*, 737.

29. William Gardner, *Life of Stephen A. Douglas* (Boston: Roxburgh Press, 1905), 12–13, 14, 15–17, 19–20, 25, 29, 48; Clark E. Carr, *Stephen A. Douglas: His Life, Public Services, Speeches, and Patriotism* (Chicago: A. C. McClurg, 1909), 7; Douglas, "Autobiographical Sketch," in *The Letters of Stephen A. Douglas*, ed. Robert W. Johannsen (Urbana, IL: University of Illinois Press, 1961), 62, 68; Robert W. Johannsen, *Stephen A. Douglas* (New York: Oxford University Press, 1973), 30–31, 56, 68, 87, 97.

Committed from the beginning of the debates to the principle of popular sovereignty, Douglas explained his détente with the figurehead of Whiggism as a
joint project for the sake of the popular sovereignty provisions in the "comprehensive scheme." Popular sovereignty, Douglas explained, is the principle "that each
community shall settle this question for itself . . . and we have no right to complain, either in the North or the South, whichever they do." Since he had never
favored the omnibus approach, Douglas craftily split the omnibus bill into five
separate bills and built separate congressional coalitions around each of them, with
his fellow Democrats cajoled and caressed into supporting them. With President
Taylor out of the way, Fillmore (in an unusual display of bipartisanship) linked
forces with Douglas and pressured congressional Whigs to back the Douglas bills.
By mid-September all five of them had been passed, and the substance of Clay's
compromise—if not the form—became law. "The difference between Mr. Clay's
Compromise Bill & my . . . Bills was a wafer," wrote Douglas before the final
votes, "and when they are all passed, you see, they will be collectively Mr. Clay's
Compromise, & separately the Bills Reported by the committee on Territories four
months ago."[30]

What, exactly, did this great Compromise of 1850 do? In general, it averted a
showdown over who would control the new western territories, and that was the
chief reason people around the country celebrated the passage of the bills with bell
ringing, and in Congress with a drunken spree. In specific terms, the Compromise
of 1850 allowed the Missouri Compromise to stand for the old Louisiana Purchase
territories, but it established the principle of popular sovereignty as the rule for organizing the Mexican Cession. California, of course, was allowed to dodge both
compromises completely and enter the Union directly as a free state without passing
through the debated stage of territorial government. The territory of Utah, which
lay above the 36°30′ line, and New Mexico, which lay below it, would be allowed
to make their own determinations about slavery or nonslavery as they saw fit. The
Compromise also added a new Fugitive Slave Law to the federal code and promised
noninterference by Congress in the interstate slave trade. After the deaths of Calhoun, Clay, and Webster, Douglas would emerge as one of the most powerful men
in the Senate.[31]

The abyss of disunion had been avoided, but only for the time being. In only six
years, a train of unsuspected consequences would throw an entirely new light on the
popular sovereignty doctrine, and both it and the Compromise of 1850 would be
wrecked with the stroke of a single judicial pen.

---

30. Douglas, "Slavery in the Territories," February 12, 1850, *Congressional Globe*, 31st Congress, 1st Session,
343; Robert W. Johannsen, "Stephen A. Douglas, Popular Sovereignty and the Territories," *Historian* 22
(August 1960): 384–85; Douglas to Charles Lanphier, August 3, 1850, in *Letters of Stephen A. Douglas*, 192.

31. Johannsen, *Stephen A. Douglas*, 296–98.

THE FAILURE OF COMPROMISE

The Compromise of 1850 had been created by a Whig (Henry Clay) and pushed through at last by the influence of a Whig president (Millard Fillmore). The laurels for this victory went to Stephen A. Douglas and the Democrats, and the Democrats used the political capital that the Compromise gave them to regain their political wind and win the presidential election of 1852. Both parties ran Mexican War heroes—the Whigs nominated Winfield Scott and the Democrats nominated Franklin Pierce of New Hampshire, who had begun the war as a private and ended up as a brigadier general—but Scott proved dull and aristocratic, while the handsome, likable Pierce stood on a pro-Compromise platform and won election easily.

There was a fly in the ointment of the Compromise of 1850, however. With all the attention in the debates of 1850 focused on the Mexican Cession territories, few people paid attention to the contents of the new Fugitive Slave Law, which Clay had included in the Compromise as a sop to wounded Southern feelings over California and popular sovereignty. There had actually been a Fugitive Slave Law on the federal books since 1793 (based on Article IV, Section 2 of the Constitution) which allowed Southern slaveholders to pursue and retrieve runaway slaves even in the free states. For that reason, until 1842 runaway slaves such as Josiah Henson had found it safer to run until they had made it to Canada and the safety of British law (where slavery was illegal and where the presumption of the law had always been in favor of freedom).

As Northern opinion turned colder and colder toward slavery, the free states offered pursuing slaveholders less and less cooperation, until in 1842 the Supreme Court (in *Prigg v. Pennsylvania*) ruled that the 1793 federal law did not necessarily require the cooperation of state magistrates and justices of the peace, especially where slave recaptures encroached on state due-process laws. The result, of course, was that numerous Northern state officials refused to cooperate at all in capturing runaways, and in some instances prosecuted slaveholders for kidnapping.

The new Fugitive Slave Law was an attempt to plug the holes *Prigg v. Pennsylvania* had put in the 1793 law. A federal enforcement apparatus was created, consisting of United States commissioners with powers to issue federal warrants for fugitive slaves and to make judgments in fugitive cases without a court hearing on the basis of as little as a simple affidavit of ownership from a slave owner (the commissioner was to receive a $10 fee for each fugitive returned to slavery and only $5 otherwise, so it was clear from the start what the preferred judgment would be). Ominously, the new law established no statute of limitations for runaways, which meant that runaways from as long as twenty years before (and more) could be captured and reenslaved. It threatened both local marshals and citizens with fines of up to $1,000 and liability for civil suits if they harbored fugitives or refused to cooperate in capture proceedings.[32]

32. "An Act to Amend, and Supplementary to the Act, Respecting an Act Entitled 'Fugitives from Justice'. . .," 31st Congress, 1st Session, *The Statutes at Large and Treaties of the United States of America, from December 1, 1845 to March 3, 1851*, ed. George Minot (Boston: Little and Brown, 1862), c. 60, 462.

This last provision was the most potentially explosive, for it virtually made every Northerner an accomplice to the betrayal and seizure of runaway slaves. Northerners who had enjoyed little or no contact with slavery, or who thought of slavery as merely an unpleasant moral abstraction, now were forced to consider how they would act if a slave owner or federal marshal in hot pursuit of a runaway should summon them to join a federal slave-catching posse.

Neither Clay nor Douglas had expected the Fugitive Slave Law to attract much controversy, if only because the actual number of runaways was fairly small compared to the entire slave population of the South. They at once learned how badly they had underestimated Northern reaction. Northerners who had never entertained a serious anti-slavery thought before were now treated to a series of public captures and extraditions of runaway slaves that only showed off slavery at its most revolting. Overeager slave owners and hired slave catchers tracked down longtime runaways such as Henry Long, who was haled before a federal judge "as the fugitive slave of John T. Smith, of Russell County, Virginia," and carted off to Richmond, Virginia, to be sold at public auction on January 18, 1851; Euphemia Williams, who had run away from "William T. J. Purnell, of Worcester County, Maryland," twenty-two years before, and whom they tried to drag, along with the six children she had raised in Philadelphia, back into slavery; or "a colored man, named Mitchum," who was arrested in Madison, Indiana, in February 1851 by "George W. Mason, of Davies County, Ky.," who had convinced a local justice of the peace that Mitchum "had left his service *nineteen years before*," and who took him back to Kentucky.[33]

Not all of these pursuits ended well for the slave hunters, however. In September 1851 a Maryland slave owner named Edward Gorsuch crossed into Pennsylvania in pursuit of four runaways. Gorsuch enlisted the aid of a federal marshal and a posse and tracked the runaways to the home of William Parker, a free black, in Christiana, Pennsylvania. There the runaways and their allies shot it out with the posse, killing Gorsuch; Parker and the runaways immediately fled for Canada. Frederick Douglass, then living and editing an anti-slavery newspaper in Rochester, New York, sheltered them and got the fugitives on board a Great Lakes steamer. At parting, one of them gave Douglass a memento that he treasured all his life: Edward Gorsuch's revolver.[34] Across the North, prisons were broken into, posses were disrupted, and juries refused to convict.

The most dramatic of these cases, and the one that added the most fuel to the fire of opposition to the Fugitive Slave Act, occurred in Boston, almost under the nose

33. Samuel May, *The Fugitive Slave Law and Its Victims* (New York: American Anti-Slavery Society, 1861), 12–15.

34. Thomas Slaughter, *Bloody Dawn: The Christiana Riot and Racial Violence in the Antebellum North* (New York: Oxford University Press, 1992), 78.

of Garrison's *Liberator*. On May 24, 1854, an escaped Virginia slave named Anthony Burns was seized by three federal deputies as he walked home from the Boston clothing store where he worked. White and black Bostonians at once assembled, and on the evening of May 26, a party of abolitionists led an assault on the prison where Burns was held, only to fail in their attempts to retrieve him. President Pierce was determined to demonstrate his support for the Compromise laws and sent in federal troops and Marines to ensure that Burns was put on a ship to carry him back to Virginia. Two Bostonians actually offered to pay Burns's market price, and more if necessary, to Burns's owner, an Alexandria merchant named Charles Suttle. The Pierce administration was determined to return Burns to Suttle for the symbolic importance of the gesture. So on June 2, 1854, while thousands of silent, pale Bostonians looked on, Burns was marched to a waiting ship between files of soldiers. The Burns affair was a massive public disgrace, and it drove many Northerners to conclude that slavery itself was a disgrace that deserved extermination rather than assurances. Amos Lawrence, a pro-Compromise Whig, remembered that after the Burns affair, "we went to bed one night old-fashioned, conservative, Compromise Union Whigs & waked up stark mad abolitionists."[35]

Even the anger stirred up by the Fugitive Slave Law was limited to the relatively small number of fugitive slave warrants that were actually issued and the even smaller number of fugitives who were actually returned to slavery (probably around eighty in all).[36] What brought the plight of the runaway under the Fugitive Slave Law into every Northern parlor was a novel, *Uncle Tom's Cabin; or, Life Among the Lowly*, written by Harriet Beecher Stowe, the wife of a theology professor at Bowdoin College in Maine. Stowe was the daughter of Lyman Beecher, a New Englander and one of the best-known Northern evangelicals; her sister, Catharine, was an educator, and her brothers, Edward and Henry Ward Beecher, were both anti-slavery clergymen.

Uncle Tom's Cabin was Stowe's first novel, but it drew on a wealth of observation she had acquired when living in Cincinnati in the 1840s while her husband was a professor at Lane Theological Seminary, and a wealth of reading she had done in slave narratives (including that of Josiah Henson, who turns up in *Uncle Tom's Cabin* as one of the models for Uncle Tom). In 1851 her sister-in-law urged her to "use a pen if you can" to denounce the Fugitive Slave Law and "make this whole nation feel what an accursed thing slavery is." "I will if I live," Stowe announced, and one Sunday shortly thereafter in church, the plot and characters of the novel broke upon her "almost as a tangible vision." The novel poured out of her pen in a matter of

---

35. Richard H. Abbott, *Cotton and Capital: Boston Businessmen and Antislavery Reform, 1854–1868* (Amherst: University of Massachusetts Press, 1991), 26.

36. Larry Gara, *The Liberty Line: The Legend of the Underground Railroad* (Lexington: University of Kentucky Press, 1999), 127–29.

weeks, sentimental and mushy and short on story line, but faultless in its character construction and perfect in its appeal to a sentimental and mushy age.[37]

The plot can be stated briefly: Tom, the faithful slave of the Shelby family, is sold away from his Kentucky home to pay the debts of his guilt-ridden master. He is purchased by a Louisiana planter, the disillusioned Augustine St. Clare, who believes that slavery is wrong but who cannot imagine a way of life without slaves. Tom wins the hearts of the St. Clare household, especially St. Clare's frail daughter, Little Eva. In what may be the most saccharine-laden chapter in American literature, Little Eva dies and the remorseful St. Clare resolves to free his slaves. Before that can happen, St. Clare is stabbed in a brawl, and when he dies, Tom is not freed. Instead, he is sold to Simon Legree, whose unalloyed villainy drives him to murder the hymn-singing Tom just before George Shelby, the son of Tom's old master, arrives to purchase to his freedom. As if this were not enough, Stowe throws in some hair-raising adventure to offset the tackiness of the plot: the escape of the runaway Eliza Harris, who eludes the slave catchers by dashing across the wintry Ohio River, her infant son in her arms, leaping precariously from ice floe to ice floe, and a shootout between Eliza's husband, George Harris, and the slave-catching posse.

The real genius of the book, however, lies in the care with which Stowe made her chief attack on slavery itself rather than merely taking quick shots at slaveholders. Slavery, for Stowe, was a nameless evil that held well-intentioned Southerners such as the Shelbys and St. Clares as much in its grip as any slave. Stowe made her readers hate slavery, and she made them hate the Fugitive Slave Law, too, for her immediate objective was to awaken Northerners to the hideous realities the new law was bringing to their own doorsteps. "His idea of a fugitive," wrote Stowe of one stunned Northern character, John Bird, who finds a half-frozen Eliza Harris in his kitchen,

> was only an idea of the letters that spell the word . . . The magic of the real presence of distress,—the imploring human eye, the frail trembling hand, the despairing appeal of helpless agony,—these he had never tried. He had never thought that a fugitive might be a hapless mother, a defenseless child,—like that one which was now wearing his lost boy's little well-known cap.[38]

Uncle Tom's Cabin began as a serial in the anti-slavery newspaper *National Era* on June 2, 1851, and ran until April 1, 1852. When it was issued in book form, 3,000 of the first 5,000 copies flew from booksellers' stalls on the first day of publication; within

---

37. Joan D. Hedrick, *Harriet Beecher Stowe: A Life* (New York: Oxford University Press, 1995), 193–223; Edmund Wilson, *Patriotic Gore: Studies in the Literature of the American Civil War* (New York: Oxford University Press, 1962), 31–32.

38. Harriet Beecher Stowe, *The Annotated Uncle Tom's Cabin*, ed. Henry Louis Gates (New York: W. W. Norton, 2007), 97.

two weeks it had exhausted two more editions, and within a year it had sold 300,000 copies.[39]

The controversial captures of runaways and the sensational impact of *Uncle Tom's Cabin* made the Fugitive Slave Law into the Achilles' heel of the Compromise of 1850. Northerners who were otherwise content to leave slavery where it was so long as it stayed where it was now found themselves dragooned into cooperation with the South in supporting and maintaining slavery. And as they turned against the Fugitive Slave Law, they began to question the entire Compromise of 1850.

They had good reason, too, especially as the much-vaunted cure-all, popular sovereignty, increasingly came to seem more like a placebo. Initially, the Compromise had allowed the organization of the New Mexico and Utah territories by the popular vote of the people of the territory, which gave some superficial hope that popular sovereignty might be the key of promise; that, in turn, tempted politicians such as Stephen Douglas to talk a little too confidently from both sides of their mouths. Although Douglas personally had little desire to see slavery taken into the territories, popular sovereignty allowed him to tell Southerners that they had no one but themselves or the climate of the territories to blame if slavery failed to take root there; while to Northern audiences Douglas could claim that since New Mexico and Utah were poor candidates for cotton growing and would be unlikely to apply for statehood for another hundred years, popular sovereignty was the safest guarantee that slavery would not be transported to the territories. To both North and South, Douglas could promise that popular sovereignty would ensure a normal and democratic result to the process of territorial organization.

It was this apparent ease with which popular sovereignty promised to charm away all difficulties that led Douglas to carry it one step too far. Eager to open up the trans-Mississippi lands to further settlement (and, incidentally, position Douglas's Illinois as a springboard for a new transcontinental railroad), Douglas and the Senate Committee on Territories (which he chaired) presented a new bill to the Senate on January 4, 1854, which would organize another new territory—Nebraska—on the basis of popular sovereignty, with "all questions pertaining to slavery in the Territories, and in the new states to be formed therefrom . . . to be left to the people residing therein, through their appropriate representatives." (After some brief reflection, Douglas agreed to split the proposed Nebraska Territory into two separate territories, with the southernmost section to be known as the Kansas Territory.)[40]

This proposal dismayed Northern congressional leaders, not only because they remained uneasy about popular sovereignty but also because the proposed Kansas and Nebraska Territories both lay within the old Louisiana Purchase lands and above

---

39. Charles Dudley Warner, "The Story of Uncle Tom's Cabin," *Atlantic Monthly*, September 1896, 315.

40. Stephen A. Douglas, *Speeches of Senator S. A. Douglas, on the Occasion of His Public Receptions by the Citizens of New Orleans, Philadelphia and Baltimore* (Washington, DC: Lemuel Towers, 1859), 5.

the old 36°30' line, in the area the Missouri Compromise had forever reserved for free settlement. The compromisers of 1850 had agreed to use popular sovereignty as the instrument for peacefully organizing the territories acquired in the Mexican Cession; no one had said anything in 1850 about applying the popular sovereignty rule to the Louisiana Purchase territories. The state of Iowa, for example, had been organized as a free territory and admitted as a free state in 1846 precisely because it lay within the Missouri Compromise lands and above 36°30', and there were many in Congress who assumed that Kansas and Nebraska ought to be organized under the same, older rule.

By 1854 popular sovereignty had whetted Southern appetites for more. Douglas knew well that the South would balk at the organization of two more free territories in the area the Missouri Compromise reserved for free settlement. They would balk even more as soon as they realized that if the proposed Kansas and Nebraska Territories were organized on the Missouri Compromise basis as free soil, the slave state of Missouri would be surrounded on three sides by free territory. It would become nearly impossible for Missouri to keep its slave population from easily decamping for freedom, and that would tempt Missouri slaveholders to cut their losses, sell off their slaves, and allow Missouri to become a free state that would block further slave state expansion westward. "If we can't all go there on the string, with all our property of every kind, I say let the Indians have it forever," wrote one Missouri slaveholder. "They are better neighbors than the abolitionists, by a damn sight."[41]

Douglas also knew equally well that Northerners would howl at the prospect of scuttling the Missouri Compromise and opening Kansas and Nebraska to so much as the bare possibility, through popular sovereignty, of slavery. Salmon P. Chase, the anti-slavery Democratic giant of Ohio, tore into Douglas's Kansas-Nebraska bill with "The Appeal of the Independent Democrats" in the *National Era* on January 24, 1854, savagely attacking Douglas and accusing him of subverting the Missouri Compromise in the interest of opening Kansas and Nebraska to slavery. "The thing is a terrible outrage, and the more I look at it the more enraged I become," Maine senator William Pitt Fessenden confessed. "It needs but little to make me an out & out abolitionist." Mass protest meetings were held in Boston's Faneuil Hall, in New York City, and in Detroit, as well as in Lexington, Ohio, and Marlborough, Massachusetts—at least 115 of them across the North—and resolutions attacking the Kansas-Nebraska bill were issued by five Northern state legislatures.[42]

41. Claiborne F. Jackson to David R. Atchison, in Nicole Etcheson, *Bleeding Kansas: Contested Liberty in the Civil War Era* (Lawrence: University Press of Kansas, 2004), 11.

42. Mark E. Neely, "The Kansas-Nebraska Act in American Political Culture: The Road to Bladensburg and the Appeal of the Independent Democrats," in *The Nebraska-Kansas Act of 1854*, ed. J. R. Wunder and J. M. Ross (Lincoln: University Press of Nebraska, 2008), 33–34, 38, 44–45.

Douglas was a gambler, and he was gambling that the song of popular sovereignty would lull enough anti-slavery sensibilities to get the Kansas-Nebraska bill through Congress. He was right. He had the ear of the Pierce administration and the whip handle of the Democratic Party in Congress, and on March 3, 1854, he success-fully bullied the Kansas-Nebraska bill through the Senate. It was a closer call in the House, where Kansas-Nebraska slipped through on a thirteen-vote margin on May 22, but it gave Douglas what he wanted. James M. Mason, who had read the dying Calhoun's demand for an open door into the territories for slavery in 1850, happily prophesied that the Kansas-Nebraska bill "bore the character of peace and tended to the establishment of peace." His fellow senator from Ohio, Benjamin Franklin Wade, could not have disagreed more. Instead, declared the acid-tongued Wade, the Kansas-Nebraska bill was "a declaration of war on the institutions of the North, a deliberate sectional movement by the South for political power, without regard for justice or consequences." As the Senate cranked ponderously toward its vote, Wade pointed to a portent of gloom: "Tomorrow, I believe, there is to be an eclipse of the sun." How appropriate that "the sun in the heavens and the glory of this republic should both go into obscurity and darkness together."[43]

True to the omen of the eclipse, it was at this point that the entire doctrine of popular sovereignty began to come unraveled.

When Stephen Douglas spoke of popular sovereignty, it was clear that he im-agined a peaceful territory filling up gradually with contented white settlers (and evicting, if necessary, any contented Indian inhabitants); eventually there would be enough white settlers on hand to justify an application for statehood and the writing of a state constitution. "The true intent and meaning of this act [is] not to legislate slavery into any territory or state, nor to exclude it therefrom, but to leave the peo-ple thereof perfectly free to form and regulate their domestic institutions in their own way." Beyond that, no one—especially not in Washington—had any business second-guessing the popular will. If a territory, declared Douglas, "wants a slave-State constitution she has a right to it . . . I do not care whether it is voted down or voted up."[44]

It seems never to have occurred to Douglas before Kansas-Nebraska that popular sovereignty might also mean that if a majority of anti-slavery settlers could camp in Kansas or Nebraska before any equal numbers of slaveholding settlers (or vice versa), that simple majority would determine the slave or free status of the territory and its

43. Fessenden, in Robert J. Cook, *Civil War Senator: William Pitt Fessenden and the Fight to Save the American Republic* (Baton Rouge: Louisiana State University Press, 2011), 86; "The Kansas and Nebraska Bill—Debate," March 2 and 3, 1854, *Congressional Globe*, 33rd Congress, 1st session, Appendix, 299, 763–65.

44. "Kansas and Nebraska Act of 1854," *The Whig Almanac and United States Register for 1855* (New York: Greeley and McElrath, 1855), 18; James A. Rawley, *Race and Politics: "Bleeding Kansas" and the Coming of the Civil War* (Philadelphia: Lippincott, 1969), 17–57; Douglas, "Kansas-Lecompton Constitution," March 22, 1858, *Congressional Globe*, 35th Congress, 1st Session, Appendix, 195, 200.

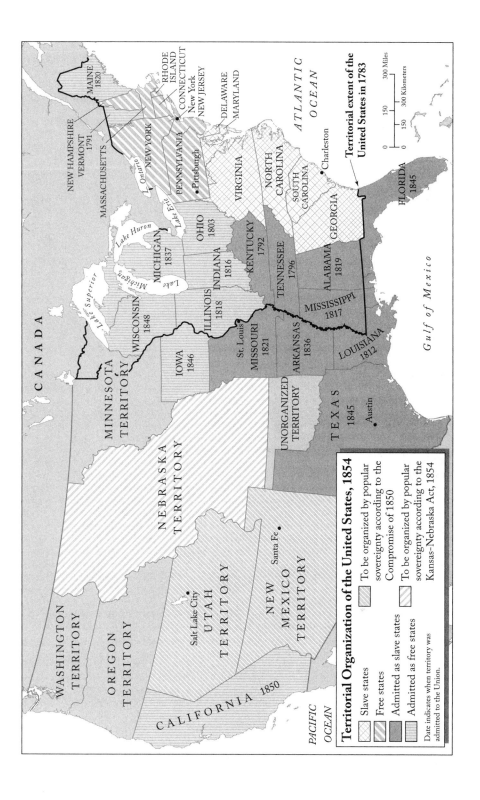

Territorial Organization of the United States, 1854

Slave states

Free states

To be organized by popular sovereignty according to the Compromise of 1850

Admitted as slave states

To be organized by popular sovereignty according to the Kansas–Nebraska Act, 1854

Admitted as free states

Date indicates when territory was admitted to the Union.

Territorial extent of the United States in 1783

300 Miles
300 Kilometers
0   150
0   150

CANADA

PACIFIC OCEAN

WASHINGTON TERRITORY

OREGON TERRITORY

CALIFORNIA 1850

UTAH TERRITORY

Salt Lake City

NEW MEXICO TERRITORY

Santa Fe

NEBRASKA TERRITORY

MINNESOTA TERRITORY

IOWA 1846

WISCONSIN 1848

MICHIGAN 1837

ILLINOIS 1818

INDIANA 1816

OHIO 1803

UNORGANIZED TERRITORY

MISSOURI 1821

St. Louis

ARKANSAS 1836

T E X A S 1845

Austin

LOUISIANA 1812

MISSISSIPPI 1817

ALABAMA 1819

TENNESSEE 1796

KENTUCKY 1792

GEORGIA

FLORIDA 1845

SOUTH CAROLINA

NORTH CAROLINA

VIRGINIA

Charleston

Pittsburgh

PENNSYLVANIA

NEW YORK

MARYLAND

DELAWARE

New Jersey

CONNECTICUT

RHODE ISLAND

MASSACHUSETTS

VERMONT 1791

NEW HAMPSHIRE

MAINE 1820

Lake Superior

Lake Michigan

Lake Huron

Lake Erie

L. Ontario

ATLANTIC OCEAN

Gulf of Mexico

future status as a state. Douglas also ignored the possibility that there might be other ways, not necessarily gradual and painless, of achieving majorities.

This, of course, is precisely what happened in the new Kansas Territory. Anti-slavery New Englanders organized a New England Emigrant Aid Society in the summer of 1854 to send trains of armed anti-slavery Northerners to Kansas; in Missouri, bands of armed pro-slavery whites crossed over the border into Kansas to claim it for slavery. In the process, both sides learned yet another way of creating majorities, namely, by killing off one's opponents, and so a fiery sparkle of violent clashes and raids between pro-slavery and anti-slavery emigrants danced along the creeks and rivers of the new territory. And by the time a territorial governor, Andrew Reeder, had been dispatched by Congress to supervise a preliminary territorial election, the Missourians had developed yet another variation on popular sovereignty— sending "border ruffians" over into Kansas on voting days to cast illegal ballots.[45]

The situation only grew worse in the spring of 1855, when Governor Reeder called for elections to create a territorial legislature for Kansas. The "border ruffians" crossed over in droves to vote for pro-slavery candidates for the legislature, and when the balloting was over and some 5,400 votes for pro-slavery candidates had materialized from the 3,000 eligible white male voters of the Kansas Territory, it was clear that the election had been stolen. The beleaguered Governor Reeder was too intimidated by the "border ruffian" gangs to invalidate the election, and the new legislature, ignoring Reeder's vetoes, enacted a territorial slave code so severe that even verbal disagreement with slavery was classified as a felony. President Pierce, still staked to popular sovereignty, refused to take any action.[46]

The angered free-soil settlers at once feared for the worst from their new legislature, and so they armed and fortified the free-soil town of Lawrence. They also organized a rival anti-slavery legislature and wrote a free-state constitution. In May 1856 the reckless and arrogant pro-slavery legislature responded by equipping a small pro-slavery army that sacked and burned Lawrence. "Gentlemen," boasted one of the pro-slavery leaders, "this is the happiest day of my life. I determined to make the fanatics bow before me in the dust . . . and I have done it—by God, I have done it."[47] Overall, two hundred people were killed in clashes between pro-slavery and anti-slavery factions in Kansas before President Pierce finally sent in John White Geary, a former army officer, as territorial governor. A more skilful arbitrator than Reeder, Geary was at last able to bring a measure of peace to what had become known to the rest of the country as "Bleeding Kansas."[48]

45. Kristen Tegtmeier Oertel, *Bleeding Borders: Race, Gender, and Violence in Pre–Civil War Kansas* (Baton Rouge: Louisiana State University Press, 2009), 91.

46. David Potter, *The Impending Crisis, 1848–1861* (New York: Harper and Row, 1976), 203–4.

47. Thomas Goodrich, *War to the Knife: Bleeding Kansas, 1854–1861* (Lincoln: University Press of Nebraska, 2004), 117.

48. Gara, *The Liberty Line*, 127–29.

What happened in Kansas was disturbing evidence that Douglas's fix-it of popular sovereignty was no help whatsoever in sorting out the complex problem of allowing the expansion of slavery into the territories. Far from bringing peace, popular sovereignty in Kansas had only brought Americans two of the most spectacular scenes of violence they had ever witnessed outside of outright war. One of them occurred in Kansas itself. A Connecticut-born abolitionist named John Brown, a man with the selfless benevolence of the evangelicals wrought into a fiery determination to crush slavery, became convinced from the reports he had heard that five anti-slavery men had died in the sack of Lawrence. Brown had moved to Kansas only in 1855, but already he had been elected captain of a free-state militia company. Seeking an eye for an eye after the sack of Lawrence, Brown, with four of his sons and two neighbors, went on a murderous rampage along Pottawatomie Creek on May 24, 1856. They dragged five pro-slavery farmers from their beds and from the arms of their wives and deliberately hacked them to death with old surplus artillery broadswords that Brown had thoughtfully bought up and brought from Ohio. "God is my judge," Brown explained with an eerie self-assurance. "It was absolutely necessary as a measure of self-defence, and for the defence of others."[49]

The second event happened almost at the same time as Brown's raid, but it took place on the floor of the United States Senate. On May 19, 1856, the anti-slavery senator from Massachusetts, Charles Sumner, rose and delivered what turned out to be a two-day diatribe: "The Crime Against Kansas." The principal burden of Sumner's complaint was directed at the attack on Lawrence, Kansas, which he portrayed in the most livid terms as the anteroom to civil war. The attack on Lawrence amounted to "the rape of a virgin Territory, compelling it to the hateful embrace of Slavery; and it may be clearly traced to a depraved longing for a new slave State, the hideous offspring of such a crime, in the hope of adding to the power of Slavery in the National Government." The ultimate meaning of the "rape" of Lawrence was the evidence it afforded that "the horrors of intestine feud" were being planned "not only in this distant Territory, but everywhere throughout the country. Already the muster has begun. The strife is no longer local, but national. Even now, while I speak, portents hang on all the arches of the horizon, threatening to darken the broad land, which already yawns with, the mutterings of civil war."[50]

This was far from the first time the elegant but pompous Sumner had thrown rhetorical caution to the winds in attacking slavery. The Southern poet William Grayson lampooned Sumner in Augustan couplets as the "supple Sumner, with the Negro cause," playing "the sly game for office and applause."

49. Evan Carton, *Patriotic Treason: John Brown and the Soul of America* (New York: Free Press, 2006), 189–93; David S. Reynolds, *John Brown, Abolitionist: The Man Who Killed Slavery, Sparked the Civil War, and Seeded Civil Rights* (New York: Knopf, 2005), 174.

50. Sumner, *The Crime Against Kansas . . . Speech of the Hon. Charles Sumner in the Senate of the United States, 19th and 20th May, 1856* (Boston: J. P. Jewett, 1856), 5–7.

What though he blast the fortunes of the state
With fierce dissension and enduring hate?
He makes the speech, his rhetoric displays,
Trims the neat trope, and points the sparkling phrase
With well-turned period, fosters civil strife,
And barters for a phrase a nation's life.[51]

But "The Crime Against Kansas" had been prepared by Sumner with unusually knife-edged care, and in the body of his speech, Sumner took time to unleash some particularly nasty personal insults at a number of Southern senators, including Andrew Butler of South Carolina. Butler, Sumner declared in some of the most virulently personal language used on the Senate floor, "has chosen a mistress to whom he has made his vows, and who, though ugly to others, is always lovely to him; though polluted in the sight of the world, is chaste in his sight . . . the harlot, Slavery." Butler was full of "incoherent phrases, discharged from the loose expectoration of his speech . . . He cannot open his mouth, but out there flies a blunder"—which was a particularly cruel play on the mild stroke that had affected Butler's speech.

Two days after Sumner finished his speech, South Carolina representative Preston Brooks, a relative of Butler's, entered the almost empty Senate chamber and found Sumner alone at his desk, franking copies of the speech for free distribution by mail. "Mr. Sumner, I have heard your speech with care and as much impartiality as was possible," Brooks said, "and I feel it my duty to tell you that you have libeled my State and slandered a relative who is aged and absent and I am come to punish you for it." Brooks then raised a gold-headed gutta-percha cane he had carried for precisely this purpose and began beating Sumner over the head, giving him "about 30 first rate stripes." Sumner, pinned into place by his desk, sank under the rain of blows until Brooks's cane broke and Brooks could only hit him with the butt end of it.

Sumner tore himself free and was rescued by New York congressman Edwin B. Morgan, but his injuries would keep him out of political life for three years. This act of wanton violence on the floor of Congress appalled the Northern states fully as much as Brown's Raid appalled the South with its equally wanton barbarism. The House of Representatives opened an inquiry into the assault, but in the end Brooks paid only a $300 fine.[52]

Both incidents were testimony to the fact that popular sovereignty, the great guarantee of the Compromise of 1850, would breed only violence, not peace. Assuming that the passage of six years had made neither the Wilmot Proviso nor Calhoun's

51. Grayson, in O'Brien, *Conjectures of Order*, 2:733.

52. Sumner, *The Crime Against Kansas*, 9; David Donald, *Charles Sumner and the Coming of the Civil War* (New York: Knopf, 1961), 285–86; Williamjames Hull Hoffer, *The Caning of Charles Sumner: Honor, Idealism, and the Origins of the Civil War* (Baltimore: Johns Hopkins University Press, 2010), 8–9, 58, 72–73, 83–84.

"common property" doctrine any more appealing than they had been in 1850 as a way of dealing with the extension of slavery in the territories, the last possible option in Congress might be a return to some form of the Missouri Compromise.

Congress was not to have any further say in the matter.

DRED SCOTT AND THE SLAVE POWER

Kansas was a double misfortune for Stephen Douglas. The Little Giant believed with all his heart that popular sovereignty was the golden key that locked up the peaceful settlement of the territories, and he had made promises to both North and South about the settlement that Kansas had shown he could not keep. Now Northerners distrusted him as the man who had carelessly torn down the old safeguard of the Missouri Compromise and allowed slavery into Kansas, and Southerners mistrusted him because the uncertainty over Kansas's future was preventing Kansas from entering the ranks of the slave states.

Douglas's reputation suffered less in the wake of Bleeding Kansas than did the reputations of the two national political parties. The Whigs had gone into the election of 1852 in poor shape to begin with. Both of their most recent presidents, Harrison and Taylor, had died in office, and in 1852 their two greatest standard-bearers, Clay and Webster, died as well. For some of the Southern Whigs, of course, those deaths could not have come sooner. Southern Whigs were especially bitter over Taylor, a slave owner and Southerner who had betrayed both slave owners and Southerners by advocating the free-state admission of California and New Mexico. So even though the Whigs still had a sitting president in 1852 in the person of Millard Fillmore, the Southern Whigs refused to allow Fillmore's nomination and held the Whig presidential convention hostage over the course of fifty-two ballots until a Virginian, Winfield Scott, was nominated. But Scott balked at wholeheartedly endorsing the Compromise, and the Southern Whigs promptly deserted. Scott carried only two of the slave states (Kentucky and Tennessee) in the 1852 election; Whig representation in the House of Representatives slipped mutely down to less than a third.[53]

The controversy over Kansas-Nebraska finished off what little fellow feeling remained between Northern and Southern Whigs, and most of the Northern Whigs wandered off to experiment with a series of short-lived anti-Nebraska "fusion" coalitions or bitter-end anti-immigrant hate groups such as the American Party (or "Know-Nothings," a name they earned from their pledge to respond, when questioned about their political loyalties, "I know nothing"). Although some of the most prominent Whigs, such as William Henry Seward of New York, openly spurned the Know-Nothings and curried the political favor of the immigrant population,

---

53. Holt, *Rise and Fall of the American Whig Party*, 754.

other Whigs found the Know-Nothing hatred for foreigners and immigrants a perfectly congenial match to their own brand of nationalism. "Every intelligent man knows full well that our country has suffered much from the too-great indulgence of foreigners, ignorant of our institutions & that their power for evil ought to be abridged," grumbled the Ohio Whig senator "Bluff Ben" Wade.

The Know-Nothings were poorly organized to function as a national political party, and their opinions were fatally divided over the slavery issue. Eventually both nativist Whigs and anti-slavery Know-Nothings would be compelled to find their way to a new free-soil party where Know-Nothing nativism could be tempered by the more moderate strains of Whig nationalism and both absorbed into the more volatile issue of slavery. It did not take long for such a new party to emerge. In May 1854 a group of thirty Northern ex-Whig and anti-Nebraska Democratic congressmen met in Washington to issue a call for a new party that would unite all the "fusion" and anti-Nebraska groups, and in July a state convention in Jackson, Michigan, nominated the first slate of candidates to run under the banner of the new Republican Party.[54]

The core of the new party was the remnants of what had once been the mainstream Northern Whigs—Seward of New York, Charles Sumner and Henry Wilson of Massachusetts, Zachariah Chandler of Michigan. Like the old Whigs, the new Republicans saw themselves as the party of an enterprising white middle class whose prosperity depended on keeping the American economy dynamic and market-oriented. "The interests of the country and its wealth are wrapped up in property in a very great degree," said William Pitt Fessenden, who quietly parted from the Whigs for the Republicans in 1856. It was simply a matter of the common good that "men should be incited in every way to accumulate,"

> because as much as they accumulate by their industry they add to the national wealth . . . and the prosperity of our country in a very great part is owing to the fact that our institutions leave the path of wealth, as of honor, open to all men, and encourage all men, whatever may be their situations in life, however they may start, to better their condition and to accumulate wealth, because the more they accumulate it the more the nation has of wealth.[55]

They resented the overly mighty power of Southern planters and Southern Democrats in Washington, believing that Democratic opposition to banks, tariffs, and "internal improvements" was little more than a strategy to starve Northern industry. They also opposed Southern plans to expand slavery into the western territories

54. William E. Gienapp, *The Origins of the Republican Party, 1852–1856* (New York: Oxford University Press, 1987), 194, 265–71.

55. William Pitt Fessenden, "Internal Revenue," May 28, 1864, in *Congressional Globe*, 38th Congress, 1st session, 2513.

because the plantation system would discourage small-scale entrepreneurs and commercial farmers from taking the risks of competition with slave agriculture. They
also had one more fear: should the territories be closed off to free settlement, the
"mechanics" who tended Northern factories would clog Northern cities and become
a permanent—and dangerous—urban underclass who owned no property of their
own and who had no real hope of access to it. So, in addition to the old project of
Henry Clay's "American System," Republicans proposed to head off the problem of
working-class poverty and the class conflict Leonidas Spratt had prophesied in 1855
by selling off public lands in the territories as homesteads at cheap prices, so that
even the poorest urban worker could, after diligent working and saving, hope to
find new life and new economic opportunity beyond the Mississippi. Governmental
power would thus come to the rescue of liberty.[56]

This, of course, is what frightened the Republicans about Kansas-Nebraska.
Mobility, development, and economic self-transformation were entirely absent from
the slave South, they argued; slaves had no real liberty to become anything other
than a slave, and the great slave moguls used the bogeyman of race and the provision
of cheap, nontaxed imports to buy off the potential resentments of nonslaveholding
whites and keep them in a state of permanent dependence. Now Douglas and the
Democrats seemed bent upon using popular sovereignty as a cheap trick to open the
territories to slavery and turn off the safety valve of opportunity that would eliminate
conflict in Northern industry. For the Republicans, slavery was no longer an economic system but a deadly conspiracy, a conscious "Slave Power" that had possessed
the soul of the Democratic Party and was determined to seize the territories and
turn them into nurseries for slavery.[57]

The Republicans were not the first to accuse the South of hatching a "Slave
Power" conspiracy. Salmon Chase claimed in 1854 that the entire Kansas-Nebraska
bill was "part and parcel of an atrocious plot" to create in the territories "a dreary
region of despotism, inhabited by masters and slaves." No one made better use of the
accusation than the Republicans, and in short order the Republicans attracted Chase
and the most anti-slavery of the Northern Democrats to their banner. Whatever
the ethnic and cultural baggage carried into the new party from the nativists among
the old Whigs or from the various cranky "fusion" and Know-Nothing groups who
lined up behind the Republicans, it was clearly dwarfed by the central position that
economic opposition to slavery and the extension of slavery into the territories came
to have for the Republicans.

The great danger in this was that by the mid-1850s, an anti-slavery party was
most likely to be an almost entirely Northern party, devoted to expressing Northern

---

56. Eric Foner, *Free Soil, Free Labor, Free Men: The Ideology of the Republican Party Before the Civil War*
(New York: Oxford University Press, 1970), 15–19.

57. Richards, *The Slave Power*, 4.

opinions and representing Northern interests. The Whigs had at least been a national party that labored to reduce sectional strife by inducing its Northern and Southern members to cooperate and compromise in the service of larger national goals. But the time for compromises between Northerners and Southerners was fast slipping away, and the Republicans had as their goal the abolition of an institution that Southerners regarded as non-negotiable. And with the death of the Whigs, one of the principal means for binding the sections of the fragile Union disappeared.

The same fate nearly overtook the Democrats. President Pierce, who had supported Kansas-Nebraska, was denounced with Douglas as a traitor by the Northern Democrats and as halfhearted by the Southern Democrats, and Democratic candidates who pledged to support their party's president were mowed down in the congressional elections in 1854. Of the ninety-one seats held by Democrats in the House of Representatives in 1854, sixty-six of them were lost in the fall congressional elections that year; only seven of the Democrats who had voted for Kansas-Nebraska survived in office.[58] When the Democratic presidential convention met in Cincinnati in 1856, the fearful Democrats jettisoned Pierce *and* rejected Douglas as their presidential candidate, and on the eighteenth ballot they nominated a Pennsylvania Democrat, James Buchanan.

Buchanan was a veteran Democratic politician who had long coveted a presidential nomination. In 1856 his chief political merit lay in the fact that he had been out of the country as American minister to Great Britain during the Kansas-Nebraska debates and so had avoided taking any side publicly. Buchanan was also a Northerner (to reassure the Northern Democrats), but one with many friends in the South (to reassure the Southern Democrats). So by nominating a party machine man who had no well-known opinions on the crying issues of the moment, the Democrats managed to avoid a North-South split.

With the old Whig Party in shambles and the Republican Party still only two years old, Buchanan's victory in the 1856 election was a foregone conclusion for most observers. Even under those circumstances, the Republicans pulled off what struck pro-slavery people as an alarmingly good show at the polls. Nominating a celebrity explorer, John Charles Frémont, for president, the Republicans scooped up a third of the nation's votes, virtually all of them from the North, where voters turned out in record numbers.[59] As many Southerners quickly realized, had the anti-slavery Northern Democrats not been mollified by Buchanan's nomination, they might have bolted to the Republicans and handed them the election on the first try, just on the strength of Northern votes alone. The next time around, the Democrats might not be so fortunate.

The political parties were not the only national institutions cracking under the strain of sectional controversy. The Protestant churches, which had for many years

58. Holt, *Fate of Their County*, 109.

59. Gienapp, *Origins of the Republican Party*, 414.

been yet another source of union within the Union, were also splitting under the stress of Southern threats and demands for assurance. Part of the strain was caused by the South's unceasing search for arguments in defense of slavery. Once slavery was being defended as a "positive good," it was only a matter of time before Southerners appealed to the Bible to show that it was a moral good as well, and had divine approval. "We assert that *the Bible teaches that the relation of master and slave is perfectly lawful and right*," declared the Presbyterian Robert Lewis Dabney; from a litany of Old Testament and New Testament examples, from Abraham to St. Paul, Dabney concluded that slavery "was appointed by God as the punishment of, and remedy for . . . the peculiar moral degradation of a part of the [human] race."[60]

When Southern divines offered these arguments, Northern evangelicals were quick to correct them, at first patiently and then angrily, as Southerners responded with accusations of apostasy and unbelief. By 1850, the year of the Compromise, one Southern Presbyterian's temper had frayed to the point where he denounced his Northern counterparts in terms fit for the Devil: "The parties in this conflict are not merely Abolitionists and Slaveholders; they are Atheists, Socialists, Communists, Red Republicans, Jacobins on the one side, and the friends of order and regulated freedom on the other."

On that other side, the greatest of the American Presbyterian theologians, Charles Hodge of Princeton Theological Seminary, at first condemned the abolitionists as troublemakers in the 1830s but then turned to accuse the South of the troublemaking; he joined the Republicans in 1856 and voted for Frémont.[61] With antagonisms of this order dividing the theologians, it was only a little time before they divided the churches as well. The Methodists split into Northern and Southern branches in 1844; in 1845 the Baptists also split; and in 1857 the Southern presbyteries of the Presbyterian Church simply walked out of the Presbyterian General Assembly, taking with them some 15,000 Southern members. These church splits were significant not only because they helped destroy vital national institutions and turn them into sectional ones but also because (as John Calhoun happily pointed out in his last speech) they demonstrated that secession could occur. The church separations provided an illusory guarantee to Southerners that, if matters warranted, secession from the Union was an easy, profitable, and moral way of putting an end to the strife over slavery.[62]

Stephen A. Douglas, however, was unconvinced that matters ever needed to come to that point. Douglas had managed to survive much of the wreckage

60. Dabney, *A Defense of Virginia, and Through Her, of the South* (Harrisonburg, VA: Sprinkle, 1977 [1867]), 103.

61. James Henley Thornwell, "The Christian Doctrine of Slavery," in *The Collected Writings of James Henley Thornwell* (Edinburgh: Banner of Truth, 1974 [1875]), 4:405–6; Archibald Alexander Hodge, *The Life of Charles Hodge* (New York: C. Scribner's Sons, 1880), 463.

62. Clarence C. Goen, *Broken Churches, Broken Nation: Denominational Schisms and the Coming of the Civil War* (Macon, GA: Mercer University Press, 1985), 113–27.

that his policies had caused, and although he once remarked that he could have traveled from Massachusetts to Illinois by the light of fires kindled to burn him in effigy, once he was back in Illinois he was able to rebuild his strength and his credibility. Swinging back at his critics, Douglas claimed that popular sovereignty would fail only where the ill will of abolitionists and radicals in both North and South made it fail.[63]

Douglas never doubted that popular sovereignty was the best method for opening the western territories, and he was confident that the soil and climate of Kansas and Nebraska would prove so hostile to slavery that the popular decision of the people of those territories would surely lean toward creating free states. Since that would be a free and open decision by the people of the territories, the Southern radicals would be deprived of any reason for complaint and for further rounds of demands and assurances. If only the agitation of the abolitionists in particular would cease, popular sovereignty could assert its strength and lay to rest the strife of North and South over slavery in the territories.

In Illinois, Douglas was speaking to an audience strongly inclined to agree with him. Illinois was part of the old Northwest, filled both with German immigrants who hated the South for trying to bring black slaves into territories that *they* desired and with Southern migrants who hated the abolitionists because they feared that emancipation of the slaves would loose free blacks into the territories; both groups feared that the result would be the closing off of the territories to free white labor. Douglas played to the fears of the small farmers and the immigrants, held up popular sovereignty as the only safe method for keeping slavery (and blacks in general) out of the territories, and blamed the uproar over the Kansas-Nebraska bill on the agitators. By October 1854 Douglas had won back the home-state loyalty he had nearly forfeited in ramming Kansas-Nebraska through Congress, and on October 3 he even used the state fair at Springfield, Illinois, as a stage for preaching the gospel of popular sovereignty and Kansas-Nebraska.

One voice was raised in dissent. A Springfield lawyer, a former member of Congress and longtime Whig named Abraham Lincoln, took up Douglas's defense of Kansas-Nebraska at the Illinois statehouse in Springfield the day after Douglas spoke at the state fair. In the course of a three-hour speech, Lincoln proceeded to tear Kansas-Nebraska and popular sovereignty to shreds. Was popular sovereignty really the most peaceful and effective method for settling the territories? Then why hadn't the Founding Fathers in 1787 thought of that when they organized the territories in the Northwest? Instead, the Northwest had been declared free territory, and the states of the Northwest did not appear to have suffered for it. "No States in the world have ever advanced as rapidly in population, wealth, the arts and appliances of life . . . as the very States that were born under the ordinance of

63. Johannsen, *Stephen A. Douglas*, 451.

'87, and were deprived of the blessings of 'popular sovereignty,' as contained in the Nebraska bill, and without which the people of Kansas and Nebraska cannot get along at all."[64]

Lincoln then pinned Douglas on the question of whether popular sovereignty was really going to keep the territories free. "It is vain," argued Lincoln, to claim that popular sovereignty "gives no sanction or encouragement to slavery." If he had a field, Lincoln shrewdly remarked, "around which the cattle or the hogs linger and crave to pass the fence, and I go and tear down the fence, will it be supposed that I do not by that act encourage them to enter?" Just so with Kansas-Nebraska: the Missouri Compromise had been the fence that kept slavery out of most of the old Louisiana Purchase, but now came Douglas, tearing down the fence in the name of popular sovereignty and expecting people to believe that slavery would not make every possible effort, climate or not, to camp there. *Even the hogs would know better,"* Lincoln sneered.

Most of all, Lincoln condemned popular sovereignty because it tried to dodge the moral issue of slavery. Douglas hoped to pacify Southern anxieties by showing how popular sovereignty gave slavery at least the appearance of a "fair chance" in the territories, and to allay Northern suspicions by pointing to how popular sovereignty was the ultimate expression of liberty. Lincoln did not believe that slavery ever deserved to have a "fair chance," and even if all the voters of a territory unanimously demanded it, their demanding it did not make it morally right. Liberty was not an end in itself, as popular sovereignty seemed to claim; it was a means, and it was intended to serve the interests of the natural rights that Jefferson had identified in the Declaration of Independence—life, liberty, the pursuit of happiness. Otherwise, liberty would itself be transformed into power, the power of a mob to do whatever it took a fancy to. It was, Lincoln declared, "a descending from the high republican faith of our ancestors" to have the United States government adopt as its territorial policy that nothing should be said or done to inhibit the "free" choice of slavery, "that both are equal with us—that we yield our territories as readily to one as the other!"[65] This was not the last time Stephen A. Douglas would hear from the tall Springfield lawyer, and those three themes—the power of Congress over the territories, the incapacity of popular sovereignty to keep slavery from any territory, and the moral injustice of slavery itself—would be Lincoln's constant hammers at Douglas's position in Illinois for the next four years.

For the moment, however, Douglas and popular sovereignty faced a more serious challenge than Lincoln, and it came in the form of the United States Supreme Court. In 1834 a United States Army assistant surgeon named John Emerson was

---

64. Goen, *Broken Churches, Broken Nation*, 113–27.

65. Lincoln, "Speech at Springfield, Illinois," October 4, 1854, in *Collected Works of Abraham Lincoln*, ed. Roy F. Basler (New Brunswick, NJ: Rutgers University Press, 1953), 2:240–47.

transferred from the Jefferson Barracks in St. Louis, Missouri, to Fort Armstrong in Illinois, where he also bought land, and with him he brought his slave Dred Scott. Two years later Emerson was transferred again to Fort Snelling, a frontier army post in what was then still the Wisconsin Territory, and once again he brought Scott with him. In both cases, Emerson had paid little attention to the details of Illinois's free-state statutes and transit laws, and even less to the Missouri Compromise (since Fort Snelling was located in a federal territory that had been part of the Louisiana Purchase). In 1840 Emerson was transferred again to Florida, and in 1842 he left the army and returned to St. Louis. The next year Emerson died, and in his will, Dred Scott and his wife and children passed into the hands of Emerson's wife, Eliza Sanford Emerson.[66]

It was at this point that Dred Scott and his family made a bid for freedom, not by running away but by filing suit against Eliza Emerson on April 6, 1846, for wrongful imprisonment, on the grounds that their residence in a state and a territory that forbade slavery had made them free. This was not an unusual suit, and the St. Louis county circuit court that heard the case in 1850 ordered Dred Scott and his family freed. Eliza Emerson then appealed to the Missouri Supreme Court, and on March 22, 1852, the Missouri high court truculently reversed the circuit ruling on the grounds that Scott was now a resident of Missouri, and Missouri was not necessarily bound to recognize the anti-slavery statutes of other states or territories.

In the meantime, Eliza Emerson remarried and moved to New York, and she transferred effective ownership of the Scotts to her brother, John Sanford, of St. Louis. Scott now filed a new suit, against Sanford, in the federal circuit court, arguing that his rights as a citizen had been violated: once on free territory, Scott claimed, he was a free man, a citizen entitled to all the privileges and immunities of citizenship specified in the Fifth Amendment to the Constitution. The Constitution was curiously vague on what actually constituted citizenship, but the federal circuit court eventually ruled against Scott in a jury trial in May 1854. Scott and his attorneys now appealed to the Supreme Court of the United States, which began hearing *Scott v. Sanford* in February 1856.[67]

The decision was handed down on March 6, 1857, two days after James Buchanan was inaugurated as the fifteenth president, and it rocked the country. First, Chief Justice Roger Brooke Taney, writing for a seven-to-two majority, denied that Scott had the privilege of appealing to the Supreme Court, on the grounds that Scott was not only a slave but also of African descent. Taney argued that on both counts, Scott could not be legally considered a citizen of the United States.

66. Don E. Fehrenbacher, *The Dred Scott Case: Its Significance in American Law and Politics* (New York: Oxford University Press, 1978), 239–49.

67. A court clerk misspelled John Sanford's name as *Sandford*, and so the case appears as *Scott v. Sandford* in the court reports.

The question is simply this: Can a negro, whose ancestors were imported into this country, and sold as slaves, become a member of the political community formed and brought into existence by the Constitution of the United States, and as such become entitled to all the rights, and privileges, and immunities, guarantied by that instrument to the citizen? . . . It is absolutely certain that the African race were not included under the name of citizens of a State . . . and that they are not included, and were not intended to be included, under the word "citizens" in the Constitution, and can therefore claim none of the rights and privileges which that instrument provides for and secures to citizens of the United States. On the contrary, they were at that time considered as a subordinate and inferior class of beings, who had been subjugated by the dominant race, and, whether emancipated or not, yet remained subject to their authority, and had no rights or privileges but such as those who held the power and the Government might choose to grant them.

The government did not choose to grant them much:

They had for more than a century before been regarded as beings of an inferior order, and altogether unfit to associate with the white race, either in social or political relations; and so far inferior, that they had no rights which the white man was bound to respect; and that the negro might justly and lawfully be reduced to slavery for his benefit. He was bought and sold, and treated as an ordinary article of merchandise and traffic, whenever a profit could be made by it. This opinion was at that time fixed and universal in the civilized portion of the white race. It was regarded as an axiom in morals as well as in politics, which no one thought of disputing, or supposed to be open to dispute; and men in every grade and position in society daily and habitually acted upon it in their private pursuits, as well as in matters of public concern, without doubting for a moment the correctness of this opinion.[68]

This rendered all questions about transit laws and the Missouri Compromise moot, and reduced the only real question in *Dred Scott* to a matter of Scott's race. Even if Scott's master had violated free-state laws by taking Scott into free territory, Scott himself had no legal standing as a citizen before the federal courts, and the federal courts had no reason to listen to his suit, justified or not.

Taney's argument from race caused only one part of the sensation; after all, Taney's notions about Scott's "inferior" race were not much different from what most white Americans and even many abolitionists believed (they merely differed as to whether that was sufficient reason to enslave someone). The political blockbuster of the *Dred Scott* decision came when Taney actually turned to consider Scott's own plea, that residence in a free territory could terminate his slave status. Taney proceeded to deny this plea in the clearest and most chilling terms. No territorial government in any federally administered territory had the authority to alter the status of a white

---

68. *A Report of the Decision of the Supreme Court of the United States and the Opinion of the Judges Thereof, in the Case of Dred Scott versus John F. A. Sandford, December Term, 1856*, comp. Benjamin C. Howard (New York: D. Appleton, 1857), 404, 423.

citizen's property, much less to take that property out of a citizen's hands, without due process of law or as a punishment for some crime.

This, of course, meant *any* property of *any* white citizen in *any* territory. In effect, Taney had resurrected John Calhoun's "common property" doctrine and overturned any federal or territorial law that in any way interfered with a citizen's "enjoyment" or use of his property—which in the case of John Emerson had been his slaves Dred and Harriet Scott. Taney then attacked the Missouri Compromise as unconstitutional on the grounds that it deprived slaveholders of the use of their slave property north of the 36°30′ line. In two sentences he destroyed popular sovereignty, the Compromise of 1850, and the Kansas Nebraska bill as well, for if it was unconstitutional for Congress to ban slavery from the territories, it was equally unconstitutional for the federal territories to do it for themselves, no matter what the majority vote of a territory on the question might be.

The two sections of the Taney opinion, running over 250 tightly printed pages in the Court's *Reports*, fit together as integral parts. The first reduced Dred Scott to a noncitizen, fit only to become some real citizen's "property," and the second denied the federal government any authority to restrain in any way the spread of slavery in any place where the federal government—as opposed to the individual state governments—had jurisdiction. In fact, only the states themselves were left by Taney with any constitutional authority to deal with slavery within their own borders, and even that might be the next safeguard to be questioned by a federal court.[69]

In terms of what the *Dred Scott* appeal actually required before the law, Taney need not have done more than declare that Scott simply had no standing before the Court. The explanation for the Taney's decision to reach beyond Dred Scott himself and strike down the great compromises lies largely in Taney and his Court. Five of the seven justices who voted in the majority were Southerners. John A. Campbell, an Alabamian, would later serve as an assistant secretary of war in the Confederacy, and Robert Wayne Grier, John Catron, and Peter Daniel were all pro-slavery partisans. Taney himself was a Marylander (and brother-in-law of Francis Scott Key, the author of "The Star-Spangled Banner") and an old Jacksonian Democrat who had served as Jackson's attorney general in the successful effort to destroy the Bank of the United States. His opinion in *Scott v. Sanford* became Taney's effort to settle the slavery question where Congress, the presidents, Clay, Webster, Taylor, and Wilmot had failed, and to settle it in favor of the South.

---

69. At the time the *Dred Scott* decision was handed down, there was already a case working its way through the New York state courts involving eight Virginia slaves who claimed that a temporary stopover in New York City in 1852 had made them free under an 1817 New York state statute. This case, *Lemmon v. New York*, might have given Taney the opportunity to overturn every anti-slavery statute in the free states on the grounds that states did not have the right to regulate interstate commerce, and paved the way for the reintroduction of slavery into the free states. The case, however, did not reach the Supreme Court before the outbreak of the Civil War, and Taney never had the chance to hand down a companion ruling to *Scott v. Sanford*.

Far from settling the slavery question, *Scott v. Sanford* only aggravated it. The game of balances had gone far beyond the point where a simple declaration from the Court could end it. The new Republican Party replied that a decision so defective in constitutional logic and so repugnant to popular opinion could never be binding as law, and Abraham Lincoln denounced Taney's attack on the natural right of blacks to freedom as a turning of the Declaration of Independence upside down. "Our Declaration of Independence was held sacred by all, and thought to include all," Lincoln declared, "but now, to aid in making the bondage of the Negro universal and eternal, it is assailed, and sneered at, and construed, and hawked at, and torn, till, if its framers could rise from their graves, they could not recognize it at all."[70] Meanwhile, Stephen A. Douglas was coming up for reelection to the Senate in 1858, and it was clear that the Illinois Republicans would be quick to challenge Douglas on how he could reconcile popular sovereignty—and the right of territories to vote slavery in or out according to their popular majorities—with Taney's declaration that neither Congress nor a federal territory had the authority to ban the transportation of slaves to those territories.

President James Buchanan, relieved at not having to deliver an opinion on the slavery controversy himself, happily announced his full intention of applying the Dred Scott decision to the trouble in Kansas, and welcomed the application of the pro-slavery legislature for the admission of the Kansas Territory to the Union as a slave state.[71]

70. Lincoln, "Speech at Springfield, Illinois," June 26, 1857, in *Collected Works*, 2:404.

71. Mark A. Graber, *Dred Scott and the Problem of Constitutional Evil* (New York: Cambridge University Press, 2006), 31–32.

CHAPTER THREE

YEAR OF METEORS

I t seems only human nature to hang the label *irrational* on what we do not understand, since it is easy for us to assume that something must be irrational if our ingenuity is unequal to the task of deciphering it. That may actually reflect more on the limits of our ingenuity than on any supposed irrationality in what we are studying. For that reason, it should come as a practical and fundamental warning not to impute irrationality to people in the study of history (or any other human endeavor) too quickly.

Nevertheless, the behavior of Northern and Southern politicians in the ten years before the Civil War is often described as irrational by many historians, as though the Civil War was a product of an undiagnosed madness, or a paralysis of communications so great as to make the tower of Babel the only worthwhile comparison. The great Allan Nevins described Southerners "in the final paroxysm of 1860–61" as being "filled with frenzy," while Northerners turned "grimly implacable" over slavery. "The thinking" of North and South alike, concluded Nevins, "was largely irrational, governed by subconscious memories, frustrated desires, and the distortions of politicians and editors." Dominated by "stereotypes" of each other, Northerners and Southerners were possessed by "fear," and "fear was largely the product of ignorance, and ignorance—or misinformation—largely the product of propaganda."[1]

Nevins's was only the mildest of historians' voices in the twentieth century who blamed the war on irrationality. Sometimes the irrationality took the form of an "egocentric sectionalism," as it did for Frank Lawrence Owsley; other times, as for James

---

1. Allan Nevins, *The Emergence of Lincoln: Douglas, Buchanan, and Party Chaos, 1857–1859* (New York: Scribner's, 1950), 15–16, 19.

Garfield Randall, it was a kind of political dementia that caused a systematic failure in the American political system and "incredible blundering" by a generation of incompetent politicians. Avery Craven believed that "sane policy" had been abandoned in the heat of unreason, and that "uncalled-for moves" and "irresponsible leadership" had doomed the nation to civil war and the wanton destruction of compromises that might have augured a better American future.[2] It did not relieve the bleakness of this interpretation that all of these historians had come of age as the Progressive movement was withering on the vine and American entry into the First World War was turning into a sucker's bad bargain. Just as it was easy to believe that irrationality had brought on the Great War and the rise of even more lethal forms of political madness, it was not difficult for embittered Progressives to cast the same dim light on the Civil War. The Civil War was, in these arguments, just one more function of political irrationality, with personal blundering in one case, structural folly in another.

The difficulty with this accusation of irrationality arises from the ease with which it permits us to discount the meaning of politics in a democracy, and perhaps even democracy itself, since the Progressives had a distinctly uneasy relationship to democracy. As much as Randall, Craven, and Owsley were not wrong to discover exaggerated rhetoric, policy blunders, and brainless leadership causing serious abrasion between North and South, it is only from the comfortable point of view of another century that all the rhetoric seems exaggerated, all the policies inarguably blunders, and all the leadership uncomprehending of the abyss toward which they were pedaling.

Looked at on their own terms, both the South's fears of territorial and economic strangulation and the North's fears of a "slave power" conspiracy are anything but irrational, and only someone who refuses to think through the evidence available to Americans in the 1850s would find either of them at all illogical. "Is it nothing to *yell* about," asked South Carolinian William Gimball in a letter to Elizabeth Gimball in 1861, "that we are prevented from carrying our property into the common territory of the United States? Is it nothing to yell for that the government is to be in the hands of men pledged to carry on the 'irrepressible conflict' against us? Is it nothing that they send incendiaries to stir up the slaves to poison & murder us? Is it nothing that our brothers at the North rob us of our property and beat us when we reclaim it?"[3]

On the Northern side, Abraham Lincoln is not usually considered a candidate for irrationality, but he was convinced of the existence of a "slave power" conspiracy and in one of his most famous speeches accused a U.S. senator, the chief justice of the U.S. Supreme Court, and two presidents of being its aiders and abettors. John Bigelow, whom

---

2. Frank L. Owsley, "The Fundamental Cause of the Civil War: Egocentric Sectionalism," *Journal of Southern History* 7 (February 1941): 16–17; James G. Randall, *Lincoln the Liberal Statesman* (New York: Dodd, Mead, 1947), 175; Avery Craven, *The Repressible Conflict, 1830–1861* (Baton Rouge: Louisiana State University Press, 1939), 5, 94; David M. Potter, "The Literature on the Background of the American Civil War," *The South and the Sectional Conflict* (Baton Rouge: Louisiana State University Press, 1968), 93–98.

3. Jimerson, *The Private Civil War*, 8–9.

Lincoln would appoint as his chargé d'affaires in Paris in 1861, reduced the contest between North and South to "a struggle . . . between the aristocratic or privileged element in our government and the democratic. The two cannot live in peace together."[4]

Similarly, only the benefit of hindsight allows us to write off the succession of compromises, from the Missouri Compromise of 1820 to the last-minute attempts to broker compromise under the nose of secession and disunion in 1861, as evidences of widening failure. Until the firing of the very first gun, Northerners and Southerners were driven not by irrationality but by the clearest political logic on offer. "As long as slavery is looked upon by the North with abhorrence; as long as the South is regarded as a mere slave-breeding and slave-driving community; as long as false and pernicious theories are cherished respecting the inherent equality and rights of every human being, there can be no satisfactory political union between the two sections," declared the *New Orleans Bee* in December 1860. While the premises of that proposition may be questionable, the logic that flowed from them was not. "If one-half the people believe the other half to be deeply dyed in iniquity; to be daily and hourly in the perpetration of the most atrocious moral offense," continued the editor of the *Bee*, "how can two such antagonistic nationalities dwell together in fraternal concord under the same government?"[5] Far from reeking of irrationality, secession and disunion were perfectly coherent and logical political choices within a political system that all along had confirmed that secession and disunion were viable options.

By the same token, the political system did not break down—the Southern states simply decided that it had fallen into the wrong hands and that they would no longer choose to use it.[6] Far from losing confidence in that system, Northerners and Southerners struggled for workable compromises right down to the last minute, even while the room for creating nation-saving compromises narrowed beyond all hope of maneuver, and they continued to agitate for them almost all the way through the war in the form of Northern and Southern peace movements. If there is anything that is genuinely appalling in the political context of the Civil War, it is the dominance of the most glittering and hard-edged political rationality. It was the hard edge of that rationality that, in the end, made a final compromise impossible.

THE LITTLE ENGINE OF ABRAHAM LINCOLN

The *Dred Scott* decision was a deep embarrassment for Stephen A. Douglas. The doctrine of popular sovereignty, on which Douglas had pegged his hopes for achieving

---

4. Bigelow, in Michael S. Green, *Freedom, Union, and Power: Lincoln and His Party During the Civil War* (New York: Fordham University Press, 2004), 37.

5. "Vain Hopes," *New Orleans Bee*, December 14, 1860, in *Southern Editorials on Secession*, 336.

6. James McPherson, "Antebellum Southern Exceptionalism: A New Look at an Old Question," *Civil War History* 29 (September 1983): 243.

sectional peace (and achieving his own nomination to the presidency), initially assumed that the inhabitants of any given territory could, if they wished, exclude slavery simply by passing the active legislation necessary to ban it from their midst. The *Dred Scott* decision, however, made it clear that no one—not Congress, not the inhabitants of a territory, not even a territorial legislature—had any power to keep any United States citizen from taking property (which had now become a euphemism for slaves) anywhere a citizen wanted and erecting the slave system in any territory of the Union. If the decision was pressed far enough, it might also open the way to claiming that no state could ban slavery, either.

Douglas was nothing if not resourceful. He "was a wonderful man with the people . . . When he came through the State, the whole Democratic party was alive and ready to rally to his support." Once the initial shock of the *Dred Scott* decision wore off, Douglas announced that the Court's decision would not contradict the operation of popular sovereignty after all. True, a territory could not pass legislation *actively* banning slavery; but the people of a territory could *passively* make it impossible for slavery to exist in their territory by refusing to enact the usual array of slave codes and police measures that slave states needed in order to keep slavery intact. The right to take slaves into the territories, claimed Douglas in a speech in Springfield in the summer of 1857, was "practically a dead letter" without "appropriate police regulations and local legislation." Withhold those, and slavery had no chance of surviving within a territory's boundaries. By Douglas's logic, *Dred Scott* not only left popular sovereignty intact but left it as the only weapon remaining by which slavery could be legally kept out of the territories.[7]

This line of reasoning did nothing to stanch the hemorrhaging of Douglas's reputation within the Democratic ranks. Southern Democrats, who were overjoyed at the *Dred Scott* decision, were furious at Douglas's refusal to submit tamely to the Supreme Court's dictum. What was more, the new president, James Buchanan, had welcomed the *Dred Scott* decision as a convenient way of declaring the Kansas problem settled. Buchanan, surrounded by a mostly Southern cabinet, was irritated that Douglas was threatening to spoil that settlement by suggesting that anti-slavery Kansans might yet have the means to obstruct a pro-slavery settlement and prolong the Kansas turmoil. As Douglas approached senatorial reelection in Illinois in 1858, it became a real question as to whether Buchanan's vengeful willingness to manipulate party patronage against Douglas might not prevent Douglas from returning to the Senate.[8]

The Republicans had been thrown into similar disarray by the *Dred Scott* decision. They had assumed that their task was the creation of a congressional coalition

7. Robert Taft, "The Appearance and Personality of Stephen A. Douglas," *Kansas Historical Quarterly* 21 (Spring 1954): 10–11, 16–17; Shelby Cullom, *Fifty Years of Public Service: Personal Recollections* (Chicago: A. C. McClurg, 1911), 62; Robert W. Johannsen, *Stephen A. Douglas* (New York: Oxford University Press, 1973), 570–72; Fehrenbacher, *The Dred Scott Case*, 379.

8. Damon Wells, *Stephen Douglas: The Last Years, 1857–1861* (Austin: University of Texas Press, 1971), 27.

large enough to block any attempt to admit Kansas or any other new territory as a slave state, and perhaps even restore the rule of the Missouri Compromise. Now the Court's decision had pulled the rug out from under them by declaring that neither Congress nor anyone else had the authority to create such an obstacle. For that reason, desperate Republicans—especially in the East—began to hearken to the song of Stephen A. Douglas. Douglas's argument that popular sovereignty (at least in its passive form) was now the only workable means of keeping slavery from the territories convinced many Illinois Republicans that, especially for the 1858 senatorial race, it was time to stymie Taney and Buchanan and throw their support behind Douglas.

There was, however, one Illinois Republican who dissented from this view of Douglas, and that was Abraham Lincoln. In 1858 Lincoln was forty-nine years old, one of the most outstanding lawyers in Illinois, and equally one of the most prominent state Republicans. Lincoln had come by his successes the hard way. Born in a crude log cabin in 1809 in Kentucky, Lincoln had known little before his twenty-fifth birthday but the poverty and hardships that formed the substance of backcountry life. "There was an unbroken wilderness there then," he recalled in an autobiographical sketch he wrote in 1859, "and an axe was put in his hand; and with the trees and logs and grubs he fought until he reached his twentieth year." Lincoln had also imbibed anti-slavery opinions almost with his mother's milk, since his parents, Thomas and Nancy Lincoln, were both members of an ultra-Calvinistic Baptist sect that banned slaveholding members from their fellowship. In fact, the spread of slavery across Kentucky was one of the motivations for Thomas Lincoln to uproot his family and move first to Indiana and then finally to Illinois.[9]

Their views on slavery may have been almost the only things Thomas and Abraham Lincoln had in common. Thomas Lincoln was content to be a farmer, only marginally literate—Lincoln recalled that his father "never did more in the way of writing than to bunglingly sign his own name"—but at least moderately successful in his calling. Abraham, however, grew up with a passion for self-education and social betterment. He rejected his father's raw Calvinistic religion; his reading turned instead to religious skeptics—Thomas Paine, Constantin Volney, Robert Burns—and the Enlightenment's rule of reason. His stepmother, Sarah Bush Johnston, whom Thomas married after the death of Nancy Lincoln in 1818, recalled in 1865 that "Abe was a good boy," but he "didn't like physical labor—was diligent for knowledge."

> He read all the books he could lay his hands on. . . . Abe read histories, papers & other books. . . . He had a copy book—a kind of scrap book in which he put down all things and this preserved them. He ciphered on boards when he had no paper or no slate and when the board would get too black he would shave it off with a drawing knife and go on again. . . . Abe, when old folks were at our house, was a silent & attentive observer—never

9. Lincoln, "Speech at Indianapolis, Indiana," September 19, 1859, in *Collected Works*, 3:463.

speaking or asking questions till they were gone and then he must understand Every thing—even to the smallest thing—Minutely & Exactly—he would then repeat it over to himself again & again—sometimes in one form and then in another & when it was fixed in his mind to suit him he became Easy and he never lost that fact or his understanding of it. Sometimes he seemed pestered to give Expression to his ideas and got mad almost at one who couldn't Explain plainly what he wanted to convey.[10]

In 1831 Abraham Lincoln struck out on his own, trying his hand at anything that offered him a way up the ladder. He tried clerking and postmastering in a store in the village of New Salem, Illinois, but succeeded at neither, and in 1832 he took his first turn at politics.

Politically, Lincoln found himself almost instinctively drawn to the Whigs rather than the Democrats. The Whigs celebrated the Union, deplored the loud demands of the states for first loyalties, and called for an enabling role for government in the economy, railroads, and internal improvements, with protective tariffs as incentives. The Whigs were the party of up-and-coming men, the businessmen, the self-improvers and self-transformers who did not want to be bound by the old loyalties of the past, and who saw at the core of American democracy the opportunity to transform themselves. Lincoln believed that what made the United States "at once the wonder and admiration of the whole world" was that, in America, "every man can make himself." Whigs such as Lincoln embraced this self-making model as the guarantee of "hope to all, and energy, and progress and improvement of condition to all." So Lincoln took Henry Clay (a fellow Kentuckian) as his political idol, as Lincoln's "beau ideal of a statesman." His first electoral platform—he ran for the state legislature but only came in eighth in a field of thirteen candidates—was dedicated to the need for tax-funded internal improvements. "He was," said Stephen T. Logan, his second law partner, "as stiff as a man could be in his Whig doctrines."[11]

In 1834 Lincoln won his first seat in the Illinois state legislature as a Whig, and served four successive terms there. In the process, he helped lead the Illinois legislature into the sponsorship of transportation projects and, in 1837, the passage of a $10 million appropriation for railroad construction. His first major speech in the Illinois legislature praised the operation of the Illinois State Bank for having "doubled the prices of the products" of Illinois farms and filled farmers' pockets "with a sound circulating medium," noting that the farmers were "all well-pleased with its operations." Democratic attacks on banks and bank charters, Lincoln explained, would

10. Sarah Bush Lincoln, interview with William Henry Herndon, September 8, 1865, in *Herndon's Informants: Letters, Interviews and Statements About Abraham Lincoln*, ed. R. O. Davis and D. L. Wilson (Urbana: University of Illinois Press, 1998), 107.

11. Lincoln, "Speech at Kalamazoo, Michigan," August 27, 1856, and "Address Before the Wisconsin State Agricultural Society," September 30, 1859, in *Collected Works*, 2:364, 3:479; "Conversation with Hon. S. T. Logan at Springfield, July 6, 1875," in *An Oral History of Abraham Lincoln: John G. Nicolay's Interviews and Essays*, ed. Michael Burlingame (Carbondale: Southern Illinois University Press, 1996), 36.

never hurt "men of wealth," who are "beyond the power of fortune," but they would "depreciate the value of its paper [currency] in the hands of the honest and unsuspecting farmer and mechanic."[12]

Having helped to put much of this program in place, Lincoln saw it promptly turned to ashes. A national economic depression, caused in large measure by the Democratic assault on the banks, crushed the American economy in 1837. Illinois had financed its railroad appropriation on bank borrowing, and the collapse of the banks saddled the state legislature (and the unforgiving taxpayers) with an indebtedness that took years to pay off.[13]

This did nothing to discourage Lincoln's urges for social betterment and education. While still a state legislator, Lincoln began teaching himself law out of an assortment of borrowed law books, and in 1836 he was licensed to practice in the state circuit courts. The choice of law as a profession was part and parcel of his Whiggish economic aspirations, since lawyers were (in the phrase of historian Charles G. Sellers) the "shock troops" of market capitalism, and from John Marshall's Supreme Court on down, American lawyers were becoming the guardians of commercial contracts and property. It was in pursuit of the market—and of the financial and social respectability that came with it—that Lincoln moved to the Illinois state capital, Springfield, and entered a law firm there with another young lawyer, John Todd Stuart. Even then Lincoln was not content. "That man," wrote his later law partner, William Henry Herndon, "who thinks Lincoln calmly gathered his robes about him, waiting for the people to call him, has a very erroneous knowledge of Lincoln. He was always calculating and planning ahead. His ambition was a little engine that knew no rest."[14]

Eventually, that "little engine" succeeded. In 1842 Lincoln married Mary Todd, the daughter of a prominent Lexington, Kentucky, family, who brought him a lifelong schooling in social graces. Even more important, Lincoln labored with ferocious intensity at becoming a successful lawyer and Whig politician. Herndon noticed that Lincoln seemed to think "that there were no limitations to the force and endurance of his mental and vital powers," and he watched Lincoln wear himself to the point of breakdown in "a continuous, severe, persistent, and exhaustive thought" on a problem. Herndon described Lincoln as "persistent, fearless, and tireless in thinking."[15]

His thoroughness, his feel for the practical in legal issues, and his remarkably retentive memory made Lincoln an outstanding courtroom performer. He was not

12. Lincoln, "Speech in the Illinois Legislature Concerning the State Bank," in *Collected Works*, 1:69.

13. Gabor Boritt, *Lincoln and the Economics of the American Dream* (Memphis, TN: Memphis State University Press, 1978), 15–22, 30–31, 47, 59.

14. Charles G. Sellers, *The Market Revolution: Jacksonian America, 1815–1846* (New York: Oxford University Press, 1991), 47.

15. Herndon to Jesse Weik, December 9, 1886, and to C. O. Poole, January 5, 1886, in *The Hidden Lincoln, from the Letters and Papers of William H. Herndon*, ed. Emanuel Hertz (New York: Viking, 1938), 124, 148.

"a learned lawyer," recalled Herndon, but he was a first-rate case lawyer with an uncanny ability to bend juries to his point of view. "He was wise as a serpent in the trial of a cause," one legal associate, Leonard Swett, recalled, "but I have got too many scars from his blows to certify that he was harmless as a dove." He was not a schemer. "Discourage litigation," was Lincoln's own advice to aspiring lawyers. "Persuade your neighbors to compromise whenever you can. Point out to them how the nominal winner is often a real loser—in fees, expenses, and waste of time." If anything, he was renowned for his scrupulous honesty. Among his fellow lawyers, "Mr. Lincoln's character for professional honor stood very high." The entire "framework of his mental and moral being was honesty," Herndon remembered, "open, candid and square in his profession, never practicing on the sharp or low." Herndon watched him warn clients with shaky cases, "You are in the wrong of the case and I would advise you to compromise, or if you cannot do that, do not bring a suit on the facts of your case because you are in the wrong and surely [be] defeated and have to pay a big bill of costs."[16]

Yet, as unbending as Lincoln could be about ends, he was surprisingly flexible about means. "Mr. Lincoln was a very patient man generally," said Herndon, "but if you wished to be cut off at the knee, just go at Lincoln with abstractions." This was a pattern that, in later years, would also characterize his political solutions. "Secret, silent, and a very reticent-minded man," Lincoln was "a riddle and a puzzle to his friends and neighbors," and in political combat he could be deceptively hard, evasive and dangerous to underestimate. "Any man," warned Leonard Swett, "who took Lincoln for a simple minded man would very soon wake [up] with his back in a ditch."[17]

The plainest example of this evasiveness was his awkward embarrassment over his crude backcountry origins. "Lincoln's ambition," remarked Herndon, was "to be distinctly understood by the common people." Yet no man wanted less to be one of them. Once Lincoln moved to Springfield, he rarely cast a backward glance at his humble origins: neither Thomas nor Sarah Lincoln was invited to their son's wedding, and Lincoln was too embarrassed and alienated by his father's crudeness even to attend the old man's funeral in 1851. His stepbrother's pleas that Lincoln come down to the Coles County farmhouse where Thomas Lincoln lay dying were met with a frosty refusal: "Say to him that if we could meet now, it is doubtful whether it would not be more painful than pleasant."[18]

When the same stepbrother tried to talk Lincoln into a loan to pay off his debts, Lincoln bluntly refused: "You are now in need of some ready money; and what

16. Lincoln, "Fragment: Notes for a Law Lecture," July 1, 1850, in *Collected Works*, 2:81.

17. Herndon to C. O. Poole and J. Henry Shaw, in *The Hidden Lincoln*, 119–20, 124, 305, 429; Davis, interview with William H. Herndon, September 20, 1866, and Swett to Herndon, January 17, 1866, in *Herndon's Informants*, 168, 350.

18. Herndon, in *The Hidden Lincoln*, 133; Lincoln, "To John D. Johnston," December 24, 1848, in *Collected Works*, 2:16.

I propose is, that you shall go to work, 'tooth and nails' for some body who will give you money [for] it. Let father and your boys take charge of things at home—prepare for a crop, and make the crop; and you go to work for the best money wages, or in discharge of any debt you owe, that you can get"—in other words, join the cash economy. Lincoln had no love for Thomas Jefferson's republic of yeoman farmers, nor would he have much use for utopian dreams of cooperative commonwealths in which all results were leveled. What he wanted for the Union was what he wanted for himself: an upwardly mobile society of successful small-scale producers and professionals, with equal liberty to pursue their own interests. "I hold the value of life is to improve one's condition," Lincoln said in 1861, and the star he navigated by was the "promise that in due time the weights should be lifted from the shoulders of all men, and that *all* should have an equal chance."[19]

The practice of law gave Lincoln his first "equal chance." Although much of his reputation as a trial lawyer was made on the state circuit courts, riding from one plank-and-shingle courthouse to another over the Illinois prairies, by the 1850s he was appearing regularly before the Illinois Supreme Court, where he handled appeals in 402 cases, and in the federal circuit court for northern Illinois, where he handled over 300 cases for bankruptcy and debt. In addition to a demanding legal practice that may have amounted to more than 5,100 cases and upward of 100,000 separate legal documents, Lincoln even managed to sit as a judge in more than a hundred cases on the state circuit courts when a regular judge was sick or unavailable. He was involved in six cases before the United States Supreme Court (one of which involved oral argument before no less than Roger B. Taney) and developed a long-term association as counsel for the Illinois Central Railroad (sublimely confident in the benefits of pushing the boundaries of markets deeper and deeper into the west, Lincoln managed to persuade the state court to have the Illinois Central declared tax-exempt as a "public work").[20]

Lincoln was not a sentimentalist about the law. "There was nothing of the milksop about him," remarked Henry Clay Whitney, who practiced alongside Lincoln on the Eighth Circuit. Although his two most famous trials—his defenses of Duff Armstrong and Peachy Quinn Harrison on murder indictments—were criminal cases, criminal law accounted for only about 6 percent of his case load over twenty-four years; the bulk of his practice was civil and commercial, and the single largest category included bankruptcies and debt collections; Whitney "never found him unwilling to appear in behalf of a great 'soulless corporation.'" Lincoln had no animus against capital: "Men who are industrious, and sober, and honest in the pursuit of their own

19. Lincoln, "To John D. Johnston," January 12, 1851, and "Speech in Independence Hall," February 22, 1861, in *Collected Works*, 2:96–97, 4:240; Jason R. Jiveden, *Claiming Lincoln: Progressivism, Equality, and the Battle for Lincoln's Legacy in Presidential Rhetoric* (DeKalb: Northern Illinois University Press, 2011), 20–21, 23.

20. *Lincoln Legal Briefs*, October–December 1996 and April–June 1998; Mark E. Steiner, *An Honest Calling: The Law Practice of Abraham Lincoln* (DeKalb: Northern Illinois University Press, 2006), 17.

interests should after a while accumulate capital, and after that should be allowed to enjoy it in peace, and also if they should choose when they have accumulated it to use it to save themselves from actual labor and hire other people to labor for them is right. In doing so they do not wrong the man they employ." Nor did Lincoln propose any "war upon capital." He took it for granted that "it is best for all to leave each man free to acquire property as fast as he can." He merely wished Americans "to allow the humblest man an equal chance to get rich with everybody else." Lincoln certainly labored to practice what he preached: by the 1850s, Lincoln was commanding an annual income of more than $5,000 per annum—approximately twenty times that figure if we reckon in today's currency—owned a large frame house in Springfield, had his eldest son in a private school in Springfield, and had investments in real estate, mortgages, notes, bank accounts, and insurance policies amounting to over $20,000.[21]

Despite his successes, Abraham Lincoln arrived at his mid-forties dissatisfied and restless. Rigidly self-controlled, Lincoln refused even the relaxation of liquor, and Robert Lincoln, his eldest son, afterward recollected that he had "seen him take a sip of a glass of ale and also of a glass of champagne . . . on two or three occasions in my life, not more." When self-control or his control of his circumstances escaped him, Lincoln had always been possessed by a strain of moody introspection, and he easily lapsed into periods of sustained and almost suicidal depression. "You flaxen men with broad faces are born with cheer and don't know a cloud from a star," he told one optimistic Iowa politician. "I am of another temperament." Whatever religion he may have been taught by his parents he had exchanged for an emotionless rationalistic deism, and he proclaimed his faith not in a personal God but in "reason, cold, calculating, unimpassioned reason," as "all the materials for our future support and defence." Yet all his life he retained a streak of the superstitious, in the form of belief in dreams and omens, and he transmuted the Calvinist predestination of his parents into "the Doctrine of Necessity—that is, that the human mind is impelled to action, or held in rest by some power, over which the mind itself has no control."[22]

One remedy for the depression lay in his peculiarly clownish sense of humor and the almost bottomless fund of jokes and funny stories he had collected from the folk humor of the Illinois frontier. His reputation as a storyteller was nearly as legendary as his eloquence as a lawyer; his jokes reeked of the cornfield, and occasionally of

21. Lincoln, "Speech at Cincinnati, Ohio," September 17, 1859, and "Speech at New Haven, Connecticut," March 6, 1860, in *Collected Works*, 3:459, 4:24; Harry E. Pratt, *The Personal Finances of Abraham Lincoln* (Springfield, IL: Abraham Lincoln Association, 1943), 52–53, 82; "Lincoln's Landholdings and Investments," *Abraham Lincoln Association Bulletin*, September 1, 1929, 1–8; Whitney, in Jesse William Weik, *The Real Lincoln: A Portrait* (Boston: Houghton Mifflin, 1922), 194.

22. Robert Todd Lincoln to Isaac Markens, February 13, 1918, in *A Portrait of Abraham Lincoln in Letters by His Oldest Son*, ed. Paul Angle (Chicago: Chicago Historical Society, 1968), 55; Lincoln, "Address Before the Young Men's Lyceum of Springfield, Illinois," and "Handbill Replying to Charges of Infidelity," in *Collected Works*, 1:115, 382; Lincoln to Josiah Grinnell, in *Recollected Words of Abraham Lincoln*, ed. Don E. Fehrenbacher and Virginia Fehrenbacher (Stanford, CA: Stanford University Press, 1996), 185.

the barnyard. Some measure of Lincoln's humor was consciously cultivated to appeal to popular audiences, and Lincoln used laughter to deadly effectiveness as a stump speaker (Douglas would later claim that he never feared Lincoln's arguments, but "every one of his stories seems like a whack upon my back"). In a larger sense, Lincoln craved the escape from melancholy offered him by the jokes he could tell to a crowd of friends and admirers, making them howl with laughter. "Some of my friends are much shocked at what I suppose they consider my low tastes in indulging in stories some of which, I suppose, are not just as nice as they might be," Lincoln admitted, "but I tell you the truth when I say that a real smutty story, if it has the element of genuine wit in its composition, as most of such stories have, has the same effect on me that I think a good square drink of whiskey has to an old toper. It puts new life into me. The fact is, I have always believed that a good laugh was good for both the mental and physical digestion."[23] It also reflected the division of Lincoln's character, one side all seriousness and ambition and Republican honesty, the other bawdy, cunning, homespun, and secretive.

Part of Lincoln's brooding was rooted in his complex and sometimes unhappy marriage to Mary Todd. Painfully aware of his own social awkwardness, Lincoln's relationships with women were tentative and uncertain. His early passion for Ann Rutledge, the daughter of a New Salem tavern keeper, has often been dismissed as a fairy tale shaped by William Herndon to discomfit Mary Lincoln, but the evidence Herndon accumulated for the Rutledge story has more substance to it than the dismissals imply. Rutledge's premature death, if we can rely on Herndon's interviews with New Salemites years afterward, devastated Lincoln. A subsequent engagement to Mary Owens in 1836 fell through due to Lincoln's hasty and not entirely becoming retreat from matrimony. For the most part, he avoided the society of women—not for lack of interest, but for fear of rejection and a strict observance of male-female proprieties. "Lincoln was a Man of strong passion for woman," said David Davis, the presiding circuit judge before whom Lincoln practiced for many years, but "his Conscience Kept him from seduction—this saved many—many a woman." In the end, only the determined intervention of friends and the equally determined strategy of Mary herself managed to tie the knot for Lincoln.[24]

As it was, Mary Todd was both a burden and a blessing to Lincoln. Criticized by her wealthy, slaveholding family for having married beneath herself, Mary constantly fed Lincoln's "little engine" and provided him with the kind of reassurance and devotion that he needed to keep himself going. She was, said Herndon, "like a toothache, keeping her husband awake to politics day and night." On the other hand, she could goad her husband into rage as easily as into politics. Mary was high-strung

23. P. M. Zall, "Abe Lincoln Laughing," in *The Historian's Lincoln: Pseudohistory, Psychohistory, and History*, ed. G. S. Boritt and Norman Forness (Urbana: University of Illinois Press, 1988), 10; J. F. Farnsworth, in *Recollected Words*, 437–38.

24. David Davis, interview with Herndon, September 20, 1866, in *Herndon's Informants*, 350.

and irritable, and Herndon (whose dislike she returned, with interest), thought her a "terror . . . imperious, proud, aristocratic, insolent, witty, and bitter"; he (and almost everyone else who knew the Lincolns personally) characterized the Lincolns' marriage as a "domestic *hell*." It was this that explained to his contemporaries why Lincoln began to spend increasing amounts of time away from Springfield on the circuit or on railroad cases. "Mrs Lincoln had notions not very agreeable to him and which so affected his domestic peace as to force him off in the circuit," wrote one Springfield neighbor. David Davis agreed: "Mr Lincoln was happy—as happy as *he* could be, when on this Circuit and happy no other place. This was his place of Enjoyment. As a general rule when all the lawyers of a Saturday Evening would go home and see their families & friends at home Lincoln would refuse to go home. It seemed to me that L was not domestically happy." By the 1850s, Lincoln was away for almost twenty weeks of the year.[25]

Further aggravating Lincoln's melancholy was his persistent failure at politics. In 1840 he had campaigned as a loyal Whig for William Henry Harrison, and in 1843 the Whig state committee recruited him to write a state party platform. He campaigned for Whig nominees in 1844, including Henry Clay, and in 1846 the Illinois Whigs successfully ran him for Congress as the representative for the Seventh Congressional District. But Lincoln's performance in Washington fell far short of impressive. Although Lincoln struggled hard to make a name for himself as a Whig, little in his solitary term as a congressman was noticed, not even his opposition to President Polk and the Mexican War. In 1848 he stepped aside in accordance with party wishes to allow another Whig, Stephen Logan, to win the Seventh District seat, and Lincoln was sent out on the stump to promote the election of Zachary Taylor, the Whig candidate for president. Despite falling on his spear so loyally, Lincoln was offered as a political reward only the governorship of the Oregon Territory, a lusterless post so far removed from real political life that Lincoln turned it down.

Thus Abraham Lincoln in the mid-1850s was a man who had accomplished much, but not nearly as much as he craved. At this point his vision shifted from the unsatisfied and ambiguous conflicts of his private world to the equally unsatisfied and ambiguous conflicts of national politics.

Lincoln had long harbored anti-slavery instincts. "I have always hated slavery," he said years later, "If slavery is not wrong, nothing is wrong. I cannot remember when I did not so think, and feel." As early as 1837, during his days as an Illinois state legislator, he had put himself on record as opposing slavery as "both injustice and bad policy." Lincoln's dislike of slavery was generated less by a concern over racial injustice and more by the arbitrary and unnatural restraint it placed on the natural rights and abilities of an individual "to make himself." Any artificial burden placed

25. Herndon to Jesse Weik, January 9, 1886, in *The Hidden Lincoln*, 131; Edgar Conkling to William Herndon, August 3, 1867, and Davis, interview with Herndon, September 20, 1866, in *Herndon's Informants*, 349–50, 565.

on the acquisition of property and the free exercise of one's natural rights, whether it be aristocracy or slavery, was an offense to Lincoln. As was the case with most Northerners through the 1830s and 1840s, his rankling at slavery never actually took the route of abolitionism, nor did he need it to: "I rested in the hope and belief that it was in course of ultimate extinction." The debate over Kansas-Nebraska and then *Dred Scott*, however, changed that: "I became convinced that either I had been resting in a delusion, or the institution was being placed on a new basis . . . for making it per-petual, national and universal." Kansas-Nebraska "took us by surprise—astounded us," and "raised such an excitement . . . throughout the country as never before was heard of in this Union," Lincoln said.[26]

Kansas-Nebraska had managed to trample on not just one but several of Lincoln's sensibilities. In the first place, it represented a reneging by the slave states on a con-tract they had agreed to in good faith in 1820. After "the South had got all they claimed, and all the territory south of the compromise line had been appropriated to slavery," the South turned its eyes on the lands reserved for freedom and attempted to "snatch that away," too. Instead of extinction, slavery had won access to the old Missouri Compromise territories, and with that, a new lease on life.[27] That, in turn, meant the spread of a planter aristocracy who meant to use the slave system to fasten a permanent system of economic dependence onto the American republic, with no more opportunity for a "poor man's son" to acquire a homestead of his own and begin the same ascent to bourgeois respectability which Lincoln had achieved.

What made this even more destructive was the way it soiled the reputation of liberal democracy before the world. "I hate [slavery] because of the monstrous injustice of slavery," Lincoln said, but even more, "I hate it because it . . . ena-bles the enemies of free institutions, with plausibility, to taunt us as hypocrites." How could Americans embrace the Declaration of Independence and Kansas-Nebraska with the same arms? The Declaration declared that all men are created equal; Kansas-Nebraska repudiated that and declared that some men might now be kept as unequals anywhere a majority decided to approve it. Lincoln could not have produced "one man that ever uttered the belief that the Declaration did not apply to negroes, before the repeal of the Missouri Compromise!" If slavery was good enough to be sanctioned, then blacks could not be good enough to be men; hence, Kansas-Nebraska has "deliberately taken negroes from the class of men and put them in the class of brutes."[28]

So he threw himself into the anti-Nebraska fight, hoping to rebuild the shattered unity of the Whig Party on a platform that offered Northern Whigs a resurrection

26. Lincoln, "Protest in the Illinois Legislature on Slavery," March 3, 1837, "Speech at Peoria, Illinois," October 16, 1854, and "To Albert G. Hodges," April 4, 1864, in *Collected Works*, 1:75, 2:282, 7:281.

27. Lincoln, "Speech at Bloomington, Illinois," September 12, 1854, in *Collected Works*, 2:232–33, 238.

28. Lincoln, "Speech at Peoria, Illinois," October 16, 1854, and "Speech at New Haven, Connecticut," March 6, 1860, in *Collected Works*, 2:255, 4:19.

of the Missouri Compromise and Southern Whigs new reassurances for the safety of slavery in the Southern states. "We rose each fighting, grasping whatever he could first reach—a scythe—a pitchfork—a chopping axe, or a butcher's cleaver."[29] That platform came near to winning him one of Illinois's U.S. Senate seats in 1855, when Lincoln outpolled a pro-Nebraska Democratic candidate, James Shields. The Whigs in Illinois no longer had the strength to push Lincoln over the finish line, however, and Lincoln was forced to throw his support to a free-soil Democrat, Lyman Trumbull, in order to keep another Douglasite out of the Senate.

Lincoln clung to the Whigs long after the party had, for all practical political purposes, asphyxiated. He had no sympathy with the Know-Nothings, and until he was convinced that another Whiggish alternative would survive as a platform for his ambitions, he was reluctant to abandon the party of Clay, which had got him elected to Congress. By the end of 1855, however, the slavery issue and Kansas-Nebraska had put the Whigs past any hope of resuscitation as far as Lincoln could see, and the mounting demands of the mysterious "Slave Power" for the extension of slavery everywhere in the territories tipped Lincoln over to the new Republican Party. In May 1856 Lincoln helped lead a coalition of anti-slavery Whigs (including his partner, William Herndon) and free-soil Democrats (such as Lyman Trumbull) into the Republican camp.

At length, in 1858, Lincoln got what he wanted most: the chance to bring down the chief perpetrator of the Kansas-Nebraska betrayal, Stephen A. Douglas, as Douglas ran for reelection in Illinois to the Senate. Not surprisingly, Lincoln was dumbfounded when he began to hear suggestions by eastern Republicans that Illinois Republicans stand aside and let Douglas be reelected without opposition. "What does the New-York Tribune mean by its constant eulogising, and admiring, and magnifying [of] Douglas?" Lincoln demanded of Lyman Trumbull during the last week of 1857. "Have they concluded that the republican cause, generally, can be best promoted by sacrificing us here in Illinois? If so we would like to know it soon; it will save us a great deal of labor to surrender at once."[30]

Lincoln need not have feared: his standing among the Illinois Republicans was too high to be jeopardized by the editorials of the *New York Tribune*. On June 16, 1858, Lincoln was endorsed by the Republican state convention in Springfield as "the first and only choice of the Republicans of Illinois for the U.S. Senate, as the successor of Stephen A. Douglas."[31] That evening Lincoln addressed the convention

29. Lincoln, "Editorial on the Kansas-Nebraska Act," September 11, 1854, "Speech at Springfield, Illinois," July 17, 1858, "Speeches at Clinton, Illinois," September 2, 1858, and "Speech at Peoria, Illinois," October 16, 1854, in *Collected Works*, 2:229–30, 2:282, 2:514, 3:82.

30. Lincoln, "To Lyman Trumbull," December 28, 1857, in *Collected Works*, 2:430.

31. "Republican State Convention of Illinois" (June 16, 1858), in *The Lincoln-Douglas Debates of 1858*, ed. E. Earle Sparks (Springfield, IL: Illinois State Historical Library, 1908), 22.

in one of his greatest speeches, the "House Divided" speech. At the very beginning, Lincoln hammered at the folly of expecting that popular sovereignty could resolve the sectional crisis:

> We are now far into the *fifth* year, since a policy was initiated, with the avowed object, and confident promise, of putting an end to slavery agitation. Under the operation of that policy, that agitation has not only *not ceased,* but has *constantly augmented.* In *my* opinion, it *will* not cease, until a *crisis* shall have been reached, and passed. "A House divided against itself cannot stand." I believe this government cannot endure, permanently half *slave* and half *free.*

He then attacked the notion that Douglas, the author of this failed policy, was now to be hailed as the adopted son of the Republicans. "*They* do *not* tell us, nor has *he* told us, that he *wishes* any such object to be effected," Lincoln observed. Just because Douglas had a quarrel with Buchanan and Taney over popular sovereignty did not mean that he had become a Republican or, more to the point, an opponent of slavery. "How can he oppose the advances of slavery?" Lincoln asked, mimicking Douglas's announcement that he didn't care whether slavery was voted up or voted down in Kansas, so long as the vote was properly conducted. "He don't *care* anything about it."

To the contrary, Lincoln argued, the entire progress of events from Kansas-Nebraska up through *Dred Scott* showed that "don't care" was merely a front, that everything in Kansas-Nebraska and *Dred Scott* had been prearranged deliberately to advance slavery, and that Douglas was as much as part of that conspiracy as Buchanan, Pierce, or Taney. "Let any one who doubts, carefully contemplate that now almost complete legal combination—piece of *machinery* so to speak—compounded of the Nebraska doctrine, and the Dred Scott decision," Lincoln declared darkly.

> When we see a lot of framed timbers, different portions of which we know have been gotten out at different times and places and by different workmen—Stephen, Franklin, Roger, and James, for instance—and when we see these timbers joined together, and see they exactly make the frame of a house or a mill, all the tenons and mortices exactly fitting . . . we find it impossible to not *believe* that Stephen and Franklin and Roger and James all understood one another from the beginning, and all worked upon a common *plan* or draft.[32]

With that, Lincoln called upon Illinois Republicans to rally to his standard and display a united front against Douglas.

Douglas cast a wary eye on Lincoln, recognizing him as "the strong man of the [Republican] party—full of wit, facts, dates—and he is the best stump speaker, with

---

32. Lincoln, "'A House Divided': Speech at Springfield, Illinois," in *Collected Works,* 2:461–62, 465–66.

his droll ways and dry jokes, in the West. He is as honest as he is shrewd, and if I beat him my victory will be hardly won."[33] Douglas's best policy would have been to stay away from Lincoln and rely on his own enormous prestige in Illinois to carry him back to the Senate. But Douglas could never resist a fight when offered, and when Lincoln challenged Douglas to a series of debates across the state, Douglas accepted—with the stipulation that the number of debates be set at seven and that Douglas be given the upper hand in rebuttals. The debates began on August 21 in Ottawa, Illinois, and ranged across the state to Freeport on August 27, Jonesboro on September 15, Charleston on September 18, Galesburg on October 7, Quincy on October 13, and Alton (where Elijah Lovejoy had been murdered twenty-one years before) on October 15.

Douglas's plan for the debates was to paint himself as the champion of a white man's democracy and Lincoln as an abolitionist fanatic whose opposition to popular sovereignty would let down Illinois's barriers to black immigration. The "House Divided" speech, in Douglas's hands, was the principal evidence that Lincoln was a reckless "Black Republican" partisan who wanted equal civil rights for blacks more than he wanted a stable and peaceful Union. "He tells you this Republic cannot endure permanently divided into Slave and Free states, as our fathers made it," Douglas roared during the third debate. "Why can it not last, if we will execute the Government in the same spirit and upon the same principles upon which it is founded?" It would last just fine, Douglas insisted, if Lincoln and the Republicans would simply leave off trying to impose abolition on the South or upon the territories. "It can thus exist if each State will carry out the principles upon which our institutions were founded . . . the right of each State to do as it pleases, without meddling with its neighbors." Giving each state active popular sovereignty over its affairs (and each territory passive popular sovereignty over its organization) was the only way to guarantee peace among the states. "There is but one path of peace in this Republic," Douglas declared, "and that is to administer this Government as our fathers made it, divided into Free and Slave States." The best signpost to that path was popular sovereignty, "allowing each State to decide for itself whether it wants slavery or not."[34]

It mattered nothing to Douglas whether slavery itself was right or wrong, or whether there was a moral imperative that justified its restriction no matter what damage that requirement did to the rights of an individual state. If each state and territory were left to "settle the slavery question for herself, and mind her own business and let her neighbors alone . . . there will be peace between the North and South, and in the whole Union." Lest this seem too much a triumph of political expediency over a question of morality, Douglas was quick to remind his white Illinois listeners of whom their moral discomforts were being lavished upon—the Negro, whose

33. Johannsen, *Stephen A. Douglas*, 640–41.

34. Douglas, "Fifth Joint Debate," October 7, 1858, in *The Lincoln-Douglas Debates of 1858*, ed. E. E. Sparks (Springfield: Illinois State Historical Library, 1908), 346.

presence they loathed anyway. He asked them to suppose that slavery was wrong, and so wrong that restriction and abolition was the only cure: what would the result be for Illinois? "Do you desire to turn this beautiful State into a free negro colony, in order that when Missouri abolishes slavery she can send one hundred thousand emancipated slaves into Illinois, to become citizens and voters, on an equality with yourselves?" Douglas asked. Thus race came to the rescue of expediency and calmed the queasy consciences of those who were wondering if peace by popular sovereignty might come at too high a price to democracy. Douglas, in fact, played the race hatred card repeatedly and shamelessly throughout the debates. "All I have to say on that subject is," Douglas announced in Freeport, "that those of you who believe that the negro is your equal and ought to be on an equality with you socially, politically, and legally, have a right to entertain those opinions, and of course will vote for Mr. Lincoln." *Down with the negro,* growled the vast throng of listeners.[35]

Lincoln was not willing to be thrown on the defensive so easily. Principally, Lincoln attacked the popular sovereignty scheme as having no meaning after *Dred Scott*. In the debate at Freeport, Lincoln forced the spotlight onto the incompatibility of popular sovereignty with *Dred Scott* by posing a question to Douglas: "Can the people of the United States Territory, in any lawful way, against the wish of any citizen of the United States, exclude slavery from its limits prior to the formation of a State constitution?" Douglas had no choice, at Freeport and elsewhere, but to answer yes, in order to preserve his own political integrity and win an election in Illinois, where white voters wanted assurances that popular sovereignty really would keep slavery out. "It matters not what way the Supreme Court may hereafter decide as to the abstract question whether slavery may or may not go into a Territory under the Constitution, the people have the lawful means to introduce it or exclude it as they please," Douglas irritably responded. The people could do this, in spite of *Dred Scott*, by passively refusing to enact slave codes, since "slavery cannot exist a day or an hour anywhere, unless it is supported by local police regulations."[36]

That meant, as Lincoln later pointed out, that what the Supreme Court had declared lawful—slavery in the territories—could somehow be rendered unlawful without the rendering being in any way contradictory. In turn, it meant that any territory that voted itself free might just as easily vote itself slave if the popular will later on altered its "police regulations." Illinoisans who hated abolition because (as Douglas put it) abolition meant an influx of freed blacks into Illinois had to be just as suspicious of popular sovereignty, since (as Lincoln put it in his own appeal to white racial prejudice) Illinoisans who emigrated to a free territory today might find it a slave territory tomorrow. "I am in favor," added Lincoln, of keeping the territories

35. Douglas, "Third Joint Debate," September 15, 1858, "First Joint Debate," August 21, 1858, and "Second Joint Debate," August 27, 1858, in *The Lincoln-Douglas Debates of 1858*, 95, 166, 223, 227.

36. Douglas, "Second Joint Debate" with "Mr. Douglas's Reply," August 27, 1858, in *Lincoln-Douglas Debates*, 161.

as "an outlet for free white people everywhere, the world over,—in which . . . all other men from all the world, may find new homes and better their condition in life."[37] This effectively reduced popular sovereignty to what Lincoln had all along insisted it was, a subterfuge.

Moreover, urged Lincoln, even if popular sovereignty could somehow ensure that the Union could peacefully endure half slave and half free, such a divided arrangement flew in the face of the real intentions of the framers of the American republic. "When this Government was first established," Lincoln said, "it was the policy of its founders to prohibit the spread of slavery into the new Territories of the United States, where it had not existed." All that Lincoln asked "is that it should be placed back again upon the basis that the fathers of our Government originally placed it upon. I have no doubt that it *would* become extinct . . . if we but re-adopted the policy of the fathers, by restricting it to the limits it has already covered,—restricting it from the new Territories." Douglas's dogma of popular sovereignty was not perpetuating the American republic; it was perverting it. And instead of popular sovereignty guaranteeing peace, it would only guarantee contention. "What right have we then to hope," Lincoln asked, "that the trouble will cease,—that the agitation will come to an end,—until it shall either be placed back where it originally stood, and where the fathers originally placed it, or, on the other hand until it shall entirely master all opposition."[38] At that point, slavery would plant itself not only in the territories but in the free states as well, and Douglas would be responsible for the very racial strife that he had fastened on Lincoln.

Lincoln had a larger point to make than merely the theoretical inconsistencies of popular sovereignty. Douglas's error lay not only in failing to see that popular sovereignty was an impractical instrument for containing slavery but also in failing to see that slavery itself was a moral wrong, a violation of the natural right to "life, liberty, and the pursuit of happiness" written into the very frame of human nature, and "made so plain by our good Father in Heaven, that all feel and understand it, even down to brutes and creeping insects." Even "the ant, who has toiled and dragged a crumb to his nest, will furiously defend the fruit of his labor, against whatever robber assails him." If the ants understood by simple instinct that the robbery of what they had worked for was naturally wrong, then it was plain that human beings must, too—"so plain, that the most dumb and stupid slave that ever toiled for a master, does constantly know that he is wronged."[39]

As a violation of natural law, slavery did not deserve, and should not claim, the protection of popular sovereignty. Douglas had advertised himself as the champion of democratic government by insisting that the people, not Congress or the Supreme Court, were the only ones who had the right to choose whether their states should

37. Lincoln, "Second Joint Debate," August 27, 1858, and "Seventh Joint Debate," October 15, 1858, in *Lincoln-Douglas Debates*, 152, 481.

38. Lincoln, "Third Joint Debate," September 15, 1858, in *Lincoln-Douglas Debates*, 230, 235.

39. Lincoln, "Fragment on Slavery," July 1, 1854, in *Collected Works*, 2:222.

be slave or free. Lincoln replied that the will of the people could never be so absolute as to vote some people into slavery and others into freedom. That would make amoral nonsense of democracy. The right of the black slave to "eat the bread, without the leave of anybody else, which his own hand earns," was so much a matter of natural law that no bare majority of white voters had the power to deny him. In that sense, the black slave was the natural equal of any other human being—"my equal, and the equal of Judge Douglas, and the equal of every living man."[40]

Democracy must be not simply the vote of the majority but the choice by the majority of what is morally right, and the position of the Republicans was that slavery was so much a moral wrong that no amount of popular sovereignty could ever make slavery right for an American territory. In the last debate of the series, Lincoln insisted that "the real issue in this controversy—the one pressing upon every mind—is the sentiment on the one part of one class that looks upon the institution of slavery as a wrong, and on another class that does not look upon it as a wrong."

> It is the eternal struggle between these two principles—right and wrong—throughout the world. . . . It is the same principle in whatever shape it develops itself. It is the same spirit that says, "You work and toil and earn bread, and I'll eat it." [Loud applause.] No matter in what shape it comes, whether from the mouth of a king who seeks to bestride the people of his own nation and live by the fruit of their labor, or from one race of men as an apology for enslaving another race, it is the same tyrannical principle.[41]

Perhaps it is worth saying, in Douglas's defense, that the Little Giant did not believe that slavery was actually right, nor did Lincoln in 1858 believe that it was wrong enough to justify direct intervention in the affairs of states where it was already domesticated, or that natural equality immediately translated into civil equality. *Natural* rights were permanent, common, and intuitive, and defined the person as a human being; *civil* rights were bestowed by communities and could be changed, altered, revoked, or bestowed as a community saw fit, without that in any way impairing the essential humanity of the individuals involved. "Society," as even one New England abolitionist wrote, "in forming its institutions and organizations has a right to with-hold [voting rights] from any person or class of persons who it believes cannot exercise it understandingly."[42] Natural rights, however, were not the gift of "society." They were possessed equally by all human beings simply by virtue of being human, and for Lincoln in 1858, black people were certainly the equals of whites in terms of their natural humanity. That made slavery a wrong that should be contained wherever there was opportunity to contain it.

40. Lincoln, "First Joint Debate," August 21, 1858, in *Lincoln-Douglas Debates*, 102.

41. Lincoln, "Seventh Joint Debate," October 15, 1858, in *Lincoln-Douglas Debates*, 482, 485.

42. Richard Sewall, *John P. Hale and the Politics of Abolition* (Cambridge, MA: Harvard University Press, 1965), 210.

For Douglas, black people were so far from being the equals of whites in any sense, natural or civil, that the misfortune of their enslavement was simply not worth antagonizing half the Union, especially when opening up half the continent was at stake. For Douglas, the question about slavery was not natural rights but workaday politics—*shall we let this quarrel over inferior beings wreck the Union?* For the time being, that was the basic outlook of most Illinoisans.

Douglas Democrats won the majority of the Illinois legislative seats on election day, November 2, and since the Illinois legislature was still the legal forum for electing the state's U.S. senators, it was the legislature and not the popular vote of the people of Illinois that on January 5 sent Douglas back to Washington.

Lincoln tried to put as jolly a face on the situation as he could. On his way home on election night, "the path" he walked "had been worn hog-backed & was slippering. My foot slipped from under me, knocking the other one out of the way, but I recovered myself & lit square: and I said to myself, 'It's a slip and not a fall.'" And that would be how he would try to understand his defeat—a slip and not a fall. In his bleaker moments, though, he could not help seeing this defeat as being of a piece with all his other political disappointments. "I have no regrets for having . . . resolutely made the struggle," he wrote to Salmon Chase of Ohio, the one Republican worthy who had come to Illinois to campaign for Lincoln in 1858—although "I would have preferred success."[43] Yet his loss really was a significant one. By forcing out into the open the inconsistencies of the popular sovereignty dogma, Lincoln had made it impossible both for anti-slavery Republicans to see Douglas as an ally and for pro-slavery Southerners to see him as a friend to slavery's unlimited expansion. Incidentally, he had also made himself a national figure, with results that people were already beginning to speculate upon.

NEVER BE PURGED BUT WITH BLOOD

When James Buchanan became president in 1856 it was fervently hoped that he would have the political tools necessary to put the slavery agitation to rest. Buchanan had to his credit almost forty years of experience in Congress, the cabinet, and most recently in diplomatic service. Although he was a Pennsylvanian by birth and a Northern Democrat by conviction, he nevertheless sympathized with the South's ever-mounting demands for reassurance, and the hope that he would be able to please everyone was the single most important factor in his victory over the fatally divided Whigs. "This question of domestic slavery is the weak point in our institutions," Buchanan admitted as early as 1836. That meant it was all the more important for him to show it the loftiest respect: "Touch this question of slavery seriously—let

---

43. John Hay, diary entry for November 8, 1864, in *Inside Lincoln's White House: The Complete Civil War Diary of John Hay*, ed. Michael Burlingame and J. R. T. Ettlinger (Carbondale: Southern Illinois University Press, 1997), 244; Lincoln, "To Salmon P. Chase," April 30, 1859, in *Collected Works*, 3:378.

it once be made manifest to the people of the South that they cannot live with us, except in a state of continual apprehension and alarm for their wives and their children, for all that is near and dear to them upon the earth,—and the Union is from that moment dissolved."[44]

This pervasive anxiety not to provoke Southerners guaranteed that Buchanan's skills as a diplomat would serve to hobble rather than help him. Anxious to obtain peace in Kansas, Buchanan allowed himself to be intimidated by the violence of Southern threats of disunion; once intimidated by the Southerners in his cabinet and in Congress, he grew spiteful and resentful when Northern Democrats—especially Stephen A. Douglas—balked at his proposals to concede virtually every demand made by the South.

Settling the bloody mess in Kansas was Buchanan's first chore. He was assisted—or so he thought—in dictating a settlement by the *Dred Scott* decision, which apparently relieved Washington of any responsibility to see that Kansas would choose slavery or freedom. However, Kansas insisted on making trouble for him anyway. The old territorial governor under President Pierce, John W. Geary, had brought a measure of peace to Kansas by the end of 1856, but the rest of the territorial government was still split between two rival legislatures, each claiming to be the legal voice of the people of Kansas. One of these was the "official" legislature, a pro-slavery body elected by fraud in 1855 and sitting in the town of Lecompton; the other was a free-soil assembly, sitting in Topeka.

On February 19, 1857, just before Buchanan's inauguration, the Lecompton legislature, anticipating that the new president would probably appoint a new territorial governor, decided to get the jump on the appointment process. The Lecomptonites authorized the election of a constitutional convention that would draw up a state constitution for Kansas, a constitution that would then be submitted to Congress for its approval and for the admission of Kansas to the Union. Geary vetoed the convention bill, rightly accusing the pro-slavery legislature of attempting to stampede a rush to statehood on pro-slavery terms. The Lecompton legislature overrode Geary's veto, however, and as soon as James Buchanan was inaugurated as president, Buchanan fired him.

Buchanan replaced Geary with a Mississippian, Robert J. Walker, which delighted the pro-slavery elements in Kansas. But Walker was no pro-slavery fire-eater. A friend of Stephen A. Douglas, Walker was convinced that slavery had no practical future in Kansas and that the territory ought to be admitted as a free state. Walker's appointment only fed the determination of the Lecompton legislature to nail together a pro-slavery state constitution as quickly as possible, and in November 1857 a constitutional convention approved a document that had something in it to offend nearly everyone.

44. Buchanan, "Remarks, March 9, 1836, on the Reception of Petitions for the Abolition of Slavery in the District of Columbia," in *The Works of James Buchanan: Comprising His Speeches, State Papers and Private Correspondence*, ed. James Bassett Moore (Philadelphia: J. B. Lippincott, 1908), 3:26–27.

In addition to protecting the 200 slaves then in Kansas, the Lecompton Constitution placed restrictions on the chartering of banks, banned free blacks from the state, and prohibited any amendments to the constitution for seven years. As a sop to the idea of popular sovereignty, the new constitution allowed for the calling of a public referendum, but only on the question of whether new slaves could be brought into Kansas, which effectively guaranteed Kansas's admission as a slave state no matter what. Even more amazing was President Buchanan's response to the Lecompton constitution. Browbeaten by Southern congressional delegations and the Southern members of his cabinet, Buchanan decided to endorse the Lecompton constitution and recommended it favorably in his first annual presidential message (his State of the Union address, as it would be called now) to Congress on December 8, 1857.

"This message," complained the unhappy Buchanan afterward, gave rise to exactly the opposite of what he had hoped: "a long, exciting, and occasionally violent debate in both Houses of Congress, between the anti-slavery members and their opponents, which lasted for three months," in which "slavery was denounced in every form which could exasperate the Southern people, and render it odious to the people of the North; whilst on the other hand, many of the speeches of Southern members displayed characteristic violence."[45]

In the light of the repeated electoral frauds in the Lecompton legislature and the refusal of the constitutional convention to submit the entire constitution for popular approval in Kansas, any congressional acceptance of the Lecompton Constitution was tantamount to repudiating the heart of popular sovereignty, as well as virtually admitting Kansas as a slave state. Stephen Douglas, righteous in his wrath against Buchanan, took his political life into his own hands and assailed the Lecompton Constitution on the floor of the Senate as a mockery of the popular sovereignty principle. When Buchanan threatened to bring down party discipline on him with all the wrath of an Andrew Jackson, Douglas belligerently replied, "Mr. President, I wish you to remember that General Jackson is dead, sir."[46]

Furthermore, free-soil Kansans boycotted the initial referendum on Lecompton on December 21, then joined in a second referendum on January 4 where they defeated it by a clear majority. But Buchanan had committed himself to the Lecompton constitution: he accepted the resignation of the disgusted Governor Walker in December and proceeded to pull every political string a president can conceivably pull, twisting approval of the Lecompton constitution out of the Senate on March 23, 1858 by a 33–25 vote, and then out of the House on April 1—but only after another full-scale donnybrook on the floor of the House that pitted two dozen congressmen against each other.

45. George Ticknor Curtis, *Life of James Buchanan: Fifteenth President of the United States* (New York: Harper and Brothers, 1883), 2:207.

46. Jeriah Bonham, *Fifty Years' Recollections: With Observations and Reflections on Historical Events* (Peoria, IL: J. W. Franks and Sons, 1883), 196–97.

Unhappily for Buchanan, the House bill contained an amendment that the Senate version lacked, and the whole question was now thrown into a House-Senate conference committee for resolution. At the urging of William H. English of Indiana, one of the three House conferees, a compromise was devised that accepted Lecompton and the statehood of Kansas—provided that the Lecompton constitution was resubmitted to the people of Kansas for a federally supervised election. Douglas, however, mistrusted Lecompton no matter who supervised an election; and his enemies in Congress foolishly persuaded Buchanan that anything that Douglas opposed was the perfect thing for the president to support. The English attachment passed both House and Senate on April 30, 1858. Accordingly, the Lecompton constitution went back to the voters of Kansas for a third time, and to the hideous embarrassment of Buchanan, the voters of Kansas turned out on August 30 and rejected Lecompton by a vote of 11,812 to 1,926.[47]

Buchanan had lost one of the most vicious political struggles in the history of Congress, Southern Democrats had seriously damaged the patience of their Northern counterparts, and Buchanan loyalists in the North were unseated wholesale by upstart Republicans in the 1858 congressional elections. In the state elections a year later, Republicans seized control of the legislatures and governorships of the New England states, Ohio, Pennsylvania, Minnesota, and Iowa. To add insult to injury, Douglas successfully won reelection to the Senate after a grueling campaign against the new rising Republican star of Illinois, Lincoln. In fact, almost the only Northern Democrats who survived Northern anger over Lecompton were anti-administration Douglasites.

Buchanan's troubles had only begun, and they were now about to be worsened by one of the weirdest episodes in the history of American politics. Few people outside Kansas knew anything about John Brown, and those within Kansas knew him only as the anti-slavery fanatic who had taken his own private revenge on the pro-slavery cause in the murders at Pottawatomie in May 1856. Brown raged against slavery with all the ill-controlled violence of his being. If Brown was a fanatic, he was also something of a visionary: profoundly moved by the injustice of slavery, a champion of the political equality of blacks, willing to break any man-made law in the interest of obeying a higher law of justice and right. "He was always an enigma," wrote one anti-slavery journalist who met Brown in 1856, "a strange compound of enthusiasm and cold, methodic stolidity,—a volcano beneath a mountain of snow."[48]

Unfortunately for Brown, the temporary peace that Governor Geary brought to Kansas after the Pottawatomie massacre dried up most of the excitement Brown had derived from butchering hapless slaveholders. He took little interest in the debate

47. Harry V. Jaffa, *Crisis of the House Divided: An Interpretation of the Issues in the Lincoln-Douglas Debates* (Chicago: University of Chicago Press, 1982), 440.

48. David S. Reynolds, *John Brown, Abolitionist: The Man Who Killed Slavery, Sparked the Civil War, and Seeded Civil Rights* (New York: Knopf, 2005), 191.

over the Lecompton Constitution, and instead he began to cast around for more substantial opportunities to wreak havoc on what he perceived as the satanic minions of the slave aristocracy. In December 1858 he participated in another raid, this time on Fort Scott, which liberated a free-state prisoner and killed a shopkeeper. Brown then raided into Missouri, liberating eleven Missouri slaves whom he then transported to Canada. But Brown got no thanks among the free-staters in Kansas, since his raids only drew the wrath of pro-slavery thugs down on their heads. "I consider it my duty to draw the scene of excitement to some other part of the country," Brown announced, and once he deposited his fugitives in Canada in March 1859, he gave no more thought to Kansas.[49]

Instead, Brown's eye fell upon Virginia. Between January 1857 and June 1859, Brown began recruiting volunteers and money for a guerilla raid into the Old Dominion. Brown's plan was to liberate as many slaves as he could find or who would flock to him, establish himself in a stronghold in the western Virginia mountains, and from there engulf all of the South in a massive slave insurrection. The initial object of the raid would be the federal arsenal at Harpers Ferry, on the upper Potomac River, where Brown would be able to seize the arms he would need to defend himself in the Virginia mountains. Listened to dispassionately, Brown's scheme was bizarre to say the least, and Frederick Douglass, who had known Brown since 1847, tried to talk him out of it, down to almost the last minute. "My discretion or my cowardice made me proof against the dear old man's eloquence," Douglass said, reporting that he attempted to convince Brown in his last meeting with him that Harpers Ferry was "a perfect steel trap and that once in he would never get out alive."[50]

Brown had made up his mind, however, and by mid-October he had managed to recruit and train twenty-two fighters, some of them free blacks, such as Dangerfield Newby, who hoped to liberate their families still in slavery. More significant, Brown had traded in on his reputation as a hero of anti-slavery militancy to approach prominent Eastern abolitionists such as Thomas Wentworth Higginson, Theodore Parker, George Luther Stearns, Franklin B. Sanborn, Gerrit Smith, and Samuel Gridley Howe, and easily hypnotized them with his fire-and-brimstone eloquence into giving him the money he needed to finance the attack on Harpers Ferry. "God has honored comparatively but a very small part of mankind with any possible chance for such mighty & soul-satisfying rewards," he assured Franklin Sanborn. "I expect to effect a mighty conquest even though it be like the last victory of Sampson."[51]

49. Oswald Garrison Villard, *John Brown, 1800–1859: A Biography Fifty Years After* (Boston: Houghton Mifflin, 1910), 366–67, 373–78; Thomas Goodrich, *War to the Knife: Bleeding Kansas, 1854–1861* (Lincoln: University Press of Nebraska, 2004), 225.

50. Frederick Douglass, *Life and Times of Frederick Douglass, Written by Himself* (New York: Pathway Press, 1941), 249–51, 352–53.

51. Merrill D. Peterson, *John Brown: The Legend Revisited* (Charlottesville: University Press of Virginia, 2002), 6–7, 11; John Stauffer, *The Black Hearts of Men: Radical Abolitionists and the Transformation of Race* (Cambridge, MA: Harvard University Press, 2001), 258.

Early in the morning of October 17, 1859, Brown and his followers descended upon the Harpers Ferry arsenal, disposed of its two guards, captured the Baltimore & Ohio railroad bridge over the Potomac, and sent squads out to gather up slave recruits. Instead of an army of slave volunteers, two companies of Virginia militia arrived to pin Brown down in the arsenal and begin picking off his men. By mid-afternoon, Brown and his beleaguered band were barricaded into the arsenal's brick firehouse. The next morning, a detachment of U.S. Marines under a lieutenant colonel of cavalry named Robert E. Lee assaulted the firehouse and captured or killed all of Brown's remaining men.[52]

It might have been best for the emotional well-being of the entire country had Brown himself died in the assault, but he was only wounded and captured, and subsequently he was put on trial for treason, murder, and insurrection against the Commonwealth of Virginia. The trial gave Brown what he had always really wanted, a public pulpit, and what he revealed about the nature of his plot, the identities of the people who had backed it, and the cold fury with which he was prepared to execute it sent a shiver of horror down the back of the South. As Frederick Douglass wrote afterward, "With the Allegheny mountains for his pulpit, the country for his church, and the whole civilized world for his audience, John Brown was a thousand times more powerful as a preacher than as a warrior."[53]

It could only have conjured up nightmares of Nat Turner, of slave rebellion, of wholesale race war, to listen to Brown's description of his planned insurrection, especially since it was evident that he had absolutely no regrets about what he had done or what he had planned to do. "I see a book kissed which I suppose to be the Bible," Brown said at his sentencing, "which teaches me that all things whatsoever I would that men should do to me, I should do to them. . . . I believe that to have interfered as I have done in behalf of His despised poor, is no wrong, but right." If the court found that sufficient grounds for his execution, then he embraced the verdict with the fervor of a Christian martyr. "Now, if it is deemed necessary that I should forfeit my life for the furtherance of the ends of justice, and mingle my blood with the blood of millions in this slave country whose rights are disregarded by wicked, cruel, and unjust enactments, I say let it be done." Brown's trial lasted seven days, during which he behaved himself with amazing composure. He was declared guilty on November 2, 1859, and hanged on December 2 in Charlestown. His last words, written on a slip of paper and handed to a jail guard, Hiram O'Bannon, hung like dark thunderclouds over the American horizon: "I John Brown am now quite *certain* that the crimes of this *guilty land* will never be purged *away*, but with Blood. I had *as I now think, vainly* flattered myself that without *very much* bloodshed, it might be done."[54]

52. Reynolds, *John Brown: Abolitionist*, 309–28.

53. David W. Blight, *Frederick Douglass' Civil War: Keeping Faith in Jubilee* (Baton Rouge: Louisiana State University Press, 1989), 97; Reynolds, *John Brown, Abolitionist*, 354.

54. Brian McGinty, *John Brown's Trial* (Cambridge, MA: Harvard University Press, 2009), 257.

Brown's raid caused an eruption in the South. Although Southern leaders publicly congratulated their slaves on their reluctance to rally to Brown's banner, the behavior of Southern whites showed something entirely different from confidence. "Never has the country been so excited before," wrote one Georgian in December 1859. "There was great feeling in 1820, but not like the present. The South is deeply stirred." Governor Andrew Barry Moore of Alabama called for passage of a bill that organized volunteer military units in every Alabama county, authorized borrowing $200,000 to buy weapons, and established scholarships for young Alabama males to attend military schools. Slave codes were toughened, slave patrols were reinstated, and violence against blacks multiplied. White Northerners were particularly suspect, since travelers and strangers from the North could easily turn out to be emissaries of some future John Brown. Nonslaveholding white Southerners were also the target of suspicion. It had not escaped the notice of the planters and their friends in the Southern state capitals that Brown had chosen western Virginia for his raid, a region of comparatively few slaves but full of resentful white yeomen. It was even more disturbing to learn that the Harpers Ferry townspeople and even the militia had been less than enthusiastic in attacking Brown (the Virginia militia had, in fact, declined Lieutenant Colonel Lee's invitation to make the final assault on Brown). "Watch Harpers Ferry people," Virginia governor Henry Wise warned his agents in mid-November, and at Brown's hanging, Wise ordered the local commander to "let no crowd be near enough to the prisoner to hear any speech he may attempt."[55]

The ultimate message of John Brown for Southerners was the lesson of distrust for the North, for Brown's raid was seized upon as argument-clinching proof that the North was only awaiting its opportunity to destroy the South by force, and the discovery of Brown's private correspondence in his temporary headquarters in Maryland underscored how much support Brown had enjoyed from prominent Northern abolitionists. Northern reactions to Brown's execution only served to redouble Southern accusations about the real intentions of Northerners. "This mad attempt of a handful of vulgar cut-throats," wrote Robert Lewis Dabney, "would have been a very trivial affair to the Southern people, but for the manner in which it was regarded by the people of the North."[56]

Although Lincoln and other Republicans hastened to wash their hands of any association with Brown, across the North Brown's steadfast and unrelenting courage at his trial dimmed the idiocy of his raid and allowed him to emerge as a hero, and abolitionism as heroic. In Chicago, church bells were tolled at the hour of Brown's

55. Clarence L. Mohr, *On the Threshold of Freedom: Masters and Slaves in Civil War Georgia* (Athens: University of Georgia Press, 1986), 7; Malcolm C. McMillan, *The Disintegration of a Confederate State: Three Governors and Alabama's Wartime Home Front, 1861–1865* (Macon, GA: Mercer University Press, 1986), 11; Simpson, *A Good Southerner*, 211–12.

56. Dabney, *Life and Campaigns of Lieut.-Gen. Thomas J. Jackson* (New York: Blelock, 1866), 144.

execution, Albany fired a 100-gun salute, immense memorial meetings were organized in Philadelphia and New York, and in Boston William Lloyd Garrison praised Brown as a model fit for repeated imitation. "Was John Brown justified in his attempt?" Garrison asked enthusiastically. "Yes, if Washington was in his . . . If men are justified in striking a blow for freedom, when the question is one of a threepenny tax on tea, then, I say, they are a thousand times more justified, when it is to save fathers, mothers, wives and children from the slave-coffle and the auction-block, and to restore to them their God-given rights." Garrison was a pacifist by conviction, "yet, as a peace man—an 'ultra' peace man—I am prepared to say 'Success to every slave insurrection at the South, and in every slave country.'"[57] No wonder the South saw Brown's raid as sinister proof that the Union was turning into an embrace with destruction.

The primary casualty of Harpers Ferry was, ironically, the Democratic Party. Persuaded that no Northerners were to be trusted after Harpers Ferry, Southern Democrats now began to demand that their voice have the preponderant weight in determining Democratic policy. Addressing the Virginia legislature in January 1860, Christopher Memminger announced that the South must secure four guarantees in the next election for its continued safety—an equal share for the South of all the Western territories, the disbanding of all anti-slavery societies, the repeal of any laws that obstructed the capture of fugitive slaves, and a ban against any amendment of the Constitution respecting slavery—while others such as Jefferson Davis of Mississippi added to that demands for a national slave code that would prevent interference by a territorial legislature "whether by direct legislation or legislation of an indirect and unfriendly nature . . . the constitutional right of any citizen of the United States to take his slave property into the common Territories."[58] They fully expected the next Democratic national convention in Charleston, South Carolina, to make these demands part of its national platform.

Douglas and the Northern Democrats were unwilling to acquiesce in a legislative program for the destruction of popular sovereignty in the territories, and certainly not for the purpose of pandering to Southern anxieties about John Brown and slavery. The stakes were made all the higher since Buchanan, bowing to Democratic tradition and weary of the burdens of the presidency, had announced his intention not to seek reelection. This left Douglas as the single most obvious candidate for the Democrats to run for the presidency in 1860. Douglas's defense of popular sovereignty and his defiance of Lecompton in the teeth of Buchanan's rage had made Douglas the champion of the Northern Democracy, and the only acceptable presidential candidate to the Northern half of the party. Moreover, Northern Democrats were convinced that only Douglas, and not the Southern fire-eaters, had the national stature to carry both

57. Garrison, "Speech of William Lloyd Garrison," December 16, 1859, in *Documents of Upheaval*, 265–66.

58. William C. Davis, *Jefferson Davis: The Man and His Hour, a Biography* (New York: HarperCollins, 1991), 268; Davis, "Relations of the States," February 2, 1860, *Congressional Globe*, 36th Congress, 1st session, 658.

Northern and Southern states in the presidential election of 1860. Consequently, they regarded Douglas as the only one capable of retaining Democratic control of the presidency and, with that, the entire apparatus of the federal bureaucracy.

The Northern Democracy's unwillingness to follow the demands of the Southern ultras, and their determination to see Douglas nominated by the Charleston convention, together with Southern demands for renewal of the slave trade and slave protection in the territories, made the destruction of the Democratic Party inevitable. Douglas "held out to us here, when we advocated and supported the Kansas-Nebraska bill . . . that the Democratic party should be a unit on the question," complained Louisiana senator Judah P. Benjamin, "but when he goes home, and is pressed in a local contest"—namely, the debates with Lincoln—"and he sees the glittering prize of a seat in this Chamber slipping from his grasp, he tells his people, as he says he has told them a hundred times before," that "he has, in the Kansas-Nebraska act, obtained . . . a perfect right to make a free Territory of every Territory in the Union, notwithstanding the decision of the court."[59]

When the Charleston convention assembled in April 1860, Southern radicals led by William Lowndes Yancey of Alabama stood for seven days agitating for a pro-slavery platform, and when it became clear that they would not get it from the Douglas men, all of the Deep South delegations except that of Georgia walked out of the convention. The Southern withdrawal made it statistically impossible for Douglas to obtain the necessary two-thirds vote for the nomination, and the shattered convention adjourned, to reconvene in Baltimore on June 18. But when the Democrats met again, the convention split once again, with still more Southern withdrawals, and Douglas, still short of the two-thirds majority of delegates, had to be nominated by the convention as part of a resolution. The same day, the Southern ultras nominated their own candidate, John Breckinridge of Kentucky, for president, thus making the party split a political reality.

Then, as if things were not already bad enough for the Democrats, a compromise movement, composed largely of old-time Southern Whigs and calling down a pox on both Douglas and Breckinridge, met in Baltimore and nominated yet another presidential candidate, the colorless Tennessean John Bell. The end result was that Douglas captured the Democratic nomination for the presidency, but both Southern support and the Democratic Party collapsed under him. "It is an utterly futile and hopeless task to re-organize, re-unite and harmonize the disintegrated Democratic party, unless this is to be done by a total abandonment of principle," editorialized the *Augusta Daily Chronicle and Sentinel.* "No, sensible people might as well make up their minds to the fact that the Democratic party is dissolved forever, that new organizations must take its place."[60]

59. J. P. Benjamin, *Defence of the National Democracy Against the Attack of Judge Douglas* (Washington, DC: National Democratic Executive Committee, 1860), 13–14.

60. "The Washington Abortion," in *Southern Editorials on Secession,* 111.

The Republicans viewed the splintering of the Democrats with glee, for the collapse of Democratic unity between Douglas and Breckinridge, and the unwillingness of Bell's supporters to vote for either as an acceptable Southern candidate, opened the way to a Republican victory in November. But precisely because victory was now within their grasp, the Republicans instantly began to hesitate about nominating their most ultra-anti-slavery standard-bearers, such as William H. Seward of New York. Seward was a longtime Whig who had once stiffened Zachary Taylor's back against slave expansion, and who was regarded by Northern Democrats as a reckless radical. Nominating Seward might be perceived as too violent an anti-slavery gesture by the Republicans, costing them the votes of the moderates within the party; even more serious, his championship of the Whig economic agenda in the Senate and as governor of New York might drive Northern and Southern Democrats back into each other's arms, depriving the Republicans of as much as a quarter of the votes they had won from Democrats in the 1856 presidential campaign.

The Republicans who assembled in Chicago in May 1860 for their national nominating convention would be looking for an anti-slavery man and a Whig economist who had managed to avoid making himself nationally notorious on either of those points, the kind of man Horace Greeley described in a letter to a friend: "I know the country is not Anti-Slavery. It will only swallow a little Anti-Slavery in a great deal of sweetening. An Anti-Slavery man per se cannot be elected; but a Tariff, River-and-Harbor, Pacific Railroad, Free Homestead man *may* succeed *although* he is Anti-Slavery."[61] Greeley thought this might mean the Missouri Whig Edward Bates, but the man who best fit Greeley's description was already at hand in Illinois in the person of Abraham Lincoln.

Lincoln's run against Douglas for the Illinois senate seat in 1858 had won him national attention. Despite his defeat, Lincoln had nearly managed to stage the political upset of the century, and Republicans across the North remembered him. "Mr. Lincoln is a man of very great ability; few men in the nation would willingly encounter him in debate," wrote the *National Era* two weeks after the election. "We have heard many men in all parts of the Union, and think, for clear statement, the simplifying of difficult points, taking into consideration his rectitude and singleness of purpose, he is our choice." An old political friend who had moved to Pennsylvania and had his ear close to the ground of national party politics told Lincoln, "Seriously, Lincoln, Judge Douglas being so widely known, you are getting a national reputation. . . . Your discussion with Judge Douglas had demonstrated your ability and your devotion to freedom; you have no embarrassing record; you have sprung from the humble walks of life, sharing in its toils and trials."[62] Invitations to stump for other

61. Jeter Allen Isely, *Horace Greeley and the Republican Party, 1853–1861: A Study of the New York Tribune* (New York: Octagon Books, 1965), 266; Philip S. Paludan, *The Presidency of Abraham Lincoln* (Lawrence: University Press of Kansas, 1994), 15.

62. "From Illinois," *National Era*, November 18, 1858; Ida M. Tarbell, *The Life of Abraham Lincoln* (New York: McClure, Phillips, 1904), 1:322.

Republican candidates now arrived from Wisconsin and Kansas, as well as from points around Illinois, and in the fall of 1859 he was invited by prominent New York Republicans to speak in New York City so that they might take his measure.

Lincoln was not at all averse to being measured. As early as February 1860 he admitted to his friends, "I am not in a position where it would hurt much for me to be nominated on the national ticket," and on February 16 he was pleased to find that the *Chicago Tribune* had openly endorsed him for the Republican presidential nomination, claiming that only Lincoln could carry the western states for the Republicans. The crucial test for Lincoln was the New York invitation, for this would clearly be his debut before the Republicans' East Coast party moguls. On February 27 about 1,500 New York Republicans turned out to hear Lincoln speak in the Great Hall of the Cooper Institute.

His address started poorly. Tall, gaunt, his wrists dangling out of his sleeves, Lincoln spoke in a shrill Kentucky drawl that made sophisticated New Yorkers wonder whether a terrible mistake had been made about this man. After a few moments, though, Lincoln warmed to his task, and in a short while the silent crowd turned increasingly more enthusiastic. He addressed himself first to Stephen A. Douglas, underscoring once again that the intention of the framers of the Constitution was to see slavery contained and gradually extinguished rather than given the tacit approval of the popular sovereignty doctrine. "Those fathers marked it," Lincoln insisted, "as an evil not to be extended, but to be tolerated and protected only because of and so far as its actual presence among us make that toleration and protection a necessity." Lincoln then turned to the Southern disunionists and warned them that the Republicans were not going to be frightened out of their principles simply because the South held the pistol of political disruption of the Union to their heads. Republican opposition to slavery was a matter of moral judgment, not just political expediency. "All they ask, we could readily grant, if we thought slavery right; all we ask, they could as readily grant, if they thought it wrong," Lincoln explained, "Their thinking it right, and our thinking it wrong, is the precise fact upon which depends the whole controversy."[63]

Yet Lincoln tempered his utterances with a large dash of caution. He insisted that he only wanted to contain slavery where it was, not to abolish it outright. "Wrong as we think slavery is, we can yet afford to let it alone where it is, because that much is due to the necessity arising from its actual presence in the nation." And he distanced himself from John Brown by referring to the Harpers Ferry raid as "peculiar" and "absurd." In short, Lincoln said everything he needed to say to make clear his moral opposition to the extension of slavery, while at the same time professing no personal animosity toward the South. Gone was the provocative rhetoric of the "House Divided" and the talk of conspiracy between Buchanan, Pierce,

---

63. Lincoln, "Address at Cooper Institute, New York City," in *Collected Works*, 3:534, 549–50.

Douglas, and Taney—Lincoln as much as conceded that the house could remain divided so long as one of the divisions could not expand, and in so doing he positioned himself as a firm but not radical anti-slavery man, the perfect Republican. The Cooper Institute audience roared its approval, and so did the major Republican newspapers.[64]

The greatest impact of the Cooper Institute speech would be felt in Illinois. On May 9, 1860, the Illinois Republican state convention at Decatur riotously pledged its national convention delegates to Lincoln for the presidential nomination, and at the height of a tremendous outburst of enthusiasm, Lincoln's cousin, John Hanks, paraded into the convention, bearing two weather-beaten fence rails bedecked with a banner reading: "Abraham Lincoln. The Rail Candidate for President in 1860. Two Rails from a Lot of 3,000 Made in 1830 by Thos. Hanks and Abe Lincoln." Though Lincoln had struggled all his adult life to put his crude origins out of sight and deeply resented anyone's attempt to address him informally as "Abe," the state convention saw at once the value of identifying him as a man "fresh from the people," especially the people of the pioneering West, and so he became not Mr. Lincoln the railroad lawyer or the Honorable Abraham Lincoln, Esq., of Springfield, but Abe Lincoln the Rail Splitter.

When the Republican national convention convened one week later in Chicago, most of the delegates arrived at the convention hall assuming that either Seward or some other party stalwart would be handed the presidential nomination. But Seward's reputation as a radical, unelectable in the West and anathema to anti-slavery Democrats, crippled him. The first ballot had Seward only sixty delegates shy of the nomination, but from that point on, the Illinois contingent (which already had been agitating and bargaining for their favorite son for weeks) now began wheeling and dealing in earnest while Lincoln remained in Springfield so as to be able to turn a blind eye to the politicking the Illinois Republicans were waging in his behalf. On the third ballot Lincoln landslided into the nomination, and the convention exploded into a pandemonium of jubilation. For a running mate, the Republicans cast a careful eye toward disheartened Northern Democrats and drafted a former Democrat from Maine, Hannibal Hamlin. "We are full of enthusiasm over Old Abe," exulted Indiana Republican Schuyler Colfax. "We feel that the battle is half won already."[65]

Southern Democrats were not nearly so jubilant. The Charleston newspapers began denouncing Lincoln as soon as he was nominated for the presidency in 1860, calling him a "horrid-looking wretch . . . sooty and scoundrelly in aspect; a cross between the nutmeg dealer, the horse-swapper, and the nightman," and

64. Ibid.; John A. Corry, *Lincoln at Cooper Union: The Speech That Made Him President* (New York: XLibris, 2003), 99–110; John Channing Briggs, *Lincoln's Speeches Reconsidered* (Baltimore: Johns Hopkins University Press, 2005), 241–50.

65. Colfax to C. H. Ray, May 28, 1860, *The Oliver Barrett Lincoln Collection* (New York, 1952), 99.

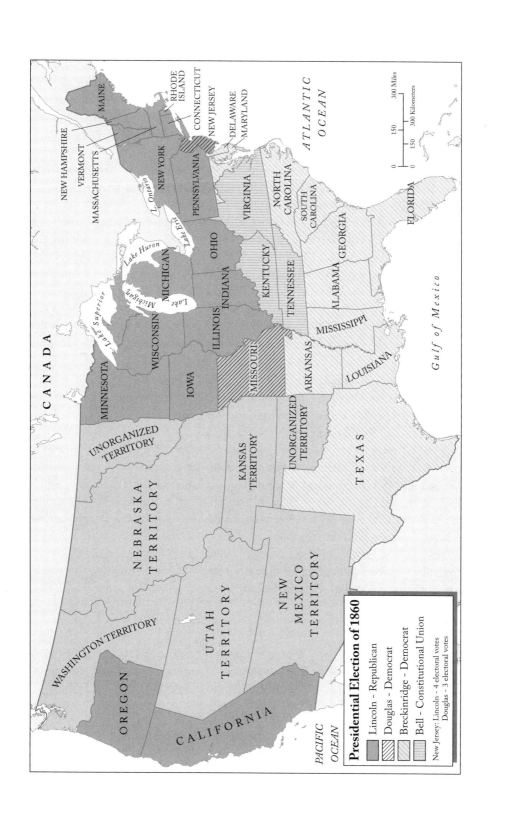

Presidential Election of 1860

Lincoln – Republican
Douglas – Democrat
Breckinridge – Democrat
Bell – Constitutional Union

New Jersey: Lincoln – 4 electoral votes
Douglas – 3 electoral votes

the Richmond papers were not much more charitable: Lincoln was an "illiterate partisan" of the abolitionists, "possessed only of his inveterate hatred of slavery." The American minister in England, George Dallas, had to fumble mentally to peg Lincoln, since he knew only that "Lincoln is as absolutely self-made as our democracy could desire. He began life as a day-labourer, and took to making fence-rails."[66]

With the Democratic Party shivered into three splinters, there was little practical hope of defeating Lincoln and the Republicans, and after a glum and lackluster campaign by most of the candidates, Lincoln successfully captured the presidential election on November 6, 1860. Ironically, he had polled almost a million votes less than the combined popular votes of his three opponents, Douglas, Breckinridge, and Bell—which meant that the Southern Democrats, by refusing to unite behind Douglas, had actually helped to bring about the very thing they had screamed against, the election of a Republican president. Even with less than a majority of popular votes, Lincoln still commanded the 180 electoral votes of the North. Those electoral votes would have given him the election even if the South had united both its popular and electoral votes entirely behind Douglas.[67]

At last the game of balances was tipping irrevocably over the edge of the table. One day after the election, interest rates on the New York money markets began to soar nervously toward 12 percent, and the New York lawyer George Templeton Strong groaned that "apprehension . . . has destroyed confidence in securities and property of every kind." That same day, Judge Andrew McGrath closed the U.S. court in Charleston, South Carolina. The outgoing governor of South Carolina, William Henry Gist, who had held the state legislature in special session to watch the outcome of the election, now urged the calling of "a convention of the people of the State . . . to consider and determine for themselves the mode and measure of redress." Gist was not reluctant about suggesting that "the only alternative left . . . is the secession of South Carolina from the Union." On November 12, the legislature complied, passing a bill calling for the assembling of a state convention that would withdraw South Carolina from the Union.[68]

66. Robert W. Johannsen, *Lincoln, the South and Slavery: The Political Dimension* (Baton Rouge: Louisiana State University Press, 1991), 104, 112; Dallas, diary entry for June 2, 1860, in *Diary of George Mifflin Dallas: While United States Minister to Russia 1837 to 1839 and to England 1856 to 1861*, ed. Susan Dallas (Philadelphia: J. B. Lippincott, 1892), 403.

67. *Tribune Almanac for 1861* (New York: New York Tribune, 1861), 64.

68. Strong, diary entry for November 17, 1861, in *The Diary of George Templeton Strong, 1860–1865*, ed. Allan Nevins (New York: Macmillan, 1962), 63; William C. Harris, *Lincoln's Rise to the Presidency* (Lawrence: University Press of Kansas, 2007), 253; Freehling, The *Road to Disunion: Secessionists Triumphant*, 398–99; Yates Snowden, *History of South Carolina* (Chicago: Lewis, 1920), 2:659.

THE SUMTER CRISIS

It will be difficult for us to appreciate the degree of desperation produced in the South by Lincoln's election unless we remember what the presidency meant on the local level in the 1860s. The creation of a professional civil service was still another thirty years in the future, and in the meantime, every federal appointive office— some 900 of them all told, from the cabinet down to the lowliest postmaster—was filled at presidential discretion and usually according to party or philosophical loyalties. Until 1860 fully half of these appointees were Southerners; in the case of the Supreme Court, nineteen out of thirty-four sitting justices appointed between Washington and Lincoln were slaveholders.[69] Much as Lincoln might protest that he was no John Brown, his identity as a Republican was enough to convince most Southerners that he would appoint only Republicans to postmasterships (where they could ensure the free flow of abolitionist literature into every Southern hamlet), only Republicans as federal marshals (who would then turn a deliberately blind eye to fugitive slaves en route to Canada), only Republicans to army commands (and thus turn the federal army into an anti-slavery militia, and federal forts and arsenals in the South into abolitionist havens), and thus make the Republicans, and the anti-slavery attitude, attractive to the nonslaveholding whites of the South without whose cooperation the survival of slavery would be impossible. These Republican intruders would "circulate insurrectionary documents and disseminate insurrectionary sentiments among [the] hitherto contented servile population." That was entirely aside from the possibility that Lincoln himself harbored hostile designs on the South. Georgia governor Joseph Brown prophesied, with remarkable foresight, that

> if Mr. Lincoln places among us his Judges, District Attorneys, Marshals, Post Masters, Custom House officers, etc., etc., by the end of his administration, with the control of public patronage, he will have succeeded in dividing us to an extent that will destroy all our moral powers, and prepare us to tolerate the running of a Republican ticket, in most of the States of the South, in 1864. If this ticket only secured five or ten thousand votes in each of the Southern States, it would be as large as the abolition party was in the North a few years ago since. . . . This would soon give it control of our elections. We would then be powerless, and the abolitionists would press forward, with a steady step, to the accomplishment of their object. They would refuse to admit any other slave States to the Union. They would abolish slavery in the District of Columbia, and at the Forts, Arsenals and Dock Yards, within the Southern States, which belong to the United States. They would then abolish the internal slave trade between the States, and prohibit a slave owner from carrying his slaves into Alabama or South Carolina, and there selling them. . . . Finally, when we were sufficiently humiliated, and sufficiently in

69. Richards, *The Slave Power*, 91–94.

their power, they would abolish slavery in the States. It will not be many years before enough of free States may be formed out of the present territories of the United States, and admitted into the Union, to give them sufficient strength to change the Constitution, and remove all Constitutional barriers which now deny to Congress this power.[70]

Lincoln, as the president-elect, tried to offer as much in the way of reassurance as he could to the South without violating his own principles or the platform of the Republican Party. Late in November Lincoln wrote that, as president, he would regard himself as bound to obey the Constitution and the laws, including the fugitive slave laws and the security of slavery in the slave states. "I have labored in, and for, the Republican organization with entire confidence that whenever it shall be in power, each and all of the States will be left in as complete control of their own affairs respectively . . . as they have ever been under any administration," Lincoln wrote calmly from Springfield two weeks after the election. "I regard it as extremely fortunate for the peace of the whole country, that this point . . . is now to be brought to a practical test, and placed beyond the possibility of Doubt." To his old Whig comrade in politics, Alexander Stephens of Georgia, Lincoln wrote on December 22 to reiterate that he had no intention of meddling with slavery in the States, where the Constitution gave him no authority to meddle with it. "Do the people of the South really entertain fears that a Republican administration would, *directly*, or *indirectly* interfere with their slaves, or with them, about their slaves?" Lincoln asked soothingly. "If they do, I wish to assure you, as once a friend, and still, I hope, not an enemy, that there is no cause for such fears."[71]

This gave little quiet to Southern jitters because, as president, Lincoln had no authority to interfere with slavery anyway; slavery was a matter of state statutes and state enactments, and while the Constitution obliquely recognized slavery's existence, it gave it no explicit guarantees, either. Lincoln was, in effect, promising not to do what he had no power to do anyway. At the same time, Lincoln made it plain that he would never countenance the extension of slavery into the territories. Territorial governments, which Lincoln insisted fell under the jurisdiction of Congress no matter what the dictum of Roger Taney, were hereby served notice that applications for statehood that legalized slavery would get no backing from him and no appointees who would

70. David Clopton to William Burton, in Charles B. Dew, *Apostles of Disunion: Southern Secession Commissioners and the Causes of the Civil War* (Charlottesville: University Press of Virginia, 2001), 57–58; "Joseph E. Brown's Secessionist Public Letter, December 7 [1860], from Milledgeville," in *Secession Debated: Georgia's Showdown in 1860*, 148–49; J. Randolph Tucker, "The Great Issue: Our Relations to It," *Southern Literary Messenger* 32 (March 1861): 174.

71. Lincoln, "Passage Written for Lyman Trumbull's Speech at Springfield, Illinois," November 20, 1860, and "To Alexander H. Stephens," December 22, 1860, in *Collected Works*, 4:142–43, 160; Harold Holzer, *Lincoln, President-Elect: Abraham Lincoln and the Great Secession Winter, 1860–1861* (New York: Simon and Schuster, 2008), 177–79.

oil slavery's wheels. "Let there be no compromise on the question of *extending* slavery," Lincoln wrote on December 10. "If there be, all our labor is lost, and ere long, must be done again." He was certainly not about to retreat to some form of the popular sovereignty doctrine in the territories in order to pacify Southern threats of disunion. "I am sorry any Republican inclines to dally with Pop. Sov. of any sort," Lincoln wrote to the Indiana Republican chairman on December 18. "It acknowledges that slavery has equal rights with liberty, and surrenders all we have contended for."[72] Beyond his promise to leave slavery alone in the slave states, Lincoln would make no further concessions.

This could have been read as Lincoln's admission that direct intervention in the slave states was out of the question, a hint he hoped Alexander Stephens and other Southerners would take to their comfort. But such an admission, however significant in Republican eyes and disappointing to the abolitionists, fell considerably short of the reassurances about a slave code and a reopened slave trade that the South was now demanding in what amounted to the final round in the forty-year-long game of balances. Exclusion of slavery from the territories meant that slave-based agriculture had no future, and since the states that would one day be formed in the territories would now be free states, then no matter what Lincoln's assurances for the present about slavery and the Constitution, the mounting number of free states in the Union would eventually permit the Republicans to create and adopt amendments to the Constitution for abolishing slavery outright, and get them ratified by an ever-increasing free-state majority.

This, at least, was the logic of the calmest slaveholders. Other Southerners, convinced that the spirit of John Brown was now about to take up residence in the White House, reached for the weapon they had so often threatened to use: unilateral secession from the Union. Within twenty-three days of Lincoln's election, five Southern states—South Carolina, Alabama, Mississippi, Georgia, and Florida—had authorized the calling of state conventions to debate withdrawal from the Union, and Louisiana's legislature was in special session in order to call such a convention. In Texas, only the stubborn opposition of Governor Sam Houston kept the legislature from calling for a secession convention, and not even Houston would be able to stave off that demand forever. Even before his state convention met, Alabama's Governor Moore mobilized the state militia, then pressured Alabama banks into suspending payments of hard cash (mostly owed to Northern banks) and made them guarantee at least $1 million in their vaults for the use of the state. Georgia governor Joseph Brown asked the Georgia legislature for $1 million to purchase weapons for the state and ordered the Georgia militia to occupy Fort Pulaski, a federal fort at the entrance to the port of Savannah.[73]

72. Lincoln, "To William Kellogg," December 11, 1860, and "To John D. Defrees," December 18, 1860, in *Collected Works*, 4:150, 155.

73. McMillan, *Disintegration of a Confederate State*, 14–15.

Leading all of the Southern states in secession fervor was South Carolina, whose grievances with the Union ran all the way back to the Nullification Crisis of 1832. Moreover, South Carolina was home to some of the most radical and eloquent voices for disunion, and they made themselves heard when the South Carolina secession convention assembled on December 17, 1860, in Columbia. After deliberating for two days, the entire convention shifted to Charleston and there, at 1:15 pm on December 20, the South Carolina convention unanimously passed a secession ordinance and declared that South Carolina had resumed its status as an independent republic.

In a document drafted by one of the most passionate of the South Carolina disunionists, Robert Barnwell Rhett, the convention rejected any notions that it was perpetrating a treasonous revolution. Instead, it asserted the provisional nature of the Union and insisted that it was simply taking back, by means of a convention, the same powers it had temporarily surrendered by means of a similar convention in 1787, when South Carolina ratified the federal Constitution. As for the possibility that the federal government might do as Andrew Jackson had done in 1832 and treat the secession as an armed insurrection, South Carolinians sniffed in contempt. South Carolina senator James Chesnut even offered to drink all the blood that would be shed in any war over the Union. From New Orleans, J. D. B. DeBow assured the readers of his *Review* that Northerners would turn out to fight each other more eagerly than they would fight the South over secession. In the North, "people have no opinions or objects in life in common. So soon as the war with the South is concluded, it is probable she will be dismembered and split up into three or four independent states or nations."[74]

South Carolina's boldness carried the other states of the Deep South before it. Mississippi passed its own ordinance of secession on January 9, 1861, with Florida adopting a secession ordinance the next day, Alabama the day after that, and Georgia on January 19. On January 26, Louisiana followed suit, and Texas joined them on February 1. In less than the short space between Lincoln's election and his inauguration, seven states had declared their union with the United States dissolved, convinced not only that the political situation of the South required disunion but also that the legal and cultural situation of the Union itself permitted it. The *Augusta Constitutionalist* explained that "the difference between North and South" had been "growing more marked for years, and the mutual repulsion more radical, until not a single sympathy is left between the dominant influences in each section." Now that the national government has fallen into the control of the Republicans, "all the powers of a Government which has so long sheltered" the South "will be turned to its destruction. The only hope for its preservation, therefore, is out of the Union."[75]

---

74. William C. Davis, *Rhett: The Turbulent Life and Times of a Fire-Eater* (Columbia: University of South Carolina Press, 2001), 394; "The Perils of Peace," *DeBow's Review* 31 (October–November 1861): 396–97.

75. "What Should Georgia Do?" in *Southern Editorials on Secession*, 242.

Yet the secessionists were not nearly as sure of themselves as their pronouncements implied. "A new confederacy, if the present Union be dissolved, it must be conceded, is a necessity," advised the *New Orleans Daily Picayune* even before South Carolina had seceded. "The history of the world proves the failure of governments embracing very small communities." The brave talk about the irreconcilable differences of North and South and the painlessness of secession notwithstanding, the South Carolinians immediately began casting around for support from their fellow Southerners. It was impossible to be sure how the federal government would actually respond; what was more, the elections of delegates to the various state secession conventions had given an uncertain sound to the enthusiasm of the Southern people for the secession movement. The Mississippi secession convention had voted strongly for secession but had also passed a resolution against reopening the African slave trade; the Alabama convention voted for secession by a bare majority of eight; in Georgia, it took ballot rigging by the secessionist governor, Joseph Brown, to ensure that enough pro-secession delegates would be elected to the secession convention. Standing alone, the seceding states might not be able to contain the forces they themselves had set loose, and as Hugh Lawson Clay of Alabama warned, something might "excite the people of N. Ala. to rebellion vs. the State and that we will have a civil war in our midst." Most significant of all, the upper South and the border states were sitting tight. Virginia, Arkansas, and Missouri each called secession conventions, only to have secession resolutions go down to defeat (in Virginia by a two-to-one margin), while North Carolina and Tennessee voted to call no secession convention at all.[76]

So on December 31, 1860, in an effort to provide security for the future of the secession movement, the South Carolina secession convention elected commissioners to meet with commissioners from the other seceding states with a view toward organizing a cooperative mutual government. On January 3, the commissioners met and discussed their situation, and concluded their deliberations with a call for a general convention of all the seceding states to meet at Montgomery, Alabama, in one month's time to form a provisional Southern government. The Montgomery convention, assembling on February 4, 1861, took just three days to create a new joint government for the Southern states. They adopted a new constitution, more or less based on the federal Constitution, but adding to the preamble the cautious reminder that "each State" was "acting in its sovereign and independent character." They chose as the new government's title (again, to underscore that it was a federation of independent powers and not a national union) the Confederate States of America. Two days later, the convention elected a president for the new Confederacy, the former West Point cadet, secretary of war, and senator from Mississippi, Jefferson Davis.

76. "New Lines of Sectionalism," in *Southern Editorials on Secession*, 312; Clement Eaton, *A History of the Southern Confederacy* (New York: Macmillan, 1954), 26.

Thus, in short order was born a Southern slave republic—but not without an ill-concealed case of nerves.[77]

The worries of the Confederates, however, were nothing compared to the woes of President James Buchanan, who became, in the lame-duck months of his unhappy presidency, the closest thing to an American Job. "Probably the unhappiest man, this day, within the whole limits of the Union, is James Buchanan, the President of these nearly disunited States," jeered the *New Orleans Daily Crescent*. "In common with nine-tenths of the people of the North, he has been accustomed to regard the threats of the South as mere idle talk, which really amounted to nothing. He finds out, now, how much mistaken he is." Wearied to death of the incessant din in Congress and in his own cabinet, Buchanan gradually lost whatever capacity he had to lay out a consistent plan of action and then follow it to the finish.

He detested the Southern disunionists and utterly repudiated any legal right to secession from the Union. In his annual message to Congress on December 3, 1860, Buchanan warned the South that the Union was more than a "mere voluntary association of states" and could not be "annulled at the pleasure of any one of the contracting parties," much less because "the election of any one of our fellow-citizens to the office of President" turns out opposite to their inclinations. If so, the Union was indeed "a rope of sand, to be penetrated and dissolved by the first adverse wave of public opinion in any of the States." Secession "is wholly inconsistent with the history as well as the character of the Federal Constitution," and therefore what the Southerners were calling secession "is neither more nor less than revolution." At the same time, he was inclined to excuse the secessionists because of "the long-continued and intemperate interference of the Northern people with the question of slavery"; anyway, he was certain that the Constitution gave him no authority as president to "coerce a State into submission" and back into the Union. The Union "rests upon public opinion," and if "it can not live in the affections of the people, it must one day perish."[78] As the weeks of his unhappy administration ran out, Buchanan sank further and further into political paralysis, desperately hoping that a crisis could be delayed long enough for him to retire gracefully and turn the government and its problems over to Lincoln.

Unfortunately for Buchanan, neither the newly triumphant Republicans in the North nor the secessionist fire-eaters in the South were willing to grant him a quiet exit. The Republicans, and especially Lincoln, refused to believe that Southern secession meant anything more than all the other temper tantrums the South had thrown since the Missouri Compromise. Senator Henry Wilson of Massachusetts, in a speech to the Senate on January 25, 1860, had heaped contempt on the secession

---

77. George C. Rable, *The Confederate Republic: A Revolution Against Politics* (Chapel Hill: University of North Carolina Press, 1994), 50–51.

78. "Meeting of Congress," in *Southern Editorials on Secession*, 293; Buchanan, "Fourth Annual Message," December 3, 1860, in *Messages and Papers of the Presidents*, 5:626, 628, 631, 635, 636.

threats as "this DISUNION FARCE," which was intended only to "startle and appall the timid, make the servility of the servile still more abject, rouse the selfish instincts of that nerveless conservatism which has ever opposed every useful reform, and wailed over every rotten institution as it fell." Lincoln himself was confidently predicting "that things have reached their worst point in the South, and they are likely to mend in the future." Part of Lincoln's peculiar confidence was due to his own overweening certainty that, as a born Kentuckian, he possessed a special insight into and empathy with Southerners. Possessed with this insight, he was sure that Unionism was a far more powerful force in the long run than the apparently illogical rush to secession.[79]

Lincoln was not the only Republican floating on a bubble of confidence. "We shall keep the border states," predicted William H. Seward in February, "and in three months or thereabouts, if we hold off, the Unionists and Disunionists will have their hands on each other's throats in the cotton states." William S. Thayer, the assistant editor of the *New York Evening Post*, noted that "the leading Republicans" were all convinced that "the seceders had no purpose of *remaining* out of the Union."[80] It was also clear to the Republicans that a stout refusal to yield to Southern threats or accommodate Southern demands was politically useful. The Southern threat of secession gave the Republicans an important issue on which to rally Northern public opinion, even while the threats of disunion divided hesitant Southerners.

Consequently, neither Lincoln nor the Republicans were going to be at all receptive when Buchanan pleaded for compromises to placate the secessionists and keep the Union together. In his December 3 message to Congress, Buchanan had called upon Congress to work out a series of compromises that would take the wind out of the secession-mongers' sails, including a constitutional convention that would consider an amendment to protect slavery in the territories and the purchase of the Spanish colony of Cuba in order to admit it to the Union as a slave state. These proposals were hardly the sort to please either Northern Democrats or Republicans, but they might have forced the secessionists to back down long enough to let the storm over Lincoln's election die down. Similarly, a constitutional convention might have been just the instrument to reawaken national interest and loyalty in the South. Congress grudgingly formed two committees, one each for the House and Senate, to discuss Buchanan's proposals for compromise, and by the end of December the Senate Committee was ready to put forth a compromise proposal that had been drafted by John J. Crittenden of Kentucky.[81]

79. Wilson, "Property in Territories," January 25, 1861, *Congressional Globe*, 36th Congress, 1st Session, 572; Johannsen, *Lincoln, the South, and Slavery*, 58ff.

80. Martin Crawford, "Politicians in Crisis: The Washington Letters of William S. Thayer, December 1860–March 1861," *Civil War History* 27 (September 1981): 232.

81. "State of the Union," December 13, 1860, *Congressional Globe*, 36th Congress, 2nd Session, 96; Philip Shriver Klein, *President James Buchanan: A Biography* (University Park: Pennsylvania State University Press, 1962), 360–63.

The Crittenden Compromise actually called for not one but a series of constitutional amendments that guaranteed the following: the old Missouri Compromise
line of 36°30′ would be revived and slavery would be forbidden in any state or territory north of the line and protected anywhere to the south; slavery in the District
of Columbia was to be protected from congressional regulation; Congress would
be prohibited from interfering in the interstate slave trade; and Congress would
compensate any slave owner whose runaways were sheltered by local Northern
courts or anti-slavery measures.

Crittenden seriously believed that his compromise could win popular support,
and he even urged Congress to submit it to a national referendum. Lincoln, who
refused to believe that the secession threats were finally serious, would have none of
it. "Entertain no proposition for a compromise in regard to the *extension* of slavery,"
Lincoln wrote on December 11. "The instant you do, they have us under again. . . .
The tug has to come & better now than later." At Lincoln's cue, the Republicans in
Congress gagged on Crittenden's guarantees for the extension of slavery into the
territories, and on January 16 they successfully killed Crittenden's compromise on
the floor of the Senate by a narrow margin, just five votes.[82]

In all fairness to Buchanan, the compromise plan had not necessarily been a bad
idea in political terms, and in February a mostly Democratic "peace convention," with
delegates from twenty states and chaired by no one less than ex-president John Tyler,
attempted to revive the Crittenden proposals. But Buchanan had lost the will and the
political force that had enabled him to carry the Lecompton constitution through an
unwilling Congress in 1858, and so his efforts at compromise, sincere but halfhearted,
died wordlessly on his own goal line. Republican intransigence was hardly Buchanan's
only problem. Buchanan might have found secession a little more tolerable, or at least
a little more ignorable, if the secessionists had not themselves kept pushing on what
was, for Buchanan, a particularly touchy question of honor: the disposition of federal
property in the seceding states. "If a separation had been sought by the slave-holding
States . . . through peaceful means alone, it might have been ultimately conceded by
the Northern States," wrote Buchanan's secretary of the Treasury, John Dix.[83]

The United States government owned and operated a mint in New Orleans, a
network of post offices throughout the South, two major arsenals full of weapons,
several storage arsenals in major cities, and nine forts—and the secessionists were
not willing to leave them alone. Since the employees of the mint, the post offices,
and the arsenals were both civilians and compliant Southerners, the seceding states

---

82. Lincoln, "To William Kellogg," in *Collected Works*, 4:150; "Vote on the Crittenden Resolutions, January 16, 1861," in *The Political History of the United States of America, During the Great Rebellion*, ed. Edward
McPherson (New York: Philp and Solomons, 1864), 64–65.

83. "Notes by John A. Dix Concerning Certain Events and Transactions in Which He Took Part During
the Civil War of 1861–'65 in the United States," in Morgan Dix, *Memoirs of John Adams Dix* (New York:
Harper and Brothers, 1883), 1:345.

simply appropriated the facilities for their own use before Buchanan or anyone else could have anything to say in the matter. The forts, however, were a different matter altogether. As U.S. military installations, they were garrisoned and commanded by the United States Army. Unless the seceders were exceptionally bold (as at Fort Pulaski) or the federal officers exceptionally unreliable, the seceders would hesitate to risk an armed confrontation with the federal government, and so the forts were left alone. In leaving them alone, the seceders only created trouble for themselves, since the continued presence of the federal government's authority in these forts only festered in the minds of the secessionists, not to mention discrediting the authority of the movement in the eyes of the other slave states, who still remained undecided about secession. And none of those forts produced more irritation than the three forts that sat quietly brooding over the harbor of Charleston, South Carolina.

Only one of the Charleston forts, Fort Moultrie, was seriously occupied by the two artillery companies that constituted Charleston's federal garrison. Of the other two, Castle Pinckney was an obsolete relic of the eighteenth century, and Fort Sumter was an incomplete brick pentagon sitting on a man-made island of granite rubble beside the main ship channel. Under pressure from the Southern members of his cabinet, Buchanan probably would have been willing to negotiate with South Carolina over the future of the forts; presumably to pave the way for those negotiations, the secretary of war, a pro-secession Virginian named John B. Floyd, sent the Charleston garrison a slaveholding Kentucky major of artillery, Robert Anderson, as its new commander in November 1860. Anderson's orders were to avoid provocations, carry out military business as usual, and make no changes in his dispositions unless he felt his garrison was actually threatened in some way. That, and a little time, would ensure that the Charleston forts could be turned over, either to Lincoln so that Buchanan could retire in peace, or to the South Carolinians without a messy confrontation.

Anderson was a Southerner, but he was also a career regular army officer whose first loyalty was to the honor of the United States. Anderson first surveyed the decaying ramparts of Fort Moultrie, then sized up the growing numbers of armed South Carolina militia keeping watch over Fort Moultrie. Six days after South Carolina uproariously adopted its secession ordinance, Anderson exercised the discretion granted him by his orders and changed his dispositions. Under cover of night, he evacuated his two companies from Moultrie and rowed them over to Sumter, where no one in Charleston had a hope of laying hands on them. The next morning Anderson raised his flag "to the top of the staff, the band broke out with the national air of 'Hail Columbia,' and loud and exultant cheers, repeated again and again, were given by the officers, soldiers, and workmen."[84]

An "outrageous breach of faith" was how the *Charleston Mercury* characterized Anderson's move. The North, by contrast, hailed Anderson as a hero, a patriot who at

84. "The Prayer at Sumter," *Harper's Weekly*, January 26, 1861, 49; Thomas Barthel, *Abner Doubleday: A Civil War Biography* (Jefferson, NC: McFarland, 2010), 62.

last had the courage to defy the secession bluster. President Buchanan was angered by Anderson's move and was inclined to order Anderson back to Moultrie. But when it appeared that Northern public opinion was solidly behind Anderson, Buchanan changed his mind and attempted to persuade the South Carolinians to accept Anderson's occupation of Fort Sumter as a legitimate exercise of federal authority. The South Carolina government, however, stopped its ears. Nothing now would satisfy their injured pride but the unconditional surrender of Sumter, and on January 9, 1861, when the steamer *Star of the West* ("a mere transport, utterly unfitted to contend with shore batteries") entered Charleston harbor with provisions and reinforcements for Sumter, South Carolina militia opened fire on it with several cannon and forced the ship to withdraw. Only Anderson's restraint in refusing to open fire himself on the South Carolinians kept civil war from breaking out at that moment.[85] From that time onward, Anderson took nothing further for granted. His eighty-five-man force of soldiers, bandsmen, and civilian workers mounted a total of sixty powerful cannon inside the fort, and he brought the uncompleted fort as close to war readiness as possible.

Anderson's refusal to take the firing on the *Star of the West* as a signal for him to bombard the city of Charleston also made it possible for Buchanan to escape from office without further incident. Lincoln formally assumed office from Buchanan on March 4, 1861, and in his inaugural address he made it as clear as he could that he had no intention of backing down in his support of Major Anderson. However, as Anderson himself informed Lincoln in a dispatch received on the evening of the inaugural, the real question was not whether the government would support Anderson but whether Anderson could support himself. When the new Confederate States government had officially taken over control of the Charleston harbor defenses on March 1, it had immediately cut Sumter off from all mail and local food supplies and begun erecting ominous batteries of cannon around the harbor perimeter. In his dispatch, Anderson warned the new president that he had only enough food for six weeks more in the fort, and at the end of that time he would be compelled to surrender.[86] What did Lincoln propose to do?

For three weeks Lincoln weighed the alternatives before him. On one hand, he could attempt to resupply Sumter, but with the example of the *Star of the West* before him, he knew that any such attempt would provoke a shooting match, which he would be held responsible for starting—contrary to all of his assurances to the slave states over the past three months, and in full confirmation of all the wild accusations about his aggressive designs on the South. That, in turn, could easily cause not only

85. Robert Hendrickson, *Sumter: The First Day of the Civil War* (Chelsea, MI: Scarborough House, 1991), 86; David Detzer, *Allegiance: Fort Sumter, Charleston, and the Beginning of the Civil War* (New York: Harcourt, 2001), 132; Abner Doubleday, *Reminiscences of Forts Sumter and Moultrie in 1860–61* (New York: Harper and Brothers, 1876), 93.

86. Joseph Holt and Winfield Scott to Abraham Lincoln, March 5, 1861, Abraham Lincoln Papers, Library of Congress.

a full-fledged civil war but also a fresh round of secessions, this time in the upper South. On the other hand, Lincoln could order Sumter evacuated; in that event, he knew, the credibility of his presidency and the Republican administration would be in pieces before either had scarcely begun.

On March 29, after polling his cabinet for the second time on the question, Lincoln decided. He ordered a supply flotilla prepared and sent to Charleston, then sat back to await the unpleasant outcome. If the flotilla succeeded in resupplying Sumter, then federal authority in South Carolina had been preserved, and Charleston could do little short of war to change it; if it failed, the failure would be due to Charleston's decision to open fire, and the onus of beginning a civil war would lie on their heads. Clearly, Lincoln was not trying to provoke war; but it was also true that either way, Charleston lost and Lincoln won, and years afterward people would become convinced that Lincoln had rigged it all deliberately to have a civil war begin that way.[87]

As it turned out, the Confederates did not wait for the flotilla to arrive. Jefferson Davis and the Confederate cabinet in Montgomery were notified of Lincoln's resupply mission on April 10, and the next day they ordered the Confederate commander in Charleston—a dashing French Louisianan named Pierre Gustave Toutant Beauregard—to demand Anderson's surrender, or else proceed to level the fort.[88] Anderson rejected Beauregard's demand, and at 4:30 am on April 12, 1861, the Confederate batteries ringing Charleston harbor opened fire on Anderson's pitiful little garrison. For thirty-four hours Anderson's two companies fought back until their ammunition was exhausted and the interior of the fort was hopelessly ablaze. On April 14 Anderson lowered his flag, and marched out of the battered fort, remarkably without having lost a single man of his garrison during the bombardment.

That night, the observatory at Harvard College noted the advent of an enormous comet. In the estimate of the venerable British astronomer Sir John Herschel, it "exceeded in brilliancy all other comets that he had ever seen," and until it passed its perihelion and faded from view in December, it was "the most brilliant that has appeared for centuries, and one of the most remarkable on record." Of course, cautioned a writer for the *Danville Quarterly Review*, people no longer regarded comets "as omens of impending evil, or messengers of an angry Deity." Looking back from the vantage point of the next four years, the *Review* might not have felt so confident.[89]

87. Russell McClintock, *Lincoln and the Decision for War* (Chapel Hill: University of North Carolina Press, 2008), 232–33; David M. Potter, *Lincoln and His Party in the Secession Crisis* (New Haven, CT: Yale University Press, 1942), 373–75.

88. Hudson Strode, *Jefferson Davis: Confederate President* (New York: Harcourt, Brace, 1959), 2:40; Beauregard to Anderson, April 12, 1861, *The War of the Rebellion: A Compilation of the Official Records of the Union and Confederate Armies*, Series One (Washington, DC: Government Printing Office, 1880), 1:14.

89. "Cometary Astronomy," *Danville Quarterly Review* 1 (December 1861): 614, 630; "Scientific Intelligence," *American Journal of Science and Arts* 32 (November 1861): 134; David Sergeant, *The Greatest Comets in History: Broom Stars and Celestial Scimitars* (New York: Springer Science, 2009), 141; *The American Annual Cyclopaedia and Register of Important Events for the Year 1862* (New York: D. Appleton, 1862), 2:174.

CHAPTER FOUR

TO WAR UPON SLAVERY

THE EAST AND EMANCIPATION, 1861-1862

On the "most exquisite morning" of April 15, 1861, Sarah Butler Wister rose early to take a bundle of letters to the post office near her home in the Philadelphia suburb of Germantown. To her annoyance, she found that their newspaper had been stolen from their doorstep. But soon she and her husband, Dr. Owen Jones Wister, found that they needed no newspapers to learn what was happening in the world. "All the world was awake & alive with the news that Ft. Sumter has surrendered," she confided to her diary.[1]

The news of the fall of Fort Sumter set off a string of contradictory emotions in Sarah Butler Wister. Her father was Pierce Butler, a Georgia planter and Democratic politician, and the mail that morning contained a letter from her father describing a guided tour he had received of the Charleston harbor batteries by "Gen. Beauregard & other officers." Her mother, however, was the celebrated English Shakespearean actress Fanny Kemble, who had married Pierce Butler in 1834 and lived to regret it. The life Kemble led on the Butler plantation was miserable beyond description, and the lot of the Butler family slaves was even more miserable. Divorcing Butler, Kemble returned to England and the stage in 1845, and would later publish a *Journal of a Residence on a Georgian Plantation*, which painted slavery in its vilest colors. Sarah Butler had been born in 1835 in Philadelphia (Pierce Butler had inherited land in both Philadelphia and Georgia from the two very different sides of

---

1. "Sarah Butler Wister's Civil War Diary," ed. Fanny Kemble Wister, *Pennsylvania Magazine of History and Biography* 102 (July 1978): 271–77.

his family) and married Owen Jones Wister there in 1859. Her opinions on slavery flowed all in her mother's direction.

Both the weather and the news turned darker through the day. While "the latter part of the day was gloomy and forbidding," she heard rumors of "thousands . . . furious at the news of the surrender," marching in the streets of Philadelphia "& swearing revenge on all disunionists or disaffected." Robert Tyler, the son of former president John Tyler, "literally fled before them," and the crowd "visited the houses, stores & offices of" Southerners who had made themselves "especially odious in the last few days." The mob was in the streets again the next day ("oh how thankful I am for Father's absence") and had to be pacified by speeches and threats from Mayor Alexander Henry. Not that Sarah Wister really minded them: "They were the most moderate, mannerly mob ever heard of." At the same time, though, she saw in their faces (when she went out to buy "radishes in the market") that "they were in the utmost state of excitement & the least thing would have fired them, & then riots must have followed." Mixed snow and rain fell the next day, but "flags large & small flaunt from every building, the dry-goods shops have red, white & blue materials draped together in their windows, in the ribbon stores the national colors hang in long streamers, and even the book sellers place the red, white, and blue bindings together."

On the day following, their newspaper was "stolen from the door step again."

Fifteen miles away, in rural Chester County, the news of the fall of Fort Sumter came over the telegraph wire to West Chester, the county seat, on Sunday evening, April 14. The next morning, the national flag was flying everywhere through the town. Across Chester County, in Upper Uwchlan Township, an immense Stars and Stripes was hoisted up an eighty-foot pole in front of the local tavern, and in the evening the county courthouse was thrown open for a mass Union rally.[2] Far to the north, at Maine's Bowdoin College, a professor and former pupil of Calvin Stowe who had once sat in the Stowe parlor listening to Harriet Beecher Stowe read drafts of *Uncle Tom's Cabin* was seized with anger that "the flag of the Nation had been insulted" and "the integrity and the existence of the People of the United States had been assailed in open and bitter war." His name was Joshua Lawrence Chamberlain, and an "irresistible impulse" came over him to abandon the teaching of rhetoric at Bowdoin and join the army to become God's minister "in a higher sense than the word."[3]

To the west, the news of the first shot fell on the Ohio legislature when "a senator came in from the lobby in an excited way" and cried out, "'The telegraph announces that the secessionists are bombarding Fort Sumter!'" There was a sick moment of

---

2. Douglas R. Harper, *"If Thee Must Fight": A Civil War History of Chester County, Pennsylvania* (West Chester, PA: Chester County Historical Society, 1990), 18.

3. Alice Rains Trulock, *In the Hands of Providence: Joshua L. Chamberlain and the American Civil War* (Chapel Hill: University of North Carolina Press, 1992), 60–61.

silence, and then "a woman's shrill voice" called out from the gallery, "Glory to God!" It was the voice of Abby Kelley, the veteran abolitionist for whose sake William Lloyd Garrison had broken up the American Anti-Slavery Society two decades before. Kelley had come to believe, with John Brown, that "only through blood" could the freedom of the slaves be won, and now the redeeming blood of the abolition martyrs could begin to flow. The next day, the news of Anderson's surrender came over the wires, and "the flag—*The Flag*—flew out to the wind from every housetop in our great cities." Ohio judge Thomas Key stopped State Senator Jacob Dolson Cox in the Ohio Senate hall: "Mr. Cox, the people have gone stark mad!" Cox, a staunch anti-slavery Whig turned Republican, replied, "I knew they would if a blow were struck against the flag."[4]

Six hundred miles to the South, the English newspaperman and war correspondent William Howard Russell had gone to church on Sunday morning, April 14, in a small Episcopal parish in Norfolk, Virginia. "The clergyman or minister had got to the Psalms" when a man slipped into the back of the church and began whispering excitedly to the first people he could speak to. The whispering rose in volume, while some of the people at the back "were stealing on tiptoe out of the church." The minister doggedly plunged on through the liturgy, and the people gradually began to heave themselves up and walk out, until at length Russell "followed the example" and left the minister to finish the service on his own. Outside in the street, Russell found a crowd running through the street. "Come along, the telegraph's in at the Day Book. The Yankees are whipped!" Russell was told. "At all the street corners men were discussing the news with every symptom of joy and gratification." That night, in Richmond, "bonfires and fireworks of every description were illuminating in every direction—the whole city was a scene of joy owing to [the] surrender of Fort Sumter"—and Virginia wasn't even then part of the Confederacy.[5]

Further south, in what was now the Confederate States of America, the Confederate president, Jefferson Davis, received a telegram from P. G. T. Beauregard at 2:00 PM on April 13, informing Davis, "Quarters in Sumter all burned down. White flag up. Have sent a boat to receive surrender." Davis wired back his congratulations, and added, "If occasion offers, tender my friendly remembrance to Major Anderson."[6] He went to bed, gloomy with the foreboding that Lincoln and the North would soon retaliate. Davis had never been able to make his fellow Southerners understand that secession would mean war with the Northern states, and a long war at that. "You

4. Cox, "War Preparations in the North," in *Battles and Leaders of the Civil War*, ed. R. U. Johnson and C. C. Buel (New York: Castle, 1956 [1887]), 1:85–86.

5. W. H. Russell, *My Diary North and South*, 49–51; Diary of Samuel H. Pendleton, Special Collections, University of Virginia.

6. Beauregard to Davis, April 13, 1861, *The War of the Rebellion*, 1:309.

overrate the risk of war," the governor of Mississippi had assured Davis. "I only wish I did," Davis replied.

Outside, in the streets of Montgomery, Alabama, the crowds cheered and cheered.[7]

WAR OF THE THOUSAND-COLORED UNIFORMS

The bombardment and seizure of Fort Sumter was an act of aggression that no one, least of all President Lincoln, could afford to ignore. What the Confederate forces had done in Charleston harbor was, technically speaking, nothing different from John Brown's assault on the Harpers Ferry arsenal, a deliberate and hostile act of war, with the added flavor of treason. It destroyed at one stroke all real hope for negotiation or compromise and left it up to Lincoln to demonstrate whether or not the federal government was prepared to back up its denial of the right to secession with force. Long ago, in 1856, Lincoln had warned the Democrats that a Republican administration would not allow the Union to be dissolved, and "if you attempt it, *we won't let you.*" At the same time he dismissed all serious talk of secession as "humbug—nothing but folly."[8] Now the talk had to be turned into iron reality.

But what means did Lincoln have at his disposal to suppress the Confederate rebellion? The United States Army consisted of only ten regiments of infantry, four of artillery, and five of cavalry (including dragoons and mounted riflemen)—in all, that worked out to 1,105 commissioned officers, a number of whom were Southerners from the seceded states, and 15,259 enlisted men.[9] Furthermore, few of the regiments were together in one place, almost all of them having been broken up piecemeal to garrison forts in the West or along the borders. It was, in truth, little more than a police force. There was no general staff to coordinate the army's various functions—recruitment, planning, training, mapmaking. The cavalry contained no heavy cavalry units, only light cavalry useful for skirmishing and scouting. Three-quarters of the army's artillery had been scrapped at the close of the Mexican War, and artillery units had been "made to serve either as infantry or cavalry, thus destroying almost completely their efficiency as artillery." No force of such tiny proportions was likely to bring the secessionists easily to heel.

What was worse, Congress was at that moment out of session, and without congressional sanction, Lincoln lacked constitutional authority to raise a national army. Nor could Congress be assembled at the drop of a hat for the emergency. Unlike

7. William C. Davis, *Jefferson Davis: The Man and His Hour, a Biography* (New York: HarperCollins, 1991), 325.

8. Lincoln, "Speech at Galena, Illinois," July 23, 1856, in *Collected Works of Abraham Lincoln*, ed. Roy F. Basler (New Brunswick, NJ: Rutgers University Press, 1953), 2:355.

9. *The American Almanac and Repository of Useful Knowledge, for the Year 1859* (Boston: Crosby, Nichols, 1859), 110–11.

the Senate, the representatives in the House were still elected in 1860 on a staggered schedule that varied from state to state, and the new Congress did not usually expect to fully assemble itself after an election year until December of the following year—which, in this case, meant December 1861. At the very best, even with speeding up some state elections, there was little hope of getting the new Congress together before July, when a number of crucial border-state elections would finally be complete. Maryland, in fact, would not hold its congressional elections until June 13, and Kentucky not until a week after that.[10]

Lincoln did have one other recourse for recruiting soldiers, and that was the 1795 federal militia statute that had originally delegated to President Washington the authority to call up the militia of the various states in the event of insurrection. So on April 15, two days after the fall of Fort Sumter, Lincoln issued a proclamation that declared the Confederate states in rebellion and called for the states of the Union to provide the federal government with 75,000 militia for three months (the statutory maximum), with the numbers to be apportioned among the states. Two weeks later, he issued a second call, this time for the recruitment of forty regiments of state volunteers (a little over 42,000 men) and the expansion of the regular army by eight regiments of infantry and one each of artillery and cavalry. Although Congress approved both acts retroactively—in fact, greatly expanded the numbers of volunteer recruitments, up to a million men—nothing in the 1795 statute had authorized either of these follow-up calls, and Lincoln would later have to justify his actions largely on the admittedly vague basis of the "war power of the government."[11]

The calls for militia, volunteers, and an expanded regular army created a parallel system in the Union armed forces, which would be composed of three kinds of military organizations. First, at the core of the army would be the old regular U.S. Army regiments, which enlisted men directly into service as long-serving professional soldiers, and which were known simply by their regimental numbers (i.e., 1st U.S. Infantry, 5th U.S. Cavalry). Second, rising into existence at the call of the various state governments would be the volunteer regiments, which were recruited by the states, marched under state-appointed officers carrying their state flag as well as the Stars and Stripes, and were identified by their state regimental number (i.e., 83rd

10. John Gibbon, "Organization of United States Artillery," *United States Service Magazine*, May 1, 1864; Horace Greeley, *The American Conflict: A History of the Great Rebellion in the United States* (Hartford, CT: O. D. Case, 1864), 1:555. Compare this level of organizational primitivism to the staff structures Helmuth von Moltke was building in Prussia at the same time; see Arden Bucholz, *Moltke and the German Wars, 1864–1871* (New York: Palgrave, 2001), 32–34, 43, 50–65.

11. "An Act to Provide for Calling Forth the Militia," February 28, 1795, in *The Public Statutes at Large of the United States of America*, ed. Richard Peters (Boston: Little and Brown, 1845), 1:424–25; McPherson, ed., *Political History of the Rebellion*, 115; Lincoln, "Message to Congress in Special Session," July 4, 1861, in *Collected Works*, 4:425.

Pennsylvania Volunteer Infantry, 1st Minnesota Volunteers, 20th Maine Volunteers, 19th Massachusetts Volunteers). These volunteers were a makeshift category, to save Congress the expense of permanently commissioning officers and mustering men into a dramatically expanded Federal service, which might prove legally difficult to disband once the wartime emergency was over.

Unlike regulars, the volunteers remained state-based, and they signed up for two- or three-year periods, after which they returned to civilian life and their units evaporated without any further fiscal obligations. The British had invented the volunteer system during the Napoleonic Wars, also to save themselves the expense of permanent expansions of their army, and the United States had taken over the example in the Mexican War, where the bulk of the U.S. forces were volunteers. In a pinch, the president was always able to call upon the supposedly vast reservoir of state militia. However, only a few states actually had a reasonably organized militia system to start with (New York's was the best, with about 45,000 men on its rolls, followed by those of Ohio and Indiana), so in practice militia units were usually employed only on emergency rear-echelon duties, to free up the volunteers and regulars.[12]

This system might have been more confusing had it not been for the fact that the regular army regiments never numbered more than a handful compared to the vast outpouring of volunteer recruits (Pennsylvania alone raised 215 volunteer infantry regiments during the course of the war), and for the fact that the volunteer regiments were frequently commanded by regular officers who were commissioned into state volunteer service. At the beginning of the war, though, it caused no end of chaos. State volunteer regiments often chose their own uniforms and weapons, elected their own noncommissioned and company officers with minimal regard for their competence, and generally behaved little better than a mob of hunters at a turkey shoot. Regiments such as the 79th New York arrived in Washington garbed in Highland kilts; the 72nd Pennsylvania copied from the daring French-Algerian colonial troops known as Zouaves the dashing Zouave uniform, complete with baggy red trousers, a cutaway monkey jacket, and a red fez and turban; the 3rd Maine reported for duty in uniforms of gray. Regimental drill often had to wait until the newly elected officers could learn, from a variety of popular handbooks or from the presence of a few old regulars, how to give the necessary orders.

Nevertheless, the volunteers were all that Lincoln at first thought he might need, for the president was sure that a show of resolute determination on the part of the federal government in raising an army would be all that was necessary to force the secessionists to back down. Still confident that Southern Unionism would reassert itself, Lincoln "questioned whether there is, to-day, a majority of the legally qualified voters of any State, except perhaps South Carolina, in favor of disunion." At least, he

---

12. Philip Howes, *The Catalytic Wars: A Study in the Development of Warfare, 1860–1870* (London: Minerva, 1998), 177–78; Robert S. Chamberlain, "The Northern State Militia," *Civil War History* 4 (June 1958): 108–9.

added weakly, "the contrary has not been demonstrated in any one of them." Only let the federal government show its resolve, and the rebellion would collapse before a rebirth of Union loyalty.

In fact, almost the exact opposite happened. Virginia had called a state convention soon after Lincoln's election to consider secession. The convention met on February 13, 1861, but debate on a secession ordinance dragged on for a month and a half before it was finally put to a vote on April 11, when secession lost, 88 to 45. The upper South, and especially Virginia, was not willing to go following the will-o'-the-wisp of secession, especially when it was led by the hotheads of South Carolina. Lincoln's call for the states to put their militia at the disposal of the federal government laid an entirely different complexion over affairs, however. Virginia would not fight the Union for South Carolina, but it would not join with the rest of the Union in suppressing its fellow Southerners and denying the principle of secession. "The militia of Virginia will not be furnished to the powers at Washington for any such use or purpose as they have in view," Virginia governor John Letcher replied to Lincoln's summons.[13] Forced by Lincoln's proclamation to choose which master it would serve, the Virginia convention reversed itself and voted to secede on April 17; the state then proceeded to seize the undefended federal navy yard at Norfolk.

Similar reactions set in across the upper South. In Maryland, pro-secession riots broke out in the streets of Baltimore a day after Lincoln issued his call for the militia, and a secessionist mob stoned the men of the 6th Massachusetts on April 19 as they changed trains in Baltimore en route to Washington. The panicky militiamen responded by opening fire, killing four civilians and wounding thirty-one. Maryland secessionists had been haranguing Maryland governor Thomas Hicks for a special session of the state legislature, which was strongly Democratic, but Hicks had so far stubbornly refused to yield to them. The Baltimore shootings momentarily unsettled Hicks and forced him to call a special session on April 26.

Hicks soon recovered his Unionist composure and designated the rural town of Frederick as the meeting place for the session, rather than in the agitated atmosphere of the state capital at Annapolis. In the peace and detachment of Frederick, Hicks was able to keep the legislature from bolting down the secession path. When the state legislature tried to reconvene in September to reconsider secession, Federal troops, now securely in control of the state, arrested twenty-seven state representatives and prevented the legislature from meeting. New state elections that fall installed a Unionist in the governor's chair and a Unionist majority in the legislature, who in turn sent Thomas Hicks to Washington as a U.S. senator.[14]

13. Lincoln, "Message to Congress in Special Session," July 4, 1861, in *Collected Works*, 4:437; McPherson, ed., *Political History of the Rebellion*, 114.

14. William Hesseltine, *Lincoln and the War Governors* (New York: Knopf, 1948), 154–56.

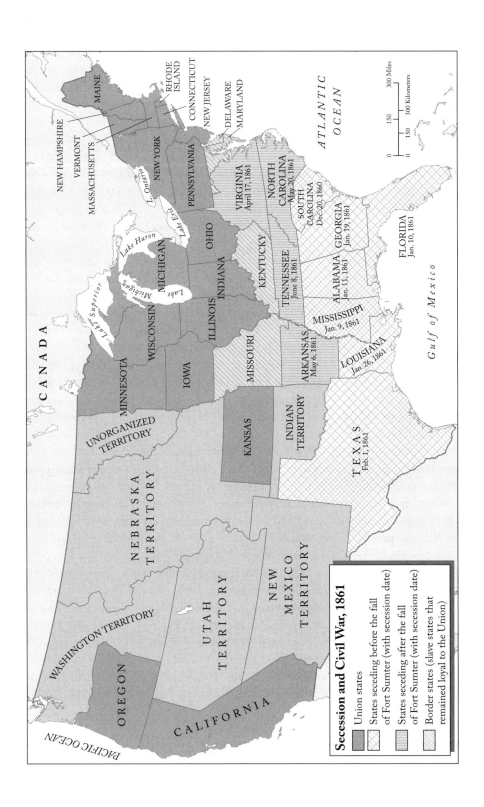

Secession and Civil War, 1861

Union states

States seceding before the fall of Fort Sumter (with secession date)

States seceding after the fall of Fort Sumter (with secession date)

Border states (slave states that remained loyal to the Union)

CANADA

ATLANTIC OCEAN

Gulf of Mexico

PACIFIC OCEAN

MAINE

RHODE ISLAND

CONNECTICUT

NEW JERSEY

DELAWARE

MARYLAND

NEW HAMPSHIRE

VERMONT

MASSACHUSETTS

NEW YORK

PENNSYLVANIA

VIRGINIA
April 17, 1861

NORTH CAROLINA
May 20, 1861

SOUTH CAROLINA
Dec. 20, 1860

GEORGIA
Jan. 19, 1861

FLORIDA
Jan. 10, 1861

L. Ontario

Lake Erie

OHIO

MICHIGAN

Lake Huron

Lake Superior

Lake Michigan

INDIANA

ILLINOIS

KENTUCKY

TENNESSEE
June 8, 1861

ALABAMA
Jan. 11, 1861

MISSISSIPPI
Jan. 9, 1861

WISCONSIN

MINNESOTA

IOWA

MISSOURI

ARKANSAS
May 6, 1861

LOUISIANA
Jan. 26, 1861

UNORGANIZED TERRITORY

KANSAS

INDIAN TERRITORY

TEXAS
Feb. 1, 1861

NEBRASKA TERRITORY

UTAH TERRITORY

NEW MEXICO TERRITORY

WASHINGTON TERRITORY

OREGON

CALIFORNIA

0   150   300 Miles

0   150   300 Kilometers

However, on May 7 the Tennessee legislature followed the example of Virginia rather than Maryland and voted to secede without even bothering to call a special convention into being. The Arkansas state convention passed a secession ordinance on the same day, and on May 20 North Carolina also seceded. In short order, Tennessee, Arkansas, Virginia, and North Carolina then joined the Confederacy, and to cement Virginia's loyalty to the new Southern republic, the Confederate government chose to move its capital from Montgomery to the Virginia capital of Richmond, only 100 miles south of Washington. Lincoln could now look out of the White House windows and see the new Confederate flag waving naughtily from housetops across the Potomac in Alexandria.

No more cheering were the deliberations Lincoln faced about what to do with the army of militia and the volunteers he had called into being. Lincoln's choice for secretary of war was a political hack from Pennsylvania, Simon Cameron, who quickly proved utterly inadequate to the task of managing a wartime army. Even if Lincoln had appointed a professional soldier to the post, the results might not have been much better. The dispersion of the regular army all over the frontier meant that virtually none of those officers had ever commanded any large military formations. Jacob Dolson Cox was appalled to find that the regular army officers whom he met knew little, read little in military science, and were woefully unprepared for the actual conduct of a war. When Cox complained to one regular whom he knew, the commonsense reply he got was: "What could you expect of men who have had to spend their lives at a two-company post, where there was nothing to do when off duty but play draw-poker and drink whiskey at the sutler's shop?" The result, as Cox could see, was that the regular army was almost useless for the war that was now breaking out, or at least not much more useful than the host of amateur military and militia units across the country. The regulars' "advantage over equally well-educated civilians is reduced to a practical knowledge of the duties of the company and the petty post," complained Cox, "and in comparison with the officers of well-drilled militia companies, it amounted to little more than a better knowledge of the army regulations and the administrative process."[15]

As it was, what little strategic wisdom there was in the regular army was divided into two conflicting schools of military thought. At the head of one of these schools stood the figure of Napoleon, or at least Napoleon as interpreted by one of the more popular of Napoleon's former staff officers, Antoine-Henri Jomini. French military practice, as a legacy of the Napoleonic wars, was considered the most advanced in the world, and a 105-page summary of Jomini's *Treatise on Grand Military Operations* was mandatory reading at West Point until 1832. Jomini believed in the virtue of the military offensive: the general who wanted a truly decisive victory (like those of

---

15. Jacob Dolson Cox, *Military Reminiscences of the Civil War* (New York: C. Scribner's Sons, 1900), 1:175, 187–88.

Napoleon) must take the war to the enemy as Napoleon did, by cutting the enemy's communications, turning the flanks of his armies, or, if all else failed, making a concentrated frontal assault on the enemy's defenses. Jomini acknowledged that the offensive was more costly in lives in the short run. Since it was more likely to achieve a decisive result more quickly, more lives would be saved in the long run.[16]

In Europe, almost all the tactical experience of the major national armies seemed to bear Jomini out. The allied British and French attack at the Alma River in 1854 during the Crimean War and the headlong French attacks upon the Austrians at Solferino in 1859 all seemed to testify that it was the army of the offense that won European battles, and at lightning speed. This was enough to convince many prewar American officers. The reigning American tactics handbooks—such as Winfield Scott's *Infantry Tactics* (1835) and William J. Hardee's *Rifle and Light Infantry Tactics* (1855)—borrowed heavily from Napoleonic sources and stressed the virtue of quick, aggressive offensive movements on the battlefield. Scott himself had put the offensive to the practical test in the Mexican War by driving an outnumbered American army straight through the gates of Mexico City on the momentum of a Napoleonic-style campaign.[17]

Beside the example of Scott's campaign operations in Mexico was the practical example of Zachary Taylor's field tactics at Buena Vista, where Taylor stood his army on the defensive and allowed Santa Anna to bleed his Mexican army to death in repeated assaults on Taylor's position. In fact, most of the great victories in American military history had been defensive ones, with Andrew Jackson's crushing defeat of the British at New Orleans in 1815 being the most famous and most politically potent example. The prolonged defiance of the Russian naval base of Sevastopol during the Crimean War was an updated notice that once a defending force had been allowed to fortify itself, head-on assaults were unlikely to budge it.

The politics of the defensive, whether on the level of grand strategy or of battlefield tactics, may have been more important to Americans than the real military value of the defensive, since the American republic retained a horror of supporting a large professional army (not only did a professional army remind Americans of British occupation during the Revolution, but a standing army represented the principle of power, the eternal enemy of republican liberty, and required heavy taxation to maintain). "The [American] government was conceived in the spirit of peace," wrote one British observer, "and framed more with a view to aid and encourage the

---

16. Herman Hattaway and Archer Jones, *How the North Won: A Military History of the Civil War* (Urbana: University of Illinois Press, 1983), 12–13; Brent Nosworthy, *Roll Call to Destiny: The Soldier's Eye View of Civil War Battles* (New York: Carroll and Graf, 2008), 26–31.

17. Russell F. Weigley, *The American Way of War: A History of United States Military Strategy and Policy* (New York: Macmillan, 1979), 78–79; Paddy Griffith, *Battle Tactics of the Civil War* (New Haven, CT: Yale University Press, 1989), 99–111; Hew Strachan, *From Waterloo to Balaclava: Tactics, Technology, and the British Army, 1815–1854* (New York: Cambridge University Press, 1985), 2–3.

development of the peaceful arts, than to promote a martial spirit in the people, or to throw the destinies of the country into a military channel."[18] So long as American armies were more likely to be made up of civilian volunteers and state militia, it was easier and safer to put nonprofessional soldiers of that sort on the defensive, rather than risking them on the offensive, where discipline, coordination, and mobility had to be of the highest order.

This preference for a strategic defensive posture in American wars was reinforced by the fact that West Point, the American military academy, was organized and run by the Army Corps of Engineers, so the education given to officers there was naturally inclined toward such defensive studies as fortification and military engineering. Then in 1832 a young meteor named Dennis Hart Mahan was promoted to the professorship of civil and military engineering at West Point, and through his classroom teaching and his publications he soon persuaded the new officers of the U.S. Army that the Napoleonic lust for the offensive had to be qualified by a realistic appreciation for the risks the offensive might run. Like Jomini, Mahan encouraged future generals to maneuver—but not, like Jomini, in order to gain advantage for an attack. Instead, fully aware that American armies were bound to the use of militia and volunteers, the principal object in Mahan's teaching was to seize and occupy enemy territory, and eventually force the enemy to launch an attack on one's own defensive fortifications. That required intensive training in the construction of major fortifications and instruction in the creation of temporary fieldworks on the battlefield, and that was what Mahan and West Point offered. The result was, as Jacob Dolson Cox remembered, that "the intellectual education at the Military Academy was essentially the same . . . as that of any polytechnic school, the peculiarly military part of it being in the line of engineering."[19]

Mahan took an academy that had been designed mostly for the defensive protection of American territory through the construction and garrison of fortification, combined it with a military tradition shaped by political mandates from Congress to favor a defensive mission, and raised the art of defense to an American science. "It has not been the policy of the country to be aggressive towards others," wrote navy secretary Gideon Welles, "therefore defensive tactics, rather than offensive have been taught, and the effect upon our educated commanders in this civil war is perceptible."[20] The American regular army officer in 1861 was thus presented with a series of

18. Alexander McKay, *The Western World; or, Travels in the United States in 1846–47* (London: Richard Bentley, 1850), 3:214–15.

19. Cox, *Military Reminiscences*, 1:179.

20. Welles, diary entry for August 17, 1862, in *Diary of Gideon Welles, Secretary of the Navy Under Lincoln and Johnson*, ed. John T. Morse (Boston: Houghton Mifflin, 1911), 1:85; Edward Hagerman, *The American Civil War and the Origins of Modern Warfare: Ideas, Organization, and Field Command* (Bloomington: Indiana University Press, 1988), 4–13.

contradictions: tactics books that encouraged officers to take the offensive and make the enemy's army their objective, and a professional military culture that looked to occupy enemy territory and fight a defensive war from behind fortifications.

In addition to these theoretical concepts, the officer of the Civil War era also would have had to come to terms with three new considerations. The first of these was supplies. From the Napoleonic Wars at the turn of the century up till the Crimean War, the size of modern armies had mushroomed from the 5,000–6,000-man forces that served under George Washington to mammoth field armies of 80,000–100,000 men, which in turn required equally mammoth numbers of horses and mules for transportation and, in the case of mounted infantry and cavalry, for combat operations. Keeping both the human and animal forces fed and armed was an increasingly difficult task and probably would have been impossible had it not been for the development of railroad technology.

Even as the railroads permitted the accumulation of ever-larger armies, they tightened a leash that limited the distance armies could afford to maneuver away from those railroads. As one British military theorist put it, war had become "not like two fencers in an arena, who may shift their ground to all points of the compass," but more like "the swordsmen on a narrow plank which overhangs an abyss."[21] At the same time, the increasing value of supply lines and railroads meant that more attention had to be paid to protecting those lines. Strategically, that meant that a general ought to take his army only along roads, rivers, or rail lines where his supply cord could not be cut, and ought to use the vulnerability of his enemy's supply lines to force him to surrender territory and advantage.

Linked to the problem of supply was the concept of lines of operations. No matter how different in size two armies might be, the only thing that mattered was the size of the force each army could bring to a battlefield at a given moment (i.e., even an army that is numerically inferior to its opponent can still achieve victory if it can manage to pick off small sections of the enemy army and defeat them piece by piece). Consequently, Mahan impressed on his West Point pupils the vital importance of operating defensively on "interior lines" and forcing the enemy to operate on "exterior lines." (What this means is that in any given strategic situation, an army occupying the interior of a position only has to move the chord of the arc surrounding that position to get from one end of it to the other; a commander on the exterior of a position has to occupy as well as move around the circumference of the arc, which forces him to spread his troops more thinly to cover the greater distance, and take more time in moving from point to point along the arc.) By taking up "interior lines," a numerically inferior army could defend itself more easily, and could move to strike at exposed positions along the enemy's arc faster than the enemy could reinforce them.

---

21. E. B. Hamley, in Strachan, *From Waterloo to Balaclava*, 6.

For an attacking army, the best way to overcome the advantage of interior lines was to outflank the enemy's lines entirely by means of *turning* or *flanking* movements. Hence, Civil War battles often found themselves determined by how successful one army was at getting hold of the other's flank and compelling a withdrawal, rather than by head-to-head attacks.[22] On the other hand, turning movements were frequently stymied by a physical problem that had never bothered Napoleon: the thickly wooded terrain of North America. Napoleon could fight Wellington across a series of neatly tended farms, but battle in the American Civil War had to deal with the fact that much of the American landscape was tangled, heavily forested, and poorly mapped. Many a clever turning movement floundered off into nowhere, slowed or lost by woods, badly mapped roads, and rivers.

All of these lessons were very much in the mind of the man to whom Lincoln initially turned for military direction and advice, the senior commanding general of the United States Army, who in this case turned out to be the apostle of the American offensive: Lieutenant General Winfield Scott. Unfortunately for Lincoln, Scott in 1861 was seventy-five years old and too badly crippled by gout to mount a horse, much less think of taking active command in the field. Scott also had little faith in the military capacities of the volunteers Lincoln was calling for. Although Scott's campaign in Mexico was the very model of the Napoleonic offensive, Scott's army in Mexico had enjoyed a much higher ratio of regulars to volunteers than the army Lincoln was calling into being, and Scott did not mind telling people how dubious he was about the quality of the volunteers. "Our militia & volunteers, if a tenth of what is said be true, have committed atrocities—horrors—in Mexico, sufficient to make Heaven weep, & every American, of Christian morals *blush* for his country," Scott wrote to the secretary of war in 1847. "Most atrocities are always committed in the absence of regulars, but sometimes in the presence of acquiescing, trembling volunteer officers."[23] Scott's doubts about the reliability of an army of volunteers had not diminished since Mexico, and without a large stiffening of regulars, Scott wanted to take as few risks with the volunteer soldier as possible.

Instead of proposing direct action against the Confederates, Scott suggested to Lincoln what derisively became known as the "Anaconda Plan" (so named for the huge snake that squeezes its prey to death), the first comprehensive strategic military plan in the nation's history. First, Scott proposed to use the Federal navy to blockade the entire length of the Southern coasts. He would then establish a strong defensive cordon across the northern borders of the Confederacy. Finally, he would mount a joint expedition of some 60,000 troops, plus gunboats, to move down the

---

22. Hattaway and Jones, *How the North Won*, 12–17.

23. David Clary, *Eagles and Empire: The United States, Mexico, and the Struggle for a Continent* (New York: Bantam Dell, 2009), 168.

Mississippi and secure the entire length of the river from the southern tip of Illinois to the Gulf of Mexico.

In effect, Scott was recognizing that the Confederacy occupied its own set of interior lines, which a motley army of volunteers would be unwise to attack; consequently, the best way to bring the Confederacy to its knees would be to turn its flank (down the Mississippi) and sever its supply lines to the outside world (with the naval blockade). With the Confederacy encircled and squeezed by land and sea, Scott believed that it would only be a matter of time before secessionist fervor would pale (and Scott was a Virginian who might have been presumed to know) and Southern Unionists would be able to seize control of their state governments again.[24]

Scott's cautious approach to waging war, however, was overwhelmed in the outpouring of aggressive chest-thumping from Congress and the Northern newspapers, which were already demanding an immediate offensive on Richmond. Even Lincoln was anxious that some kind of demonstration be made in western Virginia and eastern Tennessee, where he believed that Southern Unionists would happily rally to the old flag. Scott reluctantly authorized the 35,000 volunteers who encamped around Washington to prepare for an offensive into Virginia, and put them under the command of one of his staff officers, Irvin McDowell.

Across the Potomac, and across the Ohio, the Confederate forces were enduring similar confusions. The Confederacy had as one advantage the fact that its president, Jefferson Davis, was a West Point graduate and had served with distinction as an officer in the Mexican War and as secretary of war under Franklin Pierce. As such, Davis had the immediate advantage of being a military man with substantial military experience. In addition to Davis, 296 Southern officers serving in the United States Army (almost a quarter of the officer corps) resigned their commissions, and most returned to the South to offer their services to their respective state governments. Of the West Pointers, more than half resigned to join the Confederacy, and the bulk of those were the younger, up-and-coming officers.[25] Although a few Southerners remained with the Federal army, most of them did not, including the one officer whom Winfield Scott had set his heart upon as a possible successor as general in chief, Robert E. Lee, and the most admired and widely respected soldier in the U.S. Army, Albert Sidney Johnston.

Apart from these advantages, the Confederacy encountered the same organizational problems as the Federal army, and worse. The Confederate constitution permitted the Confederate Congress to raise and maintain armies, but its precise provisions made it clear that the Confederate government was expected to use the state militia as it existed rather than organizing a regular army of its own. Hence

24. Allan Peskin, *Winfield Scott and the Profession of Arms* (Kent, OH: Kent State University Press, 2003), 249–51.

25. Hattaway and Jones, *How the North Won*, 9; Wayne Wei-siang Hseih, *West Pointers and the Civil War: The Old Army in War and Peace* (Chapel Hill: University of North Carolina Press, 2009), 102.

the Confederacy created its Provisional Army of the Confederate States exclusively by appeal to the states to supply regiments of state volunteers, like their Northern counterparts. Only the general organization of these forces, and the commission of general officers, was kept in the hands of the Confederate government. Unlike the Federal volunteers, who were initially enlisted for two- or three-year terms, the Confederate volunteers were enlisted for only a single year (Jefferson Davis would have preferred to enlist all Confederate volunteers for the duration of the war, but in 1861 there was no hope of talking the Confederate Congress into such a measure).

Arming and equipping the new Provisional Army was another matter. In terms of men, money, and resources, the Confederacy was dwarfed by the North. The Confederacy possessed eighty-one establishments capable of turning out bar, sheet, and railroad iron in 1861, but most were small-scale and located in the vulnerable upper reaches of the Confederacy; of the ten rolling mills (for iron plate) in the Confederacy, only the Tredegar Iron Works in Richmond possessed a steam hammer for large-scale foundry work. The military-age male population of the Southern states was outnumbered five to two by that of the North, and the Confederate government was so lacking in the means to uniform and arm its new recruits that Confederate soldiers turned out in even more different varieties, styles, and colors of uniforms than their Federal counterparts. Alabama volunteers were issued dark blue frock coats and gray pants in March 1861; the 5th Georgia wore so many different styles of uniform (including a regulation navy blue U.S. Army frock coat) that they were mocked as the "Pound-Cake Regiment," while the 3rd Georgia featured a mix of red jackets and blue pants; the Louisiana "Tigers" sported brown jackets, red fezzes, and blue-and-cream-striped pantaloons; and so many Louisiana volunteers were issued blue uniforms in 1861 that the Louisianans were forced to wear red armbands to avoid being mistaken for Federal troops.[26]

Feeding the new Confederate army was an even greater problem for the state and Confederate commissaries. Private George Asbury Bruton of the 19th Louisiana found that "the first few days that we were here" at Camp Moore, Louisiana, "they fed us well," but within a few weeks the Confederate supply system broke down, and "now they feed us on old poor beef and Cast Iron pies." Armament posed some of the most serious problems of all. The Confederacy was able to provide modern rifles for only about 10 percent of its soldiers, while the rest were forced to bring "country rifles," shotguns, and even handguns from their own homes. The Virginia state arsenal at Richmond was the only facility in the South equipped to manufacture small arms, and even then it had capacity only for turning out about 1,000 rifles a month.[27]

26. Philip J. Haythornthwaite, *Uniforms of the Civil War, 1861–1865* (New York: Macmillan, 1976), 131–33, 175–76; Gary Shreckengost, *The First Louisiana Special Battalion: Wheat's Tigers in the Civil War* (Jefferson, NC: McFarland, 2008).

27. Steven Newton, *Joseph E. Johnston and the Defense of Richmond* (Lawrence: University Press of Kansas, 1998), 32.

Even if weapons and uniforms had been in generous supply, the Confederate states had less than one-third the total railroad mileage of the Northern states for moving those supplies where they were needed. Only two complete railroad systems connected Richmond with the Mississippi River. One of these was the Memphis & Charleston, which originated in Memphis, picked up connector lines through Chattanooga and up the Piedmont to the Orange & Alexandria Railroad, and then made its way to Richmond over the Richmond & Danville Railroad. The other major lateral rail line, the Memphis & Ohio, connected Memphis with Bowling Green and Louisville, then hooked onto two other connector lines to arrive in Chattanooga, but since Kentucky remained undecided about joining the Confederacy, the usefulness of the Memphis & Ohio was in some question. That left only the Mississippi Southern line as a possible alternative. But the Mississippi Southern stopped at Mobile Bay, forcing passengers and freight to ferry across the bay, and only then picked up a trunk line north to Chattanooga and to the connector lines that linked Mobile to the rest of the upper South.

Although the South had actually been an early pioneer in railroad construction in the 1830s, the Southern rail lines had been built mostly with a view toward moving cotton from the interior to the coastlines. It had never been necessary for the southern states to create interlocking east-west rail networks, and so the best Southern railroads ran north-south toward the Gulf coast, such as the Mississippi Central (which ran from New Orleans to Memphis, with the help of the Memphis & Tennessee line) and the Nashville & Chattanooga (which used connector lines to link Louisville and Nashville with Atlanta). Nor was there much likelihood that new railroad systems could now be built, since Virginia was the only Confederate state with the facilities to build locomotives. William Howard Russell watched in disbelief as a Confederate troop train arrived in a camp north of New Orleans: "Our car was built in Massachusetts, the engine in Philadelphia, and the magnifier of its lamp in Cincinnati. What will the South do for such articles in future?"[28]

There was, however, a silver lining to these logistical clouds. The South's shortages of manpower and military material dictated that the Confederacy adopt a basically defensive posture, and taking the strategic defensive would allow the Confederacy, as Winfield Scott had foreseen, to operate along interior lines. The broad heartland of the Confederate states would give the Southern armies room enough to draw the Federal armies in after them, string out their supply lines, and thus render them vulnerable to counterattack on unfriendly territory. Above all, it would force the real expense of waging war onto the Federal army, and if the Confederacy made that expense high enough through delay and resistance, the government in Washington

---

28. George Edgar Turner, *Victory Rode the Rails: The Strategic Place of the Railroads in the Civil War* (Westport, CT: Greenwood Press, 1972), 45–62; William Howard Russell, *Pictures of Southern Life, Social, Political and Military* (New York: James G. Gregory, 1861), 86.

would be forced to give up simply out of exhaustion. No matter what other material shortages the Confederacy suffered from, it was still the world's leading supplier of cotton, and Southerners fully expected that the voracious demand of European textile manufacturing for Southern cotton would draw Great Britain and France to the Southern side, as suppliers of weapons or perhaps even as open allies.

At first this Confederate war strategy seemed amply justified. By mid-July, the public outcry in the North for an invasion of Virginia had reached a pitch where Generals Scott and McDowell could afford to wait no longer. Moreover, the three-month militia enlistments would run out by the end of July, so if the militia were going to be of any use at all, it had to be now. Thus on July 16, 1861, McDowell's poorly trained, gaudily dressed, and marvelously disorganized army of newly minted volunteers and restless militia (with a sprinkling of regulars and a battalion of Marines scratched up from the Washington Navy Yard) happily marched out of Washington to crush the rebellion.

Scott and McDowell had before them two basic choices for an invasion of Virginia. They might do as Scott had done in the Mexican War and use the Federal navy to transport the army down Chesapeake Bay, deposit it on the James River peninsula on the east side of Richmond, and lay siege to the new Confederate capital without risking a pitched battle. Or they could march overland, using the Orange & Alexandria Railroad as a supply line, cross the Rappahannock River, and attack Richmond from the north, with the certainty that somewhere along the route, a stand-up, knock-down fight would have to be fought with the Confederates.

The first choice was wiser in strictly military terms, since the army was too poorly organized as yet to fight a large-scale battle, and even if they should win such a battle, the impact would disorganize the army so badly that it might have to withdraw anyway. Besides, it had been one of the first lessons of the Crimean War that it was not the one-off impact of battles that decided the outcomes of war but the fatal, unremitting grind of sieges that destroyed enemy armies. "It was in these siege-works that the strength of the Russians was worn down," wrote Sir Evelyn Wood; "the battles, glorious as they were," were "merely incidents in the struggle."[29] The second choice was what the newspapers and Congress were demanding: a sensational and decisive confrontation, straight out of a picture book of battles, that would put an end to the war at one stroke. So the long columns of Union soldiers straggled out of their Washington encampments onto the roads of northern Virginia, headed in a more or less straight line south for Richmond.

The result was a thundering humiliation for the Federal army. To defend Richmond, the Confederate government had concentrated approximately 20,000 of its own volunteers under P. G. T. Beauregard, the hero of Fort Sumter, near the village of Manassas Junction, squarely across the track of the Orange & Alexandria

29. Evelyn Wood, *From Midshipman to Field Marshal* (London: Methuen, 1906), 1:36.

railroad and behind a meandering little stream called Bull Run. There, on July 21, the hapless McDowell attempted to clinch Beauregard's army in its front with an initial punch at Beauregard's main lines behind Bull Run, and then swing a clumsy flanking maneuver around the left flank of Beauregard's defenses. It might have succeeded had not some 12,000 Confederate reinforcements under Brigadier General Joseph E. Johnston shown up at the last minute to stagger the oncoming Federals with one blow and send them reeling back to Washington. The effect of the battle of Bull Run on Union morale was crushing: more than 500 Union volunteers were dead, another 2,600 wounded or missing.

The poet Walt Whitman watched the defeated army drag itself back through the streets of Washington under a sullen and rainy sky. "The defeated troops commenced pouring into Washington over the Long Bridge at daylight on Monday, 22nd," Whitman recalled. "During the forenoon Washington gets all over motley with these defeated soldiers—queer-looking objects, strange eyes and faces, drench'd (the steady rain drizzles on all day) and fearfully worn, hungry, haggard, blister'd in the feet." Whitman found "the magnates and officers and clerks" in Washington calling for surrender and the resignation of Lincoln. "If the secesh officers and forces had immediately follow'd, and by a bold Napoleonic movement had enter'd Washington the first day, (or even the second,) they could have had things their own way."[30]

In fact, the Confederate army did not follow up its victory at Bull Run with a hot pursuit. Fully as ill-prepared for battle as the Federal army had been, the Confederates were badly disorganized by their victory and in no condition to undertake an offensive of their own. Nor did they think it was necessary, since they had achieved in this triumph all that their defensive strategy had promised. For his part, Abraham Lincoln was temporarily shaken by the defeat, but not as badly as some other Northerners. Horace Greeley's editorials in the *New York Tribune* had screamed "On to Richmond!" but now the editor decided that the rebels "cannot be beaten" and counseled Lincoln to "have Mr. Crittenden move any proposition that ought to be adopted."[31]

Within a day, the president had recovered his composure, and on July 27 Lincoln sat down to draft a more aggressive program for conducting the war, calling for a three-pronged invasion of the Confederacy in Virginia and in east and west Tennessee. To accomplish that, he needed to do some housecleaning: he relieved the unfortunate McDowell of his command and called to Washington as his replacement the commander of the Department of the Ohio, George B. McClellan, who had managed to win some small-scale victories with Ohio volunteers in western Virginia

30. Walt Whitman, "Specimen Days," in *The Portable Walt Whitman*, ed. Mark Van Doren (New York: Viking Press, 1969), 498–501.

31. William C. Davis, *Battle at Bull Run: A History of the First Major Campaign of the Civil War* (Garden City, NY: Doubleday, 1977), 245, 253.

that summer. Then in November Lincoln rid himself of the lumbering Winfield Scott and promoted McClellan to general in chief of all the Union armies, and in January 1862 he deposed Secretary of War Cameron and replaced him with a steely-eyed lawyer named Edwin M. Stanton.

The naive war, the glory-to-God war, the war of the thousand-colored uniforms, was over. The war in earnest had now begun.

THE YOUNG NAPOLEON

The arrival of George Brinton McClellan on the scene in Washington was a second wind to the demoralized Federal army. At age thirty-five, McClellan was dashing and dapper, the very storybook image of a general, a "Young Napoleon." To support that image, he brought with him from his years as a railroad executive some substantial and useful experience as an organizer. And organize he did. Numerous three-months' militia regiments that had been about to go home were reenlisted for three-year terms of service; the streets of Washington were cleared of loitering volunteers by a provost guard or regulars; the regiments were reorganized into brigades, the brigades into divisions, and the divisions into corps, and the corps were given commanders. Uniforms and weapons were given some measure of standardization, discipline and drill were imposed properly, and the bedraggled army encamped around Washington was given a name that would stick to it throughout the war—the Army of the Potomac.

The army responded by giving to McClellan its whole-souled devotion. "For the first time," wrote Adam Gurowski, a dour expatriate Pole employed by the State Department, "the army . . . looks martial. The city, likewise, has a more martial look than it had all the time under Scott. It seems that a young, strong hand holds the ribbons." McClellan made the volunteers feel like real soldiers, and at review after glorious review in the fall of 1861, the men of the Army of the Potomac shouted themselves hoarse for McClellan. "He had a taking way of returning such salutations," recalled Jacob Dolson Cox, the Ohio state senator turned officer. "He went beyond the formal military salute, and gave his cap a little twirl, which with his bow and smile seemed to carry a little of personal good fellowship even to the humblest private soldier." McClellan even acquired a portable printing press to haul around on campaign with him so that he could keep his exhortations and advice flowing constantly through the hands of his soldiers. "It was very plain that these little attentions to the troops took well, and had no doubt some influence in establishing a sort of comradeship between him and them. They were part of an attractive and winning deportment which adapted itself to all sorts and ranks of men."[32]

32. Russel H. Beatie, *Army of the Potomac: Birth of Command, November 1860–September 1861* (Cambridge, MA: Da Capo Press, 2002), 422, 425–27, 501–17; Adam G. de Gurowski, *Diary, from March 4, 1861, to November 12, 1862* (Boston: Lee and Shepard, 1862), 76; Cox, *Military Reminiscences*, 1:243; Stephen W. Sears, "Building the Army of the Potomac," *MHQ: The Quarterly Journal of Military History* 20 (Winter 2008): 80–81.

At first McClellan received the same response from Lincoln, the cabinet, and Congress. Dinner invitations poured in upon him faster than the time available to schedule them, compliments from young and old were publicly showered upon him, and in a very short while McClellan was being hailed as the savior of the Union—a view that McClellan himself began to share after old Winfield Scott was retired in November and McClellan made general in chief in his place. "By some strange operation of magic I seem to have become *the* power of the land," McClellan wrote to his wife, Ellen Marcy McClellan, soon after his appointment. "I almost think that were I to win some small success now I could become Dictator or anything else that might please me."[33] Dictator or not, McClellan found an appreciative audience in Abraham Lincoln, for at the time of McClellan's appointment, he and Lincoln saw the purpose of the war in very much the same terms. Lincoln still believed that secession was a political bubble that only required some measure of squeezing before it popped, and he advocated the application of just enough force to persuade the South that armed resistance was in vain.

Lincoln was especially careful not to drag the issue of slavery into the war, although it was a hesitation he did not enjoy. Privately, Lincoln regarded Southern secession as a blow not just against the Union but also against the most basic principles of democratic government, and for Lincoln, slavery was the uttermost negation of a people's government. No matter what Southerners might claim for their aims in secession, Lincoln was clear that "this is essentially a People's contest," in which the Union was struggling to assert the virtues of economic mobility against planter aristocracies, the hopeless caste system of the Southern backwoods and the working-class slum. "On the side of the Union, it is a struggle for maintaining in the world, that form, and substance of government, whose leading object is, to elevate the condition of men—to lift artificial weights from all shoulders—to clear the paths of laudable pursuit for all—to afford all, an unfettered start, and a fair chance, in the race of life."[34]

But Lincoln dared not push that conviction, or the war, to the point of making it an outright assault on slavery. For one thing (as he repeatedly acknowledged), he had no constitutional authority to emancipate anyone's slaves; if he tried, the attempt would be at once appealed to the federal courts, and the final desk the appeal would arrive upon would be that of Roger B. Taney, who was still the chief justice of the U.S. Supreme Court, and frankly unsympathetic to Lincoln and to emancipation.[35] Even

33. McClellan to Ellen Marcy McClellan, July 27, 1861, in *The Civil War Papers of George B. McClellan*, ed. Stephen W. Sears (New York: Ticknor and Fields, 1989), 70; Ethan Rafuse, *McClellan's War: The Failure of Moderation in the Struggle for the Union* (Bloomington: Indiana University Press, 2005), 124.

34. Lincoln, "Message to Congress in Special Session," July 4, 1861, in *Collected Works*, 4:438.

35. James F. Simon, *Lincoln and Chief Justice Taney: Slavery, Secession, and the President's War Powers* (New York: Simon and Schuster, 2006), 177–78, 194.

more to the point, Lincoln believed that if the abolition of slavery became a federal war issue, the white Southern nonslaveholders (whom Lincoln still looked upon as closet Unionists) would be backed into an irreversible racial alliance with the planters, in which nonslaveholding whites would defend the slaveholders in order to prevent being put on an equal plane with freed blacks. This situation would, he feared, make them resolve to fight to the finish, resulting in a long, bloody, and expensive war. Lincoln also had to remember that there were still four slave states—Delaware, Kentucky, Missouri, and Maryland—that had not seceded from the Union. Any attempt on his part to expand the war to include the abolition of slavery would drive these border states straight into the Confederacy and render the war unwinnable under any strategic circumstances.

This, then, was why Lincoln had taken such pains in his inaugural address in March to disassociate the federal government from any suggestion that the preservation of the Union would lead to the abolition of slavery. "Apprehension seems to exist among the people of the Southern States, that by the accession of a Republican Administration, their property, and their peace, and personal security, are to be endangered," Lincoln calmly observed. They need not worry, he assured the country, for "the property, peace and security of no section are to be in anywise endangered by the now incoming Administration." Four months later, addressing the July emergency session of Congress, Lincoln again strained to reassure the South that his aim in going to war was only to restore the Union, not to interfere with slavery in the Southern states. "Lest there be some uneasiness in the minds of candid men, as to what is to be the course of the government, towards the Southern States, *after* the rebellion shall have been suppressed, the Executive deems it proper to say . . . that he probably will have no different understanding of the powers, and duties of the federal government, relatively to the rights of the States, and the people, under the Constitution, than that expressed in the inaugural address."[36] Southern states who wanted to rethink their secession ordinances would thus find a bridge back into the Union still standing, and border states that still suspected the intentions of the Republican president would have a reassuring incentive not to join the Confederacy.

George McClellan, as both general in chief of all the Union armies and the commander of the Army of the Potomac, had no argument with Lincoln's conception of the war's purposes. He was relieved to find that "the president is perfectly honest & is really sound on the nigger question." Born and raised in comfortable circumstances in Philadelphia, and a Douglas Democrat by conviction and habit, McClellan genuinely disliked slavery, but without feeling the slightest desire to free African Americans. "When I think of some of the features of slavery I cannot help shuddering," he wrote to his wife in November 1861, and he vowed that "when the

---

36. Lincoln, "First Inaugural Address—Final Text," March 4, 1861, and "Message to Congress in Special Session," July 4, 1861, in *Collected Works*, 4:262–63, 438–39.

day of adjustment comes I will, if successful, throw my sword into the scale to force an improvement in the condition of those poor blacks."

McClellan looked only for a day of adjustment, not a day of judgment; for "improvement," not freedom. He scorned the secessionists and the abolitionists in equal parts, and promised his wife that "I will not fight for the abolitionists." He begged his fellow Democrat Samuel Barlow to "help me to dodge the nigger—we want nothing to do with him. I am fighting to preserve the integrity of the Union & power of the Govt" and "on no other issue."[37] On those grounds, McClellan was happy to agree with the president that the purpose of waging war was to nudge the Confederacy back into the Union, not to punish the South, seize its property, or subjugate its people.

To that end, McClellan proposed to incorporate most of the features of Scott's passive Anaconda Plan into his own strategic initiative. First, McClellan authorized a combined army-navy operation that would secure critical locations along the Atlantic seaboard of the Confederacy. On November 7, 1861, Captain Samuel F. Du Pont steamed into Port Royal Sound, fifty miles south of Charleston, landed a small contingent of Federal soldiers, and cleared the islands of Hilton Head, Port Royal, and St. Helena of Confederates. Two months later, a Federal force of 15,000 men under a Rhode Island inventor, manufacturer, and railroad man named Ambrose E. Burnside landed on Roanoke Island in Hatteras Sound and easily drove off a scattering of Confederate defenders. In April, another naval expedition bombarded Fort Pulaski, at the mouth of the Savannah River, into submission.[38]

In five months' time, Federal naval and land forces controlled virtually all of the Atlantic coastline between Savannah and Norfolk, except for Charleston harbor and Wilmington, on the estuary of North Carolina's Cape Fear River. At the same time, McClellan also authorized Major General Don Carlos Buell, now commanding McClellan's old Department of the Ohio, to march a small Federal army of 45,000 men through Kentucky and into eastern Tennessee, where (it was assumed) loyal Tennesseans would rise in support of the Union and overthrow the secessionist state government in Nashville. Then McClellan proposed to lead the Army of the Potomac in a major invasion of Virginia, aimed at the capture of Richmond. The result would be "to advance our centre into South Carolina and Georgia; to push Buell either towards Montgomery, or to unite with the main army in Georgia."[39]

37. McClellan to Samuel Barlow, November 8, 1861, and to Mary Ellen McClellan, November 14, 1861, in *Civil War Papers of George B. McClellan*, 128, 132.

38. McClellan to E. M. Stanton, February 3, 1862, in *McClellan's Own Story: The War for the Union* (New York: C. L. Webster, 1887), 234.

39. Donald Stoker, *The Grand Design: Strategy and the U.S. Civil War* (New York: Oxford University Press, 2010), 55, 58–60.

This was not a bad plan, and in fact it conformed rather handsomely to the indirect methods of campaigning Dennis Hart Mahan had championed at West Point (McClellan had been one of Mahan's prize pupils at the academy). It aimed at the acquisition of territory, not the expensive confrontation of armies, and even though the Union forces would be forced to operate on exterior lines in coordinating these movements, the Union's superiority in terms of ships and railroad support would help to overcome that deficit. Politically speaking, McClellan's plan also had the advantage of carrying the war to those areas that had shown the least fervor for secession and probably would show the least resistance.

There were two factors working against McClellan that no one in a West Point classroom could easily have anticipated, much less corrected, and both of them would help to undercut McClellan and his plan. One of these was McClellan's simple personal vanity. McClellan had at first been flattered by the attention paid to him by official Washington, but the more he listened and believed the complimentary nonsense heaped upon him by the press, the bureaucrats, and the politicians, the more he began to believe himself superior to all three. "I am becoming daily more disgusted with this administration—perfectly sick of it," he wrote to his wife, "There are some of the greatest geese in the Cabinet I have ever seen." Even "the President is an idiot."[40]

Two weeks after McClellan succeeded Winfield Scott as general in chief, Lincoln called at McClellan's temporary headquarters in Washington, only to be told that McClellan was out, though he "would soon return." Lincoln waited for an hour. But when McClellan at last arrived, the general paid no "particular attention to the porter who told him the President was waiting to see him, went up stairs," and went to bed. Lincoln's secretary, John Hay, took this as a "portent of evil to come . . . the first indication I have yet seen, of the threatened supremacy of the military authorities." It would not be the last, either. "I have no ambition in the present affairs," McClellan claimed, "only wish to save my country—& find the incapables around me will not permit it!" His conclusion that the administration was incapable was precisely what fired his ambition, and he began to entertain fantasies about "the Presidency, Dictatorship &c."[41]

He grew increasingly uncooperative with the cabinet, especially Lincoln's new secretary of war, Edwin M. Stanton, and increasingly contemptuous of and uncommunicative with Lincoln. "The Genl: it seems, is very reticent," complained Attorney General Edward Bates. "Nobody knows his plans. The Sec of war and

40. McClellan to Mary Ellen McClellan, August 16 and October 10, 1861, in *Civil War Papers of George B. McClellan*, 85, 106.

41. Hay, diary entry for November 13, 1861, in *Inside Lincoln's White House*, 32; McClellan to Mary Ellen McClellan, August 9, 1861, in *Civil War Papers of George B. McClellan*, 82.

the President himself are kept in ignorance of the actual condition of the army and the intended movements of the General—if indeed they intend to move at all." McClellan rationalized this as a necessary security precaution. "If I tell [Lincoln] my plans," McClellan assured Quartermaster General Montgomery C. Meigs, "they will be in the *New York Herald* tomorrow morning. He can't keep a secret." At this point Republicans in Congress began to wonder if McClellan was keeping secrets about more plans than just military ones. On December 31, the newly formed Joint Congressional Committee on the Conduct of the War complained to Lincoln about McClellan's inertia, and in a meeting with the entire cabinet on January 6, the committee urged Lincoln to remove McClellan and reinstate Irvin McDowell.[42]

There was also a problem with McClellan's fussiness. One railroad executive remembered that in civilian life McClellan had been "constantly soliciting advice, but he knows not more about a situation and has no more confidence in his own judgment after he has received it, than before." This characteristic was not going to disappear from McClellan "as a soldier."[43] The debacle at Bull Run had demonstrated the foolishness of rushing untrained soldiers into combat, and so Congress had been willing to give McClellan what it had not given McDowell, the time to train and equip an army. As the summer of 1861 faded into autumn, and autumn into winter, McClellan showed no desire to do more than train and equip, plus organize elaborate reviews.

Part of the politicians' impatience with McClellan was generated by a persistent unwillingness on the part of the politicians to recognize the immense difficulties in arming, feeding, clothing, and then moving an army that was larger than the entire Mexican War enlistments. A good deal of it was also the result of a West Point engineer's love for perfecting technical details. McClellan's first plan for Virginia, which he formulated in late 1861, dismissed the notion of assaulting the Confederates at Manassas Junction directly and called for an ambitious joint army-navy landing operation that would unload Federal forces at Urbanna, on the Rappahannock River in Virginia, and march from there overland to Richmond, only fifty miles away. By January 1862 McClellan had changed his mind: he would need to wait on Buell's advance into Kentucky before doing anything in Virginia, and he even considered moving his army to Kentucky and abandoning all notion of a Virginia invasion.

Neither of these plans produced any movement on McClellan's part, and by the end of January Lincoln was so exasperated with his general in chief that on January 27

42. Bates, diary entry for January 3, 1862, in *The Diary of Edward Bates, 1859–1866*, ed. Howard K. Beale (Washington, DC: Government Printing Office, 1933), 220; "General M. C. Meigs on the Conduct of the Civil War," *American Historical Review* 26 (1920–21): 292–93; Bruce Tap, *Over Lincoln's Shoulder: The Committee on the Conduct of the War* (Lawrence: University Press of Kansas, 1998), 105–6.

43. Steven S. L'Hommedieu, in Beatie, *Army of the Potomac: Birth of Command*, 403.

he issued a presidential order mandating a "general movement of the land and naval forces of the United States against the insurgent forces" on February 22, followed by a second order on January 31 that assigned McClellan particular responsibility for "an expedition for the immediate object of seizing and occupying a point upon the railroad southwestward of what is known as Manassas Junction."[44]

McClellan, incensed at what he saw as unprofessional meddling on Lincoln's part, replied by resurrecting the Urbanna plan and proposing to move down to the Rappahannock instead of Manassas. "The Lower Chesapeake Bay . . . affords the shortest possible land route to Richmond, and strikes directly at the heart of the enemy's power in the east," McClellan argued. "A movement in force on that line obliges the enemy to abandon his intrenched position at Manassas, in order to hasten to cover Richmond and Norfolk. . . . During the whole movement our left flank is covered by the water. Our right is secure, for the reason that the enemy is too distant to reach us in time. He can only oppose us in front. We bring our fleet into full play." By March 8 McClellan was no closer to moving on Urbanna than he was to the moon, and Lincoln called him onto the White House carpet for an explanation. The prodding finally worked, and on March 10 McClellan and his grand army marched out of Washington to attack what McClellan was sure would be a Confederate Sevastopol, filled with abundant Confederate soldiers who would inflict thousands of casualties that his Urbanna plan would have avoided.[45]

To McClellan's unspeakable surprise, the Confederate entrenchments at Manassas turned out to be empty. Confederate General Joseph E. Johnston, who now had sole command of the Confederacy's northern Virginia army, had far fewer men than McClellan thought, and he prudently eased himself out of the Manassas lines before McClellan's hammer fell, withdrawing to the Rappahannock. The next day McClellan read in the newspapers that Lincoln had relieved him of his post of general in chief, ostensibly to allow McClellan to concentrate his energies on the Virginia theater.[46]

For McClellan, this was a humiliation of the first order. But Lincoln had by now learned that humiliation was a remarkably effective medicine for McClellan's case of "the slows": the next day McClellan laid out yet another plan for invading Virginia. He had no interest in an overland campaign from Manassas, and the original Urbanna campaign was now impossible with Joe Johnston sitting behind the Rappahannock. McClellan insisted that the basic idea of a combined army-navy operation was still feasible, provided one changed the target area to the James River,

44. General War Orders No. 1, January 27, 1862, and Special War Orders No. 1, January 31, 1862, in *War of the Rebellion*, 5:41.

45. Stephen W. Sears, *George B. McClellan: The Young Napoleon* (New York: Ticknor and Fields, 1988), 131, 148–49, 160–61.

46. "President's War Order No. 3," March 11, 1862, in *War of the Rebellion*, 5:54.

where the federal government still retained possession of Fortress Monroe, at the tip of the James River peninsula. He would load the 120,000 men of the Army of the Potomac onto navy transports and, relying on the superiority of the Federal navy in the waters of Chesapeake Bay and the strategic cover provided by Fortress Monroe, land his soldiers on the James River peninsula just below Richmond, then draw up to the Confederate capital and besiege it before Johnston's Confederate army on the Rappahannock knew what was happening.[47]

In McClellan's mind, this plan had all the proper advantages to it. By using Federal seapower, he would overcome the Confederate advantage of interior lines in Virginia, constitute a gigantic turning movement that would force the Confederates to abandon everything north of Richmond without a shot, and take the rebel capital rather than the rebel army as the real object of the campaign, thus avoiding unnecessary battles and unnecessary loss of life. To Lincoln, who had borrowed books on military science from the Library of Congress in an effort to give himself a crash course on strategy and tactics, this looked instead like an unwillingness on McClellan's part to advance to a decisive Napoleonic battle, and it was only a matter of time before Lincoln's administration began to impute political as well as strategic motives to McClellan's indirect methods. Secretary of War Stanton at once objected that the James River plan merely demonstrated how unaggressive McClellan was. And since piloting the Army of the Potomac down to the James River would leave Washington almost undefended, it also left a question in Stanton's suspicious mind as to whether McClellan was deliberately opening the national capital to a Confederate strike from northern Virginia.

Still, McClellan was the expert, and the army was solidly behind him, so Lincoln (despite Stanton's reservations) decided to authorize the venture—provided that McClellan left approximately 30,000 men under the rehabilitated Irvin McDowell in front of Washington to protect the capital. When McClellan discovered this caveat, he protested that he needed every last man of the Army of the Potomac for his offensive. Lincoln was adamant, however: he would release McDowell's troops only if Washington was safe beyond doubt, and even then McDowell would need to march overland, down to the James, to link up with McClellan.[48] On March 17, 1862, McClellan began the laborious process of transporting nearly 90,000 men of the Army of the Potomac to the tip of the James River peninsula at Fortress Monroe, leaving the remainder behind in scattered commands and forts around Washington, and McDowell at Alexandria.

The resulting Peninsula Campaign confirmed everyone's worst fears about McClellan's vanity and slowness, and for a few others raised fears about his loyalty

---

47. For Lincoln on "the slows," see *Recollected Words of Abraham Lincoln*, 32; Rowena Reed, *Combined Operations in the Civil War* (Annapolis, MD: Naval Institute Press, 1978), 121–30.

48. Lorenzo Thomas to McClellan, April 4, 1862, in *War of the Rebellion*, 11(III):66.

to a Republican administration. True to McClellan's prediction, the Army of the Potomac's landing on the James peninsula caught the Confederate army in Virginia totally by surprise. Only a thin force of 15,000 rebel infantry, under the command of former West Pointer and amateur actor John Magruder, held a defensive line across the James peninsula at the old Revolutionary War battlefield of Yorktown, and if McClellan had but known the pitiful numbers opposing him, he could have walked over Magruder and into Richmond without blinking. What Magruder lacked in terms of numbers, however, he more than made up for with theatrical displays of parading troops and menacing-looking artillery emplacements, and he successfully bluffed McClellan into thinking that a major Confederate army stood in his path. By the time McClellan was finally ready to open up a major assault on the York-town lines on May 5, 1862, Joe Johnston's Confederate army in Virginia had been regrouped around Richmond and was prepared to give McClellan precisely the kind of defensive battle he had hoped to avoid. To make matters worse, Johnston enjoyed the reputation of being one of the finest defensive strategists in the old army.

For the next three weeks, McClellan slowly felt his way up the peninsula, growing more and more convinced that Johnston had as many as 200,000 rebels defending Richmond (Johnston actually had only 60,000) and demanding that Lincoln send him more reinforcements, starting with McDowell's troops, whom he wanted to move overland across the Rappahannock to join him around Richmond. By the last half of May, McClellan and the Army of the Potomac were beside the Chickahom-iny River, six miles from Richmond, with his right flank sitting to the northwest and expecting to be joined by McDowell. As he finally worked himself up to planning an assault on Richmond, he began feeding his army, corps by corps, across to the south side of the Chickahominy, closer to Richmond.

Unfortunately for McClellan, torrential spring rains swept away the Chickahom-iny bridges after only two of his five army corps had crossed the Chickahominy. On May 31, hoping to crush these two isolated corps before the river subsided, Johnston wheeled out his entire army and struck the exposed Federals at the battle of Seven Pines.[49]

For two days Johnston and the Confederates hammered at the two vulnerable Federal corps. The Federal generals handled their untested men well, and the Con-federates drew off with the loss of more than 6,000 men, including Joe Johnston, who was severely wounded. Far from this putting spirit back into McClellan, howev-er, the outcome of Seven Pines only operated against him. Frightened by Johnston's unaccountable aggressiveness, McClellan cautiously slowed his advance across the Chickahominy. Far more ominous was the replacement of the wounded Johnston by an infinitely more skillful and aggressive Confederate general, Robert Edward Lee.

---

49. "Memorandum," May 17, 1862, in *War of the Rebellion*, 11(III):176–77; Newton, *Joseph E. Johnston and the Defense of Richmond*, 151, 168.

In Lee, the Confederacy possessed one of the purest examples of American military culture. The consummate Virginia gentleman, the son of a Revolutionary War general and grandson-in-law of George Washington, Lee had enjoyed a spotless career in the old army in Mexico and on the western plains, and had even served briefly as superintendent of West Point. Despite his faultless aristocratic bloodlines, Lee had actually spent a lifetime living down the dissipated reputation established by his dashing but improvident father, "Light-Horse Harry" Lee, who had been the commandant of George Washington's cavalry. Chronically in debt and chronically in flight from his creditors, Light-Horse Harry abandoned his family for refuge in the West Indies and died in 1818, leaving his wife, Anne Carter Lee, and family to the tender mercies of his wife's relatives and the open-armed community of Alexandria, Virginia.

Struggling to efface these stains on the family name, Robert Lee committed himself to the life of the army and to education at West Point. All of the Lees had a certain debonair wildness in their makeup, but Robert fought it back with a consciously cultivated aloofness and reserve that might almost have seemed arrogant had it not been wedded to a softness and gentility of manner. His four years at West Point were close to flawless—he had no behavioral demerits and was ranked second (by a fraction) in his class academically—and so he was commissioned in the army's premier service, the Corps of Engineers.[50]

Behind the shield of Virginia gentlemanliness, Lee could be as aggressive as the most Napoleonic of generals. He had become one of Winfield Scott's most trusted subordinates in Mexico. By the beginning of 1861 Lee had risen to the post of lieutenant colonel of the 2nd U.S. Cavalry, and he was promoted to full colonel by Abraham Lincoln on March 30, 1861. Old General Scott had wanted to give Lee even more: the full command of the Federal armies, which eventually went to George McClellan.

But Lee, unlike Scott, who was also a Virginian, could not tear himself away from his old family and state loyalties, especially when he owed so much of his boyhood redemption to them. He could not agree with Lincoln's decision to "pin the States in the Union with the bayonet," and on April 20, 1861, he resigned his commission. Lee had told Frank Blair, Lincoln's personal emissary, that if it were up to him, he would free all the slaves in the South in order to avert civil war, but he could not "draw my sword . . . save in defense of my native State." No Southerner went into rebellion with more professed reluctance. As he explained to his sister the same day, "With all my devotion to the Union, and the feeling of loyalty and duty of an American citizen, I have not been able to make up my mind to raise my hand against my relatives, my children, my home." He offered his services instead to Virginia, where he

---

50. Elizabeth Brown Pryor, *Reading the Man: A Portrait of Robert E. Lee Through His Private Letters* (New York: Viking, 2007), 17, 32–33, 60, 63.

was made a major general of state volunteers; when Virginia was accepted into the Confederacy on May 7, Lee was commissioned a brigadier general in the Confederate forces, and for a year he served in a variety of capacities, especially as Jefferson Davis's de facto chief of staff.[51] With Johnston wounded, Davis would entrust the defense of Richmond to no one but Lee.

Lee had already made more than enough trouble for McClellan even before taking the field. In March Lee prevailed upon Davis to allow Thomas Jonathan Jackson, a former Virginia Military Institute professor and minor hero of the Bull Run battle, to take command of the small Confederate force in Virginia's Shenandoah Valley and make a threatening feint down the Valley toward Harpers Ferry and the poorly defended Federal capital. Jackson, who had acquired the nickname "Stonewall" for his courage at Bull Run, moved menacingly toward the Potomac River, confirming all of Lincoln's and Stanton's fears that McClellan's Peninsula operation was going to lay Washington open to capture. Lincoln threw three separate Federal forces of about 40,000 men after Jackson's 16,000 "foot cavalry," but Jackson easily eluded or trounced all three, and left all the Federal soldiers in northern Virginia tied securely in knots and unavailable to the increasingly nervous McClellan—including McDowell's troops, whom McClellan was still awaiting on the Chickahominy.[52]

Now Lee took personal command of the Richmond defenses, and, in complete contrast to McClellan, he at once advanced to the offensive and opened what became known as the Seven Days' Battle. On June 26, finding the Federal army still straddling the Chickahominy, Lee decided to strike at Federal troops on the north side of the river at Mechanicsville. Lee's attacks were repulsed and his forces suffered more than 1,400 casualties, but the next day Lee attacked the same Federal troops again at Gaines Mill, and this time the Confederate forces inflicted nearly 6,800 casualties on the Union troops and forced them to withdraw.[53]

McClellan's communications with his supply base at White House Landing on the York river were now bare, and McClellan, imagining himself to be outnumbered and endangered by untold hosts of rebel fiends, concluded that he had no choice but to fall back to a safe spot on the James River and set up a new base there. Lee, scenting blood, harried and snapped at McClellan's retreating army at Allen's Farm and Savage's Station (on June 29) and Glendale, or Frayser's Farm, and White Oak

51. Lee to Anne Marshall, April 20, 1861, in *The Wartime Papers of Robert E. Lee*, eds. Clifford Dowdey and Louis Manarin (Boston: Little, Brown, 1961), 10; Alan Nolan, *Lee Considered: General Robert E. Lee and Civil War History* (Chapel Hill: University of North Carolina Press, 1991), 40–41, 50–58.

52. Lincoln to McClellan, May 24, 1862, in *War of the Rebellion*, 11(I):30; Peter Cozzens, *Shenandoah 1862: Stonewall Jackson's Valley Campaign* (Chapel Hill: University of North Carolina Press, 2008), 344–45.

53. Matt Spruill, *Echoes of Thunder: A Guide to the Seven Days Battles* (Knoxville: University of Tennessee Press, 2006), 307.

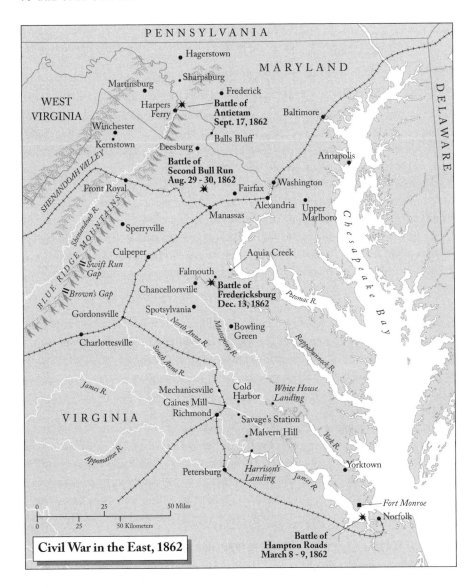

Civil War in the East, 1862

Swamp (both on June 30), hoping to pick off and crush isolated Federal brigades and divisions, until at last he was handed a bloody repulse by the Federal rear guard at Malvern Hill (July 1). All in all, the Seven Days' Battle cost Lee's army 3,494 men killed and 15,758 wounded—but he had saved Richmond.[54] McClellan, still believing himself outnumbered and blaming his defeat on Lincoln's unwillingness to send him

---

54. Sears, *To the Gates of Richmond: The Peninsula Campaign* (New York: Ticknor and Fields, 1992), 208, 249, 294, 343–45; Clifford Dowdey, *The Seven Days: The Emergence of Lee* (Boston: Little, Brown, 1964), 273.

McDowell, dug the Army of the Potomac into an impregnable defensive position at Harrison's Landing, on the James River. The great Peninsula Campaign was over.

And so, it seemed, was McClellan's career. McClellan, of course, saw no blame in himself; in fact, he expected Lincoln to grant him reinforcements so that he could move from the new base at Harrison's Landing along the south side of the James River and clamp Richmond into a siege from below. But on July 8, when Lincoln himself came down to Harrison's Landing to speak with McClellan, the president was in no mood for petting the Young Napoleon. Even as McClellan was still struggling back to Harrison's Landing, Lincoln had decided to appoint a new commander for the scattered Union forces that had been beaten black and blue by Stonewall Jackson in the Shenandoah Valley. He selected a hard-fighting, no-compromise, anti-slavery westerner named John Pope and had the forlorn remnants of McDowell's corps and the troops Jackson had led merrily up and down the Shenandoah reorganized as a new army, the Army of Virginia. He then sent them off to launch a fresh invasion—an overland invasion, not one of McClellan's fancy but fruitless combined land-and-sea operations.

Under Pope, there would be no observances of polite niceties by Union troops in rebel territory. In a series of general orders, Pope freely authorized his troops to forage from the population at will, to shoot any civilians guilty of taking potshots at Federal soldiers while "not forming part of the organized forces of the enemy nor wearing the garb of soldiers" and confiscate their property, and to impress local civilians into military road work. There would be no more studious protection of Southern property: "Soldiers were called into the field to do battle against the enemy, and it is not expected that their force and energy shall be wasted in protecting private property of those most hostile to the Government." When Pope's men flooded into northern Virginia's Culpeper County, Jefferson Davis was astounded to learn that the Yankees "are systematically destroying all the growing crops and everything the people have to live on"; on July 31 Davis ordered Lee to treat any of Pope's officers he might capture as "robbers and murderers" rather than prisoners of war.[55]

While Pope was spreading premeditated devastation into northern Virginia, McClellan remained motionless at Harrison's Landing, demanding that Lincoln supply him with another 100,000 men for his new drive at Richmond. Even if Lincoln had wanted to give them to McClellan, the time it would take to reinforce and reequip McClellan for another campaign on the Peninsula would allow Lee and his victorious Confederates to slip northward and menace Washington in force. Lincoln could not risk another close call like the one Stonewall Jackson had given the capital

55. Daniel E. Sutherland, "Introduction to War: The Civilians of Culpeper County, Virginia," in *Civil War History* 37 (June 1991): 124–25; "General Orders No. 5," July 18, 1862, "General Orders No. 7," July 10, 1862, "General Orders No. 11," July 23, 1862, and "General Orders No. 13," July 25, 1862, in *War of the Rebellion*, 12(II):50–52, 12(III):509.

in March. Yet Lincoln hesitated to cashier McClellan outright. Although Lincoln might have wanted to rid himself of "Little Mac" right on the dock at Harrison's Landing, McClellan had become too clearly identified with Democratic political interests in the North. With critical state elections in New York, New Jersey, and Pennsylvania, and with the 1862 congressional elections hanging over the horizon in November, Lincoln could not afford to alienate Northern Democratic sympathies. He was "tired" of McClellan's "excuses [and] said he'd remove him at once but for the election."[56]

What was even more dangerous, McClellan still possessed the loyalty and admiration of the ordinary soldiers of the Army of the Potomac, and he had had fully a year to fill up the officer corps of the army with his friends and subordinates. Not only might those officers refuse to serve under a McClellan replacement, but Lincoln could not be certain that they might not attempt a political action of their own if McClellan was summarily relieved of command. Quartermaster General Montgomery Meigs, who accompanied Lincoln to Harrison's Landing, was appalled to hear "mutterings of a march on Washington."[57] Hence Lincoln chose not to dismiss McClellan but to ease the Army of the Potomac out from under him. On August 3 McClellan was ordered to begin putting elements of the Army of the Potomac back onto their transports to return to Washington, where one by one McClellan's proud formations were fed over to General Pope to become part of the Army of Virginia.

This delicate outmaneuvering might have gone off smoothly if it had not been for the ferocious aggressiveness of Robert E. Lee and the simple inadequacy of John Pope. Even before taking command of the Army of Northern Virginia, Lee had become convinced of the necessity of moving the center of campaigning north of the Potomac, into Maryland and Pennsylvania. The thin-soiled dispersion of agriculture everywhere in Virginia except the Shenandoah Valley could not feed his army indefinitely, and as soon as he was installed at the head of the Army of Northern Virginia, he began pressing Jefferson Davis to allow him to strike northward, through Maryland, to the Susquehanna, where he could "change the character of the war."

First, though, he would have to deal with John Pope's Army of Virginia. After the Malvern Hill fight, Lee decided to gamble on the likelihood of McClellan's inactivity and catch Pope before he could be further reinforced. "I want Pope to be suppressed," Lee wrote in a rare burst of contempt. "The course indicated in his orders . . . cannot be permitted." Lee and Stonewall Jackson bounded back up into northern Virginia, and on August 30, 1862, Jackson and Lee trapped the hapless Pope between them on the old Bull Run battlefield. The second battle of Bull Run was an even greater disaster for the Union than the first one: Pope's army of 60,000 men suffered 16,000 casualties and was left a hopeless wreck. Meanwhile, the triumphant

56. Adams Hill, in Louis Starr, *Bohemian Brigade: Civil War Newsmen in Action* (New York: Knopf, 1954), 152.

57. "General M. C. Meigs on the Conduct of the Civil War," 294.

Lee was now free to lunge across the Potomac into Maryland, hoping to parlay his victories into a massive pro-secession uprising among slaveholding Marylanders and perhaps reach far enough across the Mason-Dixon Line into Pennsylvania to disrupt the North's vital east-west railroad junction on the Susquehanna River at Harrisburg.[58]

With Pope utterly discredited and the now defunct Army of Virginia in pieces, Lincoln had no choice but to put McClellan back in charge, transfer Pope's command back into the structure of the Army of the Potomac, and order them to pursue Lee into Maryland. The soldiers in the ranks were elated, and the unhappy Pope had to listen as "tired fellows, as the news passed down the column, jumped to their feet, and sent up such a hurrah as the Army of the Potomac had never heard before. Shout upon shout went out into the stillness of the night; and as it was taken up along the road and repeated by regiment, brigade, division and corps, we could hear the roar dying away in the distance."[59]

Few generals ever get a second chance to redeem themselves, and McClellan's gratitude to Lincoln spurred him on after Lee with unaccustomed vigor—gratitude, that is, plus the unlooked-for gift of a copy of Lee's campaign orders (Special Orders No. 191) for the Maryland campaign, which a private and a corporal in the 27th Indiana discovered in the grass near Frederick, Maryland, on September 13, 1862. The lost orders were in McClellan's hands by noon that day, and he was elated: "Now I know what to do!" They revealed that Lee's army was actually dangerously dispersed along Maryland's roads and could easily be destroyed piece by piece if McClellan hopped to it. For once, McClellan did just that. The Federals surprised Confederate screening forces at South Mountain on September 14, and three days later McClellan had pinned Lee's army in between the Potomac and one of the Potomac's little tributary streams, the Antietam Creek, near the town of Sharpsburg, Maryland.[60]

The subsequent battle of Antietam ought to have been McClellan's win-it-all opportunity to redeem his reputation. Once again, his slowness and his discomfort with the headlong offensive were his undoing. In a terrible, bitter all-day battle on September 17—a battle that cost a total of 23,000 casualties from both armies— McClellan launched a series of poorly coordinated attacks on Lee's army that not only failed to deliver the sledgehammer blow that might have flattened the Confederates but even failed to prevent Confederate reinforcements from arriving from Harpers Ferry. At the end of the day, Lee's men were only barely holding on to their

---

58. Lee to Davis, June 5, 1862, and to Jackson, July 27, 1862, in *Wartime Papers of Robert E. Lee*, 183–84, 239; Joseph L. Harsh, *Confederate Tide Rising: Robert E. Lee and the Making of Southern Strategy, 1861–1862* (Kent, OH: Kent State University Press, 1998), 54–60.

59. Pope, "The Second Battle of Bull Run," *Battles and Leaders*, 2:489–90.

60. Stephen W. Sears, "Last Words on the Lost Order," in *Controversies and Commanders: Dispatches from the Army of the Potomac* (Boston: Houghton Mifflin, 1999), 114–15.

positions, but McClellan showed no disposition to send in a final knockout assault, even though he had at least 15,000 fresh troops in reserve. Instead, Lee was allowed to creep back across the Potomac into Virginia. A Confederate band that tried to cheer up Lee's troops at the river crossings by playing "Maryland, My Maryland" was hooted down until they struck up "Carry Me Back to Old Virginny."[61] McClellan, meanwhile, went into camp to lick his wounds, and there he stayed, through September and into October. Lincoln tried in vain to move him, even visiting McClellan personally to urge him to pursue Lee. McClellan waited until the end of October before putting his columns back onto the roads southward. By then, Lincoln had already nerved himself to fire his truculent general. The president waited until the day after the New York and New Jersey congressional elections, to mute the political damage, and then on November 5, 1862, Lincoln dismissed McClellan.

The reactions were bad, especially in the Army of the Potomac, where loyal McClellanite officers whispered plots for a coup into the general's ear. "Nay, there was considerable swearing indulged in, and threats of marching on Washington, should McClellan but take the lead," remembered Captain Amos Judson of the 83rd Pennsylvania.[62] But whatever else McClellan was, he was not a traitor, and even if he had once talked foolishly about dictatorships, he silenced the gossip in his headquarters and rode away from the army he had built, never to return.

The slaughter at Antietam had not been without its merits. Although in military terms the battle had been something of a draw, Lincoln was prepared to treat Lee's withdrawal afterward as evidence of a Union victory. On the strength of that victory, just six days after Antietam, Lincoln issued the preliminary announcement of a dramatic shift in war policy: as of January 1, 1863, "all persons held as slaves within any State or designated part of a State . . . in rebellion against the United States, shall be then, thenceforward, and forever free," and the United States military forces "will recognize and maintain the freedom of such persons, and will do no act or acts to repress such persons . . . in any efforts that may make for their actual freedom."[63]

Lacking any means for dealing directly with slavery, Lincoln had assumed from the start that anything he did on the slavery issue must necessarily be on a political track, separate from the military track on which he proposed to win the war and restore the Union. Events had created a new set of circumstances, however. As he told Congress a month later in his annual message, "The dogmas of the quiet past are inadequate to the stormy present. The occasion is piled high with difficulty, and

61. James V. Murfin, *The Gleam of Bayonets: The Battle of Antietam and Robert E. Lee's Maryland Campaign, September 1862* (New York: T. Yusoloff, 1965), 298, 303–4, 374–77.

62. "McClellan Relieved," November 5, 1862, in *War of the Rebellion*, 19(II):545; Amos M. Judson, *History of the Eighty-Third Regiment, Pennsylvania Volunteers* (Dayton, OH: Morningside Bookshop, 1986 [1865]), 98.

63. Lincoln, "Emancipation Proclamation," in *Collected Works*, 6:29.

we must rise with the occasion. As our case is new, so we must think anew and act anew." It was not only the slaves who must be freed, but Lincoln and Congress who must free themselves of thinking about slavery purely as a political problem. "We must disenthrall ourselves, and then we shall save our country."[64]

LINCOLN AND EMANCIPATION

No other single document, except perhaps the Gettysburg Address, has done so much to fix Lincoln permanently in the constellation of American history as the Emancipation Proclamation. Lincoln himself believed that "as affairs have turned, *it is the central act of my administration, and the great event of the nineteenth century.*"[65] Yet debate has not ceased to rage since the day of the Proclamation's preliminary publication over what its meaning was to be, or what Lincoln's real intentions in issuing it were.

Much of that debate was, and still is, fueled by Lincoln himself. This was, after all, the man who criticized abolitionists for rocking the anti-slavery boat, who in 1858 had affirmed that he had "no purpose to introduce political and social equality between the white and the black races" because of the "natural disgust in the minds of nearly all white people, to the idea of an indiscriminate amalgamation of the white and black races."[66] And it was he who had asserted that his paramount intention in the war was always to save the Union, and not to do anything one way or the other about slavery unless the doing of it would assist the federal government in restoring the Union:

> I would save the Union. I would do it the shortest way under the Constitution. . . . My paramount object in this struggle is to save the Union, and is not either to save or destroy slavery. If I could save the Union without freeing any slave I would do it; and if I could save it by freeing all the slaves I would do it; and if I could save it by freeing some and leaving others alone I would also do that. What I do about slavery and the colored race, I do because I believe that it helps save the Union.[67]

How are we to understand the Emancipation Proclamation when the president who wrote it held beliefs on race that fly straight in the face of equality? And especially when the words of the Emancipation Proclamation seem suspiciously lacking in the

---

64. Lincoln, "Annual Message to Congress," December 1, 1862, in *Collected Works*, 5:537.

65. Francis B. Carpenter, *Six Months at the White House with Abraham Lincoln: The Story of a Picture* (New York: Hurd and Houghton, 1866), 90.

66. Lincoln, "Speech at Springfield, Illinois," June 26, 1857, and "First Debate with Stephen A. Douglas," August 21, 1858, in *Collected Works*, 2:404, 3:16.

67. Lincoln, "To Horace Greeley," August 22, 1861, in *Collected Works* 5:388.

eloquence that produced Lincoln's other great state papers? "Had the political strategy of the moment called for a momentous human document of the stature of the Declaration of Independence, Lincoln could have risen to the occasion," snarled Columbia University historian Richard Hofstadter in 1948; instead, "the Emancipation Proclamation of January 1, 1863, had all the moral grandeur of a bill of lading."[68]

There are actually two questions involved in the debate over the Emancipation Proclamation, one of them about ends and the other about means. There is no reason to doubt the sincerity of Lincoln's oft-repeated statement that "I have always thought that all men should be free." Slavery was "founded in the selfishness of man's nature," in his desire to shift the burden of work onto the shoulders of others and appropriating the full value of another's labor to oneself. "Its ownership betokened not only the possession of wealth but indicated the gentleman of leisure who was above and scorned labour." The right to freely enjoy the fruits of one's own labor was as much a matter of liberty as any other natural right, and denying it made slavery "a great & crying injustice, an enormous national crime, and that we could not expect to escape punishment for it." Lincoln might regard a discussion of the *civil* rights of the freed slaves *after* slavery as being in a totally different universe of rights (and in this, nineteenth-century writing on law and rights tended to support him), but there was never any real question about the slave's natural right to liberty and to whatever happiness his labor could bring him.[69]

Lincoln's election to the presidency—and as an anti-slavery candidate who needed no electoral votes from the South to get elected—convinced him that the opportunity to put slavery on the path to extinction was now at hand. Emancipation, wrote his Illinois political ally Isaac Arnold in 1866, was Lincoln's "deepest, strongest desire of the soul," and from the time of his election Lincoln "hoped and expected to be the Liberator of the slaves." Another longtime Illinois political friend, Joseph Gillespie, was convinced that Lincoln "had it in his mind for a long time to war upon slavery until its destruction was effected."[70]

If the end was clear in Lincoln's mind, the means were very much another matter. So long as slavery was a matter of individual state enactments and individual state legalization, there was nothing he could do as a citizen to touch it, and not much more he could do as president. "Some of our northerners seem bewildered

68. Hofstadter, "Abraham Lincoln and the Self-Made Myth," in *The American Political Tradition and the Men Who Made It* (New York: Knopf, 1973 [1948]), 131.

69. Joseph Gillespie to W. H. Herndon, January 31, 1866, in *Herndon's Informants*, 183, 197.

70. Lincoln, "Speech at Peoria, Illinois," October 16, 1854, and "Speech to One Hundred Fortieth Indiana Regiment," March 17, 1865, in *Collected Works*, 2:271, 8:361; Isaac Newton Arnold, *The History of Abraham Lincoln and the Overthrow of Slavery* (Chicago: Clarke, 1866), 300, 685–86; Joseph Gillespie to W. H. Herndon, December 8, 1866, in *Herndon's Informants*, 507.

and dazzled by the excitement of the hour," Lincoln remarked, even to the point of thinking "that this war is to result in the entire abolition of slavery." But presidents are only presidents; they do not have plenary powers to do anything they wish. Announcing an end to slavery purely on his own authority would accomplish about as much as if he were "to open that window and shout down Pennsylvania Avenue."[71]

Even some of the most ardent abolitionists recognized how difficult state legalization made it for any federal agency or officer to touch slavery. Thaddeus Stevens, the Pennsylvania congressman and radical abolitionist, admitted in 1860 that there was no "desire or intention, on the part of the Republican party . . . to interfere with the institutions of our sister States"; Owen Lovejoy, the Illinois congressman whose brother had been abolitionism's first martyr back in 1837, likewise conceded that "I have no power to enter the State of North Carolina"—or any other state, for that matter—"and abolish slavery there by an act of Congress."[72]

If no direct path to emancipating slaves beckoned, that did not mean that Lincoln was ignoring indirect paths. He had long believed that any workable notion of emancipation would have to involve "three main features—gradual—compensation—and the vote of the people." *Gradual*, so that "some practical system by which the two races could gradually live themselves out of their old relation to each other, and both come out better prepared for the new" and thus "spares both races from the evils of sudden derangement." *Compensated*, so that the disappearance of some $6 billion invested in slave ownership did not wipe out the capital necessary to begin paying wages to now-free workers or capsize the entire economy. And with the *vote of the people*, so that individual state legislatures undid what their own statutes had created, and insulated emancipation from any appeals by disgruntled slave owners to the federal courts.[73]

This might be a tedious process, Lincoln conceded. But "emancipation will be unsatisfactory to the advocates of perpetual slavery," no matter how it was packaged, and allowing for it to take effect gradually "should greatly mitigate their dissatisfaction." During the Lincoln-Douglas debates in 1858, he estimated that gradual emancipation might take "a hundred years, if it should live so long, in the States where it exists"; by 1862, he had shrunk that estimate to thirty-eight years. The example of previous emancipation plans in the West Indies, and even in the early days of the new American republic, was that such plans invariably took on their own speed

---

71. Lincoln, in *Recollected Words*, 206, 449.

72. Stevens, "Speech on Republican Aims," January 25, 1860, in *The Selected Papers of Thaddeus Stevens*, ed. B. W. Palmer (Pittsburgh: University of Pittsburgh Press, 1997), 1:165; Lovejoy, in Mitchell Snay, "The Emergence of the Republican Party in Illinois," *Journal of the Abraham Lincoln Association* 22 (Winter 2001): 94–95.

73. Lincoln, "To Horace Greeley," March 24, 1862, and "To Nathaniel P. Banks," August 5, 1863, in *Collected Works*, 5:169, 6:365.

and finished far ahead of the estimates. So, even while Lincoln professed to have no direct designs on slavery, by November 1861 he was already pressing a gradual, compensated emancipation scheme on the border slave state of Delaware, funded by U.S. bonds. If Delaware took the buyout bait, then the other three border slave states—Maryland, Kentucky, and Missouri—would do likewise; and once the Union was restored, the same process could be set in motion in all the rest of the slave states. By these means, Lincoln explained, "it seemed to him that gradual emancipation and governmental compensation" would bring slavery "to an end."[74]

To make this work, however, Lincoln would have to hold back some of the more zealous of his anti-slavery colleagues. Charles Sumner, the abolitionist senator who had survived his beating at the hands of Preston Brooks in 1856 and was now chair of the Senate Foreign Relations Committee, argued that "under the war power the right had come to [Lincoln] to emancipate the slaves" unilaterally. In time of peace, Lincoln might have no authority to touch slavery, but in time of war, all restraints dropped away in the name of emergency action. "The civil power, in mass and in detail, is superseded, and all rights are held subordinate to this military magistracy."[75]

The problem was that no such "war power" might actually exist. The Constitution designated Lincoln as "Commander-in-Chief of the Army and Navy of the United States . . . when called into the actual Service of the United States" (Article II, Section 2), but no one knew precisely what that meant, much less what war powers it might entail. There was, in fact, no constitutional clarity even on what martial law might mean if commanders in the field had to impose it. On August 31, 1861, one of Lincoln's most recently minted major generals, the onetime Republican presidential candidate John Charles Frémont, not only declared martial law across the state of Missouri but confiscated the property of anyone "who shall take up arms against the United States" and declared their slaves "free men." Eight months later, Major General David Hunter issued a similar martial law declaration, declaring any slaves in his district "forever free."[76] Lincoln revoked their proclamations, rebuked both generals, and eventually removed them. Without a firm constitutional plank to rest upon, Lincoln was wary of invoking war powers or martial law as means for freeing slaves, if only because any actions he or his generals might take would then be appealed to the federal courts. Sitting atop those courts was still the grim-visaged Roger B. Taney, who would seize on any opportunity to strike down any form of

74. Lincoln, "Annual Message to Congress," December 1, 1862, in *Collected Works*, 5:530–31, 534; Lincoln, "First Joint Debate," in *The Lincoln-Douglas Debates of 1858*, 105; Davis, in *Recollected Words*, 132, 182.

75. David Donald, *Charles Sumner and the Coming of the Civil War* (New York: Knopf, 1961), 388; "The Hon. C. Sumner on a War for Emancipation," *The Anti-Slavery Reporter*, November 1, 1861, 246.

76. Frémont, "Emancipation Proclamation of General Fremont," August 31, 1861, and Hunter, "General Orders No. 11," May 9, 1862, in *Political History of the Rebellion*, 245–46, 250.

emancipation in the same way he had struck down attempts to exclude slavery from the territories in *Dred Scott.*

Other generals tried to evade the legal armor around slavery in more creative ways. In May 1861 a group of three runaway slaves showed up at the gate of Fortress Monroe, where they were interrogated by the fort's commandant, Major General Benjamin F. Butler. Swiftly a representative from their owner, Confederate colonel Charles King Mallory, appeared with a request that Butler return the slaves, as provided for by the Fugitive Slave Law. Like Frémont, Butler was a political appointee, but he was also a lawyer with a sardonic sense of humor, and the prospect of a Confederate officer demanding the return of his "property" under a law of the same government the Confederate was fighting against amused Butler in the worst way. Butler declared that he would detain the slaves at Fortress Monroe—not only had the officer repudiated the authority of the government whose law he was now expecting Butler to enforce, but since Mallory regarded the slaves as "property," Butler would also regard them as war-related "property" to be seized in time of war, and so declared the slaves "contraband." By July, Butler had 900 "contrabands" on his hands.[77]

This created almost as much legal danger for Lincoln as Frémont and Hunter would with martial law. Lincoln had insisted from the beginning that secession was a legal impossibility; ergo, what was called the "Confederate States of America" was in fact not a nation at all but merely a domestic insurrection. Every textbook on international law and the laws of war taught that seizure of enemy property as "contraband of war" could only take place between sovereign and equal *nations.* Even then, there was nothing in the rules governing contraband of war that actually made the human "contraband" free. "The possession of real property by a belligerent," warned Henry Halleck, Frémont's replacement in Missouri and himself a former lawyer, "gives him a right to its use and to its products, but not a completely valid and indefeasible title, with full power of alienation." Once the war was over, slave owners would have full right to claim the return of their slaves, and emancipation would be a dead letter.[78]

Congress also tried to put a legislative oar into the emancipation waters. On July 15, 1861, Lyman Trumbull, the chair of the Senate Judiciary Committee, introduced a bill to authorize the confiscation of the property of anyone "aiding, abetting or promoting insurrection" open to seizure as "prize and capture." Trumbull's confiscation bill was immediately denounced as a de facto "act of emancipation, however limited

77. "The Contrabands at Fortress Monroe," *Atlantic Monthly* 8 (November 1861): 626–27; Robert F. Engs, *Freedom's First Generation: Black Hampton, Virginia, 1861–1890* (Philadelphia: University of Pennsylvania Press, 1979), 18–22; Adam Goodheart, *1861: The Civil War Awakening* (New York: Knopf, 2011), 296–338.

78. Henry Halleck, *International Law; or, Rules Regulating the Intercourse of States in Peace and War* (San Francisco: H. H. Bancroft, 1861), 447.

and qualified." After furious debate and an unseemly amount of to-ing and fro-ing between the Senate and the House of Representatives, the bill was finally passed. Lincoln signed it on August 6, but reluctantly. "The President had some difficulty in consenting to approve the act of Congress," wrote Treasury Secretary Chase, and according to the *New York Times*, Lincoln "finally consented only upon the most urgent entreaties of prominent members of the Senate."[79]

Lincoln was as unconvinced of the constitutionality of the Confiscation Act as he was of the notion of war powers, especially since the Constitution expressly forbade permanent confiscations of property "except during the life of the person attainted" (Article III, Section 3). If the Confiscation Act confiscated slaves, the federal government would be constitutionally obligated to hold them in trust for the heirs of those punished under its terms, not to free them. Trumbull admitted that the bill was more for political effect than a practical instrument of emancipation, and Maine senator William Pitt Fessenden conceded that it was a "humbug" that Congress adopted only because "something must pass."[80] In July 1862 Congress passed another, more stringent Confiscation Act, which Lincoln also signed, with the same misgivings.

Lincoln did not have any illusions about the usefulness of the Confiscation Acts, and he put little legal muscle behind them. Instead, Lincoln preferred to await the outcome of his legislative solution in Delaware. "Should the experiment inaugurated by this measure of deliverance be crowned by wholesome consequences," editorialized the *Washington Sunday Morning Chronicle*, "all the Border States will gradually accept the proposition of the President, and prepare for emancipation." Lincoln himself assured Charles Sumner that compensated, gradual emancipation would obtain the same ends as martial law, only with greater legal permanence. "The only difference between you and me," Lincoln told Sumner when he briefed Sumner of the Delaware plan on November 30, "is a difference of a month or six weeks in time." He assured another impatient abolitionist that the Delaware plan was not unlike the Irishman in the prohibitionist state of Maine, who asked for a glass of soda water but "with a drop of the creature put into it unbeknownst to myself."[81]

Lincoln was due for a cruel disappointment. The "Act for the Gradual Emancipation of slaves in the State of Delaware" passed the Delaware state senate, but only by

79. Trumbull, "Army Appropriations Bill," July 15, 1861, *Congressional Globe*, 37th Congress, 1st Session, 120; "The Last of Congress," *New York Times*, August 7, 1861.

80. Henry Wilson, *History of the Antislavery Measures of the Thirty-Seventh and Thirty-Eighth United-States Congresses, 1861–1864* (Boston: Walker, Wise, 1864), 4–5; J. W. Schuckers, *The Life and Public Services of Salmon Portland Chase* (New York: D. Appleton, 1874), 428; Cook, *William Pitt Fessenden*, 146.

81. "The Emancipation Act," *Washington Sunday Morning Chronicle*, April 26, 1862; Edward Everett Hale, memorandum of conversation with Sumner, April 26, 1862, in "The War," *Memories of a Hundred Years* (New York: Macmillan, 1903), 2:191–92; Moncure Conway, in *Recollected Words*, 119.

a 5–4 vote, but in the Delaware statehouse a straw poll showed that the bill would fail, and its backers withdrew it. Undeterred, on March 6, 1862, Lincoln proposed to Congress a general compensated emancipation scheme:

> RESOLVED that the United States ought to co-operate with any state which may adopt gradual abolishment of slavery, giving to such state pecuniary aid, to be used by such state in its discretion, to compensate for the inconveniences public and private, produced by such change of system.[82]

But the Border State representatives in Congress were no more enthusiastic for Lincoln's scheme than the Delaware legislature had been. Charles Wickliffe of Kentucky, a Unionist but also a slave owner, demanded to know in "what clause of the Constitution" Lincoln "finds the power in Congress to appropriate the treasure of the United States to buy negroes, or to set them free."[83]

Then came the debacle on the Peninsula, and the rising mutterings from Harrison's Landing that McClellan was contemplating some form of military intervention, which would surely kick emancipation over into who-knows-when land. On July 12, 1862, with renewed urgency, Lincoln called in the border states' congressional delegations and warned them that he could not wait forever for them to act. "Our country is in great peril," Lincoln argued, "demanding the loftiest views and boldest actions to bring it speedy relief." If they did not take action on their own "to emancipate gradually," then the "friction and abrasion" of war would do it for them. Referring to a biblical metaphor of cataclysm, he told them they must read "the signs of the times."[84]

Lincoln himself was long past caution on this point. On July 13, Lincoln confided to the secretary of the navy, Gideon Welles, that if the Southern states persisted in their rebellion, it would be "a necessity and a duty on our part to liberate their slaves," and if that meant resorting to some sort of war powers for justification, he would do it. "We had about played our last card," Lincoln decided, "and must change our tactics or lose the game." A week later, on July 22, Lincoln read to an astounded cabinet a preliminary draft of an Emancipation Proclamation, which would free all the slaves in the rebel states.[85]

82. "Joint Resolution Declaring That the United States Ought to Cooperate with, Affording Pecuniary Aid to Any State Which May Adopt the Gradual Abolishment of Slavery," April 10, 1862, in *The Statutes at Large Treaties, and Proclamations of the United States of America from December 5, 1859 to March 3, 1863*, ed. George Sanger (Boston: Little and Brown, 1863), 617.

83. J. W. Crisfield, in *Conversations with Lincoln*, ed. Charles M. Segal (New York: Putnam, 1961), 165–68; Wilson, *History of the Anti-Slavery Measures*, 81–85.

84. Lincoln, "Appeal to Border State Representatives," July 12, 1862, in *Collected Works*, 5:318–19.

85. Welles, diary entry for July 13, 1862, in *Diary of Gideon Welles*, 1:70; Welles, "The History of Emancipation," in *Civil War and Reconstruction: Selected Essays by Gideon Welles*, ed. Albert Mordell (New York: Twayne, 1959), 237; Carpenter, *Six Months at the White House*, 21.

As with the compensated emancipation proposal, Lincoln's Proclamation sounded like a good deal less than what the old-line abolitionists wanted. It provided only for the emancipation of slaves still inside Confederate-held territory, leaving untouched slaves in the border states and in areas of the South already occupied by Federal forces. If Lincoln really had the war powers Charles Sumner thought he had, then constitutionally they could apply only to the places where there was a war in progress; since the border states had never been at war with the federal government, no war powers could be asserted there, unless Lincoln wanted to see his Proclamation end up in Roger Taney's lap. Since it had been Lincoln's argument all along that secession from the Union was a legal impossibility, the reclaimed occupied districts were not at war, either. If Lincoln wanted his Proclamation to stick, he would have to zone off the border states and the occupied districts—and their slaves.

But the states of the Confederacy—"any state or states, wherein the constitutional authority of the United States shall not then be practically recognized" was how he insisted on describing them—were another matter. Having removed themselves from civil jurisdiction, the Confederate states were now under the jurisdiction of the president as commander in chief of the army and navy of the United States. Under the rubric of those powers, Lincoln was prepared to do what no president under any other circumstances could have done legally, and that was declare general emancipation of all the slaves, without exception, in all rebellious areas; the emancipated slaves were "permanently free, thenceforward, and forever."

On the advice of his cabinet, Lincoln waited to publish the preliminary Proclamation until the Federal armies had won some significant victories, so that the Proclamation would not appear as a counsel of despair on Lincoln's part. This delay frustrated abolitionist editors such as the *New York Tribune*'s Horace Greeley, and Greeley (who had evidently caught up a rumor that Lincoln had some sort of edict ready to hand) wrote his provocative "Prayer of Twenty Millions" in August as an expression of that frustration. Lincoln's reply that the "paramount object in this struggle is to save the Union" has often been read as a refusal to consider outright emancipation. But given that the Proclamation was already, literally, sitting in a pigeonhole in his desk, the very fact that Lincoln would almost nonchalantly announce that "if I could save it by freeing all the slaves I would do it" was actually a radical statement, bundled into the most diffident possible language. No president in the previous six decades, from Jefferson to Buchanan, would ever have dreamt of suggesting that he might consider "freeing all the slaves," or any slave at all, under any circumstances.

On September 17, the battle at Antietam gave Lincoln all he needed in the form of a victory, and on September 22, 1862, Lincoln released the text of the Proclamation with the warning that unless Southern resistance ceased before January 1, the terms of the Proclamation would automatically go into effect on that date.

The Confederates did little more than rain curses on Lincoln's head, and on January 1, 1863, the Proclamation became official.

No one found the wait for emancipation more unbearable than the people who longed to be free. "How long! How long! O Lord God of Sabaoth!" Frederick Douglass exclaimed in 1847. Not long, if the outbreak of the war seemed to mean anything. When a Union naval flotilla steamed into South Carolina's Port Royal Sound in November, 1861, the slaves on the Sea Islands in the sound thought they knew exactly what the rumble of the Federal naval guns meant. "Son, dat ain't no t'under," whispered one slave boy's mother, "dat Yankee come to gib you Freedom."[86] When the preliminary Proclamation was released in September 1862, Frederick Douglass greeted it with a yelp of jubilation: "Ye millions of free and loyal men who have earnestly sought to free your bleeding country from the dreadful ravages of revolution and anarchy, lift up now your voices with joy and thanksgiving for with freedom to the slave will come peace and safety to your country."

When Lincoln finally signed the Proclamation in midafternoon on January 1, it touched off wild celebrations of rejoicing. In Philadelphia, where a 100-gun salute broke the night's stillness "in honor of the President's Proclamation," Mother Bethel Church "was crowded to overflowing, at least one-fourth of the congregation being whites, who seemed to take a deep interest in the exercises. . . . until a few minutes of twelve o'clock, when the whole congregation knelt in silent prayer to welcome in the new-born day of liberty." In Boston's Tremont Temple, the citadel of the free Massachusetts black community, Douglass, Charles Lenox Redmond, William Wells Brown, and John S. Rock spoke in celebration of the Proclamation. "In the evening when the Proclamation came to hand," it was read aloud to the audience "who received it with uproarious applause, shouting, tossing up their hats, rapping on the floor with their canes, and singing 'Blow ye the trumpet, blow.'"[87]

Thirty years before, white Bostonians "deemed it a duty that they owed to God" to harass abolitionists, but now *"things was a-workin."* When the news came over the wires that the Proclamation had indeed been signed, "the joyous enthusiasm manifested was beyond description. Cheers were proposed for the president and for the Proclamation, the whole audience rising to their feet and shouting at the tops of their voices, throwing up their hats and indicating the gratification in every conceivable manner." Douglass wrote, "The fourth of July was great, but the first of January, when we consider it in all its relations and bearings is incomparably greater. The one respect to the mere political birth to a nation, the last concerns the national life

86. Frederick Douglass, "Farewell Speech to the British People," March 30, 1847, in *Selected Speeches and Writings*, ed. P. S. Foner and Y. Taylor (Chicago: Lawrence Hill Books, 1999), 58; Willie Lee Rose, *Rehearsal for Reconstruction: The Port Royal Experiment* (New York: Oxford University Press, 1964), 12.

87. "City Items," *Christian Recorder*, January 10, 1863; Douglass, "Emancipation Proclaimed," "Rejoicing over the Proclamation," in *Douglass' Monthly*, January 1863 and February 1863.

and character, and is to determine whether that life and character shall be radiantly glorious with all high and noble virtues, or infamously blackened, forevermore, with all the hell-darkened crimes and horrors which attach to Slavery."[88]

If the Proclamation answered one question—*What shall we do about slavery?*—the answer only opened the door to another: *What shall be done with the freed slaves?* "How shall we deal with four millions of liberated blacks?" asked William Grosvenor in the *New Englander*. "Rightly considered, it is the most awful problem that any nation ever undertook to solve." Frederick Douglass hoped that the war would show white Americans how "the fate of the Republic and that of the slave" were tied together "in the same bundle."[89] But neither Lincoln nor the federal government seemed to give Douglass much hope that emancipation would do more than leave the freed slave in a sort of civic limbo—no longer a slave, but now . . . what? A citizen? The political equal of every white citizen? But what exactly was a citizen? The Constitution offered only vague hints about whether citizenship was a privilege bestowed and defined by the individual states or by the United States as a whole.

Lincoln, still hoping to evade a punishing white backlash against emancipation, at first hoped that he could dodge the question by promoting several schemes for colonizing emancipated blacks elsewhere—in effect, suggesting that they find political equality someplace other than the United States. Colonization had been one of the pet solutions of the Whigs for slavery ever since the days of Henry Clay, and in August 1862 Lincoln the ex-Whig tried to persuade a delegation of free black leaders led by Edward M. Thomas that it would be all for the best if African Americans could find a new life for themselves in Liberia, Central America, or the Caribbean, rather than trying to raise themselves to political equality in white America. Few black leaders saw any reason why they should have to abandon the only country they had known. Frederick Douglass was outraged when he heard of Lincoln's plans for colonization. "Mr. Lincoln assumes the language and arguments of an itinerant Colonization lecturer," Douglass stormed on the pages of his newest publication, *Douglass' Monthly*, in September 1862, "showing all his inconsistencies, his pride of race and blood, his contempt for Negroes and his canting hypocrisy." A mass meeting of free blacks in Philadelphia denounced the colonization plans: "Shall we sacrifice this, leave our homes, forsake our birthplace, and flee to a strange land to appease the anger and prejudice of the traitors now in arms against the Government?"[90]

88. Douglass, "January First 1863," in *Douglass' Monthly*, October 1862; "The Emancipation Proclamation," *Philadelphia Inquirer*, January 2, 1863. See also *Boston Evening Transcript*, January 2, 1863; *Boston Daily Advertiser*, January 2 and 3, 1863; and *Philadelphia Daily North American*, January 2 and 5, 1863.

89. Grosvenor, "The Rights of the Nation and the Duty of Congress," *New Englander* 24 (October 1865): 757; "Nemesis," in *The Life and Writings of Frederick Douglass*, ed. Foner, 3:99.

90. Blight, *Frederick Douglass' Civil War*, 138–40.

Nevertheless, Lincoln persisted. Congress appropriated funds, and a developer, Bernard Kock, was contracted to organize a freedmen's colony on Île-à-Vaches, an island off the southern coast of Haiti, in 1863. Kock was only ever able to recruit fewer than 500 volunteers for the project, and he mishandled so many aspects of the settlement that in March 1864 Lincoln finally ended support for the colony and evacuated all the colonists. Lincoln's "distress" over the "mistakes" of the Île-à-Vaches project was "as keen as it was sincere," wrote Chaplain John Eaton, who was in charge of the "contraband camps" the army was setting up across the South for newly freed slaves. "The spectacle of the President of the United States, conducting the affairs of the Nation in the midst of civil war," worrying over the fate of the hapless colonists he had dispatched there "was a spectacle that has stayed with me all my life."[91]

So, in the end, it came back to Lincoln to persuade a nation whose basic racial theories were usually little more than variations on bigotry that they were going to have to accept black people, free as well as newly freed, as their political and social brethren. In August 1863, when Frederick Douglass came to the White House to meet Lincoln for the first time, he was sure that he would still meet a president who was "preeminently the white man's president, entirely devoted to the welfare of white men." Douglass came away with a view of Lincoln very different from what he had expected. Lincoln was "the first great man that I talked with in the United States freely who in no single instance reminded me of the difference between himself and myself, or the difference of color."[92]

Nor did Lincoln mean to allow others to remind Douglass of the issue of color, and Lincoln was soon implementing a series of measures that would at last bring African Americans closer to the mainstream of American life. The first of these measures came in the form of an economic experiment. When the Federal navy seized the islands in the Port Royal Sound in the fall of 1861, the navy expected only to use the islands as a coaling station for the blockade of the Carolina coast. Slave owners on the islands fled from the Northern occupation, leaving their plantations, and in many cases their slaves, behind. Since the slaves could now be deemed "contraband," Treasury officials at Port Royal began putting the slaves to work harvesting the cotton on the abandoned plantations. Then, with the backing of anti-slavery societies in Boston, New York, and Philadelphia, a small army of "Gideonites" descended upon Port Royal with evangelical fire in their hearts and schoolbooks in their hands to preach, to teach, to heal, and to divide up the old plantations into farm plots for the newly free slaves to manage as their own property. The results were extremely

91. Gary Gallagher, "The A'Vache Tragedy," *Civil War Times Illustrated* 18 (February 1980): 5–10; John Hay, diary entry for July 1, 1864, in *Inside Lincoln's White House*, 217; Eaton, *Grant, Lincoln and the Freedmen: Reminiscences of the Civil War* (New York: Longmans, Green, 1907), 91–92.

92. Douglass, *Life and Times*, 347–49.

gratifying—one of the new cotton-planting operations easily cleared $80,000 in one year—and they demonstrated that free black people had the full capacity to compete equally with white people in the free-labor society of the North, without requiring subsidies or preferment.[93]

The second measure was military. At the beginning of the war, thousands of free blacks had volunteered to serve in the Union army. "The prejudiced white men North or South never will respect us until they are forced to do it by deed of our own," declared the *Weekly Anglo-African,* and Frederick Douglass urged the readers of *Douglass' Monthly* to put "the keen knife of liberty" to "the throat of slavery" and "deal a death-blow to the monster evil of the nineteenth century":

> Friends of freedom! be up and doing;—now is your time. The tyrant's extremity is your opportunity! Let the long crushed bondman arise! and in this auspicious moment, snatch back the liberty of which he has been so long robbed and despoiled. Now is the day, and now is the hour![94]

Three days after Lincoln's April 15, 1861, militia proclamation was issued, a company of "Hannibal Guards" from Pittsburgh offered its services, declaring that "although deprived of all political rights, we yet wish the government of the United States to be sustained against the tyranny of slavery, and are willing to assist in any honorable way or manner to sustain the present administration." One hundred and fifteen black students from Wilberforce University offered themselves as a company to Ohio governor William Dennison in 1861, and when Federal forces occupied New Orleans in the spring of 1862, three regiments of black and Creole Louisianans who made up the Louisiana Native Guards proposed to volunteer as entire units for Federal service.

In every case, the black volunteers were turned away. "My belief is that any attempt to make soldiers of negroes will prove an ignominious failure and should they get into battle the officers who command them will be sacrificed," reflected the artist turned cavalry colonel David Hunter Strother in May 1862. A Pennsylvania sergeant was more blunt: "We don't want to fight side and side by the nigger. We think we are too superior a race for that."[95]

93. Rose, *Rehearsal for Reconstruction,* 306.

94. Douglass, "The Fall of Sumter," *Douglass' Monthly,* May 1861.

95. "The Civil War Letters of Quartermaster Sergeant John C. Brock, 43rd Regiment, United States Colored Troops," ed. Eric Ledell Smith, in *Making and Unmaking Pennsylvania's Civil War,* ed. William Blair and William Pencak (University Park: Pennsylvania State University Press, 2001), 143; James G. Hollandsworth, *The Louisiana Native Guards: The Black Military Experience During the Civil War* (Baton Rouge: Louisiana State University Press, 1995), 12–15; Versalle F. Washington, *Eagles on Their Buttons: A Black Infantry Regiment in the Civil War* (Columbia: University of Missouri Press, 1999), 2–3; Jimerson, *The Private Civil War,* 92, 93.

Not until Congress amended the Militia Act in July 1862 did Lincoln have the presidential discretion to begin enlisting black soldiers as he saw fit, and only after the Emancipation Proclamation became official was black recruitment begun in earnest. At first black recruits were mustered into state volunteer regiments such as the 5th Massachusetts Colored Cavalry, the 29th Connecticut Colored Infantry, and the 54th and 55th Massachusetts Infantry, and they limited blacks to service in the ranks (as a result of border state opposition in Congress, commissions as officers were reserved for whites). In May 1863 the War Department created a Bureau of Colored Troops to organize and muster black troops directly into Federal service as the 1st through the 138th United States Colored Troops (USCT), along with six regiments of U.S. Colored Cavalry, fourteen of heavy artillery, and ten batteries of light artillery. The USCT units remained racially segregated ones, and not until the end of the war did the War Department agree to pay them on an equal plane with white soldiers. All the same, they promised to treat the disease of rebellion "in the shape of warm lead and cold steel, duly administered by two hundred thousand black doctors."[96]

In the process, they shocked a number of white Union soldiers out of their smug bigotry. "I never believed in niggers before," wrote one Wisconsin cavalryman, "but by Jesus, they are hell in fighting." Lincoln was confident that the biggest surprise would be the one experienced by the rebels. "The bare sight of fifty thousand armed and drilled black soldiers on the banks of the Mississippi would end the rebellion at once," Lincoln wrote to Andrew Johnson, the Unionist military governor of Tennessee. "And who doubts that we can present that sight if we but take hold in earnest."[97] Eventually 178,000 African Americans enlisted in the Union army, and almost 10,000 served in the navy.

Lincoln was fully conscious, when he issued the Emancipation Proclamation, that he was sending the war and the country down a very different road than people had thought they would go. If he seems to have taken an unconscionably long time about taking that turn, and if he made a number of ambiguous utterances about the relationship of the war and slavery beforehand, it was largely because all of Lincoln's instincts led him to avoid tumultuous challenges over issues and seek evasions or compromises that would allow him to get the decision he wanted without paying the costs. He had yet to confront for himself the full implications of some of the issues of black freedom and black equality, and he knew that the North was even further from having come to grips with them. Nevertheless, "no human power can subdue this rebellion without using the Emancipation lever as I have done," Lincoln realized.

96. "The Black Military Experience, 1861–1867," in Ira Berlin et al., *Slaves No More: Three Essays on Emancipation and the Civil War* (New York: Cambridge University Press, 1992), 199.

97. Jimerson, *The Private Civil War*, 106; Lincoln, "To Andrew Johnson," March 26, 1863, in *Collected Works*, 6:149–50.

To bring African Americans out of slavery and into the war to save the Union meant that the Union, if victorious, had an immense obligation to grant them full political equality as Americans. In his mind, it had become "a religious duty" to see that "these people, who have so heroically . . . demonstrated in blood their right to the ballot," get the "humane protection of the flag they have so fearlessly defended."[98]

The problem Lincoln would now face would be finding a general for the Army of the Potomac with a similar vision for the war. And when he finally dismissed George B. McClellan in November 1862, he had no idea that it would take two more bloody years before he would find one.

98. Lincoln, "To James Wadsworth," January 1864, in *Collected Works*, 7:100.

CHAPTER FIVE

ELUSIVE VICTORIES

EAST AND WEST, 1862-1863

The Mississippi is well worth reading about," wrote Mark Twain in the opening lines of *Life on the Mississippi*. "It is not a commonplace river, but on the contrary is in all ways remarkable." For Twain, who was born beside it and worked upon it, most of that remarkableness was a matter of the colorful characters who populated the river, the clusters of peculiar towns along its banks, and the eccentricities of the broad, slow-winding river itself. For foreign travelers in the South, it was the sheer dimensions of the river and the vast cross section of life it contained that regularly left their mouths agape. When British war correspondent William Howard Russell arrived in Memphis in 1861, he was bewildered by how the river embraced "this strange kaleidoscope of Negroes and whites, of extremes of civilisation in its American development . . . of enormous steamers on the river, which bears equally the dug-out or canoe of the black fisherman" and "all the phenomena of active commercial life . . . included in the same scope of vision which takes in at the other side of the Mississippi lands scarcely settled." The Mississippi was almost more than a river: as Twain remembered it, the Mississippi was "the great Mississippi, the majestic, the magnificent Mississippi, rolling its mile-wide tide along, shining in the sun" with "the dense forest away on the other side" and "the 'point' above, and the 'point' below, bounding the river-glimpse and turning it into a sort of sea, and withal a very still and brilliant and lonely one."[1]

---

1. Mark Twain, *Life on the Mississippi* (New York: Harper & Bros., 1901), 1, 31; W. H. Russell, *My Diary North and South*, 139, 161.

Twain and Russell were not the only ones in 1862 concerned with the grandeur of the Mississippi River. Both Jefferson Davis and Abraham Lincoln had traveled, worked, and lived on the Mississippi and knew it well. Lincoln had grown up in Indiana and Illinois with the talk of the river and its great tributaries all around him, and in his youth Lincoln had conveyed cargoes of goods downriver on flatboats. Jefferson Davis's sprawling plantation, Brierfields, occupied a portion of Davis Bend, eighty miles on the river above Natchez, Mississippi. But the immediate concern of both Davis and Lincoln with the river in 1862 was practical, not aesthetic or romantic. Whatever else the river was to Americans, it had been the great commercial highway of the American republic ever since Thomas Jefferson's Louisiana Purchase had acquired undisputed title to the territories it watered.

Before the Revolution, the economy of Britain's North American colonies was hooked into Britain's transatlantic trading networks, and the economic geography of that trade ran eastward, to the Atlantic seaboard. With the creation of the United States, and Britain's surrender of all of its former colonial territory over the Appalachian Mountains, white settlers poured over the mountain passes into Kentucky, Tennessee, the Northwest territories, and eventually (after Andrew Jackson had ruthlessly cleared out the Cherokee, Creek, and Seminole Indians) the Alabama and Mississippi territories. Rather than attempting to trade their agricultural surpluses back over the Appalachians, the new settlers discovered instead that it was much easier to trundle their goods down to the broad navigable rivers that drained the trans-Appalachian territories—the Ohio, Cumberland, Tennessee, and Missouri Rivers. All of those rivers flowed west and south, away from the old Atlantic seaboard trading centers, and all of them emptied into the even broader southward flow of the Mississippi.

Taken together the entire Mississippi River system pulled into itself the commerce of 1.25 million square miles in a gigantic net that stretched to include Pittsburgh in the east and St. Louis in the west. The Mississippi was the commercial highway of the old Northwest and the new cotton lands of the Mississippi Delta, and it tied westerners and southerners into closer economic units than westerners enjoyed with the old East Coast. Pittsburgh, Wheeling, St. Louis, Louisville, Memphis, Natchez, and Cincinnati all grew rich on their trade southward on the river system. It was the river, too, that helped to throw Southerners into the lap of the Democratic Party in the 1830s and 1840s, since they had no wish to help the Whigs build canals and highways in the North when the river brought the nation's commerce their way simply by force of nature. The South had in the Mississippi River system all the cheap water transportation it needed without the taxation necessary for funding "internal improvements," and Southerners had no wish to see their western trading partners lured back toward the East by artificial networks of canals or turnpikes.

The river, however, was only a river until Americans actually learned how to use it, and the key to opening up the potential of the Mississippi River system was the steamboat. In 1811, the first steam-powered vessel on the Mississippi River system was built at Pittsburgh and sent down the Ohio to the Mississippi. It easily beat out the travel time needed by flatboats to work down the rivers, and within a decade newer and faster steamboats cut the travel time from the Gulf to Louisville to under a week. By 1820, there were 89 steamboats operating on the Ohio and Mississippi; by 1840, there were 536. They could penetrate even the smaller rivers in the Mississippi system and cut the costs of shipping every kind of marketable good. In particular, the steamboats were a godsend to cotton agriculture. Baled cotton was bulky and expensive to ship to markets, and before the steamboats, shipping costs cut severely into its profitability. Prior to the 1820s, it cost as much as $5 to move 100 pounds of cotton downriver from Louisville. With the coming of the steamboats, the freight rates fell in 1830 to only $2 per 100 pounds, and in 1840 to only 25¢. Steam made cotton worth transporting to market, and cotton profits, in turn, underwrote the growth of steam navigation on the western rivers. Even the peculiar design of the riverboats was dictated largely by the need to build large, flat-bottomed river craft that could accommodate the space needed for shipping cotton.[2]

If the steamboat provided the means for getting the agricultural produce of the west to market, it was the port of New Orleans that provided the greatest marketplace—provided, in fact, one of the great international entrepôts of the world. Down the long river network to New Orleans went most of the grain, hogs, cattle, cotton, and other goods of Ohio, Minnesota, Illinois, and Louisiana; then, in the 1850s, as Tennessee and the border states developed new iron and textile industries, the South's infant industrial potential poured out onto the rivers and down to New Orleans as well. Up the river from New Orleans, beating against the sluggish brown current of the Mississippi, came the imported goods and manufactures that Southern and western agriculture depended on.

By the outbreak of the Civil War, New Orleans was the sixth-largest city in the United States and the third-largest importer of goods, and it had to accommodate more than 3,500 steamboat arrivals during the year, with more than 2 million tons of freight that earned more than $185 million. It was from New Orleans that William Howard Russell could see "a grand slave confederacy enclosing the Gulf in its arms, and swelling to the shores of the Potomac and Chesapeake, with the entire control of the Mississippi and a monopoly of the great staples on which so much of the manufacture and commerce of England and France depend."[3]

2. Dan Elbert Clark, *The Middle West in American History* (New York: Thomas Crowell, 1966 [1937]), 107; Louis C. Hunter, *Steamboats on the Western Rivers: An Economic and Technological History* (Cambridge, MA: Harvard University Press, 1949), 22–33.

3. Paul Johnson, *The Birth of the Modern: World Society, 1815–1830* (New York: HarperCollins, 1991), 195–96; *The American Almanac and Repository of Useful Knowledge for the Year 1859*, 169, 214; Russell, *My Diary North and South*, 137.

It was scarcely noticed that by 1860 some of the Mississippi River system's grand predominance over the West was already beginning to slip away. Southerners in Congress could block the massive appropriations needed for building the rival systems of national roads and canals that would divert western trade back toward eastern markets, but they could not prevent state legislatures in the North from building canals of their own, such as New York's Erie Canal, which linked the entire Great Lakes water system with the Hudson River and New York City. Nor could they prevent private railroads—the steam-powered mate of the riverboat—from extending their fingers over the Alleghenies into Ohio and Illinois and across the Mississippi into Missouri. The first commercial rail line began construction on July 4, 1828, with the laying of what would become the 73-mile track of the Baltimore & Ohio rail line; two years later, with the rail line complete, a former brewer and brickmaker named Peter Cooper put his own locomotive, *Tom Thumb*, on the B&O line and hauled the first load of thirty passengers around Baltimore. Within ten years, there was more railroad mileage in the United States than canal mileage, and over the next twenty years the railroads grew to the length of 30,626 miles of track.[4]

The first warning bell for New Orleans's slipping control over the commerce of the continent rang on May 5, 1856, when the 430-ton side-wheel steamboat *Effie Afton* rammed a newly opened railroad bridge over the Mississippi at Rock Island, Illinois. The boat burned, and the vessel's owners—her captain, clerk, and engineer—sued the owners of the bridge—the Rock Island Bridge Company, a subsidiary of the Illinois Central Railroad—on the grounds that the bridge was a hazard to navigation. The case came to trial in federal court in Chicago in July 1857 over whether "the defendants have constructed . . . a permanent obstruction to commerce on the river." The real question was whether New Orleans river traffic deserved a better right-of-way than a Yankee railroad. The jury could not come to a verdict, however, and subsequent efforts to appeal the non-verdict to the Supreme Court (in 1863) and the Illinois state courts (in 1875) failed. The steamboat (and New Orleans) had lost.[5]

One of the lawyers for the Rock Island Bridge Company was Abraham Lincoln.

WAR ON THE BORDER

At the outbreak of the war, the importance of controlling the Mississippi River and its vast system of tributary rivers was obvious to both the Union and the Confederate governments. Indeed, the only really aggressive feature of General

4. Daniel Walker Howe, *What Hath God Wrought: The Transformation of America, 1815–1848* (New York: Oxford University Press, 2007), 562–69; Maury Klein, *Unfinished Business: The Railroad in American Life* (Hanover, NH: University Press of New England, 1994), 11.

5. "Hurd et al v. Rock Island Bridge Company," in *The Papers of Abraham Lincoln: Legal Documents and Cases*, ed. Daniel W. Stowell et al. (Charlottesville: University Press of Virginia, 2007), 3:308–83.

Winfield Scott's Anaconda Plan had been its insistence on redeeming the Mississippi River valley for the Union. So long as the Confederacy controlled the lower Mississippi River and New Orleans, the prevailing wisdom dictated that Northern farmers everywhere west of the Appalachians would suddenly face ruin, and angered farmers were very likely to take their anger with them to the ballot box at the next congressional elections unless Lincoln and his soldiers did something about it very quickly. By the same token, Jefferson Davis realized that the Confederacy would never be secure unless it could control not just New Orleans and the lower Mississippi but also the great tributaries, the Ohio and the Missouri.

The Ohio was, in Davis's judgment, the natural northern boundary of the Southern Confederacy. The Ohio would offer a natural defensive moat for southern armies to resist invasion by the Federals. A Confederate presence on the south bank of the Ohio would further paralyze Northern commerce and force the Lincoln government to the negotiating table. Most important of all, the Ohio was fed, near its confluence with the Mississippi, by two vital rivers, the Tennessee and the Cumberland, which led deep into Tennessee, Mississippi, and Alabama. Unless the south bank of the Ohio was firmly in Confederate hands, Federal steam-powered transports, supply ships, and gunboats could enter the Tennessee and Cumberland Rivers without obstruction and use them as easy invasion routes into Confederate heartland.

In order to control the Ohio, the Confederates needed to control the border states, especially Kentucky and Missouri, and that was precisely what Abraham Lincoln was determined to prevent. He still hoped, well into 1862, that Confederate control of the upper South could be disrupted by appealing to pro-Union sentiment in eastern Tennessee, western Virginia, and northern Alabama and Arkansas. None of that would be possible, however, if Kentucky and Missouri, by falling into Confederate hands, stood in the way. "To lose Kentucky is nearly the same as to lose the whole game," Lincoln wrote to Orville Browning in September 1861. "Kentucky gone, we cannot hold Missouri, nor, as I think, Maryland. These all against us, and the job on our hands is too large for us."[6]

Thus the political race to woo the border states became the first round of the Civil War in the West, and in the case of both Missouri and Kentucky, it was a round won largely by the Union. At first all the advantages in the race seemed to belong to the Confederacy. Both Missouri and Kentucky were slave states and had important social and economic ties to the South, and every natural appearance indicated that they would join the Confederacy. Yet appearances proved deceiving, and for two reasons. The first was Lincoln's carefully cultivated assertions that he

6. Lincoln, "To Orville H. Browning," September 22, 1861, in *Collected Works*, 4:532.

had no intention of touching slavery in the states where it was sanctioned by the Constitution. Those assurances, however much they grated on the ears of abolitionists, persuaded border state Unionists not to risk their slave property on the shaky chances of a rebellion. Second, in both states, slavery was not nearly as powerful an institution as in the Deep South, and slaveholding and strong Unionist sentiments often existed hand in hand.

Missouri quickly became a case in point. Although Missouri had been a slave state since the days of the Missouri Compromise in 1820, slavery had actually flourished in Missouri only along a fairly narrow belt of counties stretching across the center of the state. In St. Louis, Missouri's principal Mississippi river town, the population was increasingly taking on a free-soil flavor from immigrants from across the Mississippi River in Illinois, and from a flourishing community of German refugees and exiles who had found a home there after fleeing political oppression in Germany in the wake of the revolutions of 1848 and who had no sympathy at all with slavery. As the Deep South began to secede from the Union, the pro-slavery governor of Missouri, Claiborne F. Jackson, strong-armed a special session of the state legislature into calling a secession convention. "The destiny of the slave-holding States of this Union is one and the same," Jackson insisted.

> . . . . The identity, rather than the similarity, of their domestic institutions; their political principles and party usages; their common origin, pursuits, tastes, manners, and customs; their territorial contiguity and commercial relations—all contribute to bind them together in one sisterhood. And Missouri will in my opinion best consult her own interests, and the interests of the whole country, by a timely declaration of her determination to stand by her sister slave-holding States, in whose wrongs she participates, and with whose institutions and people she sympathizes.[7]

But the report of the convention backed away from secession for Missouri, and it adjourned in March 1861 leaving Missouri still in the Union. Lincoln's call for volunteers after Sumter set off another demand for a secession convention in April, and as an extra measure to support secession, Governor Jackson called out the state militia, established a training camp near St. Louis (named Camp Jackson), and prepared to seize the Federal arsenal in St. Louis. As it turned out, Jackson had not reckoned with either the strength of the Missouri Unionists or the boldness of the arsenal's commander, Captain Nathaniel Lyon, a onetime Democrat whom the Kansas-Nebraska bill had converted into an ice-cold opponent of slavery. On May 10, Lyon surrounded the state militia encampment with 7,000 regulars and pro-Union volunteers, capturing

---

7. Christopher Phillips, *Missouri's Confederate: Claiborne Fox Jackson and the Creation of Southern Identity in the Border West* (Columbia: University of Missouri Press, 2000), 235.

the entire encampment without a shot. But when Lyon attempted to parade his prisoners through the streets of St. Louis to the arsenal, he was attacked by a pro-slavery mob and his men opened fire. Twenty-eight people, including many innocent bystanders, were killed.[8]

Jackson hoped that this would be understood as the signal for the state legislature at last to act and "place the State at the earliest practicable moment in a complete state of defence." As Jackson realized, though, Lyon's preemptive strike had also rendered the secessionist movement in Missouri militarily powerless. After a month of fruitless political jockeying between himself and Lyon, Jackson fled to southwestern Missouri with a pro-slavery remnant of the legislature, and there declared Missouri out of the Union. The rest of the legislature remained firmly pro-Union, and Jackson's rump assembly never really amounted to more than a government in exile. A provisional Unionist governor, Hamilton Gamble, was appointed in July. Although Missouri would be repeatedly invaded by Confederate forces loyal to Jackson, and large areas of the backcountry were turned by Confederate guerillas under William Quantrill, Cole Younger, and "Bloody Bill" Anderson into no-go areas for Federal troops, they never seriously threatened the hold that Missouri Unionists retained on St. Louis and the strategic dock and riverbank areas along Missouri's stretch of the Mississippi and its confluence with the Ohio River.

The story in Kentucky was fundamentally the same. The governor, Beriah Magoffin, was pro-slavery and called the Kentucky legislature into special session to arrange for a state secession convention. When the legislature met on January 17, 1861, it turned down Magoffin's request and instead chided the Southern states for reacting too hastily to Lincoln's election. A Unionist mass rally in Louisville on April 19 warned that if Kentucky seceded, "all is lost. There will then be no breakwater, but instead, Kentucky will be the battle-ground—the scene of a conflict between brethren—such a conflict as no country has yet witnessed." Magoffin again begged the legislature in May to call a secession convention; again the legislature refused, but it did allow Magoffin to resort to the unusual expedient of declaring Kentucky neutral on May 20: in "the deplorable war now waging between the United and Confederate States I solemnly forbid any movement upon Kentucky soil, or occupation of any post or place therein for any purpose whatever, until authorized by invitation or permission of the legislative and executive authorities." Both Lincoln and Davis were anxious not to push the Kentuckians too hard. Davis, like Lincoln, wanted "to treat Kentucky with all possible respect," while Lincoln promised Kentucky congressman Garrett Davis that he would send no troops into Kentucky "unless she or

---

8. Thomas L. Snead, *The Fight for Missouri: From the Election of Lincoln to the Death of Lyon* (New York: C. Scribner's Sons, 1888), 21–22, 65–66, 88, 122–23, 163, 170–71; Louis S. Gerteis, *Civil War St. Louis* (Lawrence: University Press of Kansas, 2001), 97–125.

her people should make it necessary by a formidable resistance of the authority and laws of the United States."[9]

So for several months both the Union forces on the other side of the Ohio and Confederate forces below the Kentucky border fumed and waited. A convention of border state representatives met in Frankfort, Kentucky, on May 27, chaired by the venerable compromiser John J. Crittenden. The convention pledged that Kentucky and Missouri would "purpose to take no part in this war . . . our sense of honor and of duty requires that we should not allow ourselves to be drawn or driven into a war in which other States, without consulting us, have deliberately chosen to involve themselves." On August 5, however, the Kentucky legislative elections gave a resounding majority to pro-Union delegates.[10]

Reading what he presumed was Union-slanted handwriting on the wall, the Confederate commander in western Tennessee, Major General Leonidas Polk, decided that the Confederacy could wait no longer to secure the Ohio River line, and on September 3, 1861, Polk's troops moved into Kentucky and occupied Columbus. At first the Confederate government was tempted to repudiate Polk's violation of Kentucky's neutrality. But Jefferson Davis supported Polk's action, and Confederate troops moved over into Kentucky to occupy Bowling Green. The Kentucky legislature angrily voted to end state neutrality and reconfirm its allegiance to the Union. An unhappy Governor Magoffin resigned his office in August 1862 and retreated into private law practice.[11]

Keeping Kentucky and Missouri in the Union saved the Ohio River line for the North by the end of 1861. The question then was what the federal government proposed to do next about it, and on that score both President Lincoln and his new general in chief, George B. McClellan, had very clear ideas. Lincoln wanted Kentucky occupied at once and cleared of Confederates, followed by a thrust into eastern Tennessee to rally Tennessee Unionists to the Federal armies. McClellan also advocated a movement into Kentucky and eastern Tennessee as part of the three-way pincer movement in the spring of 1862 from Virginia and the Carolina coast, which he hoped would bite off the upper third of the Confederacy at one stroke. Unfortunately, the Federal forces along the Ohio River line were badly organized and equipped; what was more, the length of the Ohio River was divided between

9. "Mr. Dixon's Speech" and "Governor Magoffin's Proclamation," in *The Rebellion Record: A Diary of American Events*, ed. Frank Moore (New York: G. P. Putnam, 1862), 1:76, 264–65; Elizabeth Leonard, *Lincoln's Forgotten Ally: Judge Advocate General Joseph Holt of Kentucky* (Chapel Hill: University of North Carolina Press, 2011), 138; Davis, in *Recollected Words of Abraham Lincoln*, 133; Hesseltine, *Lincoln and the War Governors*, 209–10.

10. "Addresses of the Convention of the Border States," in *Rebellion Record*, ed. Moore, 1:352.

11. Steven E. Woodworth, "The Indeterminate Qualities: Jefferson Davis, Leonidas Polk, and the End of Kentucky Neutrality, September 1861," *Civil War History* 38 (December 1992): 289–97.

two military departments whose commanders were either unwilling or unable to cooperate.

The first of these departments, the Department of the Ohio, running from western Virginia to the mouth of the Cumberland River, consisted of about 45,000 men commanded by Brigadier General Don Carlos Buell. It was to Buell that McClellan looked to spearhead the drive into eastern Tennessee. In January 1862 he wrote anxiously to Buell that "my own advance cannot, according to my present views, be made until your troops are soundly established in the eastern portion of Tennessee." But Buell was hampered by his men's rawness, a lack of experienced officers, and the difficulties of the terrain that lay before him. Although he defeated a small Confederate force at Logan's Crossroads, in southern Kentucky, on January 19, 1862, Buell's men had neither roads nor railroads to operate upon, and they proceeded to bog themselves down in the impenetrable wild mountains north of Knoxville.[12]

This provided an unlooked-for opportunity to Buell's neighbor, Major General Henry Wager Halleck, the commanding general of the Department of Missouri, whose military jurisdiction stretched from the Cumberland River into Missouri itself. Halleck was "a black-browed saturnine man, heavy of figure and of feature; suspicious of everybody and incapable of friendship." An 1839 graduate of West Point and one of the prizes of the Corps of Engineers, Halleck was nevertheless a capable administrator, "a man of great capacity, or large acquirements, and at the time possessed the confidence of the country, and of most of the army." After leaving the army as a captain in 1854, he had served as secretary of state for California, practiced law in San Francisco, and wrote several outstanding textbooks on legal and military affairs. The outbreak of the war brought him back to the army as a major general, and on November 9, 1861, he inherited the troubled Department of Missouri. His appointment as the department head was largely prompted by Halleck's considerable legal and administrative skills, since Missouri in 1862 was still a large political black hole, and no one expected much from him in the way of fighting.[13]

However, Halleck had no intention of playing second fiddle to Buell. In January 1862 Halleck suggested to McClellan that a more direct route into the Southern heartland lay in western, rather than eastern, Tennessee. There, Halleck pointed out, an army willing to borrow the steamboats that carried river commerce could use the broad, navigable Cumberland and Tennessee Rivers to move upon instead of getting

12. McClellan to Buell, January 6, 1862, in *The Civil War Papers of George B. McClellan*, 148; R. M. Kelly, "Holding Kentucky for the Union," in *Battles and Leaders*, 1:387–92; Thomas L. Connolly, *Army of the Heartland: The Army of Tennessee, 1861–1862* (Baton Rouge: Louisiana State University Press, 1967), 96–98.

13. John F. Marszalek, *Commander of All Lincoln's Armies: A Life of General Henry W. Halleck* (Cambridge, MA: Harvard University Press, 2004), 48–82, 109; William T. Sherman, *Memoirs of General W. T. Sherman*, ed. Charles Royster (New York: Library of America, 1990), 274; *The Military Memoirs of General John Pope*, ed. Peter Cozzens and R. I. Girardi (Chapel Hill: University of North Carolina Press, 1998), 13.

as bogged down as Buell was in eastern Tennessee. What was more, the Tennessee River was navigable to steam-powered transports and gunboats all the way south through Tennessee into Alabama, while the Cumberland wound eastward into the eastern Tennessee mountains. An army that controlled these rivers could force three things to happen. First, using steamboats to seize control of the Tennessee River would isolate the occupation force that the Confederates had installed at Columbus, Kentucky, and compel them to retreat in order to keep their lines of operation open. That could clear all of western Kentucky of rebels at one stroke. Second, a similar steamboat movement up the Cumberland would force whatever Confederate forces were in the eastern mountains of Kentucky to withdraw into middle Tennessee, compelling the Confederates to abandon eastern Tennessee without a battle. And third, such an operation would have the additional advantage of severing the Memphis & Ohio Railroad, one of the Confederacy's two east-west railroad lines, because the Memphis & Ohio relied on bridges over the Tennessee River, as well as the Cumberland River at Clarksville, which gunboats could easily destroy. By moving into western Kentucky and Tennessee on the rivers, rather than marching overland through eastern Kentucky and Tennessee, a Federal army could turn the Confederacy's uppermost flank and easily peel open the upper South like ripe fruit. "Move up the Cumberland and Tennessee, making Nashville the first objective point," Halleck recommended. "This line of the Cumberland or Tennessee is the great central line of the Western theater of war, with . . . two good navigable rivers extending far into the interior of the theater of operations."[14]

It went without saying, of course, that both the Cumberland and Tennessee Rivers flowed through Halleck's department rather than Buell's, and that any such operation would be under Halleck's command and not Buell's. But Halleck had a point. Even Buell conceded that it might be a wise move to try to crack the Confederacy's shell further to the west than he himself was operating. So, in January 1862, even while he was still haranguing Buell to move into eastern Tennessee, McClellan acceded to Halleck's proposal to push up the two rivers into western Tennessee, with Nashville as the ultimate objective.

Halleck's plan succeeded beyond anyone's wildest dreams, and that was chiefly because he enjoyed two advantages that, it is safe to say, no one else in the world possessed. The first was a fleet of ironclad gunboats ideally designed for river warfare. Prior to the nineteenth century, and for almost as long as ships had been used as weapons of war, navies had been content to build their warships—and all their other ships—of wood, and relied on lofts of sail to move them. Even if the navies of Europe had seriously desired to plate their wooden ships with protective iron, the technology of iron making was too primitive and too expensive before the nineteenth

---

14. Halleck to McClellan, January 20, 1862, in *The War of the Rebellion*, Series One, 8:509.

century to provide iron that would not shatter upon impact, while the inability of sail to move ships weighted down with iron armor would leave an ironclad warship almost dead in the water. In 1814, at about the same time that steam-powered riverboats first appeared on the Mississippi River system, the British navy began experimenting with steam propulsion in its warships, first in the form of paddlewheel steamers, and then in conjunction with new screw-type propellers. Then, in the 1820s, the French navy began developing explosive shells for use by its warships, so even the best-built wooden warship could be turned into a roaring holocaust with only one hit by a naval gun. With steam propulsion at last able to move heavier and heavier ships, and pressed with the urgent necessity of protecting their wooden warships from the fiery impact of explosive shell, both the French and the British navies began tinkering with the use of protective iron armor. The Crimean War of 1854–56, in which France and England were allied against Russia, gave the two navies the chance to try out their ideas under fire. They constructed five "floating batteries," awkward and unseaworthy monstrosities that were little more than large wooden packing cases with sloping sides sheathed in wrought iron four and a half inches thick. Although these gunboats could only crawl along at the antediluvian speed of 4 knots, their iron sides proved invulnerable to anything the Russian artillery could do to them, and they were a tremendous success. "Their massive wrought-iron sides, huge round bows and stern, and, above all, their close rows of solid 68- and 84-pounder guns, show them at once to be antagonists under the attacks of which the heaviest granite bastions in the world would crumble down like contract brickwork." When in 1859 the British launched the first full-size, seagoing armored warship, *Warrior*, the age of the ironclad had at last arrived.[15]

The lessons taught by the "floating batteries" were not lost on American designers, and in August 1861 the War Department contracted with John B. Eads to build seven ironclad gunboats for use on the western rivers. Eads and his chief designer, Samuel Pook, built what amounted to a series of 512-ton floating batteries like those used in the Crimea, with flat bottoms, slanting armored sides of two and a half inches of iron plate, and an assortment of cannon. Known as "Pook's Turtles," the gunboats handled awkwardly, were badly overweight, and (since no one seems to have thought of who was going to operate them) had no crews. However, the naval officer detached to bring them into service, a stern anti-slavery Connecticut salt named Andrew Foote, managed to get the boats finished and launched, rounded up crews (with Halleck's authorization), and otherwise provided Halleck with an armored naval flotilla. "Pook's Turtles" were far from being great warships, but they were more than anything the Confederates had on the Tennessee or the Cumberland.

---

15. "On Floating Batteries: A Lecture Given by Capt. Fishbourne, R.N., on Monday 19 April 1858," *United Services Institute Journal* 2 (1858); "The Grand Review—The Fleet at Spithead," *News of the World*, April 27, 1856; D. K. Brown, *Warrior to Dreadnought: Warship Development, 1860–1905* (London: Chatham, 1997), 11–13.

Still, nothing that Foote or the gunboats achieved along the rivers would have amounted to much if Halleck had not also possessed another, less obvious advantage, and that was an officer who could take command of the Union land forces, work in tandem with Foote, and win Halleck's campaign for him. The name of that officer was Ulysses Simpson Grant.

No one in American history has ever looked less like a great general than Ulysses Grant. He was the sort of person one would have to stare at very intently just to be able to describe him, and there had been nothing in his life up to this point that in any way suggested that he was going to be a great general. He was born in Ohio in 1822 as Hiram Ulysses Grant, and his father managed to wangle him an appointment to West Point in 1839. (The congressman who made out the appointment papers somehow confused Grant's name with the names of some of Grant's relatives, and this turned him into Ulysses Simpson Grant.) No brilliant student, Grant graduated in 1843, twenty-first in a class of thirty-nine cadets, and although he was a talented horseman with a penchant for mathematics, he was shunted off as a lieutenant to the 4th U.S. Infantry. The Mexican War brought him his first action and first promotion to captain. But after the war, peacetime boredom and separation from his family drove him to alcohol, and in July 1854 he resigned from the army.

For the next seven years, Grant failed at nearly everything he tried, until his father finally gave him a job as a clerk in the family leather goods store in Galena, Illinois. Having been in the army most of his life, and with simple economic survival occupying all of his attention since leaving the army, Grant "had thought but little about politics," he later recalled. Although he was (like Lincoln) "a Whig by education and a great admirer of Mr. Clay," the disintegration of the Whigs left him with no one to vote for in 1856, and for a while he indulged a brief fling with the Know-Nothings. He soon enough grew weary of the Know-Nothings' ethnic hate-mongering, but his fear that a Republican presidential victory in 1856 would trigger civil war threw him to the Democrats. He had not lived in Galena long enough to vote in the 1860 election, which (he reflected later) was just as well, for if he had voted, it would have been for Douglas.[16] When the war broke out, Grant unhesitatingly wrote to the War Department to try to get a commission in the regulars to fight secession. He never received a reply (the letter was found years later in "some out-of-the-way place" in the adjutant general's office), but a month later the governor of Illinois appointed Grant colonel of the 21st Illinois Volunteers, and from then on, Grant went nowhere but up. In September a friend in Congress obtained a brigadier general's commission for him, and in November he found himself under Halleck's command in the Department of Missouri.[17]

16. Grant, "Personal Memoirs," in *Memoirs and Selected Letters*, ed. M. D. McFeely and W. S. McFeely (New York: Library of America, 1990), 142, 144–45; Joan Waugh, *U. S. Grant: American Hero, American Myth* (Chapel Hill: University of North Carolina Press, 2009), 45.

17. Grant, "Personal Memoirs," 142, 158.

Grant and Halleck had both seen at virtually the same time the opportunity presented by the Tennessee and Cumberland Rivers. However, the Confederates in Kentucky also realized the vulnerability of the river lines and had constructed two forts at points on the rivers just below the Kentucky-Tennessee border, Fort Henry on the Tennessee River and Fort Donelson on the Cumberland. Both were in good position to bottle up the rivers pretty securely. Flag Officer Foote was confident that his gunboats could beat down the fire of the forts if Grant could bring along enough infantry to take the forts from their landward sides. So Halleck gave Grant 18,000 men, and on February 3, 1862, Grant put them onto an assortment of steamboats and transports, and along with Foote's gunboats, entered the Ohio and then the Tennessee River for the turn up to Fort Henry. Built in 1861, Fort Henry was a small but powerful nut to crack: it mounted seventeen guns facing upriver, including a big 10-inch Columbiad, protected by fifteen-foot-wide earthen parapets. There were only a hundred men detailed to garrison Fort Henry, however, and heavy early spring rains put Fort Henry's parade ground under two feet of Tennessee river overflow. Grant moved to the attack on the morning of February 6. Smothered by the fire of Foote's four ironclad gunboats—*Carondolet*, *Cincinnati*, *St. Louis*, and *Essex*—the Confederates kept up a halfhearted fight at Fort Henry for three hours, and then abandoned it.[18]

Almost any other Federal commander in 1862 would have sat down at once and begged alternately for reinforcements, more supplies, and a promotion. Grant now began to demonstrate to what degree he resembled no other Federal general in 1862 or any other year, for as soon as Fort Henry had surrendered, he sent one gunboat downriver to destroy the Memphis & Ohio railroad bridge over the Tennessee, and then he casually telegraphed Halleck that he was going to move over to Fort Donelson at once.

Fort Donelson was a considerably bigger target than Fort Henry: a twelve-foot-high earthen parapet enclosed fifteen acres of ground, plus a separate pair of "water batteries" at river's edge with eight 32-pounder guns and another 10-inch Columbiad. Taken together, Donelson bristled with sixty-seven big guns and had a combined garrison of some 19,000 men, and the water batteries proved themselves quite capable of badly damaging Foote's gunboats when they tried to duplicate their earlier success at Fort Henry. The Confederate command at Fort Donelson was divided unevenly between two incompetents, former secretary of war John B. Floyd and Gideon Pillow, and even more badly divided over its options. Floyd and Pillow threw away, by inaction, an opportunity to beat Grant piecemeal while his troops were still strung out on the roads between the two forts. They then threw away an

18. Manning Ferguson Force, *From Fort Henry to Corinth* (New York: Charles Scribner's Sons, 1881), 28, 30–31; Benjamin Franklin Cooling, *Forts Henry and Donelson: The Key to the Confederate Heartland* (Knoxville: University of Tennessee Press, 1987), 101–8; "Attack on Fort Henry," February 6, 1862, in *War of the Rebellion*, 7:133–35; Ron Field, *American Civil War Fortifications*, vol. 3: *The Mississippi and River Forts* (Oxford: Osprey, 2007), 14.

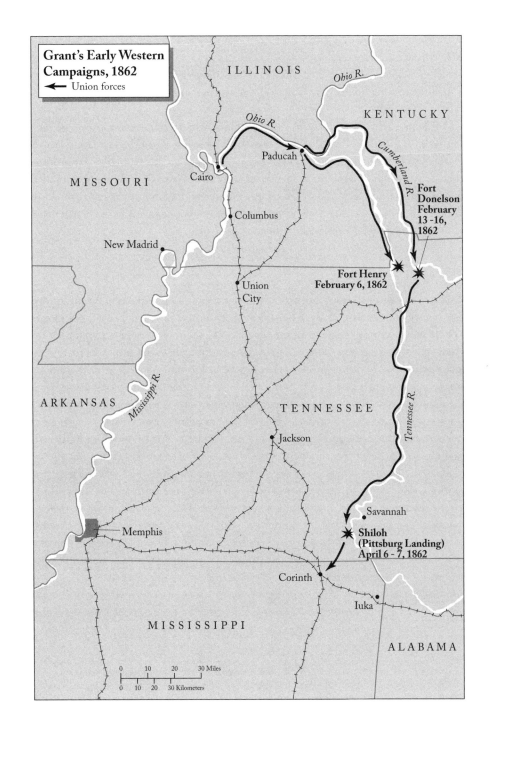

Grant's Early Western Campaigns, 1862

← Union forces

ILLINOIS

Ohio R.

Ohio R.

KENTUCKY

Cumberland R.

Paducah

MISSOURI

Cairo

Fort Donelson
February 13-16, 1862

Columbus

New Madrid

Fort Henry
February 6, 1862

Union City

ARKANSAS

Mississippi R.

TENNESSEE

Tennessee R.

Jackson

Savannah

Memphis

Shiloh
(Pittsburg Landing)
April 6-7, 1862

Corinth

Iuka

MISSISSIPPI

ALABAMA

0   10   20   30 Miles

0   10   20   30 Kilometers

opportunity to evacuate Fort Donelson on February 15 when they punched an escape hole through Grant's lines and then turned around and walked back to their entrenchments. The next day Fort Donelson finally surrendered to Grant. About 5,000 Confederates (including Floyd and Pillow) made off in the night, leaving 14,000 to fall into Union hands.[19]

Little more than a single week's campaigning had driven an ominous wedge into the upper South. It also made Grant a national hero, for when the last Confederate commander at Donelson, Simon Bolivar Buckner, sent out his white flag, suggesting that he and Grant negotiate for terms of surrender, Grant bluntly replied that he would consider "no terms at all except immediate and unconditional surrender."[20] It was with a genuine sense of relief that the Northern public at last heard of a general who was concerned simply with winning.

KEEP MOVING ON

When the news of the surrender of Forts Henry and Donelson struck Washington, the victory-starved capital went berserk with joy. Guns boomed all day, and in the Senate the frock-coated solons of the republic violated their own procedural rules by cheering and applauding like schoolboys. Grant suddenly found himself a man with a reputation for fighting, and on March 7 he was rewarded with a promotion to major general, while Foote won promotion to rear admiral when Congress created the new rank that summer. Grant's aggressiveness was certainly a welcome departure from the attitude other Northern generals had brought to the battlefield, although this was certainly not because of what he had learned at West Point. Grant himself ruefully admitted that he "had never looked at a copy of tactics from the time of my graduation," and even then, "my standing in that branch of studies had been near the foot of the class." In this case, however, Grant's ignorance only meant that he had less to unlearn and more readiness to adapt to the realities of his situation as a commander. "War is progressive," Grant wrote in his *Memoirs*, and for an officer trained in an engineering-and-fortifications school and whose only war experience was the diminutive war in Mexico fifteen years before, Grant turned out to be a surprisingly progressive military thinker.[21]

One way in which war had become very progressive, and very swiftly, was the use of the railroads and the telegraph. Electrical telegraphy was only seventeen years old

---

19. "Capture of Fort Donelson, Tennessee," in *War of the Rebellion*, 7:157–253; Field, *American Civil War Fortifications*, 14; Kendall D. Gott, *Where the South Lost the War: An Analysis of the Fort Henry-Fort Donelson Campaign, February, 1862* (Mechanicsburg, PA: Stackpole, 2003), 256–58; Spencer C. Tucker, *Unconditional Surrender: The Capture of Forts Henry and Donelson* (Abilene, TX: McWhiney Foundation Press, 2001), 84–95.

20. Grant to Buckner, February 16, 1862, in *War of the Rebellion*, 7:161.

21. Grant, "Personal Memoirs," 166.

at the outbreak of the Civil War, and its first use had been to convey commercial news; the railroads were only slightly older, and they had been designed first for moving people, then freight. Both soon showed how easily they could be turned to military purposes, and especially for strategic communication and movement. Less than ten years after the first successful commercial railroad line opened, the Prussian army learned how to simplify deployment schedules by moving troops on rail lines. "Every new development of railways is a military advantage," wrote the Prussian military reformer Helmuth von Moltke as early as 1843. "A few million [spent] on the completion of our railways is far more profitably employed than on our fortresses."

Both the railroads and the telegraph were put to their first test for the British army in the Crimean War, when a newly formed Land Transport Corps built a track from the supply port of Balaklava to the siege lines around Sevastopol, accompanied by twenty miles of telegraph wire. Five years later Napoleon III took the railroads one step further and used them for troop transportation into northern Italy against the Austrians. French railroads moved 76,000 men in just ten days, and in the run-up to the battles at Magenta and Solferino, it took some of Napoleon's regiments only five days to reach their concentration point in northern Italy from Paris.[22]

Almost from the start, Grant sized up the capacity of the telegraph to gather and transmit information, and to allow generals to coordinate and redeploy scattered forces. He stayed in telegraphic communication with Halleck all during the Henry-Donelson campaign, laying down miles of telegraph wire as he advanced, and in later campaigns Grant stayed in constant touch with his subordinates over telegraph networks as long as 1,500 miles. Grant also grasped the potential of the railroads, largely because Grant was a mover. Indeed, hardly anyone in the Civil War demonstrated a greater skill in swiftly moving large bodies of infantry from one place to another. When Dr. John Brinton asked Grant, early in the war, what he thought of great tactical theorists such as Baron Jomini, Grant surprised him by claiming that he had never read Jomini. Rather, he had his own self-hewn alternative: "The art of war is simple enough. Find out where your enemy is. Get at him as soon as you can. Strike him as hard as you can, and keep moving on."[23]

In the West, he had fewer rail lines to rely upon, but much more in the way of riverborne transport, and of all the major commanders in the Civil War, only Grant and McClellan seem to have had a real grasp of how to use the rivers and inland

22. Orlando Figes, *Crimea: The Last Crusade* (London: Allen Lane, 2010), 355–56; Michael Howard, *The Franco-Prussian War* (London: Rupert Hart-Davis, 1961), 2; Richard Brooks, *Solferino 1859: The Battle for Italy's Freedom* (Oxford: Osprey, 2009), 23, 25; Michael I. Handel, *War, Strategy, and Intelligence* (Totowa, NJ: F. Cass, 1989), 57; Alexander William Kinglake, *The Invasion of the Crimea, Its Origin and an Account of Its Progress down to the Death of Lord Raglan: The Winter Troubles* (Edinburgh: W. Blackwood, 1880), 384–85.

23. John Hill Brinton, *Personal Memoirs of John H. Brinton, Major and Surgeon, U.S.V., 1861–1865* (New York: Neale, 1914), 239.

waterways in conjunction with the army. (If only McClellan had also had a little of Grant's combativeness, it would have been McClellan who ended the war in 1862, and McClellan's name rather than Grant's would be the one celebrated in the textbooks.) The river lines became Grant's way of overcoming the Confederacy's advantage of interior lines, and his cooperation with Foote in the movement down the Tennessee and Cumberland was so smooth that the sheer innovation of using the navy to transport troops on the inland rivers often gets overlooked. Later in the war, when his campaigns took him away from the rivers to the East, Grant would turn to the railroads to give him the same edge, and in almost every case they would get Grant and his men to a particular point before the Confederates ever had any notion of movement. In 1864, he would supply his troops with a purpose-built military railroad, twenty-one miles long, with twenty-five locomotives and 275 cars, connecting a 3,500-acre supply zone with his front lines.[24]

Grant also possessed an advantage over other old regulars such as Winfield Scott in his commonsense empathy for the volunteer. Although Grant was a West Point man and an ex-regular himself, he conceded from the start that the real burden of the war was going to have to be carried by the volunteers—by civilians in uniform who remained civilians in temperament even after they donned their uniforms. Unlike the regulars, the volunteers could not simply be expected to shoot straight, keep clean, and obey orders. They would have to be reasoned with, sorted out gently, and kept from turning a parade ground into a debating society. Yet, as Grant quickly realized, for all his pigheaded independence the volunteer soldier really wanted to get on with the war, finish it up, and go home, and he would do so if only he could be put into the right hands.

When Grant was made colonel of the 21st Illinois, he learned that he had been put there to replace an earlier colonel, foolishly elected by popular ballot of the regiment, who had done nothing to teach them anything useful. To bring the regiment around, Grant was careful to appeal to the volunteers' desire to be led, not driven, into battle. "My regiment was composed in large part of young men of as good social position as any in their section of the State," Grant wrote. "It embraced the sons of farmers, lawyers, physicians, politicians, merchants, bankers, and ministers, and some men of maturer years who had filled such positions themselves." These men knew nothing of discipline, and in their own democratic way, they all imagined that they were the equal of any officer. Grant "found it very hard work for a few days to bring all the men into anything like subordination." Once Grant made it clear that discipline in battle was what saved lives and won wars—and that discipline was not the humiliating business of kowtowing to some idiot in shoulder straps—then "the great majority favored discipline, and by the application of a little regular army

24. Waugh, *U. S. Grant*, 53; Howes, *The Catalytic Wars*, 574–76.

punishment all were reduced to as good discipline as one could ask." What marked Grant from the beginning, wrote the editors of the *Chicago Tribune*, was that "he understands Northern character, and reposes entire confidence in the pluck and endurance of his soldiers."[25]

The question now for Grant was whether his immediate superior in St. Louis, Henry Wager Halleck, would let him keep on moving, for in this spring of 1862, Grant was as optimistic as nearly everyone else in the North that with a little energy the war could be wrapped up right then, and especially on the rivers. "'Secesh' is about on its last legs in Tennessee," Grant calmly predicted, and he clearly remembered twenty-five years later the confidence he had had then that "after the fall of Fort Donelson the way was opened to the National forces all over the South-west without much resistance."[26]

The Confederate forces in the West were thrown into a panic by the speed of Grant's movement and the embarrassing loss of Forts Henry and Donelson. The Confederates had pinned their hopes on using the Ohio River as their northern line of defense, and their eagerness to stake out the Ohio line as a Confederate moat was what had led them to take the risk of violating Kentucky's neutrality in 1861. Once having invaded Kentucky, the Confederates tried to make sure they could hold it. All Confederate forces between the Mississippi and the Appalachians were consolidated into one department, and overall command of that department was given in September 1861 to Albert Sidney Johnston, one of the most highly regarded officers of the old regular army and one of the dearest military friends of Jefferson Davis. "If he is not a general," said Davis, "we have no general." With 43,000 men at his disposal, with the two forts (Henry and Donelson) on the Tennessee and Cumberland, with another fort on Island No. 10 in the Mississippi, with Confederate forces already holding the Ohio River line at Columbus, and with convenient railroad links along the Memphis & Ohio to assure him of the advantage of interior lines—with all this, Johnston certainly began the war in the west holding what appeared like the all the best strategic cards.[27]

The problem was that Johnston's cards were actually of less value than they seemed. Johnston's forts were either incomplete or poorly constructed, his men and his officers were badly undertrained and underequipped, and Johnston himself turned out to be something less of a general than his reputation had suggested. He failed utterly to anticipate Grant's vicious strike at Henry and Donelson, and by the time

25. John Keegan, *The Mask of Command* (New York: Viking, 1987), 187–94, 210–11; Grant, "Personal Memoirs," 160–61; Gary W. Gallagher, *The Union War* (Cambridge, MA: Harvard University Press, 2011), 134.

26. Grant to Julia Dent Grant, March 21, 1862, in *The Papers of Ulysses Simpson Grant*, ed. John Y. Simon (Carbondale: Southern Illinois University Press, 1972), 4:406; Grant, "Personal Memoirs," 214.

27. Albert Castel, *Articles of War: Winners, Losers, and Some Who Were Both in the Civil War* (Mechanicsburg, PA: Stackpole, 2001), 142; Charles P. Roland, *Albert Sidney Johnston: Soldier of Three Republics* (Lexington: University Press of Kentucky, 2001 [1964]), 347.

Johnston realized what had happened, Federal gunboats were controlling the Tennessee and Cumberland, the Memphis & Ohio had been cut, and Johnston had lost all ability to concentrate his troops anywhere in Kentucky or Tennessee. Recalling the garrisons at Columbus and Bowling Green, and hastily gathering what forces he could lay his hands on, Johnston abandoned all of Kentucky and what remained to him of Tennessee, and selected as a concentration point the town of Corinth, a railroad junction just below the Tennessee-Mississippi border on the last remaining east-west Confederate rail line, the Memphis & Charleston.

The other Confederate outposts left in Tennessee, including Island No. 10 in the Mississippi River, simply dropped into the hands of Halleck's other forces. "Secession is well-nigh played out—the dog is dead," trumpeted "Parson" William G. Brownlow, who defied Confederate authorities in Tennessee to stop publication of his pro-Union newspaper, the *Knoxville Whig*. "Their demoralized army are on their way back to the Cotton States," Brownlow advised Halleck, "where they can look back at you, as you approach their scattered lines. . . . You will overtake them at the Tennessee River,—sooner if they come with new supplies of mean whiskey."[28]

The jubilation Halleck felt at these military successes was matched only by the pleasure of the political rewards he reaped. The afternoon after Fort Donelson surrendered, Halleck wired McClellan: "Give me command in the West. I ask this for Forts Henry and Donelson."[29] The War Department did even better: it promoted Halleck to the top Federal command in the west *and* demoted McClellan to field command in the East. Don Carlos Buell, who was supposed to be carrying the real war in the west into eastern Tennessee, suddenly became Halleck's subordinate, and Halleck was now set free to prosecute the western war as he wished—not by invading the mountains of eastern Tennessee and rallying some vague body of Tennessee Unionists, but by pursuing the Confederacy's western army down to Corinth and smashing it up for good. With that tantalizing object in mind, Halleck ordered Grant to push south along the Tennessee River toward Corinth with the force he had used to capture Henry and Donelson. At the same time, and with ill-concealed satisfaction, Halleck ordered Buell to bring his men down to the Tennessee River for a rendezvous with Grant. By the time the two forces had rendezvoused on the Tennessee, Halleck would have come up the river by steamboat to take personal command and push on overland to Corinth.

The Federal army began moving up the Tennessee River on March 5, unloading first at Savannah, Tennessee, on the east bank of the river. On March 17 Grant began moving them again and steamed nine miles further upstream to a scrawny little steamboat tie-up called Pittsburg Landing on the west bank of the Tennessee,

---

28. Brownlow, *Sketches of the Rise, Progress, and Decline of Secession*, 388–89.

29. Halleck to McClellan, February 17, 1862, in *War of the Rebellion*, 7:628; Stephen D. Engle, *Struggle for the Heartland: The Campaigns from Fort Henry to Corinth* (Lincoln: University of Nebraska Press, 2001), 83.

which Halleck had designated as the rendezvous point with Buell and the forward depot for the big push on Corinth. There Grant sat, waiting for Halleck to come up from departmental headquarters in St. Louis, and waiting for Buell (who spent twelve days building a bridge across the Duck River) to make it to the ferry point at Savannah. In the meantime, Grant's 33,000 men were allowed to sprawl out from the river landing, in no particular order, for almost three miles (all the way to a little log meetinghouse innocently known as Shiloh Church), just as though there were no Confederates worthy of notice within a thousand miles.[30]

Grant was wrong. In fact, he had committed the worst error in strategic judgment he would ever make during the war, for Grant and Halleck alike had sadly underestimated Albert Sidney Johnston's determination to win back what he had lost in Kentucky. The ease with which Grant had walked over Fort Henry and Fort Donelson and put half of Johnston's western army out of commission had frightened and angered the Confederacy, and in this case it galvanized the Confederates into frantic action. Jefferson Davis hurriedly stripped every Confederate garrison along the Gulf coastline, and all other points between there and Corinth, of every soldier he could lay hands on, and concentrated them at Corinth, until by April 1 Johnston had an army of about 40,000 men at his disposal. Additionally, in February Davis sent Johnston the Confederacy's most successful general to date, P. G. T. Beauregard, as a sort of auxiliary commander to help plan a counterblow at the Federal forces.

Downriver, on the other hand, Grant's victories bred a slaphappy complacency, which allowed Grant's command to sit motionless at Pittsburg Landing until the morning of Sunday, April 6, when Johnston's army came crashing through the underbrush around Shiloh Church and rolled up to within half a mile of the Federals.

What happened over the next forty-eight hours has been sufficient to give the name *Shiloh* an eerie, wicked ring that still sends shivers down the American spine. In some respects, it was hardly a battle. Johnston had only the barest hold over his green and undisciplined rebel soldiers, and it is one of the great marvels of military history that he ever managed to assemble them at Corinth, get them over the flood-soaked Tennessee roads to Pittsburg Landing, and do it all without inducing much alarm among the Federals, from Grant on down to the lowliest cavalry pickets. But Johnston was a desperate man in a desperate strategic situation, and marvels are sometimes what desperation is capable of conjuring up. In the exact obverse of Grant's optimism, Johnston knew that unless he got to Grant before Buell and Halleck did, then the war in the west was as good as over.

It was that fear as much as anything else that got Johnston moving and got him to Shiloh Church that morning, while the Federal army was still rubbing sleep from its eyes. "I would fight them if they were a million," Johnston grimly remarked after one last parley with Beauregard and his subordinates. "The more men they

---

30. James Lee McDonough, *Shiloh—in Hell Before Night* (Knoxville: University of Tennessee Press, 1977), 52.

crowd in there, the worse we can make it for them."[31] That determination, and the stupendous indifference of the Federals (Grant was actually nine miles downriver at Savannah, sitting down to breakfast), gave the Confederacy its best and biggest chance of evening up, and maybe bettering, the score set at Henry and Donelson.

Once the battle began, however, the terrain and the rawness of Johnston's troops took matters out of his hands. Shiloh became a huge grappling match, with disconnected pieces of each army standing, breaking, and running in almost every direction. "Parts of regiments," wrote an appalled reporter for the *Cincinnati Enquirer*, "ran disgracefully." One Federal division, under Benjamin Prentiss (with half of another commanded by W. H. L. Wallace), backed itself around the lip of a sunken road that became known as "the Hornet's Nest," and fought to cover the pell-mell retreat of the other four Union divisions until it was "completely cut off and surrounded," and finally surrendered. Grant wrote afterward that "more than half the army engaged . . . was without experience or even drill as soldiers," while the officers, "except for the division commanders and possibly two or three of the brigade commanders, were equally inexperienced in war."[32]

By nightfall, Albert Sidney Johnston himself was dead, killed by a stray bullet that severed an artery and left him to bleed to death, and the two bleary, punch-drunk mobs of soldiers that had been armies that morning now faced each other by the river landing without much idea of what was coming next. More than one high-ranking Union officer thought it was the end and counseled a retreat across the Tennessee. Grant, who raced upriver to Pittsburg Landing by steamboat at the first faint thump of artillery, saw at once that it was the Confederates who had failed, not the Federals. So long as they held the landing, the Federals still had the key to the Shiloh battlefield, and no one was quicker to realize that than Grant. "He had," said John Russell Young, "the woodcraft of an Indian, knew places, localities, the lay of the ground, what the skies had to say as to the weather and other mysteries," and it was plain to Grant that the Confederates had spent their last strength just getting as far as they had. One of Grant's officers, an Ohioan named William Tecumseh Sherman, found Grant that night in the pouring rain, standing under a tree with a cigar clenched between his teeth. Sherman had lost most of his division that morning, and he had come to advise Grant that a pullout was the only hope. Still, Sherman, who had been at West Point with Grant and knew him well enough to nod to before the

31. William Preston Johnston, *The Life of Gen. Albert Sidney Johnston, Embracing His Services in the Armies of the United States, the Republic of Texas, and the Confederate States* (New York: D. Appleton, 1879), 569.

32. Force, *Fort Henry to Corinth*, 144, 146; Whitelaw Reid, "The Battle of Pittsburg Landing, Tennessee," April 19, 1862, in *A Radical View: The "Agate" Dispatches of Whitelaw Reid, 1861–1865*, ed. J. G. Smart (Memphis, TN: Memphis State University Press, 1976), 1:130–31, 133; Timothy B. Smith, *The Untold Story of Shiloh: The Battle and the Battlefield* (Knoxville: University of Tennessee Press, 2006), 24, 48; Grant, "Personal Memoirs," 239; Kenneth P. Williams, *Grant Rises in the West: The First Year, 1861–1862*, ed. Mark Grimsley (Lincoln: University of Nebraska Press, 1997 [1952]), 371–73.

war, sensed something in Grant's brooding imperturbability that prompted Sherman to change his tune. "Well, Grant," Sherman said, "we've had the devil's own day, haven't we." "Yes," Grant replied, "yes. Lick 'em tomorrow, though."[33]

By the next morning, Grant had reorganized his forces (as best he could), called in reinforcements (the advance elements of Buell's column had begun arriving at Savannah the day before), and proceeded to shove back at the battered Confederates. By 3:00 PM on April 7, Beauregard, who had taken over command from the fallen Johnston, had pulled the remains of the Confederate army back onto the road to Corinth. Five days later Halleck arrived at Pittsburg Landing to take command of Grant's and Buell's newly combined armies and to find out exactly what had happened.

The most obvious fact was the casualty list: Grant's army had lost almost 13,000 men killed, wounded, or missing, more than a third of his force, while the Confederates had lost 10,000 of their own. Wits as well as lives had been lost, as the untested soldiers of both armies were unhinged by the appalling and concentrated carnage. "I have heard of wars & read of wars," wrote George Asbury Bruton, of the 19th Louisiana, two days after the battle, "but never did I think it would be to my lot to participate in such a horrible scene. . . . I never want to witness any other such scene. It seems as if I can hear the groans of the dying & wounded men and the cannons roaring all the time worse than any thunderstorms that ever was heard." Far away, in New York, Herman Melville (who had already sunk into a twilight of critical neglect after the failure of his sprawling novel *Moby-Dick, or The White Whale* in 1851) wrote of

> the pause of night
> That followed the Sunday fight
> Around the church of Shiloh—
> The church, so lone, the log-built one,
> That echoed to many a parting groan
> And natural prayer
> Of dying foeman mingled there—
> Foeman at morn, but friends at eve—
> Fame or country least their care:
> (What like a bullet can undeceive!)[34]

A sergeant from the 9th Indiana named Ambrose Gwinnett Bierce (whom Melville would join in the front rank of American writers once Melville's reputation was exhumed in the 1920s) went cold with horror when he found that gunfire had

33. John Russell Young, *Men and Memories: Personal Reminiscences*, ed. M. D. R. Young (New York: F. Tennyson Neely, 1901), 2:474; Larry J. Daniel, *Shiloh: The Battle That Changed the Civil War* (New York: Simon and Schuster, 1997), 266; Bruce Catton, *Grant Moves South* (Boston: Little, Brown, 1960), 242.

34. Melville, "Shiloh, A Requiem," in *Selected Poems of Herman Melville*, ed. Robert Penn Warren (Jaffrey, NH: Nonpareil, 2004), 122.

ignited the underbrush where part of the battle had raged and incinerated dead and wounded alike: "At every point . . . lay the bodies, half-buried in the ashes; some in the unlovely looseness of attitude denoting sudden death by the bullet, but by far the greater number in postures of agony that told of the tormenting flame." Bierce stumbled over another Federal sergeant, shot in the head but still alive, "taking in his breath in convulsive, rattling snorts, and blowing it out in sputters of froth which crawled creamily down his cheeks" while "the brain protruded in bosses, dropping off in flakes and strings."[35]

Most of the loss was blamed squarely on Grant's lack of preparedness. Not only had Grant not organized his camp for defense, but he himself had been nowhere near it when the fighting began, and at that point the old story of Grant's alcohol problems resurfaced and the word began to circulate that Grant had been drunk. Actually, Grant had been stone sober, and he had been at Savannah for the very good reason that he would be needed there as Buell's column finally arrived on the Tennessee. Although it was true he had been caught dangerously by surprise, he had nevertheless managed to pull victory out of the jaws of defeat. Shiloh also taught Grant a very effective lesson about the war: that the Confederates were deadly in earnest about winning and were not going to go away merely because a Federal army and a gunboat or two showed up to remind them who was supposed to be in charge. "Up to the battle of Shiloh, I, as well as thousands of other citizens, believed that the rebellion against the Government would collapse suddenly and soon if a decisive victory could be gained over any of its armies," Grant recollected, but after that, "I gave up all idea of saving the Union except by complete conquest."[36]

At the same time, however, Halleck would be taking no more chances. Now that Halleck and Buell were on the scene, Grant ceased to be a semi-independent operator and became just another part of Halleck's command along with Buell, and the dazzling thrust that had brought a Union army to the Mississippi border in two months slowed to a crawl. Turning inland from the river toward Corinth, Halleck's advance took a month and a half (during which he stopped every night to entrench) to move over to Corinth, and when Halleck finally arrived there on May 29, Beauregard took the counsel of prudence and abandoned Corinth without a fight. With the fall of Corinth into Federal hands, the Confederacy's last direct east-west rail line, the Memphis & Charleston Railroad, was cut, and in June the outflanked Confederate garrisons along the Mississippi at Fort Pillow and Memphis collapsed. The Mississippi (at least down to Vicksburg), Tennessee, and Cumberland Rivers were all now securely under Halleck's control.

---

35. Bierce, "What I Saw of Shiloh," in *Shadows of Blue and Gray: The Civil War Writings of Ambrose Bierce*, ed. B. M. Thomsen (New York: Forge, 2002), 212.

36. Grant, "Personal Memoirs," 246; Grant, "The Battle of Shiloh," in *Battles and Leaders*, 2:485–86.

At that point the Union army in the west ran out of steam for several reasons, the first and most important of which had to do with the Confederates. In June, the luckless Beauregard fell ill—or at least claimed to be feeling unwell—and departed from the army to go on sick leave. Jefferson Davis, who had grown increasingly unhappy with the Confederacy's first military hero, gladly replaced Beauregard with a scrappy, hot-tempered regular army veteran named Braxton Bragg. "Tall and erect, with thick, bushy eyebrows and black, fierce eyes" and a "naturally abominable temper," Bragg fought in Mexico as an artillery officer under Zachary Taylor and quarreled thereafter with nearly every other officer he served beside; John Pope thought Bragg "seemed even to detest himself." To Davis's delight, Bragg immediately determined to regain the initiative in the west that summer. He overhauled the organization of Beauregard's disheveled army, and took what "was little better than a Mob" and put them to five hours of drill a day. Commanding a force of about 30,000 men, Bragg swung around the edges of the Federal penetration into Tennessee and raced up through eastern Tennessee, where he picked up another 18,000 reinforcements under Edmund Kirby Smith. By the end of August, Bragg was aiming at the Kentucky border and stood in a fair way to undo everything that had been won by the Union since February.[37]

Halleck immediately detached Buell's troops to try to head off Bragg. But Buell was no faster a mover in the summer of 1862 than he had been the previous winter, and instead of pursuing Bragg pell-mell, Buell proceeded to retrace his original path through Tennessee, rebuilding the Nashville & Chattanooga Railroad as he went. That was slow enough work on its own terms, but it was made slower by the activities of two of the Confederacy's most successful raiders, John Hunt Morgan and Nathan Bedford Forrest. Bragg had given both Morgan and Forrest cavalry brigades and orders to create as much havoc as possible between himself and Buell. This Forrest and Morgan did effortlessly. Forrest, a former millionaire slave trader, was a natural military genius who possessed the killer instinct in spades, and in the middle of July Forrest's raiders struck at Buell's patiently rebuilt railroad line at Murfreesboro, Tennessee, and put it out of commission for two weeks. Meanwhile, Morgan swept up through Nashville in August, destroying rail lines and a railroad tunnel and further delaying Buell. Bragg, meanwhile, rolled into Kentucky and occupied Glasgow, Kentucky, on September 14. He then began recruiting volunteers for the Confederate army and commenced a leisurely move on Frankfort, the capital of Kentucky, where he scattered the Unionist legislature and inaugurated a Confederate governor on October 4, 1862.

By that time, Buell had finally managed to catch up with Bragg, and on October 8 the two armies collided near Perryville, Kentucky. The battle that resulted was a happenstance affair, like Shiloh, with neither Bragg nor Buell fully in control of the day's events. After a day of pitiless slugging, the battle of Perryville ended with Buell

37. *Military Memoirs of General John Pope*, 79; Grady McWhiney, *Braxton Bragg and Confederate Defeat*, vol. 1: *Field Command* (New York: Columbia University Press, 1969), 265, 267–68.

in command of the field, while Bragg withdrew into Tennessee. Buell had saved the Ohio River for the Union, but he received small thanks for it. Like McClellan, he failed to pursue the fleeing Confederates. Even more like McClellan, Buell unwisely announced that he "would not lend his hand to such an act as the emancipation of the slave," and on October 24, 1862, he was relieved of his command.[38]

If the distraction afforded by Bragg's abortive offensive into Kentucky was one reason why the Federal offensive in the west came to halt, then the other reason was Halleck himself. Once Halleck occupied Corinth, he was determined not to risk the troops under his command on further offensive moves, and began parceling up his forces into small garrisons to keep the likes of Forrest and Morgan away from his supply lines. Although Halleck retained Grant as his deputy, Grant fumed and sputtered in frustration, his mind burdened with the tide of press criticism still flowing in his direction over Shiloh. One of Halleck's subordinates complained that, after Corinth, "this great army . . . could have marched anywhere through the South without effective opposition . . . yet in less than two months," Halleck had dissipated its strength in penny-ante garrison duties "to such an extent that the war was half over before it was again reunited." In June, feeling that "I am in the way here" and "can endure it no longer," Grant would have resigned his commission had not Sherman talked him out of it. Then, in July, Halleck was called to Washington to assume the post of general in chief of the Federal armies, the job Lincoln had taken away from McClellan in March. Halleck reconfigured the departmental boundaries and in October designated Grant as commander of the Department of the Tennessee (effectively this meant that Grant was responsible for policing all the newly occupied Confederate territory between the Tennessee and Mississippi Rivers).[39]

By that time Grant was ready to approach Halleck with a proposal for a new campaign. During the spring campaign up the Tennessee, the upper stretches of the Mississippi River had fallen into Union hands simply because the Confederates could no longer hold them once they had lost the Tennessee River. What was worse for the Confederates was that they had also lost New Orleans. The Federal navy had been planning its own operation against New Orleans as early as November 1861, and in February 1862 command of an assault flotilla was given to a hard-eyed and aggressive fleet captain named David Glasgow Farragut. With four steam-powered sloops—the *Hartford*, *Brooklyn*, *Richmond*, and *Pensacola*—and a collection of small gunboats and mortar schooners, Farragut began the ascent of the Mississippi on April 16, stopping below New Orleans on the eighteenth for six days so that his mortar schooners could pound the two forts that guarded the river.

38. *Military Memoirs of General John Pope*, 100; Stephen D. Engle, *Don Carlos Buell: Most Promising of All* (Chapel Hill: University of North Carolina Press, 1999), 300.

39. Sherman, *Memoirs*, 276; *Military Memoirs of General John Pope*, 75; Carl R. Schenker, "Ulysses in His Tent: Halleck, Grant, Sherman, and 'The Turning Point of the War,'" *Civil War History* 56 (June 2010): 175–221.

Impatient with the results of the bombardment, at two in the morning of the twenty-fourth Farragut arranged his ships in two columns and swept up the river past the fire of the forts. Farragut anchored for the day just above the forts, and the next morning he ran his ships past the last small Confederate batteries below New Orleans. At noon on April 25, Farragut dropped anchor in the river by the city and sent ashore an officer to raise the United States flag over the New Orleans mint. The downriver forts, abandoned by most of their disheartened garrisons, surrendered on April 28.[40]

The fall of New Orleans was probably the severest single blow the Confederacy sustained in the war. New Orleans was the Confederacy's great port, its doorway to the rest of the world, and its commercial and financial equivalent of New York City. In addition to losing the city itself, 15,000 bales of cotton (worth over $1.5 million) were burned by the retreating Confederates, along with more than a dozen river steamboats, a half-completed ironclad gunboat, and the entire city dock area. "The extent of the disaster is not to be disguised," wrote Edward Pollard of the *Richmond Examiner*. "It annihilated us in Louisiana . . . led by plain and irresistible conclusion to our virtual abandonment of the great and fruitful Valley of the Mississippi," and cost the Confederacy "a city which was the commercial capital of the South, which contained a population of one hundred and seventy thousand souls, and which was the largest *exporting* city in the world."[41]

Serious though the loss of Tennessee was that spring, the Confederacy could have survived it so long as it held New Orleans and the lifeline New Orleans offered to the outside world. However, Albert Sidney Johnston had convinced Jefferson Davis that the real threat to New Orleans was from the Yankees on the Tennessee River and the upper Mississippi, and Johnston's determination to throw Grant and Halleck out of Tennessee had led him to clear out all the Gulf coast garrisons, including New Orleans, of men and equipment, including a squadron of river gunboats that might have made a significant difference in Farragut's ability to maneuver upriver. When the Federal navy burst through the back door into New Orleans only two weeks after Shiloh, New Orleans was simply too weak to defend itself.

With the Union suddenly holding both the upper and lower ends of the river, it seemed to Ulysses Simpson Grant a worthwhile effort to move over and seize the remaining parts in the middle, around the fortified town of Vicksburg. Grant could not have known it, but at that very moment Halleck was already under pressure from Lincoln to make precisely that kind of move. The November midterm congressional elections would soon be upon Lincoln, and the farmers of the Union West were restless at the prospect of a longer and longer war that kept the Mississippi shipping network closed to them. John A. McClernand, a powerful Illinois Democrat and

40. Alfred Thayer Mahan, *The Gulf and the Inland Waters* (New York: Scribner, 1883), 73–88.

41. Pollard, *Southern History of the War* (New York: C. B. Richardson, 1866), 1:326–27.

now a major general of volunteers in Grant's district, had gone off on his own to Washington demanding that Lincoln let him recruit his own army to take down the Mississippi and blow open the Vicksburg bottleneck; to placate the Northern Democrats, Lincoln had given him a curiously worded authorization in October to raise a force of volunteers. Halleck looked upon McClernand as a nuisance, and rather than take the risk that Lincoln would actually allow an inexperienced politician to take a Federal army on a joyride down the Mississippi, Halleck sanctioned Grant's plan to move on Vicksburg, with McClernand parked safely under Grant's command.

This time almost nothing went right for Grant. At first he hoped simply to march overland from Corinth with a force of 72,000 men and quickly seize Vicksburg and its garrison, but once under way in November, Grant changed his mind and detached Sherman and 32,000 men to advance down the Mississippi in another combined army-navy operation. He might have saved himself the trouble: Confederate raiders under Earl Van Dorn struck at Grant's supply base at Holly Springs, Mississippi, on December 20, destroying the bulk of Grant's supplies and stopping his overland march in its tracks. Meanwhile, Sherman's men arrived before Chickasaw Bayou, northeast of Vicksburg, on December 26 to find that the Confederate troops from Vicksburg had dug themselves in along the hills on the other side of the bayou. After a series of futile attacks, Sherman withdrew and the whole endeavor went up in smoke.[42]

Grant would not give up on Vicksburg that easily. He would admit only that the idea of an overland march on Vicksburg from above the city was impractical, and during the winter of 1862–63 he mounted no fewer than five attempts to find a way to move his men downriver, past Vicksburg, and land them on the other side of the city, where he could cut off supplies and reinforcements to the city from points south and east. None of his ideas (which included attempts to dig canals around Vicksburg, to navigate the back bayous, and to reroute the Mississippi) worked, though, and by March 1863 he was no closer to taking Vicksburg than ever. Finally, in April, Grant decided to gamble on the riskiest of all the possible approaches to Vicksburg. He ferried his men across the Mississippi, marched them down below Vicksburg on the Louisiana side of the river, and on the moonless night of April 16–17, 1863, ran a fleet of eight navy gunboats and three transports (plus some coal barges) past the four-mile-long line of Confederate naval artillery on the Vicksburg waterfront. Every one of the gunboats was hit, but only one transport was sunk, and once below Vicksburg they provided cover for Grant to safely ferry his men back across the Mississippi, this time *below* Vicksburg.[43] Within a month Grant had cut off all of Vicksburg's outside communications and had bottled up Vicksburg's 30,000 Confederate

42. Michael B. Ballard, *Vicksburg: The Campaign That Opened the Mississippi* (Chapel Hill: University of North Carolina Press, 2004), 121–26, 129–44.

43. William L. Shea and Terrence J. Winschel, *Vicksburg Is the Key: The Struggle for the Mississippi River* (Lincoln: University of Nebraska Press, 2003), 98–99.

soldiers into an airtight siege. After six weeks the Confederates were reduced to near starvation, and on July 4, 1863, Vicksburg surrendered to Grant.

With Vicksburg the Confederacy had lost a citadel, an army, and an additional measure of its self-confidence. "The surrender was the stab to the Confederacy from which it never recovered," remembered one of Vicksburg's citizens. "No rational chance of its triumph remained after the white flag flew on the ramparts of the terraced city."[44] With Vicksburg, Ulysses Simpson Grant had redeemed a reputation. He also set a president to wondering whether he had at last found a general who could win his war for him.

THIS IGNORANT MAN

At the beginning of the Civil War Abraham Lincoln was fifty-two years old, and the numerous photographs that were taken of him during his first year as president reveal a man thin and spare, but erect and powerful, with a strongly etched face and the familiar whiskers (which he had grown as a fashionable whim shortly after his election) encircling his jaw. By the end of the war, Lincoln's face had grown aged and careworn, his cheeks sunken into ashen hollows, his coarse black hair showing tufts of white, and his beard shrunken to a pitiful tuft at the chin. As the conflict dragged on and the casualty lists began to lengthen, Lincoln descended deeper into a peculiar variety of religious mysticism in which he began to view himself as merely "a humble instrument in the hands of our Heavenly Father," powerless to guide events on his own terms. As the offspring of parents who were hard-shell Calvinistic Baptists, Lincoln had already imbibed a brooding certainty that all human activity was predestined to some mysterious end. Now that sense of helplessness in the face of events intensified: "I have all my life been a fatalist," Lincoln remarked to one congressman, and added, quoting Hamlet, "'There's a divinity that shapes our ends.'"[45]

Other burdens conspired to further drain Lincoln's energies and blacken his impenetrable moods. He received a glut of hate mail, much of it threatening him with various kinds of death, which he filed in an envelope marked "Assassination." "Soon after I was nominated in Chicago," Lincoln said, "I began to receive letters threatening my life. The first ones made me feel a little uncomfortable; but I came at length to look for a regular installment of this kind of correspondence in every mail." Eventually the threats preyed so much on his mind that he began to dream of assassination and funerals in the White House, and his friend Ward Hill Lamon pestered him so badly to protect himself that Lincoln made Lamon federal marshal

44. Edward Gregory, "The Siege of Vicksburg," in *The Annals of the War Written by Leading Participants* (Philadelphia: Times Publishing, 1879), 133.

45. Lincoln, "To Eliza P. Gurney," October 26, 1862, in *Collected Works*, 5:478; Isaac N. Arnold, *The Life of Abraham Lincoln* (Chicago: Jansen, McClurg, 1885), 81; William J. Wolf, *The Almost Chosen People: A Study of the Religion of Abraham Lincoln* (Garden City, NY: Doubleday, 1959), 36–37, 77–78, 147.

of the District of Columbia, and let him and Stanton provide regular guards. Lincoln himself made no attempt at protection. As he explained resignedly to Francis Carpenter, there was no security in this life from fate: "If . . . they wanted to get at me, no vigilance could keep them out. We are so mixed up in our affairs, that—no matter what the system established—a conspiracy to assassinate, if such there were, could easily obtain a pass to see me for any one or more of its instruments." Besides, Lincoln added, democracy imposed a certain amount of risk on its leaders. "It would never do for a President to have guards with drawn sabres at his door, as if he fancied he were, or were trying to be, or were assuming to be, an emperor."[46]

As it turned out, it was not for Lincoln that the bell tolled. In February 1862 Lincoln's third son, William Wallace Lincoln, died of typhoid fever in the White House, and grief over the boy's death nearly tipped Mary Todd Lincoln over the brink into insanity. Lincoln, himself "worn out with grief and watching," could explain the death only as yet another visitation of the inscrutable power that held human destinies in a powerful and inescapable grip. "My poor boy," Lincoln murmured, "he was too good for this earth . . . but then we loved him so. It is hard, hard to have him die." After Willie Lincoln's death, Lincoln's own health began to suffer. Mary only made matters worse with spendthrift habits and a weakness for flattery by schemers and poltroons looking to acquire insider information about administration policies. "Many times," recalled his old friend Orville Hickman Browning, "he used to talk to me about his domestic troubles" and "was constantly under great apprehension lest his wife should do something which would bring him into disgrace." Unable to sleep, he paced the White House through the night, or sat up into the wee hours of the morning in the telegraph room of the War Department to receive the latest news of the war. He gradually lost weight, until his clothes seemed to hang from him, and in the fall of 1863 he contracted a mild form of smallpox. There was, he complained, a tired spot in him that no rest could ever touch.[47]

Over and above all these reasons for the haggard look of Lincoln's face was the crushing weight of having to conduct what amounted to two separate wars. In addition to the shooting war, Lincoln was also compelled to wage a political war behind the lines to keep up civilian support and morale, to enable the armies to keep on fighting, and to implement the long-term agenda of domestic policies he had inherited from Henry Clay and cherished ever since his first days as a Whig politician. The initial consensus of 1861–62 was that Lincoln was no more successful in winning the

46. Carpenter, *Six Months at the White House with Abraham Lincoln*, 62–63, 65–67; Charles G. Halpine, in *Recollected Words*, 194.

47. Elizabeth Keckley, *Behind the Scenes, or, Thirty Years a Slave and Four Years in the White House* (New York: G. W. Carleton, 1868), 103; Brooks, *Lincoln Observed*, 43; Browning, in *An Oral History of Abraham Lincoln*, 3.

political war than he was in winning the military one. On the eve of his inauguration, one longtime Washingtonian shook his head over Lincoln: "He certainly does not seem to come much to the level of the great mission" before him "& I fear that a weak hand will command the ship." "My opinion of Mr. Lincoln," wrote Orestes Brownson to Charles Sumner at the end of 1862, "is that nothing can be done with him. . . . He is wrong-headed . . . the petty politician not the statesman & . . . ill-deserving the *sobriquet* of Honest." The New York lawyer George Templeton Strong confided to his diary in 1862, "Disgust with our present government is certainly universal. Even Lincoln himself has gone down at last. Nobody believes in him any more."[48]

Of course, the benefit of hindsight suggests that Lincoln's critics were wrong and that Lincoln eventually succeeded in rallying the political morale of the North around even the most radical of his policies, emancipation. But it is also true that Lincoln accomplished that goal only very slowly, and at the cost of terrific political turmoil. The reasons lying behind that turmoil are twofold. The first is bound up with Lincoln's inexperience in national politics. Although Lincoln had been involved in state and local politics for almost his entire adult life, he had never actually been elected to an office of any consequence in Illinois beyond the state legislature, and his only experience on the national level before 1861 consisted of his solitary and undistinguished term as a representative from Illinois's Seventh District. Had there been such a thing as executive search firms in Lincoln's day, none of them would have given him a second look. His work habits had been shaped by the experience of local politics and a two-man law practice, and as a result, Lincoln only grudgingly delegated even routine correspondence to his secretaries. "His methods of office working were simply those of a very busy man who worked at all hours," Robert Todd Lincoln recalled.

> He never dictated correspondence; he sometimes wrote a document and had his draft copied by either [John] Nicholay [*sic*] or [John] Hay; sometimes he himself copied his corrected draft and retained the draft in his papers. . . . He seemed to think nothing of the labor of writing personally and was accustomed to make many scraps of notes or memoranda. In writing a careful letter, he first wrote it himself, then corrected it, and then rewrote the corrected version himself.[49]

That same inexperience made many of the old Republican hands look at him askance, as a quirk in an electoral process that ought to have elected a Seward, a Chase, or a Douglas instead. Elihu Washburne, meeting Lincoln on the railroad

48. Montgomery Meigs, in Russell F. Weigley, *Quartermaster General of the Union Army: A Biography of M. C. Meigs* (New York: Columbia University Press, 1959), 131; J. G. Randall, *Lincoln the President* (New York: Dodd, Mead, 1945), 2:241; Strong, diary entry for September 13, 1862, in *Diary of George Templeton Strong*, 256.

49. Robert Lincoln to Isaac Markens, February 13 and June 18, 1918, in *A Portrait of Abraham Lincoln in Letters by His Oldest Son*, ed. Paul Angle (Chicago: Chicago Historical Society, 1968), 56, 62.

platform when the president-elect arrived in Washington on February 23, 1861, could not help thinking that Lincoln "looked more like a well-to-do farmer from one of the back towns . . . than the President of the United States." Fully as much as George McClellan, Republican senator Benjamin Wade of Ohio dismissed "Old Abe" as a "fool," and curtly declined an invitation to a White House ball in February 1862 with the acid question, "Are the President and Mrs. Lincoln aware that there is a civil war?" Newspaper editors foamed angrily over Lincoln's election, asking, "Who will write this ignorant man's state papers?" The historian George Bancroft burst out, in a letter to his wife, "We suffer for want of an organizing mind at the head of the government. We have a president without brains."[50]

Although Lincoln was elected president as a Republican, he still carried over into the Republican Party many of the political principles of the old Whigs, and chief among those principles was the Whiggish suspicion of putting too much power into the hands of the national president. The Whigs, wrote John Pendleton Kennedy, "fearing this administrative arm, and believeing [sic] that the safety of free institutions is best secured by watching and restraining the Executive, disdain to seek its favor by any act of adulation or by any relaxation of their distrust," and "naturally put great faith in the National Legislature." Lincoln, of course, wanted to act the Whiggish part. In his first major political speech in Springfield in 1838, Lincoln had warned his hearers against the emergence of a "towering genius" who would disdain the "beaten path" of republican institutions and erect a despotism on the ruins of "the temple of liberty," and it was plain that Lincoln had Democrats such as Jackson in view. After his own election as president, Lincoln insisted in consistently Whiggish terms that he intended to take a backseat to Congress in running the country. "My political education strongly inclines me against a very free use of . . . the Executive, to control the legislation of the country," Lincoln declared in 1861. "As a rule, I think it better that congress should originate, as well as perfect its measures, without external bias."[51]

However, a civil war changed all normal expectations, and Lincoln reserved to himself exactly how to construe that "use" of the Executive. What deceived political spectators about Lincoln was his preference for moving indirectly, relying on private embassies performed by staffers or old Illinois friends such as Leonard Swett. Even before arriving in Washington, Lincoln sent Swett ahead to map the political landscape,

50. Washburne, in William C. Harris, *Lincoln's Rise to the Presidency* (Lawrence: University Press of Kansas, 2007), 318; Hans L. Trefousse, *Benjamin Franklin Wade: Radical Republican from Ohio* (New York: Twayne, 1963), 154, 167; Louis A. Warren, *Lincoln's Gettysburg Declaration: "A New Birth of Freedom"* (Ft. Wayne, IN: Lincoln National Life Foundation, 1964), 48; Mark DeWolfe Howe, *The Life and Letters of George Bancroft* (New York: C. Scribner's Sons, 1908), 2:132.

51. David Donald, "Abraham Lincoln: A Whig in the White House," in *Lincoln Reconsidered: Essays on the Civil War Era* (New York: Knopf, 1956), 187–208; John Pendleton Kennedy, "A Defence of the Whigs," in *Political and Official Papers* (New York: Putnam, 1872), 320–21; Lincoln, "Speech at Pittsburgh, Pennsylvania," February 15, 1861, in *Collected Works*, 214–15.

and Swett dutifully reported back, "From all I can learn of the Town I think by the time you had been here a week you would either be bored to death or in a condition in which you never could sensibly determine any thing." Swett "tried by all means in my power, to induce" one politician "to adopt the course you requested"; another proposal couldn't even be discussed by letter and "any decisive measures" would have to wait "until I arrive for I think I have important considerations to present to you." Other old friends were converted into listening posts to gauge public opinion, particularly in Kentucky, where long-time friend Joshua Speed's ears were close to the political wires. Lincoln's private secretaries, Nicolay and Hay, were sent on missions to Missouri, South Carolina, Ohio, Florida, New York, Illinois, Indiana, Kentucky, and Tennessee, as well as up to Capitol Hill whenever any business in Congress was pending. "When the President had any rather delicate matter to manage at a distance," recalled Hay, "he . . . sent Nicolay or me." In critical cases, Lincoln called senators to the White House for some presidential talking-to.[52]

The wise heads in the Senate criticized Lincoln's "back-kitchen way of doing this business." So did the wise heads in the cabinet, since Lincoln hardly ever involved his cabinet secretaries in policy-making decisions, except to confirm a conclusion he had already reached. Though he gave his cabinet secretaries wide enough room to use their own talents in managing those responsibilities, it was plain that Lincoln regarded them as little more than clerks, rather than partners in the great business of managing the war. This was not, of course, what his cabinet had expected: from Jefferson's day forward, cabinet secretaries had been growing in power and independence, to the point where under Franklin Pierce's secretary of war—a figure no less than Jefferson Davis—had been regarded as a greater power in the administration than Pierce himself.[53]

The discretion cabinet secretaries had in making patronage appointments (in these days before a professional civil service) was "enormous, so enormous that when not discreetly dispensed, it tears a party to pieces." That was a development Lincoln stopped cold in its tracks. Salmon Chase was indignant to discover that, in his role as secretary of the Treasury, Lincoln regarded him as no more than an extension of the presidential will. "We . . . are called members of the Cabinet," Chase raged in disappointment, "but are in reality only separate heads of departments, meeting now and then for talk on whatever happens to come uppermost, not for grave consultation on matters concerning the salvation of the country." But it gave no end of amusement to John Hay, who wrote in 1863 that Lincoln "sits here and wields like a backwoods

52. Swett to Lincoln, January 5, 8, and 19, 1861, and Thurlow Weed to Swett, January 20, 1861, in Abraham Lincoln Papers, Library of Congress; John Hay, "Letter to William H. Herndon, Paris," September 5, 1866, in *At Lincoln's Side: John Hay's Civil War Correspondence and Selected Writings*, ed. Michael Burlingame (Carbondale: Southern Illinois University Press, 2000), 110.

53. Benjamin Wade, "Confiscation of Rebel Property," July 16, 1862, "Confiscation and Emancipation," July 16, 1862, "Confiscation," July 17, 1862, in *Congressional Globe*, 37th Congress, 2nd Session, 3375, 3400, 3406.

Jupiter the bolts of war and the machinery of government with a hand equally steady & equally firm."[54]

Lincoln might not have been able to deal so independently had he not enjoyed substantial Republican majorities in both the 37th Congress (elected with him in 1860) and the 38th Congress (elected in 1862). As it was, Republicans on Capitol Hill turned the Civil War Congresses into an engine of legislative activity: House resolutions and congressional joint resolutions alone more than doubled during the war. Most of them emerged from a plethora of new House and Senate committees organized by the Republicans in 1861 to investigate disloyalty, war contracts, the New York City Customs House, and so on; still more were produced by the powerful Republican Party caucus, where the most radical measures on emancipation, confiscation of Southern property, and postwar reconstruction were hatched.[55]

Lincoln would need those majorities particularly for handling the needs of war finance and the impact the war would have on the Northern economy. From the first call for volunteers, it was clear that some way had to be found to harness the North's unquestioned industrial and financial superiority to the task of winning the war. Lincoln professed to have no expertise in finance. "Money," remarked Lincoln, when Treasury Secretary Chase brought a group of New York bankers to the White House to discuss war finance, "I don't know anything about 'money.' I never had enough of my own to fret me, and I have no opinion about it any way." In truth, Lincoln had been interested in fiscal issues as far back as his days in the Illinois legislature, when he had been the point man for the Illinois state bank, and he had been bitterly critical of the Democrats' national financial policies all through the 1840s. "Finance will rule the country for the next fifty years," Lincoln predicted to William Pitt Kellogg, and with that in mind, he wanted "the Capital of the country to become interested in the sustaining of the national credit." He "had taken an especial interest" in Chase's financial strategy, and "Mr. C. had frequently consulted him in regard to it."[56]

It was actually not Lincoln but Chase who lacked experience in "money." Chase was a onetime Democrat who had thrown his allegiance to the Republicans over slavery and Kansas-Nebraska, and he had never fit comfortably with the Whigs or the Whiggish economic views that abounded in the new party. Chase was skeptical on tariffs, hesitant about the virtues of federally financed "internal improvements,"

54. Robert Bruce Warden, *An Account of the Private Life and Public Services of Salmon Portland Chase* (Cincinnati: Wilstach, Baldwin, 1874), 484; John Hay, "To John G. Nicolay," September 11, 1863, in *At Lincoln's Side*, 54.

55. Allan G. Bogue, *The Congressman's Civil War* (New York: Cambridge University Press, 1989), 44–59, 63, 74–88, 114, 118, 121–32.

56. Carpenter, *Six Months at the White House*, 252; Kellogg, in *Recollected Words*, 277; Hay, diary entry for December 25, 1863, in *Inside Lincoln's White House*, 133–34.

and so resolutely set against banks that in 1853 he had supported a restructuring of the Treasury to prevent the Treasury from borrowing money (Congress should exercise the sole right to authorize borrowing), setting interest rates on Treasury securities, or using commercial bank accounts for government payables or receivables. He opposed "a mere paper money system of currency," had railed "against the frauds and undue expansions of banks and their suspensions of payment on their issues and deposits," and had criticized tariffs "in favor of free trade."[57] Now he was in charge of them all.

Of course, part of the rationale for appointing Chase as secretary of the Treasury was precisely that he was a former Democrat and so could assuage the fears of other Democrats for the nation's fiscal policy. Still, that did nothing to ease the pains of Chase's distaste for such responsibilities, or the flimsy structures of government finance that he inherited from his erstwhile Democratic friends. The nation's financial and banking system was in 1861 still very largely what Andrew Jackson and the Democrats had made it in the 1830s. Suspicious of the market revolution and of finance capitalism, Jackson demolished the federally sponsored Bank of the United States, and the Treasury became little more than a warehouse for government cash and customs receipts. This meant that banking became a matter for individual state governments to charter, which each state did mostly by its own lights. Jackson also took the added precaution of restricting all federal government monetary transactions to specie (which the Democrats regarded as the only real money), so the Treasury would neither accept paper money for itself nor print its own. No such restriction applied to the state-chartered banks, and so by 1861 the American economy was riding on a crazy quilt of banknotes and bonds issued by more than 5,000 state-chartered institutions (including canal companies). No merchant could do business without publications like *Day's New-York Bank Note List, Counterfeit Detector and Price Current*, *Bicknell's Reporter, Counterfeit Detector, and Philadelphia Prices Current*, or the *Cincinnati Price Current* to learn which banknotes were worth the value printed on their faces, which had to be discounted, and which were no longer anything more than paper.[58]

The great virtue of this system in Democratic eyes was that it kept economic power dispersed and ensured that the national government would remain small and fiscally weak. However, whatever that might have meant as an asset in peacetime politics, it became another matter entirely in war. Northern banks that had acted as the South's financial brokers for decades often had nothing more than Southern

57. Warden, *An Account*, 299.

58. Harry L. Watson, *Liberty and Power: The Politics of Jacksonian America* (New York: Hill and Wang, 1990), 35–38; William H. Dillistin, *Bank Note Reporters and Counterfeit Detectors, 1826–1866: With a Discourse on Wildcat Banks and Wildcat Bank Notes* (New York: American Numismatic Society, 1949), 99; Q. David Bowers, *Obsolete Paper Money Issued by Banks in the United States, 1782–1866: A Study and Appreciation for the Numismatist and Historian* (Atlanta, GA: Whitman, 2006), 185.

banknotes and bonds in their vaults as backing for their own accounts and banknotes, and with the secession of the Southern states, Northern bankers suddenly found that they no longer had any guarantee that Southerners would stand by those notes and bonds, or redeem them for specie. Southern bond prices in New York City plummeted like dead pigeons; of the 913 mercantile and banking firms in New York at the beginning of 1861, only 16 were still in business by year's end. At the same time, as secession loomed larger and larger on the horizon, confidence in U.S. bonds and notes spiraled downward; by December 1860 the Treasury had to offer interest rates as high as 12 percent to sell its notes, and U.S. 6 percent bonds could only be sold at a steep 11 percent discount.

The unlooked-for blessing in this disaster was that the collapse of Southern bonds and notes wiped out any fiscal leverage the Confederates might have had on the Northern financial markets in 1861, something that was made worse by the Confederate decision to sequester loans owed by Southerners to Northern finance for the duration of the war. Northern businessmen who might otherwise have hesitated to support Lincoln in making what amounted to war on their investments now swung behind the war as the only hope of reclaiming what the Southerners owed them. At the same time, European financiers who had invested in American bonds and notes now hurriedly unloaded them for whatever they could get on the open market, thus telescoping American foreign indebtedness and leaving American businesses with more unobligated gold in their reserves than they had expected.[59]

All of this was a voyage of discovery for Chase, and notwithstanding Lincoln's confidence that Chase could learn his way around fiscal matters, it took Chase time to figure out what was happening, how much money he would have to get to pay for the war, and where (and in what form) he was going to get it. At the very beginning, Chase greatly underestimated the amount of money needed to fund the war (he thought $320 million ought to do the job), and he was reluctant to ask Congress to raise more than a quarter of it by taxation, which in Democratic eyes was the unpardonable political sin. But Chase soon found that the war was costing the federal government $1 million a day, and by the end of 1861 he could foresee the price tag on the war hitting $350 million just to get to the end of the fiscal year in June 1862. As the war's bills multiplied, the enthusiasm of bankers and investors for government securities cooled, and Chase did not help matters by irritably questioning their patriotism. As he did so, Chase found himself in the peculiarly un-Democratic posture of supporting Republican senator John Sherman's Omnibus Revenue Act in August 1861, which allowed the levying of a direct income tax

59. Philip S. Paludan, *"A People's Contest": The Union and the Civil War* (New York: Harper and Row, 1988), 108–10; Richard F. Bensel, *Yankee Leviathan: The Origins of Central State Authority in America, 1859–1877* (New York: Cambridge University Press, 1990), 243–54; Theodore E. Burton, *John Sherman* (Boston: Houghton, Mifflin, 1906), 90.

and the issue of $150 million in short-term Treasury notes and another $100 million in long-term bonds.[60]

The old Democratic insistence that Treasury transactions be made only in gold hobbled the sale of these notes, and what was actually raised from the marketing of these securities turned out to be hopelessly inadequate. By February 1862 all the proceeds had been spent, and a further issue of bonds and notes would be taken by the financial markets as a confession of desperation. At this point Congress stepped in with its own measures for war finance, on February 25, 1862, passing the Legal Tender Act, which authorized Chase to print $150 million in paper money to pay government debts. The issue of paper money was a particularly difficult pill for Chase to swallow, since Jacksonian economics confidently predicted that the use of notes, bonds, and especially unsecured paper money rather than specie would destroy public confidence in the economy, feed financial speculation on the money markets, and send prices through the roof. In fact, successive issues of another $300 million of legal tender notes (or "greenbacks," from the green ink used to print their reverse sides) helped to inflate prices in the North by almost 80 percent during the war. Chase had little choice, however: "It is true that I came with reluctance to the conclusion that the legal-tender clause is a necessity," he admitted, "but I came to it decidedly and I support it earnestly. The Treasury is nearly empty. . . . You will see the necessity of urging the bill through without more delay."[61]

In July, at the prompting of Thaddeus Stevens as chair of the House Ways and Means Committee, Congress carefully propped up the Treasury's paper issues with the Internal Revenue Act of 1862, which used a graduated income tax to bring in $600 million in new revenue and take the inflationary steam out of the greenbacks. In fact, Congress eventually began to take its financial cues more from Stevens (a longtime Whig) than Chase, and at Stevens's prodding Congress took another step away from the era of Jacksonian finance in 1863 when it passed the National Banking Act. The act resurrected the issuance of federal charters for banks, which had been killed when Jackson destroyed Nicholas Biddle's Second Bank of the United States in the 1830s, and created a national banking system, which effectively turned private banks into depositories and receivers for federal funds. The new national banking system adopted greenbacks as their national banknotes, and Congress drove the old state banknote issues permanently out of existence by slapping a ruinous 10 percent tax on their use.[62]

60. J. W. Schuckers, *The Life and Public Services of Salmon Portland Chase* (New York: D. Appleton, 1874), 216, 238; Paludan, *"A People's Contest,"* 111; Heather Cox Richardson, *The Greatest Nation of the Earth: Republican Economic Policies During the Civil War* (Cambridge, MA: Harvard University Press, 1997), 45.

61. Burton, *John Sherman*, 105, 112–13; Ellis Paxson Oberholtzer, *Jay Cooke: Financier of the Civil War* (Philadelphia: G. W. Jacobs, 1907), 1:172–73.

62. Frederick J. Blue, *Salmon P. Chase: A Life in Politics* (Kent, OH: Kent State University Press, 1987), 160–62; Schuckers, *Life and Public Services of Chase*, 239–41.

For long-term borrowing, Chase wisely and conveniently washed his hands of the un-Jacksonian chore of hawking government securities through the Treasury by designating a fellow Ohioan, Jay Cooke, as the Treasury's bond agent. Cooke, a natural-born financier, had made his fortune in banking before retiring at the tender age of thirty-seven, and in 1861 Chase had actually offered him the post of assistant secretary of the Treasury. Cooke preferred a free hand, and in July 1861 he countered Chase's offer with an ambitious proposal for funding the war through the sale of a new and complicated series of government securities. With Chase's hesitant approval, Cooke opened a Washington office at 452 15th Street, across from the Treasury building, and oversaw the issuing of a bewildering variety of government bonds and notes, carrying variable interest rates over varying terms. In October 1862 Chase made Cooke the Treasury's general subscription agent for selling bonds across the country.

The most popular of these securities was the "5-20" bond (rather like modern federal savings bonds, these were discounted bonds that were redeemable after a minimum of five years but came to full maturity in twenty years), and through his network of 2,500 subagents Cooke was able to sell $362 million of them in their first year of offering. Not only were the redemption dates reasonable and the minimum purchase low (anyone with $50 could purchase 5-20s with interest rates as high as 7.5 percent), but the direct taxes enacted by Congress assured investors that the Treasury would have the money in hand to redeem the bonds at time of maturity. "Talk not of Taxes!" announced one bond sale circular, "they *secure* the Loans. Take the Loans! and the Taxes will fall more lightly—and they supply the ready, *present* and *required* means to strike the death blow at rebellion and the foul disturbers of the Nation's peace!"

By skillfully juggling the dynamic of notes, bonds, paper money and taxation, Chase, Cooke, and Congress succeeded in raising the money needed for the war without sapping the Northern economy. They also hooked the nation's private finance capital to the interests of the federal government, for as private investors bought the new securities, they were also buying an interest in the success of the North in the war (after all, if Lincoln and Chase failed, investors would probably never recover their investments). In return, as the federal government inched toward victory, Northern financiers such as Cooke, J. Pierpont Morgan, and A. J. Drexel found themselves mounting a rising tide of financial power and experience. Over the 1860s, the number of New York City banking houses would leap from 167 in 1864 to 1,800 in 1870, and the New York Stock Exchange would open its own building in 1863. The war would thus produce a temporary transfer of the nation's private capital into government hands (the nightmare of the old Jacksonians) and the rise of a new class of American financiers who brokered this transfer.[63]

63. Schuckers, *Life and Services of Chase*, 229; Bensel, *Yankee Leviathan*, 251–52; Oberholtzer, *Jay Cooke*, 1:137, 142–43, 187, 232–52; Paludan, *"A People's Contest*,*"* 115–17; Richardson, *The Greatest Nation*, 31–56; Michael S. Green, *Freedom, Union, and Power: Lincoln and His Party During the Civil War* (New York: Fordham University Press, 2004), 317–26.

Successful though these fiscal measures were, there remained some question as to whether they were actually constitutional, and the need to deal with the constitutionality of a broad spectrum of wartime policies soon became a major headache for Lincoln and Congress. At the very beginning of the war, on April 27, 1861, Lincoln authorized General in Chief Scott to suspend the writ of habeas corpus along the insecure railway lines running into Washington through Maryland, and to imprison anyone suspected of threatening "public safety" there. The "Great Writ" of habeas corpus means, in the simplest terms, that a civil court can demand to "have the body"—it can require a ruler or a government who has imprisoned someone purely on his own authority to surrender the prisoner to the courts for a full and fair trial of his offense, instead of being locked forever in a dungeon with no notice to anyone and the key thrown away.

Habeas corpus has been part of English common law since the Magna Carta in 1215, and part of English statute law since 1679. The very first statute adopted by the new federal Congress under the Constitution empowered all federal courts to issue the writ. The Constitution itself mentioned the writ only once (Article I, Section 9), to permit its suspension "when in Cases of Rebellion or Invasion the public Safety may require it." But the provision for suspension was located in the article concerning Congress, which implied that the suspension power lay there. When Andrew Jackson suspended the writ while preparing to defend New Orleans from the British in 1815, he was punished for his presumption with a $1,000 fine from a federal judge once the threatened British invasion was over.[64]

Roger Taney, who was still sitting as the chief justice of the United States despite his eighty-four years, was deeply antagonistic to Lincoln. He was convinced that Lincoln had no authority to repress secession, and he now looked for an opportunity to stymie Lincoln's self-claimed war powers by contesting the suspension of the writ in Maryland. Taney got his chance in the case of John Merryman, a Confederate sympathizer and Maryland militia officer who had helped put to the torch railroad bridges leading into Baltimore during the uproar over troop passage in April 1861. Merryman, a substantial landowner in Cockeysville, was arrested on May 25, 1861, and imprisoned without a warrant in Fort McHenry. On May 26, Merryman's brother-in-law and family lawyer hurried to Taney's home in Washington to petition him for a writ of habeas corpus for Merryman.

Each Supreme Court justice was, in 1861, responsible not only for sitting on the high court but also for administering one of the federal circuits of appeal; Taney's responsibility was for the Fourth Circuit Court of Appeals, which included Baltimore, and Taney promptly issued a writ of habeas corpus for Merryman to be delivered to his district courtroom in Baltimore. George Cadwalader, the commandant at Fort McHenry, refused to honor the writ, and when Taney issued a contempt citation, the

64. Rollin C. Hurd, *A Treatise on the Right of Personal Liberty: and on the Writ of Habeas Corpus* (Albany, NY: W. C. Little, 1858), 136.

U.S. marshal who carried it to Fort McHenry was refused admittance. Taney then read aloud a condemnation of Lincoln and Cadwalader, based on Taney's conviction that "the privilege of the writ could not be suspended, except by act of Congress" and that Merryman's arrest constituted a violation of the safeguard against "unreasonable searches and seizures." On June 3 Taney filed his objections as *Ex parte Merryman*.[65]

For several days it seemed that Lincoln might be legally incapable of keeping pro-Southern agitators off the streets. Lincoln argued that the Constitution merely located the suspension clause among the articles describing the functions of Congress; it did not actually specify who had the authority to do the suspending, and since Congress was at that moment out of session, Lincoln saw no reason why he should let the situation in Maryland come crashing down around his ears. It was folly to dillydally over legal niceties when Confederate sympathizers were bent on committing sabotage against the Union war effort—folly to wait until the sabotage had taken place before arresting Merryman, and folly to turn Merryman over to a civil jurisdiction that would, in all likelihood, set him loose with a wink. Action to prevent this by suspending the writ lay fully within his war powers as commander in chief. "Ours is a case of Rebellion," Lincoln argued, "in fact, a clear, flagrant, and gigantic case of Rebellion; and . . . in such cases, men may be held in custody whom the courts acting on ordinary rules, would discharge."[66] In the end, Lincoln ignored Taney, and the case of *Ex parte Merryman* became a dead letter.

This was only the beginning of a lengthy series of legal challenges (based on both constitutional and international law) generated by the war, any one of which might have interposed obstacles to the war effort that Lincoln could not ignore as easily as he had *Ex parte Merryman*. Two of the most famous of these challenges were the *Prize Cases* of 1863 and *Ex parte Milligan*. *Prize Cases* was actually a collection of suits brought against the federal government by the owners of four cargo-carrying ships stopped by the federal blockade of Southern ports in May, June, and July of 1861 and turned over to federal prize courts. Blockades were, in legal terms, something like laying a port or even an entire nation's coastline under siege from the sea. An effort at regulating the operation of blockades had been attempted at the end of the Crimean War in 1856, when the participants in the peace negotiations in Paris drafted a four-point protocol that specified what constituted a blockade and what ships and cargoes could be seized by it. Although the United States was not a signatory to what became known as the Declaration of Paris, most of the other European nations were, and they would expect their ships to be treated under its terms by any U.S. blockade.

Prize Cases questioned the legality of the stoppage of the ships in question on two grounds. The Declaration of Paris assumed that blockades were imposed by one sovereign nation upon the ports and coasts of another sovereign nation. If (as Lincoln

---

65. Brian McGinty, *Lincoln and the Court* (Cambridge, MA: Harvard University Press, 2008), 65–83.

66. Lincoln, "To Erastus Corning and Others," June 12, 1863, in *Collected Works*, 6:264.

claimed) the southern states were not in fact a belligerent nation but only an insurrection, then a blockade of international commerce had no legal standing, and ships seized by such a blockade could not be turned over to prize courts. If the blockade was indeed legal, it would be considered an act of war, but no declaration of war had been made by Congress, the only branch of the U.S. government empowered by the Constitution to do so. Only when Congress convened in its special July 1861 session and confirmed Lincoln's unilateral actions against the Confederacy could a blockade come into legal effect. Hence the four ships seized by the Federal navy before that time had been taken illegally.

The case was decided by the Supreme Court on March 20, 1863, with a bare 5–4 majority declaring that although the Confederacy could not be recognized as a belligerent nation on its own, the federal government could still claim belligerent rights for itself in attempting to suppress the Confederacy. Writing for the majority, Justice Robert C. Grier agreed with Lincoln that "it is not necessary that the independence of the revolted province or State be acknowledged in order to constitute it a party belligerent in a war according to the law of nations." Justice Samuel Nelson (speaking for Taney) wrote a blistering dissent for the minority arguing that "the President does not possess the power under the Constitution to declare war . . . within the meaning of the law of nations . . . and thus change the country and all its citizens from a state of peace to a state of war." Nothing would have pleased Taney more, or more quickly have struck a major strategic weapon from Lincoln's hand, than if the Court had agreed with Nelson's passionate contention that the blockade's "capture of the vessel and cargo in this case, and in all cases before us . . . are illegal and void. . . ."[67]

The Republicans were shocked by how easily the change of one vote on the high court could have undercut the operation of the blockade, and calls began to go up in Congress for either a new court or the replacement of the current justices. Most of this criticism was aimed at Roger Taney, who despite his poor health insisted on holding on to his seat on the Court in an undisguised search to find more ways of checking Lincoln's "excesses." Taney especially yearned to hear an appeal that would give him the opportunity to issue an opinion on emancipation, which he denounced as an unconstitutional interference with property rights. But death came to Taney before an appeal did, and when Taney died in Washington on October 12, 1864, Lincoln quickly replaced him with Salmon Chase.[68]

The High Court gave Chase's old Democratic inclinations freer rein than his cabinet post had, and his opinions did not actually greatly differ in substance from

67. *Reports of Cases Argued and Determined in the Supreme Court of the United States at December term 1862* (Washington, DC: U.S. Government Printing Office, 1863), 2:669, 698–99; Stephen C. Neff, *Justice in Blue and Gray: A Legal History of the Civil War* (Cambridge, MA: Harvard University Press, 2010), 24–27, 32–34; Simon, *Lincoln and Chief Justice Taney*, 224–32.

68. Mark E. Neely, *Lincoln and the Triumph of the Nation: Constitutional Conflict in the American Civil War Era* (Chapel Hill: University of North Carolina Press, 2011), 190.

Taney's, especially in the case of *Ex parte Milligan*. Lambdin Milligan was an Indiana Democrat who had gone beyond mere criticism of Lincoln's policies; he had actually joined a clandestine organization, the Sons of Liberty, which smuggled supplies to the Confederacy and planned raids on Federal arsenals to obtain weapons, and in 1864 he had been the Sons' candidate for governor of Indiana. Milligan was arrested by the military commander of the District of Indiana in October 1864 and then tried and condemned to death for treason by a military tribunal, not by the civil courts. Milligan petitioned for a writ of habeas corpus, and since the war was effectively over by the time of his filing in May 1865, the federal circuit court for Indiana agreed to certify the presentation of three inquiries to the U.S. Supreme Court: Should a writ be issued? Should Milligan be released from military custody? And could he be tried by a military tribunal when the civil courts in Indiana were open and operating?

When the Chase court handed down its ruling in April 1866, it unanimously held that the writ should be issued, Milligan should be released, and military tribunals had no business trying civilians. "The guarantee of trial by jury, contained in the Constitution, was intended for a state of war as well as a state of peace," announced the Court, "and is equally binding upon rulers and people, at all times and under all circumstances."[69] As *Ex parte Milligan* was not finally decided until long after the close of the war, however, it had no impact on the course of the wartime policy.

However, the Milligan case does point to another area of political difficulty Lincoln encountered, and that was the ever-increasing opposition of the Northern Democrats to the war. From the beginning of the secession crisis, pro-Union Northern Democrats had strained to support the Union cause and distance themselves from their Southern counterparts, whom they denounced as the source of so much of the secession trouble. Stephen Douglas, who wore himself into an early grave in June 1861, stumping against secession, declared, "There are but two parties, the party of patriots and the party of traitors. [Democrats] belong to the first."

> It was not a party question, nor a question involving partisan policy; it was a question of government or no government; country or no country; and hence it became the imperative duty of every Union man, every friend of constitutional liberty, to rally to the support of our common country, its government and flag as the only means of checking the progress of revolution and of preserving the Union of States.[70]

---

69. Robert Bruce Murray, *Legal Cases of the Civil War* (Mechanicsburg, PA: Stackpole, 2003), 75–84; John A. Marshall, *American Bastile: A History of the Illegal Arrests and Imprisonment of American Citizens During the Late Civil War* (Philadelphia: T. W. Hartley, 1869), 84; "Ex Parte in the Matter of Lambdin D. Milligan, Petitioner," December 17, 1866, in *Cases Argued and Decided in the Supreme Court of the United States, December Terms 1865–1867*, ed. Stephen Williams (Rochester, NY: Lawyers Co-operative Publishing, 1901), 281–303.

70. Jacob Dolson Cox, "War Preparations in the North," *Battles and Leaders*, 1:87; Douglas, "To Virgil Hickox," May 10, 1861, in *Letters of Stephen A. Douglas*, 512; Adam I. P. Smith, *No Party Now: Politics in the Civil War North* (New York: Oxford University Press, 2006), 37–38.

Lincoln, recognizing that the Democrats had garnered a healthy 44 percent of the vote in a three-way race in 1860, struggled to appease them with political and military appointments. But the spirit of Democratic-Republican bipartisanship lasted only a short while. The Northern Democrats' view of the war was summed up in their slogan "The Constitution as it is; the Union as it was"—and, some of them were inclined to add, "the Negroes where they are." As the Republican-dominated Congress began to issue unsecured greenbacks, raise tariffs, and gradually move toward emancipation and abolition—to enact, in other words, the Whig domestic agenda—Democratic support began to crumble. "The enormity of this bill," wailed the *Cincinnati Enquirer* after the passage of the National Banking Act in 1863, "is sufficient to make General Jackson, who killed the old Bank of the United States, turn over in his coffin. . . . The design is to destroy the fixed institutions of the States, and to build up a central moneyed despotism." Protective tariffs were "a great fiscal tyranny," managed on the backs of midwestern farmers by "the iron-masters of Pennsylvania and the cotton millionaires of New England." It was as though Henry Clay and Andrew Jackson had once more arisen to do political combat.[71]

The Democratic Party's fragments fell into two basic piles. The first, known as the "War Democrats," had no real organized leadership after the premature death of Stephen Douglas, but War Democrats such as Edwin Stanton of Pennsylvania, Joseph Holt of Kentucky, Benjamin Butler of Massachusetts, and Andrew Johnson of Tennessee were as forward as any Republican in their support for the war. However, many of them carefully defined the war they were supporting as a war to reunite the nation and suppress treason, not a war against slavery to result in racial equality. Robert C. Winthrop, a Massachusetts independent who ended up siding with the Democrats during the war, protested that

> I, for one, have never had a particle of faith that a sudden sweeping, forcible emancipa-
> tion could result in anything but mischief and misery for the black race, as well as the
> white. . . . The idea that the war is not to be permitted to cease until the whole social
> structure of the South has been reorganized, is one abhorrent to every instinct of my
> soul, to every dictate of my judgment, to every principle which I cherish as a statesman
> or as a Christian. It is a policy, too, in my opinion, utterly unconstitutional; and as much
> in the spirit of rebellion as almost anything which has been attempted by the Southern
> States. . . . We are not for propagating philanthropy at the point of the bayonet. We
> are not wading through seas of blood in order to reorganize the whole social structure
> of the South.[72]

71. Frank J. Klement, "Economic Aspects of Middle Western Copperheadism," in *Lincoln's Critics: The Copperheads of the North*, ed. Steven K. Rogstad (Shippensburg, PA: White Mane, 1999), 48–49.

72. Robert C. Winthrop, "Great Speech of Hon. Robert C. Winthrop at New London, Conn.," in *Union Pamphlets of the Civil War, 1861–1865*, ed. Frank Freidel (Cambridge, MA: Harvard University Press, 1967), 2:1098, 1101.

It became increasingly difficult for many War Democrats to keep that line up: Stanton and Butler both moved over to the Republicans at a very early stage of the war and became ardent supporters of emancipation; Joseph Holt served as Lincoln's judge advocate general. Increasingly, political momentum in the party passed to the "Peace Democrats." Rallying around prominent Democrats such as Samuel Tilden, Horatio Seymour, and Fernando Wood of New York, Samuel S. Cox, Alexander Long, and George H. Pendleton of Ohio, George Woodward of Pennsylvania, and James Bayard and Willard Saulsbury of Delaware, the Peace Democrats reversed the War Democrats' order of priorities: end Lincoln's war before it destroyed the country, even if it meant conceding Southern independence.[73]

The Republicans looked on the agitation of the Peace Democrats as just more evidence of the same dangerous Democratic policies that had brought on the war in the first place, and so it was not long before partisanship yielded to howling accusations of treason. "These men make the conditions of peace the humiliation of the North," protested the *Philadelphia Press*. "If they will not serve the country, they should not become the enemies of those in the country's service." At first it was only a matter of name-calling: in the fall of 1861, Ohio Republicans began comparing leading Peace Democrats to copperhead rattlesnakes, and "Copperhead" became the standard Republican way of talking about Democrats. Few of these opposition Democrats were really cut from the same cloth: even Peace Democrats were divided between peace-at-any-price extremists and moderates who wanted to end the war but not at the price of outright disloyalty. Little in these distinctions got much attention in the fevered atmosphere of the war, however. As Confederate agents attempted to manipulate Democratic dissent into outright resistance, army generals began removing Democratic judges from their benches, Democratic preachers from their pulpits, and Democratic newspapers from the mail. Estimates of the actual number of arrests by military authorities vary, from only about 4,400 all the way up to 35,000. But each one of these was treated as an insufferable violation of civil liberties, and each one only heightened Democratic resentments at Lincoln's administration.[74]

The most sensational and illuminating of these civil liberties cases concerned the Democratic candidate for governor of Ohio in 1863, Clement Laird Vallandigham. Forty-three years old and the most handsome politician in America, Vallandigham sat in Congress from 1858 until 1863, when Republicans in the Ohio legislature successfully gerrymandered his district out from under him. It was not hard to see why. Vallandigham wore the "Copperhead" tag as a badge of honor, even to the point of

73. Joanna D. Cowden, *"Heaven Will Frown on Such a Cause as This": Six Democrats Who Opposed Lincoln's War* (Lanham, MD: University Press of America, 2001), 15–17.

74. "Harmony in the Future," *Philadelphia Press*, July 1, 1863; Mark E. Neely, *The Union Divided: Party Conflict in the Civil War North* (Cambridge, MA: Harvard University Press, 2002), 89–111; Thomas S. Mach, *"Gentleman George" Hunt Pendleton: Party Politics and Ideological Identity in Nineteenth-Century America* (Kent, OH: Kent State University Press, 2007), 60–63.

fashioning a lapel pin made from the head of a copper penny. "I am not a Northern man. I have little sympathy with the North, no very good feeling for, and I am bound to her by no tie whatsoever, other than what once were and ought always to be among the strongest of all ties—a common language and common country," Vallandigham said in 1859. If anything, he was as much a secessionist and sectionalist as the Calhounites. "I am a Western Man, by birth, in habit, by education . . . and . . . wholly devoted to Western interests," even "a Western Sectionalist, and so shall continue to the day of my death."[75]

In January 1863 Vallandigham decided to run for governor of Ohio, and thereupon he ran afoul of Major General Ambrose Burnside. A thoroughgoing War Democrat and now commander of the Department of the Ohio, Burnside issued a general order that forbade "the habit of declaring sympathies for the enemy" and threatened that "persons committing such offenses will be at once arrested, with a view to being tried . . . or sent beyond our lines into the lines of their friends"—"their friends," of course, meaning the Confederates. Vallandigham became an obvious target for Burnside's order, and on May 1, 1863, Burnside planted several spies in an election crowd that Vallandigham was due to address. Vallandigham made numerous incautious remarks about a "wicked, cruel, and unnecessary war" that was "not being waged for the preservation of the Union" but for "the purpose of crushing out liberty and erecting a despotism," and he declared "that he was at all times, and upon all occasions, resolved to do what he could to defeat the attempts now being made to build up a monarchy upon the ruins of our free government." In peacetime this sort of rhetoric would hardly have gotten Vallandigham more than a few column-inches in the newspapers, but now it was enough to set General Burnside off like a Roman candle. Four days later, a company of Federal soldiers broke down the door of Vallandigham's house and hauled him off to Cincinnati for a military trial.[76]

Vallandigham was no fool: though a military commission easily found him guilty of violating Burnside's general order and sentenced him to imprisonment in Fort Warren, in Boston harbor, he appealed for a writ of habeas corpus and cast himself as a martyr in the cause of the Constitution. Sensing the political Pandora's box that Vallandigham's arrest could easily open, Lincoln changed his sentence from imprisonment to banishment in the Confederacy. But Lincoln was unable to escape the eruption of attack and abuse from Northern Democrats that followed, and when the Ohio Democrats met in Columbus in June to select a nominee for the Ohio governorship, a crowd of as many as 100,000 showed up to demand Vallandigham's

---

75. Clement Vallandigham, "There Is a West; For the Union Forever; Outside of the Union, for Herself," December 15, 1859, in *Speeches, Arguments, Addresses and Letters of Clement L. Vallandigham* (New York: J. Walter, 1864), 210, 212.

76. *The Trial of Hon. Clement L. Vallandigham: By a Military Commission* (Cincinnati: Rickey and Carroll, 1863), 7, 11; McGinty, *Lincoln and the Court*, 186–90; Jennifer L. Weber, *Copperheads: The Rise and Fall of Lincoln's Opponents in the North* (New York: Oxford University Press, 2006), 96–99.

nomination. Vallandigham's absentee campaign slowly evaporated without his magnetic presence, however, and a daring Confederate raid into Ohio under John Hunt Morgan frightened Ohioans into a clearer sense of their wartime priorities. When the votes were tallied in the fall elections, Vallandigham lost his long-distance bid for the governorship by 100,000 votes. Relieved, Lincoln turned his attention to matters other than Vallandigham, and when he was advised in the summer of 1864 that Vallandigham had slipped back into Ohio, disguising himself with a set of false whiskers and a cape, Lincoln merely recommended that the new departmental commander leave Vallandigham alone. "Watch Vallandigham and others closely," Lincoln advised, but "otherwise do not arrest without further order. . . ."[77]

The oddity of the Democratic protests over Lincoln's suspension of the writ of habeas corpus and the Vallandigham arrest was how atypical the Vallandigham, Merryman, and Milligan cases were. When historians have looked closely at the record of civil arrests under Lincoln's administration, most of them have turned out to be arrests for wartime racketeering, the imprisonment of captured blockade runners, deserters, and the detention of suspicious Confederate citizens, not the imprisonment of political dissenters; most of the cases concerning the notorious military commissions occurred, in fact, in areas of the occupied Confederacy, not in the North.[78] The Vallandigham case notwithstanding, Lincoln was as undisposed to erect a political despotism over the North as he was to fashion a legislative despotism over Congress. When measured against the far vaster civil liberties violations levied on German Americans and Japanese Americans in America's twentieth-century world wars, Lincoln's casual treatment of Vallandigham appears almost dismissive.

Lincoln's presidency has often been characterized as a "war presidency," and indeed Lincoln's four years as president are unique for having coincided almost in their entirety with a condition of war. Still, that should not distract attention from the very considerable energy he devoted to domestic issues. In addition to rebuilding the national banking system, Lincoln and his Congress introduced a sweeping new tariff plan—the Morrill Tariff, named for Vermont senator Justin Smith Morrill—that would offer the shield of import duties not only to American manufacturing but to agriculture and mining as well. The Morrill Tariff, which came into effect even before Lincoln took office, pegged tariffs as high as 36 percent; thus it "radically changed the policy of our customs duties," wrote Maine congressman James Blaine, "and put the nation in the attitude of self-support in manufactures." A Homestead Act, introduced by the abolitionist Owen Lovejoy at the opening of

77. Frank L. Klement, *The Limits of Dissent: Clement L. Vallandigham and the Civil War* (New York: Fordham University Press, 1998 [1970]), 252, 272–77; Lincoln, "To John Brough and Samuel L. Heintzelman," June 20, 1864, in *Collected Works*, 7:402.

78. Mark Neely, *The Fate of Liberty: Abraham Lincoln and Civil Liberties* (New York: Oxford University Press, 1991), 24–28, 60, 98, 133–37.

the first regular session of the 37th Congress, opened up 160-acre blocks of federal lands in the western territories at the fire-sale price of $1.25 an acre. No longer could pro-slavery propagandists such as George Fitzhugh boast that Northern factory workers were just as enslaved to their benches as black slaves were to their plantations; the way was now open for every immigrant, every day laborer, every "penniless beginner in the world" to acquire "a patch of wild, vacant public land, and convert it into a homestead and productive farm." In July 1862 Lincoln signed the Pacific Railroad Bill, which put government-backed loans at the disposal of the single greatest internal improvements project in American history: the transcontinental railroad.[79]

Lincoln and his Congress understood both the war and the politics of the war to be devoted to a single goal, and that was the ushering in of a great free-labor millennium in which middle-class culture in the form of free schools, small-town industry, and Protestant moralism would spread peace, prosperity, and liberal democracy across the continent. "Commerce and civilization go hand in hand," proclaimed Pennsylvania Republican James H. Campbell, "civilization of that high type which shall spread the cultivated valley, the peaceful village, the church, the school-house, and thronging cities."[80] In that respect, Lincoln was as much the last Whig president as the first Republican one, and his presidency marked the triumph of most of Henry Clay's old "American System" over the political legacy built up since 1800 by successive Democratic administrations.

---

79. Richardson, *The Greatest Nation*, 2, 105–6, 109, 146, 187; Green, *Freedom, Union and Power*, 307–8; James Blaine, *Twenty Years of Congress: From Lincoln to Garfield, with a Review of the Events Which Led to the Political Revolution of 1860* (Norwich, CT: Henry Bill, 1884), 1:399.

80. James H. Campbell, "Pacific Railroad—Again," April 8, 1862, in *Congressional Globe*, 37th Congress, 2nd Session, 1580.

CHAPTER SIX

THE SOLDIER'S TALE

The ordinary soldier of the Civil War was in almost every case a temporary volunteer. Unlike most of the European nations, which either used a universal military draft and a trained national reserve (as did France or Prussia) or relied upon an army of long-serving professionals (Britain), the armies of the American Civil War were filled with untutored amateurs who had left their plows in their fields or their pens by their inkwells and fully expected to return to them as soon as the war was over. What their officers knew about tactics, combat, and war in general could have been fitted onto a calling card without crowding. Although both the Union and the Confederacy eventually resorted to a compulsory draft to keep their ranks filled, the number of men who were actually drafted for war service was comparatively small. Even when the draft itself was a motivation, right down to the end of the war it was the volunteer, signing the enlistment papers of his own volition, who shouldered the burden of war.

These volunteers had almost as many reasons for enlisting as there were ordinary soldiers to volunteer. In the first weeks of conflict, Confederate secretary of war Leroy P. Walker was swamped with offers from 300,000 men to serve in the Confederate army, and not a few of them were straightforward in their frank willingness to fight for slavery. When asked why he had enlisted, Douglas J. Cater, a musician in the 3rd Texas Cavalry, "thought of the misguided and misinformed fanatical followers of W^m. Lloyd Garrison and Harriet Beecher Stowe" who had driven the issue of slavery through Congress until the Southern states "saw no other solution than a peaceful withdrawal and final separation." Cater owned no slaves himself, but he was convinced that slavery was the right condition for blacks. Northerners "had now become fanatical, and wrote and preached about it, without considering the condition of the Negro in the jungles of Africa as compared to his happy condition (of course there were exceptions) with his master in the cultivation of the fields of the southern states." As a result, secession was merely the South's "exercise of Constitutional rights in their desire for harmony and peace."[1]

For many more Southerners, it was individual local patriotisms rather than the defense of slavery or even the Confederacy that tipped the tide toward enlistment. Joseph Newton Brown, who enlisted in the 1st South Carolina Rifles in 1861, dismissed secessionist political rhetoric as claptrap and insisted, "The war was brought on by the politicians and the newspapers." He enlisted anyway, and stayed in the Confederate army all through the war out of a sense of responsibility to his community. Similarly, Patrick Cleburne, a well-born Protestant immigrant from Ireland, owned no slaves and had no interest in slavery, but he enlisted in the 1st Arkansas in 1861 because "these people have been my friends and have stood up to me on all occasions."[2]

Others cast the war in dramatic terms as a war of national self-defense, protecting hearth and home from invaders. However protracted the debates over secession had been before the war, the Confederacy was no slaveholders' coup. Texas lieutenant Theophilus Perry believed that he "was standing at the threshold of my door fighting against robbers and savages for the defense of my wife & family." Georgian William Fleming declared that he was fighting "not only for our country—her liberty & independence, but we fight for our homes, our firesides, our religion—every thing that makes life dear." Then there was Philip Lightfoot Lee, of Bullitt County, Kentucky, who offered a whole calendar of loyalties as his reason for joining the Confederacy. At first, he explained, he was for the Union; if that split apart, he was for Kentucky; if Kentucky failed, he would go for Bullitt County; if Bullitt County collapsed, he would fight for his hometown, Shephardsville; and if Shephardsville was divided, he would fight for his side of the street. And of course there were always those such as John Jackman, who enlisted simply on the impulse of a friend's suggestion while walking to the local railroad station to buy a newspaper.[3]

Northern soldiers found themselves enlisting for an equally wide variety of reasons. For some Northerners, the war was a campaign to keep the American republic from being torn in two and made vulnerable to the hungry ambitions of foreign aristocracies. Ulysses S. Grant was moved by the fear that "our republican institutions were regarded as experiments up to the breaking out of the rebellion, and monarchical Europe generally believed that our republic was a rope of sand that would part the moment the slightest strain was brought upon it." Wilbur Fiske, who enlisted in the 2nd Vermont, believed that "slavery has fostered an aristocracy of the rankest

1. Douglas John Cater, *As It Was: Reminiscences of a Soldier of the Third Texas Cavalry and the Nineteenth Louisiana Infantry*, ed. T. Michael Parrish (Austin, TX: State House Press, 1990), 67–68, 69, 173.

2. Varina Davis Brown, *A Colonel at Gettysburg and Spotsylvania: The Life of Colonel Joseph Newton Brown and the Battles of Gettysburg and Spotsylvania* (Baltimore, MD: Butternut and Blue, 1988 [1931]), 12; Howell and Elizabeth Purdue, *Pat Cleburne: Confederate General* (Hillsboro, TX: Hill Jr. College Press, 1973), 74.

3. Jimerson, *The Private Civil War*, 24–25; William C. Davis, *The Orphan Brigade: The Kentucky Confederates Who Couldn't Go Home* (Garden City, NY: Doubleday, 1980), 1, 29, 57.

kind," and unless it was rooted up, it would choke the last stand of democracy. Walt Whitman, who found part-time government work in Washington so that he could serve as a nurse in the army hospitals, wrote in 1863 that a divided America would reduce the world's greatest liberal experiment to the level of a third-rate power, which would then lie prone at the feet of England and France. "The democratic republic," groaned Whitman, has mistakenly granted "the united wish of all the nations of the world that her union should be broken, her future cut off, and that she should be compell'd to descend to the level of kingdoms and empires." So long as the war raged, Whitman believed, "there is certainly not one government in Europe but is now watching the war in this country, with the ardent prayer that the United States may be effectually split, crippled, and dismember'd by it."[4]

The war not only endangered the possibility of popular government by inviting foreign intervention but also raised the question of whether, if the Confederacy succeeded, popular government could ever be made to work again at home. "If the ground assumed by the States in revolt is yielded, what bond is there to hold together any two States that may remain—North or South, East or West?" asked Ezra Munday Hunt, a surgeon in the 19th New Jersey. "What becomes of our national power, or title to respect? In such an event, must not the wealth and enterprise and energy of this young nation become the prey of contending factions, and our very name be a hissing and a byword among other nations?" On the other hand, declared one Union colonel at a mass Union rally in Indianapolis in February 1863, if the Union was saved, it would keep the principle of republican government alive for the benefit of every other nation yearning to throw off the shackles of aristocracy. It "would be to not only strengthen our own government, but to shed a radiating light over all the other nations of the world by which the down-trodden people could see their way to liberty." As a Harvard student named Samuel Storrow (who enlisted in the 44th Massachusetts) explained to his disapproving parents, "What is the worth of this man's life or of that man's education if this great and glorious fabric of our Union . . . is to be shattered to pieces by traitorous hands . . . If our country and our nationality is to perish, better that we should all perish with it." This was nationalism of a very ideological sort—not the Romantic nationalism of race and blood, but a highly intellectualized, universal nationalism, based on the open-ended promise of the Declaration of Independence and the Constitution.[5]

---

4. Ulysses S. Grant, "Personal Memoirs," in *Memoirs and Selected Letters*, ed. M. D. McFeely and W. S. McFeely (New York: Library of America, 1990), 774; Wilbur Fiske, in Warren B. Armstrong, *For Courageous Fighting and Confident Dying: Union Chaplains in the Civil War* (Lawrence: University Press of Kansas, 1998), 114; Walt Whitman, "Attitude of Foreign Governments During the War," in *The Portable Walt Whitman*, ed. Mark Van Doren (New York: Viking Press, 1969), 562–63.

5. Ezra Munday Hunt, "About the War" and "The Great Union Meeting Held in Indianapolis, February 26th, 1863," in *Union Pamphlets of the Civil War*, 1:562, 2:602; Bell I. Wiley, *The Life of Billy Yank: The Common Soldier of the Union* (Baton Rouge: Louisiana State University Press, 1978 [1952]), 39.

For many other men in the Northern armies, as in the Confederate armies, there were considerations that impelled them to sign their lives away that had nothing to do with politics or ideology. Like his Southern counterparts Patrick Cleburne and Joseph Newton Brown, Edward King Wightman of the 9th New York enlisted out of a simple sense of civic obligation. "It is not only desirable that our family should have a representative in the army, but where we are so well able to furnish one, it would be beyond endurance disgraceful for young men [to be] living peacefully and selfishly at home, while the land is rent by faction and threatened with ruin by violence." Oliver Wendell Holmes Jr. was a "pretty convinced abolitionist," but he remembered as his prevailing reason for joining the 20th Massachusetts the need to demonstrate his manhood to his generation. "As life is action and passion," Holmes wrote twenty-five years later, "it is required of a man that he should share the passion and action of his time at peril of being judged not to have lived." Samuel Hinckley, a Massachusetts mill owner, heartily approved of his son's enlistment in the 5th Massachusetts Cavalry, believing that "this civil war will work good to the young men of this age & land." Peace and prosperity had led to softness and effeminate self-indulgence; now, "money-making & peddling give place to higher aspirations and this war is marking a distinctly manly character in our young men."[6]

Few of the white Union recruits listed any interest in destroying slavery as a motivation for enlistment. The 24th Michigan Volunteers gave as their collective reason for enlistment to "fight for the Union and maintain the best government on earth," not the abolition of Southern slavery. Indiana sergeant Samuel McIlvaine wrote his parents to explain that he had enlisted to defend "this Government, which stands out to the rest of the world as the polestar, the beacon light of liberty & freedom to the human race." So in February 1862 Sergeant McIlvaine made no effort to stop "three or four slave hunters" from entering the regiment's campsite and seizing two runaway slaves who "got mixed with the Negro cooks and waiters and were thus endeavoring [to] effect their escape to the North." Even though the runaways had armed themselves with a pistol and a butcher knife, "they had evidently counted on being protected in the regiment but they were sadly disappointed, as they were disarmed by their pursuers and taken back without molestation on our part."[7]

6. Edward King Wightman, *From Antietam to Fort Fisher: The Civil War Letters of Edward King Wightman, 1862–1865*, ed. E. G. Longacre (Madison, NJ: Fairleigh Dickinson University Press, 1985), 24; Liva Baker, *The Justice from Beacon Hill: The Life and Times of Oliver Wendell Holmes* (New York: HarperCollins, 1991), 97; Samuel Hinckley to Henry Hinckley, March 11, 1862, in *Yankee Correspondence: Civil War Letters Between New England Soldiers and the Home Front*, ed. Nina Silber and Mary Beth Sievens (Charlottesville: University Press of Virginia, 1996), 59.

7. Donald L. Smith, *The Twenty-Fourth Michigan of the Iron Brigade* (Harrisburg, PA: Stackpole, 1962), 18; Samuel McIlvaine, *By the Dim and Flaring Lamps: The Civil War Diaries of Samuel McIlvaine*, ed. C. E. Cramer (Monroe, NY: Library Research Associates, 1990), 32, 147.

Some Union soldiers were, in fact, even more hostile than their Confederate counterparts to the notion that the war had anything to do with slavery. "If *anyone* thinks that this army is fighting to free the Negro, or that that is any part of its aim, they are *terribly mistaken*," declared Massachusetts sergeant William Pippey. "I don't believe that there is *one abolitionist* in *one thousand*, in the army." Indianan John McClure had enlisted because he thought "we were fighting for the union and constitution" and not "to free those colored gentlemen." He was enraged by the Emancipation Proclamation and Lincoln's apparent aim of having "all the niggars on an equality with you" and wished that "if I had my way about things I would shoot every niggar I cam across." Even William Tecumseh Sherman was at best indifferent to making the war a crusade against slavery. "I would prefer to have this a white man's war and provide for the negroes after the time has passed," Sherman wrote to his wife, Ellen Ewing Sherman, "but we are in revolution and I must not pretend to judgment. With my opinion of negroes and my experience, yea, prejudice, I cannot trust them yet."[8]

As the war brought more and more Northerners into close contact with the brutal realities of the slave system, the urge to destroy slavery gradually became an important part of the soldiers' motivations. "I had thought before that God had made the Negro for a slave for the whites," Elisha Stockwell of the 14th Wisconsin recalled, but after seeing one slave owner abuse two female slaves, "my views on slavery took a change." Marcus Spiegel, a German Jew who rose to command an Ohio regiment before his death in battle in 1864, enlisted as a pro-Union Democrat, believing that "it is not necessary to fight for the darkies, nor are they worth fighting for." By early 1864, Spiegel had seen enough of slavery in Louisiana to change his mind. "Since I am here I have learned and seen more of what the horrors of Slavery was than I ever knew before and I am glad indeed that the signs of the time show towards closing out the accused institution." Never again would Spiegel "either speak or vote in favor of Slavery; this is no hasty conclusion but a deep conviction." Later in the war, a white Iowa regiment captured twenty-three prisoners from a Confederate unit that had participated in the massacre of black federal soldiers at Fort Pillow; the angry whites interrogated the prisoners, asked them if they remembered Fort Pillow, and then shot them all.[9]

Sometimes both Union and Confederate volunteers would be led by more pragmatic motives to join the armies. Some simply wanted to get away from home. The

8. Jimerson, *The Private Civil War*, 41, 43; Lloyd Lewis, *Sherman: Fighting Prophet* (New York: Harcourt, Brace, 1932), 303.

9. *Private Elisha Stockwell, Jr., Sees the Civil War*, ed. Byron R. Abernathy (Norman: University of Oklahoma Press, 1985), 39; *Your Own True Marcus: The Civil War Letters of a Jewish Colonel*, ed. Frank L. Byrne and Jean Soman (Kent, OH: Kent State University Press, 1984), 62, 315–16; Marvin R. Cain, "A 'Face of Battle' Needed: An Assessment of Motives and Men in Civil War Historiography," *Civil War History* 28 (March 1982): 23.

Federal army set eighteen as the minimum age for its recruits, but recruiting officers did not mind winking at restless teenagers in order to fill a recruiting quota.[10] Henry C. Matrau was just fourteen when he joined Company G of the 6th Wisconsin in 1862, but the mustering officer simply treated the boy's presence on the line as a pleasant joke:

> More than a hundred men who had become interested in the little chap stood around to see if he would pass muster. He had picked out a pair of large shoes into which he stuffed insoles that would raise him up a half inch or more, higher heels and thicker soles had been added to the shoes. The high crowned cap and the enlarged shoes lifted the little fellow up. . . . I can see him as he looked when he started to walk past the mustering officer. I can see Captain McIntyre of the Regular Army, who mustered our regiment. The minute the boy started down the line, his eyes were fixed upon him, and he watched him until he reached the left of the company. I can see the captain's smile of approval as the little fellow took his place. He had won the day. He was mustered into Uncle Sam's service for three years or during the war.[11]

As many as 10,000 boys below the age of eighteen managed to join the army legally, as drummer boys or musicians. Johnny Clem was a ten-year-old runaway who attached himself to the 22nd Michigan as a drummer boy and whose pay had to be anted up by the regiment's officers. Clem grew up into a reliable soldier, eventually exchanging his drum for a rifle and actually wangling an officer's commission after the close of the war (he retired in 1916 as a major general). Besides the legally enrolled Johnny Clems, it is entirely possible that as many as 800,000 underage soldiers, many as young as fifteen, slipped past cooperative recruiters. Elisha Stockwell was one of these fifteen-year-olds when he signed up to join Company I, 14th Wisconsin Volunteers, and though his father successfully voided the enlistment, in February 1862 the boy took the first chance he had and ran away to join the regiment. Stockwell admitted that he thought of politics as "only for old men to quarrel over." He just wanted to get off the farm and see the wider world.[12]

Getting away from home, however, could easily serve as the solution to other problems. Amos Judson of the 83rd Pennsylvania had a sharp eye for the kind of men who filled the ranks of his company, and he sketched a few of the more amusing reasons they had for enlisting. "There goes a man who knocked his wife down with a wash board, and then ran off and joined the army to spite her, looking

---

10. William J. Wray, *History of the Twenty Third Pennsylvania Volunteer Infantry, Birney's Zouaves* (Philadelphia: Survivors Association, 1903), 151.

11. L. J. Herdegen and W. J. K. Beaudot, *In the Bloody Railroad Cut at Gettysburg* (Dayton, OH: Morningside Press, 1990), 65.

12. *Private Elisha Stockwell, Jr., Sees the Civil War*, 15.

behind him all the time to see if she would call him back." And when "in melt-ing letters" she "forgave him and called him back to her bosom . . . he wished the army and the war were at the devil. But it was too late and he is now a patriot." Or consider the "young man who got into a woman-scrape at home; and in order to save himself from being shot or from suffering the penalty of the law, he left the young woman in her sorrow, ran off and became a soldier." This was all well and good until "he came to realize that there was as much danger of getting shot in the army as there was at home," and shortly "he, too, wished that the army was at the devil and that he had staid home and married the girl. But it was too late, and he also became a patriot." On it went, in inglorious detail—the jealous husband who "in a moment of despair and rage left home and went to the wars," the foreigner, the professional gambler, and the runaway teenager, guilty of "some outrageous breach of domestic discipline, for which his parental ancestor had taken down the old cow skin [and] with it warmed the seat of his pantaloons"—all of them, said Amos Judson with a grin, are "the patriots upon whom we are depending to conquer the rebellion."[13]

Whatever the reason for enlisting, by 1865 the Union had sworn in 2,128,948 men, approximately one-third of the military-age male population of the northern states, while the Confederacy probably enrolled a little under 1 million men, about four-fifths of its military-age male population. They represented not simply a sta-tistical percentage of the American population but also a healthy cross section of classes and occupations. The Civil War was by no means merely a "poor man's war." The Virginia brigade first commanded by "Stonewall" Jackson at Bull Run in 1861 carried on its rolls 811 farmers, 477 ordinary laborers, 107 merchants, 41 lawyers, 26 printers, 142 students, 75 blacksmiths, six bakers, five distillers, two dentists, and four "gentlemen." The 2nd South Carolina enrolled fifty-three sets of brothers and forty-nine individuals whose net worth in the 1860 census had been listed as greater than $1,000. The same regiment enlisted lawyers, a mathematics professor, three civil engineers, a druggist, and students from Furman College, Erskine College, and South Carolina College, plus fifteen immigrants (from Ireland, France, Eng-land, Germany, Scotland, and Sweden). Slaveholders, and those from slaveholding households, accounted for 36 percent of the soldiers of the Confederate army of 1861; more than half the officers were slaveholders, with a combined average wealth of nearly $9,000.[14]

13. Judson, *History of the Eighty-Third Regiment, Pennsylvania Volunteers*, 180–81, 184.

14. James I. Robertson, *The Stonewall Brigade* (Baton Rouge: Louisiana State University Press, 1963), 15–16; Mac Wykoff, *A History of the Second South Carolina Infantry, 1861–1865* (Wilmington, NC: Broad-foot, 2011), 441–596; Joseph Glatthaar, *General Lee's Army: From Victory to Collapse* (New York: Free Press, 2008), 19–20.

The 11th Ohio boasted that it had enlisted workmen from approximately a hundred trades and occupations, "from selling a paper of pins to building a steamboat or railroad." The 19th Massachusetts had six Harvard graduates in its ranks, while the 23rd Ohio carried two men on its regimental rolls who would later be president of the United States, Rutherford B. Hayes and William McKinley. One study of 1,337 Union recruits from Newburyport, Massachusetts, has shown that high-status skilled workers and professionals were actually overrepresented in the Union army; the rates of enlistment for those in the poorest and wealthiest categories among the Newburyport troops was almost even.[15] Similar studies of Concord, Massachusetts, and Claremont and Newport, New Hampshire, have also shown that white-collar workers and independent artisans (the segments of the Northern population with the greatest openness to the Republican free-labor ideology) formed the largest segment of recruits, while soldiers from the lowest and highest wealth categories enlisted at approximately the same rates.[16]

Taken as a whole, skilled laborers and professionals made up approximately 25 percent and 3 percent, respectively, of the Union Army, which works out to almost exactly the same proportions these groups occupied in the entire male population of the North in the 1860 census. Unskilled laborers made up about 15 percent of the Federal recruits, which means that poor workers were actually slightly underrepresented in the Union Army. As for the Confederates, unskilled laborers composed only 8.5 percent of the recruits, a substantial underrepresentation of this group, which otherwise accounted for almost 13 percent of the white Southern population.[17]

THE MAKING OF THE VOLUNTEERS

Since so much of the responsibility for recruitment fell upon the individual states, and since so few of the states were really equipped to handle recruitment in any systematic fashion, the actual process of raising and organizing a regiment often became a matter of local or personal initiative. The 28th Virginia had actually been born before the war started, as a response in the Lynchburg area to John Brown's raid

---

15. Maris A. Vinovskis, "Have Social Historians Lost the Civil War? Some Preliminary Demographic Speculations," in *Toward a Social History of the American Civil War: Exploratory Essays*, ed. Maris A. Vinovskis (New York: Cambridge University Press, 1990), 1–30.

16. William J. Rorabaugh, "Who Fought for the North in the Civil War? Concord, Massachusetts, Enlistments," *Journal of American History* 73 (December 1986): 695–701; Thomas R. Kemp, "Community and War: The Civil War Experience of Two New Hampshire Towns," in *Toward a Social History of the American Civil War: Exploratory Essays*, ed. Maris A. Vinovskis (New York: Cambridge University Press, 1990), 31–77.

17. See the tables James M. McPherson created from data on Union enlistees and on Confederate soldiers (based on profiles assembled by Bell I. Wiley) in James M. McPherson, *Ordeal by Fire*, 359.

by ad hoc companies such as the Blue Ridge Rifles, the Roanoke Grays, and the Craig Mountain Boys. Ten of these companies were organized as a regiment on May 17, 1861, and nine days later they were en route by train to Manassas Junction to become part of the hastily assembled Confederate army that defeated Irvin McDowell at Bull Run. The 3rd Virginia began life as a militia company in Norfolk County in 1856, then expanded to become a four-company battalion, and finally was enlarged to become the 3rd Regiment of Virginia militia the following year. They were called out on April 20 to participate in the capture of the Norfolk Navy Yard, and in July were mustered into Confederate service as the 3rd Virginia Volunteers. The Hibriten Guards were recruited as a company from Caldwell County, North Carolina, in the foothills of the Blue Ridge, and sent off on July 31, 1861, with ceremonies in the town square of the county seat, Lenoir and the presentation of a handmade state flag. On August 27 they were baptized along with nine other companies as the 26th North Carolina.

It was no different on the Union side. The 24th Michigan was recruited in July 1862 after a war rally in Detroit organized by Judge Henry Morrow and Sheriff Mark Flanigan of Wayne County. Morrow and Flanigan, together with a group of recruiting officers, scoured Wayne County for recruits, holding meetings in churches and town halls, and after ten days the regimental quota of 1,030 officers and men had been met. The 17th Maine was recruited that same summer by individuals commissioned by the state governor and state adjutant-general to open recruiting offices and hold recruiting meetings in Portland and the surrounding counties of Cumberland, Oxford, York, Franklin, and Androscoggin; recruiters who were successful in raising full companies would be commissioned by the state as regimental officers, irrespective of whether they had any previous military experience. The 83rd Pennsylvania was originally a three-months regiment, raised single-handedly in April 1861 by John W. McLane, who had been handed a colonel's commission by the governor of Pennsylvania and authorized to recruit a regiment from his native Erie County. It took McLane only four days of war rallies and buttonholing to enlist 1,200 men; another 400 had to be turned away due to the governor's limitations on the size of the regiment.[18]

Recruitment rallies were a ritual of the early days of the war, and like religious revivals, they had the capacity to bring the full social pressure of local communities to bear on potential recruits. John D. Billings, who served in the 10th Massachusetts Artillery, came to recognize a fairly predictable pattern in recruitment rallies that appealed to the social self-definition of white males. "The old veteran of 1812 was

18. Frank E. Fields, *28th Virginia Infantry* (Lynchburg, VA: H. E. Howard, 1985), 1–4; Lee A. Wallace, *3rd Virginia Infantry* (Lynchburg, VA: H. E. Howard, 1986), 1, 2, 7, 16; Rod Gragg, *Covered with Glory: The 26th North Carolina Infantry at Gettysburg* (New York: HarperCollins, 2000), 9–10; William B. Jordan, *Red Diamond Regiment: The 17th Maine Infantry, 1862–1865* (Shippensburg, PA: White Mane, 1996), 3–4.

trotted out, and worked for all he was worth, and an occasional Mexican War veteran would air his non-chalance at grim-visaged war," Billings remembered, but the
clearest challenge of all would come from "the patriotic maiden who kept a flag or
handkerchief waving with only the rarest and briefest of intervals, who 'would go in
a minute if she was a man.'" The town newspaper in Cornwall, Connecticut, actually
urged the "Women of Cornwall" to "hurry along your husbands, sons, and brothers
to the field! The exigencies of the hour demand the sacrifice: let it be made." The
same charms worked on Confederate volunteers as well. "If men were all like the
Ladies we would Whip old lincon before Tomorrow night," marveled one Georgia
private.[19] The pressure to be a man, or to avoid becoming a "woman" while women
were becoming "men," put a substantial squeeze on any townsman's reluctance to
enlist. At other points, the recruitment meeting would apply the fervor, as well as the
structure, of an evangelical revival:

> . . . Sometimes the patriotism of such a gathering would be wrought up so intensely by
> waving banners, martial and vocal music, and burning eloquence, that a town's quota
> would be filled in less than an hour. It needed only the first man to step forward, put
> down his name, be patted on the back, placed upon the platform, and cheered to the
> echo as the hero of the hour, when a second, a third, a fourth would follow, and at last
> a perfect stampede set in to sign the enlistment roll, and a frenzy of enthusiasm would
> take possession of the meeting.[20]

To enlist was a conversion to true manhood; to skulk was a fall from social grace.

Recruits usually moved from the recruiting meeting or office to a "camp of rendezvous," which could be almost anything from a city park to a county fairground. The
quartermaster of the 121st New York simply leased part of a farm "for the season . . .
for the purpose of allowing the same to be used as a military camp." Since most
recruits in the early stages of the war arrived as companies rather than fully formed
regiments, the "camp of rendezvous" was the place where the plethora of local companies were sorted out into regiments for the first time. The largest of these camps
in the North was Camp Curtin, outside Harrisburg, Pennsylvania. Harrisburg was
the single most important east-west junction point for the northern railroad system,
and Camp Curtin's location one mile north of the Pennsylvania Railroad's main
Harrisburg depot made it the prime location for the organization of Pennsylvania
troops as well as a major supply dump for military equipment for the Army of the
Potomac. All in all, 106 regiments were organized at Camp Curtin. But close behind
Curtin in organizational numbers were Camp Chase at Columbus, Camp Morton

---

19. John D. Billings, *Hardtack and Coffee, or The Unwritten Story of Army Life* (Boston: G. M. Smith, 1887),
38; Glatthaar, *General Lee's Army*, 38.

20. Billings, *Hardtack and Coffee*, 41.

in Indianapolis, Camp Butler in Springfield, Illinois, and Camp Harrison and Camp Dennison in Cincinnati.[21]

There recruits were issued blankets, tin plates and cups, forks and knives, and, once they had been officially mustered into United States or Confederate States service, uniforms. The official uniform of the United States Army in 1861 included a long dark blue frock coat with matching wool pants and a broad-brimmed hat known by the name of its designer as the "Hardee." These regulation hats "were neither useful nor ornamental," remembered a soldier in the 13th Massachusetts. "They were made of black felt, high-crowned, with a wide rim turned up on one side, and fastened to the crown by a brass shield representing an eagle with extended wings, apparently screaming with holy horror at so base an employment."[22] There were few enough of these outfits available in 1861 to issue to the volunteers, but the shortages went unlamented since the volunteers preferred to show up in their own homegrown varieties of uniforms anyway. Italians who had fought under Garibaldi in the Italian wars of national unification organized the 39th New York under a collection of former Garibaldini officers—Ercole Salviatti, Luigi Delucchi, Luigi Roux, and Amborgio Bixio—and kitted themselves out in uniforms inspired by Garibaldi's Italian revolutionaries.

> The officers' uniforms were dark blue cloth, single breasted, bordered, and its seams were faced, with gold braid. Its deep cuffs and its standing collar were scarlet cloth. . . . The trousers had double broad red stripes down the outer seam. The hat was of stiff black felt, round in the crown and very wide in the brim, and loaded with a massive cluster of drooping dark green cock-feathers on the left, *a la Bersaglieri.* . . .[23]

The gaudier the uniform or the less in conformity it was to regulations, the less likely it was to win favor in the eyes of army quartermasters or West Point regulars, and the harder it was to replace them when, after a few months, they wore out.

By the spring of 1862, the general uniform pattern of the Union armies had settled into the use of a navy blue frock coat or sack coat, with sky-blue or robin's-egg-blue trousers, and either a black felt slouch hat or a baggy-looking flat-topped forage cap sometimes called (after its French pattern) a *kepi.* Only four sizes of this standard uniform were manufactured for Union army use, which compelled most soldiers to develop some kind of crude sewing skills in order to make them fit, and

21. Isaac O. Best, *History of the 121st New York State Infantry* (Chicago: J. H. Smith, 1921), 3; William J. Miller, *The Training of an Army: Camp Curtin and the North's Civil War* (Shippensburg, PA: White Mane, 1990), 237–38.

22. Charles E. Davis, *Three Years in the Army: The Story of the Thirteenth Massachusetts* (Boston: Estes and Lauriat, 1893), 9.

23. Michael Bacarella, *Lincoln's Foreign Legion: The 39th New York Infantry, The Garibaldi Guard* (Shippensburg, PA: White Mane, 1996), 31.

shoes were simply hard leather brogans, square-toed and ill-fitting at best. "My first uniform was a bad fit," remembered Warren Lee Goss, a Massachusetts volunteer. "My trousers were too long by three or four inches; the flannel shirt was coarse and unpleasant, too large at the neck and too short elsewhere. The forage cap was an ungainly bag with pasteboard top and leather visor; the blouse was the only part which seemed decent; while the overcoat made me feel like a little nubbin of corn in a large preponderance of husk."[24]

The Confederate dress regulations adopted in September 1861 specified a uniform of similar design, but adopted cadet gray as the official uniform color, largely since many state militia units were already clothed in gray uniforms of their own design and purchase. As the blockade progressively cramped Confederate supplies, Confederate uniforms became shabbier and more improvised; by the end of the war, some Confederate soldiers were dressed in old farm clothes and captured Federal uniforms. What was worse, supplies of chemical dye had become so scarce that Southerners were forced to resort to common vegetable dyes to color what uniforms they could make, and so produced frock coats and trousers not in gray but in a brownish, mousy color nicknamed "butternut." "Dirt and tatters seemed to be the rule in their clothing," thought a Union prisoner captured by Stonewall Jackson's men, "from their rusty slough hats, sandy beards, sallow skins, butternut coats, and pantaloons down to their mud-stained shoes."[25]

If the "camp of rendezvous" was too small, then the next stop for a newly organized regiment would be a larger "camp of instruction," where the volunteer was supposed to learn the basics of drill and discipline. At the beginning of the war, the "camp of instruction" frequently turned into a local entertainment. "Crowds of ladies and gentlemen repair every afternoon to the 'Camp of Instruction' of the Virginia Volunteers, at the Hermitage Fair Grounds," reported one Richmond newspaper. "The proficiency of the Lexington Cadets . . . is something wonderful to behold, and worth going a long distance to see." Henry Handerson joined the Stafford Guards on June 17, 1861, near Alexandria, Louisiana; he spent ten days putting his affairs in order, then joined his company on board a river steamer that brought them to "Camp Moore, the camp of instruction," sixty miles north of New Orleans. "Here we were fairly initiated into the mysteries and miseries of a soldier's life, though the miseries of this camp were bliss itself when compared with the more serious discomforts of our later experience." Handerson and

24. Goss, "Going to the Front," in *Battles and Leaders*, 1:152.

25. Clay McCauley, "From Chancellorsville to Libby Prison," in *Glimpses of the Nation's Struggle: A Series of Papers Read before the Minnesota Commandery of the Military Order of the Loyal Legion of the United States* (St. Paul, MN: St. Paul Book and Stationery, 1887), 1:191.

Stafford Guards were then united with several other companies to form the 9th Louisiana, under the command of Richard Taylor, the son of former president Zachary Taylor.[26]

Unfortunately, since the United States had fought its last major war more than thirteen years before in Mexico and had kept up only the tiniest regular army since then, most young Americans of military age had never in their lives encountered the reality of military life, and knew next to nothing of military drill and discipline. Everything had to be taught from the very beginning, including something as simple as how to stand at attention. Moreover, few of the volunteers seemed inclined to take drill, discipline, or the military itself with the spit-and-polish seriousness it demanded. The volunteer never ceased to think of himself as an independent American and experienced a good deal of confusion and irritation at being made to obey orders he could see no sense in. Charles S. Wainwright, a Federal artillery officer, was exasperated by "how little snap" the first volunteers he met in 1861 "have generally." Michigan lieutenant Charles Haydon was annoyed to find that "many of the men seem to think they should never be spoken to unless the remarks are prefaced by some words of deferential politeness. Will the gentlemen who compose the first platoon have the kindness to march forward, or will they please to halt, &c. is abt. what some of them seem to expect."[27]

Discipline in the Confederate armies was, if anything, even worse. As Robert E. Lee ruefully admitted, "Our people are so little liable to control that it is difficult to get them to follow any course not in accordance with their inclination." He acknowledged to the Prussian army observer Justus Scheibert that Confederate soldiers were second to none to terms of bravery, but "give me also Prussian discipline and Prussian forms, and you would see quite different results!" One major difficulty in imposing discipline on Southern soldiers was that the discipline, regimentation and authoritarianism of camp life was very nearly identical to that of the plantation, and Southern whites resented and resisted efforts to impose on them what looked for all the world like the discipline they imposed at home on black slaves. One Georgia private insisted that "I love my country as well as any one but I don't believe in the plan of making myself a slave. . . ." When he wrote home, he did not hesitate to compare military life with plantation slavery: "A private soldier is nothing more than a slave and is often treated worse. I have during the past six months gone through

26. Richmond *Daily Whig,* May 22, 1861, in *Richmond in Time of War,* ed. W. J. Kimball (Boston: Houghton Mifflin, 1960), 8; Henry E. Handerson, *Yankee in Gray: The Civil War Memoirs of Henry E. Handerson with a Selection of His Wartime Letters,* ed. C. L. Cummer (Cleveland, OH: Press of Western Reserve University, 1962), 29–30.

27. Charles S. Wainwright, *A Diary of Battle: The Personal Journals of Colonel Charles S. Wainwright, 1861–1865,* ed. Allan Nevins (New York: Harcourt, Brace and World, 1962), 22; Jimerson, *The Private Civil War,* 201.

more hardships than anyone of ours or Grandma's negroes; their life is a luxury to what mine is sometimes."[28]

This situation was all the more galling to nonslaveholding whites, who had grudgingly supported the slave system precisely because black slavery was the one social fact which gave them any sense of equality with white planters. Military life forced slaveholders and nonslaveholders into a relationship of class and command that denied race-based equality among whites. Frank Robinson, a Louisiana soldier, complained that "the life of a common soldier . . . is a great deal worse than that of a common field hand. . . . Those commissioned officers . . . are just like the owners of slaves on plantations, they have nothing to do but strut about, dress fine, and enjoy themselves."[29]

In many cases, the discipline problem lay not so much with the volunteer soldier as with the volunteer system itself, since volunteer regiments were usually allowed to elect their own officers from among themselves, officers who might be popular as good fellows but who knew neither how to give orders and get them obeyed nor even what kind of orders to give. "In the sense in which the term is understood in the regular armies of Europe," admitted John William Jones, a Southern Baptist chaplain, "we *really had no discipline.*" At his worst, the volunteer officer could be fully as ignorant and irresponsible as the men he was supposed to command. Thomas Hyde began the war as an officer by "drilling as much as possible by day and studying by candle light in the evenings." Charles Wainwright was more exasperated at the officers the volunteers elected than at the volunteers themselves. "Their orders come out slow and drawling, then they wait patiently to see them obeyed in a laggard manner, instead of making the men jump to it sharp. . . ." This was because, as Wainwright realized, the officers had "raised their own men and known most of them in civil life." A Northern missionary at Port Royal was shocked to see "officers and men . . . on terms of perfect equality socially" in the Union army. ". . . Off duty they drink together, go arm in arm about the town, call each other by the first name, in a way that startles an Eastern man."[30]

28. Lee to Jefferson Davis, July 29, 1863, in *The War of the Rebellion*, 27(III):1048; Justus Scheibert, *Seven Months in the Rebel States During the North American War*, ed. W. M. S. Hoole (Tuscaloosa: University of Alabama Press, 2009 [1958]), 75; James I. Robertson, *Soldiers Blue and Gray* (Columbia: University of South Carolina Press, 1988), 124.

29. Jimerson, *The Private Civil War*, 206.

30. J. William Jones, "The Morale of General Lee's Army," in *Annals of the War*, 200; Thomas W. Hyde, *Following the Greek Cross; or, Memories of the Sixth Army Corps* (Columbia: University of South Carolina Press, 2005), 37; Reid Mitchell, "The Northern Soldier and His Community," in *Toward a Social History of the American Civil War: Exploratory Essays*, ed. Maris A. Vinovskis (New York: Cambridge University Press, 1990), 82; Joseph T. Glatthaar, *The March to the Sea and Beyond: Sherman's Troops in the Savannah and Carolinas Campaigns* (New York: New York University Press, 1985), 26.

Time and the Confederate and Federal governments eventually weeded out the worst of the incompetent officers. The Federal army imposed qualifying exams for commissioned officers after First Bull Run, and the Confederacy followed in 1862. The qualifying exams were woefully easy to pass, but even so, some were not able to do so. Dillon Bridges of the 13th Indiana Cavalry was examined by a three-man board after being elected captain of Company M in 1864 and failed to answer some of the most obvious of the thirty-nine questions on the exam:

Q. How are battalions placed?
A. Can't tell. . . .
Q. Moving in column of fours and you wish to form platoons, what command?
A. Can't tell. . . .
Q. What course would you pursue in sending or receiving a flag of truce?
A. I do not know. . . .
Q. Have you ever studied the tactics or Army regulations?
A. Not half an hour. All I have learned has been from observation.

Bridges was eventually prevailed upon to resign his captaincy. Company M's second lieutenant, John A. Chapman, who confessed that he was "not capable of standing an examination," was passed by the examining board after a few perfunctory questions about picket duty.[31]

Even if Dillon Bridges had studied "the tactics or Army regulations," none of that might have made him a more effective officer. The prevailing tactics books—by Winfield Scott, William Hardee, and, after 1862, Silas Casey's *System of Infantry Tactics*—were long on the technicalities of drill, such as basic weapons handling and movement in and out of formations, but painfully short on real instruction for combat. Given the inexperience of the average volunteer officer, the limitations of the tactics books, and the disposition of the handful of available regular army officers toward a war of fortification and maneuver, the result for the average soldier was that drill *became* his training for realities of actual battlefield fighting. One Ohio colonel, Jacob Ammen, recorded how he handled and instructed both his volunteer officers and men: "Daily drills—daily recitations in tactics—take the starch out of some, and others are learning fast. And now I superintend—select an officer to drill the others in the morning, one squad drill, company drill, and Battalion drill in the afternoon. . . . I drill the sergeants daily, in length of step, time and preserving distance."

All of this was effective for bringing large and unwieldy bodies of men to the battlefield itself, but it generally turned out to be useless once the shooting started, especially as units lost cohesion and started to take casualties. When the 24th Michigan came under fire for the first time in December 1862, the regiment's colonel could

---

31. John W. Powell, "How to Pick Out Bad Officers," *Civil War Times Illustrated* 30 (March/April 1991): 46–49.

This 1864 lithograph of Abraham Lincoln is based on an earlier oil sketch by Frances Carpenter. Beginning his political career as a Whig in the 1830s, Lincoln emerged as a major national opponent of slavery after his sensational challenge to Stephen A. Douglas for the U.S. Senate in 1858. He was elected president in 1860 with only 39 percent of the popular vote but a majority in the Electoral College. He was re-elected in 1864 with resounding majorities in both, plus overwhelming support from the soldier vote in the Union armies. *Photographs and Prints Division, Schomburg Center for Research in Black Culture, New York Public Library*

Although often rigid and aloof, Jefferson Davis managed the Confederacy's limited resources and cantankerous political figures with surprising skill. This prewar photograph was taken while Davis was still a U.S. senator from Mississippi. *Library of Congress*

The Hutchinson Family Singers, nine siblings from New Hampshire who staged concert tours from 1840 until 1867, popularized the song "Slavery Is a Hard Foe to Battle." Their sheet music and concerts were part of the abolitionist movement's effort to spread the anti-slavery message through popular culture as well as moral and political argument. *Library of Congress*

This portrait of Frederick Douglass was made in 1848, three years after he published his first autobiography, *Narrative of the Life of Frederick Douglass, an American Slave.* Born in slavery in Maryland as Frederick Bailey, Douglass fled to Pennsylvania in 1838 and subsequently became the most prominent black orator and activist of his day. *Chester County Historical Society, West Chester, PA*

RALLY, BOYS, FOR THE UNION

Goodwin's Battery of Breech-Loading
LIGHT ARTILLERY!

SOON TO TAKE THE FIELD!

THE OLD FLAG FOREVER!

LET THE REBELS TAKE WARNING!
NOW IS THE TIME TO SERVE YOUR COUNTRY!

NO SKEDADDLERS WANTED! FALL IN, BOYS!

The Union MUST and SHALL BE preserved! The Rag of Treason must not longer defy us!

Young and Able-Bodied Men who are willing to sustain our Government and Fight for the Soil and Liberty so dear to us all, can join this Battery, assured that New York will feel proud of us if we but do our duty as Soldiers.

All the Bounties offered by City, State and Nation will be given for Recruits if soon filled up. Good Quarters and Camping Grounds provided. Fall in, Boys!

WM. F. GOODWIN, Commanding Battery.

BAKER & GODWIN, Printers, Printing-House Square, opposite City Hall, N. Y.

The single largest category of troops serving in the Civil War was the Volunteers (in contrast to the Regular Army and the state militias), whose regiments were raised by the sort of strenuous state recruiting efforts evident in this giant recruitment poster. Later in the war, recruitment posters would add inducements of large state and Federal bounties for enlisting. *New-York Historical Society*

Robert Edward Lee had enjoyed a long career in the U.S. Army when, in 1861, he decided to follow his home state, Virginia, into the Confederacy. After four years as the Confederacy's most aggressive and successful general, the once-dark-haired, handsome Lee had been worn down to a gray-haired old man, as seen in this photograph taken shortly after he surrendered the Army of Northern Virginia at Appomattox Courthouse. *Library of Congress*

This popular photograph of Ulysses S. Grant captures both his stubborn "pertinacity" and imperturbable calm. Having failed at nearly every career he attempted before the war, he found natural and almost unbroken success as a Union field commander, and he rose to the unheralded rank of Lieutenant-General in 1864. *Library of Congress*

A bronze-barreled "Napoleon" gun-howitzer, designed by the Emperor Napoleon III and capable of firing a 12-pound solid shot on a flat trajectory (as a "gun") or in a high, descending arc (as a howitzer), on outdoor display at Harpers Ferry National Historical Park. The 12-pounder Napoleon was so versatile that it eventually accounted for half of the artillery used by both armies in the Civil War. *Author's collection*

The color guard of the 1st Delaware Volunteer Infantry, with its national and state flags. A regiment's flags served the practical purpose of marking position amid the smoke and confusion of combat, and the symbolic purpose of embodying the regiment's esprit de corps. *Delaware Public Archives, Dover, Delaware*

The U.S. Navy's blockade of the Southern coastlines forced the Confederacy to employ fast, purpose-built cargo vessels to slip back and forth through the blockade to points in the Caribbean where they could pick up cargo. Originally built as a steam-powered packet in Scotland, this ship was bought by the Confederacy and named *Robert E. Lee*. It made twenty-one successful trips through the blockade before being captured in November 1863. *U.S. Naval History Center*

In May 1863, women in Richmond, Mobile, and elsewhere in the South staged riots to protest food shortages. This image of the Richmond Bread Riot, showing angry and militant Southern women looting a store, appeared in *Frank Leslie's Illustrated Newspaper* on May 23, 1863. *Library of Congress*

A key element in the success of the Union war effort was the innovative finance measures deployed by Treasury Secretary Salmon Chase and his chief financial agent, Jay Cooke. This advertisement for "5-20" U.S. bonds showcased the most popular form of federal government bond during the war. *Historical Society of Pennsylvania*

Dead horses of the 9th Massachusetts Artillery were left in the farmyard of the Trostle House in Gettysburg in July 1863. The 9th Massachusetts made a desperate stand in the Trostle farmyard on the second day of the battle of Gettysburg, until Confederate soldiers shot down the battery's horses to immobilize it and then overran the battery's guns. *Library of Congress*

Four score and seven years ago our fathers
brought forth, upon this continent, a new nation, conceived in Liberty, and dedicated to the proposition
that all men are created equal.

Now we are engaged in a great civil war, testing whether that nation, or any nation, so conceived,
and so dedicated, can long endure. We are met
here on a great battlefield of that war. We have
come
~~And~~ to dedicate a portion of it as ~~the~~ a final resting place for those who here gave their lives that
that nation might live. It is altogether fitting
and proper that we should do this.

But in a larger sense we can not dedicate—
we can not consecrate— we can not hallow this
ground. The brave men, living and dead, who struggled here, have consecrated it far above our poor power
to add or detract. The world will little note,
nor long remember, what we say here, but
can never forget what they did here. It is
for us, the living, rather to be dedicated
here to the unfinished work, which they have,
thus far, so nobly carried on. It is rather

In the fall of 1863, Lincoln was invited to deliver what were originally designed to be a only a "few appropriate remarks" to dedicate the new Soldiers National Cemetery at Gettysburg. His short address became one of the most effective explanations of the war's purposes ever written. *Library of Congress*

The frontispiece of Sara Emma Edmonds's autobiography, *Nurse and Spy in the Union Army: Comprising the Adventures and Experiences of a Woman in Hospitals, Camps and Battle-fields.* Edmonds alternately volunteered for war service as a nurse, darkened her skin to pass as a slave in order to spy behind Confederate lines, and enlisted as a soldier in male disguise. *Courtesy of Special Collections / Musselman Library, Gettysburg College, Gettysburg, Pennsylvania*

1   2   3   4   5   1   2   3   1   2   3   1
note, not, move, love, book--tube, tub, full--type, hymn, myrrh--dew.

No. 46.—XLVI.

A *battery* is used in war to protect the gunners. *Cavalry* are soldiers who fight on horseback, and *infantry* are those who travel on foot.

An *enemy* is one who hates us. The Yankees are enemies to the Southern people.

We are commanded to love our enemies.

A *gallery* is the upper story of a Church.

A *rarity* is something which we do not have every day.

Modesty is very becoming to young ladies.

The burglar breaks into people's houses to rob them of their goods. The Bible says, "Thou shalt not steal."

A *mystery* is someting hard to understand ; a *novelty* is something new and strange, and a *prodigy* is something very wonderful.

Gluttony is eating to excess; the glutton makes himself sick, and often shortens his days by eating too much.

An *artery* is a large blood vessel.

A canopy is a fine covering for a throne or bed. The sky is sometimes called the canopy of blue.

Ebony is a fine black wood.

A *luxury* is something very good

Felony is a crime often punished with death.

We erect tomb-stones to the *memory* of our departed friends.

This page from the *Dixie Speller,* a Southern wartime textbook, instructs children, "An *enemy* is one who hates us. The Yankees are enemies to the Southern people." Lessons in Southern schoolbooks were frequently rewritten to glorify a distinctively Southern culture. *Virginia Historical Society*

The Confederate commerce-raider *Alabama* was one of seven raiders built or purchased by the Confederate Navy to prey on Union shipping around the world in order to even scores with the U.S. Navy's blockade of the Confederacy's ports. This illustration depicts the sinking of the *Alabama* by the USS *Kearsarge* off Cherbourg, France, in June 1864. *Library of Congress*

Newspaper artist William Waud sketched "Gen Sherman reviewing his army in Savannah before starting on his new campaign" as he observed the triumphant parade that marked William Tecumseh Sherman's capture of the Georgia port city at the end of his notorious "March to the Sea" in December 1864. Sherman was soon to launch a new raid into the Carolinas that would end in the surrender of Joseph Johnston and what was left of the Confederate Army of Tennessee in April 1865. *Library of Congress*

Robert E. Lee's staff selected the Wilmer McLean House, at Appomattox Courthouse, as the best location for Lee to meet Ulysses S. Grant and surrender the Army of Northern Virginia. McLean had lived near the Bull Run battlefield at the beginning of the war and now found himself hosting the war's end in his front parlor at Appomattox. *Library of Congress*

Hd Qrtrs U.S. Army
Appomattox C.H. Va
Apr 10th 1865

Genl R E Lee
Comdg C.S. Army
Genl
In accordance with
the substance of my letter to you of the 8th inst. I propose
to receive the Army of N.V. on the following terms (to
wit) Rolls of all the officers & men to be made
in duplicate, one copy to be given to an officer to be
designated by me & the other to be retained by such
officer or officers you may designate.
The officers to give their individual parole not to
take up arms against the Government of the United
States, untill properly exchanged & each company
or Regt. commder to sign a like parole for the men of
their commands
The arms Artillery & public property to be
parked, stacked & turned over to the officer appointed
by me to receive them — This will not include the side
arms of the officers, nor the private Horses or baggage
This done each officer & man will be allowed to return to
their homes, not to be disturbed by the United States
authorities as long as they observe their Paroles & the laws
inforce of where they reside
Very Respectfully
U.S. Grant
Lt Genl

Jack Boyer,
dinner & liquor crowd (2.)
Forsythe

Ulysses S. Grant presented these surrender terms to Robert E. Lee at the McLean house. Much to Lee's relief, Grant proposed surprisingly mild conditions: no march to prisoner-of-war camps, officers were allowed to keep personal side-arms, and soldiers were allowed to keep horses or mules for their own use. *Auburn University Libraries Department of Special Collections & University Archives*

In this symbolic image, an agent of the Freedmen's Bureau intervenes in a dispute between black freedmen and disgruntled Southern whites. Although designed as an agency for uplifting the economic status of the freed slaves, the bureau was never permitted to exercise real powers of intervention on behalf of the freedpeople and was phased out of existence by 1871. *Library of Congress*

President Warren G. Harding meets with Confederate veterans from Beauvoir, Mississippi, outside the West Wing of the White House, June 24, 1922. The urge to promote North–South reconciliation in the decades after the war frequently led to the downplaying of Northern veterans' desire to remember the war as a triumph for Union and emancipation. A month before, Harding had presided at ceremonies for the dedication of the Lincoln Memorial in Washington, DC, which confined black spectators to a segregated seating area. *Library of Congress*

think of nothing better at that moment to steady his men than to put them through the manual of arms. "His sonorous orders: 'Attention, battalion! Right dress! Front! Support arms . . .' were heard over the field, and with all the precision of a parade, the orders were obeyed . . . while the air was torn with cannon balls and the very hills seemed to rock with the reverberations." It made a grand sight, but it was also a telling testimony to the real inability most Civil War officers suffered in not knowing how to direct their men under the terrifying conditions of real combat. "Instead of practising the men in the simple flank and line movements used in battle, or at targets, or in estimating distances," complained Union artilleryman Frank Wilkeson, "they were marched to and fro and made to perform displayful evolutions," which would have been commendable if war had been a "competitive drill for a valuable, and maybe, sacred prize," but which were worse than useless "in a rugged, wooded country where the clearings were surrounded by heavy forests . . . and where practice and practice and still more practice in estimating distances was required, if we were to fire accurately and effectively."[32]

The most important result of this preoccupation with drill was that few units, either North or South, were actually prepared to carry an attack forward under fire. Captain Edward Hewett, a British observer from the Royal Engineers, was annoyed to find that "neither side can be manoeuvred under fire, and this is about the secret of the whole present American War." The volunteers can "be brought under fire, and when there will stand well," but they were too undertrained "either in morale or field movements to advance, change position or retire—The moment they have to manoeuvre, they get into confusion and break, this their own officers admit. . . ."

Their own officers *did* admit it. "It is astonishing how soon, and by what slight causes, regularity of formation and movement are lost in actual battle," remembered David L. Thompson of the 9th New York. "Disintegration begins with the first shot. To the book-soldier all order seems destroyed, months of drill apparently going for nothing in a few minutes." For one thing, the American terrain, with its thick woods and comparatively poor system of internal roads made battlefield maneuver by the book an impossibility. William Tecumseh Sherman observed:

> We . . . had to grope our way over unknown ground, and generally found a cleared field or prepared entanglements that held us for a time under a close and withering fire. Rarely did the opposing lines in compact order come into actual contact, but when . . . the lines did become commingled, the men fought individually in every possible style, more frequently with the musket clubbed than with the bayonet, and in some instances

32. T. Harry Williams, *Hayes of the Twenty-Third: The Civil War Volunteer Officer* (New York: Knopf, 1965): 30–31; Alan T. Nolan, *The Iron Brigade: A Military History* (Madison: Wisconsin State Historical Society, 1975), 182; Frank Wilkeson, *Recollections of a Private Soldier of the Army of the Potomac* (New York: G. P. Putnam's Sons, 1887), 21–22.

the men clinched like wrestlers, and went to the ground together. Europeans frequently criticised our war, because we did not always take full advantage of a victory; the true reason was, that habitually the woods served as a screen, and we often did not realize the fact that our enemy had retreated till he was already miles away and was again intrenched, having left a mere skirmish-line to cover the movement, in turn to fall back to the new position.

Confederate general Daniel Harvey Hill put the matter even more simply: the Confederate soldier "was unsurpassed and unsurpassable as a scout and on the skirmish line," but "of the shoulder-to-shoulder courage, born of drill and discipline, he knew nothing, and cared less. Hence, on the battlefield, he was more of a free lance than a machine. Whoever saw a Confederate line advancing that was not crooked as a ram's horn? Each ragged Rebel yelling on his own hook and aligning on himself."[33]

Still fewer officers were trained in how to use their regiments' firepower properly. Target practice was almost unknown in both armies, and when it was tried, the results were usually too pitiful to be encouraging. The 14th Illinois tried to practice target shooting at a barrel set up 180 yards away from the firing line: out of 160 tries, only four shots hit the barrel. The 5th Connecticut scored even more poorly: forty men firing at a barn fifteen feet high from a distance of only a hundred yards managed to score only four hits, and only one below the height of a man. At Bull Run, Col. William B. Franklin was exasperated even by the regulars of his 12th U.S. Infantry: "It is my firm belief that a great deal of the misfortune of the day at Bull Run is due to the fact that the troops knew very little of the principles and practice of firing. . . . Ours was very bad, the rear files sometimes firing into and killing the front ones."[34]

George Eminhizer of the 45th Pennsylvania received no weapons training at all at Camp Curtin in 1862, and was greatly embarrassed by the command to load his rifle. "I did not know how," Eminhizer recalled. "I turned to my comrade on the right and said: 'Can you tell me which end of the cartridge I must put in first?' He loaded the gun for me." At least Eminhizer did not have to learn his lesson under fire. Ulysses Grant remembered seeing raw Federal soldiers coming under attack at Shiloh who had been issued weapons only days before, on the way up the Tennessee, "and were hardly able to load their muskets according to the manual." Their officers knew no

33. Hewett, in Jay Luvaas, *The Military Legacy of the Civil War: The European Inheritance* (Lawrence: University of Kansas Press, 1999 [1959]), 27; David L. Thompson, "With Burnside at Antietam," in *Battles and Leaders*, 2:660; Sherman, *Memoirs of General W. T. Sherman*, 885–86; "Address of General D. H. Hill," October 22, 1885, in *Southern Historical Society Papers* 13 (January–December 1885): 261.

34. Bell I. Wiley, *The Life of Billy Yank*, 51; Brent Nosworthy, *The Bloody Crucible of Courage: Fighting Methods and Combat Experience of the Civil War* (New York: Carroll and Graf, 2005), 144–45; "Report of Col. William B. Franklin," July 28, 1861, in *War of the Rebellion*, Series One, 2:407.

better, and Grant could only concede that it was perfectly natural "that many of the regiments broke at the first fire."[35]

The weapon which the volunteer was expected to master, on his own or otherwise, would depend largely on which branch of the service he volunteered to serve in: the infantry, the service of the common foot soldier; the cavalry, that of the horse-mounted soldier; or the artillery, which serviced the various sizes and shapes of cannon that supported the infantry or protected fortifications. Both armies also recruited engineering and medical services and attracted a plethora of chaplains, clerks, and civilian peddlers known as sutlers, who accompanied the combat soldiers on campaign. The infantry was the backbone of the army, and the burden of winning a battle or a campaign invariably rested on the skills and endurance of the infantryman. Approximately 80 percent of the entire Union army was infantry, with 14 percent serving in the cavalry and 6 percent in the artillery. In the Confederate army, the differential was much the same: 75 percent of all enlisted Confederates served in the infantry, with another 20 percent in the cavalry and the remaining 5 percent in the artillery.[36]

The basic infantry weapon was the Model 1861 United States Rifle Musket, frequently known as the "Springfield" (from the Springfield, Massachusetts, armory where most of them were made), a 58.5-inch-long, single-shot, muzzle-loading rifle, weighing 9 pounds 4 ounces and fitted to carry a 21-inch-long triangular socket bayonet, which converted the rifle into an improvised pike for close-at-hand fighting. The rifle musket was, in theory, a distinct improvement over the inaccurate and short-range smoothbore muskets that had been the common weapon of armies from the mid-eighteenth century up through the wars of Napoleon Bonaparte. The standard British Army's "Brown Bess" musket was dependable for hitting a target only up to 40 yards, useful for hitting things in general only up to 80 yards, and little more than guesswork at 140 yards. (During Wellington's campaigns in Spain, it was estimated that one casualty was inflicted for every 459 shots fired.) For that reason, musket fire was best delivered in simultaneous-fire volleys, propelling a large cloud of bullets at an oncoming enemy force, which would compel it to stop, return fire, or go to ground (in which case it was unlikely to start moving forward again).[37]

The rifle musket, however, featured spiral grooving on the inside of the musket barrel that gripped the bullet as it was fired, gave it a spiral twist, and thus straightened its flight to its target. Rifles had been in military use for almost a hundred years, but their loading process was tedious and difficult, a problem not solved until the

35. Miller, *Training of an Army*, 115; Ulysses S. Grant, "The Battle of Shiloh," in *Battles and Leaders*, 1:473.

36. Robertson, *Soldiers Blue and Gray*, 19.

37. Philip Haythornewaite, *British Napoleonic Infantry Tactics, 1792–1815* (Oxford: Osprey, 2008), 23; Strachan, *From Waterloo to Balaclava*, 32.

1840s by French army captains Louis-Etienne de Thouvenin and Claude-Etienne Minié, who experimented with cone-shaped bullets that made the loading process substantially easier. Due to the deadly slow spin imparted by the grooves (the rifling, which gave the weapon its name), a rifle musket firing one of Minié's conical, soft-lead slugs (hilariously misnamed the "minnie ball" after its designer) could hit an eleven-inch bull's-eye at 350 yards and could penetrate six inches of pine board at 500 yards.

The rifle musket received its first practical tests in North Africa in 1846, the Crimean War (1854–56), and the North Italian War of 1859, and in short order the British Army reequipped its soldiers with a British-made version of the Minié-system rifle, the .577 caliber Enfield, followed by the Austrians (who developed the .54 caliber Lorenz rifle in 1854), the Russians, and the United States, with then secretary of war Jefferson Davis presiding over the development of the .58-caliber Springfield. Federal arsenals manufactured almost 700,000 of the 1861 Model Springfields for use during the war, while twenty private Northern arms manufacturers supplied 450,000 more. Approximately 400,000 Enfields were run through the blockade to equip the Confederate armies, who had no access to the Springfield rifle beyond what could be scavenged from battlefields, along with an assortment of Austrian Lorenz rifles, Belgian-made Minié rifles, and smoothbore conversions.[38]

The rifle, however, remained slow to load, requiring a sequence of nine separate steps (known as "load in nine times"). Each Minié ball, packed into a cigar-shaped paper tube along with sixty grains of black powder, had to be removed from the soldier's cartridge box, torn open with the teeth, emptied into the barrel through the muzzle (which required standing the weapon upright on its stock), and rammed home with a long thin steel ramrod. Then the infantryman would have to raise the musket, fit a percussion cap onto the nipple of the lock plate above the trigger, and pull the trigger, exploding the percussion cap and igniting the powder charge in the barrel. Although the optimal firing rate was three rounds per minute, the practical reality under battlefield conditions was closer to one round every four to five minutes.

The Sharps Rifle, a .52 caliber rifle that could be loaded from the rifle's breech rather than by the muzzle, was invented by Christian Sharps in 1844, and was favored as a sharpshooter's rifle. But even the Sharps rifle was still a single-shot, one-by-one affair. It remained for Christopher Miner Spencer, a Connecticut inventor, to develop a seven-shot repeating rifle, firing manufactured brass cartridges from a magazine in the stock of the rifle, which streamlined the tedious and dangerously exposed process of loading and reloading. Alongside Spencer's rifle, the Colt Patent Firearms company introduced a repeating rifle with a peculiar five-chambered

---

38. Earl J. Hess, *The Rifle Musket in Civil War Combat: Reality and Myth* (Lawrence, KS: University Press of Kansas, 2008), 24–25; Joseph G. Bilby, *Civil War Firearms: Their Historical Background, Tactical Use and Modern Collecting and Shooting* (Conshohocken, PA: Combined Books, 1996), 62–66.

revolving cylinder, while the New Haven Arms Company's Henry repeating rifle could carry fifteen rounds in its magazine, and could reload a new cartridge and eject a spent one with a single lever motion.[39]

Oddly, the repeating rifles failed to get the approval of the army's chief of ordnance, James Wolfe Ripley. Part of this distrust may have been simple obstinacy on the part of the sixty-seven-year-old Ripley. Ripley had at least some justification in fearing that the move to rapid-fire repeating rifles would put too much stress on the federal arsenals' ability to supply the repeaters' ammunition in sufficient quantities to the Union armies. Breech-loading repeating rifles encouraged soldiers to blaze away without regard for supply, and Ripley had enough trouble supplying soldiers with sufficient ammunition for their muzzle-loaders without having to think of the quantities of expensive, brass-encased repeating cartridges he would have to supply for an army full of repeaters (Spencer cartridges cost more than two dollars apiece). As it was, an early government contract for 10,000 Spencer repeaters was nearly lost by Spencer when his small factory was unable to keep up a supply of the weapons or their ammunition. Whatever else was wrong with the Springfield, it was a simple and durable weapon and cost little more than half the price of a Henry repeater or a Spencer, while the Enfield and Springfield both accepted the same standardized Minié ball.

These arguments were perfectly plausible to an army bureaucrat; they meant a good deal less to the soldier in the field. In 1861, Colonel Hiram Berdan went over Ripley's head to the president to get authorization to arm his two regiments of United States Sharpshooters with the Sharps breech-loading rifle; and in 1863 Colonel John T. Wilder offered to buy Spencer repeating rifles for his brigade out of the contributions of the men themselves. (Ripley relented on this occasion and refunded the cost of purchase to Wilder's men.) Wilder's men got the first test of their repeaters in June 1863, when they easily outshot both Confederate cavalry and infantry at Hoover's Gap, Tennessee. In August Spencer got an opportunity to display his repeating rifle before Abraham Lincoln, and on September 15 Ripley was officially retired. By January 1865, the Ordnance Bureau was no longer even considering new models of muzzle-loaders. By contrast with Union hesitancy, the Confederates were much more willing to experiment with new weapons and were happy to capture as many Spencers as they could. But the South lacked the technology to manufacture its own copy of the Spencer, and it had no way at all to manufacture the special metal cartridges for use in captured repeaters.[40]

39. Hess, *The Rifle Musket in Civil War Combat*, 17–18; W. W. Greener, *Modern Breech-loaders: Sporting and Military* (London: Cassell, Petter and Galpin, 1871), 186–87.

40. Charles Augustus Stevens, *Berdan's United States Sharpshooters in the Army of the Potomac, 1861–1865* (St. Paul, MN: Price-McGill, 1892), 7; Roy M. Marcot, *U.S. Sharpshooters: Berdan's Civil War Elite* (Mechanicsburg, PA: Stackpole, 2007), 47–48; Robert V. Bruce, *Lincoln and the Tools of War* (Urbana: University of Illinois Press, 1956), 252–56, 261–64.

The most common tactical formation that the volunteer infantryman fell into was the "line of battle": a regiment drawn up in two long ranks, one behind the other, with a thin curtain of skirmishers in front to clear the advance and another thin curtain of sergeants and lieutenants in the rear to give orders and restrain cowards and shirkers. Attack in line of battle had been the formula for the British army's successful assault against the Russians at the Alma River in 1854, and the received wisdom was that "the formation in line—that is to say, the extended volley, followed by the charge—is the most effective" at winning victories.[41]

As the line moved forward, alignment was maintained by sergeants and corporals on the flanks of the lines, bearing small flags called guidons in their musket barrels; and by a color guard in the center of the front line, bearing the regiment's national and state flag. In the midst of movement and battle, these regimental colors could be the most important markers and pointers of all, since they could be seen and followed when drums and orders could not be heard. The position regimental colors occupied in battle also made them the most potent emotional symbol of the Civil War soldiers' group identity. Attempts to capture or defend regimental colors under near-suicidal conditions became appallingly routine in Civil War combat, and the example of the 19th Massachusetts, which lost thirteen color-bearers within ten minutes of fighting at Fredericksburg, is a case in point:

> The two color-bearers, Sergt. Ronello B. Creasey, of Co. I, and Corp. Winfield Rappell, of Co. B, were among the first to fall, but the colors were instantly picked up and the line hastily withdrew. Re-forming under cover of the canal bank, the regiment again advanced. . . . Again the color bearers were shot down. Sergt. Charles B. Brown, of Company G, was the seventh man to grasp the colors and he quickly received a wound in the head which stunned him. Lieut. Hume, thinking the wound a mortal one, told him to give up the colors, but he refused saying, "I will not give them to any man." Finding that he was fast becoming weak, Brown rushed out in advance of the line, staggered and fell, driving the color lance into the earth; and there he lay, dizzy and bleeding, still grasping the lance with both hands until Lieut. Hume caught them up. A color corporal then took it, while Edgar M. Newcomb grasped the other, the bearer of which had also fallen. Lieut. Newcomb shouted "Forward" and the quivering line sprang on again, but as he spoke the brave lieutenant was hit by a shot which passed through and shattered the bones of both legs below the knees. As he fell, he handed his color to Second Lieut. J. G. B. Adams, who was then in command of Co. I. "Don't let them go down!" exclaimed Newcomb. ("It seemed as if I grasped for death, expecting every moment to be my last," said Lieut. Adams afterward.) Instantly the color corporal with the

41. "The Column of Attack," *Colburn's United Service Magazine and Military Journal* 70 (1852): 199; Ian Fletcher and Natalia Ishchenko, *The Battle of the Alma: First Blood to the Allies in the Crimea* (South Yorkshire: Pen and Sword, 2008), 140; Michael Barthorp, *The British Army on Campaign, 1816–1902: The Crimea, 1854–1856* (Oxford: Osprey, 1987), 3, 9–10, 11.

other flag was felled by a wound and it was grasped by Sergt. Chas. L. Merrill, of Co. C . . . and he, too, fell wounded. The man who seized the flag when Sergt. Merrill fell was at once struck down by a ball and as the color again dropped, Lieut. Adams caught that also. He now held the two flags of the regiment in his hands. . . . Realizing that it meant sure death and probably the loss of both colors if he stayed where he was, Lieut. Adams rushed across the field to the left and reached the shelter of a fence.[42]

No wonder that, when the colonel of the 51st New York asked his regiment "if they would exchange" their old bullet-shredded state color for a new one, "the boys let up such a yell as convinced the Colonel that the City would have a good time getting that old Flag." Lieutenant George Washington Whitman (Walt Whitman's brother) of the 51st added, "It has 15 or 20 bullet holes in it and the staff was shot in two at New Bern, and we think a great deal of it." James Madison Williams had a similar reaction when the 21st Alabama was sent a new flag to replace the one damaged at Shiloh: "I like the ragged old flag torn with the enemy's shot, that we carried through the fight, better than all the flags in the Confederacy. . . ."[43]

Heroic as all this seems, it also appears to modern eyes as puzzlingly suicidal, since few things seem more counterintuitive on a battlefield than soldiers standing up in plain view in neat, tightly bunched lines, as if on parade instead of in combat, offering themselves as perfect targets to their enemy. And it would have been, had the new weapons technology of the rifle musket been as revolutionary as it seemed. While the rifle musket offered increased range and accuracy to its users, the increases were limited by two factors. First, rifle muskets, like the old smoothbores, still used black powder as a propellant, which not only quickly fouled the barrel with caked powder residue but also kicked out billowing clouds of whitish gray smoke. These banks of powder smoke "hung pall-like over the fields and woods all day along the battle lines," often becoming "so thick and dense sometimes during the day that it was impossible to discern anything fifty paces away, and at midday the smoke was so thick overhead that I could just make out to see the sun, and it looked like a vast ball of red fire hanging in a smoke-veiled sky."[44] All the technological improvements in accuracy and range would mean nothing if a target could not be seen.

---

42. *History of the Nineteenth Regiment, Massachusetts Volunteer Infantry, 1861–1865*, ed. E. L. Waite (Salem, MA: Salem Press, 1906), 180–81.

43. George Washington Whitman, *Civil War Letters of George Washington Whitman*, ed. Jerome M. Loving (Durham, NC: Duke University Press, 1975), 56; James M. Williams, *From That Terrible Field: Civil War Letters of James M. Williams, Twenty-first Alabama Infantry Volunteers*, ed. John Kent Folmar (University: University of Alabama Press, 1981), 60.

44. George Michael Neese, *Three Years in the Confederate Horse Artillery* (New York: Neale, 1911), 261; Earl J. Hess, *Pickett's Charge: The Last Attack at Gettysburg* (Chapel Hill: University of North Carolina Press, 2001), 197–98.

Second, the rifling in the barrel slowed the speed of the round (the old Brown Bess smoothbore had a muzzle velocity of 1,500 feet per second; the new Enfield's rifling dropped the muzzle velocity to 1,115 feet per second). Lacking that speed, the rifle's Minié ball followed a curved trajectory that could drop as much as fourteen feet over 300 yards. A rifleman had to be carefully trained to make allowance for the drop of the bullet by aiming *above* the actual target (which is why rifle muskets were fitted with backsights, to induce the rifleman to raise his rifle above the line of sight while seeming to aim straight at the target) and by mentally calculating the distance and speed of his target, since the bullet would drop onto its target rather than hitting it in a straight line in front of him.[45]

The rifle may have had the potential for greater accuracy and longer range, but only under ideal conditions, with clear lines of sight and exact knowledge of the range of the target at each moment. That meant that the actual improvements in killing power offered by the rifle musket remained limited. One South Carolina officer thought the hitting rate of the rifle came down to only 1 in 400. Lt. Cadmus Wilcox, who was commissioned in the 1850s to write a handbook on the use of the rifle musket (and who would later serve as a Confederate general), insisted that "a Rifle, whatever may be its range and accuracy, in the hands of a soldier unskilled in its use, loses much of its value." It required "the most detailed and thorough practical instruction as to the means of preserving the piece, and . . . teaching the soldier the art of firing"—little of which was ever possible under the actual conditions of combat.[46]

The only practical way to make the infantry's firepower count, even armed with rifle muskets, was the old-fashioned method of delivering simultaneous-fire volleys. That, in turn, required bunching infantrymen into lines so as to maximize the concentration of fire and sufficiently multiply the likelihood of hitting enough targets to give an attacker second thoughts. The musket's only real offensive use was as a means of suppressing a defending enemy's fire until the attacker had moved near enough to close with the bayonet. It was the sharp, menacing bayonet that would crack a defending enemy's courage and send the enemy fleeing pell-mell to the rear. The bayonet also required bunching and drilling of its own so that a unit of attacking infantrymen could drive through a defender's volley and be on top of them with the bayonet before the defender could reload. "No troops," declared Sir Charles Napier, "stand a charge of bayonets, and whoever charges first has the victory." No wonder, then, that the goal of combat was still to close with the bayonet as quickly as possible. British experience in the Sepoy Rebellion of 1857 had shown the value

45. William Valmore Izlar, *A Sketch of the War Record of the Edisto Rifles, 1861–1865* (Columbia, SC: State, 1914), 55–57; Nosworthy, *Bloody Crucible of Courage*, 30–34; Hess, *The Rifle Musket*, 30.

46. Cadmus M. Wilcox, *Rifles and Rifle Practice: An Elementary Treatise upon the Theory of Rifle Firing* (New York: D. Van Nostrand, 1859), 238.

of the bayonet over and over again, and as he exhorted his troops before the battle of Solferino in 1859, Napoleon III warned them, "In battle, remain closed-up and do not abandon your ranks to run forward. Avoid too great an élan: that is the only thing I fear. The many arms of precision are only dangerous from afar; they will not prevent the bayonet from being, as it was before, the terrible arm of the French infantry . . ."[47]

Every battlefield of the 1850s seemed to reinforce the lesson that the bayonet would cause defending formations to disintegrate, even when armed with rifles. At the battles of Montebello (May 20, 1859) and Magenta (June 4, 1859), French bayonet charges still won the day against Austrian units armed with rifle muskets. A sublieutenant in Patrice de MacMahon's 2nd Corps at Magenta described how "we were in column by platoons at section distance; we advanced in echelons, with the second battalion a little bit back, a company of skirmishers in front . . . Reaching within 150 meters of the Austrians, one could distinctly see wavering in their lines; the first ranks were throwing themselves back on the rear ranks." No one less than Karl Marx's partner in writing *The Communist Manifesto*, Friedrich Engels, announced that "the Italian War proved to all who could see, that the fire from modern rifles is not necessarily so very dangerous to a battalion charging with spirit . . . passive defense, if ever so well armed, is always sure of defeat."[48]

The task of a good line officer, therefore, was to master the combat algorithm—to be able to calculate, on the spot, the distance and oncoming speed of an attacking force and understand how many volleys might be needed to halt or disrupt the attackers, and how to keep his troops well in hand. On the offensive, the officer would be able to calculate the depth of the enemy's force, their rate of fire, how much distance he could cover at a speed which would shorten the defenders' opportunities to fire, and how fast he could push his troops until they are ready to close with the bayonet. He would also understand when reinforcement was required and how artillery could best support his troops. All of this would require elaborate training in drill, bayonet, and firing procedures, both for officers and for men in the ranks—a finishing school in training that the volunteer armies of the Civil War lacked the leadership and the time to acquire. The raw inexperience of Civil War officers, the poor training in firearms offered to the Civil War recruit,

47. Napier to Sir John Pennefather, March 11, 1846, in Henry Knollys, *Life of General Sir Hope Grant: With Selections from His Correspondence* (Edinburgh: W. Blackwood, 1894), 1:97; Saul David, *The Indian Mutiny: 1857* (New York: Viking, 2002), 250; Brooks, *Solferino 1859*, 26.

48. Patrick Marder, "The French Campaign of 1859," *Military History Online*, www.militaryhistoryonline. com/19thcentury/articles/frenchcampaignof1859.aspx; Friedrich Engels, "The History of the Rifle," December 29, 1860, in *Engels as Military Critic: Articles Reprinted from the Volunteer Journal and the Manchester Guardian of the 1860s*, ed. W. H. Chaloner and W. O. Henderson (Manchester: Manchester University Press, 1959), 64.

and the obstacles created by the American terrain generally cut down the effective range of Civil War fire combat to little more than eighty yards, at which point the technological advantage of a rifle over a smoothbore musket shrank to the vanishing point.

Five years before the Civil War broke out, a three-man U.S. military commission (whose junior member was none other than George B. McClellan) warned, "As a nation, other than in resources and general intelligence of our people, we are without the elements of military knowledge and efficiency of sudden emergency. . . . We possess a nucleus of military knowledge in the country barely sufficient for the wants of our army in time of peace." Sure enough, in 1861 officers and men who were unschooled in the need to close with the enemy ended up slugging matters out in short-range firefights, piling up bullet-riddled corpses until one side or the other collapsed and retreated. Instead of pressing attacks home and accepting the higher danger of the assault for a shorter period of time, Civil War volunteers were more likely to go to ground, and as the war grew longer, soldiers on both sides entrenched more and more—a development that West Point–trained regular officers were not reluctant to applaud.[49]

The American volunteer, remarked the British army's Capt. Henry Charles Fletcher (an officer in the elite Scots Guards, and a veteran of the Crimea), possessed "indomitable perseverance, cheerfulness under fatigue and hardship, diligence in entrenching, and stubbornness in defending these entrenchments." But "the rapid, well sustained attack, which in many of the great European combats has led to important success, does not appear adapted to the qualities" of the American soldier. That, in turn, was what made so many of the immense and bloody battles of the Civil War surprisingly resultless. Elisha Paxton, a lieutenant in Stonewall Jackson's brigade, complained in 1862 that "our victories . . . seem to settle nothing; to bring us no nearer the end of the war. It is only so many killed and wounded, leaving the work of blood to go on with renewed vigor."[50]

The terrific rates of death in the infantry might have persuaded more men to seek service in the cavalry or artillery had those components not had their problems, too. Artillery in the nineteenth century could be roughly divided into two groups, field artillery and heavy artillery. The field artillery was organized into regiments composed of ten batteries, with each battery made up of six cannon, and each cannon pulled by a team of six horses, along with ammunition chests and portable forges. The guns themselves were hitched to limbers, and they were served by crews of up

---

49. Nosworthy, *Roll Call to Destiny*, 20.

50. Henry Charles Fletcher, *History of the American War* (London: R. Bentley, 1866), 3:366; Gerald F. Linderman, *Embattled Courage: The Experience of Combat in the American Civil War* (New York: Free Press, 1987), 250; Elisha Paxton, October 12, 1862, in John G. Paxton, *Memoir and Memorials: Elisha Franklin Paxton, Brigadier-General, C.S.A.* (New York: Neale, 1907), 66.

seven men who aimed, fired, and loaded them in a sequence even more complex than the "load in nine times" required for a rifle musket.

The size and tasks of the guns varied almost as much as the infantry's weapons, and they could vary from the light, portable mountain howitzer (with a bronze barrel only thirty-seven inches long) to the big cast-iron 10-pounder and 20-pounder Parrott rifled guns (so named from their inventor, Robert Parker Parrott, as well as from the weight of the shot they fired and the rifling grooves in their barrels). The most popular field guns were the easily handled 3-inch wrought-iron Ordnance rifle and the 12-pounder bronze smoothbore Napoleon (named for Napoleon III, its designer). The smoothbore Napoleon, which could alternately do the work of a high-trajectory howitzer or a line-of-sight field gun, was the Civil War battlefield's maid of all work. "Nothing surpasses . . . the impression of a battery of 12-pound smoothbores which approaches to within 400–600 paces of the enemy," Robert E. Lee assured the Prussian military observer Justus Scheibert. "In such moments rifled artillery, the advantages of which in open country I fully appreciate, cannot replace the smoothbore." By 1863, half of the artillery force of Civil War armies was composed of 12-pounder Napoleons.[51]

The kinds of ammunition used varied as well, depending on the need of the moment. Most Civil War field batteries fired four basic kinds of shot. The artilleryman's standby was solid shot, a solid iron ball, either wrought or cast iron, which relied on its weight and the speed of its impact to destroy a target. Solid shot had the terrifying capacity of "bounding like rubber balls" along a line of battle, and could "come right at the line with the sound of a huge circular saw ripping a log." Civil War artillery also turned to shell, a hollow sphere or cone containing powder or other explodables ignited by a charge in the base of the cone, with the fuse cut to a predetermined length to ensure the shell enough flying time to reach its target before exploding and shredding anything around it with razor-sharp white-hot splinters. Case shot (or shrapnel, so named after its British inventor, Lt. Henry Shrapnel) was a shell filled with eighty musket balls and "a small charge of powder," which "scattered scores of cast-iron bullets when it exploded."[52]

51. Fairfax Downey, *Sound of the Guns: The Story of American Artillery from the Ancient and Honorable Company to the Atom Cannon and Guided Missile* (New York: D. McKay, 1956), 121; William E. Birkhimer, *Historical Sketch of the Organization, Administration, Matériel and Tactics of the Artillery, United States Army* (Washington, DC: J. J. Chapman, 1884), 286–87; *The Ordnance Manual for the Use of the Officers of the United States Army* (Philadelphia: J. B. Lippincott, 1862), 14, 18–21; J. G. Benton, *A Course of Instruction in Ordnance and Gunnery Compiled for the Use of the Cadets of the United States Military Academy* (New York: D. Van Nostrand, 1862), 112–13, 166–68, 516–23; Scheibert, in Luvaas, *Military Legacy of the Civil War*, 66.

52. William W. Strong, *History of the 121st Regiment Pennsylvania Volunteers: "An Account from the Ranks"* (Philadelphia: Catholic Standard and Times, 1906), 31; "The Rifle and the Spade, or the Future of Field Operations," *Journal of the United Service Institution* 3 (1860): 173–74; Henry Nichols Blake, *Three Years in the Army of the Potomac* (Boston: Lee and Shepard, 1866), 217; R. L. Murray, *E. P. Alexander and the Artillery Action in the Peach Orchard* (Wolcott, NY: Benedum Books, 2000), 7–8; Richard Holmes, *Sahib: The British Soldier in India, 1750–1914* (London: HarperCollins, 2005), 337; Joseph A. Frank and George A. Reaves, *Seeing the Elephant: Raw Recruits at the Battle of Shiloh* (New York: Greenwood Press, 1989), 103, 136.

The most fearsome load in the artillery limber was canister, a tin cylinder packed with balls or slugs. Canister was a short-range item that could turn a cannon into a giant sawed-off shotgun. Used on masses of infantry at close ranges, it could be hideous in its effect. A Napoleon gun triple-shotted with three canister tins could blow 650 lead balls into an oncoming enemy unit, equivalent to the fire of an entire infantry brigade. A New York infantryman in 1864 watched, horrified, as a single Napoleon, packed to the muzzle with tins of canister, fragmented the attack of an entire Confederate infantry column:

> As soon as the enemy had moved his column out of the cover of the woods and was advancing along the road, the gun of the Twelfth New York battery was fired into the head of the column with a triple charge of canister. The road over which the enemy advanced was hard and smooth and the best possible for the effective use of canister, as the bullets which did not strike the enemy directly did so on the rebound. The column melted away under the fire, and when the smoke arose no trace of it appeared.[53]

More often, however, artillery was used in the Civil War mostly to disorganize and disrupt attacking infantry formations, rather than actually to kill or maim individuals, and it served its purpose best by preventing enemy formations from getting close enough to do damage to one's own infantry. "The principal object of artillery," wrote the artillerists' guru, John Gibbon, "is, to sustain the troops in attack and defense; to facilitate their movements and oppose the enemy's; to destroy his forces as well as the obstacles which protect them; and to keep up the combat until an opportunity is offered for a decisive blow." To that end, Civil War artillery, which at the opening of the war was parceled out battery by battery in piecemeal fashion to infantry brigades and divisions, increasingly came to be used in mass formations like those of Bonaparte's grand battery at Waterloo or the French artillery at Solferino in 1859. Likewise, the ratio of artillery to infantry spiraled upward. In 1844, the British army stipulated a distribution of two guns per 1,000 men, but by the middle of the Civil War the ratio in the Army of the Potomac had risen to four guns per 1,000 infantrymen.[54]

The Union's industrial resources gave it the technical edge in artillery all through the Civil War. However, the rural and agrarian structure of Southern society gave the Confederacy an equal edge in terms of cavalry. The Confederacy also possessed

---

53. George K. Dauchy, "The Battle of Ream's Station," May 8, 1890, in *Military Essays and Recollections: Papers Read Before the Commandery of the State of Illinois, Military Order of the Loyal Legion of the United States* (Chicago: A. C. McClurg, 1899), 136.

54. Paddy Griffith, *French Napoleonic Infantry Tactics, 1792–1815* (Oxford: Osprey, 2007), 52–53; John Gibbon, *The Artillerist's Manual, Compiled from Various Sources and Adapted to the Service of the United States* (New York: D. Van Nostrand, 1860), 389; J. M. Spearman, *The British Gunner* (London: Parker, Furneval and Parker, 1844), n.p.

several great natural cavalry leaders: in the west, Nathan Bedford Forrest used his cavalry to burn and pillage Union supply lines with virtual impunity; in the east, J. E. B. Stuart, the twenty-eight-year-old commander of Lee's cavalry, easily rode circles around McClellan's clumsy Northern cavalrymen—on the Peninsula, he literally rode around McClellan's entire army—and created an image of the Confederate cavalry as banjo-strumming knights-errant dressed in plumes and capes. The great difficulty with cavalry was that it was costly to maintain—the Union's quartermaster general, Montgomery Meigs, had to keep up a supply of 35,000 horses to the Army of the Potomac for just the six months between May and October 1863 at a cost to the government of $144 to $185 a head—and the South was forced to restrict the size of its cavalry arm simply through its inability to provide mounts (much of the Confederate cavalry was actually mounted on horses owned by the troopers themselves). The average life expectancy of a horse in the Army of Northern Virginia was less than eight months, and every fifteen months a supply of 7,000 horses and 14,000 mules was required just to keep the army mobile.[55]

If the combat training of Civil War volunteer infantry left a great deal to be desired, the training of Civil War volunteer cavalryman was even worse, and also because it, too, involved time and costs that neither army was willing to absorb. In the British army, cavalry training required at least 120 hours of riding drill, plus training in stable work, saddling, and packing. "The difficulty of converting raw men into soldiers is enhanced manifold when they are mounted," complained Richard Taylor, who rose from commanding Harry Handerson's 9th Louisiana to lead the Confederate Department of East Louisiana, Mississippi and Alabama, and this seemed especially and painfully true when it came to dealing with Taylor's own Confederate cavalry.

> Both man and horse require training, and facilities for rambling, with temptation to do so, are increased. There was but little time, and it may be said less disposition, to establish camps of instruction. Living on horseback, fearless, and dashing, the men of the South afforded the best possible material for cavalry. They had every quality but discipline, and resembled Prince Charming, whose manifold gifts, bestowed by her sisters, were rendered useless by the malignant fairy. Scores of them wandered about the country like locusts, and were only less destructive to their own people than the enemy. . . . Assuredly, our cavalry rendered much excellent service, especially when dismounted and fighting as infantry. Such able officers as Stuart, Hampton, and the younger Lees in the east, Forrest, Green, and Wheeler in the west, developed much

55. Stephen Z. Starr, *The Union Cavalry in the Civil War: The War in the East from Gettysburg to Appomattox, 1863–1865* (Baton Rouge: Louisiana State University Press, 1981), 14; Weigley, *Quartermaster General of the Union Army*, 257; J. Boone Bartholomees, *Buff Facings and Gilt Buttons: Staff and Headquarters Operations in the Army of Northern Virginia, 1861–1865* (Columbia: University of South Carolina Press, 1998), 62–63.

talent for war; but their achievement, however distinguished, fell far below the standard that would have been reached had not the want of discipline impaired their efforts and those of their men.

North Carolina governor Zebulon Vance grew so exasperated with the indiscipline of Confederate cavalry wandering through his state that he cried out in 1863: "If God Almighty had yet in store another plague worse than all others which he intended to have let loose on the Egyptians in case Pharaoh still hardened his heart, I am sure it must have been a regiment or so of half-armed, half-disciplined Confederate cavalry."[56]

If the Civil War departs from the pattern of the Napoleonic wars at any major point, it is in its failure to use cavalry to achieve the kinds of decisive victories on the battlefield that the Napoleonic pattern had taught generals to expect. From the seventeenth century onward, cavalry had been taught to charge home with the sword or lance at the first sign of wavering on the part of enemy infantry. The sheer weight of an oncoming rush of horses and men could strike the final amount of terror needed to convince infantrymen to break and bolt. And when they did, the cavalry could cut them down and scatter them almost at its ease. This sort of cavalry—known as heavy cavalry, from the outsize weight and height of the horses and men chosen for the task—was expensive to equip and time-consuming to train, and one penny-pinching Congress after another had shown no interest in it. Moreover, in the uneven overgrowth of the American landscape, heavy cavalry had little room to develop the momentum needed for its climactic charges; and in the American West, where most of the army's cavalry was deployed, its enemy were mounted Indians, who required lightness and speed to pursue.[57]

So, strictly speaking, the army did not even bother to create a cavalry arm until the 1850s; its few mounted units were organized and trained as dragoons and mounted rifles who would use their horses more as a means of transportation than for combat, and dismount in battle to fight on foot with their short-barrel carbines rather than sabers or lances. Cavalry units in the Civil War were also deployed in smaller ratios to infantry than in Europe, and concentrated almost exclusively on the traditional occupations of light cavalry, including scouting, raiding, and skirmishing. The introduction of the Spencer repeating carbine (the downsized version of the rifle issued for cavalry use) only accelerated this trend, making the classical

56. Michael Asher, *Khartoum: The Ultimate Imperial Adventure* (New York: Viking, 2005), 112; Richard Taylor, *Destruction and Reconstruction: Personal Experiences of the Late War*, ed. Charles P. Roland (Waltham, MA: Blaisdell, 1968 [1879]), 53; Zebulon Vance to James Seddon, December 21, 1863, in *The War of the Rebellion*, 2:1061–62.

57. Strachan, *From Waterloo to Balaclava*, 75, 77.

cavalry saber useless as a field weapon. "The only real use I ever heard of their being put to was to hold a piece of meat over a fire for frying," snorted John Singleton Mosby, the most famous of the Confederacy's mounted scouts. "I dragged one through the first year of the war, but when I became a commander, I discarded it." Sabers came out of their scabbards only on the infrequent occasions when cavalry clashed headlong with cavalry; on the even rarer occasions when cavalrymen actually engaged enemy infantry, they dismounted and fought on foot with their carbines. Lt. Col. Arthur Fremantle, yet another British observer from the Guards brigade, had no opinion whatsoever of the legendary J. E. B. Stuart's horsemen. Their battles "are miserable affairs" in which "neither party has any idea of serious charging with the sabre." Instead, "they hesitate, halt, and commence a desultory fire with carbines and revolvers," which hardly qualified them to "be called cavalry in the European sense of the word."[58]

THE MAKING OF THE ARMIES

The volunteer who mastered the intricacies of his weapon and drill would leave his "camp of instruction" with the rest of his regiment and be shipped off to wherever the main armies might be at that moment. From that point on, the basic organizational unit, and the unit most soldiers used to identify themselves, was the regiment. Unlike the regimental system of the British army, the volunteer regiments of the Civil War had no previous history. They were the creations of 1861, having no existing traditions or institutions with which to shelter and socialize the new recruit, no already existing cadres of officers or non-commissioned officers, and no barracks or recruiting depots. It fell on the volunteers themselves to turn their regiments into either livable facsimiles of home life or freewheeling moral carousels. Some units, like the two regiments of Hiram Berdan's United States Sharpshooters, prided themselves on living "like a band of brothers, imbued with the one feeling of patriotism in their voluntary enlistment for three years." Others converted the long stretches of empty camp time into study halls, as did a young lieutenant in the Confederate Army, Basil Gildersleeve, who improved his command of "his English classics" and "his ancient classics." In the 7th Ohio, the company recruited from the pious students of Charles Finney at Oberlin College made sure that "daily prayer meetings were established." St. Clair A. Mulholland described the camp of his 116th Pennsylvania as a religious idyll where "seldom was an obscene word or an oath heard in the camp" and "meetings for prayer were of almost daily occurrence, and the groups of

---

58. Weigley, *The American Way of War*, 71; *Memoirs of Colonel John S. Mosby* (Nashville, TN: J. B. Sanders, 1995 [1917]), 30; Fremantle, *Three Months in the Southern States—April-June 1863* (Lincoln: University of Nebraska Press, 1991 [1864]), 284–85; Griffith, *Battle Tactics of the Civil War*, 181–86.

men sitting on the ground or gathered on the hill side listening to the Gospel were strong reminders of the mounds of Galilee when the people sat upon the ground to hear the Savior teach."[59]

In other regiments, the abrupt transition from domestic routine to the poorly structured life of an army camp meant crossing over a social line where the customary behavioral restraints might mean very little. Prostitution, drunkenness, gambling, and thievery were rife in both Federal and Confederate regiments. "Gen. Meagher got up this morning & drank about a quart of whiskey," wrote a disgusted Theodore Gates in his diary in 1864, "& went to bed again & has been there all day drunk." The 154th New York were "good companions" for the most part, "but at the same time there is much going on in camp that is not intended to improve the morals nor the manners or the mind." Army life "seems adapted to make a man coarse & rough," and "many a man does that here that he would be utterly ashamed to do at home and excuses himself by saying that others do it or that it is customary in the Army to do it." Edward King Wightman found that "most of our common soldiers are scarcely above brutes by nature."

> The privates, of course, are not such people as you or any sensible man would choose, or perhaps I should say could endure, as associates. As a mass, they are ignorant, envious, mercenary, and disgustingly immoral and profane. Being as they are here free from the restraints of civil law, they give loose rein to all their vices and make a boast of them. In our whole regiment, I know no private who will not curse and swear and but few who will not, when circumstances favor, rob and steal or, as they more euphon[i]ously style the operations, "briz things."[60]

On paper, Civil War regiments were supposed to contain eight to ten companies of approximately 100 enlisted men and officers each, commanded by a colonel, so the full strength of a regiment ought to have been, more or less, 1,000 men. In the Union Army, however, regiments were often allowed to dwindle down to between 200 and 300 men, as the ranks were thinned by sickness and casualties. The reason for this neglect was nakedly political. Since the volunteer regiments were raised by the states, it was easier for many Northern governors to create new regiments, and thus create new openings for cronies whom they wished to reward with officers' commissions, than to keep refilling the old regiments.

59. Stevens, *Berdan's United States Sharpshooters*, 20; Basil L. Gildersleeve, "A Southerner in the Peloponnesian War," *Atlantic Monthly* 80 (September 1897): 338; Theodore Wilder, *The History of Company C, Seventh Regiment, O.V.I.* (Oberlin, OH: J. B. T. Marsh, 1866), 6; St. Clair A. Mulholland, *The Story of the 116th Regiment, Pennsylvania Infantry* (Baltimore, MD: Butternut and Blue, 1991 [1895]), 184.

60. *The Civil War Diaries of Col. Theodore B. Gates, 20th New York State Militia*, ed. Seward R. Osborne (Hightstown, NJ: Longstreet House, 1991), 152; Mark H. Dunkelman, *Brothers One and All: Esprit de Corps in a Civil War Regiment* (Baton Rouge: Louisiana State University Press, 2004), 181; Wightman, *From Antietam to Fort Fisher*, 74, 97; Scott Nelson and Carol Sheriff, *A People At War: Civilians and Soldiers in America's Civil War, 1854–1877* (New York: Oxford University Press, 2007), 221.

The result was an army of shadow units. When Union general John A. Dix reviewed George Washington Whitman's 51st New York at Newport News, Virginia, in February 1863, the 51st "could only muster 140 men," and "when we came along with our old flag all torn to pieces, I saw the old. Gen. eye the flag and Regt. and shake his head."[61] In many cases, it was up to the regimental commanding officer to keep up a supply of new enlistments from back home for his regiment, but most commanders could ill afford to detail their precious supply of junior officers for recruiting duty behind the lines. The Confederates armies, on the other hand, recognized the value of integrating new recruits and replacements with veteran combat regiments, and so the Confederate regiments were more likely to maintain their organizational integrity throughout the war than Union regiments.

If the regiment was the basic unit of identity, the brigade was soon recognized as the basic unit of maneuver on the Civil War battlefield, and most of the movement and action in Civil War combat occurred in groups of brigades. The average brigade consisted of four or five regiments, commanded by a brigadier general, and sometimes they acquired an identity of their own to rival the individual regimental identities— the Iron Brigade of the Army of the Potomac was composed of five western regiments that all retained the use of the black Hardee hat as their badge. The Irish Brigade, another Army of the Potomac unit, was composed of an odd amalgam of Irish-born New Yorkers and Protestant Pennsylvanians who carried a green flag emblazoned with a gilded harp into battle. The Philadelphia Brigade, also in the Army of the Potomac, was the only brigade in either army that took its name from its hometown.

Brigades were themselves usually organized into divisions, comprising two or three brigades, and commanded by either a senior brigadier general or a major general. Finally, the divisions were organized into corps, with both armies making up a corps from two or three divisions. The corps was the real innovation of this war for the American military, and like so much else, it was a borrowing from Napoleon Bonaparte's determination to create a *corps d'armée*, an all-arms unit big enough to fight anything except the entirety of an enemy's army but still small enough to be within the grasp of a single commander and nimble enough to march separate from the other parts of an army. Wellington had briefly adopted the corps model before Waterloo, but it never took serious hold in British military thinking, and in the Crimea, the British Army never organized itself at a higher level than the division. Napoleon III resurrected the *corps d'armée* in the North Italian War, and like so much else that was French, it proved irresistible to American borrowing.[62]

Confederate corps were generally identified by the name of their commanding general, while Union corps were assigned numbers. The corps commanders, usually

61. *Civil War Letters of George Washington Whitman*, 88.

62. Robert M. Epstein, "The Creation and Evolution of the Army Corps in the American Civil War," *Journal of Military History* 55 (January 1991): 21–46; Lawrence Kreiser, *Defeating Lee: A History of the Second Army Corps, Army of the Potomac* (Bloomington: Indiana University Press, 2011), 4–5.

senior major generals, were expected (unlike division or brigade commanders) to be able to exercise a large measure of independent judgment and initiative, and the measure of any army's effectiveness could be reliably prophesied from the quality of its corps commanders. In Lee's army in 1863, the corps commanders—James Longstreet and Stonewall Jackson—were probably the best pair of military talents on the North American continent. The Army of the Potomac also boasted equally outstanding combat soldiers in the commanders of the 1st Corps (John F. Reynolds) and the 2nd Corps (Winfield Scott Hancock).

To the ordinary volunteer, however, the principal concern was not with generals or even weapons but with the experience of war service itself. Much as enlistment propaganda might have initially convinced the volunteer that the Rebel or the Yankee was his sworn enemy, the volunteer soon recognized that the soldier opposite him was an American like himself. No matter how much Southerners and Northerners tried to persuade themselves that they were fighting an alien from an alien culture, soldiers from both armies quickly found that both were usually Protestant in religion, democratic in politics, and fond of the same music.

So, to the despair of their commanders (who feared the leakage of important information on troop movements), they fraternized freely in the quiet periods between battles. Edward King Wightman described such a meeting near Fortress Monroe in May 1863, with a "johnny Reb" who had "laid aside his piece and crossed over in a skiff to exchange papers with our pickets." Wightman looked over this "very lean black-eyed fellow with long straight hair" and noticed that he "was well clothed in a gray jacket and pants and so forth." Wightman "bantered him the best I knew how, but he took it very well." A year later, Wightman saw a more general truce break out between Confederates and Federals on the James River, who created a temporary market for swaps of goods. "One of our men, laying aside his rifle, would walk out boldly half-way to the enemy's line, leave a little bag of coffee on a stump, and return," while "Johnny Reb would then issue forth, take the coffee and substitute in its place a big plug of tobacco, which was speedily secured for the service of the Union." Eventually the "ballygogging" attracted the notice of a Confederate officer, who "determined to make a demonstration."

> All at once the rebs started for cover, but not before they had called out warningly, "Take care, Yanks, we're going to shell ye." To this our boys replied by flopping into pits, leaving but one eye exposed and crying with equal friendship, "Lay low, Rebs!" The artillery fire opened on the right, intermingled with rapid volleys of musketry, and worked gradually around to us. In our immediate neighborhood shells were dropped in profusion, spiced with a few rifle balls; but no advance was made and no one was hit. In an hour everything was quiet again, and we all came forth whistling and laughing as before, to cook our supper. The rebs did likewise.[63]

---

63. Wightman, *From Antietam to Fort Fisher*, 132, 196–97.

Wartime fraternization had its limits, and the principal limit was race. White soldiers might profess any amount of fellow feeling, but unsleeping hostility was the rule between black Federals and white Confederates. A Confederate soldier imprisoned at Point Lookout, Maryland, wrote that the "negro troops" guarding rebel prisoners were "as mean as hell," and Confederates captured at Cold Harbor in 1864 were taunted "revengefully" by black Union soldiers as the Confederates were marched away to a prisoner-of-war camp.[64]

Soldiers black and white soon learned that the real enemy in the war was not the other soldier but disease, wounds, and the fear of wounds. Disease in fact, turned out to be the real killer of the Civil War. For every soldier who died in battle, another two died of disease in camp, and overall, more than 10 percent of the Union Army and 20 percent of the Confederate Army were killed off by disease rather than by bullets. One principal cause for the ravages of disease was the nature of military camp life in the nineteenth century, which in clinical terms acted as little better than a disease funnel. Americans of the Civil War era knew little or nothing of bacteriology, and so neither the volunteer nor his officers had any idea of the communicative and infectious nature of malaria, typhus, bronchitis, or pneumonia. As a result, men were taken into the armies carrying a number of diseases with them, and then packed into teeming military camps where they could easily spread a vast sampling of pathogens among themselves.

The volunteers unwittingly added to the odds against them by responding to sanitary discipline with the same contemptuous independence they displayed toward military discipline, and only with the greatest difficulty could they be persuaded to take appropriate health precautions. Camp life, for white American males in the nineteenth century, created an inversion of social roles, since male soldiers now found themselves responsible for a range of domestic labors—sewing clothes, cooking meals, cleaning—which were normally assigned at home to women, and many soldiers were unable to make the cognitive adjustment to the performance of these tasks even when their lives depended on it. "I am most heartily sick of this kind of life," wrote Jacob W. Bartness, an Indiana soldier, to his wife in 1865. "Oh, what a pleasant retreete from the repulsive scenes of this man-slaughtering life, would be the society of my family in some secluded spot, shut out from the calamities of war."[65]

On campaign, the constant exposure to all varieties of weather, and the vulnerability of northern-bred systems to the drastic ecological difference of the deep South's climate and environment, made Northern soldiers particularly vulnerable to

---

64. Robert N. Rosen, *The Jewish Confederates* (Columbia: University of South Carolina Press, 2000), 182; Mark A. Grimsley, *And Keep Moving On: The Virginia Campaign, May–June 1864* (Lincoln: University of Nebraska Press, 2002), 174.

65. Glatthaar, *The March to the Sea and Beyond*, 43.

sickness. Charles Jewett of the 2nd New Hampshire wrote home in July 1862 warning a family friend of the rough living that would await him if he enlisted. "If he thinks it would be any Benefit to his health, tell him to try it at home first. Tell him to go out dores and sleep on the ground through two or three rain storms without any thing to put over or under him. If that don't dishearten him put [a] half Bushel of corn on his back and march all day, then take a Shovel and shovel all night without any thing to eat or drink."

The impossibility of washing and cleaning on long marches made the volunteer an easy target for infestations of lice, fleas, ticks, and other pests. For John Billings, the constant presence of lice was a great leveler of pretensions, the butt of a good soldiers' joke. "Like death," Billings wrote, lice were "no respecter of persons." The pest "inserted its bill as confidingly into the body of the major-general as of the lowest private. I once heard the orderly of a company officer relate that he had picked fifty-two graybacks from the shirt of his chief at one sitting." Soldiers in the 154th New York wrote home in exasperation that "when we were on the march, we had every time we stopped to take off our shirts and drawers and kill the lice, to keep them from carrying us off." Few soldiers suspected that these pests also helped to transmit bacteria through bites and open sores. In camp, the volunteers carelessly continued to make trouble for themselves. Water contaminated by poorly dug latrines, along with piles of waste and garbage that attracted flies and rodents, brought on waves of dysentery, diarrhea, and typhoid fever, but little could convince the volunteer to protect himself. "Our poor sick, I know, suffer much," sighed Robert E. Lee, but "they bring it on themselves by not doing what they are told. They are worse than children, for the latter can be forced."[66]

The army medical services compounded these problems instead of curing them. Like the army itself, army medical practice, at the outbreak of the war, was almost nonexistent. In 1861, the Union surgeon-general was Colonel Thomas Lawson, an eighty-four-year-old veteran of the War of 1812 who had only 113 other surgeons on the army rolls to assist him (26 of whom resigned to join the Confederacy). Medical screening of enlistees was virtually nonexistent. The volunteers who enlisted in the 143rd Pennsylvania in the summer of 1862 were examined "by a trio of surgeons who told the men "to strip to natures habiliments," given a cursory inspection lasting no more than three or four minutes," then told to dress "and get out of there." The recruits of the 1st Minnesota were asked to walk, "face to the right or the left, and to march a few paces further, then face about," and that was it. No provision had been made for a system of army general hospitals; not until August 1862 did McClellan recommend the creation of a military ambulance corps for the Army of the Potomac.

66. Billings, *Hardtack and Coffee*, 80; Dunkelman, *Brothers One and All*, 103; Jewett to "Brother and Sister," July 18, 1862, in *Yankee Correspondence*, 37; Lee to Mary Custis Lee, September 17, 1861, in Robert Edward Lee Jr., *Recollections and Letters of General Robert E. Lee* (New York: Doubleday, Page, 1904), 46.

Even those surgeons and doctors who were on hand were liable to make matters worse instead of better. Not only were they necessarily as ignorant as everyone else of the most basic notions of bacteriology, but they relied on cures that were often worse than the disease. "God save me from being sick and having hospital care such as I have seen," wrote one officer of the 154th New York. "Those in Washington perhaps are not as bad," but in the field and in camp, "the medical treatment is a damning one. Blisters, then diarrhea powders next, then cough powders & damning and so on." In addition to alcoholic stimulants, opium-based painkillers were unwisely ladled out in fantastic amounts: one estimate suggests that more than 10 million opium pills, plus 2.8 million ounces of opium-related medicines, were handed out by Federal medical officers during the war. The result was widespread addiction, either to opiates or to alcohol, in order to cope with pain and illness, and in some cases with battle fatigue and anxiety. Braxton Bragg's erratic behavior as a Confederate field commander may have been related to opium addiction; John Bell Hood, an aggressive Confederate field general who suffered a mangled arm and an amputated leg, sustained himself on alcohol and opiates, and they in turn probably helped him lose his luckless campaign in Tennessee in 1864 by sapping his strength and deadening his judgment.[67]

What made all of this worse was the reluctance of the army medical services to issue medical discharges. Fearing abuse of the discharge system by conniving soldiers, regimental surgeons in the Civil War turned themselves into the first line of defense against military "malingering." William Fuller, Second Assistant Surgeon of the 1st Michigan Volunteers, seems to have treated men who reported on sick call to a classic case of military catch-22—the more serious an illness, Fuller reasoned, the more likely it was faked. "Vast strides have been made in the proficiency of malingering in this country since the first year of the war," Fuller intoned solemnly. "When a surgeon has reason to think that a man has an object or a motive for feigning, no statement of his should be accepted as true. . . ."[68] The result of Fuller's zeal, however, was that sick men were sent back into camp or onto the march, where they only managed to infect other men and further spread sickness.

Eventually, much of the neglect and malpractice in both the Federal and Confederate army medical systems was ironed out. A new Federal surgeon-general, Lieutenant William Alexander Hammond, was appointed in 1862, and from then on Union army medical care drastically improved: 190 new army hospitals with 120,000

67. *Avery Harris' Civil War Journal*, ed. Peter Tomasak (Luzerne, PA: Luzerne National Bank, 1999), 15; James A. Wright, *No More Gallant a Deed: A Civil War Memoir of the First Minnesota Volunteers*, ed. S. J. Keillor (St. Paul: Minnesota Historical Society Press, 2001), 23; Dunkelman, *Brothers One and All*, 116; David T. Courtwright, "Opiate Addiction as a Consequence of the Civil War," *Civil War History* 24 (June 1978): 101–11; James Street, "Under the Influence," *Civil War Times Illustrated* 27 (May 1988): 30–35.

68. Albert Castel, ed., "Malingering," *Civil War Times Illustrated* 26 (August 1977): 29–31.

beds were established under Hammond's aegis, and 15,000 new surgeons were recruited. Even the Confederates, shorthanded and undersupplied as they were, created 28 military hospitals in and around Richmond and took over 57 other buildings, the largest of which, Chimborazo Hospital, could hold 4,300 men (making it the largest hospital in the world at that time), and treated more than 77,000 cases during the war.

In the Army of the Potomac, Jonathan Letterman (who was appointed the army's medical director in June 1862) organized a three-tiered system of field hospitals, post hospitals, and general hospitals for processing battle casualties. The reformer Dorothea L. Dix lobbied successfully to have women recruited as army nurses, and was herself appointed superintendent of army nurses, after the model of Florence Nightingale, in 1861. Additionally, the federal War Department authorized the operation of the civilian-run United States Sanitary Commission and the Christian Commission to act as voluntary auxiliaries for providing nursing and hospital care. As a result, actual disease mortality rates fell from 73 percent of all wartime deaths in the Revolution and 86 percent of all war-related deaths during the Mexican War to little more than 61 percent in the Civil War (the rates of death from disease would actually go back up in the Spanish-American War to over 84 percent of all wartime deaths among American soldiers). The disease statistics are appalling all the same, and sickness often decimated a regiment long before it ever fired a gun in anger.[69]

Without question, the greatest damage to the volunteers' health was done by the soldiers' diet. Food preservation was only in its infancy in the 1860s, and as a result, the soldier on campaign was issued only the most portable—and most indigestible—of rations. The marching ration of the Federal soldier in the Army of the Potomac was "one pound of hard bread; three-fourths of a pound of salt pork, or one and one-fourth pounds of fresh meat; sugar, coffee, and salt." The bread was, in the most literal sense of the word, hard, and so it went by the name of hardtack.[70] John Billings described it as "a plain flour-and-water biscuit" measuring "three and one-eighth by two and seven-eighths inches, and . . . nearly half an inch thick." Hardtack resembled a large, hard cracker more than anything that could be called bread, and "they may have been so hard that they could not be bitten" and "required a very strong blow of the fist to break them."

69. Michael A. Flannery, *Civil War Pharmacy: A History of Drugs, Drug Supply and Provision, and Therapeutics for the Union and Confederacy* (Binghamton, NY: Pharmaceutical Products Press, 2004), 92; Thomas J. Brown, *Dorothea Dix: New England Reformer* (Cambridge, MA: Harvard University Press, 1998), 290; Carol C. Green, *Chimborazo: The Confederacy's Largest Hospital* (Knoxville: University of Tennessee Press, 2004), 5–8; Rebecca Barbour Calcutt, *Richmond's Wartime Hospitals* (Gretna, LA: Pelican, 2005), 20; William W. Kern, "Before and After Lister," *Science*, June 11, 1915: 851–52.

70. David Madden, *Beyond the Battlefield: The Ordinary Life and Extraordinary Times of the Civil War Soldier* (New York: Simon and Schuster, 2000), 138; Palmer H. Boeger, "Hardtack and Burned Beans," *Civil War History* 4 (March 1958): 84; Billings, *Hardtack and Coffee*, 113–14.

On the other hand, Billings admitted that "hardtack was not so bad an article of food . . . as may be supposed," and devising ways of eating it stretched the soldiers' imaginations in odd ways. "Many of them were eaten just as they were received— hardtack *plain*," while others were "crumbed in coffee" and "furnished the soldier his breakfast and supper." Others "crumbled them in soups for want of other thickening" or "crumbed them in cold water, then fried the crumbs in juice and fat of meat," and still others simply "liked them toasted, either to crumb in coffee or . . . to butter." The invariable accompaniment to hardtack, and to any other circumstances, was the soldier's coffee.

> One of the most interesting scenes presented in army life took place at night when the army was on the point of bivouacking. As soon as this fact became known along the column, each man would seize a rail from the nearest fence, and with this additional arm on the shoulder would enter the proposed camping-ground. In no more time than it takes to tell the story, the little camp-fires, rapidly increasing to hundreds in number, would shoot up along the hills and plains, and as if by magic acres of territory would be luminous with them. Soon they would be surrounded by the soldiers, who made it an almost invariable rule to cook their coffee first, after which a large number, tired out with the toils of the day, would make their supper of hardtack and coffee, and roll up in their blankets for the nights. If a march was ordered at midnight, unless a surprise was intended, it must be preceded by a pot of coffee; if a halt was ordered in mid-forenoon or afternoon, the same dish was inevitable, with hardtack accompaniment usually. It was coffee *at* meals and *between* meals; and men going on guard or coming off guard drank it at all hours of the night, and to-day the old soldiers who can stand it are the hardest coffee-drinkers in the community, through the schooling which they received in the service.

Last in the soldier's estimate was the army's standard meat ration, salt pork, which Billings found "musty and rancid . . . flabby, stringy, 'sow-belly'" that was frankly indigestible to anyone but a hungry soldier. "We ignored the existence of such a thing as a stomach in the army."[71]

There were, at times, exceptions to this diet. In the Union army's permanent camps, the soldier's ration was usually expanded to add vegetables and fresh meat. If possible, the armies would drive their own beef herds along with them on the march to provide more fresh beef. A correspondent marching with William Tecumseh Sherman in 1864 noticed that

> every corps has with it its own droves of beeves, which are kept in good condition by foraging, and which have a way of absorbing all that are found by the roadside, so that the men have little to complain of in this particular. All along the lines of battle,

---

71. Billings, *Hardtack and Coffee*, 116, 129–30, 135.

when the armies were confronting each other, a few rods in the rear, were little pens of cattle from which the men in the trenches were well reinforced with smoking steaks, added to their coffee and pilot bread; while two or three miles in the rear could be seen large droves, under guard, serenely grazing in the pastures—forming the best possible reserve forces upon which the army could fall back.[72]

And there were always boxes and packages from home with varieties of good things that the government had no interest in issuing. But even with these additions, the average soldier's diet did little except further reduce his resistance to infection and exhaustion, and wreak immeasurable havoc with his digestive system.

As for the Confederate armies, the food was not only bad but sometimes nonexistent. The impact of the blockade and the breakdown of the Confederacy's internal transportation system meant that its volunteers frequently went hungry on campaign, and it could be said without the guilt of exaggeration that through most of the Civil War, the average Confederate soldier lived on raw courage and endurance more than on food and drink. George Asbury Bruton wrote to his brother and sister in 1864, "Our rations is small. We get ¼ pound of bacon per day and 1 pound of corn meal. Sometimes we get a little rice & sometimes we get a spoon full of soap to wash our hands." Seven months later, Bruton lectured his brother James for not appreciating "home as you ought." At home, "you have good clothes to put on and good socks to put on before you put on your clothes & best of all a good hot breakfast with plenty of ham & eggs, potatoes, & butter & milk." Unlike his brother James, George Bruton and the 19th Louisiana were living on "a little piece of half-cooked beef about as big as my 3 fingers for a days ration & 4 doggers of corne bread about the size of a grand mother biscuit. . . ." In addition to poor rations, there were "thousands without a blanket & more bairfotted & all without socks." Every stop on the march, wrote one amazed surgeon, was the signal for "every corn field and orchard within two or three miles" to be "completely stripped."[73] Mary Bedinger Mitchell, a Virginia woman, watched in disbelief as Lee's army passed by her house in September 1862 on its way to Antietam:

> When I say that they were hungry, I convey no impression of the gaunt starvation that looked from their cavernous eyes. All day they crowded to the doors of our houses, with always the same drawling complaint: "I've been a-marchin' an' a-fightin' for six weeks stiddy, and I ain't had n-a-r-thin to eat 'cept green apples an' green cawn, an' I wish you'd please to gimme a bite to eat." . . . I know nothing of numbers, nor what was or was not engaged in any battle, but I saw the troops march past us every summer for four years,

72. "Another Account," July 7, 1864, in *The Rebellion Record: A Diary of American Events*, ed. Frank Moore (New York: G. P. Putnam, 1868), 11:207.

73. Hortense Herman, "Rank and File of the Confederate Armies," *Confederate Veteran* 22 (May 1914): 203; Bartholomees, *Buff Facings and Gilt Buttons*, 56.

and I know something of the appearance of a marching army, both Union and South- ern. There are always stragglers, of course, but never . . . were want and exhaustion more visibly put before my eyes, and that they could march or fight at all seemed incredible.[74]

The most fearsome thing the volunteer faced, however, was actual combat. The Civil War battlefield presented the volunteer with a frightening variety of sensa- tions, the first of which was the sheer unfamiliarity of the ground he was fighting on. Soldiers' accounts of Civil War battle are notorious for their uncertain geographical references. Robert Lewis Dabney's memoir of his commander "Stonewall" Jackson is peppered with bland descriptions of terrain—"alternate woods and fields," "abrupt little ravines," "a wide expanse of fertile meadows"—which betrayed how unfamiliar Dabney was with the Shenandoah Valley territory he was fighting over. The colonel of the 19th Virginia described the lay of the land at Gaines Mill on June 26 in terms so vague they could have been applied to almost any ten acres on the North Ameri- can continent: "Passing through woods we soon reached a large, open, undulating field, with heavy timber on all sides, where we were formed in line of battle and awaited a few minutes the approach of the enemy, which was momentarily expected, as they were exactly in our front." The Army of the Potomac's chief of staff, Daniel Butterfield, admitted that even on campaign, "maps, wherever possible, must be ob- tained from citizens," since no comprehensive topographical survey of the United States existed.[75]

The noises of the battlefield were even more disorienting, since the concussive impact of artillery and massed rifle fire created an amphitheater of noise unlike any- thing within the experience of any nineteenth-century American. One Union gen- eral tried to re-create the sonic environment of a battlefield by inviting his daughter to imagine, "in fancy, the crashing roll of 30000 muskets mingled with the thunder of over a hundred pieces of artillery; the sharp bursting of shells and the peculiar whizzing sound of its dismembered pieces, traveling with a shriek in all directions; the crash and thud of round shot through trees and buildings and into earth or through columns of human bodies; . . . the uproar of thousands of voices in cheers, yells, and imprecations . . . riderless horses rushing wildly about; now and then blow- ing up of a caisson and human frames thrown lifeless into the air."[76]

The low velocity of the Minié bullet gave it a particularly noticeable humming whir, and soldiers devoted considerable time to trying to explain the sound of rifle

---

74. M. B. Mitchell, "A Woman's Recollections of Antietam," in *Battles and Leaders*, 2:687–88.

75. "Testimony of Major General Daniel Butterfield," March 25, 1864, in *Report of the Joint Committee on the Conduct of the War* (Washington, DC: Government Printing Office, 1865), 4:421–22; "Report of Gen. John B. Strange, Nineteenth Virginia Infantry," July 15, 1862, in *The War of the Rebellion*, Series One, 11(II):767.

76. Alphaeus Williams, in Dora L. Costa and Matthew E. Kahn, *Heroes and Cowards: The Social Face of War* (Princeton, NJ: Princeton University Press, 2008), 76–77.

fire in letters and diaries. "You never heard such whooping," wrote private Bruton after Shiloh, "the bullets whistled worse & faster than pouring peas on a dry cow hide." Another Confederate soldier at Shiloh wrote that rifle bullets sang angrily around him "worse then ever bees was when they swarm." When a bullet struck a man, it made what Amos Currier of the 8th Iowa called "a peculiar spat." For others, the sheer volume of unlooked-for terror and confusion in the environment of nineteenth-century battle was so vast that the provincial and localized vocabulary of most Americans was simply beggared by it. "I have not time nor disposition to attempt a description," wrote James Madison Williams of the 21st Alabama after Shiloh. "When I go home it will take me months to describe what I saw on that terrible field."[77]

The most frightening aspect of combat was the chance of being seriously or mortally wounded. Not only was the general inexperience of the volunteer officer more likely to expose a soldier to lethal amounts of fire for longer periods of time than in any other nineteenth-century war, but the soft lead Minié ball (unlike the brass-jacketed bullets of later wars) mushroomed upon impact, smashing up bones and cartilage, and making dreadful exit wounds. "Often did I see a simple gunshot wound," wrote one surgeon, "scarcely larger than the bullet which made it, become larger and larger until a hand would scarcely cover it, and extend from the skin downward into the tissues until one could put half his fist into the sloughing wound."

Artillery rounds could deliver even more horrifying forms of death, adding to the terror of every soldier nearby, as shell splinters could slice a body into a bloody pulp. A shell plowed through Company E of the 9th Vermont during an attack on Confederate entrenchments below Richmond in 1864, and Colonel Edward H. Ripley looked over to see a favorite corporal "lying on his side and face . . . his buttocks clear to the thigh bones were both carried away, showing a raw mass of torn flesh with the crushed bones protruding. He was alive, conscious, and brave." A few moments later another shell crashed near Ripley and "I was dashed in the face with a hot streaming mass of something horrible which closed my eyes, nose and mouth. I thought my head had gone certainly this time." It hadn't; instead, it was the "brains, skull, hair and blood" of an artilleryman who had been standing nearby. Ripley had to be cleaned off by a staff officer who "just then came up and happened to have a towel in his boot leg."[78]

Nothing in Civil War field medicine was able to deal with the wounds or the trauma inflicted by the rifles and artillery of the era, and not until after the turn of

---

77. Bell I. Wiley, *The Life of Johnny Reb: The Common Soldier of the Confederacy* (Baton Rouge: Louisiana State University Press, 1982 [1943]), 34; Frank and Reaves, *Seeing the Elephant*, 105; Williams, *From That Terrible Field*, 53.

78. William W. Keen, "Surgical Reminiscences of the Civil War," in *Addresses and Other Papers* (Philadelphia: W. B. Saunders, 1905), 431; "Charging New Market Heights: Edward Ripley Recalls," ed. Edward Longacre, *Civil War Times Illustrated* 20 (February 1982): 42.

the century would surgical skill and surgical instruments develop to the point where gunshot wounds to main body parts could even become routinely operable. "We had no clinical thermometers; our only means of estimating fever was by touch," lamented one surgeon. "We had no hypodermatic syringes," and so "the mouth and the bowel were the only avenues for the administration of remedies." This meant that for the badly wounded soldier, the common regimental surgeon was little better than death itself.[79]

Wounds to the extremities could be treated only by amputation, in order to head off the onset of gangrene and blood poisoning, and at the height of any major battle, a surgeon's field or division hospital would resemble nothing so much as a butcher's shop on market-day—an unventilated tent or barn, with an old door set up on two barrels for an operating table, an unending line of wounded men in various degrees of shock, a pile of amputated limbs that reminded observers of a cord of wood, and a corner full of men with wounds to the abdomen or chest who had simply been set aside as surgically hopeless. Sergeant Hiram Lathe of the 9th New Hampshire lost two fingers of his right hand, but counted himself fortunate compared to what he saw in the field hospital he walked back to. The "hospital" was nothing more than "a field of I should say about fifty acres, where the surgeons were busily at work . . . on rudely constructed benches, on old tables, or anything that could be extemporized for an operating table." All around him were men who were wounded

> in every conceivable way, from cannon and shell wounds, and burns from exploding shells, with bowels torn out and bodies gashed and mangled from bayonet thrusts, or with heads and faces smashed almost beyond recognition by blows from a musket-breech, though by far the greater part of the wounds were made by the deadly Minie balls. . . . The ambulances kept coming onto the field loaded up with men, and some of them would be dead when they were taken out, but altogether there must have been several thousand of the wounded there in that field.[80]

If this horrified the men, it did not have much different effect on the surgeons. "I am not out of [hearing] much of the groans of the wounded from morning till night," wrote Claiborne Walton, a surgeon with the 21st Kentucky who was clearly teetering on the mental brink in 1864.

> My hands are constantly steaped in blood. I have had them in blood and water so much that the nails are soft and tender. I have amputated limbs until it almost makes my heart ache to see a poor fellow coming in the Ambulance to the Hospital. . . . I could tell you of many yes—of the [most] distressing cases of wounds. Such as arms

---

79. Keen, "Surgical Reminiscences of the Civil War," 435–36.

80. Edward O. Lord, *History of the Ninth Regiment, New Hampshire Volunteers in the War of the Rebellion* (Concord: Republican Press Association, 1895), 508.

shot off—legs shot off. Eyes shot out—brains shot out. Lungs shot through and in a word *everything* shot to pieces and totally maimed for all after life. The horror of this war can never be half told.[81]

Wounds to the abdomen, especially the stomach or the bowels, were simply hopeless—the Minié ball caused too much internal damage, and surgical skills were as yet too poorly developed, to make recovery possible. "Wounds . . . involving the viscera were almost uniformly fatal," wrote one Union surgeon. "Opium was practically our only remedy and death the usual result." He could not remember "more than one incontestable example of recovery from a gunshot wound of the stomach and not a single incontestable case of wound of the small intestines." Consequently, the Civil War soldier became a quick study in analyzing what wounds meant. Frank Wilkeson, an artilleryman in the Army of the Potomac, observed in 1864 how swiftly a soldier knew what his end might be:

> Wounded soldiers almost always tore their clothing away from their wounds, so as to see them and to judge of their character. Many of them would smile and their faces would brighten as they realized that they were not hard hit, and that they could go home for a few months. Others would give a quick glance at their wounds and then shrink back as from a blow, and turn pale, as they realized the truth that they were mortally wounded. The enlisted men were exceeding accurate judges of the probable result which would ensue from any wound they saw. They had seen hundreds of soldiers wounded, and they had noticed that certain wounds always resulted fatally. They knew when they were fatally wounded, and after the shock of discovery had passed, they generally braced themselves and died in a manly manner. It was seldom that an American or Irish volunteer flunked in the presence of death.[82]

Perhaps not. But a large number of Civil War soldiers certainly quailed at the prospect of combat, and they deserted the Union and Confederate armies in record-setting droves. More than 200,000 Federal soldiers deserted during the war, nearly 12 percent of the entire total of Union enlistments, while 104,000 Confederates, as much as 16 percent of the Confederate armies, took French leave. In many cases, it was a risk-free solution. Only about 80,000 Union deserters were ever actually arrested; of the even smaller number who appeared before courts-martial, only 147 received the traditional punishment for desertion: a firing squad or the gallows.[83]

81. "One Continued Scene of Carnage: A Union Surgeon's View of War," *Civil War Times Illustrated* 15 (August 1976): 34, 36.

82. Keen, "Surgical Reminiscences of the Civil War," 433; Wilkeson, *Recollections of a Private Soldier*, 206–7.

83. Ella Lonn, *Desertion During the Civil War* (Lincoln: University of Nebraska Press, 1998 [1928]), 226; Mark A. Weitz, *More Damning than Slaughter: Desertion in the Confederate Army* (Lincoln: University of Nebraska Press, 2005), 14; Vinovskis, "Have Social Historians Lost the Civil War?" 10; Judith Lee Hallock, "The Role of the Community in Civil War Desertion," *Civil War History* 29 (June 1983): 126; Nelson and Sheriff, *A People at War*, 203–4.

Others who might have lacked the will to face enemy fire were set up on their legs by the free use of alcohol. A Confederate newspaper complained that "officers with gold lace wound in astonishing involutions upon their arms" as well as "private soldiers in simple homespun . . . all seem to drink whisky . . . in quantities which would astonish the nerves of a cast-iron lamp-post, and of a quantity which would destroy the digestive organs of the ostrich." Many of the Civil War's legendary charges into the face of the enemy were made by soldiers who had been drugged into near insensibility by the liberal dispensing of hard liquor before battle. The 16th North Carolina went into action at Seven Pines after the company commissary "hobbled down with several canteens of 'fire water' and gave each of the men a dram. He knew we needed it, and the good angels only smiled." Confederate prisoners taken by Berdan's Sharpshooters at Malvern Hill had been "unduly excited by frequent rations of whisky . . . their canteens, some half full of this stimulant." Members of Confederate general George Pickett's staff, and even one of his brigadiers, downed a bottle of whiskey over a lunch of cold mutton just before Pickett's famous charge at Gettysburg.[84]

On the other hand, officers who prodded men too hard into battle, with or without whiskey, were likely to become targets for disgruntled enlisted men, especially on a battlefield where it was difficult to establish whether an officer's death was a normal combat fatality or a covert assassination. It was not at all unusual, wrote New Jersey private Alfred Bellard, for overbearing Yankee martinets to receive "a stray ball occasionally on the field of battle." The major of the 33rd Virginia was described as a "tyrannical little puppy" who "would have been riddled with bullets and not yankee ones either."[85]

The most obvious evasion of combat was simple, and usually temporary, flight to the rear. "The *sneaks* in the army are named *Legion*," remarked Edward King Wightman. "When you read of the number of men engaged on our side, strike out at least one third as never having struck a blow." Oliver Wendell Holmes reminded his fellow veterans of the 20th Massachusetts years after the war that "We have stood side by side in a line—we have charged and swept the enemy—and we have run away like rabbits—all together." Sometimes the "sneaks" did not need to resort to the humiliation of running in order to evade battle. Any wounded comrade in a fight became an excuse for one or two others to break ranks and assist the wounded man to a field hospital, and unless a brigade or division commander was unusually diligent in posting a provost guard in the rear of his units, a wounded man's helpers would simply remain out of sight and sound of the action for the rest of the day.

84. Moore, ed., *Rebellion Record*, 4:65; George Henry Mills, *History of the 16th North Carolina Regiment in the Civil War* (Hamilton, NY: Edmonston, 1992 [1903]), 14–15; Stevens, *Berdan's United States Sharpshooters*, 151; George R. Stewart, *Pickett's Charge: A Microhistory of the Final Attack at Gettysburg, July 3, 1863*, 2nd ed. (Dayton, OH: Morningside Press, 1980), 106.

85. Alfred Bellard, *Gone for a Soldier: The Civil Memoirs of Private Alfred Bellard*, ed. David Donald (Boston: Little, Brown, 1975), 188; Glatthaar, *General Lee's Army*, 190.

Only by 1864 were serious efforts to keep able-bodied men from leaking rearward out of a fight really working, as Frank Wilkeson discovered when he strolled too far away from his artillery unit in the Wilderness and was prodded into frontline infantry combat by a provost guard who demanded that he "show blood" before being allowed to move to the rear. Yet however easy it may be to point out the failings of the volunteer under fire, it is also true that the volunteer in the Civil War—Union or Confederate, black or white, however untrained or uncomprehending he might be of the niceties of military life—was being asked to stand up to some of the most savage combat ever met by soldiers in the nineteenth century. War would be easy, Holmes wrote before Antietam, if one could "after a comfortable breakfast . . . come down the steps of one's home, putting on one's gloves and smoking a cigar, to get on a horse and charge a battery up Beacon Street." The reality, however, was that the soldier faced "a night on the ground in the rain and your bowels out of order and then after no particular breakfast to wade a stream and attack an enemy."[86] If Holmes and his companions sometimes ran "like rabbits," they had more than enough incentive.

What, then, accounts for the "will to combat" among the green volunteers at a place such as Shiloh, where individual groups of raw soldiers continued to fight on and on despite the dissolution of all direction from above? There were some soldiers who found that they were enthralled by war and the exhilaration of combat. "I love war," wrote Philip Kearny, one of the most combative of the Army of the Potomac's division commanders. "It brings me indescribable pleasure, like that of having a woman." For more than a few, combat was simply a risk to be exchanged for the chance to loot. One officer of the famed Louisiana Tiger battalion was shocked after First Bull Run to find "30 or 40" of his men "marching up with new uniforms on, gold rings on their fingers, and their pockets filled with watches and money that they had stolen." Henry Blake of the 11th Massachusetts was disgusted by the legion of "army thieves" who "plundered the slain" or "grasped with their remorseless hands the valuables, clothing, and rations of the unwary, wounded soldiers."

For others, a willing entrance into battle was due to the bravery and example of a regimental or company leader; sometimes it was the powerful incentive of following the colors forward. At other times a strange, hysterical killer instinct took over and banished any consideration of personal safety. Frank Holsinger admitted that in combat, "you yell, you swing your cap, you load and fire as long as the battle goes your way. . . . It is a supreme minute to you; you are in ecstasies." Colonel Rufus Dawes of the 6th Wisconsin spoke of seeing men at Antietam "loading and firing with demoniacal fury and shouting and laughing hysterically," while David Thompson wrote of the "mental strain" of combat in which "the whole landscape for an instant

---

86. Wightman, *From Antietam to Fort Fisher*, 91; Holmes, "The Fraternity of Arms," December 11, 1897, in *The Essential Holmes: Selections from the Letters, Speeches, Judicial Opinions and Other Writing of Oliver Wendell Holmes, Jr.*, ed. R. A. Posner (Chicago: University of Chicago Press, 1992), 73; Baker, *Justice from Beacon Hill*, 131–32.

turned slightly red." Michael Hanifen of the 1st New Jersey Artillery, remembered that "it is a terrible sight to see a line of men, two deep, coming up within 300 or 400 yards of you, with bayonets flashing and waving their colors, and you know that every shot you fire into them sends some one to eternity, but still you are prompted by a devilish desire to kill all you can."[87]

For Amos Judson, the shrewd observer of the 83rd Pennsylvania, the ultimate answer to the murderous question of courage in battle lay hidden within each soldier. "In my opinion, what is called courage is very much a matter of pride or principle with others, and a compound of both with all men." Sometimes it was a result of fear, sometimes a result of being fed sufficiently, and sometimes it was really no more than "a proper sense of duty on the field of battle, and you will consequently find men of the most quiet and apparently timid dispositions at home, to be the most resolute and reliable men in action."[88] The only thing, said Judson, which he had never seen in the war was "any manifestations of absolute fear of trepidation or trembling during a fight, or during even the anticipation of one." Judson was, of course, telling less then he knew. It might have been more accurate to say that the only shame which the American volunteer of 1861 to 1865 had to endure was that his enemy was another American.

87. Linderman, *Embattled Courage*, 74; "The Diary of Corporal Westwood James," ed. Michael Musick, *Civil War Times Illustrated* 17 (October 1978): 35; Blake, *Three Years in the Army of the Potomac*, 292; Holsinger, "How Does One Feel Under Fire," May 5, 1898, in *War Talks in Kansas: A Series of Papers Read Before the Kansas Commandery of the Military Order of the Loyal Legion of the United States* (Kansas City, MO: Franklin Hudson, 1906), 294; Nolan, *The Iron Brigade*, 140; David Thompson, "With Burnside at Antietam," in *Battles and Leaders*, 2:661–62; Michael Hanifen, *History of Battery B, First New Jersey Artillery* (Hightstown, NJ: Longstreet House, 1991 [1905]), 53.

88. Judson, *History of the Eighty-Third Regiment, Pennsylvania Volunteers*, 186–87.

CHAPTER SEVEN

THE MANUFACTURE OF WAR

A s the thin winter sunlight faded over the outer sand islands of the Cape Fear River, an iron-hulled side-wheel steamer slowly slipped away from the dark protection of the inlet. The steamer nudged cautiously down into the ship channel that broadened toward the Atlantic Ocean, her captain anxiously scanning the dark horizon of the moonlit ocean.

Beyond the bar, the masts of ships poked up in the silvery light. These ships wanted nothing so much as to run down the slender steamer, her master, and her crew and put them under lock and key for as long as the law of the sea would allow. For the steamer's name was *Cecile*, and she was the property of John Fraser & Company, who had fitted her out on behalf of the Confederate States of America to run war supplies through the U.S. Navy's blockade of Southern ports and rivers. Her captain was Lieutenant John Newland Maffitt, a forty-two-year-old North Carolinian and former U.S. Navy officer whose fifteen years of duty with the United States Coastal Survey had made him the master of virtually every shoal, sandbar, and inlet on the Gulf and Atlantic coastlines of North America. On board the *Cecile* were 700 fat bales of Southern cotton that would buy the Confederacy rifles, shoes, clothing, and food for its armies. Maffitt and the *Cecile* were vital strands in the Confederacy's lifeline to the outside world, and so the Federal navy hung close to the mouth of the Cape Fear River, hoping to choke Maffitt and his ship and the future of the Confederacy all at once.

The moon sank, and Maffitt urged the *Cecile* over the bar and out to sea, counting on the inky darkness to cloak her stealthy passage through the net of the Federal blockade. Every light had been extinguished, and every command was whispered; even the steamer's upper works, formerly white, had been repainted in drab or dark colors. But Maffitt could not disguise the splashing of the steamer's side-wheel paddles, and as he crept past the Federal ships, a large gas-fired spot-light shot a beam of light across the *Cecile*. There was no need for stealth now. Maffitt roared for full speed as the guns of the blockade ships leapt to life, throw-ing shells over the *Cecile* and striking her a glancing blow that knocked several bales of cotton into the sea.

The Federal ships had the guns and the spotlights, but Maffitt had the advantage of speed and surprise, and together Maffitt and the *Cecile* slithered away into the night. The next afternoon, another U.S. Navy warship appeared over the horizon and set off after the *Cecile*. This ship was fast and gained on the Confederate ship. While he prayed for the coming of darkness, Maffitt had his chief engineer feed coal dust into the engines. The coal dust sent up a sooty cloud of smoke from the *Cecile*'s funnel, trailing behind the steamer in a fat black plume. Once the smokescreen was thick enough to conceal him, Maffitt switched back to clean-burning anthracite coal and changed course, leaving his befuddled Federal pursuer chasing the smoke. The next day, Maffitt and the *Cecile* were in Nassau.

Lying only 570 miles from Wilmington, Nassau was the chief port of call in the British-held Bahamas. There, agents, brokers, importers, and exporters flocked from England and the Confederacy with weapons and supplies to be run through the blockade. There, too, Southern cotton could be transshipped to British steamers to be ferried to England or France to pay for the Confederacy's purchases and feed Europe's cotton-hungry textile mills. In the heyday of blockade-running in 1863, a blockade-runner would clear Nassau every other day, on average. St. George in Bermuda, the Spanish-held port of Havana, and the Danish island of St. Thomas all contributed their share of low-slung, quick-driving steamers to pierce the Federal blockade. Meanwhile, Federal navy vessels could only hover impotently off the limits of British territorial waters in the Bahamas or Bermuda, or off the Spanish or Dan-ish Caribbean islands, while the Confederate agents negotiated for the weapons the Confederacy would use against the Federal armies.

Once his ship had been emptied of its cotton cargo, Maffitt was ready to take on military freight from John Fraser & Company's agents for the return run to Wilm-ington. In this case, he would carry 900 pounds of gunpowder, purchased in England through the partner firm Fraser, Trenholm & Company. As Maffitt realized, it was a cargo that required only one well-placed shell from a Federal blockader "to blow our vessel and all hands to Tophet." Maffitt, however, was unworried. Under cover of night, the *Cecile* glided out of Nassau. At daybreak, three Federal ships were waiting for her, and sent several shells screaming through her rigging. Nevertheless, the *Cecile*'s superior speed soon left them far behind. Sixty miles from Wilmington, Maffitt slack-ened speed to take his bearings on the coastline he knew so well, and with a final burst of the *Cecile*'s engine power, he boldly stormed through the blockade line outside Wilmington at 16 knots, with Federal shells dropping around him. Nothing touched the *Cecile*, and the ship crossed the bar at Wilmington with her precious cargo, which would soon be heading for Albert Sidney Johnston's waiting soldiers in the west.[1]

The *Cecile* was only one of 286 blockade-runners that cleared the port of Wilmington during the Civil War. Taken together, ships such as the *Cecile* brought out 400,000 bales of cotton, which the Confederate government and private Southern entrepreneurs parlayed into loans, purchases, and acquisitions that helped to keep the Southern war effort running long after Southern sources of supply had been depleted. These same blockade-runners brought 400,000 rifles into the Confederacy, along with 2.25 million pounds of ingredients for gunpowder and 3 million pounds of lead for bullets, in addition to clothing, blankets, shoes, and medicines. The blockade-runners also bound Great Britain and the markets of Europe into a tight web of finance and diplomatic intrigue with the Confederacy, and kept the threat of European intervention in the war hanging like a sword over the head of the Union.[2]

Lieutenant Maffitt continued to run the *Cecile* into Nassau and Wilmington for the next three months. In May, Maffitt was posted to a twin-screw steamer that he used to raid and burn Yankee commercial shipping. He was never caught by the U.S. Navy.

The *Cecile* ran aground on the Abaco reef in the Bahamas on June 17, 1862, and was abandoned.

THE WATCHERS OVERSEAS

Five days after the surrender of Fort Sumter, President Lincoln took his first directly hostile step against the Confederacy by proclaiming a blockade of all Confederate ports. "Whereas an insurrection against the Government of the United States has broken out in the States of South Carolina, Georgia, Alabama, Florida, Mississippi, Louisiana, and Texas," Lincoln declared, it was now "advisable to set on foot a blockade." Any ships—and this included ships under a foreign flag, not just ships registered as Confederate vessels—attempting to penetrate the blockade "will be captured and sent to the nearest convenient port, for such proceedings against her and her cargo as prize, as may be deemed advisable."[3] In the strict sense, Lincoln announced the measure only as a military decision. Nevertheless, the blockade immediately embroiled both the Union and the Confederacy in an ongoing battle of international diplomacy that lasted for the length of the war and for years beyond.

This diplomatic tangle persisted for the Union because, whether Lincoln had clearly recognized it or not in 1861, imposing a blockade posed three thorny and potentially disastrous foreign policy problems for the blockaders. In the first case, a

1. E. C. Boykin, *Sea Devil of the Confederacy: The Story of the Florida and Her Captain, John Newland Maffitt* (New York: Funk and Wagnalls, 1959), 3–9.

2. Stephen R. Wise, *Lifeline of the Confederacy* (Columbia: University of South Carolina Press, 1988), 59–60, 166, 180, 221, 226.

3. Lincoln, "Proclamation of a Blockade," April 19, 1861, in *Collected Works*, 4:338–39.

naval blockade of the South might anger the South's major trading partners. Fully a quarter of the British workforce was in some way connected to the cotton-textile manufacturing trade, and as much as half of all British exports were some form of finished cotton goods. Any attempt to disrupt the transatlantic flow of cotton might easily invite Britain to conclude that its national interests were at stake, and that might provoke the British to either break the blockade by force (at the least) or (at worst) actively intervene in the course of the war to secure Southern independence and bring the war and the blockade to an end.

For their part, the Confederates were fully aware of the value of the cotton export trade, and they expected that the loss of cotton would compel Britain, and perhaps France, to intervene before a few months had passed. Henry L. Benning of Georgia confidently declared, "We have an article which England must have."

> To deprive England of cotton would be the same as to deprive 4,000,000 of her sub-
> jects of the means of subsistence, and to throw them out to work anarchy and revolu-
> tion. This she would never consent to. . . . She has ships enough to destroy the entire
> navy which the North would have, and to enter the harbor of New York and Boston,
> and with the improved artillery of the day destroy these cities in a few hours.[4]

A week and a half after Lincoln's blockade proclamation, the English newspaper correspondent William Howard Russell noticed an advertisement in a Charleston merchant's office for direct sailings between Charleston and Europe, and when Russell wondered whether that might be a little premature due to the blockade, he was quickly told that cotton would solve that problem in a short while.

> "Why, I expect, sir," replied the merchant, "that if those miserable Yankees try to block-
> ade us, and keep you from our cotton, you'll just send their ships to the bottom and
> acknowledge us. That will be before autumn, I think." It was in vain I assured him he
> would be disappointed. "Look out there," he said, pointing to the wharf, on which were
> piled some cotton bales; "there's the key will open all our ports, and put us into John
> Bull's strong box as well."[5]

Southerners were also convinced that it was worth Britain's while to remember that the South, which had always needed to import British manufactured goods as badly as Britain needed to import Southern cotton, would continue to be an important market for the sale of British exports. The Confederate states, freed from the federal government's high import tariffs, would be in an even better position to buy British goods than if they had still been in the Union. The logic of commerce alone would seem to dictate that any attempt by the Federal navy to stopper

---

4. Sven Beckert, "Emancipation and Empire: Reconstructing the Worldwide Web of Cotton Production in the Age of the Civil War," *American Historical Review* 109 (December 2009): 1408; "Henry L. Benning's Secessionist Speech," in *Secession Debated: Georgia's Showdown in 1860*, 131.

5. W. H. Russell, *My Diary North and South*, 69.

the Confederacy's ports would sooner or later invite some kind of unpleasant action from the vastly superior British navy, and to help that conclusion along, the Confederacy sent its first set of commissioners to Europe in the summer of 1861 to appeal to France and Britain for formal diplomatic recognition and military aid.

Entirely apart from the realpolitik of cotton, the status of blockades in international law was a highly technical and tricky affair that posed problem of its own. Lincoln insisted from the beginning of the war that the Southern states had no constitutional right to secede from the Union, and when the Confederates insisted that their republic was a legitimate and independent nation and the civil war a conflict of two belligerent nations, Lincoln would reply that it was really only an insurrection against Federal authority. This involved more than simple bandying about. For the British in particular, with their outsize naval power, it was possible for a blockade to cut off an enemy nation's inflow of supplies, serve as an early-warning tripwire in the event of an attempted invasion, and act as a net to apprehend an enemy nation's privateers before they could escape onto the world's oceans and damage British commerce—all at once. The more complex blockades became, the more urgent the need to define how they operated, since the seizure of ships and cargoes attempting to penetrate the blockade included the shipping of neutrals whose antagonism the British might not want to inflame.

The first serious attempt at defining the operations of blockades—the Declaration of Paris—bound its adherents to four rules. Privateering must be abolished—in other words, letters of marque and reprisal (government licenses to private shipping to prey on the commerce of an enemy nation) must end. The ships and cargoes of neutral-nation owners must be protected from confiscation if stopped by a blockade (provided the cargoes were not actual contraband of war). The cargoes of neutral-nation owners must be protected from confiscation even if they were being shipped in vessels owned by the blockaders' enemy (although no such protection was extended to the ships or the cargoes actually owned by that enemy). And blockades, to be legal, must be effective, not mere token or "paper" blockades. The Declaration of Paris offered no actual definition of what an *effective* blockade would look like, but the presumption was that everyone would know it when they saw it.

The first point operated very much to the favor of Great Britain, since it removed a threat that British commerce around the world dreaded; the second and third bought the adherence of the other major European powers, since it guarded their seaborne commerce from arbitrary seizure by British warships. However, the United States declined to endorse the Declaration of Paris. The secretary of state at the time, William Marcy, was happy to agree to the second and third points, but the United States had always looked to fall back on privateering as a way to augment its naval forces in the event of war, without having to pay for the privateers' upkeep in time of peace; the absence of any working definition of an *effective* blockade provided another annoyance that Marcy objected to. Marcy proposed an amendment that would have exempted even the private property of belligerents from seizure by a blockade. But the British government would not agree to Marcy's amendment, and there the matter rested until the outbreak of the Civil War.[6]

The customary alternative to blockade in the case of insurrections was a declaration of closure of ports (since any sovereign nation has the prerogative of closing its ports to foreign shipping). Closure of ports assumed that the insurrection was a localized and small-scale affair; ships of foreign nations might defy the closure and trade in those ports, but they were served notice that, at the end of the insurrection, ships that ignored the closure would be assessed for duties otherwise owed to the original government. It did not actually prevent outside supplies from reaching the ports and hands of rebels, and the most that the Federal navy could have done under those terms was stop a ship trying to enter a closed port, register a warning on the ship's log, and then again stop the ship when it made a second attempt to enter. This left Lincoln with the problem of defining and imposing a blockade upon an insurrection—which was a contradiction in terms of international law.[7]

At the same time, though, Lincoln carefully avoided any use of terms suggesting that the Confederacy was a legitimate sovereign nation. Never would he use the term "Confederate States," and he would describe them only as a "combination" that federal authority found "too powerful to suppress" by normal police action. He would *act* by blockade, as though the Confederacy were a sovereign nation, but he would *talk* insurrection, as if the Confederacy didn't exist. In the eyes of the European powers, however, a blockade was a blockade, and in that case, other nations had one of three options open to them. They could agree to the pretense that the Confederacy was only an insurrection and forbid their own shipping to have any contact with rebel-held ports. They could agree that the Confederacy was not exactly a sovereign nation, but they could also point to the fact that it was a large-scale affair with a functioning government of its own, conducting what amounted in fact to a civil war. Under those circumstances, they might declare neutrality and concede belligerent rights to the Confederates. Conceding belligerent rights recognized that the conflict had moved from the realm of a mere uprising, to be suppressed as a police action, to a full-scale war, to be conducted by the international laws of war; this, in turn, would allow Confederate agents, emissaries, and suppliers to operate on foreign shores within certain limited spheres of action. Or they could go all the way up to formal diplomatic recognition of the Confederacy. Recognition might then trigger a

6. Sir Francis Taylor Piggott, *The Declaration of Paris, 1856* (London: University of London Press, 1919), 116, 142–46; Mountague Bernard, *A Historical Account of the Neutrality of Great Britain During the American Civil War* (London: Longmans, 1870), 41–48, 106–21.

7. T. H. Lee and M. D. Ramsay, "The Story of the *Prize Cases*: Executive Action and Judicial Review in Wartime," in *Presidential Power Stories*, ed. C. H. Schroeder and C. A. Bradley (Eagan, MN: Foundation Press, 2009), 60.

Confederate appeal, as a nation to other nations, for allies, for international mediation, or for foreign intervention.

The neutrality/belligerent-rights option was, in fact, what the United States itself had practiced in the 1820s by conceding belligerent rights to Spain's rebellious colonies in South America, and the British took swift advantage of this fact in May 1861, when the Foreign Office simultaneously proclaimed its neutrality in the American conflict but also extended belligerent rights to the Confederacy (even before the new American minister to Great Britain, Charles Francis Adams, had arrived to take up his duties). Adams protested this concession to the British foreign secretary, the crusty and dismissive Lord John Russell, but Russell had only to point out that this was the price the Americans were going to have to pay if they wanted to impose a blockade. "It was . . . your own government which, in assuming the belligerent right of blockade, recognized the Southern states as belligerents," Russell later explained; in fact, the United States "could lawfully interrupt the trade of neutrals with the Southern States upon one ground only—namely, that the Southern States were carrying on war against the government of the United States; in other words, that they were belligerents."[8]

Lincoln was not happy with the British decision, but he was unhappier still with the unsolicited attempts of his secretary of state, William Henry Seward, to respond to that decision on his own. Before his inauguration, Lincoln had been confronted with the need to placate the major Republican front-runners who had been passed over by his nomination, which was why he handed the Department of the Treasury to Salmon P. Chase, and why he gave the Department of State to William H. Seward, the most famous political name in the Republican Party. Seward had been the most prominent voice among the anti-slavery Whigs long before Lincoln had ever been heard of outside Illinois, and in 1860 he had confidently expected to win the Republican Party's nomination without much contest. Of course he hadn't, but when Lincoln offered the State Department to Seward as a sop to Seward's political vanity and to cement the unity of the Republican Party, the New Yorker interpreted the proposal as a concession of weakness on Lincoln's part.

Seward promptly cast his tenure in the role as a grand secretaryship, on the model of John Quincy Adams, James Monroe, and Henry Clay. That led him to make on-the-spot decisions and bottomless promises that he lacked authority to

8. Charles Francis Adams Jr., *Charles Francis Adams* (Boston: Houghton Mifflin, 1899), 146–48, 170–71, 175–76; Martin Duberman, *Charles Francis Adams, 1807–1886* (Boston: Houghton Mifflin, 1961), 264; Russell to Adams, May 4, 1865, in *Das Staatsarchiv: Sammlung der offiziellen Aktenstücke zur der Geschichte der Gegenwart—Achter Band 1865, Januar bis Juni*, ed. L. K. Aegidi and A. Klauhold (Hamburg: Otto Meissner, 1865), 135–36, 137–39; Ludwell H. Johnson, "The Confederacy: What Was It? The View from the Federal Courts," *Civil War History* 32 (March 1986): 6.

make: on April 1, Seward actually presented a memorandum to Lincoln, seriously urging the president to provoke a war with France and Spain in the Caribbean as a way of reunifying the states in the face of a foreign threat. Lincoln ignored Seward's proposal and made it clear that, so far as the war was concerned, the president would be responsible for foreign policy, not Seward.[9] However, Lincoln did not anticipate Seward's penchant for composing incontinent dispatches and firing them off to American diplomats to present to other governments. The worst of these dispatches went out to Charles Francis Adams a week after the British neutrality proclamation.

Seward entertained little affection for Great Britain, and British recognition of Confederate belligerency brought out the worst in him. On May 21, Seward drafted a violent protest against the British action that actually threatened the British with war if they made any attempt to intervene in the blockade or the American conflict. "The true character of the pretended new State is . . . a power existing in *pronunciamento* only," Seward announced, and British recognition of belligerent rights would have no effect unless the British also meant to intervene militarily to "give it body and independence by resisting our measures of suppression." In that case, Seward trumpeted, "we, from that hour, shall cease to be friends and become once more, as we have twice before been . . . forced to become, enemies of Great Britain."[10]

It was not clear from Seward's logic whether the British proclamation was to be treated as an intervention itself, whether the next British ship to try its chances on the blockade would constitute such an intervention, or whether intervention meant the formal use of warships and troops on U.S. soil. That unsteadiness of focus only made the dispatch more inflammatory, and Seward's little manifesto might have been enough, all by itself, to bring on a war had not Charles Francis Adams took it upon himself to delete the most provocative passages in the document before reading it to Lord Russell. Russell merely reminded Adams that the United States itself had granted belligerent status to the Latin American republics when they rose in rebellion against their Spanish colonial masters, and he added that the United States had tried to extend similar status to French Canadian rebels in a revolt against British authority in Canada in 1837. As for the belligerent status of the Confederacy, the Lincoln government might claim that the Confederacy was merely an insurrection, but to British eyes the Confederacy was an organized government with its own constitution, congress, and president, with an army and

9. William H. Seward, "Some Thoughts for the President's Consideration," in *Dear Mr. Lincoln: Letters to the President*, ed. Harold Holzer (Reading, MA: Addison-Wesley, 1993), 239; Lincoln, "To William H. Seward," in *Collected Works*, 4:316–18.

10. Seward to Adams, May 21, 1861, in *Neutrality of Great Britain in the Civil War: Senate Document No. 18, 58th Congress* (Washington, DC: Government Printing Office, 1903), 25.

9 million citizens behind it. In the end, all that Seward's note served to create was a dangerous and highly charged diplomatic atmosphere that would require only a small spark to ignite an explosion.[11]

The greatest difficulty the imposition of a blockade posed for Lincoln was a practical one: how was the U.S. Navy to enforce it? In 1864, Denmark's tiny navy struggled to enforce a blockade of the coast of Prussia during its brief and unhappy war with Prussia and Austria and succeeded only intermittently, despite the inability of the Prussians to float more than a handful of gunboats and corvettes in their own defense.[12] On the day Lincoln proclaimed the blockade to be in effect, the U.S. Navy listed only forty-two ships in commission, and of them only twenty-four were modern steam-powered vessels (and just three of those were in Northern ports at the outbreak of the war and thus available immediately for blockade duty). Before them stretched 3,550 miles of Southern coastline, with 189 openings for commerce and nine major ports—Charleston, Wilmington, Mobile, Galveston, New Orleans, Savannah, Pensacola, Norfolk, and Jacksonville.

The suggestion that a blockade of the Confederacy now existed with these ships seemed preposterous. In short order, the aggressive secretary of the navy, Gideon Welles, chartered or commissioned 200 vessels of various sizes and descriptions, while 23 specially designed steam-powered blockade gunboats (which became known as the ingenious "ninety-day gunboats") were laid down and completed by March 1862. On April 30, Norfolk was officially blockaded, followed by Charleston on May 28, New Orleans on May 31, and Wilmington on July 21.[13]

The speed of the navy's mobilization stunned the Confederacy. Yet that speed presented a problem for the Federal navy, too, for in addition to the logistical problems of supplying and organizing these vessels, few Federal naval officers were prepared to deal with the even more incendiary difficulties in international diplomacy that blockade duty might present. In November 1861 one of those officers struck off the fireball that almost created war between the United States and Great Britain.

On November 8, 1861, the Federal steam sloop *San Jacinto* stopped a British mail steamer, the *Trent*, en route from Havana, Cuba, to St. Thomas in the West Indies. The *San Jacinto*'s master, Captain Charles Wilkes, had learned through a U.S. consul in Cuba that two new Confederate commissioners, James M. Mason and John Slidell, had slipped through the blockade to Nassau and from there to Cuba, and

11. Duberman, *Charles Francis Adams*, 268; Brian Jenkins, *Britain and the War for the Union* (Montreal: McGill-Queen's University Press, 1974), 1:104–9.

12. Michael Embree, *Bismarck's First War: The Campaign of Schleswig and Jutland 1864* (Solihull, UK: Helion, 2006), 272–86.

13. Donald L. Canney, *The Old Steam Navy*, vol. 1: *Frigates, Sloops, and Gunboats, 1815–1885* (Annapolis, MD: Naval Institute Press, 1990), 91–94; Stephen R. Taaffe, *Commanding Lincoln's Navy: Union Naval Leadership During the Civil War* (Annapolis, MD: Naval Institute Press, 2009), 26.

had purchased passage on the British mail packet *Trent* for St. Thomas, where they planned to board another steamer for England. "Probably no two men in the entire South were more thoroughly obnoxious to those of the Union side than Mason and Slidell," wrote Charles Adams's son, Henry, serving as his father's secretary in the American legation in London. The vision of these two Confederate diplomats sailing serenely to England to plot the destruction of the Union alternately maddened and excited Wilkes, who pulled down every book on the law of the sea in his possession, pored over them in his cabin, and decided that the presence of the Confederates on the *Trent* provided sufficient reason for stopping and searching an unarmed neutral ship and seizing the diplomats. "I carefully examined all the authorities on international law to which I had access, which bore upon the rights of neutrals and their responsibilities," Wilkes reported to Gideon Welles, and he convinced himself that "it became my duty to make these parties prisoners, and to bring them to the United States."[14]

Wilkes waited for the *Trent* in the Bahama Channel, and when the *Trent* hove into view, Wilkes fired a shot across her bow, then boarded the ship with an armed party. He demanded to see a list of the passengers and was refused, but Mason and Slidell identified themselves, and were manhandled (along with their two secretaries, J. E. McFarland and George Eustis) over the side of the *Trent* and into the *San Jacinto*'s waiting cutter.[15]

Northern public opinion was at first jubilant at Wilkes's daring pinch of the two Confederate emissaries, and Congress voted to grant Wilkes a gold medal. The British government was substantially less enthused: an unarmed British ship flying the British flag under a declaration of British neutrality and carrying British mail had been fired upon, stopped, and boarded by an American war vessel, and four passengers had been hauled off without so much as a by-your-leave. The deck of a ship is considered an extension of the territory of the nation under whose flag it flies, and so Wilkes might as well have sailed up the Thames and kidnapped four diplomats right off the docks.

So when news of the *Trent* boarding reached Britain on November 28, 1861, the prime minister, Lord Henry John Temple Palmerston, immediately drafted an ultimatum and ordered a squadron of steamers and 7,000 troops readied to send to Canada. On December 19 the British minister in Washington, Lord Richard Lyons, handed Seward a note from Earl Russell (who had by this point inherited the family earldom) demanding immediate redress—"namely, the liberation of the four gentlemen and their delivery to your lordship, in order that they may again be placed under

---

14. Wilkes to Gideon Welles, November 16, 1861, in *The Rebellion Record: A Diary of American Events*, ed. Frank Moore (New York: G. P. Putnam, 1868), 3:323–24.

15. Charles Francis Adams Jr., *The Trent Affair: An Historical Retrospect* (Boston: Massachusetts Historical Society, 1912), 7; D. M. Fairfax and Charles Wilkes (November 12, 1861), in *Rebellion Record*, 3: 328–30.

British protection, and a suitable apology for the aggression which has been committed"—or else Lyons was instructed to break off diplomatic relations and return to London. "If Commodore Wilkes designed making a sensation he succeeded to his heart's content," wrote Edwin de Leon, the Confederacy's chief propagandist in Britain. "The usually apathetic Englishmen were roused to a sudden frenzy by this insult to their flag, such as I had never witnessed in them before."[16]

Seward was always happy to talk about war with Britain, but with the reality of the situation staring him in the face, he reluctantly proceeded to eat his words. Seward consulted with McClellan, who advised him that the United States was in no position to fight the Confederates along the Ohio and the Potomac and simultaneously fight a British army along the St. Lawrence. There was no doubt that the British could muster more than sufficient forces in Canada to cause serious trouble. Up until the 1840s, the British government had left the defense of Canada largely in the hands of local militia, and much of that militia was as disorganized and ragtag as its counterparts across the border. The Crimean War taught the British the valuable lesson of relying on well-organized colonial auxiliary forces to sustain its far-flung empire, and in 1855 the Canadian Militia Act allowed the governor-general of Canada to reorganize the Canadian militia around a core of 5,000 volunteers who were to be armed and uniformed on a par with British regulars.[17]

When the *Trent* affair exploded, the Canadian Volunteer Militia was immediately called out, and Palmerston's troops were shipped to New Brunswick; another 35,000 Canadian volunteers were called up, and an additional 11,000 British regulars were soon on their way across the Atlantic. These were not forces that either Lincoln or Seward wanted to tangle with, and on December 25, Lincoln met with his cabinet and decided to swallow their humiliation. Mason and Slidell were released and placed on board a ship bound for Southampton, England, Wilkes was made to bear the blame for the seizure of the *Trent* for having acted "upon his own suggestions of duty," and the crisis relaxed. Mason and Slidell, who had been incarcerated at Fort Warren in Boston harbor, were retrieved by a British steamer on January 8 and made their way to London without any further interruptions. Still, it had been a near thing.[18]

The international ill temper created by the Federal blockade and its problems seemed to set every diplomatic wind blowing in the Confederacy's favor. The landed

16. Russell to Lyons, November 30, 1861, *London Gazette* 22589 (January 14, 1862): 196–97; Edwin De Leon, *Secret History of Confederate Diplomacy Abroad*, ed. William C. Davis (Lawrence: University Press of Kansas, 2005), 80.

17. David Ross, *Canadian Campaigns 1860–70* (New York: Osprey, 1992), 5; George Taylor Denison, *Soldiering in Canada: Recollections and Experiences* (London: Macmillan, 1900), 33–34; Hereward Senior, *The Last Invasion of Canada: The Fenian Raids, 1866–1870* (Toronto: Dundurn, 1991), 26–27.

18. Virgil Carrington Jones, *The Civil War at Sea: The Blockaders, January 1861–March 1862* (New York: Holt, Rinehart, Winston, 1960), 292–310; John A. Williams, "Canada and the Civil War," in *The Shot Heard Round the World: The Impact Abroad of the Civil War*, ed. Harold Hyman (New York: Knopf, 1969), 269; Ernest J. Chambers, *The Royal Grenadiers: A Regimental History of the 10th Infantry Regiment of*

English aristocracy sympathized with what they saw as a corresponding plantation aristocracy in the South, and they were not sad at the prospect of the American republic demonstrating what they had all along insisted was the inevitable fate of all popular democracies—instability, faction, division, civil war, and dismemberment. The aristocratic regimes of Europe were determined to put down anything which looked like liberal revolutions—in Spain, in Poland, in Russia, and all across Europe in 1848. In Britain, the traditional powers of an elected Parliament exerted the strongest check on monarchical authority, and liberalism there had great champions in the philosopher John Stuart Mill and the free-market capitalists of the Manchester School, Richard Cobden and John Bright. But Britain remained a far cry from liberal democracy. Despite a widening of voting rights in the Great Reform Act of 1832 and the repeal of the Tory aristocracy's chief economic bulwark, the Corn Laws, in 1848, it remained true that "the great institutions of society, the church . . . primogeniture, the house of peers, though threatened, are not overthrown."[19]

Not only not overthrown, but the American Civil War seemed likely to remove the principal bad example in the path of Tory privilege. In the House of Commons, Sir John Ramsden happily greeted the American Civil War as the bursting of "the great republican bubble," and the *Times* of London, the great mouthpiece of Tory reaction, offered its considered opinion that the self-destruction of "the American Colossus" would be the "riddance of a nightmare" for all monarchies. Henry Adams found that "British society had begun with violent social prejudice against Lincoln, Seward, and all the Republican leaders except Sumner. . . . Every one waited to see Lincoln and his hirelings disappear in one vast *debacle*." On Commemoration Day at Oxford, the custom "of cheering and hissing the different names of popular or odious public men as they are proposed" earned Jefferson Davis "tumultuous and unanimous applause" while the name of Lincoln "was greeted with hisses and groans."[20]

"The American Eagle," remembered the Confederate propagandist Edwin de Leon, "was a bird, they thought, whose wings would bear clipping," and to the aristocrats, "the supposed failure of the American experiment was a source of joy." British soldiers, among them Lieutenant Colonel Garnet Wolseley (who would eventually rise to become the most famous British general of the Victorian age) and Lieutenant Colonel Arthur Fremantle, slipped through the Union blockade to

---

the *Active Militia of Canada* (Toronto: E. L. Ruddy, 1904), 13–14; Robin W. Winks, *The Civil War Years: Canada and the United States* (Toronto: McGill-Queen's University Press, 1998 [1960]), 82.

19. John Ramsden, *An Appetite for Power: A History of the Conservative Party Since 1830* (London: HarperCollins, 1999), 51.

20. Duberman, *Charles Francis Adams,* 264; Frank Lawrence Owsley, *King Cotton Diplomacy: Foreign Relations of the Confederate States of America* (Chicago: University of Chicago Press, 1931), 186; Adams, *The Education of Henry Adams: An Autobiography* (Boston: Massachusetts Historical Society, 1918), 122–23; "English and American Aristocracy," *New York Times,* July 30, 1862.

attach themselves to the Confederate army as military observers. There they came to admire the lofty and chivalric principles of war they thought they saw practiced by the Southern generals. Fremantle found Robert E. Lee the very embodiment of a proper British officer, even down to his religion. "General Lee is, almost without exception, the handsomest man of his age I ever saw. . . . He is a perfect gentlemen in every respect." Fremantle added with evident gratification that Lee "is a member of the Church of England." Wolseley, too, was struck with admiration for Lee, and one of Wolseley's aides described Lee in terms that bordered on beatification:

> Every one who approaches him does so with marked respect, although there is none of that bowing and flourishing of forage caps which occurs in the presence of European generals; and, while all honor him and place implicit faith in his courage and ability, those with whom he is most intimate feel for him the affection of sons to a father. . . . When speaking of the Yankees he neither evinced any bitterness of feeling nor gave utterance to a single violent expression, but alluded to many of his former friends and companions among them in the kindest terms. He spoke as a man proud of the victories won by his country and confident of ultimate success under the blessing of the Almighty, whom he glorified for past successes, and whose aid he invoked for all future operations.[21]

Fremantle, after leaving the Confederacy in 1863, happily declared that "a people which in all ranks and in both sexes display a unanimity and a heroism which can never have been surpassed in the history of the world is destined sooner or later, to become a great and independent nation."[22]

Nor were the British rejoicing alone. Eugénie, the French empress, laughed at the impossibility of taking the Union cause seriously: "Why is [the French-American scientist] Du Chaillu searching Africa for the missing link when a specimen was brought from the American backwoods to Washington?" Leopold of Belgium, the power broker among European monarchs, ardently hoped that the war would make it possible "to raise a barrier against the United States and provide a support for the monarchical-aristocratic principle in the Southern states." In Prussia, Otto von Bismarck, who was only beginning the ascent to power which would make him and Germany the colossus of central Europe, admitted that "there was something in me that made me instinctively sympathize with the slaveholders as the aristocratic party." He could not understand "how society could be kept in tolerable order where the powers of the government were so narrowly restricted and where there was so little reverence for the constituted or 'ordained' authorities." Paul von

---

21. Garnet Wolseley, "A Month's Visit to the Confederate Headquarters," *Blackwood's Magazine* 93 (January 1863): 20.

22. De Leon, *Secret History of Confederate Diplomacy*, 12, 35; Arthur Fremantle, *The Fremantle Diary*, ed. Walter Lord (New York: Andre Deutsch, 1954), 197–99; J. R. Jones, *Life and Letters of Robert Edward Lee: Soldier and Man* (Harrisonburg, VA: Sprinkle, 1978 [1906]), 203–4.

Hindenburg, who would serve in 1870 as a Prussian army subaltern and in World War I as one of the principal German overlords, could recite even in the 1930s "every detail" and "every place" involved in the campaigns of the Army of Northern Virginia; in the post–Civil War years "Lee, Jackson and Stuart" were "the favorite heroes" of Prussian officers.[23]

It was not just the aristocrats and generals who sympathized with the Confederacy. After all, the Confederacy could claim that its war was being waged on the basis of national independence and free trade. As a result, many English liberals admired the South's fight as a struggle against money-grubbing Yankee overlordship and high protective tariffs, while others feared the political instability that massive unemployment and the disruption of trade would cause in England. The liberal stalwart and chancellor of the exchequer William Ewart Gladstone told a political dinner in Lancashire in October 1862 that they might as well recognize the inevitable success of the Confederacy now, rather than wait for the blockade to inflict more of its "frightful misery on British workers." "We may have our own opinions about slavery; we may be for or against the South; but there is no doubt that Jefferson Davis and other leaders of the South have made an army; they are making, it appears, a navy; and they have made what is more than either, they have made a nation." (In Paris, John Slidell bolted upright on hearing about Gladstone's speech: "If this means anything, it means immediate recognition!")[24]

Nor was Gladstone seeing ghosts for bedsheets in that "frightful misery." Only 497 of the 1,678 cotton-spinning mills in Manchester had enough cotton to operate at full capacity; 298 were shuttered entirely, and 80,000 mill workers were out of work. "I need hardly say that now there is great distress from want of employment—the result of your horrid war," a Methodist preacher wrote to the American evangelist Charles Grandison Finney. Another English friend advised Finney, "We have been working short time at the mill . . . & we seem to get worse & worse weekly & from all human appearances we can see no end to it after all." By December 1862, almost 15 percent of English textile workers were out of work entirely, and another 70 percent were working reduced shifts. "Better fight Yankees," read one workers' newspaper, "than starve operatives."[25]

The blockade also inflicted damage on the French economy, and with some of the same results in French public opinion. And the French emperor, Napoleon III,

23. Bismarck, in Louis L. Snyder, *The Blood and Iron Chancellor: A Documentary-Biography of Otto von Bismarck* (Princeton, NJ: Van Nostrand, 1967), 176–77; A. R. Tyrner-Tyrnauer, *Lincoln and the Emperors* (London: Rupert Hart-Davis, 1962), 61, 66; Luvaas, *The Military Legacy of the Civil War*, 72, 206.

24. Richard Shannon, *Gladstone, 1809–1865* (Chapel Hill: University of North Carolina Press, 1984), 468; Beckles Wilson, *John Slidell and the Confederates in Paris, 1862–1865* (New York: Minton, Balch, 1932), 91.

25. Howard Jones, *Abraham Lincoln and a New Birth of Freedom: The Union and Slavery in the Diplomacy of the Civil War* (Lincoln: University of Nebraska Press, 1999), 73; Paludan, *"A People's Contest,"* 269.

had reasons based on colonial ambition for preferring an independent Southern Confederacy. In December 1861 England, France, and Spain sent troops into Mexico to enforce the collection of debts owed by the bankrupt Mexican Republic. This was not the first time the European monarchies had schemed to reestablish themselves in the New World: the British had established a protectorate in Nicaragua, the Belgians set up a quasi-colony in Guatemala, both the French and the Spanish had repeatedly put their oars into Mexican affairs, and even the north German states had their eyes on Central America for "emigration and colonization" in the 1850s. But intervention in Mexico in 1861 was the most serious effort yet, since Napoleon intended to use the debt crisis as a pretext for deposing the Mexican president, Benito Juárez, and installing a puppet ruler who would rule Mexico, for all intents and purposes, as a French colony. The English and the Spanish withdrew once it became clear that this was Napoleon's game, and in 1863, Napoleon recruited an Austrian archduke, Ferdinand Maximilian (the brother of the Austrian emperor, Franz Josef), as the new "emperor" of Mexico.[26]

The chief threat to this scheme was the United States, which publicly warned Napoleon not to intervene in Mexican affairs. By 1862 the United States was in no position to obstruct Napoleon's ambitions in Mexico, and Napoleon hoped that the division of the American republic would permanently eliminate the United States as an obstacle to French colonization in Central America. The Confederate agents in Europe, headed by John Slidell, decided to play on Napoleon's desires and offered Confederate support for his Mexican adventure, plus a renewed supply of cotton, if the emperor would grant French diplomatic recognition to the Confederacy and aid the Confederates in breaking the blockade. Napoleon pulled shy of accepting the Confederate offer, but he did create a favorable climate in France for Confederate agents to obtain loans and other assistance. The French banking house of Emile Erlanger underwrote the sale of $14.5 million of Confederate bonds in March 1863, and Confederate purchasing agents were able to buy up substantial amounts of war supplies to run through the blockade.[27]

The most damaging pieces of war equipment that the British and French allowed the Confederates to buy from them were ships, especially armed commerce raiders. In March 1861 the Confederate government appointed a former U.S. naval

26. Thomas Schoonover, "Napoleon Is Coming! Maximilian Is Coming? The International History of the Civil War in the Caribbean Basin," in *The Union, the Confederacy, and the Atlantic Rim*, ed. Robert E. May (West Lafayette, IN: Purdue University Press, 1995), 101, 107, 118–19; Joan Haslip, *The Crown of Mexico: Maximilian and His Empress Carlota* (New York: Holt, Rinehart and Winston, 1972), 211; John Metcalf Taylor, *Maximilian and Carlotta: A Story of Imperialism* (New York: G. P. Putnam, 1894), 75.

27. Judith Fenner Gentry, "A Confederate Success in Europe: The Erlanger Loan," *Journal of Southern History* 36 (May 1970): 159, 160; Richard C. Todd, *Confederate Finance* (Athens: University of Georgia Press, 2009 [1954]), 48–51.

officer named James Bulloch as its civilian naval agent, and by June Bulloch had set himself up in Liverpool to arrange contracts for building or buying ships for the Confederacy. Bulloch turned out to be an extremely adroit and successful bargainer, as well as a careful reader of the terms of Britain's Foreign Enlistment Act of 1819, which forbade even recognized belligerents to "equip, furnish, fit out, or arm . . . any Ship or Vessel, with Intent or in order that such Ship or Vessel shall be employed in the Service of any Foreign Prince, State, or Potentate." The act threatened violators of the law with seizure of these vessels, but the law also provided little in terms of the proof required beforehand to demonstrate that a ship was being built or fitted out with belligerent intent. It became easy, therefore, for Bulloch to build or purchase English ships through registered agents or English partners, sail them out of British waters, and then outfit them for their real military purposes somewhere else.[28]

Bulloch's first commission, a steamer named *Oreto*, sailed from Liverpool in March 1862 as a merchant ship with what appeared on the records as an English captain and crew and registry with the tiny Kingdom of Palermo. The builders "may . . . have had a tolerably clear notion that she would at some future time, and by some subsequent arrangement, pass into the possession of the Confederate Government," Bulloch snickered, "but they never mentioned their suspicions, and they undertook nothing more than to build and deliver in Liverpool a screw-steamer, according to certain specified plans and conditions, fitted for sea in every respect, but without armament or equipment for fighting of any kind whatever." Having fulfilled the letter of British neutrality, Bulloch then ordered the *Oreto* to a rendezvous on a deserted island in the Bahamas, where she was equipped with naval guns, a Confederate crew, and a new name, CSS *Florida*. The *Florida* then set off on a two-and-a-half-year career of commerce raiding that sent thirty-eight Yankee merchant ships to the bottom or into refit to emerge as Confederate raiders themselves.[29]

The *Florida* was not the only ship Bulloch would slip out of England through the cracks in the laws. In the summer of 1861 Bulloch negotiated with another firm, Laird Brothers, for the construction of a sleek steam cruiser known only by its yard number, *290*. The U.S. consul in Liverpool, Thomas Haines Dudley, suspected from the beginning that Bulloch was planning another *Oreto*, and amassed considerable evidence that the *290* was intended for purposes other than peaceful trade. The British government was slow to follow up on the charges, and by the time an

28. Frederick Waymouth Gibbs, *The Foreign Enlistment Act* (London: William Ridgway, 1863), 72 (otherwise 59 George III. c. 69).

29. James D. Bulloch, *The Secret Service of the Confederate States in Europe: or, How the Confederate Cruisers Were Equipped* (London: Bentley and Son, 1884), 1:54–58.

order to impound the ship was issued in July 1862, Bulloch had already bundled it out to sea.

It was now the turn of Charles Francis Adams to send barely contained statements of outrage to the Foreign Office. Given the *290*'s "peculiar adaptation to war purposes, there could have been no doubt by those engaged in the work, and familiar with such details, that she was intended for other purposes than those of legitimate trade," in blithe disregard of the Foreign Enlistment Act. Even worse, the *290*, "although commanded by Americans in her navigation of the ocean . . . is manned almost entirely by English seamen, engaged and forwarded from that port by persons in league with her Commander"—yet another violation of the Act. It was all to no avail. The *290* sailed blithely to the Azores, where this vessel, too, was outfitted with guns and stores and took on the most dreaded name in the entire gallery of American ships—CSS *Alabama*.[30]

By the autumn of 1862, the Confederacy had come as close as it was ever to come to obtaining outright cooperation and recognition from France and Britain. The effects of the cotton blockade, the unpleasant consequences of the *Trent* affair, and other blockade incidents, and especially the surprising success of the Confederate armies under Lee and Bragg in Virginia and Kentucky, persuaded both Lord Palmerston and Napoleon III that the time had at last arrived to intervene in the American mess. Palmerston knew that recognition of the Confederacy could easily bring on the war with the United States that he had avoided in 1861, since the Confederacy would not be "a bit more independent for our saying so unless we followed up our Declaration by taking Part with them in the war."[31]

But by late summer 1862 the North appeared exhausted anyway. In June Palmerston had surprised Charles Francis Adams with a savage note denouncing Union occupation practices in New Orleans, and Adams took the note as a signal that the Palmerston government was about to open a campaign for intervention and mediation. In July, James Mason, as the Confederacy's representative in London, pressed Earl Russell with "a direct and vigorous effort to obtain recognition of the Confederacy . . . ending with a formal demand." Later in June and again in July, debate erupted in Parliament over Southern recognition, with one pro-Southern member of Parliament, William Lindsay, loudly proclaiming that he wanted Britain to grant diplomatic recognition to the Confederacy and then present an ultimatum for mediation because he "*desired the disruption of the American Union, as every honest*

---

30. C. F. Cross, *Lincoln's Man in Liverpool: Consul Dudley and the Legal Battle to Stop Confederate Warships* (DeKalb: Northern Illinois University Press, 2007), 37; Frank J. Merli, *Great Britain and the Confederate Navy, 1861–1865* (Indianapolis: Indiana University Press, 2004 [1970]), 92–93; Adams to Earl Russell, November 20, 1862, in *Papers Relating to Foreign Affairs, Accompanying the Annual Message of the President to the First Session of the Thirty-Eighth Congress* (Washington, DC: Government Printing Office, 1864), Part I, 5–7.

31. Jenkins, *Britain and the War for the Union*, 2: 66.

Englishman did, because it was too great a Power and England sh'd not let such a power exist on the American continent."

In August, Earl Russell began sounding out the French about the possibility of a joint Anglo-French intervention to stop the war. Finally, on September 14, 1862, Palmerston drafted a short note to Russell that asked whether it might not "be time for us to consider whether . . . England and France might not . . . recommend an arrangement upon the basis of separation?" If mediation was rejected by the Lincoln administration, would it not be time for Britain "to recognize the Southern States as an independent State" and force some kind of arbitration on the North? Three days later Russell responded favorably to Palmerston's suggestion, observing that "the time is come for offering mediation to the United States Government, with a view to the recognition of the Independence of the Confederates." Palmerston should call for a cabinet meeting on October to discuss the offer, Russell said, and he added hopefully that "if the Federals sustain a great defeat, they may be at once ready for mediation."[32]

The Federals did not sustain a great defeat, however. On the same day that Russell yielded to Palmerston's suggestion about recognizing Southern independence, Lee and McClellan fought each other to a bloody standstill at Antietam. When Lee retreated afterwards, Palmerston decided to shelve his proposal. And there the matter rested, for whatever abstract or emotional sympathies the British might feel for the Confederacy, none of them was so burning that Palmerston would commit his government to backing a loser. Nor is there any substantial evidence that the British government had gotten to the point of calculating what force it would take to get the North to the peace table. Russell and Palmerston talked of mediation only if it could be jointly arranged with the French and the Russians. Despite the effect of the cotton blockade in 1862, British textile merchants soon found new sources of cotton in Egypt, Brazil, and India, and the British economy gradually recovered, thus removing a major agitation for intervention.[33]

Also, as Palmerston acknowledged, any form of intervention could very likely mean a war at sea. While the British navy was undoubtedly the most powerful in the world at that time, the American navy had grown by leaps and bounds since 1861, and since the United States was not a signatory of the Declaration of Paris, it could unleash a cloud of privateers, which, as the example of the *Florida* and the *Alabama* demonstrated, could easily create serious trouble for British commerce, sending

---

32. De Leon, *Secret History of Confederate Diplomacy*, 125; Howard Jones, *Union in Peril: The Crisis over British Intervention in the Civil War* (Chapel Hill: University of North Carolina Press, 1992), 134. The Palmerston-Russell correspondence is contained in Appendix E of James V. Murfin, *The Gleam of Bayonets: The Battle of Antietam and Robert E. Lee's Maryland Campaign, September 1862* (New York: T. Yoseloff, 1965), 394, 396–97, 399–400.

33. Jones, *Union in Peril*, 210–26; Douglas R. Egerton, "Rethinking Atlantic Historiography in a Postcolonial Era: The Civil War in a Global Perspective," *Journal of the Civil War Era* 1 (March 2011): 82–84.

insurance rates as well as losses in ships and cargoes beyond acceptable limits. In the event of armed intervention, the British army would be compelled to operate from the Canadian border, and to do so under the disadvantage of having to supply it across three thousand miles of Atlantic Ocean.

Even if the military situation had not been enough to give the British pause, there was the business of President Lincoln's preliminary Emancipation Proclamation, issued a week after Antietam in September 1862. At first emancipation actually looked as though it might drive the British even more quickly toward mediation, since Palmerston and Russell read the Proclamation as an incitement to John Brown–style slave rebellion. Such incitement, they were sure, would result in a race war that would not only disrupt the transatlantic cotton flow beyond repair but also set an uncomfortable example for Britain's colonial subjects about the possibilities of non-Europeans rising in revolt against white European rulers. (The British had only just endured such a conflict in the Sepoy Rebellion in India in 1857–58, and prospect of an American slave rebellion reviving the specter of the racial antagonisms that generated violence in India was not reassuring to British minds.)[34]

However, Lincoln's decision to make even partial abolition of slavery a stated aim of the war operated in exactly the other direction on the British public's view of intervention. No matter what opinion an English aristocrat had of Southern planters, or what opinion English merchants or workingmen had of cotton, few Englishmen wanted to set themselves up as the enemies of a war against slavery, which had been abolished in the British empire in 1833. From the moment Lincoln announced the Proclamation, wrote Richard Cobden to Charles Sumner, "our old anti-slavery feeling began to arouse itself, and it has been gathering strength ever since." Cobden, who originally lacked confidence in Lincoln, now came decisively down from the fence himself and embraced the Union for "the lofty motive of humanity that has induced them to risk the longer continuance of the war rather than allow the degrading institution of slavery to continue." Once the Proclamation was in place, John Bright (Cobden's great partner in the promotion of the Manchester School) jubilantly demanded to know "who they are who speak eagerly in favour of England becoming the ally and friend of this great conspiracy against human nature." Who, he asked, are the men in England "eager to admit into the family of nations a State . . . more odious and more blasphemous than was theretofore dreamed of in Christian or in Pagan, in civilized or in savage times"?[35]

34. Jones, "History and Mythology: The Crisis over British Intervention in the Civil War," in *The Union, the Confederacy, and the Atlantic Rim*, ed. Robert E. May (West Lafayette, IN: Purdue University Press, 1995), 33, 43–50; Elizabeth Kelly Gray, "'Whisper to Him the Word India': Transatlantic Critics and American Slavery, 1830–1860," *Journal of the Early Republic* 28 (Fall 2008): 403, 405.

35. John Morley, *The Life of Richard Cobden* (Boston: Roberts Bros., 1881), 560–61, 583; Richard Cobden, "Foreign Policy IX," November 23, 1864, in *Speeches on Questions of Public Policy by Richard Cobden, M.P.*, eds. J. Bright and J. E. T. Rogers (London: Macmillan, 1880), 490; John Bright, in George Barnett Smith, *The Life and Speeches of the Right Honourable John Bright, M.P.* (London: Hodder and Stoughton, 1881), 2:57.

One week after the preliminary Proclamation was issued, a meeting staged by pro-Confederate British sympathizers at Staleybridge, outside Manchester, was broken up by a pro-Union workers' group; in Manchester, a New Year's Day workers' meeting forwarded to Abraham Lincoln a series of resolutions that affirmed that "since we have discerned . . . that the victory of the free north, in the war which has so sorely distressed us as well as afflicted you, will strike off the fetters of the slave, you have attracted our warm and earnest sympathy." On January 29, 1863, a pro-Union meeting at Exeter Hall in London drew overflow crowds that spilled out into the streets and snarled traffic. Great as the suffering of the unemployed mill workers was, they saw in the Emancipation Proclamation an unambiguous blow against oppression and tyranny of every kind. "The distress in Lancashire is & has been very great," admitted one of Charles Grandison Finney's correspondents in March 1863, but all the same, "I would be very sorry & so I am persuaded would the bulk of our Lancashire people to see you patch up a peace with the South upon the basis of protection of slavery."

> We are Sure the mass of our people [are] Sympathetic with the Northern interest, especially since the Emancipation Policy has been adopted. I cannot tell you how glad I felt & how I shouted Hurrah for Lincoln when news reached here that he had confirmed that Proclamation on the 1st Jan[uar]y. . . . The reason why many of our people did not sooner sympathize with the North was a feeling that they were not fighting for the destruction of slavery but merely for the Union with or without slavery.[36]

So when Gladstone unwisely attempted to raise the subject of Confederate recognition in Cabinet, Palmerston quashed the motion and Russell turned to rap Gladstone sharply on the knuckles for going "beyond the latitude which all speakers must be allowed when you say that Jefferson Davis had made a nation."[37] On October 9, 1863, Russell stepped in and seized two powerful ironclad warships that Bulloch had contracted for at Laird Brothers and appropriated them for the British navy as HMS *Wivern* and HMS *Scorpion*.

The Confederacy still had hopes for the French. Napoleon III was less moved by the Emancipation Proclamation than Palmerston was, and he continued to make hopeful noises about European support and recognition for the Confederacy. The negotiation of the Erlanger loan in March 1863, and the emperor's private approval of a plan by Bulloch to build two ironclads and two wooden steam cruisers in France, gave further encouragement to Confederate agents to hope that Napoleon III might yet act on his own. But Napoleon was unwilling to act for the Confederacy without British support, and that support never had much hope of materializing

36. James Barlow to Finney, March 17, 1863, in Finney Papers, Oberlin College Archives.

37. Charles Francis Adams, *The Crisis of Foreign Intervention in the War of Secession, September-November 1862* (Boston: Massachusetts Historical Society, 1914), 23; Russell, in *Europe Looks at the Civil War*, ed. B. B. Sideman and L. Friedman (New York: Orion Press, 1960), 186.

after September 1862, if it had ever had any. On November 10, 1862, Napoleon proposed to Palmerston that Britain, France, and Russia impose a cease-fire in America, along with a lifting of the blockade. What he had in mind was "an armistice of six months, with the Southern ports open to the commerce of the world," the emperor explained to John Slidell—and added, with a wink and a nod, that "hostilities would probably never be resumed." Palmerston's cabinet rejected the proposal. In June 1863, the emperor met with two pro-Confederate members of Parliament and made more veiled suggestions about cooperative intervention to end the war—but Parliament refused to listen. And with that, the emperor's interest in American affairs wandered. By 1867 he had even abandoned his luckless puppets in Mexico. In January 1864 the French government withdrew permission for the construction of Bulloch's ships, and only a phony sale of one of the ironclads to Denmark allowed Bulloch to salvage at least one of his prizes. By the time the ship (named CSS *Stonewall*) could be repurchased from the Danes, fitted for service, and sailed to the West Indies, the war was over.[38]

By the end of 1863, the once-bright confidence of the Confederacy that Europe would be forced by economic necessity to step in and guarantee Southern independence lay in the dust. John L. Peyton, North Carolina's state agent in Paris, warned his home-state governor, Zebulon Baird Vance, that "the people of the South" must "realize that they have no friends among the crown heads of Europe—that they must rely upon themselves for deliverance from the hated thralldom of the Yankee Union."[39] In August 1863 the Confederate government recalled Mason from London, effectively conceding the hopelessness of winning over British opinion; in October Jefferson Davis and the Confederate Cabinet concurred in expelling all British consuls from Southern ports on the grounds that the consuls had been obstructing Southern military draft laws.

Much of the credit in frustrating Confederate foreign policy lies with the American minister to Britain, Charles Francis Adams. The perfect statesman, Adams not only tirelessly represented the Union cause to the British government and the British people but also financed an active network of spies and agents who relentlessly exposed Confederate violations of the British neutrality laws and hobbled Confederate efforts to raise money and buy arms. Even the Confederate propagandist de Leon had to admit that Adams "played well his part, and by his singular moderation of language and action . . . sustained his own dignity and that of the people he represented . . . and won reluctant admiration from many who loved not the cause

---

38. Bulloch, *Secret Service of the Confederate States*, 2:63–64, 73–74, 76, 83–86; John Bigelow, *France and the Confederate Navy, 1862–1868: An International Episode* (London: S. Low, Marston, Searle and Rivington, 1888), 56; Lynn M. Case and Warren F. Spencer, *The United States and France: Civil War Diplomacy* (Philadelphia: University of Pennsylvania Press, 1970), 269–71, 475–77; Wilson, *John Slidell*, 105.

39. Peyton to Vance, January 15, 1863, in *The Papers of Zebulon Baird Vance*, ed. Joe A. Mobley (Raleigh, NC: State Department of Archives and History, 1995), 2:18.

or the Government he sustained."[40] William L. Dayton, the American minister to France (who died in harness in 1864), was equally active in pushing the French to stay within their own neutrality laws, and Dayton's shrewd exposures of the shakiness of Confederate finance critically depressed the value of the Confederate bond sale by the Erlangers. The two rocks on which Confederate hopes for foreign intervention unavoidably foundered were the fatal timing of its military defeats in 1862, and the moral capital Lincoln earned for the Union with the Emancipation Proclamation. After Antietam, and after Emancipation, the Confederacy was simply no longer believable.

THE WAR AT SEA

Lincoln's decision to impose a naval blockade of the Confederacy broadened, at one stroke, the scope of the American Civil War to take in the seven seas as well as the Confederate heartland. By the same token, the Confederacy could ill afford to stand by and allow the Federal navy to put its hands around the Confederacy's neck and wring it. So between the Federal navy's determination to choke the Confederates inside their own harbors and the Confederacy's desperation to find some way of forcing the Federal navy to loosen its grip, the Civil War spread outward from land to sea, and from there around the world.

In 1861, the U.S. Navy carried 1,500 officers and about 7,500 sailors on its active list; the cream of the fleet were the six big 5,000-ton steam frigates, *Niagara*, *Roanoke*, *Colorado*, *Merrimack*, *Minnesota*, and *Wabash*, launched in 1855 and carrying batteries of up to forty 9-inch, 10-inch, and 11-inch smoothbore cannon (and with room for some specialty armament as well, such as the *Minnesota*'s 150-pound Parrott rifle and the *Niagara*'s twelve 12-inch shell guns). Following the steam frigates were the twelve steam sloops of 1857 and 1858, the biggest of which—*Hartford*, *Brooklyn*, and *Richmond*—displaced 2,500 tons and carried sixteen to twenty 9-inch guns.[41]

None of these ships, however, had been designed for blockade duty. As it was, the outbreak of the war found all of the frigates in various navy yards undergoing all sorts of refitting and overhaul. One of them, the *Merrimack*, suffered from chronic engine trouble and was in dry dock for machinery repairs at Gosport Navy Yard at Norfolk when Virginia passed its secession ordinance. Despite the entreaties of Benjamin Isherwood, an army engineer sent expressly to Norfolk to get the *Merrimack* out of danger, the commandant of the yard ordered the steam frigate burned and scuttled to prevent it from falling into the hands of the Rebels. As with the ships, there was also some question about the reliability of the navy's

---

40. De Leon, *Secret History of Confederate Diplomacy*, 85.

41. James Russell Soley, *The Blockade and the Cruisers* (New York: C. Scribner's Sons, 1885), 241–42.

officers. Although only 237 of the navy's officer corps resigned and went South at the beginning of the war, Federal admiral Samuel F. Du Pont was keenly aware of the fact that "not a single officer" in his South Atlantic Blockading Squadron in 1862 had "voted for Lincoln." At the same time, Du Pont was also aware that "there is not a proslavery man among them," and the officers who had some chance ashore to see the remains of the slave system for themselves experienced great awakenings. The aristocratic Du Pont, whose home was in the border slave state of Delaware, confessed that he had "been a sturdy conservative on this question, defended it over the world, argued for it as patriarchal in its tendencies . . . that the condition of the slaves was far in advance of the race in Africa." Nevertheless, he was horrified by the conditions he found on the coastal plantations. Having seen "the *institution* 'de pres,'" Du Pont wrote feelingly to a friend in Philadelphia, "may God forgive me for the words I have uttered in its defense as intertwined in our Constitution."[42]

In terms of both ships and personnel, the federal government clearly was going to have to find ways to improvise a navy, as much for the blockade as to maintain the navy's high-seas profile. That the government did, in fact, manage to improvise such a navy was largely due to Gideon Welles, the secretary of the navy, an ex-Democrat and former naval bureau chief. Welles and his assistant secretary, Gustavus Fox, realized from the beginning that it was much more important to put ships of any size or description outside a Southern port as soon as possible to make the blockade visible than to wait until a specially designed blockading fleet could be built. So Welles chartered one of almost everything that would float, armed them in make-shift fashion, and sent them off to pound a beat outside Southern rivers and harbors. As early as May 11, 1861, Welles had the frigate *Niagara* stationed outside Charleston harbor. By January 1862 Welles had organized four blockading squadrons, two along the Gulf and two along the Atlantic, to guard the Confederate coastline; and by the end of the war he would have bought, borrowed, deployed, or built over 600 warships, merchantman, steamboats, and ordinary tugs and turned them into a blockading fleet.[43]

The principal objective of the blockade was to prevent any shipping, Southern or otherwise, from entering or leaving the Confederacy. That meant, for much of the time, that blockade duty was an incessant string of empty, passive and depressingly boring days, waiting for the possible blockade-runner to appear over the horizon. "Dull! Dull! Dull! is the day," wrote the surgeon of the Federal blockader *Fernandina* in his diary. "Nothing to do." On top of the boredom, sailors had to endure

42. Du Pont to Mrs. Du Pont, April 10–13, 1862, and Du Pont to James Stokes Biddle, December 17, 1861, in *Samuel Francis DuPont: A Selection from His Civil War Letters*, ed. John D. Hayes (Ithaca, NY: Cornell University Press, 1969), 1: 281, 413.

43. Robert M. Browning, *Success Is All That Was Expected: The South Atlantic Blockading Squadron During the Civil War* (Dulles, VA: Brassey's, 2002), 11; Taaffe, *Commanding Lincoln's Navy*, 170–71.

many of the same routine annoyances and bad food that soldiers onshore suffered. The *Fernandina*'s unhappy surgeon explained that "'a life on the ocean wave' is not a very pleasant one unless a person is fond of feasting every day on salt junk and hard tack, reading papers a month after they are published, hearing from home once a month, etc., etc." Add to the boredom and discomfort the fierce Southern heat, and it quickly became apparent that blockade duty was anything but romantic. One sailor stationed off Wilmington, North Carolina, explained in his diary how adventurous blockade duty really was.

> I told her [his mother] she could get a fair idea of our "adventures" if she would go on the roof of the house, on a hot summer day, and talk to half a dozen hotel hallboys, who are generally far more intelligent and agreeable than the average "acting officer." Then descend to the attic and drink some tepid water, full of iron rust. Then go on to the roof again and repeat this "adventurous process" at intervals, until she has tired out and go to bed, with every thing shut down tight, so as not to show a light. Adventure! Bah! The blockade is the wrong place for it.[44]

Yet for all its discomforts, blockade duty was still preferred over service on the inland rivers or on foreign stations, chiefly because blockade duty offered the prospect of prize money to any ship's crew that captured a merchantman trying to run the blockade. The USS *Magnolia* bagged a blockade-runner named *Memphis* in 1863, and when the *Memphis* was sold off as a prize, the crew divided up the staggering sum of $510,000. The naval lieutenant in command, who enjoyed the Melville-esque name of William Budd, took home $38,318.55 as his share, and the *Magnolia*'s ordinary seamen realized $1,350.88 each. When the ninety-day gunboat *Kennebec* could lap up over $1.5 million in prize money for its 100 officers and crewmen, and when Rear Admiral Samuel Philips Lee could pocket between $110,000 (Lee's reported figure) and $150,000 (what Gideon Welles believed he had raked in) in prize money over the two years he commanded the North Atlantic Blockading Squadron, blockade duty could suddenly seem appealing after all.[45]

The blockade came to involve more than merely sitting in ambush for Confederate blockade-runners. A surprisingly large proportion of blockade seizures were made by the little Potomac Flotilla, which ran small expeditions up the Potomac and the other Chesapeake Bay rivers to disrupt Confederate coastal trade and the smuggling of medicines and weapons through Confederate lines in Virginia.

---

44. William Still, "The Common Sailor: The Civil War's Uncommon Man," *Civil War Times Illustrated* 23 (February 1985): 38–39.

45. "How Fortunes Are Made in the Navy," *The Big Blue Union* [Marysville, KS], December 5, 1863; Canney, *The Old Steam Navy*, 94; Virginia Jeans Laas, "'Sleepless Sentinels': The North Atlantic Blockading Squadron, 1862–1864," *Civil War History* 31 (March 1985): 33; Dudley Taylor Cornish and Virginia Jeans Laas, *Lincoln's Lee: The Life of Samuel Phillips Lee, United States Navy, 1812–1897* (Lawrence: University Press of Kansas, 1986), 123.

At the other end of the scale, the navy also aimed to shut down as many major Southern ports as it could. In November 1861 the navy seized Beaufort and the Carolina Sea Islands, and the following January the army and navy together established a foothold on the North Carolina coast. In April 1862 another joint army-navy operation recaptured Fort Pulaski on the Savannah River and closed the Georgia coastline to blockade-running, while the next month Farragut and his steam sloops pushed their way past the Confederacy's Mississippi River forts and steamed up to New Orleans. Farragut also sealed off Mobile Bay in August 1864, and in January 1865 Wilmington surrendered to yet another joint expedition led by Farragut's stepbrother, Rear Admiral David Dixon Porter. Only Charleston managed to resist the onslaught of the Federal navy. Throughout the summers of 1863 and 1864, both the army and navy attempted to capture the Charleston harbor defenses and bombard Fort Sumter (now in Confederate hands) into submission. But Sumter, and the rest of Charleston harbor, held out until February 1865, when the approach of a Federal army from Georgia finally forced the Charleston garrison to evacuate the city.

The Confederates had been aware from the beginning of the war that the blockade represented a noose that would strangle them if they could not first find a way to cut through it. "The blockade is breaking up the whole South," wrote "Parson" Brownlow, the Unionist Tennessean in the spring of 1862. "It has been remarked in the streets of Knoxville that no such thing as a fine-toothed comb was to be had, and all the little Secession heads were full of squatter sovereigns hunting for their rights in the territories." So if maintaining the blockade was the item of first importance for the Federal navy, then rendering it ineffective as soon as possible became a top priority for the Confederates.[46]

Unfortunately, the Confederates had very little at hand to use as a weapon against the Federal ships. At least the Union started out with *some* kind of a navy; the Confederates had none, except for a few small sloops and revenue cutters that they were able to seize at the time of secession. By February 1862 the Confederate navy still only amounted to thirty-three ships. Nor did the Confederates have much to build with. The South had little or nothing in the way of a shipbuilding industry: it possessed few of the raw materials or manufacturing facilities for fitting and arming warships, and lacked building and repair facilities. The only naval construction yard was in the Florida harbor of Pensacola, but the waters of the harbor were controlled by Fort Pickens, whose Union garrison had clung to control of the fort even after Fort Sumter had been bombarded into surrender. Of course, Virginia had occupied the navy yard at Norfolk in April 1861, but the Norfolk yard could easily be sealed off by Federal blockading ships in Hampton Roads and at the mouth of the Chesapeake. If the South had any hope of breaking the blockade, it was going to have to be by some unexpected and unconventional means.

46. Brownlow, *Sketches of the Rise, Progress, and Decline of Secession*, 423.

However, the unexpected and unconventional seem to have come naturally to the Confederate secretary of the navy, Stephen Russell Mallory, whose technical ingenuity single-handedly created a Confederate navy, which in turn almost broke up the Union blockade. Very much like his opposite number, Gideon Welles, Mallory laid hands on any possible weapon, any proposed invention, no matter how unlikely—mines made from beer kegs, submarines made from boilerplate, gunboats laminated with railroad iron—and floated them out to do battle with the Federal steam frigates. It was in that last category, ironclads, that Mallory came the nearest to succeeding in his schemes. Mallory, a former U.S. senator from Florida and formerly the chairman of the Senate Naval Affairs Committee, was fully abreast of the latest developments in building ironclad gunboats and warships. He was aware that, however imposing the Federal steam frigates and steam sloops might seem, not a single one of them was ironclad, and the Federal ironclad gunboats being built for use on the Mississippi were strictly for the river, too small to venture out on the ocean. Let the Confederacy manage, somehow, to construct even one ironclad warship capable of steaming on the high seas, then that one ship would be more than a match for each and every one of the Federal frigates. "I regard the possession of an iron-armored ship as a matter of the first necessity," wrote Mallory. "Such a vessel at this time could traverse the entire coast of the United States, prevent all blockade, and encounter, with a fair prospect of success their entire navy. . . . Naval engagements between wooden frigates as they are now built and armed will prove to be the forlorn hopes of the sea—simply contests in which the question, not of victory, but who shall go to the bottom first is to be solved."[47]

The difficulty, for Mallory, was that nowhere in the Confederacy was there the capability of building such a ship, even if he could find enough iron plate or iron rails to armor her. Then, on June 23, 1861, two of Mallory's lieutenants at Norfolk reminded Mallory about the scuttled steam frigate *Merrimack* in the Norfolk Navy Yard. They pointed out that a salvage company had pumped out the half-sunken shell of the frigate and placed her in dry dock, and as it turned out, the hull and boilers of the *Merrimack* were still relatively intact. It would be possible to cut away her burned-over masts and useless upper decks, rebuild her upper works with an iron casemate like one of the Crimean "floating batteries," and arm her with enough guns to sink anything the Federal navy could send against her. Mallory bought the idea at once: he had the sunken frigate inspected, and in July 1861 work began on reconstructing the *Merrimack* as a seagoing ironclad.

On February 17, 1862, the rebuilt *Merrimack* was launched and commissioned—and given a new name, *CSS Virginia*. The reborn steam frigate now looked nothing like its first form—or, for that matter, like anything else afloat. The Confederate engineers had cut the hull of the ship down to the waterline and then erected a

47. James Russell Soley, "The Union and Confederate Navies," in *Battles and Leaders*, 1:631.

thirteen-and-a-half-foot-high iron-plated casemate on top of the hull, using two layers of two-inch-thick wrought-iron plates, eight feet long by eight inches wide; the armored casemate would be rounded at each end and with sides sloping outwards at a 36-degree angle, and roofed over by an iron grille with three hatches. Four gunports with iron shutters gaped in each side, and at each rounded end of the casemate were three more gunports for a 7-inch rifled pivot gun. Just beneath the waterline at her bow was a 1,500-pound cast-iron ram, which the ironclad could use to smash the timber hulls of the Federal blockading fleet. On February 24 the *Virginia* was given a captain, Franklin Buchanan, and on March 8 Buchanan nosed the makeshift ironclad's way out of Norfolk and down the ten-mile-long channel into Hampton Roads.[48]

Standing out in the Roads, sealing off Confederate access to Chesapeake Bay and the Atlantic, were seven ships of the North Atlantic Blockading Squadron— the prize steam frigates *Minnesota* and *Roanoke*, the twenty-four-gun sail-powered sloop *Cumberland*, an obsolete forty-four-gun sail frigate named *Congress*, and an assortment of supporting craft. Shortly after 1:00 PM, the *Virginia* bore down on them, selecting the *Cumberland* as its target as the most heavily armed ship in the line. As the startled Federal seamen beat to quarters, the *Virginia* cruised ominously past the antiquated frigate *Congress*, which unleashed a twenty-five-gun broadside at the passing monster. The broadside banged and rattled on the *Virginia*'s side, bouncing harmlessly off the iron plates and splashing hugely into the waters of the Roads. The *Virginia* then opened up on the *Congress* with a point-blank broadside of her own, dismounting an 8-inch gun and turning her "clean and handsome gun-deck into a slaughter-pen, with lopped-off legs and arms and bleeding, blackened bodies scattered about by shells." But the *Virginia*'s real object was the *Cumberland*. The Confederate behemoth bore down remorselessly on the Federal sloop as shot from the *Cumberland*'s 9-inch pivot gun made no more impression on the ironclad than the *Congress*'s guns had. The *Virginia* returned the fire, then drove directly at the *Cumberland*, crushing its ram into the *Cumberland*'s side. The stricken sloop sank bow first, its gun crews still trying to bang shot off the *Virginia*'s sides until the water closed over the ship's unlowered flag. One hundred and twenty-one of her crew went down with her.[49]

The rest of the Federal squadron, having watched the easy destruction of the *Cumberland*, attempted to escape. But the *Congress*, *Minnesota*, and *Roanoke* all managed to run aground in the shallow waters of the Roads. The *Virginia* drew up behind its first antagonist, the old frigate *Congress*, and pounded it into a blazing shambles in half an hour; one of her few surviving officers struck her colors. The *Virginia* would

48. Carl D. Park, *Ironclad Down: USS* Merrimack–*CSS* Virginia, *from Construction to Destruction* (Annapolis: Naval Institute Press, 2007), 135–36, 142–43, 160; Raimondo Luraghi, *A History of the Confederate Navy*, trans. Paolo E. Coletta (Annapolis, MD: Naval Institute Press, 1996), 93–99.

49. Edward Shippen, "Pictures of Two Battles," *United States Service Magazine* 4 (July 1865): 53.

probably have done the same to the rest of the Federal ships had not the tide started to ebb. Anxious not to be caught aground themselves, the Confederates turned their triumphant experiment around and the *Virginia* slowly steamed back up the Roads, intending to finish off the stranded *Minnesota* the next morning. Despite being hit ninety-eight times on her armor plate, she had suffered only two of her crew killed (by a Federal shell exploding near one of *Virginia's* gun ports) and a handful (including Captain Buchanan) wounded.

With the *Virginia's* capabilities proven, the Confederates had only to choose how to deploy the ship next. In his original orders to Captain Buchanan, and in a follow-up letter on March 7, Mallory grandly suggested that once the *Virginia* finished off the Federal ships in Hampton Roads, she should steam out into the Chesapeake and then up the Potomac to bombard Washington. "Could you . . . make a dashing cruise on the Potomac as far as Washington, its effect upon the public mind would be important to the cause." The *Virginia* could then continue on to New York and "burn the city and the shipping." With that, "peace would inevitably follow. Bankers would withdraw their capital from the city. The Brooklyn navy yard and its magazines and all the lower part of the city would be destroyed, and such an event, by a single ship, would do more to achieve our independence than would the results of many campaigns." Whether the *Virginia's* unwieldy bulk ever could have survived the first pitch and roll of the open ocean, much less navigate the shallow reaches of the Potomac River, is debatable. However, Mallory *thought* she could, and what was more, so did Lincoln's cabinet.[50]

The next morning, the *Virginia* steamed back down to Hampton Roads to destroy the *Minnesota* and perhaps put an end to the war. As the Confederate ironclad bore down on the stranded *Minnesota*, the officers of the *Virginia* noticed that the Federal ship was not alone. At first they thought a raft had been brought alongside the *Minnesota* to take off the steam frigate's crew. Then the raft began to move, and as it did, the Confederate sailors and gunners got their first good look at what they could only describe as "a tin can on a shingle." It was, said one of the Virginia's officers, "the queerest-looking craft afloat" and reminded him of "a cheese box on a raft." It was in fact a Federal warship, an ironclad that floated almost flush on the surface of the water except for a single round gun turret in the middle. Its name was *Monitor*.[51]

The Federal navy had actually found out about the Confederate plans to re-build the *Merrimack* as early as August 1861, and in February 1862 "a negro woman,

50. Rodman L. Underwood, *Stephen Russell Mallory: A Biography of the Confederate Navy Secretary and United States Senator* (Jefferson, NC: McFarland, 2005), 97–98; Frank M. Bennett, *The Monitor and the Navy Under Steam* (Boston: Houghton, Mifflin, 1900), 102–4; A. A. Hoehling, *Thunder at Hampton Roads: The U.S.S.* Monitor—*Its Battle with the* Merrimack *and Its Recent Discovery* (New York: Da Capo, 1993), 80.

51. John V. Quarstein, *C.S.S.* Virginia: *Mistress of Hampton Roads* (Appomattox, VA: H. E. Howard, 2000), 108.

who . . . had closely watched the work upon the 'Merrimac'. . . passed through the lines at great risk to herself" and brought Navy Secretary Welles word "that the ship was nearly finished." Although Welles himself was skeptical of the usefulness of ironclads on the high seas, the threat of what the *Merrimack* might be turned into forced him to ask Congress for an appropriation of $1.5 million to experiment with three ironclad prototypes. Two of the designs Welles commissioned were little more than conventional steam frigates with various kinds of iron plating; the third prototype came from a Swedish inventor named John Ericsson, and it was so bafflingly different that one officer advised taking the model of the ship home and worshipping it. "It will not be idolatry," the officer quipped. "It is the image of nothing in the heavens above, or the earth beneath, or the waters under the earth."[52]

Certainly it was peculiar. Ericsson's plans called for an iron-plated raft 173 feet long and 41 feet 6 inches wide, with a small armored pilot house at the bow, two portable smokestacks that could be taken down for combat purposes, and, in the center, a revolving gun turret (with two 11-inch smoothbore guns) that could be turned to face in any direction. The 9-foot-high steam-powered turret, protected by eight layers of inch-thick iron plate, was the greatest marvel in this little ship of marvels (although in truth, the original plan for an armored cupola on a turntable belonged to the British gunnery expert Captain Cowper Coles, who had patented a design in 1859 and conducted trials on a prototype in September 1861), and it took the fancy of both Welles and Lincoln. On October 4, 1861, Welles and Ericsson signed the contract for the weird little ironclad, and less than four months later Ericsson launched the vessel from a private shipyard at Greenpoint, Brooklyn. At the invitation of assistant navy secretary Gustavus Fox, Ericsson named the ship USS *Monitor*. Formally commissioned on February 25, 1862, at the Brooklyn Navy Yard, the *Monitor* steamed down the East River on March 4, bound for Hampton Roads to search out and destroy the rebuilt *Merrimack* before the Confederates could turn their ironclad loose.[53]

The *Monitor* arrived one day too late. But for the *Minnesota*, and the rest of the Federal blockade, her timing could not have been more exquisite. For the next three hours the two strangest ships in the world battered each other with their guns, each unable to hurt the other. The captain of the *Minnesota* watched in a mixture of delight and disbelief as the little *Monitor*, "completely covering my ship as far as was

52. William Chapman White and Ruth Morris White, *Tin Can on a Shingle* (New York: E. P. Dutton, 1957), 36.

53. Richard S. West, *Gideon Welles: Lincoln's Navy Department* (Indianapolis, IN: Bobbs-Merrill, 1943), 150, 153; Gideon Welles, "The First Iron-Clad Monitor," in *Annals of the War*, 20; Olav Thulesius, *The Man Who Made the* Monitor: *A Biography of John Ericsson, Naval Engineer* (Jefferson, NC: McFarland, 2007), 98; D. K. Brown, *Warrior to Dreadnought: Warship Development, 1860–1905* (London: Chatham, 1997), 41; Quarstein, *C.S.S.* Virginia, 105.

possible with her dimensions . . . laid herself right alongside of the *Merrimack*, and the contrast was that of a pigmy to a giant."

> Gun after gun was fired by the *Monitor*, which was returned with whole broadsides from the rebels with no more effect, apparently, than so many pebblestones thrown by a child. After a while they commenced maneuvering, and we could see the [*Monitor*] point her bow for the rebels, with the intention . . . of sending a shot through her bow porthole; then she would shoot by her and rake her through her stern. In the meantime the rebel was pouring broadside after broadside, but . . . when they struck the bomb-proof tower [the *Monitor's* turret] the shot glanced off without producing any effect, clearly establishing the fact the wooden vessels can not contend successfully with iron-clad ones; for never before was anything like it dreamed of by the greatest enthusiast in maritime warfare.

The *Virginia* tried to ram the *Monitor*, but the nimble little turret ship dodged aside. The *Virginia's* replacement captain, Catesby Jones, assembled a boarding party and tried to lay his unwieldy ship alongside the *Monitor* to board her, throw a coat over the *Monitor's* pilothouse to blind her, and then toss grenades down her vents, but the *Monitor* dodged away again. Then each ship, baffled at the other's invincibility, drew off. The tide was running out, and the *Virginia* could not afford to be stranded on the shoals with this shallow-drafted terrier nipping at her. The *Virginia's* plans to burn Washington and New York would have to be shelved. The *Minnesota* had been saved, and so had every other wooden warship in the Federal fleet.[54]

The two ironclads never fought again; in fact, neither of them survived the year. When McClellan began his movement up the James River peninsula later in April, the Confederates were forced to evacuate Norfolk. The *Virginia*, drawing too much water to retreat up the James River, was blown up on May 10 to keep it from capture. The *Monitor* remained on station in Hampton Roads until November 1862, when it was ordered to join the blockading squadron off North Carolina, where it was rumored that the Confederates were constructing another blockade-breaking ironclad. On December 30, in treacherous water off Cape Hatteras, the *Monitor* was caught in a severe storm and sank with the loss of four officers and twelve men.

Despite their short lives, the *Monitor* and the *Virginia* had written their own chapter in naval history: their combat was the first occasion in which ironclad warships fought each other. Both ships also became the model for further experiments in building ironclads. The success of the *Monitor's* design induced the U.S. Navy to build sixty *Monitor*-type vessels, some of them big enough to carry two turrets, and even one, the *Roanoke*, with three, and from that point until after World War

---

54. "Report of Captain Van Brunt, U.S. Navy, Commanding U.S.S. *Minnesota*," in *The War of the Rebellion: A Compilation of the Official Records of the Union and Confederate Navies*, Series One (Washington, DC: Government Printing Office, 1880), 7:11; John Taylor Wood, "The First Fight of the Iron-Clads," in *Battles and Leaders*, 1:702–3; Quarstein, *C.S.S. Virginia*, 115.

II, the turret design dominated naval ship building. The Confederates clung to the casemate design of the *Virginia*, and with its limited resources, the Confederate navy scraped together enough men and material during 1862 to have four large ironclads built by private firms on the Mississippi River: the *Arkansas*, the *Tennessee*, the *Mississippi*, and the *Louisiana*. None of them, however, was used well or wisely by the Confederate navy, and all of them were eventually destroyed by the Confederates to avoid Federal capture.[55]

Undaunted, the Confederate navy laid down twenty more casemate-style ironclads, and three new facilities for rolling iron plate were developed in Richmond, Atlanta, and northern Alabama. The overall scarcity of materials in the Confederacy, and the inadequacy of even three new mills to roll enough iron, doomed most of these ships to rot on the stocks. One of the most fearsome of them, the *Albemarle*, was sunk at her moorings in the North Carolina sounds by a daring nighttime Federal raid, while the 216-foot *Tennessee* (the second rebel ironclad to bear that name) was pounded into surrender by the combined gunnery of Farragut's fleet at Mobile Bay in 1864.

The Confederates continued to experiment with a variety of exotic naval weapons. Commander Matthew F. Maury developed the first electrically detonated harbor mines, and between these mines and other improvised naval explosives, the Confederates sank thirty-seven Federal ships, including nine ironclads, on the waters of the Confederacy's rivers and harbors. A four-man "torpedo-boat," appropriately named the *David* and closely resembling a floating tin cigar, puttered out of Charleston on the night of October 5, 1863, with 100 pounds of high explosive rigged on a ten-foot spar that jutted out from the little metal boat's bow. Lieutenant William T. Glassell maneuvered the *David* up to the side of one of the Federal blockade ships—which just happened to be one of the other Federal ironclad prototypes, the *New Ironsides*—and detonated the spar "torpedo." The explosion cracked iron plates and struts in the *New Ironsides*'s hull, while the wash from the detonation swamped the *David* and drowned its small boiler fire. Glassell ordered his men to abandon ship and swim for their lives (Glassell himself was fished out of the water by a Federal schooner and made a prisoner). But his quickthinking engineer relit the boiler and navigated the unlikely little vessel back into Charleston harbor.

Far stranger than the *David* were the projects submitted for building submarines. The most famous of these submersibles was the *H. L. Hunley*, the eponymous brainchild of a civilian, Horace Lawson Hunley. Hunley's primitive submarine successfully destroyed the Federal sloop *Housatonic* outside Charleston on February 17, 1864. Unhappily, the *Hunley* never made it back to port (her resting place on the ocean

55. William N. Still, *Iron Afloat: The Story of the Confederate Armorclads* (Columbia: University of South Carolina Press, 1985), 41–61.

bottom, four miles offshore, would not be found until 1995), and any serious further Confederate interest in submarines went down with her.[56]

Even with all the inventiveness in the world at its disposal, it was apparent after the failure of the *Virginia* to disrupt the blockade that the Confederacy could not wait for the development of some other secret weapon to pry the blockade ships loose. So, unable to break the Federal navy's hold on the Confederate throat, they responded by trying to get their own grip around the Federal throat by sending out commerce raiders to prey on Northern shipping.

The first great success in commerce raiding was scored by John Newland Maffitt in the *Florida*.[57] But by far the most daring of the Confederate raider captains was Raphael Semmes, a fifty-two-year-old lawyer and former naval officer. Semmes was a strong advocate of the use of commerce raiders, and even took it upon himself in 1861 to convert an old New Orleans steamer into the raider *Sumter*. He made his first capture, the *Golden Rocket*, as early as July 3, 1861, and over the next six months he captured eighteen U.S. merchant ships, burning one and either sending the others off as prizes or releasing them on the payment of a bond. Cornered by three Federal warships in the British outpost of Gibraltar in January 1862, Semmes simply sold the *Sumter*, paid off his crew, and disappeared. Six months later Semmes turned up in the Azores, where he took command of James Bulloch's newest purchase from British shipbuilders, a sleek, deadly 1,040-ton cruiser that Semmes named the *Alabama*.[58]

Over the next two years, Semmes sailed his beautiful ship, with her 144-man crew, two big pivot guns, and eight 32-pounders, across the Atlantic and Indian Oceans, never calling at a Confederate port, always replenishing her supplies from captured Yankee ships or from stores purchased by Confederate agents in Cape Town, Singapore, and the French port of Cherbourg. "She was built for speed rather than for battle," wrote her executive officer. "Her lines were symmetrical and fine; her material of the best." By the time Semmes brought the *Alabama* into Cherbourg for a badly needed refitting in June of 1864, he had sunk or captured 64 Union merchantmen worth more than $6.5 million, and had even sunk a Federal blockade ship, the *Hatteras*—all this at an original building cost of £47,500. While anchored in Cherbourg harbor, however, the *Alabama* was trapped by the Federal steam sloop *Kearsarge*, and when Semmes and the *Alabama* attempted to fight

56. William T. Glassell, "Reminiscences of Torpedo Service in Charleston Harbor," *Southern Historical Society Papers* 4 (November 1877): 231–32; John Thomas Scharf, *History of the Confederate States Navy: From Its Organization to the Surrender of Its Last Vessel* (New York: Rogers and Sherwood, 1887), 759; Charles Ross, *Trial by Fire: Science, Technology and the Civil War* (Shippensburg, PA: White Mane, 2000), 83–106; Mark K. Ragan, *Submarine Warfare in the Civil War* (Cambridge, MA: Da Capo Press, 2002), 187–210.

57. David W. Shaw, *Sea Wolf of the Confederacy: The Daring Civil War Raids of Naval Lt. Charles W. Read* (New York: Free Press, 2004), 56–57; Emma Martin Maffitt, *The Life and Services of John Newland Maffitt* (New York: Neale, 1906), 343.

58. Raphael Semmes, *The Cruise of the Alabama and the Sumter from the Private Journals and Other Papers of Commander R. Semmes* (London: Saunders, Otley, 1864), 1:257–62.

their way free, the *Kearsarge*'s two 11-inch pivot guns sent the *Alabama* to the bottom. "The *Alabama* settled stern foremost, launching her bows high in the air" and staying "graceful even in her death-struggle." Semmes was rescued by an English yacht and managed to make his way back to the Confederacy in October, 1864, where he was promoted to rear admiral in 1865 and, ironically, given river-defense duty below Richmond.[59]

The *Alabama* and *Florida* were only the most successful of the Southern commerce raiders. Together with some twenty smaller cruisers, the Confederate commerce raiders accounted for the destruction of at least 261 U.S.-registered ships. After the war, the United States demanded that the British government pay reparations as a way of taking responsibility for the raiders its shipyards had built, and in 1872 the British settled the so-called *Alabama* Claims for $15.5 million. But that figure cannot begin to account for the millions expended in chasing the raiders down (Welles had to devote the attentions of seventy-seven warships and twenty-three other chartered vessels to chasing the raiders), for the trade that was frightened off the seas by the Confederate raiders, or for the 715 other American vessels that were transferred (either for safety or for the opportunity to evade Federal prohibitions on trade with the Confederacy) to other flags. The American merchant marine, which before 1861 held first place in the Atlantic carrying trade with 2.4 million tons of shipping under the Stars and Stripes, was toppled from its preeminence, falling to 1.3 million tons by 1870, and to this day it has never recovered from the blows dealt it by the *Alabama* and the Civil War.[60]

For all the destruction wrought by the commerce raiders, the one thing they failed to do was force any lightening in the pressure the Federal blockade was gradually twisting around the Confederacy. That meant that, in the end, the most effective way of dealing with the Federal blockade was to evade it. At the beginning of the war, the creation of a special blockade-running flotilla was beyond the power of the Confederacy, which had all it could do to build its few ironclads and buy its handful of commerce raiders. Instead, the Confederate government designated the Charleston firm of John Fraser & Co. (and its Liverpool branch, Fraser, Trenholm & Co.) as its European financial agents and left blockade-running up to the entrepreneurial ingenuity of the company. Fraser, Trenholm & Co. assumed all the risks of hiring

59. Warren F. Spencer, *Raphael Semmes: The Philosophical Mariner* (Tuscaloosa: University of Alabama Press, 1997), 112–36; Raphael Semmes, *Memoirs of Service Afloat, During the War Between the States* (Baltimore: Kelly, Piet, 1869), 344–45; Charles Grayson Summersell, *CSS* Alabama: *Builder, Captain, and Plans* (University: University of Alabama Press, 1985), 12, 72, 74, 78–90; John McIntosh Kell, "Cruise and Combats of the 'Alabama,'" in *Battles and Leaders*, 4:600, 611.

60. Kenneth J. Blume, "The Flight from the Flag: The American Government, the British Caribbean, and the American Merchant Marine, 1861–1865," *Civil War History* 32 (March 1986): 44–55; Brown, *Warrior to Dreadnought*, 18; H. H. Wilson, *Ironclads in Action: A Sketch of Naval Warfare from 1855 to 1895* (London: S. Low, Marston, 1896), 168.

their own ships and their own crews to run the blockade with Southern cotton or European weapons, but were also able to make immense profits.

The example of Fraser, Trenholm & Co. soon showed other British and Southern entrepreneurs how quickly a path to wartime fortunes could be blazed, and a series of private import-export firms based either in England or in Nassau sprang up to run cotton, weapons, supplies, and costly consumer goods in and out of Southern ports. The Importing and Exporting Company of South Carolina was created by a consortium of Charleston businessmen and run by William C. Bee and Charles T. Mitchel, who bought up two blockade-runners, the *Cecile* and the *Edwin*, in April 1862 to make the company's first dash through the blockade. The *Cecile* made a successful round-trip from Charleston to Nassau and back, but the *Edwin* ran aground outside Charleston harbor on its way back from Nassau and had to be abandoned. Nevertheless, the venture was a smashing success for the company. The Charleston cotton that the two vessels dropped in Nassau netted the company $18,000, while the goods that were brought back were either sold to the Confederate government or auctioned off to the public for $90,000. The company had no trouble recovering its expenses (or the stockholders' investment), and the endeavor paid Bee and Mitchell a handsome commission of $5,000. On its next voyage, the *Cecile* brought 2,000 Enfield rifles through the blockade, along with a rich cargo of private goods that netted the company another $100,000.[61]

One reason why private entrepreneurs were willing to risk their necks and their ships in this way is that at first there was comparatively little neck to risk in running the blockade. In 1861, the Union navy still had only a few ships on blockade duty, and not many of them had much idea of what they were doing; as a result, at least nine out of ten blockade-runners made it through. "So loose . . . is the blockade," boasted Robert Warneford,

> that running pays uncommonly well on the average. The capital employed in the trade, already enormous—there never being less than contraband of war to the value of two millions sterling at Nassau alone, ready for shipment—is rapidly increasing, and our seamen like the business immensely. The excitement inseparable from such enterprises,— the high wages paid,—an instinctive contempt and dislike of the bragging Yankees— attract them to, and retain them in the service; and there appears to be little doubt that, should the suicidal war continue many months longer, a new and formidable brotherhood of the coast will have been created, who will practically nullify the blockade.[62]

By the end of 1862, the only major ports still open to blockade-runners were Mobile, Charleston, and Wilmington, and Federal sailors (with visions of prize money dancing through their heads) had become more skilled at ship catching. Of course, as the risks went up, so did the costs, and in the interests of maintaining their profit

---

61. Wise, *Lifeline of the Confederacy*, 69–70.

62. Lt. Warneford, *Running the Blockade* (London: Ward and Lock, 1863), 1.

margins, the entrepreneurs turned to the design and construction of ships specially designed for fooling Federal navy observers: the vessels were long, lean, and rakish, and burned smokeless coal. The longer and leaner the ships, however, the less capable they were of carrying heavy war matériel as cargo, and since the entrepreneurs mistrusted the Confederate government's procurement policies anyway, the hulls of the purpose-built blockade-runners filled up with luxury goods that commanded fairy-princess prices on the consumer markets but did little or nothing to support the Confederate war effort. "It did not pay merchants to ship heavy goods, the charge for freight per ton at Nassau being $80 to $100 in gold," wrote one blockade-runner, and so "a great portion of the cargo generally consisted of light goods, such as silks, laces, linens, quinine, etc., on which immense profits were made."[63] Eventually this compelled the Confederate government to begin operating its own line of blockade-runners, and in 1864 the Confederate Congress imposed a series of new regulations that forbade the import of high-cost luxuries and forced private shippers to yield half their cargo space to government use.[64]

Neither private ventures nor government regulations were ever able to deliver to the South the kind of triumph over the blockade that the Confederacy needed. In terms of simple numbers, the successes of the blockade-runners appear impressive: over the course of the war, some 300 blockade-running steamers made approximately 1,300 attempts to run the blockade and made it through unscathed more than 1,000 times; even in 1865 103 of the 153 attempts to penetrate the blockade were successful.[65] But the real success of the blockade has to be measured not in terms of how many cleverly designed blockade-runners squeezed through it but by how many ordinary ships from around the world never tried it at all. By comparison with the South's prewar import-export trade, the blockade-runners amounted to little more than a trickle. The South exported fifty times as much cotton in 1860 as it was able to pass through the blockade during all four years of the war; nearly five times as many ships called at Southern ports in 1860 as made it through during the four years of blockade.[66]

63. Thomas E. Taylor, *Running the Blockade: A Personal Narrative of Adventures, Risks, and Escapes During the American Civil War* (London: J. Murray, 1896), 18. Robert B. Ekelund Jr. and Mark Thornton dubbed this trend "the Rhett Butler effect," after the self-centered blockade-running hero of Margaret Mitchell's *Gone with the Wind*; see their "The Union Blockade and Demoralization of the South: Relative Prices in the Confederacy," *Social Science Quarterly* 73 (December 1992): 891–900.

64. "An Act to Prohibit the Importation of Luxuries, or of Articles Not Necessaries or of Common Use," February 6, 1864, in *Public Laws of the Confederate States of America, Passed at the Fourth Session of the First Congress, 1863–4*, ed. James M. Mathews (Richmond: R. M. Smith, 1864), 179.

65. Wise, *Lifeline of the Confederacy*, 221; Joseph McKenna, *British Ships in the Confederate Navy* (Jefferson, NC: McFarland, 2010), 210, 213.

66. Lance Edwin Davis and Stanley L. Engerman, *Naval Blockades in Peace and War: An Economic History Since 1750* (New York: Cambridge University Press, 2006), 146; David G. Surdam, *Northern Naval Superiority and the Economics of the American Civil War* (Columbia: University of South Carolina Press, 2001), 5–6, 155.

The blockade was a lethal drain on the South simply by the fact of its existence, irrespective of how many blockade-runners wriggled out of the hands of Federal sailors. It drove the costs of goods within the Confederacy to astronomical levels, wrecked the Confederate currency, and demoralized its people. Although by itself the blockade may not exactly have won the war for the Union, there it is no question that it seriously constricted the South's ability to make war, much less to win it.

SUPPLYING THE WAR

American society and government before 1861 were utterly unprepared for the organizational demands placed upon it by a major war. As late as 1830, the entire Federal bureaucracy in Washington consisted of exactly 352 people, and in 1861 the total number of government employees (including non-Washingtonians such as postmasters and customs officers) numbered less than 40,000. The entire army Quartermaster's Department civilian workforce in Washington embraced thirteen clerks. Up until 1854, the city of Philadelphia was still governed as a collection of twenty-seven separate colonial-era municipalities; it pumped its city water through wooden pipes until 1848, and pigs were still scavenging in the city streets in the 1860s. Backyard trenches served as toilets for much of New York City, and garbage and wastewater ended up in street gutters, where it bred cholera, typhus, and other contagious diseases. Louisiana did not possess a single macadamized road before 1861.[67]

The Civil War thus threw into the laps of the Richmond and Washington governments an immense and hitherto inconceivable problem in management. "Let the people know that we are desperately in want of men, desperately in want of arms, desperately in want of money, desperately in want of clothing, desperately in want of medicines and food for our sick," Frederick Law Olmsted complained to a Northern official in 1861. It seemed to Olmsted that it ought to be possible for the North, with its resources, to "be relieved of our difficulties as a suffocating man is relieved by opening a window." But in many cases the windows Olmsted needed to open did not even yet exist in American society, and a whole new apparatus for government and administration would have to be created to put those windows in place. "We have more of the brute force of persistent obstinacy in Northern blood than the South has," Olmsted wrote hopefully, "if we can only get it in play."[68]

67. Paul P. Van Riper and Keith A. Sutherland, "The Northern Civil Service: 1861–1865," *Civil War History* II (December 1965): 351; Weigley, *Quartermaster General of the Union Army*, 224; Elizabeth M. Geffen, "Industrial Development and Social Crisis, 1841–1854" and Russell F. Weigley, "The Border City in the Civil War, 1854–1865," in *Philadelphia: A 300-Year History*, ed. Russell F. Weigley (New York: W. W. Norton, 1982), 317, 373; Ernest A. McKay, *The Civil War and New York City* (Syracuse, NY: Syracuse University Press, 1990), 217.

68. Olmsted to H. W. Bellows, September 29, 1861, and to Oliver Wolcott Gibbs, January 31, 1863, in *The Papers of Frederick Law Olmsted: Volume IV, Defending the Union*, ed. Jane Turner Censer (Baltimore: Johns Hopkins University Press, 1986), 210, 505.

The ultimate means for getting a Federal supply system in play was the secretary of war, Edwin McMasters Stanton. "He was in no sense an imposing person, either in looks or manner," wrote John Pope, who briefly led the short-lived Army of Virginia in 1862. "He was below the medium stature, stout and clumsy," with a "shaggy, belligerent sort of look, which, to say the least, was not encouraging to the man in search of favors." A former attorney general (in the closing months of the Buchanan administration), Stanton possessed an immense, coarse black beard threaded with white, rude and dictatorial manners, and "a perpetually irritable look in his stern little eyes."[69] His appointment as secretary of war on January 20, 1862, to replace Simon Cameron, came as a surprise, and to no one more than Stanton. Not only was he a lifelong Democrat, but in 1855 he had personally snubbed Lincoln as "that giraffe" and that "creature from Illinois" when both were retained as counsel in a patent case involving the McCormick Reaper Company.[70] Stanton was a solid Union man, however, and heartily anti-slavery. The fact that he was a Democrat could actually have been considered an advantage to Lincoln in trying to garner increased Democratic support for the war. And he had what few of the Republicans had: extensive experience in the inner workings of national government.

Whatever Lincoln's reasons were, time soon justified them, for Lincoln could not have chosen a better foreman to run his wartime workshop. Within a week of assuming office, Stanton wrote to Charles A. Dana that as soon as he could "get the machinery of the office working, the rats cleared out, and the rat holes stopped we shall *move*." Move is precisely what Stanton did. He became the "black terrier" of the cabinet. He drove himself and his staff of undersecretaries with maniacal fury and animation, auditing government contracts, reviewing and digesting military data for Lincoln's use, intimidating army contractors, barking orders, and banging on his stand-up writing desk to make his point. He also took it as his duty to keep the Union army's generals in line with administration policy. Where they did not, they found Stanton an implacable and unforgiving enemy, and sooner or later he had them sacked; where they did, they found themselves promoted. It was Stanton more than anyone else who would help bring Ulysses Simpson Grant to the command of all the Union armies in 1864; it was also Stanton who helped destroy George Brinton McClellan. "This army has to fight or run away," Stanton growled to Dana, and Stanton took it upon himself to ensure that "while men are striving nobly in the West, the champagne and oysters on the Potomac must be stopped."[71]

---

69. *The Military Memoirs of General John Pope*, 115; George S. Bryan, *The Great American Myth* (New York: Carrick and Evans, 1940), 129–30.

70. Fletcher Pratt, *Stanton, Lincoln's Secretary of War* (New York: Norton, 1953), 62.

71. Benjamin P. Thomas and Harold Hyman, *Stanton: The Life and Times of Lincoln's Secretary of War* (New York: Knopf, 1962), 63–66, 141–68; Ethan Rafuse, *McClellan's War: The Failure of Moderation in the Struggle for the Union* (Bloomington: Indiana University Press, 2005), 177; A. Howard Meneely, *The War Department, 1861: A Study in Mobilization and Administration* (New York: Columbia University Press, 1928), 318.

Determined to sweep up the entire War Department as his private fiefdom, Stanton began welding the various parts of the Department together into a unified and coherent machine. His first move in that direction was to have McClellan deposed as general in chief of the Federal armies in March 1862 and replaced in July with Henry Wager Halleck. In the process, Stanton sharply redefined the job of general in chief, so Halleck spent the rest of the war as little more than the means of transmitting Stanton's policy directives down to commanders out in the field. To be fair to Halleck, there really was a need, in a civilian-run republic, for a reliable and competent organizer who could serve as that kind of liaison between the civilian leadership at the War Department and the military at the front, and Halleck performed the job superbly throughout the war. "Halleck was not thought to be a great man in the field," wrote Dana, who joined the War Department as one of Stanton's assistant secretaries of war, "but he was nevertheless a man of military ability, and by reason of his great accomplishments in the technics of armies and of war was almost invaluable as an adviser to the civilian Lincoln and Stanton."[72]

In addition to the general in chief, Stanton next brought securely under his dictate the heads of the three most important War Department supply bureaus: the quartermaster general, Montgomery C. Meigs; the commissary general, Joseph P. Taylor; and the truculent chief of ordnance, James Wolfe Ripley. None of these men was more important to Stanton than Meigs, a forty-six-year-old Georgian who had only been promoted to brigadier general in 1861. The quartermaster-general was responsible for supplying the Federal armies with all of their basic hardware, including uniforms, tents, ambulance wagons, supply wagons, mules, cavalry and transport horses, and the forage to feed them—everything from hospitals to tent pins. And supplying the immense variety of the army's goods was only half the challenge. The sheer volume of what was required of each of these items staggered belief. Already in September 1861, the Army of the Potomac needed 20,000 cavalry horses and a further 20,000 transportation horses just to do its daily business. On the peninsula, the Army of the Potomac needed 14,000 horses and mules (along with 26 wagons for every 1,000 men) to haul baggage and supplies. By the middle of 1862 that requisition had swollen to 1,500 horses weekly in six depots across the North, and by 1864 the demand had risen to 500 horses a day, with the government shelling out $170 per horse. Outfitting a new regiment with uniforms cost $20,000 per regiment (Brooks Brothers won a contract for 12,000 uniforms for New York state volunteers in 1861 at the discount price of $19.50 per uniform), and the uniforms could easily be worn out after three months of campaigning. Shoes were by far the worst problem, since

72. Charles A. Dana, *Recollections of the Civil War with the Leaders at Washington and in the Field in the Sixties* (New York: D. Appleton, 1898), 187.

the army could scarcely move without them, and when it did move, it consumed them at a rate of 25,000 pairs weekly.[73]

Since so much of this had to be done virtually at once, and by officers and clerks who had never before in their lives administered anything like it, the opportunities for mistake and oversight were legion. Individual states muddied the picture by launching their own procurement initiatives—Pennsylvania's quartermaster general, R. C. Hale, set up a shop to cut and sew uniforms in Philadelphia, Illinois created a state arsenal, Massachusetts governor John Andrew sent a state agent to England to purchase 19,000 rifles—and Meigs had to struggle to wrench control from their hands in order to guarantee some semblance of standardization.[74]

At the same time, Meigs shied away from committing the government to the actual manufacture and production of its own supplies. Meigs was strictly a retailer; the actual production of the army's goods remained in the hands of private civilian contractors. It also went without saying that, under these circumstances, the opportunities for fraud, kickbacks, and corruption were great. Nevertheless, Montgomery Meigs proved to be both tireless and incorruptible as quartermaster general. He reorganized the Quartermaster's Department into nine division (for animals, clothing, transportation, forage, barracks, hospitals, wagons, inspection, and finance) and expanded the workforce in his office to 591 by the end of the war, with 130,000 other employees in depots across the North. At the same time, his expenditures rose over the course of the war from $40,631,000 in 1861–62 to $226,199,000 in 1864–65, and by the end of the war his department was spending nearly half a billion dollars a year. Despite the gargantuan size and frantic demands of his department, a congressional audit could not find so much as one penny unaccounted for in any major contract authorized by Meigs.[75]

Keeping the Federal armies clothed and equipped was one thing. Keeping them fed and armed was quite another, and those responsibilities fell to Commissary General Taylor and Chief of Ordnance Ripley. Neither Ripley nor Taylor ever won the praise awarded to Montgomery Meigs—Ripley because of his stubborn refusal to permit the introduction of the breech-loading repeating rifle into the war, and Taylor because Union army food was so consistently bad by civilian standards. Taylor was up against the fact that the technologies of food preservation, including meatpacking, canning, and condensed liquids, were still relatively new. What critics missed was the happier fact that although army food was bad, the Union armies

73. Hagerman, *The American Civil War and the Origins of Modern Warfare*, 45; Weigley, *Quartermaster General of the Union Army*, 234–35, 268–69; "Interrogatories to Edwin D. Morgan," in *Documents of the Assembly of the State of New York, Eighty-Fifth Session, 1862* (Albany, NY: Charles van Benthuysen, 1862), 2:168–69.

74. Mark R. Wilson, *The Business of War: Military Mobilization and the State, 1861–1865* (Baltimore: Johns Hopkins University Press, 2006), 12–13, 78.

75. Weigley, *Quartermaster General of the Union Army*, 317, 358; Hattaway and Jones, *How the North Won*, 120–24.

rarely lacked for sufficient quantities of it. Something of the same could be said about Ripley. The ordnance chief's insistence on sticking by the muzzle-loading rifle as the standard infantry arm, rather than introducing the breech-loading repeating rifle, was one of the most wrongheaded administrative decisions of the war. In spite of this one majestic failure of judgment, Ripley turned into a surprisingly competent administrator. Once having made up his mind against the breech-loading repeaters, Ripley never failed to deliver sufficient supplies of muzzle-loaders or their ammunition to the Union army, and that was no small accomplishment.

Like Meigs, Ripley relied heavily on civilian contracting for weapons, including foreign contractors in England and Austria. At the beginning of the war Ripley had only about 437,000 muskets and rifles in his inventory of government weapons, with only 40,000 being of any recent vintage, and virtually no procedure for getting them into soldiers' hands. He could count on only two armories capable of manufacturing arms, one at Harpers Ferry and the other at Springfield, Massachusetts. The Springfield arsenal could be pushed to manufacture 3,000 to 4,000 rifles a month, but the Harpers Ferry arsenal (with most of its manufacturing equipment) had to be abandoned to the Confederates after the secession of Virginia from the Union. With no other alternative but outside contracting and foreign purchases, Ripley managed to acquire 727,000 arms from foreign dealers over the next year, and let out contracts to a variety of smaller arms manufacturers who subsequently built their fortunes on wartime government purchases: Remington, New Haven Arms (which in 1866 changed its name to Winchester), Smith & Wesson, and Samuel Colt. Ripley also expanded the armory at Springfield to a production level of 300,000 weapons a year, and opened or enlarged nine other arsenals across the North. By the end of 1862 the Federal government was making enough weapons to meet its own needs without more foreign imports, and by September 1863 Ripley was able to report that the Springfield arsenal was now actually stockpiling surplus rifles.[76]

None of these success stories about the supply of weapons or clothing or food might have amounted to much if the War Department had had no way of moving them to where they were needed. As it was, though, the greatest administrative success story of them all was Stanton's shrewd manipulation of the Northern railroad system. The North began the war with 22,000 miles of railroads compared to the Confederacy's 9,000, and the rail lines carried with them the capacity to transport men and supplies at a cost almost a tenth of that of horse-and-wagon transport. Although Congress initially gave Lincoln authority to seize control of the northern railroads in 1862, Stanton instead set about striking a deal with the major rail operators, and less than a month after taking over the War Department, Stanton sat down in a Washington hotel room with McClellan, Meigs, and the most important northern railroad presidents. They set a basic troop transportation rate (they agreed

76. Bruce, *Lincoln and the Tools of War*, 48–49, 61, 252.

on two cents per mile per soldier, with eighty pounds of baggage each) and agreed on standardizing gauges among the lines (they settled for the English gauge of 4 feet 8.5 inches), signaling systems, and freight rates.

These arrangements effectively discouraged rate wars and their attendant disruption by guaranteeing full-time operations to the rail lines, kept the military out of the railroad business by leaving all of the railroad companies' officers in place to direct operations as normal, and moved the Union army and its supplies around the frontiers of the Confederacy fast enough to overcome the Confederacy's advantage of interior lines. By 1865, Stanton's deal with the railroads was moving 410,000 horses and 125,000 mules each year, plus 5 million tons of quartermaster, ordnance, and commissary stores.[77]

With the successful creation of a working staff within the War Department and the extraordinary accomplishments of Meigs, Ripley, and Taylor as the major department heads, the Union forces never seriously lacked for the materials necessary to win the war. On the Confederate side of the ledger, however, the case was less happy. Taking the inventories of all the small depot arsenals in the South, the Confederacy could lay its hands on no more than 159,000 firearms of all sorts, many of them obsolete. In a March 4, 1862, report to the Confederate Congress, Jefferson Davis estimated that the Confederate armies would need 300,000 more men than they then had enlisted, 50 ironclad gunboats, "ten of the most formidable war vessels to protect our commerce upon the high seas," 750,000 rifles, 5,000 cannon, and 5,000 tons of gunpowder, but at the same time he had to admit that "it cannot be foreseen" how the Confederacy was going to obtain them. The Confederacy had only one-ninth of the industrial capacity of the North, and only a relative handful of major industrial plants—the Tredegar Iron Works in Richmond, employing some 700 hands, the Shelby Iron Works and the Brierfield Furnace in northern Alabama, and the complex of ironworks begun in Selma, Alabama, later in 1861. The Confederacy might have drawn some consolation from the fact that its lack of industrial promise was compensated for by the South's substantial agricultural resources. Even then, much of the South's agricultural produce was committed to cotton in order to pay for the Confederacy's foreign imports, and its principal grain-growing and meat-producing areas lay in the upper Confederacy, which fell into Union hands early in the war.[78]

Not only was the Confederacy seriously deficient in railroad mileage at the onset of the war, but the two east-west rail systems that did manage to offer a fairly direct

77. Paludan, "*A People's Contest*," 141–43; Wilson, *The Business of Civil War*, 135; Robert G. Angevine, *The Railroad and the State: War, Politics and Technology in Nineteenth-Century America* (Stanford, CA: Stanford University Press, 2004), 130–39; John Elwood Clark, *Railroads in the Civil War: The Impact of Management on Victory and Defeat* (Baton Rouge: Louisiana State University Press, 2001), 35–36; Thomas Weber, *The Northern Railroads in the Civil War* (Bloomington: Indiana University Press, 1999 [1952]), 102–3.

78. Davis, "To the Speaker of the House of Representatives," March 4, 1862, in *Messages and Papers of Jefferson Davis and the Confederacy, Including Diplomatic Correspondence, 1861–1865*, ed. J. D. Richardson, A. Nevins, and W. J. Cooper (Philadelphia: Chelsea House, 2001), 1:194–95; Frank E. Vandiver, *Ploughshares into Swords: Josiah Gorgas and Confederate Ordnance* (Austin: University of Texas Press, 1952), 60.

route across most of the Confederacy were both cut by the Union army before the summer of 1862. Furthermore, since so many of these lines had been built with only limited use in view, they had been allowed to make do with poor sidings and fuel facilities and even poorer-quality track, and by 1863 the excessive wear of wartime rail movement was chewing up the southern rail lines. With the southern ironworks already fully committed to manufacturing weapons, there were no means of also manufacturing new rail iron. Confederate officials were reduced to cannibalizing iron from unused branch lines to make repairs.[79]

These problems were exacerbated by a sheer lack of organizational talent in the upper echelons of the Confederate government. As a former soldier and secretary of war himself, Davis was easily the superior of Lincoln in simple military experience. But Davis found it difficult locate competent officers and cabinet secretaries of the quality of Stanton or Meigs. Davis ran through four secretaries of war by November 1862, and the personal military acquaintances whom Davis appointed to the Quartermaster and Commissary Departments were far from the standards set by their Federal counterparts. Abraham Myers, whom Davis appointed as quartermaster general of the Confederacy on March 25, 1861, was convinced by May that "the resources of the Southern States cannot supply the necessities of the Army of the Confederate States with the essential articles of cloth for uniform clothing, blankets, shoes, stockings and flannel."[80]

The Confederate solution was to retreat from providing uniforms and award a $21 uniform allowance to Confederate soldiers every six months that they could spend themselves—which resulted in either a confusing "medley of garments which would hardly be called a uniform" or else no uniforms at all, as the soldiers spent the money on more interesting goods and services. The problems this created led to the abandonment of the clothing allowance scheme in October 1862. Myers, as he had predicted, found it impossible to meet the Confederate armies' clothing needs from the Confederate government's resources. Southern mills failed to produce an adequate supply of wool cloth; worse, state governments in North Carolina, Georgia, and Alabama embargoed any export of wool or leather beyond state boundaries and set about clothing their own troops themselves. The Georgia state legislature actually appropriated $1.5 million to create a Georgia Soldiers Bureau at Augusta to clothe Georgia's troops; North Carolina did likewise, and managed to end the war with a surplus of 92,000 uniforms.[81]

79. Robert C. Black, *The Railroads of the Confederacy* (Chapel Hill: University of North Carolina Press, 1952, 1998), 9–15, 58–59.

80. Harold S. Wilson, "Virginia's Industry and the Conduct of the War in 1862," in *Virginia at War, 1862*, ed. William C. Davis and James I. Robertson (Lexington: University Press of Kentucky, 2007), 23.

81. "Reports of Gen. G. T. Beauregard, C. S. Army, and Resulting Correspondence," August 4, 1861, in *War of the Rebellion*, 2:508; Harold S. Wilson, *Confederate Industry: Manufacturers and Quartermasters in the Civil War* (Jackson: University Press of Mississippi, 2002), 24, 35; Thomas D. Arliskas, *Cadet Gray and Butternut Brown: Notes on Confederate Uniforms* (Gettysburg: Thomas, 2006), 8–9, 43, 54, 60.

Even more of a magnet for discontent was the Confederate commissary general, Lucius Bellinger Northrop, "an erratic old personage" whose "coat hangs as loosely as if it were four sizes beyond his measure" and whose chief recommendation for the job seemed to be his friendship with (and perhaps also his unusual physical resemblance to) Jefferson Davis. Two months after assuming his office, Northrop warned Davis that he might not be able to sustain the Confederate army's food requirements, especially if he had to compete with state authorities in purchasing edibles. Until the spring of 1862, Confederate troops were sufficiently well fed to ward off criticism. It was not until mid-1862, after the Confederacy had lost control of the wheat- and meat-producing areas of the upper South, that Northrop began to signal the onset of shortages. Northrop was forced to start cutting the standard rations of the Confederate volunteer, and by the fall of 1864 it had fallen to one-third of a pound of meat and a pound of bread a day; even with this reduction, the Commissary's main depot in Richmond was often as low as only nine days' supply for the army. Northrop was forced to bear most of the blame for this situation as "the most cussed and vilified man in the Confederacy" and the "poorest of all apologies for a Chief Commissary," and the vilification was aggravated by his 1863 enforcement of the Impressment Act, which authorized his agents to seize food supplies when farmers refused to sell them at the government rate.[82]

Even if we take Northrop's critics at face value, the fundamental cause of the shortages lay less with Northrop than with the deficiencies of the Confederate rail system. The South did not so much lack food supplies—both Grant and Sherman found plenty of food to pillage in their invasions of Mississippi and Georgia in 1863 and 1864—as it lacked a means for getting them where they were needed. The unhappy Northrop was driven to distraction in August 1862 when he discovered that a shipment of meat from Nashville to Richmond had been delayed on the railroads by twenty days, during which the meat slowly spoiled into uselessness. Northrop vigorously defended his bureau as "near perfection as is possible under the general plan that has been adopted for all purchases," but "its working has been constantly crippled" by the unwillingness of farmers to sell the goods and produce at government rates. "If the Army is not as well fed as the condition of the country will allow, or if at any time it should be without food, it will be the result of these influences in overruling an efficient and comprehensive system which has proved and maintained itself against constant and potent opposition"—which was as much as saying, in the eternal fashion of all good bureaucrats, that if the Confederate government would only apply more stringently the impressment policies that had caused the shortages in the first

82. Jeremy P. Felt, "Lucius B. Northrop and the Confederacy's Subsistence Department," *Virginia Magazine of History and Biography* 69 (April 1961): 182, 185–86, 188; Richard D. Goff, *Confederate Supply* (Durham, NC: Duke University Press, 1969), 51, 65–66; Chestnut, *Mary Chestnut's Civil War*, 124.

place, all would be well. The Confederate Congress demanded his removal. But Davis protected Northrop until almost the very end; he was not cashiered until February 1865.[83]

The one major exception to this gloomy schedule of inability in Davis's war administration was the hard-driving chief of ordnance, Josiah Gorgas. A northerner by birth and director of the Frankford Arsenal in Philadelphia, Gorgas had married a daughter of the governor of Alabama and threw in his lot with the Southern cause. Resigning his commission in the U.S. Army, Gorgas took over the gun-manufacturing machinery captured at Harpers Ferry, seized the cannon abandoned at the Norfolk Navy Yard, and proceeded to build a Confederate ordnance supply from scratch. He hired agents to scour Europe for weapons and successfully ran 600,000 arms through the blockade on ships he had either bought or subsidized for the Confederate War Department.[84]

Gorgas also established new arsenals and workshops across the South. He built a chemical laboratory, a major gunpowder factory in Augusta, Georgia, and a new cannon foundry in northern Georgia, and organized a string of eight new arsenals from Richmond to Selma, along with several other smaller gunworks in the Carolinas. Together, the new plants were manufacturing 170,000 rifle cartridges a day, and his gunpowder factory produced 2.7 million pounds of gunpowder over the course of the war. He had what one subordinate called "a gift of prescience, which enabled him to provide for the wants of every battlefield," and by 1864 Gorgas was the only member of the Confederate War Department who could really describe himself as an unqualified success—which he did not hesitate to do. "I have succeeded beyond my utmost expectations," he happily confided to his diary in 1864, "Where three years ago we were not making a gun, a pistol nor a saber . . . we now make all these in quantities to meet the demands of our large armies. In looking over all this I feel that my three years of labor have not been passed in vain."[85]

The dark side of Gorgas's endeavors was the fact that, as chief of ordnance, he found himself directly intervening in the production as well as the administration of war matériel. Edwin Stanton, for all his driving determination to get the war moving, was respectful and cautious in dealing with the North's industrial potential. As a former railroad lawyer (like Lincoln), Stanton wanted "the aid of the highest business talent . . . this country can afford," and his arrangements with the north-

83. Northrop to James A. Seddon (December 12, 1864), in *Official Records*, series four, 3:932; Eaton, *A History of the Southern Confederacy*, 143; Goff, *Confederate Supply*, 156.

84. Owsley, *King Cotton Diplomacy*, 290.

85. Frank E. Vandiver, *Their Tattered Flags: The Epic of the Confederacy* (New York: Harper's Magazine Press, 1970), 240–42; Vandiver, *Ploughshares into Swords*, 61, 77; Bayne, "A Sketch of the Life of General Josiah Gorgas, Chief of Ordnance of the Confederate States," *Southern Historical Society Papers* 13 (January–December 1885), 222; Gorgas, diary entry for April 8, 1864, in *The Journals of Josiah Gorgas 1857–1878*, ed. Sarah Woolfolk Wiggins (Tuscaloosa: University of Alabama Press, 1995), 98; Ross, *Trial by Fire*, 54–80.

ern railroads were carefully constructed to harness the military power of railroad technology, while leaving the actual direction of the railroads to the private sector.[86] Similarly, Stanton's quartermaster and commissary heads contracted out their needs for weapons, horses, and clothes by bid on the open market, rather than by appropriating existing industries for government use.

By contrast, the Confederate War Department struggled to nationalize Confederate industries, set official prices for goods, and even compete against its own citizens with government-owned blockade-runners. And those businesses that the government did not nationalize outright it tried to regulate into submission: in April 1863 the Confederate Senate actually passed a bill limiting businesses to a 20 percent profit margin (it failed to pass the Confederate House, however). None of these problems is entirely surprising in a society whose plantation elites felt little desire to see any emergence of a powerful industrial middle class in their new nation. Although the Confederate government's reach into the economy fell considerably short of being state socialism or state corporatism, and a great deal of its resort to nationalization was really more in the nature of an improvisation in the face of desperation, the Confederate government still came to exercise an unprecedented degree of control over Southern industrial production and prices in just the way it had always assumed it could control Southern slave labor. The ruling Southerners' plans may not have been consciously illiberal, but their instinct was.[87]

What the Confederate elite did not count upon was that, like their slaves, the vast pool of nonslaveholding whites might find ways to elude submission—hoarding, black-marketeering (which was routinely denounced as "extortion"), and simple withdrawal from the market. Quartermaster General Myers increasingly resorted to outright confiscation of wool, which in turn led to manufacturers cutting back on production. Manufacturers who did sign Confederate contracts soon found their production monopolized by government orders, leaving the states, suppliers, and merchants empty-handed. "If Congress and the State Governments desired to limit production," raged the *Charleston Mercury* in June 1863, "they could not pursue a more certain policy to effect that end, than that of restricting prices, and every such step taken by our rulers will tend to embarrass and ruin our country." Myers, unlike Northrop, was eventually superseded in August 1863, by Alexander Lawton, but the overall policies did not change. When Samuel Bassett was commissioned by the

86. Hattaway and Jones, *How the North Won*, 121.

87. "Secret Session" (April 6, 1863), in *Journal of the Congress of the Confederate States of America, 1861–1865* (Washington, DC: Government Printing Office, 1904), 3:250; Raimondo Luraghi, *The Rise and Fall of the Plantation South* (New York: New Viewpoints, 1978), 123; John Majewski, *Modernizing a Slave Economy: The Economic Vision of the Confederate Nation* (Chapel Hill: University of North Carolina Press, 2009), 7; Michael Brem Bonner, "Expedient Corporatism and Confederate Political Economy," *Civil War History* 56 (March 2010): 48–53.

Virginia General Assembly to acquire a half million dollars' worth of cotton cloth, he had to report back that "the universal response has been that the working capacity of every mill is entirely absorbed by the Confederate Government."[88]

Nothing illustrates this conflict between the attitude of the plantation and the fluidity of the market than Confederate railroad policy. In April and again in October 1861 Secretary of War Leroy Walker attempted to bargain with Southern railroad presidents for a quid pro quo arrangement not unlike the one Stanton hammered out with the Northern railroads a year later. In February 1862 the Confederate quartermaster department urged Jefferson Davis to disregard Walker's initiative and militarize the railroads "under the direction of an efficient superintendent, free from local interests, investments, or connection with special railroads," and in March the Confederate Congress authorized Davis to take "absolute control and management of all railways and their rolling stock." Davis hesitated to seize control of the railroads outright, and railroad company presidents begged and parried for exemptions, advantages, and special orders prohibiting military interference with their railroads. However, Davis did appoint a "superintendent," William R. Wadley, to coordinate "supervision and control of the transportation for the Government on all the railroads of the Confederate States" in December 1862.[89]

This muddle of directives served no real purpose except to signal to departmental Confederate military commanders that there was no coherent railroad policy and that they were free to offer abysmally low rates for transportation, disrupt freight schedules with claims for military priority, and generally run the South's limited supply of locomotives and boxcars until they fell apart. As early as 1862 the president of the Virginia Central railroad had to confess to his stockholders that "much anxiety is felt to know whether our railroads can be kept in safe running order if the war shall continue a few years longer, and it is hardly to be doubted that the rapid decline in the efficiency of our roads is soon to diminish our means of successfully maintaining our struggle for independence." By the end of the war, the feeble Southern railway system had been run into the ground by the unsure policies of the Confederate government and military.[90]

88. Richard E. Beringer, Herman Hattaway, Archer Jones, and William Still, *Why the South Lost the Civil War* (Athens: University of Georgia Press, 1986), 213–21; Wilson, *Confederate Industry*, 38, 54, 64, 88, 116; Goff, *Confederate Supply*, 143.

89. "Open Session," March 19, 1862, in *Journal of the Congress of the Confederate States of America* (Washington, DC: Government Printing Office, 1904), 5:122; Mary A. DeCredico, *Patriotism for Profit: Georgia's Urban Entrepreneurs and the Confederate War Effort* (Chapel Hill: University of North Carolina Press, 1990), 76–90; Bonner, "Expedient Corporatism," 57–61; Charles W. Ramsdell, "The Confederate Government and the Railroads," *American Historical Review* 22 (July 1917): 796, 800, 805–6, 809–10.

90. George E. Turner, *Victory Rode the Rails: The Strategic Place of the Railroads in the Civil War* (Indianapolis: Bobbs-Merrill, 1953), 172; Jeffrey N. Lash, *Destroyer of the Iron Horse: General Joseph E. Johnston and Confederate Rail Transport, 1861–1865* (Kent, OH: Kent State University Press, 1991), 186; Goff, *Confederate Supply*, 107–11, 195–99, 247; Charles W. Turner, "The Virginia Central Railroad at War, 1861–1865," *Journal of Southern History* 12 (November 1946): 511.

The struggle of the Union and Confederate economies to supply and support their armies thus became a reflection of the prewar antagonism between liberal democracy and slavery. The free-labor ideology of the Republican Party, with its confidence that a "harmony of interests" naturally existed between capital and labor, found convenient expression in Stanton's decision to step back from drastic economic interventions and allow Northern capitalism to lay its own golden eggs for the war effort. The Confederacy, insensibly obeying the logic of an authoritarian labor system, conscripted, confiscated, and imposed state-ordered controls. And within that logic lay many of the seeds of the Confederacy's destruction.

CHAPTER EIGHT

THE YEAR THAT TREMBLED

EAST AND WEST, 1863

E arly on the morning of April 1, 1863, an angry group of women gathered in the small, squat brick building of the Belvidere Hill Baptist Church in the Confederate capital of Richmond. They met for complaint, not for prayer. Some of the women had husbands in the Confederate army and were fending for themselves on the pittances they could earn and the broken promises of assistance made by the Confederate government. Others had husbands in the Tredegar Iron Works whose pay fell woefully short of subsistence levels. Food supplies in the Confederate capital had dwindled as the fruits of the last year's harvest were consumed by Robert E. Lee's army and the civilian population of the city. What was now offered for sale by Richmond's merchants, bakers, and butchers went for astronomical prices. One woman, Mary Jackson (who was variously described as a farmer's wife, a sign painter's wife, and the mother of a soldier), stood up behind the pulpit of the church and demanded action: let the working-class women of Richmond assemble the next day, march to Governor John Letcher's mansion on Capitol Square, and force the governor to make good on the promises of assistance. If assistance was not forthcoming, then let them turn on the "extortioners" in the shops and levy their own brand of fairness by ransacking the bakeries and market stalls for what they needed.

The next morning, a crowd of 300 women joined Mary Jackson at a city marketplace four blocks from Capitol Square. Armed with a Bowie knife and revolver, Jackson led a seething procession through the streets to the governor's mansion, where Letcher met them on the front steps. The governor, however, had nothing to offer them but a few expressions of personal concern, and after a short speech the governor retreated behind his door and left the dissatisfied crowd milling around in his front yard. Another woman named Mary Johnson, "a tall, daring Amazonian-looking woman" with a "white feather, standing erect from her hat," took the lead of the crowd and pointed them down Richmond's Main Street. "Clubs and guns and stones" appeared, and the crowd surged down the street toward Richmond's shops.[1]

Over the next several hours, all semblance of order disappeared in Richmond's commercial district as the enraged women broke down doors and windows, seized bread and meat, and then went on to loot jewelry, clothing, hats, "and whatever else they wanted." The hapless Governor Letcher and Richmond's mayor, Joseph Mayo, appeared on the scene to calm the mob, but the women were beyond listening to the words of the politicians. At last a company of soldiers, normally detailed for service at the Tredegar Ironworks, filed into Main Street. Someone or some people in the crowd pulled a wagon into the street as a hasty barricade, and at that moment, all that was needed for Confederate soldiers to begin shooting down Confederate women in the middle of Richmond was one reckless gesture, one careless word.[2]

No one had ever thought of Jefferson Davis as possessing a dramatist's sense of timing, but on this occasion the president of the Confederacy appeared at precisely the right moment. It is not clear whether someone summoned Davis (who lived only a few blocks away) or whether he was simply following his own ear for trouble, but he found the mob and the soldiers at the point where each was ready to begin a me-lee. Coolness under pressure had been Davis's long suit ever since his army days, and he quickly mounted the barricade wagon and began to speak. His speech was con-ciliatory, reproachful, and threatening by turns. He knew the people of Richmond were hungry, but he pointed out that farmers in the countryside would only be more unwilling to bring their produce to market in Richmond if they knew that it would be stolen by rioters there. He shamed them by pointing to the stolen jewelry and clothing in their hands when their protest was supposed to be for bread. He even offered them money from his own pockets. He closed by taking out his pocket watch and announcing that if the crowd had not dispersed in five minutes, he would order the soldiers to open fire. A minute or two crawled past, and then the crowd slowly began to break up and drift away. Eventually forty-one women, including Mary Jackson, and twenty-four men were arrested on theft and riot charges.[3]

The Richmond bread riot was not an isolated case. During 1863, similar riots broke out in Georgia, North Carolina, and Alabama; in Mobile, a crowd of wom-en carrying banners with slogans such as "Bread or Blood" and "Bread and Peace"

---

1. "Richmond's Bread Riot—Jefferson Davis Describes a Wartime Incident," *New York Times*, April 30, 1889; "Reported Bread Riot at Richmond," *Harper's Weekly*, April 18, 1863, 243; Emory Thomas, "Wartime Richmond," *Civil War Times Illustrated* 16 (June 1977): 33–34.

2. Stephanie McCurry, "Bread or Blood!" *Civil War Times* 49 (June 2011): 37–41.

3. Michael B. Chesson, "Harlots or Heroines? A New Look at the Richmond Bread Riot," *Virginia Magazine of History and Biography* 92 (April 1984): 131–75.

marched down Dauphine Street, smashing shop windows as they went. A group of "Soldiers' Wives" wrote to North Carolinian Zebulon Vance to complain that with "our Husbands & Sons . . . now separated from us by this cruel War not only to defend our humble homes but the homes & property of the rich man," he should understand that "there are few of us who can make over a dollar a day. . . . Many of us work day after day without a morsal of meat to strengthen us for our Labours and often times we are without bread. Now, Sir, how We ask you in the name of God are we to live."[4]

By 1863, the war that Southerners had entered into so confidently two years before was imposing strains on Southern society that few had imagined in the heady spring of Sumter and the high summer of First Bull Run. The creation of a workable Southern nation required more than enthusiasm—it required time to resolve the numerous contradictions in Southern society between slaveholders and non-slaveholders, between the Romantic image of the South as a society of plantation aristocrats and the grubby rationality of cotton capitalism, between states' rights and the urgency of centralizing every Southern resource in order to win the war. Unfortunately, time was in short supply in the Confederacy. Southern armies were losing territory, Southern men were quietly avoiding war service, and Southern families were going hungry. If Southerners were ever to have the time they needed to understand why they were fighting this war, then the Confederate armies must strike and strike quickly to secure Confederate independence, or else the stress of performing this experiment in nation building under the sword would push the Southern nation into collapse.

The day after the Richmond bread riot, the lead editorial in the Richmond *Dispatch* was resolutely headlined, "Sufferings in the North."[5]

SOMEONE MORE FIT TO COMMAND

On November 7, 1862, President Lincoln finally dismissed George Brinton McClellan from command of the Army of the Potomac. The immediate reason for McClellan's dismissal was his slowness in pursuit of Lee's battered Army of Northern Virginia after its hammering at Antietam the previous September. Looming behind that was the larger conflict between Lincoln and McClellan over slavery and emancipation. But getting rid of McClellan only solved half the problem; it now became necessary for Lincoln to find a more politically reliable replacement who would be aggressive enough to pursue and defeat the Army of Northern Virginia.

4. "Soldiers' Wives" to Vance, March 21, 1863, in *The Papers of Zebulon Baird Vance*, 2:92; "The Bread Riot in Mobile," *New York Times*, October 1, 1863; "Another Bread Riot," *Harper's Weekly*, October 10, 1863.

5. Emory Thomas, *The Confederate Nation, 1861–1865* (New York: Harper & Row, 1979), 204.

At first Lincoln thought he had found such a man in another of McClellan's corps commanders, Major General Ambrose Burnside. A floridly bewhiskered, six-foot-tall midwesterner, Burnside was admired by one reporter as "the very *beau ideal* of a soldier." A West Point graduate of 1847, Burnside had served briefly in the Mexican War (he arrived the day Mexico City fell, so he saw no action) and then resigned from the army in 1853 to go into the arms business, where he patented a breech-loading rifle known as the Burnside carbine. When the war broke out, he was appointed to command the 1st Rhode Island Volunteers and led the expedition that captured Roanoke Island in February 1862. The Roanoke Island expedition made Burnside's reputation as an aggressive leader, and when McClellan's Peninsula campaign collapsed that July, Lincoln offered Burnside command of the Army of the Potomac on the spot. But Burnside had known McClellan since West Point, counted him as a friend, and felt too much personal gratitude to McClellan for past favors to take advantage of McClellan's failure. By November, however, there was no question that McClellan had to leave the army, and Burnside reluctantly obeyed Lincoln's summons to replace him.[6]

That reluctance should have warned Lincoln that all was not what it seemed with Burnside. Despite the reputation he had won as a fighter in the Roanoke expedition, Burnside was actually hesitant and unsure of himself as a general, and the higher he ascended the ladder of command responsibilities, the more hesitant and unsure he grew. At Antietam, McClellan had ordered Burnside to send the four divisions of Burnside's 9th Corps across a bridge on the Antietam Creek and attack Lee's right flank. Burnside found getting across the creek and across the bridge far more difficult than anyone had imagined, and not until after noon did the Federals finally storm across and drive off the thin curtain of Confederate skirmishers who had been defending it. He then paused for two hours to straighten out the alignment of his divisions, allowing just enough time for a full Confederate division under A. P. Hill to arrive pell-mell from Harpers Ferry and knock the 9th Corps back to the creek. Caution and uncertainty caused Burnside to throw away a golden opportunity to crush Lee's army, and he escaped criticism only because so much of Lincoln's disappointed wrath after Antietam was poured out on McClellan's head instead. Replacing McClellan with Burnside, Lincoln imagined, would give the Army of the Potomac an aggressive commander, but it would also placate any unrest among McClellan's stalwarts in the senior officer ranks by selecting someone who was supposed to be one of McClellan's friends.[7]

6. William Marvel, *Burnside* (Chapel Hill: University of North Carolina Press, 1991), 5, 11–12, 14–15, 50–61, 99–100, 159–60.

7. Ethan Rafuse, *Antietam, South Mountain and Harpers Ferry: A Battlefield Guide* (Lincoln: University of Nebraska Press, 2008), 101–6; Ethan S. Rafuse, "'Poor Burn'? The Antietam Conspiracy That Wasn't," *Civil War History* 54 (June 2008): 169–73.

Burnside was aware that despite the lateness of the year, Lincoln and the War Department would expect him to mount a campaign as soon as possible to make up for the time McClellan had wasted in the fall. He also understood that there would be no patience with any plans for another flanking campaign down to the James River peninsula, with a careful and bloodless siege of Richmond. Lincoln wanted confrontation and he wanted it now, and anything less than a head-on over-land drive would be interpreted politically as weakness of will. Lee and the Army of Northern Virginia, not Richmond, must be the real object of attack. So within a week of taking over the Army of the Potomac, Burnside called the army's major generals together and unveiled his plan. Abandoning McClellan's James River route, he would march overland, cross the Rappahannock River at Fredericksburg, and draw Lee into a knock-down, drag-out fight in the flat country somewhere between Fredericksburg and Richmond. Since the bridges across the Rappahannock at Fre-dericksburg had been destroyed as the city changed hands through 1862, Burnside would surprise Lee by building bridges of pontoon boats there, and be on the south side of the Rappahannock before Lee knew what was happening.[8]

The critical point in this plan was getting across the Rappahannock quickly, for if Lee got wind of what was going on and moved the Army of Northern Virginia to Fredericksburg first, the Army of the Potomac would have to fight its way across the Rappahannock and out of Fredericksburg at a decided disadvantage. Unhappily for Burnside, this was precisely what happened. Although Burnside took only three days, from November 14 to November 17, to march the Army of the Potomac down to the Rappahannock opposite Fredericksburg, his pontoons were nowhere to be found. By the time the first elements of Burnside's pontoon train finally arrived from Washington on November 24, Lee had frantically assembled the scattered parts of the Army of Northern Virginia and dug them in along a ridge known as Marye's Heights, just below Fredericksburg, covering the approaches south toward Rich-mond. Burnside had lost the advantage of surprise.[9]

In any other circumstances, a commander of the Army of the Potomac would have been well advised to give up the campaign as lost and gone into winter quarters until spring brought fairer weather. Burnside was under too much pressure from Washington to stop now, though, and as if to prove that he really was the aggres-sive general everyone thought he was, Burnside ordered the river crossing forced and the pontoon bridges built under fire. Remarkably, his soldiers and engineers pulled it off, and by December 12, 1862, a shaky trio of bridges was thrown over the

8. Frank A. O'Reilly, *The Fredericksburg Campaign: Winter War on the Rappahannock* (Baton Rouge: Loui-siana State University Press, 2003), 49.

9. George C. Rable, *Fredericksburg! Fredericksburg!* (Chapel Hill: University of North Carolina Press, 2002), 81, 87–88; E. J. Stackpole, *The Fredericksburg Campaign: Drama on the Rappahannock* (Mechanics-burg, PA: Stackpole, 1991 [1957]), 84–87.

Rappahannock through a curtain of harassing rebel fire, and the town of Fredericksburg was secured. But the Confederates remained on the heights beyond the town. Burnside planned to tackle them on December 13 by staging a large-scale demonstration in front of Marye's Heights, while swinging a third of his army around Lee's right flank.[10]

Planning an operation of this scale, however, proved beyond Burnside's grasp. The flanking maneuver was checked by "Stonewall" Jackson, and, as if to annihilate all memory of any hesitancy at Antietam, Burnside ended up making not one or two but *six* perfectly formed but ghastly frontal assaults on Marye's Heights. From behind a stone wall at the foot of the heights, the Confederates mowed down the thick, slow-moving Federal formations all day, until more than 12,000 Union soldiers were dead or wounded, 6,000 of them piled in front of Marye's Heights alone. "We had to advance over a level plane, and their batteries being on high ground and they being behind breastworks, we had no chance at them, while they could take as deliberate aim as a fellow would at a chicken," wrote George Washington Whitman to his brother three weeks after the battle, "The range was so short, that they threw percussion shells into our ranks that would drop at our feet and explode, killing and wounding Three or four every pop." The next day Burnside wanted to make one more attack, which he would lead personally, but his disgusted corps commanders talked him out of it.[11]

Burnside withdrew to the north bank of the Rappahannock, hoping for a second chance to get at Lee. However, when he started a new campaign on January 20, 1863, to get across the Rappahannock several miles further west, winter rains turned the roads into bottomless morasses, and Burnside's infamous "Mud March" slopped to a halt. It "was the meanest . . . the most 'ornery' time the Army of the Potomac ever had," remembered one Maine captain. "For mud, rain, cold, whiskey drowned-out men, horses, mules, and abandoned wagons and batteries, for pure unadulterated demoralization . . . this took the cake." With soldiers demoralized and deserting in record numbers, with most of Burnside's corps commanders publicly criticizing his ineptitude, Lincoln had no choice but to relieve Burnside.[12]

Lincoln's second choice for a general for the Army of the Potomac was yet another soldier with a reputation for aggressiveness, Major General Joseph Hooker, a handsome, happy-go-lucky brawler with an alcoholic's red nose and an awesome command of old army profanity. By appointing Hooker Lincoln showed that he

10. William B. Franklin, "The Battle of Fredericksburg," in *The Rebellion Record: A Diary of American Events*, ed. Frank Moore (New York: G. P. Putnam, 1867), 10:160.

11. O'Reilly, *The Fredericksburg Campaign*, 431–32, 436, 440; *Civil War Letters of George Washington Whitman*, ed. Jerome M. Loving (Durham, NC: Duke University Press, 1975), 78.

12. Robert G. Carter, "Four Brothers in Blue," *Maine Bugle* 5 (October 1898): 357; Daniel E. Sutherland, *Fredericksburg and Chancellorsville: The Dare Mark Campaign* (Lincoln: University of Nebraska Press, 1998), 91.

had lost patience with the army's McClellan loyalists, since Hooker was one of the few anti-McClellan officers in the upper echelons of the Army of the Potomac and one of the even fewer to have endorsed the Emancipation Proclamation. He was also a surprisingly good administrator, and he spent the first three months of 1863 restoring the shattered morale and organization of the Army of the Potomac until, by April 1863, Hooker was able to invite Lincoln down to the army's camps on the Rappahannock for a grand review. While Hooker was an uncommon organizer and a popular division and corps commander, there was some question in the mind of Darius Couch, the senior corps commander in the Army of the Potomac, about whether he possessed "the weight of character" needed to "take charge of that army." Hooker was, in fact, a braggart and a show-off. Henry Slocum, who commanded the 12th Corps in the Army of the Potomac, had "no faith whatever in Hooker's ability as a military man, in his integrity or honor." Instead, "whiskey, boasting, and vilification have been his stock in trade." Nevertheless, Hooker deliberately played up to the press to swell his image as a stern, remorseless campaigner, and he reveled in the nickname the newspapers happily bestowed upon him, "Fighting Joe."[13]

Despite the image, Hooker grew unsteady and unsure under pressure. "He could play the best game of poker I ever saw," commented Hooker's chief of cavalry, George Stoneman, "until it came to the point where he should go a thousand better, and then he would flunk." Far worse than this, Hooker was also grasping and loyal only to his own ambitions. "Gen. Hooker," wrote Colonel Theodore Gates of the 20th New York, "is reputed a very ambitious & some what unscrupulous man." Hooker had privately damned McClellan behind the general's back to members of the Cabinet, and undercut Burnside's authority so often by criticism and innuendo that the normally placid Burnside beseeched Lincoln to have Hooker court-martialed for insubordination. He liked to hear himself talk, whether it was about how he intended to thrash Lee—"May God have mercy on General Lee, for I will have none"—or how the country needed to get serious about winning the war and, like the old Roman republic, create a temporary dictatorship to finish things up.[14]

Lincoln struggled to bring Hooker to heel by reminding him that it was only with serious reservations that he had been appointed to command the Army of the Potomac. "I have heard, in such way as to believe it, of your recently saying that both the Army and the Government needed a Dictator," wrote Lincoln in a letter he quietly handed to Hooker after summoning the general to the White House to appoint him as commander of the Army of the Potomac.

13. Darius N. Couch, "Sumner's 'Right Grand Division,'" in *Battles and Leaders*, 3:119; Slocum, in Stephen R. Taaffe, *Commanding the Army of the Potomac* (Lawrence: University Press of Kansas, 2006), 120.

14. Alexander K. McClure, *Recollections of Half a Century* (Salem, MA: Salem Press Company, 1902), 348; *The Civil War Diaries of Col. Theodore B. Gates, 20th New York State Militia*, ed. Seward R. Osborne (Hightstown, NJ: Longstreet House, 1991), 60; Stephen W. Sears, *Chancellorsville* (New York: Houghton-Mifflin, 1996), 120.

Of course it was not *for* this, but in spite of it, that I have given you the command. Only those generals who gain successes, can set up dictators. What I now ask of you is military success, and I will risk the dictatorship. . . . I much fear that the spirit which you have aided to infuse into the Army, of criticizing their Commander, and withholding confidence from him, will now turn upon you.[15]

Hooker now proceeded to confirm every one of those reservations. To begin with, his plans were little more than a variation on Burnside's: the Army of the Potomac would again attempt to cross the Rappahannock and force a fight with the Army of Northern Virginia above Richmond. Since the Fredericksburg crossing was obviously too dangerous, Hooker left two of his infantry corps opposite Fredericksburg as decoys under Major General John Sedgwick and actually crossed the Rappahannock about twelve miles to the west with his remaining five corps (between 70,000 and 80,000 men). In theory, this would bring the bulk of the Army of the Potomac across the Rappahannock and down onto Lee's left flank at Fredericksburg before the Confederates could act; Lee would be forced to fight pinned against the Rappahannock or else fall back on Richmond. In that case, Hooker trumpeted, "our enemy must either ingloriously fly, or come out from behind his defences and give us battle on our own ground, where certain destruction awaits him."[16]

When Hooker crossed the Rappahannock on April 29, 1863, the country on the other side of the river turned out to be a dark, unsettled tangle of woods and scrub underbrush, crisscrossed by few usable roads. Hooker plunged firmly into this impassable and spooky terrain, known as the Wilderness, and within twenty-four hours had managed to penetrate all the way to a little country crossroads called Chancellorsville (which was not much of a town at all, but actually a large, rambling hostelry owned by the Chancellor family). "This is splendid," cried George G. Meade, the commander of the 5th Corps, "Hurrah for old Joe; we are on Lee's flank, and he does not know it." If Slocum and the 12th Corps would "take the Plank Road toward Fredericksburg," Meade claimed, "I'll take the Pike, or vice versa, as you prefer, and we'll get out of this Wilderness" and hit Lee before he knew what was coming. Hooker's real plan was nothing so venturesome. He hoped that his advance through the Wilderness would entice Lee to attack *him* rather the other way round, and so Hooker decided over the protests of his corps commanders to entrench the army around Chancellorsville. Slocum was aghast: "Nobody but a crazy man would give such an order when we have victory in sight!" But Hooker was convinced that "I have got Lee just where I want him; he must fight me on my own ground." So he waited

15. Lincoln, "To Joseph Hooker," January 26, 1863, in *Collected Works*, 6:78–79.

16. "General Orders No. 47," April 30, 1863, in *The War of the Rebellion*, Series One, 25(I):171.

to see what would happen—which was usually a fatal thing to do in the vicinity of Robert E. Lee.[17]

Lee had been as surprised by Hooker's move as by Burnside's back in December, but he took full advantage of Hooker's hesitancy the same way as he had of Burnside's difficulty with his pontoon bridge. While Hooker pulled back to Chancellorsville, Lee left only a thin line of Confederate troops to guard Fredericksburg and pulled the rest over to confront Hooker in the Wilderness. He had only 43,000 men (one entire corps of the Army of Northern Virginia was absent on detached service) to face Hooker. Yet Lee scarcely hesitated before throwing the single most dramatic gamble of the Civil War. Dividing his already understrength army into two parts, he yielded to the prompting of "Stonewall" Jackson to allow him to march his 29,000-man corps entirely around the right flank of Hooker's army and use the advantage of surprise to crumple Hooker's line like a piece of paper.[18]

Jackson began his flank march late on the morning of May 2, 1863, and after twelve hours of marching under the shadows of the Wilderness's impenetrable tree cover, his men were in position on the edge of the unsuspecting flank of the Army of the Potomac. Shortly after five o'clock, Jackson pulled his watch from his pocket and serenely informed his lead division commander, Robert Rodes, "You can go forward, then." As Jackson's men came bounding through the woods, yip-yipping their dreaded rebel yell, the unprepared Federals fell to pieces. The Army of the Potomac's entire 11th Corps dissolved into "a dense mass of beings who had lost their reasoning faculties, and were flying from a thousand fancied dangers . . . battery wagons, ambulances, horses, men, cannon, caissons, all jumbled and tumbled together in an apparently inextricable mass, and that murderous fire still pouring in upon them." Only the fall of darkness prevented Jackson from rolling right over Hooker's headquarters. Over the next two days, Lee pressed home his attack again and again, while Hooker simply drew his lines in tighter, abandoning a position at Hazel Grove, which allowed Confederate artillery to bombard his own headquarters in the Chancellorsville tavern. One solid shot smashed into a porch pillar that Hooker was leaning against, temporarily concussing Hooker, and drawing a veil of paralysis over his decisions.[19]

Finally, on May 5, Hooker had had enough and pulled his army back over the Rappahannock. He had lost nearly 17,000 men and a major battle; what was more, he had lost them to a force nearly half the size of his own, and had done it while nearly

17. Edward G. Longacre, *The Commanders of Chancellorsville: The Gentleman vs. the Rogue* (Nashville, TN: Rutledge Hill Press, 2005), 160; John Bigelow, *The Campaign of Chancellorsville: A Strategic and Tactical Study* (New Haven, CT: Yale University Press, 1910), 259.

18. John Selby, *Stonewall Jackson as Military Commander* (New York: Barnes and Noble, 1999), 191–93.

19. James I. Robertson, *Stonewall Jackson: The Man, the Soldier, the Legend* (New York: Macmillan, 1997), 171; *Life of David Bell Birney, Major-General United States Volunteers* (Philadelphia: King and Baird, 1867), 144.

one-third of his own army stood idle for want of orders from its confused and vacillating commander. It was now Hooker's turn to fall prey to the same rumor mill he had so often turned himself, and on May 13 Lincoln informed Hooker that his corps and division commanders were already muttering loudly behind the general's back. Not that Lincoln intended to do anything about it. The grim news from Chancellorsville crushed Lincoln. "One newly risen from the dead could not have looked more ghostlike," wrote the correspondent Noah Brooks. Lincoln vetoed a proposal for a new crossing of the Rappahannock that Hooker telegraphed to him on May 13, and the following month, seeing the handwriting on the wall, the exasperated Hooker resigned.[20]

By this time a certain paranoia had begun to set in among the officers of the Army of the Potomac: could the Army of Northern Virginia ever be beaten? By the summer of 1863, it seemed not. "Everywhere but here success crowns our arms," complained Theodore Gates. "The Army of the Potomac which has been petted & lauded ad nauseam & drilled & dressed more and better than any other in the service has accomplished absolutely nothing. . . . So our Generals rise & fall one after another."[21] Even the Army of Northern Virginia was becoming convinced of its own invincibility. George Henry Mills of the 16th North Carolina went cheerfully into camp with his regiment after Chancellorsville, "where we put in the time drilling on the beautiful fields of the Rappahannock and waiting for Halleck to put up another General for us to whip."[22]

The magnetic pole of that confidence, beyond any question, was the figure of Lee himself, and by the summer of 1863, Lee enjoyed a degree of adulation from his own army that few generals have ever seen. Confederate propagandist Edwin De Leon met Lee briefly in Richmond in 1862 and was struck by the "stately figure" who "induced one who passed by to turn and look again." At Chancellorsville, Lt. Francis Hillyer of the 3rd Georgia saw Confederate "troops opened to the right and the left" around Lee and his staff, "and as the old Hero passed through, the line greeted him with tremendous cheers."[23] Wesley Lewis Battle of the 37th North Carolina watched Lee return the salute of his regiment at a review on May 29, 1863, and Lt. Battle's reaction surprised even himself:

> After the review was over & we were marching back to Camp, Gen. A. P. Hill rode
> up to Col. Barbour & told him to make his Regt. give three cheers for Gen. Lee. It is

20. Brooks, "The Effect," May 8, 1863, in *Lincoln Observed*, 50; Michael Burlingame, *Abraham Lincoln: A Life* (Baltimore: Johns Hopkins University Press, 2008), 2:498–500; Ernest B. Furgurson, *Chancellorsville 1863: The Souls of the Brave* (New York: Knopf, 1992), 332.

21. *Civil War Diaries of Theodore Gates*, 60, 63.

22. George Henry Mills, *History of the 16th North Carolina Regiment in the Civil War* (Hamilton, NY: Edmonston, 1992 [1903]), 33.

23. Sears, *Chancellorsville*, 365; Edwin De Leon, *Secret History of Confederate Diplomacy Abroad*, ed. William C. Davis (Lawrence: University Press of Kansas, 2005), 107.

impossible for me to describe the emotions of my heart as the old silver-headed hero acknowledged the salute by taking off his hat, thereby exposing the most noble countenance I ever beheld. I felt proud that the Southern Confederacy could boast of such a man. In fact I was almost too proud for the occasion, for I could not open my mouth to give vent to the emotions that were struggling within.[24]

Actually, Lee's success as a commander was due to more than just the inspiration he generated. The first important factor in that success was clearly his adroit choice and management of his subordinate officers. Lee succeeded in gathering around him a remarkable collection of military talent, especially "Stonewall" Jackson and James Longstreet, and he communicated with them on an almost intuitive level. With officers such as this on hand, it became Lee's style only to give general shape to plans for a campaign or battle and to leave the actual execution to his subordinates, confident that they understood his intentions so perfectly that on-the-spot decision making could be left entirely to their own discretion. He told one of his corps commanders, "I only wish you therefore to keep me advised of your movements that I may shape mine accordingly, and not to feel trammeled in your operations, other than is required by the general plan of operations." "I think and work with all my powers to bring my troops to the right place at the right time; then I have done my duty," Lee explained to the Prussian observer Justus Scheibert. "My supervision during the battle would do more harm than good. I would be unfortunate if I could not rely upon my division and brigade commanders."[25]

It was just as well that he could, for few of Lee's senior officers—Jackson, Hill, Longstreet, Richard Ewell—showed much capacity to get along with each other. Jackson and Hill in particular carried on a spiteful and venomous vendetta against each other, culminating in 1863, when Jackson attempted to have Hill cashiered. Lee alone seemed exempt from the friction of the talented and prickly personalities in the upper command levels of the Army of Northern Virginia, partly because of his own personal reticence and partly because Lee could rely on his immaculate prewar service record and his membership in one of the preeminent families in Southern society to quell the flood of argument around him. For Lee, unlike his senior officers, was the only major representative of the planter aristocracy in the top hierarchy of the Army. "Stonewall" Jackson was an orphan, raised in the yeoman farmer counties of western Virginia, and most observers were struck by how much he looked like a farmer rather than a general. Captain William Seymour of the Louisiana Tiger

24. "In the Words of His Own Men: As They Saw General Lee," ed. Everard H. Smith, *Civil War Times Illustrated* 25 (October 1986): 22.

25. Douglas Southall Freeman, *Lee's Lieutenants: A Study in Command*, vol. 2: *Cedar Mountain to Chancellorsville* (New York: C. Scribner's Sons, 1943), 510–14; Justus Scheibert, *Seven Months in the Rebel States During the North American War*, ed. W. M. S. Hoole (Tuscaloosa: University of Alabama Press, 2009 [1958]), 75; Lee to James Longstreet, March 21, 1863, in *The Wartime Papers of Robert E. Lee*, eds. Clifford Dowdey and Louis Manarin (Boston: Little, Brown, 1961), 416.

battalion noticed that Jackson regularly wore nothing more impressive than "an old rusty, sunburnt grey coat and a faded blue cap of a peculiar pattern, the top of which fell forward over his eyes." From his appearance, wrote George Henry Mills, "no one would have suspected that he was more than a Corporal in a cavalry company."[26]

James Longstreet, another son of yeoman farmers, also lost his father at an early age and labored under the added disadvantage (in this army) of having no Virginia connections (born in South Carolina, Longstreet had grown up in Georgia under the tutelage of his slave-owning uncle, Augustus Baldwin Longstreet). Richard Ewell, a pop-eyed eccentric who lisped vulgarities and profanity, was the son of an alcoholic physician from a once-prosperous Virginia family. Only Ambrose Powell Hill's family came close to conferring any kind of recognizable social status on any of these subordinates, and even then, Powell Hill's father was a townsman and a merchant rather than a landholder. Hill was also known to be as rakish and irreligious as "Stonewall" Jackson was a severe and devout Presbyterian.[27]

Lee, by contrast, came from the elite of Virginia Tidewater society and low-church Virginia Episcopalianism (even though much of his land and slaves had come from his wife's family and not through Lee's spendthrift and bankrupt father). Although Lee had repeatedly expressed before the war his personal preference for seeing slavery brought to an end at the right time, like most Virginia slaveholders Lee found that the right time was never within the foreseeable future, and Lee began the war as committed to the defense and preservation of slavery as any other slaveholder. In every respect, Lee was the embodiment of the ideal Virginia planter—decent, gentlemanly, religious, and immovably convinced that slavery was, for the unending present, the best of all possible worlds for black people.[28] And he expected, demanded, and received from his subordinate officers precisely the unarguable deference that his middle-class lieutenants were conditioned and expected to give.

Another key to Lee's successes on the battlefield was his cultivation of good relations with Jefferson Davis. The Confederate president originally intended to use Lee in much the same way that Lincoln used Henry Halleck, as a general military adviser and liaison between the army and the government, and from March to June 1862 Lee worked behind a desk in Richmond as an informal military chief of staff to the Confederate President. Although Joseph E. Johnston's wound in the Peninsula

26. William Seymour, *The Civil War Memoirs of Captain William J. Seymour: Reminiscences of a Louisiana Tiger*, ed. Terry L. Jones (Baton Rouge: Louisiana State University Press, 1991), 49; Mills, *History of the 16th North Carolina*, 18.

27. William Garrett Piston, *Lee's Tarnished Lieutenant: James Longstreet and His Place in Southern History* (Athens: University of Georgia Press, 1987), 2–5; Donald C. Pfanz, *Richard S. Ewell: A Soldier's Life* (Chapel Hill: University of North Carolina Press, 1998), 7–8, 33; James I. Robertson, *General A. P. Hill: The Story of a Confederate Warrior* (New York: Random House, 1987), 5–7, 303.

28. Nolan, *Lee Considered*, 9–29.

campaign forced Davis to put Lee into field command, the two remained in very close communication throughout the war, and Lee's victories in the Peninsula convinced Davis to yield to Lee's strategic judgment throughout the ensuing eighteen months. By 1863, Lee had become indispensable to Davis: as Davis wrote to Lee, to find "someone in my judgment more fit to command, or who would possess more of the confidence of the army, or of the reflecting men of the country, is to demand an impossibility."[29] Thus, Lee was able to exercise, through Davis, an outsize influence over the shape of Confederate military operations and logistics.

The most important key to Lee's successes was his aggressiveness. Beneath the marble-like calm and dignity that his soldiers and enemies so admired, Lee was a volcano of aggressive impulses. The "evenness and self-control in General Lee's bearing and habits of thought . . . prevented the ordinary observer from realizing the boldness and energy held reserve under cover of his composed demeanor," warned William Preston Johnston, one of Jefferson Davis's military aides (and the son of the fallen Albert Sidney Johnston). "Lee was the most aggressive man I met in the war," wrote John Singleton Mosby, "and was always ready for an enterprise." In the spring of 1862, when Lee was still a relatively new and untried article, one man asked Colonel Joseph Ives, who knew Lee, whether the general possessed sufficient vigor and audacity to defend Richmond. "If there is one man in either army, Confederate or Federal, head and shoulders above every other in *audacity* it is General Lee. His name might be audacity. He will take more desperate chances, and take them quicker than any other general in this country, North or South; and you will live to see it, too."[30]

Ives's prediction was amply borne out, for Lee easily turned into a different man on the battlefield than he was in the drawing room. In the early months of the war, Lee favored a cautious, defensive strategy. "Our policy should be purely on the defensive," he advised in the first two weeks of the war, believing that it was still possible that "Reason" will "resume her sway" and convince the Lincoln administration to turn to negotiations rather than conflict. That confidence melted away before the end of the year, and he soon came to realize that the South's resources were too feeble to prevent the Northern juggernaut from gradually crushing a passive Confederacy. Nor did he look for salvation from Britain or France. "You must not build your hopes on peace on account of the United States going into a war with England," he warned in 1861, "Expect to receive aid from no one." Only by quickly meeting the Yankee armies straight on, using surprise and dexterity to defeat and embarrass them, and thus rapidly depressing Northern war morale to the point where disheartened

29. Davis to Lee, August 11, 1863, in *War of the Rebellion*, Series One, 29(II):640.

30. "Memoranda of Conversations Between General Robert E. Lee and William Preston Johnston, May 7, 1868, and March 18, 1870," ed. W. G. Bean, *Virginia Magazine of History and Biography* 73 (October 1965): 475; *Memoirs of Colonel John S. Mosby* (Nashville, TN: J. B. Sanders, 1995 [1917]), 374; Douglas Southall Freeman, *R. E. Lee: A Biography* (New York: C. Scribner's Sons, 1935), 2: 92.

Northerners would declare the war unwinnable, did the Confederacy stand a chance. "I am aware that there is difficulty & hazard in taking the aggressive," he warned the Confederacy's Secretary of War in 1863, James A. Seddon. Apart from inducing a swift Northern collapse, however, Lee privately considered the Confederacy to be doomed. "He knew [in 1861] the strength of the United States Government," wrote William Preston Johnston.[31]

On the other hand, Lee knew that democracies do not easily bear the burdens of long wars. Democracies are geared to peace, and public opinion in a democracy cannot be regimented and drummed up repeatedly. If the Confederates were wise, they would "give all the encouragement we can, consistently with truth, to the rising peace party of the North." Let Lincoln's Northern opposition declare the war to be lost, let them wax eloquent about their desires for an armistice and negotiations "for a restoration of the Union," and let their constant yammering for peace talks finally compel Lincoln to agree to an armistice. Once a truce was announced and the talks begun, Lincoln would never be able to convince war-weary Northerners to restart the war; the Confederates could then dismiss any talk about "bringing us back to the Union" and demand a "distinct and independent national existence." That, of course, meant allowing Lincoln's Northern opposition to think that the goal of peace talks would be reunion when in fact the Confederates never intended any other outcome than independence, but "it is not the part of prudence to spurn the proposition in advance, merely because those who wish . . . to believe that it will result in bringing us back to the Union." Cynical, perhaps, but "should the belief that peace will bring back the Union become general, the war would no longer be supported, and that after all is what we are interested in bringing about."[32]

Looking to wear down Northern morale before Northern numbers could overwhelm him, Lee leaped to the attack at every opportunity he could, invading the North twice in 1862 and 1863 and taking the tactical offensive in every major battle he fought in those years (except for Antietam and Fredericksburg). The cost in lives for this aggressiveness was not cheap—Lee's men sustained 42,000 casualties in his first four months in command of the Army of Northern Virginia (almost as many men as Albert Sidney Johnston commanded at Shiloh)—but Lee at least achieved in the process the most extraordinary combat victories of the war, and at Second Bull Run he came as close as any other Civil War general to the complete annihilation of an opposing army. Lee was prepared to fight the Civil War in Virginia as a great Napoleonic conflict, and even after the terrible pounding his army took at Antietam, Lee was ready four days afterward to "threaten a passage into Maryland, to occupy

31. "Memoranda of Conversations between General Robert E. Lee and William Preston Johnston," 479.

32. Lee to Mary Custis Lee, December 25, 1861, G. W. C. Lee, January 4, 1862, and James A. Seddon, June 8, 1863, in *Wartime Papers of Robert E. Lee*, 12, 96, 98, 505; Lee to Jefferson Davis, June 10, 1863, in *War of the Rebellion*, Series One, 27(III):882.

the enemy on this frontier, and, if my purpose cannot be accomplished, to draw them into the [Shenandoah] Valley, where I can attack them to advantage."[33]

Ultimately, though, it was not in Virginia that Lee wanted to fight Yankees. "Stonewall" Jackson began pressing Lee in the summer of 1862 to take the war northward, across the Potomac, "and transfer this campaign from the banks of the James to those of the Susquehanna" in Pennsylvania. Lee could not have agreed more. "After much reflection," he told Jefferson Davis, "I think if it was possible to reinforce Jackson" and send him to "cross Maryland into Pennsylvania," it would relieve the pressure on northern Virginia's threadbare farms and pastures, and "call all the enemy from our Southern coast & liberate those states." When Joe Johnston's wounding put command of the Army of Northern Virginia into his hands, Lee wasted little time in taking his own advice, and the 1862 Maryland campaign would have been a Pennsylvania campaign had it all not ended so abruptly at Antietam.[34]

The subsequent victories at Fredericksburg and Chancellorsville he regarded as little more than distractions from his larger plan for a second attempt at invading Pennsylvania. "At Fredericksburg," Lee admitted, "our people were greatly elated," but "I was much depressed. We had really accomplished nothing; we had not gained a foot of ground, and I knew the enemy could easily replace the men he had lost." The same thing happened after Chancellorsville. "Our people were wild with delight—I, on the contrary, was more depressed than after Fredericksburg; our loss was severe, and again we had gained not an inch of ground and the enemy could not be pursued. . . . I considered the problem in every possible phase, and to my mind it resolved itself into the choice of one of two things—either to retire on Richmond and stand a siege, which must ultimately have ended in surrender, or to invade Pennsylvania."[35]

However, each of these three parts of Lee's success as a commander also carried within it the seeds of Lee's destruction. Lee's heavy reliance on the talents of his corps commanders to win battles rendered him much too vulnerable, emotionally and strategically, should any of them fall to wounds or death. At Chancellorsville, this was exactly what happened to "Stonewall" Jackson. Accidentally wounded by his own men while performing a risky nighttime reconnaissance, Jackson suffered the amputation of his left arm, and then eight days later died of complications from the

33. Grady McWhiney and Perry D. Jamieson, *Attack and Die: Civil War Military Tactics and the Southern Heritage* (University: University of Alabama Press, 1982), 19; Lee to Davis, September 21, 1863, in *War of the Rebellion*, Series One, 19(I):143.

34. A. R. Boteler, "Stonewall Jackson in the Campaign of 1862," *Southern Historical Society Papers* 40 (September 1915): 165; Henry Kyd Douglas, *I Rode with Stonewall, Being Chiefly the War Experiences of the Youngest Member of Jackson's Staff* (Chapel Hill: University of North Carolina Press, 1968), 113; Lee to Jefferson Davis, June 5, 1862, and September 4, 1862, in *Wartime Papers of Robert E. Lee*, 183–84, 288.

35. "Letter from Major General Heth, of A. P. Hill's Corps, A.N.V.," *Southern Historical Society Papers* 4 (October 1877): 153–54.

amputation. With Jackson's death, Lee lost one of the few men capable of turning Lee's audacious plans for offensive warfare into tactical victories, and he never found a satisfactory replacement. "There never were such men in an army before," Lee told John Bell Hood, one of his up-and-coming division commanders and a personal pet. "They will go anywhere and do anything if properly led. But there is the difficulty— proper commanders. Where can they be obtained?"

Similarly, Lee's influence over Davis tended to operate to the advantage of Virginia, but at the expense of the rest of the Confederacy. By 1863 Davis was under substantial pressure from within his own government (and especially Secretary of War Seddon) to shift the weight of the Confederate war effort to the west and reduce the war in Virginia to a holding action. Lee, however, had sacrificed his first career in the United States Army for the sake of Virginia, and he was not about to see his second career in the Confederate army compel him to make a similar choice. Lee tenaciously fought every suggestion that the Army of Northern Virginia be denuded to reinforce the west, and his influence over Davis guaranteed, at least until the fall of 1863, that the defense of Virginia would always be able to outweigh the demands for help from the Confederate forces in the West.[36]

Lee's tactical judgment was inevitably going to be affected by the increasing deterioration of his health and by the deepening sense of fatalism caused by the losses his incessant urge for the offensive produced. By the spring of 1863, Lee was fifty-six years old, prematurely white-haired and already suffering from severe arthritis. During the Maryland campaign, his horse bolted while Lee was seated on the ground, holding his reins, and the general was dragged over the ground by the frightened animal, spraining both wrists and breaking bones in his hands. Then, on March 30, 1863, Lee suffered the first of a series of heart attacks, a premonition of the heart disease that would, after the war, eventually kill him. All of these ills and accidents took a severe toll on Lee's energies, both in camp and in battle. "Old age & sorrow is wearing me away," Lee wrote to his wife, Mary Custis Lee, in March 1863, "& constant anxiety & labour, day and night, leaves me but little repose."[37]

Along with the physical wear and tear of his command, Lee had to cope with the deaths of irreplaceable subordinates such as Jackson, and the deaths of his beloved daughter Anne Carter Lee and daughter-in-law Charlotte Wickham. "In the hours of night, when there is nothing to lighten the full weight of my grief, I feel as if I should be overwhelmed," Lee wrote after Annie Lee died in 1862. "I had always counted, if God should spare me a few days of peace after this cruel war was ended, that I should have her with me. But year after year my hopes go out, and I must be resigned." Lee's sense of resignation increasingly found shape in a mystical submission to the mysterious workings of an all-controlling Providence. "The ties to earth

---

36. Lee to Hood, May 21, 1863, in *Wartime Papers of Robert E. Lee*, 490; Thomas L. Connelly, *The Marble Man: Robert E. Lee and His Image in American Society* (New York: Knopf, 1977), 202–3.

37. Lee to Mary Custis Lee, March 9, 1863, in *Wartime Papers of R. E. Lee*, 413.

are taken, one by one, by our Merciful God to turn our hearts to Him and to show us that the object of this life is to prepare for a better and brighter world." Yet, as in so many similar cases (including Lincoln's), Lee's sense of divinely ordered purpose in these afflictions only made him more willing than ever to throw himself and his army into the balances of battle. "Our country demands all our strength, all our energies," Lee wrote. "If victorious, we have everything to hope for in the future. If defeated, nothing will be left for us to live for. . . . My whole trust is in God, and I am ready for whatever He may ordain."[38]

Affliction was now, in the summer of 1863, about to be visited on Lee in unprecedented amounts. In September 1862 the Confederate Congress authorized Lee to subdivide the Army of Northern Virginia into two corps, commanded by Jackson and James Longstreet (who would be awarded the rank of lieutenant general). The size of these corps had proven, in practice, "too large for one commander," and in the weeks after Chancellorsville and Jackson's death, he redistributed the units of the two corps to make three, retaining Longstreet as commander of one and turning command of the other two over to Richard Ewell and A. P. Hill. Ewell was "an honest, brave soldier, who has always done his duty well," and Hill "is the best soldier of his grade with me." But Longstreet was a moodier and more truculent subordinate than "Stonewall" Jackson, and neither Ewell nor Hill ever matched Jackson's raw hitting power. What was worse, Ewell had only just recovered from a wound at Second Manassas that had cost him his leg, and neither he nor Hill was given much time to become accustomed to their new responsibilities before Lee was once more turning his head toward Pennsylvania.[39]

Lee opened his new campaign northward on June 3, quietly pulling Ewell's corps off the Army of Northern Virginia's defensive line behind the Rappahannock River and slipping it into the Shenandoah Valley, where Ewell easily overran a Union occupation force at Winchester. Longstreet and Hill followed, and by June 22 the advanced elements of Ewell's corps had crossed the Potomac and were already in Pennsylvania, leaving the baffled Federals to hop belatedly after them. Despite orders from Lee that discouraged foraging and looting, Lee's underfed soldiers were a visitation of famine on the Pennsylvania countryside. Amos Stouffer, a Swiss-German farmer from Chambersburg, Pennsylvania, wrote in his diary that "the Rebs . . . are scouring the country in every direction. . . . They take horses, cattle, sheep, hogs, &c.," and even took over a Chambersburg mill and forced the farmers to grind wheat for them. The Confederates also made off with what they regarded as yet another form of moveable property: not only Chambersburg's "horses and cattle" but also its "Negroes." Out of a free black population of 451 in and around

38. J. R. Jones, *Life and Letters of Robert Edward Lee: Soldier and Man* (Harrisonburg, VA: Sprinkle, 1978 [1906]), 200, 207; Freeman, *R. E. Lee*, 3:268.

39. Lee to Jefferson Davis, May 20, 1863, in *Wartime Papers of Robert E. Lee*, 488; "Special Orders No. 146," May 30, 1863, in *War of the Rebellion*, Series One, 25(II):840.

Chambersburg, more than fifty were rounded up by Confederate soldiers and started south to be sold into slavery.[40] On June 27, an advance column of Ewell's corps was in Carlisle, Pennsylvania, a short distance across the Susquehanna River from Harrisburg; the next day, one of Ewell's divisions was in York.

Once again, however, Lee's plans were thwarted, this time by the loss not of orders but of his cavalry. Lee's cavalry commander, J. E. B. Stuart, slipped the long leash Lee kept on his trusted subordinates and managed to become hopelessly separated from the main body of Lee's infantry. So, instead of providing Lee with scouting and reconnaissance, Stuart effectively rode right off the map, leaving Lee strategically blind. No matter; Lee's general plan was "to push boldly forward . . . to Harrisburg, Pennsylvania, seize the capital of the commonwealth and fight a decisive battle somewhere upon her soil." He assured Longstreet that whatever battle he fought, he would assume the tactical defensive and allow the Army of the Potomac to immolate itself the same way it had at Fredericksburg. But Lee also reserved to himself a more aggressive alternative: if the Army of the Potomac strung itself out in an attempt to pursue him northward, he would wait for the first moment that the separate parts of the Union army pulled far enough away to become isolated from each other, then turn on them, one after the other, and crush them in detail.[41]

That, Lee told Isaac Trimble, might occur somewhere in the open country between Harrisburg and the Potomac, near the crossroads town of Gettysburg, Pennsylvania. In that event, the much-beaten and demoralized Army of the Potomac would probably disintegrate (as John Pope's Army of Virginia almost had after Second Bull Run) and perhaps allow him to threaten Baltimore or Washington. The most optimistic view held that the public outcry in the North would be so great that Lincoln might finally be forced to open negotiations, and for that purpose Jefferson Davis had asked his vice president, Alexander H. Stephens, to be on hand to represent Confederate interests in a face-to-face meeting with Lincoln. If the Army of the Potomac shunned battle and concentrated on shielding Washington, Lee could still "subsist his army" on the fat Pennsylvania countryside "for two months" and allow the battered farmlands of northern Virginia a brief respite.[42]

Without Stuart's cavalry to provide intelligence, Lee was thrown back on what little he could glean from spies, captured newspapers, and Southern sympathizers. He did not discover from them until June 28—when his own army was itself strung

40. "The Rebs Are Yet Thick Around Us: The Civil War Diary of Amos Stouffer of Chambersburg," *Civil War History* 38 (September 1992): 214–15; Wilbur Sturtevant Nye, *Here Come the Rebels!* (Dayton, OH: Morningside Press, 1984), 184–85; Ted Alexander, "A Regular Slave Hunt," *North and South* 4 (September 2001): 84–88.

41. William Swallow, "From Fredericksburg to Gettysburg," in *Gettysburg Sources*, ed. J. and J. Mclean (Baltimore: Butternut and Blue, 1987), 2:2–3; Stephen Sears, *Gettysburg* (Boston: Houghton Mifflin, 2003), 202.

42. Kent Masterson Brown, *Retreat from Gettysburg: Lee, Logistics, and the Pennsylvania Campaign* (Chapel Hill: University of North Carolina Press, 2005), 16.

out in an awkward triangle between Carlisle, Chambersburg, and York—that the Army of the Potomac had made uncommonly fast time in its pursuit of him out of Virginia and was closer to parts of the Confederate army than those parts were to each other. Lee at once ordered a concentration of the Army of Northern Virginia on Cashtown, a small village eight miles west of Gettysburg.

In the process, A.P. Hill allowed one of his divisions to become entangled in a firefight with Federal cavalry just west of Gettysburg on the morning of July 1, without realizing that two Federal army corps (1st and 11th) were only a few miles south of the town. The Yankee infantry pounced on Hill's troops, and in turn, Hill committed more of his corps to the fight. Lee, at Cashtown, heard the sound of fighting in the distance and rode out to see for himself. Caution might have dictated that he break off the engagement until he could find out if more federal infantry was lurking nearby. But by the time he arrived at the scene of the battle that afternoon, Richard Ewell's corps had shown up from Carlisle on its own, and Hill and Ewell together were successfully driving the Federal infantry through the town and to a low, flat plateau known as Cemetery Hill, just south of Gettysburg. Unwilling to back off from a battle his men were clearly winning, Lee summoned Longstreet's corps to come up from Chambersburg, ordered Ewell to secure the other hills south of the town if Ewell thought it "practicable," and in general behaved as though he had just had the battle he had hoped to fight near Gettysburg delivered to him on precisely his own terms.[43]

This might have been a fairly reasonable procedure, given what had happened at Chancellorsville, and provided the Army of the Potomac was still commanded by someone like Hooker. By this time, however, Hooker was no longer at the head of the Army of the Potomac. Angered over slights he had received from the War Department, Hooker resigned on June 27, and Lincoln replaced him with the commander of the Army of the Potomac's 5th Corps, George Gordon Meade. Meade was a throwback to the McClellanites (Meade was a Philadelphian, from the same social circle as the McClellans, and a Democrat), and his selection may have been a compromise on Lincoln's part to forestall calls to restore McClellan to command once again. In any case, Lincoln hurriedly shoved command of the army's 95,000 men into Meade's hands to take care of the invasion emergency.[44]

Meade's first instinct would have played right into Lee's plans. Given command on such short notice, Meade proposed to adopt a defensive posture, digging the Army of the Potomac into a line behind Pipe Creek, in northern Maryland, and then sitting down to protect Washington. But the engagement at Gettysburg

43. Harry W. Pfanz, *Gettysburg: The First Day* (Chapel Hill: University of North Carolina Press, 2001), 21, 344.

44. Freeman Cleaves, *Meade of Gettysburg* (Norman: University of Oklahoma Press, 1960), 122–24; George Meade Jr., *The Life and Letters of George Gordon Meade, Major-General, United States Army* (New York: Charles Scribner's Sons, 1913), 2:2–5; Ethan S. Rafuse, *George Gordon Meade and the War in the East* (Abilene, TX: McWhiney Foundation Press, 2003), 24.

on July 1 forced Meade's hand fully as much as it had forced Lee's, and Meade hurriedly ordered the Army of the Potomac to converge as rapidly as possible on what was left of the 1st Corps and 11th Corps on Cemetery Hill. During the night, Meade assembled almost all of the Army of the Potomac there, and rendered null any prospect that Ewell would be able to capture Cemetery Hill by just walking up and taking it.[45]

This was still the Yankee army Lee had twice defeated in the last seven months, and on the morning of July 2, Lee decided to launch an imitation of the blow that had floored the Yankees at Chancellorsville. He sent James Longstreet's newly arrived corps in a long flanking hook to hit the Union left, and when Longstreet did so late that afternoon, the results almost perfectly mirrored Stonewall Jackson's attack exactly two months before. Union troops managed to save the most prominent high ground, a rock-littered hill known locally as Little Round Top, throwing back Confederate brigades of Alabamians and Texans with little more than grit and bluff. (One Union regiment, the 20th Maine Volunteers, and their colonel, the former Bowdoin college rhetoric professor Joshua Lawrence Chamberlain, surprised the Alabamians by launching a counterattack of their own at Little Round Top, catching the Confederates so completely by surprise that they broke and ran.) In every other respect, however, Longstreet wrecked half the Army of the Potomac by the time the sun set on July 2, and only vigorous protests from his corps commanders prevented Meade from throwing in the towel and ordering a retreat.[46]

Just as had happened at Chancellorsville, Lee now had the Army of the Potomac on the ropes and was ready to deliver the knockout blow. This time, though, he had sustained so many losses in killed, wounded, and missing that the blow would have to be struck with the only uncommitted division he had left, one of Virginians from Longstreet's corps under Major General George E. Pickett, supported by North Carolinians from Hill's depleted corps—approximately 10,500 men in all—against the center of the Union line of battle. By the example of the British attack on the Alma in 1854, this should have swept the Army of the Potomac from the heights of Gettysburg. Instead, Pickett's charge turned into a reverse of Fredericksburg. The Confederates were compelled to cross almost a mile of open ground under a murderous fire of artillery, then confront the fire of Federal infantry from the 2nd Corps of the Army of the Potomac, who were convinced that the outcome of the war was resting on their shoulders. Although a few Confederates managed to reach the Union line and punch a small hole in it, the overall attack collapsed, with the loss of more than 1,100 killed and 4,500 wounded. By the end of the day, it was at last evident to Lee

45. Douglas Craig Haines, "'Lights Mingled with Shadows': Lt. Gen. Richard S. Ewell—July 1, 1863," *Gettysburg Magazine* 45 (July 2011): 68–70.

46. Harry W. Pfanz, *Gettysburg: The Second Day* (Chapel Hill: University of North Carolina Press, 1987), 486; John J. Pullen, *The Twentieth Maine* (Philadelphia: Lippincott, 1957), 124.

that he could not dislodge Meade from his position at Gettysburg. With his supplies and ammunition badly depleted, and almost 28,000 casualties from the three days of fighting, Lee wearily ordered the Army of Northern Virginia to retreat.[47]

After ten months of almost unrelieved bad news from the battlefield, the news of Gettysburg came as welcome relief to the North. In the Confederacy, it shattered the image of Lee's invincibility and raised questions for the first time about Lee's capabilities as a field commander. On August 8, assuming full responsibility for the defeat at Gettysburg, Lee offered Jefferson Davis his resignation. Davis refused, but at the same time, Lee would never again have complete control of Davis's military policy, and in September Davis would detach Longstreet's corps from the Army of Northern Virginia and send it west to reinforce Braxton Bragg. "One brief month ago," wept Josiah Gorgas into his journal on July 28, "we were apparently at the point of success. Lee was in Pennsylvania, threatening Harrisburgh, and even Philadelphia. Vicksburg seemed to laugh all Grant's efforts to scorn." Now, the "picture is just as somber as it was bright then. . . . The Confederacy totters to its destruction."[48] At almost the same time, a Confederate officer in the Army of Northern Virginia wrote a similar lament in his diary:

> Another month has passed and the results are perhaps more disastrous than even Feby. '62. Vicksburg, Port Hudson & Gettysburg have been fought and leave a gloom on the country. Unless unceasing success attends the Confederate arms, fits of despondency at once overhang every community. Even the army grows despondent, and evidence of demoralization are visible. More desertions than usual are occurring. Rumors of renewed difficulties in the South are circulating.[49]

For Lincoln, however, Gettysburg offered only limited consolations. Although he was jubilant at Meade's victory, he waited in vain to hear of Meade pursuing and destroying the defeated Lee. Instead, Meade, in a manner tiringly reminiscent of McClellan, rested his men and then cautiously set off in a perfunctory pursuit of the Army of Northern Virginia. Lee and the Army of Northern Virginia crossed the Potomac River on July 14, and after that, any hope that Meade would finish him off disappeared. Lincoln would have to keep on looking for the general who would fight and win the kind of war that he had in mind.

47. Hess, *Pickett's Charge*, 9–19; Scott Bowden and Bill Ward, *Last Chance for Victory: Robert E. Lee and the Gettysburg Campaign* (New York: Da Capo, 2001), 427–70; George R. Stewart, *Pickett's Charge: A Microhistory of the Final Attack at Gettysburg, July 3, 1863* (Dayton, OH: Morningside Press, 1980), 263, 295–97.

48. Gorgas, diary entry for July 28, 1863, in *The Journals of Josiah Gorgas*, 75.

49. Capt. Frank Imboden, diary entry for July 17–18, 1863, in Spencer C. Tucker, *Brigadier General John D. Imboden: Confederate Commander in the Shenandoah* (Lexington: University Press of Kentucky, 2003), 150, 172.

ADVANCE INTO THE CONFEDERATE HEARTLAND

Vicksburg fell to Grant the day after Meade's victory at Gettysburg, and the conjunction of the two events gave the North its happiest weekend in two years of war. Still, the repulse of Lee's invasion of Pennsylvania and the reopening of the Mississippi probably meant a good deal less in strategic terms than they seemed to. Although Gettysburg had inflicted severe wounds on the Army of Northern Virginia, Meade's failure to pursue Lee only ensured that the same cycle of invasions, retreats, and counterinvasions would have to begin all over again in the fall of 1863 or the spring of 1864. As for the Mississippi River, the anxiety Lincoln felt about reopening the entire length of the river to the Gulf was generated by his youthful memories of how dependent Western farmers had always been on the Mississippi for transporting their surpluses to market, and by the croaking of western governors such as Oliver Perry Morton of Indiana, who was convinced that his legislature would vote to secede and join the Confederacy unless the Mississippi was reopened.[50]

Lincoln's memories were a generation old in 1863, and the mature Lincoln's association as a lawyer with the railroads provided telling evidence of a dramatic shift in market transportation away from the north-south axis of the Mississippi River Valley and toward the east-west axis of the railroads, which now brought goods more swiftly to Chicago and New York than the steamboat could bring them to New Orleans. Even as Vicksburg bitterly surrendered to Grant, resourceful Northern farmers had already begun to turn to the railroads as their preferred means of shipment to market, and Mississippi River traffic never again regained the heights it had attained before 1861.

Of course, the conquest of the Mississippi did pay the Union a few dividends. The Confederates surrendered an entire army at Vicksburg—nearly 29,000 men—and the loss of the Mississippi cut them off from Texas, Arkansas, and most of Louisiana. But Braxton Bragg's rebel Army of Tennessee was still intact and dangerous in middle Tennessee; what was more, none of the regions cut off by the capture of the Mississippi had been a critical source of supply for the Confederacy anyway. Whatever their loss did to damage the Confederate war effort, it did not prevent the Confederacy from waging war for almost two more years. In fact, the real heart of the Confederacy's power to carry on the war—its factories, its granaries, its rail centers—never had lain along Halleck's or Grant's lines of operation on the Tennessee or the Mississippi. They lay, instead, in upper Alabama and Georgia, around the critical rail centers of Chattanooga and Atlanta, where the remaining pieces of the Confederacy's two lateral rail lines still intersected, and around the new government-run gun foundries and ironworks at Selma and the great powder works in Augusta. This meant that the real line of successful operations for the Union in 1862 and 1863

---

50. William Hesseltine, *Lincoln and the War Governors*, 312.

would have to be the same eastern Tennessee line that McClellan had vainly urged Buell to follow back in January 1862.

A good deal more might have been made of this had not Buell shown himself no more eager to pursue his chances in 1862 than McClellan had been. In the spring of 1862, he had pretty much taken McClellan's view of the war by announcing, "We are in arms, not for the purpose of invading the rights of our fellow-countrymen anywhere, but to maintain the integrity of the Union and protect the Constitution." He had defeated Braxton Bragg at Perryville in October 1862, only to let Bragg retreat unscathed while Buell composed criticisms of the Emancipation Proclamation. Lincoln and the War Department had seen all they wanted to see of this kind of behavior from field officers, and on October 24, 1862, Buell was unceremoniously replaced by Major General William Starke Rosecrans. It would now be up to Rosecrans to finish the long-delayed conquest of eastern Tennessee, seize Chattanooga and Atlanta, and drive a stake into the heart of Georgia and Alabama.[51]

Like so many other high-ranking Union officers, Rosecrans was a West Point graduate, class of 1842, who served in the prestigious Corps of Engineers until 1854 (including a stint teaching at West Point from 1843 to 1847), when he resigned and opened up his own business as an architect and engineer. Unlike many of the others, however, Rosecrans was a Democrat and a Roman Catholic (his brother was a bishop), which made him an object of suspicion in an overwhelmingly Protestant culture. James A. Garfield, one of Rosecrans's brigadiers and a radical evangelical preacher, sat up into the wee hours of many mornings with Rosecrans, "talking constantly and incessantly for hours on religion." To Lincoln, any Union man with those credentials was a political godsend who could be used to rally Northern Democrats and working-class immigrants, and Rosecrans suddenly found himself rewarded in 1861 with a brigadier general's commission. He served briefly (and not entirely happily) under Grant, and conducted a successful defense of Corinth from a rebel attempt to recapture that key Mississippi railroad junction in 1862. A serious student of strategy, paternal and well loved by every brigade and division he had ever commanded, Rosecrans now took over Buell's 46,900 men, gave them the name "Army of the Cumberland," and on December 26 moved south out of Nashville after Bragg.[52]

Braxton Bragg, meanwhile, had nearly gone the same way as Buell. Bragg was gravely hampered by an assortment of physical ills, ranging from nightmarish

51. "Occupation of Nashville," February 26, 1862, in *The Rebellion Record: A Diary of American Events*, ed. Frank Moore (New York: G. P. Putnam, 1862), 4:205; Engle, *Buell*, 185, 316–20.

52. Whitelaw Reid, *Ohio in the War: Her Statesmen, Her Generals, and Soldiers* (New York: Moore, Wilstach and Baldwin, 1868), 1:313–14, 325–26, 328–29; Garfield to Lucretia Garfield, February 13, 1863, in *The Wild Life of the Army: Civil War Letters of James A. Garfield*, ed. F. D. Williams (East Lansing: Michigan State University Press, 1964), 233.

headaches to abdominal cramps, which made him quarrelsome with subordinates and a disciplinary fiend to his soldiers. After Perryville, rather than risk chances with a fresh invasion of Kentucky, Bragg went into winter quarters at Murfreesboro, Tennessee, approximately forty miles south of Nashville along Stone's River. When Davis visited Bragg and the Army of Tennessee at Murfreesboro in early December 1862, Davis was delighted to see that Bragg's men were "in good condition and fine spirits."[53]

Bragg was soon given a chance to use the Army of Tennessee to redeem his reputation. The combative Rosecrans and the Army of the Cumberland moved down to within two miles of Bragg's lines around Murfreesboro on December 30, and the next day, both armies planned to leap at each other's throats in simultaneous attacks. In the event, however, the Confederates moved first, catching Rosecrans's right flank still at breakfast and scattering it backward for three miles. The battle might well have been lost right there had not Rosecrans personally rode down the lines and rallied his men in the face of Confederate fire. When his chief of staff protested against exposing himself, Rosecrans merely replied, "Never mind me. Make the sign of the cross and go in." As for Bragg, the Confederate commander kept on feeding his divisions into the fight piece by piece, feeling all along Rosecrans's battered lines for a weakness. Somehow the Federals held on: one Federal division under a scrappy Irishman named Philip Sheridan lost all three of its brigade commanders and almost one-third of its men, but it slowed Bragg's attack on the center of the Union line to a halt by midday. At other points, the Federals managed to repel Confederate attacks with nothing more than odds and ends of cavalry and, in one instance, members of Rosecrans's own headquarters escort. By the time darkness fell, each army had lost close to a third of its men as casualties.[54]

Bragg immediately jumped to the conclusion that he had won a great victory, and he telegraphed Richmond that Rosecrans was falling back. Rosecrans himself was inclined to agree. But his three corps commanders disagreed; one of them, George Henry Thomas, snapped, "This army can't retreat. . . . I know of no better place to die than right here." When Bragg awoke the next morning, New Year's Day, the Army of the Cumberland was still there. On January 2, Bragg launched a second series of attacks, hoping to prod Rosecrans into the withdrawal that Bragg presumed he ought to be making. Instead, by the end of the day, it was Bragg who became convinced that he had lost the fight and ought to retreat, and during the night of

53. Davis to J. A. Seddon, December 18, 1862, in *Jefferson Davis, Constitutionalist: Letters, Papers and Speeches*, ed. Dunbar Rowland (Jackson: Mississippi Department of Archives and History, 1923), 5:386; Hudson Strode, *Jefferson Davis: Confederate President* (New York: Harcourt, Brace, 1959), 2:344–45.

54. James Lee McDonough, *Stones River—Bloody Winter in Tennessee* (Knoxville: University of Tennessee Press, 1980), 118–22; William M. Lamars, *The Edge of Glory: A Biography of General William S. Rosecrans, U.S.A.* (Baton Rouge: Louisiana State University Press, 1999), 213–14, 219, 223, 225, 233–36.

January 3, 1863, Bragg began pulling out of Murfreesboro for another camp twenty miles south.[55]

Murfreesboro was, like Shiloh, more like a simple slugfest than a model of tactical brilliance, but it temporarily made Rosecrans a national hero all the same. Bragg, meanwhile, was assailed by a mounting tide of criticism from his own officers for uselessly throwing away a victory. Just as at Perryville, at Murfreesboro Bragg demonstrated a fatal incapacity to perform under the stress of combat, and his abrupt decision to retreat was due at least in part to a simple loss of nerve. As one of Bragg's disgusted subordinates remarked, Bragg could easily fight his way straight up to the gates of Heaven, but once there would doubtless order a withdrawal. One division commander in the Army of Tennessee, Benjamin F. Cheatham, vowed never to serve under Bragg again. Another, the Irish-born Patrick Cleburne, politely informed Bragg that no one really trusted his military judgment anymore: "I have consulted all my Brigade commanders . . . and they write with me in personal regard for yourself, in a high appreciation of your patriotism and gallantry . . . but at the same time they see, with regret, and it has also met my observation, that you do not possess the confidence of the Army, in other respects, in that degree necessary to secure success."[56]

At this point, even President Davis was ready to relieve him of command, and in March 1863 Davis tried to persuade Joseph E. Johnston to take over Bragg's command. Johnston declined Davis's suggestion, however, and Davis took that as a sign that Bragg had been severely misjudged by his subordinates. Accordingly, Davis decided to grant Bragg one more reprieve, and in March he even allowed Bragg to court-martial one of his critics, Major General John Porter McCown, who had loudly threatened to leave the Army of the Tennessee and go back to farming potatoes until Bragg was relieved.[57]

The situation for the western Confederacy might have looked even bleaker had not Bragg's failures been partly compensated for by the spectacular achievements of one of Bragg's cavalry brigadiers, Nathan Bedford Forrest. By the end of 1862, Forrest had emerged as the single most daring and successful light cavalry officer of the Civil War: in July 1862, leading only 1,400 cavalry troopers, Forrest raided Buell's supply lines, "captured two brigadier-generals, staff and field officers, and 1,200 men; burnt $200,000 worth of stores; captured sufficient stores with those burned to amount to $500,000, and brigade of 60 wagons, 300 mules, 150 or 200 horses, and field battery of four pieces." In December 1862, he led a new brigade of

55. Peter Cozzens, *No Better Place to Die: The Battle of Stones River* (Urbana: University of Illinois Press, 1990), 172–74; Robert P. Broadwater, *General George H. Thomas: A Biography of the Union's "Rock of Chickamauga"* (Jefferson, NC: McFarland, 2009), 100–101; Wilson J. Vance, *Stone's River: The Turning-Point of the Civil War* (New York: Neale, 1914), 56–57.

56. Cleburne to Bragg, January 13, 1863, in *War of the Rebellion*, Series One, 20(I):684.

57. McWhiney, *Braxton Bragg and Confederate Defeat*, 374, 378.

2,100 cavalrymen on a destructive joyride through middle Tennessee that, in two weeks, destroyed fifty bridges along the Mobile & Ohio Railroad, killed or captured 2,500 Federal pursuers, captured ten pieces of artillery and enough Enfield rifles to reequip his own men (with 500 rifles to spare), and generally made a shambles of the Federal occupation of middle Tennessee. "Forrest's cavalry seemed to be ubiquitous," rejoiced one Tennessee rebel. "The Federals never knew when he would appear upon their flanks or in their rear."[58]

Nevertheless, Forrest was an embarrassment to Braxton Bragg. A self-made man, Forrest smacked of the slave market (where before the war he had made a fortune in slave dealing), and his grammar invariably left something to chance. He had no formal military schooling (or any other schooling, for that matter), and made up his own earthy maxims of war as he went. Always strike first, he counseled his artillery commander, the twenty-two-year-old John Watson Morton; "in any fight, it's the first blow that counts; and if you keep it up hot enough, you can whip 'em as fast as they can come up." Then, never let the enemy regain his balance, or, as Forrest put it, "Get 'em skeered and then keep the skeer on 'em." His final piece of advice was never to be intimidated by professional soldiers, since, as Forrest had discovered, "Whenever I met one of them fellers that fit by note, I generally whipped hell out of him before he got his tune pitched."[59]

Forrest was utterly indifferent to drill and urged his men to attack the enemy directly and without regard for the niceties of the tactics books. "General Forrest, as a commander, was, in many respects, the negative of a West Pointer," wrote Morton. "He regarded evolution, maneuvers, and exhaustive cavalry drill an unnecessary tax upon men and horses." Forrest's untutored lust for combat might have merely resulted in more casualty-laden melees had it not been for his natural, baffling gift—a gift possessed by only a few generals in the Civil War, including Ulysses Grant—for sizing up a given tactical situation and instinctively knowing what to do in response. According to Morton:

> [Forrest] had absolutely no knowledge or experience of war gleaned from the study of what others had wrought. General Forrest grasped intuitively and instantaneously the strategic possibilities of every situation which confronted him. . . . His knowledge of men was in most cases unerring; and his ability to inspire and bring out the greatest power and endurance of his men was unsurpassed. . . . His eye for position was almost

---

58. J. P. McCown to Braxton Bragg, July 17, 1862, and "Special Orders No. 3," September 25, 1862, in *War of the Rebellion*, Series One, 16(I):801, 16(II):876–77; Thomas Jordan and J. P. Pryor, *The Campaigns of Lieut.-Gen. N.B. Forrest, and of Forrest's Cavalry* (New Orleans: Blelock, 1868), 162, 172–81; John Allan Wyeth, *That Devil Forrest: The Life of General Nathan Bedford Forrest* (New York: Harper, 1959), 92–125; Thomas A. Head, *Campaigns and Battles of the Sixteenth Regiment, Tennessee Volunteers, in the War Between the States* (Nashville, TN: Cumberland Presbyterian, 1885), 425.

59. Morton, *The Artillery of Nathan Bedford Forrest's Cavalry* (Paris, TN: Guild Bindery Press, 1988 [1909]), 12, 13.

infallible, and his knowledge of the effect of a given movement on the enemy was intuitive and seemed to come rather from an inner than an outer source of information.[60]

Forrest was a fairly good inkling of what could be done by pressing relentlessly for decisive combat conclusions on the battlefield. Unfortunately, he was also everything that a tightly buttoned regular (such as Bragg) ought not to be, and Forrest never ceased to suspect that Bragg had authorized his raids chiefly as a means of getting him out of the way.

Forrest's raids were almost the only activity Bragg, or anyone else, would indulge in after Murfreesboro. For six months, the Confederate and Union armies, exhausted and bloodied by the battle at Stone's River, were content to rest and refit. Rosecrans's self-confidence had been badly shaken by the carnage at Murfreesboro (his closest friend and adjutant, Colonel Julius Garesché, had been decapitated by a shell while riding beside Rosecrans, spattering the general with a mess of blood and brains), and instead of pushing on toward Chattanooga, he carefully fortified himself in Murfreesboro and began demanding reinforcements and supplies. Stanton and Halleck refused. "You have already more than your share of the best arms," Halleck replied, "Everything has been done, and is now being done, for you that is possible by the Government. Your complaints are without reason." When Stanton instead began prodding Rosecrans to get the Army of the Cumberland moving southward, Rosecrans went over Stanton's head and began whining to Lincoln in March 1863 about enemies in the War Department who were denying him the promotion he deserved, the staff members he wanted, and so forth.[61]

Then, on June 23, 1863, Rosecrans's old aggressiveness resurfaced, and the Army of the Cumberland suddenly lurched into action. Bragg's Army of Tennessee was entrenched around Tullahoma, Tennessee, almost halfway between Rosecrans and Chattanooga, inviting an attack as a sure way of revenging itself for Murfreesboro. But Rosecrans deftly feinted to Bragg's left, smartly zigzagged to Bragg's right, and then slipped around behind Bragg in a skillfully executed turning movement that forced Bragg to retreat in confusion to Chattanooga. Rosecrans then paused and waited until more telegrams from Washington caught up with him, demanding more advances.

On August 16, Rosecrans set off again, this time to turn Bragg's position in Chattanooga, too. Finding an unguarded ferry on the Tennessee River about thirty miles below Chattanooga, Rosecrans threw the entire Army of the Cumberland across the Tennessee on the back of a single pontoon bridge and an assortment of rafts and boats. He then swept around behind Chattanooga and compelled Bragg to

60. Ibid., 16–17.

61. Louis Garesché, *Biography of Lieut. Col. Julius P. Garesché, Assistant Adjutant-General, U.S. Army* (Philadelphia: J. B. Lippincott, 1887), 439; Halleck to Rosecrans February 1, 1863, in *War of the Rebellion*, Series One, 22(II):31; Lamars, *The Edge of Glory*, 267–68.

abandon the city on September 8 without firing a shot in its defense. In only ten weeks, Rosecrans had moved the Army of the Cumberland almost a hundred miles southward, had outmaneuvered Bragg into abandoning all of eastern Tennessee and Chattanooga, and had done it all at the price of less than a thousand casualties.[62]

What Rosecrans did not know, however, was that in Richmond, an anxious Jefferson Davis had finally decided that the threat to Chattanooga was dangerous enough to justify desperate measures. At the very same moment that Rosecrans was crossing the Tennessee, Davis overrode Robert E. Lee's objections and sent James Longstreet's corps of the Army of Northern Virginia to reinforce Bragg at LaFayette, Georgia, about twenty-five miles south of Chattanooga. The southern railroads were in such poor condition that it took the first of Longstreet's men ten days to make the 952-mile trip from Richmond to northern Georgia. By September 19, Longstreet and five of his nine brigades were with Bragg, and Bragg now determined to use his newly reinforced strength of 47,000 men (not counting Forrest's dismounted cavalry) to strike back at Rosecrans. All unsuspecting, Rosecrans kept on rolling along merrily after Bragg into northern Georgia under the delusion that Bragg was still retreating, and not until September 10 did he realize that Bragg had actually turned and was moving in for the kill. Rosecrans hastily concentrated his four corps—approximately 56,000 men—in the valley of Chickamauga Creek, a dozen miles south of Chattanooga. Before he could devise a plan of action, Bragg struck first.[63]

Chickamauga is a Cherokee word meaning "river of death," and for two days, September 19 and 20, Chickamauga Creek fully lived up to its name. The fighting on the nineteenth was a cautious draw, with Bragg hesitantly testing Rosecrans's defensive lines behind Chickamauga Creek. The next morning, Bragg threw caution to the winds and launched a furious series of frontal assaults on the Federal corps that lasted for two hours without gaining much ground. But at 11:00 AM, Rosecrans mistakenly pulled one of his divisions out of line and sent them in the wrong direction, just as Longstreet's three divisions came avalanching down upon the 600-yard gap so conveniently left for them. The Federal left flank simply turned and fled in panic, sweeping Rosecrans and two of his corps commanders with it. "I saw our lines break and melt away like leaves before the wind," wrote Charles Dana, who was traveling with Rosecrans as an observer. "Then the headquarters around me disappeared. . . . The whole road was filled with flying soldiers. . . . Everything was in the greatest disorder."[64]

62. "General Halleck's Report of Operations in 1863," November 15, 1863, in *The Rebellion Record: A Diary of American Events*, ed. Frank Moore (New York: G. P. Putnam, 1865), 8:181; Freeman Cleaves, *Rock of Chickamauga: The Life of General George H. Thomas* (Norman: University of Oklahoma Press, 1948), 149–50.

63. Steven E. Woodworth, *Six Armies in Tennessee: The Chickamauga and Chattanooga Campaigns* (Lincoln: University of Nebraska Press, 1998), 65.

64. Dana, *Recollections of the Civil War*, 115, 117.

By 1:00 PM, all that was left of Rosecrans's army at Chickamauga was the single corps commanded by George H. Thomas, who had so stoutly rebuked the idea of retreating from Murfreesboro the preceding December. Thomas's corps stood its ground against Longstreet on a small hill beside the road to Chattanooga, and gave the rest of the beaten Army of the Cumberland time to retreat. Thomas's valiant rearguard action earned him the nickname "The Rock of Chickamauga," but Thomas was almost the only senior Federal officer to emerge from the defeat at Chickamauga with any semblance of reputation intact. The Federals lost 16,000 men that afternoon (fully half of them as prisoners) plus 51 cannon and 15,000 rifles, not to mention innumerable horses, wagons, and supplies.[65]

Rosecrans never recovered from the shock of Chickamauga. A disgusted Lincoln told John Hay that "Rosecrans has seemed to lose spirit and nerve since the battle of Chickamauga," and he imagined Rosecrans waddling in circles, "confused and stunned like a duck hit on the head." Curling up in the defenses of Chattanooga, Rosecrans allowed Bragg to close off the Tennessee River and move his army onto Missionary Ridge and Lookout Mountain, the heights that loomed over Chattanooga. Without full control of the Tennessee, Rosecrans was in a very bad supply position, and within a month the despondent Army of the Cumberland was facing either starvation or surrender. Charles Dana anxiously wired Stanton, "It does not seem possible to hold out here another week without a new avenue of supplies." Soldiers working on entrenchments hooted at their generals and shouted for hardtack. Nor did it seem that Rosecrans was likely to pull himself together in time to avoid the disaster. "The practical incapacity of the general commanding is astonishing, and it often seems difficult to believe him of sound mind. His imbecility appears to be contagious, and it is difficult for any one to get anything done." Here was Vicksburg in reverse, and at last Lincoln decided that it was time to bring Grant onto the scene.[66]

Grant believed that Vicksburg had more than made up for the damage done to his military reputation at Shiloh, and he fully expected that he ought to be given a free hand in mounting a new campaign into the vital interior of Alabama. But Halleck had other plans, none of which included independent action for Grant. "The possession of the trans-Mississippi by the Union forces seemed to possess more importance in his mind than almost any campaign east of the Mississippi," Grant

---

65. "Report of Brigadier-General B. R. Johnson," October 26, 1863, in *Rebellion Record*, 10:407–16; Peter Cozzens, *This Terrible Sound: The Battle of Chickamauga* (Urbana: University of Illinois Press, 1992), 357–73; Glenn Tucker, *Chickamauga: Bloody Battle in the West* (Indianapolis: Bobbs-Merrill, 1963), 250–77.

66. John Hay, diary entry for October 19 and October 24, 1863, in *Inside Lincoln's White House*, 94, 98; James Lee McDonough, *Chattanooga—A Death Grip on the Confederacy* (Knoxville: University of Tennessee Press, 1984), 45–46; Charles A. Dana to Stanton, October 18, 1863, in *War of the Rebellion*, Series One, 30(I):221.

wrote, and Grant found himself reduced to policing the Vicksburg area "against guerilla bands and small detachments of cavalry which infested the interior."

This, however, was not what Lincoln and Stanton had in mind for Grant. Both the president and the secretary of war had been keeping a close and inquisitive eye on Grant ever since the capture of Forts Henry and Donelson in February 1862, and Lincoln defended Grant after the Shiloh debacle. When Alexander McClure accused Grant of drunkenness and incompetence at Shiloh and urged Lincoln to cashier him, Lincoln "gathered himself up in his chair and said in a tone of earnestness that I shall never forget, '*I can't spare this man; he fights.*'" Francis Carpenter remembered one "self-constituted committee" that visited Lincoln in 1863 to warn the president against Grant's reputed alcoholism. "By the way, gentlemen," Lincoln remarked after hearing them out, "can either of you tell me where General Grant procures his whiskey? because, if I can find out, I will send every general in the field a barrel of it!"[67]

Behind the jokes, Lincoln remained unsure about Grant, and in 1863 Stanton sent Charles Dana to keep an eye on Grant during the Vicksburg campaign and report anything untoward. As it turned out, Dana gave Grant the highest possible praise: "the most modest, the most disinterested, and the most honest man I ever knew, with a temper that nothing could disturb, and a judgment that was judicial in its comprehensiveness and wisdom . . . whom no ill omens could deject and no triumph unduly exalt." That clinched the matter for Lincoln and Stanton. In October, unwilling to face the prospect of the destruction of an entire Federal army at Chattanooga, Stanton wired Grant to come up the Mississippi to Cairo, and thence to Louisville, and meet with him personally. Their trains crossed instead in Indianapolis on October 17, with Stanton boarding Grant's car, mistaking Grant's medical attaché for Grant, and confidently informing the aide that he recognized him from his photographs. Once the proper identities had been sorted out, Stanton informed Grant that Lincoln had decided to consolidate all Federal military operations in the west (except for the occupation of Louisiana) and put Grant in command of them all. Next, Grant was to take himself and whatever troops he had at hand over to Chattanooga to rescue the Army of the Cumberland. Grant never hesitated. Three days later, he relieved Rosecrans of command of the Army of the Cumberland and turned it over to the hero of Chickamauga, George Thomas. Three days after that, Grant himself was in Chattanooga.[68]

67. Ulysses S. Grant, "Personal Memoirs," in *Memoirs and Selected Letters*, ed. M. D. McFeely and W. S. McFeely (New York: Library of America, 1990), 388–89; Alexander K. McClure, *Lincoln and Men of War-Times* (Philadelphia: Times, 1892), 196; Carpenter, *Six Months at the White House with Abraham Lincoln*, 247.

68. Dana, *Recollections of the Civil War*, 61; Wiley Sword, *Mountains Touched with Fire: Chattanooga Besieged, 1863* (New York: St. Martin's Press, 1995), 53; Bruce Catton, *Grant Takes Command* (Boston: Little, Brown, 1968), 34–35.

What Grant did to lift the siege of Chattanooga looks almost ludicrously simple from a distance, but that only underscores the real genius of his accomplishment. First, Grant reopened the Tennessee River supply line to Chattanooga on October 28. Then Grant brought up substantial reinforcements, including two army corps shipped by railroad from the Army of the Potomac under Fighting Joe Hooker in October, and two more from the Mississippi under William Tecumseh Sherman by mid-November. With these forces in hand, and with Thomas's Army of the Cumberland, Grant now turned on the complacent Bragg and prepared to drive him off his positions atop Lookout Mountain and Missionary Ridge. The inevitable confrontation came on November 24 and 25. After a preliminary skirmish the day before, Grant sent Hooker's men up the steep sides of Lookout Mountain (on Bragg's left flank) and threw Sherman's men at a railroad grade and tunnel on Bragg's other flank. Thomas's Army of the Cumberland, angered and humiliated, was held in reserve in the center to await the results.

As it turned out, Hooker's men easily cleared the Confederates off Lookout Mountain, but Sherman's attack on the tunnel stalled. To relieve pressure on Sherman, Grant ordered Thomas's men to seize the trenches the Confederates had dug along the base of Missionary Ridge. But when the Army of the Cumberland finally got moving, it scarcely bothered to stop at the trenches but kept right on going up the 200-foot-high face of Missionary Ridge and over the top. The Confederates up on the ridge were taken completely by surprise. The colonel of the 24th Mississippi watched in slow-motion disbelief as "under a galling and destructive fire the Federal army climbed up the steep sides of the mountain. I thought they could never reach the summit, but a short time before night set in I had the bitter mortification of seeing our line, about one hundred and fifty or two hundred yards to the left of our brigade, give way and run in confusion. I heard the triumphant shout of the Federals as they placed their colors on the ridge." The center of Bragg's line caved in, and the rest of the Army of Tennessee stumbled back along the roads down to Georgia, with Bragg berating his men for the disaster.[69]

This time, however, no amount of shifting and excuse could disguise Bragg's incompetence. Instead of crushing Rosecrans in Chattanooga when he could have, Bragg had settled into a comfortable and indolent siege. He had quarreled with the best of his officers again, including a wrathy Nathan Bedford Forrest, who finally descended on Bragg and shook his fist in Bragg's face:

> I have stood your meanness as long as I intend to. You have played the part of a damn scoundrel, and are a coward. . . . You may as well not issue any more orders to me, for I will not obey them, and I will hold you personally responsible for any further indignities

69. W. F. Dowd, "Lookout Mountain and Missionary Ridge," *The Southern Bivouac* 1 (November 1885): 399; Larry J. Daniel, *Days of Glory: The Army of the Cumberland, 1861–1865* (Baton Rouge: Louisiana State University Press, 2004), 375–76; Thomas L. Connelly, *Autumn of Glory: The Army of Tennessee, 1862–1865* (Baton Rouge: Louisiana State University Press, 1971), 275–76.

you endeavor to inflict upon me. You have threatened to arrest me for not obeying your orders promptly. I dare you to do it, and I say to you that if you ever again try to interfere with me or cross my path it will be at the peril of your life.[70]

Then, as though the presence of Grant in Chattanooga meant nothing, Bragg had sent Longstreet's corps off on a wild-goose chase to recapture Knoxville. In short, Bragg had done almost everything necessary to destroy the morale and order of the Army of Tennessee, and Chattanooga just about finished it. Five days after the battle, Bragg was officially relieved by President Davis and recalled to Richmond, where he would finish out the war behind a desk. Between Gettysburg, Vicksburg, and Chattanooga, it was now beginning to be a good question in Confederate minds whether there was much of a war left to win.

THE PROBLEM OF THE CONFEDERATE NATION

For many Southerners, the secession of the southern states from the Union was the ultimate solution to the political and economic problems that confronted them inside the Union. On the other hand, it was also true that, like the soldiers in their armies, the Southern people were not always of one mind about which of those problems was the most important. For the Georgia secession convention, secession was an act of racial revolution, a necessary reconstruction of the republican ideology along racial lines so as to secure the existence of "a white man's Republic" and keep African American slaves firmly in their place as slaves. Alexander H. Stephens told an enthusiastic audience in Savannah in 1861 that "our Confederacy is founded upon . . . the great truth that the negro is not equal to the white man. That slavery—subordination to the superior race, is his natural and normal condition. Thus our new government is the first in the history of the world, based upon this great physical and moral truth." One lonely Georgia Unionist was shocked to find how strongly Southern women agreed with Stephens. "I had rather every one of my children should be laid out on the *cooling board*," snorted one, "than to have Yankees get my niggers." One Georgian, interviewed in the 1930s after he had spent a lifetime drifting from one poorly paid farm job after another, still felt that "I'd rather git killed than have these niggers freed and claimin' they's as good as I is." In the delirium of the hour, recalled John Singleton Mosby, "we all forgot our Union principles in our sympathy with the pro-slavery cause, and rushed to the field of Mars."[71]

70. McDonough, *Chattanooga*, 35.

71. "Speech of A. H. Stephens," in *The Rebellion Record: A Diary of American Events*, ed. Frank Moore (New York: G. P. Putnam, 1861), 1:45; Marilyn Mayer Culpeper, *Trials and Triumphs: Women of the American Civil War* (East Lansing: Michigan State University Press, 1991), 21; Jim Jeffcoat, in Armstead L. Robinson, *Bitter Fruits of Bondage: The Demise of Slavery and the Collapse of the Confederacy, 1861–1865* (Charlottesville: University Press of Virginia, 2005), 82; Mosby, *Memoirs*, 19.

Other Southerners pulled shy of justifying secession from the Union solely for the sake of protecting slavery. Even among the elite of the planter class, there remained an acute sense of embarrassment over slavery as a necessary but unpleasant economic necessity. Robert E. Lee claimed after the war that he had seen "the necessity at first of . . . a proclamation of gradual emancipation and the use of negroes as soldiers." Instead, Southerners such as Edward A. Pollard spoke about the preservation of a Romantic agrarianism, a culture of leisured and independent agriculture that was standing deliberately aloof from the hard-handed industrial money grubbing of the North. "No one can read aright the history of America," said Pollard, the editor of the *Richmond Examiner*, "unless in the light of a North and a South: two political aliens in a Union imperfectly defined as a confederation of states." The North, envious of the South's "higher sentimentalism, and its superior refinements of scholarship and manners," chose to divert attention away from its real animosity toward Southern culture "in an attack upon slavery," but this was "nothing more than a convenient ground of dispute between two parties, who represented not two moral theories, but hostile sections and opposite civilizations." In that light, it was the North that represented revolution against the past, and secession was the South's cultural antidote to it.[72]

Then there were those for whom the basic justification for secession arose from neither slavery nor culture but from the more practical considerations of profits and politics. Southerners such as Alabama governor John Gill Shorter argued that for too long, Northern politicians and bankers had been fattening themselves off the tariffs they charged on the imports Southerners needed and the cotton Southerners consigned to their commission houses. Dissolving the Union, declared Shorter, would result in "deliverance, full and unrestricted, from all commercial dependence upon, as well as from all social and political complicity with, a people who appreciate neither the value of liberty nor the sanctity of compacts." Once independent, the Southern states could solve the tariff problem for themselves, and swing firmly into the great network of transatlantic free-trade that was centered on the British textile economy.[73] Henry L. Benning of Georgia was sure that

> the South would gain by a separation from the North, for [by] the mere act of separation all these drains would stop running, and the golden waters be retained within her own borders. And the grand option would be presented to her of adopting free trade, by

72. Gary W. Gallagher, "An Old-Fashioned Soldier in a Modern War? Robert E. Lee as Confederate General," *Civil War History* 45 (December 1999): 311–12; Lee, in "Memoranda of Conversations Between General Robert E. Lee and William Preston Johnston, May 7, 1868, and March 18, 1870," 479; Pollard, *The Lost Cause*, 46, 49.

73. Shorter, in *War of the Rebellion*, Series Four, 1:773; Malcolm C. McMillan, *The Disintegration of a Confederate State: Three Governors and Alabama's Wartime Home Front, 1861–1865* (Macon, GA: Mercer University Press, 1986), 33.

which her consumers would gain eighty millions a year clear money in the consequent lower price at which they could purchase their goods or a system of protection to her own mechanics and artisans and manufactures by which they would soon come to rival the best in the world.[74]

Or else, in a similar vein, Southerners simply complained that the Union they had played so large a role in creating in the eighteenth century was no longer listening to their concerns. Northerners "know that the South is the main prop and support of the Federal system," declared the *New Orleans Daily Crescent* in January 1861. "They know that it is Southern productions that constitute the surplus wealth of the nation, and enables us to import so largely from other countries." Knowing that, "they know that they can plunder and pillage the South, as long as they are in the same Union with us, by other means, such as fishing bounties, navigation laws, robberies of the public ands, and every other possible mode of injustice and peculation." On those terms, it was high time for the Southern states to reclaim their individual sovereignty as states, assert the supremacy of "states' rights," and resume an independent status in which they could be sure of putting their own affairs first.[75]

But the southern states were not permitted the luxury of a peaceful and uncontested separation from the Union. So Southerners found themselves compelled to do two things that, as it turned out, flew straight in the face of the principles they held so dear. First, in the interests of survival, the Southern states were forced to cooperate with each other; so they began their war for state sovereignty by immediately subordinating themselves to a confederation arrangement and the authority of a central government in Richmond. Second, they were forced to wage a major war of national defense, which would strain their resources to the breaking point in simple economic terms, but which would also strain their own self-perception, as more and more nonslaveholding whites balked at the sacrifices they increasingly had to make to defend the planter elite, and as Southerners who valued independence even more than slavery began tinkering with the slave system so that the Confederate nation might survive. At first, neither of these undertakings appeared difficult. The convention that assembled in Montgomery, Alabama, in February 1861 to form a Confederate government for the first wave of seceding states worked hard to avoid any suggestion of ultra-Jeffersonian radicalism and seemed to give remarkably small place to the states'-rights fire-eaters. The convention, in fact, turned itself into the Confederacy's first Provisional Congress, and the constitution that the Provisional Congress adopted for the Confederacy was a close replica of the U.S. Constitution. Just like the old Constitution, it provided for a president, a bicameral Congress, and an independent judiciary. Though the Confederate constitution explicitly recognized

---

74. "Henry L. Benning's Secessionist Speech," in *Secession Debated: Georgia's Showdown in 1860*, 142.

75. *Southern Editorials on Secession*, ed. Dumond, 408.

the principle of state sovereignty in its preamble, stressing that each state was "acting in its sovereign and independent character," its announced intention was to form a "permanent federal government." The states were given authority to initiate constitutional conventions (with consent from only two-thirds of the states needed to ratify amendments) and to remove Confederate officials operating within their boundaries, but no mention about a right to secession or to nullification was added. The principle of judicial review was restricted to specific constitutional questions (and not "all cases in Law and Equity," as in the U.S. Constitution), and the Confederate Congress was forbidden to "appropriate money for any internal improvement intended to facilitate commerce." Yet, at the same time, the Confederate president was granted powers that even the federal president lacked, such as a line-item veto over appropriations, a six-year term of office, and the provision for cabinet members to be allowed a voice on the floor of the Confederate Congress. Even more to the point, the decision to elect Jefferson Davis as provisional president and Alexander H. Stephens as provisional vice president neatly skipped over the slavery and state-sovereignty ideologues.[76]

The principal challenge to making this constitution operate was that it would have to do so under the immediate pressure of outside attack, although even on that point, the Confederacy appeared to have a major advantage in the person of Jefferson Davis, its president.

Despite Davis's reputation as the ideological heir apparent of John Calhoun, Davis's political outlook on banking, tariffs, and internal improvements had sometimes been as close to Whiggery as a Democrat's could be. From the very beginning (and to the disgust of the states' rights fire-eaters), Davis warned the Southern people to stop thinking of themselves as citizens of states and start seeing themselves as the members of a new political nation whose overall survival was of greater importance than the survival of any of the separate parts—slavery, culture, states' rights—which made it up. "To increase the power, develop the resources, and promote the happiness of the Confederacy, it is requisite that there should be so much of homogeneity that the welfare of every portion shall be the aim of the whole," Davis warned. "Our safety—our very existence—depends on the complete blending of the military strength of all the States into one united body, to be used anywhere and everywhere as the exigencies of the contest may require for the good of the *whole*."[77] That led Davis to stretch his war powers as president of the Confederacy in precisely the same ways Lincoln stretched his: Davis acted to extend Confederate control over former

76. "Constitution of the 'Confederate States of America,'" March 11, 1861, in *Rebellion Record*, 2:321–27; "Constitution of the 'Confederate' States," in *Political History of the Rebellion*, 98–100; Marshall L. DeRosa, *The Confederate Constitution of 1861: An Inquiry into American Constitutionalism* (Columbia: University of Missouri Press, 1991), 23, 40–44, 91–101.

77. Davis, "Inaugural Address of the President of the Provisional Government," February 18, 1861, in *Messages and Papers of Jefferson Davis and the Confederacy*, 1:35.

U.S. arsenals and navy yards within the Confederate states, to justify Confederate military control over Southern rail lines, and to secure presidential oversight of the Confederate army's officer selection process, and all before the end of 1862.

Davis's political flexibilities surprised many observers even within his administration, since in many ways Davis was not a particularly charming or attractive personality. Erect in his bearing, rigid in his conception of his own correctness, thin to the point of emaciation, and virtually blind in one eye, Davis was crippled throughout the war by bouts of illness that would have killed most people and by levels of political catcalling that would have killed most politicians. The raw willpower that kept him at the helm of state through all these storms was his greatest asset, but it also made him impatient, unforgiving of failure, and excessively sensitive to criticism. Still, no portrait of the Confederate president can ignore his political canniness, his ability to draw all but his most violent critics back into cooperation, and his sterling dedication to the idea of a Confederate nation. "There may have been among them some equal to or even superior to President Davis in some one department or study or branch of knowledge," wrote John H. Reagan, the Confederate postmaster general, "but taking into view the combined elements of character and ability I regard him as the ablest man I have known. . . . In all my association with him, I found him thoughtful, prudent, and wise." Like Lincoln, Davis ruthlessly overworked himself and failed to delegate responsibilities; like Lincoln, he turned most of his attention to managing the war effort rather than domestic politics; like Lincoln, he was notoriously inclined to issue pardons to condemned soldiers; and like Lincoln, he tasted tragedy in his presidency in the death of a young son.[78]

If Davis turned out to be a more calculating politician than his enemies imagined, he also turned out to be a far more lackluster commander in chief than his friends had expected. Although Davis frequently insisted that the Confederacy was not interested in waging a war of aggressive conquest, he fully shared Robert E. Lee's preference for offensive over defensive warfare, "that reviled policy of West-Pointism," and he committed the Confederate armies in 1861 to the well-nigh impossible task of policing (and in the case of Kentucky, seizing) every inch of the slave South's immense Ohio and Potomac River boundary lines with the North. After the fall of Forts Donelson and Henry, Davis acknowledged "the error of my attempt to defend all the frontier," and he would later sanction Lee's raids north of the Potomac and lend eastern troops to Bragg so that he could go on the offensive against Rosecrans.[79]

Far more serious than his strategic misjudgments, though, were Davis's personnel misjudgments. If Lincoln was overly prone to appoint incompetent politicians

---

78. Reagan, *Memoirs with Special Reference to Secession and the Civil War* (New York: Neale, 1906), 252; William J. Cooper, *Jefferson Davis, American* (New York: Knopf/Random House, 2000), 351–57; Morris Schaff, *Jefferson Davis: His Life and Personality* (Boston: J. W. Luce, 1922), 76.

79. Steven E. Woodworth, *Jefferson Davis and His Generals: The Failure of Confederate Command in the West* (Lawrence: University Press of Kansas, 1990), 305–16.

to generalships, Davis was overly willing to appoint and defend incompetents—Leonidas Polk, Theophilus Holmes, Braxton Bragg—who were either personal friends or else men he believed had been unfairly condemned by unscrupulous and self-interested rivals (as Davis was convinced he himself had been). At the same time, though, in many cases Davis made these appointments knowing full well that he was dealing from the bottom of the deck, and he stood by them through one blunder after another simply because the supply of real military talent in circulation was so limited. "A *General* in the full acceptation of the word is a rare product, scarcely more than one can be expected in a generation," Davis grimly observed to his brother, "but in this mighty war in which we are engaged there is need for half a dozen."[80]

Davis's military miscues were not nearly as harmful to the Confederacy as were the lamentable failures of his cabinet and the Confederate Congress. Most of Davis's first choices for the Confederate Cabinet were dictated by the need to assure the various states that their interests were being represented in the government. His first secretaries of state and war, Leroy Pope Walker of Alabama and Robert Toombs of Georgia, were both brainless political appointees, and neither of them survived the first year of the war in office. Davis's most talented cabinet member, Judah P. Benjamin, was also, unfortunately, his most unpopular. With a Cheshire-cat smile playing around his lips, Benjamin was described by John S. Wise as overfull of "oleaginous" slickness, with a "keg-like form and over-deferential manner suggestive of a prosperous shopkeeper," and "more brains and less heart than any other civic leader in the South."[81] But Davis could not spare Benjamin, and each time Benjamin's political enemies demanded that he be removed, Davis would simply shift him to another post within the cabinet, moving him from attorney general to secretary of war, and then to secretary of state.

The weakest link in Davis's chain of cabinet secretaries was the secretary of the Treasury, Christopher Memminger. Born in Württemberg, Germany, and brought to America with his grandfather as an orphan, the wealthy South Carolina politician's only real fiscal experience was his chairmanship of the old House Committee on Finance. He had been an important standard-bearer for secession in South Carolina, however, and the need to accommodate the South Carolinians in the Confederate government compelled Davis to make room for him in the cabinet. It is hard to know where Memminger would have done the least damage, and it was probably Davis's own naiveté in fiscal matters that led him to park Memminger at the Treasury.[82]

80. Davis to W. M. Brooks, March 13, 1862, and to Varina Davis, June 11, 1862, in *Jefferson Davis: Letters, Papers and Speeches*, 5: 216–17, 272; Davis, *Jefferson Davis: The Man and His Hour*, 504.

81. John Sergeant Wise, *The End of an Era* (Boston: Houghton, Mifflin, 1901), 401–2; Eli N. Evans, *Judah P. Benjamin: The Jewish Confederate* (New York: Free Press, 1988), 147–48.

82. Burton Jesse Hendrick, *Statesmen of the Lost Cause: Jefferson Davis and His Cabinet* (New York: Literary Guild, 1939), 188; Jon L. Wakelyn, "Christopher Gustavus Memminger," in *Leaders of the American Civil War: A Biographical and Historiographical Dictionary*, ed. C. F. Ritter and Jon L. Wakelyn (Westport, CT: Greenwood Press, 1998), 288–95.

As it turned out, Memminger's tenure as the Confederate Treasury chief was as close as one could come to unrelieved disaster. Overconfident as a result of the Confederacy's initial military successes in 1861, Memminger scoffed at Judah Benjamin's proposal that the Confederate government buy up all available Southern cotton with Confederate bonds and notes, hoard the white gold to drive up the price on foreign markets, then sell it and (once the principal was repaid) use the gigantic profits to purchase the weapons and ships the Confederacy needed. In 1861, Southern credit seemed sound on the world's financial market (an initial Confederate loan of $5 million was snapped up, even oversubscribed, at face value), and Memminger could not imagine when such good financial times would ever fail. He made no effort to prevent Northern merchants from removing hard currency from their Southern bank accounts, and allowed the specie in the vital New Orleans banks to fall into Federal hands while hardly stirring in concern when New Orleans was captured by Farragut's ships in April 1862.[83]

Not until the war had dragged on into 1862 did Memminger reverse himself and attempt to buy up cotton for government use. By then, however, cotton was commanding much steeper prices, and even when he was able to purchase it, he found himself unable to find enough blockade-runners willing to ship the cotton at government prices. Memminger was not able to ensure a regular means for exporting cotton until 1863, when the Confederate Congress acted to regulate the blockade-runners. Even though this was much too little much too late, the export of Confederate cotton still helped underwrite the Erlanger loan, and it is anyone's guess how much other financial support a cotton-starved Europe might have lent to Memminger if he had acted as decisively in 1861. This forced Memminger to resort more and more to the printing presses to print the money he needed, and he helplessly flooded the Confederate economy with notes and bonds that had little or no backing in either specie or cotton.[84]

If there was any single nonmilitary matter that must stand before all the others in leading to the defeat of the Confederacy, it was the stunning failure of Memminger and the Treasury to make the Confederate economy work. As late as the fall of 1863, Josiah Gorgas was confident that "there is breadstuff enough" and "war material sufficient—men, guns, powder . . . to carry on the war for an indefinite period." None of it was going to change hands for the worthless shinplasters Memminger was offering, though. "The great fear of every patriot at this moment relates to our currency," groaned Gorgas. "The fear is that a swift national bankruptcy is coming upon us." Considering "the absolute wealth of the South," Gorgas thought it all the more "amazing that our finances should have been allowed to run into this ruinous condition." He knew whom to blame: "The real pinch is in the Treasury."[85]

83. Strode, *Jefferson Davis*, 2:17–18; Henry Dickson Capers, *The Life and Times of C. G. Memminger* (Richmond, VA: Everett Waddey, 1893), 10–11.

84. Douglas B. Ball, *Financial Failure and Confederate Defeat* (Urbana: University of Illinois Press, 1991), 85–98, 128–29; Eaton, *A History of the Southern Confederacy*, 135.

85. Gorgas, diary entry for October 29, 1863, in *Journals of Josiah Gorgas*, 85.

Davis's difficulties in assembling a competent cabinet were overshadowed by several factors over which he had no control, starting with the political turbulence of the Confederate Congress. The Provisional Congress that first sat in Montgomery was composed of only fifty members, appointed by the state secession conventions and including some of the South's most distinguished men (including a former secretary of war and a former president of the United States, John Tyler). Forty-two of them were lawyers and seventeen were planters. But once the new constitution was formally adopted and the capital moved to Richmond, a new Confederate Congress had to be elected, and when it assembled in November 1861, it turned out to be a very different assembly. The Confederate armies had sucked up a good deal of the Confederacy's experienced leadership, with the result that only about a third of the 257 men who sat in the Confederate Congress during the war possessed any previous service in the U.S. Congress. The rest were either political amateurs or else men with nothing more than the limited experience of serving in state legislatures, who would be likely to speak only for the most narrow and local state interests. "The extremist and ultra friends of state rights, appear to have lost their reasoning," wailed Burgess Gaither, one of North Carolina's representatives. "They [had] shown high capacity for the destruction of the old government," but "now exhibit none for the construction of the new one."

Even those who could boast some experience in the old House were men whose long struggle to defend slavery there had turned them temperamentally into political outsiders, more inclined to oppose and criticize than to construct. Georgia representative Warren Aiken was "amazed to see the differences of opinion that exist among the members. It seems, sometimes, that no proposition, however plain and simple could be made that would not meet with opposition." Absenteeism, drunkenness, and outright brawling on the floor of the House further crippled the effectiveness of the Confederate Congress. Georgia Senator Benjamin Hill hurled an inkstand at the head of William Yancey of Alabama, and when he missed, he picked up a chair to attack him again; on February 13, 1863, Henry Foote of Tennessee was attacked by a member from Alabama with a Bowie knife; an outraged female constituent of Missouri senator George Vest horsewhipped him in the lobby of the Capitol. "Some malign influence seems to preside over your councils," complained James Henry Hammond to Virginia senator R. M. T. Hunter. "Pardon me, is the majority always drunk?"[86]

---

86. Thomas Alexander and Richard Beringer, *The Anatomy of the Confederate Congress: A Study of the Influences of Member Characteristics on Legislative Voting Behavior, 1861–1865* (Nashville, TN: Vanderbilt University Press, 1972), 406ff.; Wilfred Buck Yearns, *The Confederate Congress* (Athens: University of Georgia Press, 1960), 9–10, 15–16; Gaither to Zebulon Vance, April 24, 1863, in *Papers of Zebulon Baird Vance*, 2:131–32; John E. Gonzales, "Henry Stuart Foote: Confederate Congressman and Exile," *Civil War History* 11 (December 1965): 390; Clement Eaton, *Jefferson Davis* (New York: Free Press, 1977), 211; Eaton, *A History of the Southern Confederacy*, 63; Peter J. Parish, *The American Civil War* (New York: Holmes and Meier, 1975), 218–19.

Mercifully for Jefferson Davis, few challenges to his calls for greater central authority in Richmond emerged from Congress during the first ten months of the war. But the sudden loss of Forts Henry and Donelson, followed by the failure to redeem the Tennessee River at Shiloh and the fall of New Orleans, badly jolted Southern complacency. On February 27, 1862, only five days after his formal inauguration as Confederate president under the new constitution, Davis suspended the writ of habeas corpus around Norfolk and Portsmouth, Virginia, and he eventually widened his suspension of the writ to include any Southern districts threatened by invasion. On March 28 he appealed to the Confederate Congress to institute a selective military draft for all males between the ages of eighteen and thirty-five "not legally exempt for good cause." The Congress blinked, and on April 16 it passed Davis's Conscription Act (with some important exemptions) by a margin of two to one. On August 18, 1862, Davis called on the second session of the Confederate Congress for a second conscription act that would raise the age of liability to forty-five. A third Conscription Act in February 1864 expanded the age limits yet again, from seventeen to fifty.[87]

The grasp of the conscription bills over the rights of the individual Southern states was greater than anything anyone had seen, even in the old Union. Georgia governor Joseph E. Brown protested the draft in pure Democratic terms as a "bold and dangerous usurpation by Congress of the reserved rights of the States . . . at war with all the principles for which Georgia entered into the revolution." To Alexander Stephens, Brown added that "I entered into this revolution to contribute my humble mite to sustain the rights of the states and prevent the consolidation of Government, and I am a rebel till this object is accomplished, no matter who may be in power." To the delight of his constituents, Brown defied the draft in the state courts and promptly appointed large numbers of eligible Georgia males to fictitious state offices in order to exempt them. In South Carolina, Governor Francis W. Pickens was trying to impose a state draft of his own and attempted to exempt South Carolina draftees from any liability to the Confederate draft. Even in Virginia, the otherwise cooperative Governor John Letcher ordered the superintendent of the Virginia Military Institute to refuse any movement to draft Virginia Military Institute cadets.[88]

The Conscription Acts also alienated a far more dangerous segment of Southern society in October 1862 by exempting certain classes of skilled workers, and (in response

87. Davis, "To the Senate and House of Representatives of the Confederate States," March 28 and August 18, 1862, *Messages and Papers*, 1:205–6, 236; "The Rebel Conscription Law," in *The Rebellion Record: A Diary of American Events*, ed. Frank Moore (New York: G. P. Putnam, 1864), 1(Supp.):324–25; David J. Eicher, *Dixie Betrayed: How the South Really Lost the Civil War* (New York: Little, Brown, 2006), 104, 217.

88. Joseph H. Parks, *Joseph E. Brown of Georgia* (Baton Rouge: Louisiana State University Press, 1977), 204; Brown to Stephens, July 2, 1863, in *The Correspondence of Robert Toombs, Alexander H. Stephens, and Howell Cobb*, ed. U. B. Phillips (Washington, DC: American Historical Association, 1913), 598; Albert Burton Moore, *Conscription and Conflict in the Confederacy* (New York: Macmillan, 1924), 24, 298–99; Yearns, *The Confederate Congress*, 83.

to planter anxieties over the possibility of slave revolts when so many Southern white men were being pulled into the armies) the owners, agents, or overseers of plantations with more than twenty slaves. The intentions behind the exemption were plausible enough, but linking slave ownership to exemption from war service was a spark to the tinder of the nonslaveholders of the South. In effect, this "twenty-nigger law" protected large-scale slave-owning planters—the very people who had the most at stake in this war—from military service, while drafting the small-scale slaveholders and the nonslaveholders who had the least interest in fighting to defend slavery.

That, in turn, caused Southern yeomen who were ambivalent about the planters and their slaves anyway, and who rallied to the defense of the Confederacy only because it promised to keep the demons of abolition and black amalgamation from their doors, to wonder whether they had more to lose at the hands of the Yankees or those of the planters. "Never did a law meet with more universal odium than the exemption of slave owners," wrote Alabama senator James Phelan to Davis. "Its influence upon the poor is most calamitous, and has awakened a spirit and elicited a discussion of which we may safely predicate the most unfortunate results." Unless Davis agreed to "reorganize the whole system, and let popular attention be started and attracted by the prominent, rich, and influential men being swept into the ranks," then Phelan could only promise that "it only needs some daring man to raise the standard to develop a revolt."[89]

Jefferson Davis turned out to be both stubborn and resourceful in getting his legislative way with the draft. Since the Confederate Congress had declined to organize even the rudimentary Supreme Court that the Confederate constitution allowed, Davis took his defense of the conscription into the Georgia state courts, where he won, to the amazement of onlookers. There was no real debate over Davis's suspension of the writ of habeas corpus, and only one of the thirty-seven state supreme court justices in the Confederacy saw any contradiction between states' rights and national conscription. In Richmond, Davis kept a working majority behind his bills and lost only one veto to an override in Congress. In time, as Confederate military fortunes died away after Antietam and Perryville, he persuaded Congress to hand him even more vital powers. In March 1863 Congress authorized quartermaster and commissary officers to confiscate food and animals for the use of the Confederate army and to offer reimbursement at well below market values. A month later, in an effort to raise more revenue and pull some of Memminger's worthless paper currency out of circulation, Congress imposed a broad range of stiff direct taxes on the Confederate people, including a 10 percent sales tax, another 10 percent tax in kind on livestock and produce, an 8 percent value-added tax on all other agricultural products, and a

89. Phelan to Davis, December 9, 1862, in *War of the Rebellion*, Series One, 17(II):790; Robinson, *Bitter Fruits of Bondage*, 183–87; Paul D. Escott, *After Secession: Jefferson Davis and the Failure of Confederate Nationalism* (Baton Rouge: Louisiana State University Press, 1978), 120; Moore, *Conscription and Conflict in the Confederacy*, 71.

graduated income tax, up to 15 percent on all yearly incomes over $10,000. "This is no time for making nice distinctions between the laws of the Confederate Government and the laws of any State," urged the *Richmond Dispatch*. "We want soldiers to fight, not lawyers to talk," and "State Governments that will conform their laws to those of the Confederate Government, not raise opposition to them."[90]

This did not entirely eliminate the howls of the state sovereignty loyalists against the "Aristocratic and demanding Horse leeches of the Confederate Service." R. M. T. Hunter, once one of Davis's cabinet members and now a senator from Virginia, turned on the Confederate president, and even Davis's own vice president, Alexander Stephens, became a bitter critic of Davis's national policies. But the critical factor exerting downward pressure on confidence in Davis's government was its strategic failures. The tightening of the blockade and the gradual collapse of the Confederacy's own internal transportation system spelled increasing want and dislocation for Southern society. Governor John Milton of Florida had 13,000 destitute families on the public dole by 1864, in a state that had only cast 14,000 votes (and therefore had about as many white households) in the 1860 election. Although Davis and the governors urged cotton planters to switch to planting grains and cereals for the war, much of what they might grow had no way to reach vital Confederate markets.[91]

The shortages, combined with the unreliability of Memminger's unceasing flood of unbacked bonds and notes, drove prices on goods to astronomical levels. In Richmond, John B. Jones, a War Department clerk, found that "a dollar in gold sold for $18 Confederate money" on November 21, 1863, while "a genteel suit of clothes cannot be had for less than $700" and "a pair of boots, $200—if good." Two weeks later, after Bragg had been driven off Missionary Ridge, one gold dollar was fetching twenty-eight Confederate ones. On a combined family income of $7,200 in 1864, Jones was forced to buy "flour at $300 a barrel; meal, $50 per bushel; and even fresh fish at $5 per pound." By the end of the year, Richmond hospital steward Luther Swank found flour going at $400 a barrel, sweet potatoes at $40 a bushel, and butter at $11 a pound. In the Treasury Department, Jones confided to his diary, "some of the clerks would shoot Mr. Memminger cheerfully."[92]

90. John Christopher Schwab, *The Confederate States of America, 1861–1865: A Financial and Industrial History of the South During the Civil War* (New York: C. Scribner's Sons, 1901), 202–8; Emory Thomas, *The Confederate Nation, 1861–1865* (New York: Harper and Row, 1979), 198; Neely, *Lincoln and the Triumph of the Nation*, 319–20.

91. William A. Smith to Zebulon Vance, January 3, 1863, in *Papers of Zebulon Baird Vance*, 2:3; Wilfred Buck Yearns, "Florida," in *The Confederate Governors* (Athens: University of Georgia Press, 1985), 36, 68.

92. Gregory P. Downs, *Declarations of Dependence: The Long Reconstruction of Popular Politics in the South, 1861–1908* (Chapel Hill: University of North Carolina Press, 2011), 35; John B. Jones, *A Rebel War Clerk's Diary*, ed. E. S. Miers (New York: Sagamore Press, 1958), 309, 316, 345, 349; "Inflation Grips the South: Luther Swank Reports from a Field Hospital," ed. Horace Mathews, *Civil War Times Illustrated* 22 (March 1983): 46.

As the price for creating an independent Confederate nation rose higher and higher, more and more Southern hearts grew faint with war-weariness, and more and more began to kick against the goads. George Pickett, occupying his time with garrison duties on the Rappahannock, warned that while "a greater portion of our loyal men, the chivalry and high-toned gentlemen of the country, have volunteered, and are far from their homes," there remained "a strong element among those who are left either to be non-combatants or to fall back under the old flag. . . . We have to fear them most" who "have refused to volunteer, while the proprietors of the country are actually in the field . . . and would join the enemy should an occasion occur." William W. Holden, the editor of the Raleigh *Standard*, began editorializing for a negotiated peace in 1863, only to have soldiers of the Army of Northern Virginia, stopping in Raleigh on September 9, 1863, on the their way to reinforce Braxton Bragg in the West, destroy his press. Undaunted, Holden resumed publication of the *Standard* and in 1864 ran for governor of North Carolina against Zebulon Vance on the unspoken promise to take North Carolina out of the war or out of the Confederacy.

In the Carolinas and northern Alabama, secret anti-war movements with names such as the Order of the Heroes of America (in western North Carolina and southwestern Virginia), the Peace and Constitutional Society (in the hill country of Arkansas), and the Peace Society (in northern Alabama) sprang into existence. The yeomen of the piney woods of Alabama had been reluctant secessionists to start with, and by the spring of 1862 Unionists in Winston County were raising recruits for the *Union* army. Overall, at least 100,000 Southerners ended up enlisting to fight against the Confederacy.[93]

Those who weren't actually volunteering to fight the Confederates were concealing Confederate army deserters; before the end of the war, Winston County had sheltered between 8,000 and 10,000 deserters. "The Conscript law . . . has filled the mountains with disaffected desperadoes of the worst character, who joining with the deserters from our Army form very formidable bands of outlaws," complained North Carolina governor Zebulon Vance, and one of Vance's advisers warned him that he might as well leave them alone, since "the deserters are more numerous & better armed and drilled than the Militia is, consequently there is more danger of their banding themselves together for armed resistance."[94] Some Southern counties simply deserted the Confederacy en masse: in western Virginia, the nonslaveholding mountain counties created their own new state, Kanawha, in August 1861—effectively seceding from secession—and in 1863 they were formally admitted to the Union as the state of West Virginia.

93. Pickett to D. H. Maury, December 10, 1861, in *War of the Rebellion*, Series One, 5:991–92; Richard N. Current, *Lincoln's Loyalists: Union Soldiers from the Confederacy* (Boston: Northeastern University Press, 1992), 195–97.

94. Vance to James A. Seddon, January 5, 1863, and L. S. Fash to Vance, June 1, 1863, in *Papers of Zebulon Baird Vance*, 2:5, 180.

The Confederate government was not slow to retaliate. An elaborate internal passport system was created, starting in 1861 and becoming general throughout the Confederacy by 1864. In early 1863, Confederate troops swept down on Unionists in Shelton Laurel, in rural Madison County, and shot thirteen of them after being told by a senior officer, "I want no reports from you about your course at Laurel," nor "to be troubled with any prisoners." In Arkansas, Confederate general Thomas Hindman authorized the destruction of "all the cotton" on the Arkansas River and "its tributaries or the country beyond" and to arrest "as Traitors to the confederacy all persons resisting the execution of this order." Nine resisters were shot, "Hindman himself witnessing the execution."[95] In the spring of 1864, George Pickett captured twenty-two North Carolinians who had been members of the state militia but then deserted to join Union forces along the occupied Carolina coast. Pickett refused to treat them as Union prisoners of war. Instead, he court-martialed them and hanged them all, over the protests of their Union commandant, Major General John Peck. After each hanging, Pickett allowed the bodies to be stripped of clothing and shoes by his own men, and as the prisoners were sent one by one to the gallows, Pickett leered, "God damn you, I reckon you will hardly ever go back there again, you damned rascals; I'll have you shot, and all other damned rascals who desert." That April, Confederate cavalry under Col. Robert Lowry rode through Jones County, Mississippi, which had a reputation for Unionism, hanging ten men for "armed resistance."[96]

The ebbing of the Confederacy's military and financial fortunes did little to endear the Davis administration to the Confederate voter, and the Confederacy's congressional elections in the fall of 1863 showed a significant drop in confidence in Davis's policies. The number of anti-administration representatives in the Confederate House rose from 26 to 41 out of a total of 106, while in the Confederate Senate, Davis clung on to a thin majority of 14 pro-administration members out of 26. None of the new members from North Carolina had voted for secession two years before, and one of the Alabama representatives was so plainly in favor of an immediate peace that the Congress voted to expel him. Alexander Stephens, who had become so alienated from Davis that he spent most of his vice presidency at home in Georgia, issued a public letter on September 22, 1864, calling for "a peaceful adjustment of our present difficulties and strife through the medium of a

---

95. Philip S. Paludan, *Victims: A True Story of the Civil War* (Knoxville: University of Tennessee Press, 1981), 84–98; Mark E. Neely, *Southern Rights: Political Prisoners and the Myth of Confederate Constitutionalism* (Charlottesville: University Press of Virginia, 1999), 18–22.

96. Seddon to Vance, May 23, 1863, in *Papers of Zebulon Vance*, 2:167; Lesley J. Gordon, *General George E. Pickett in Life and Legend* (Chapel Hill: University of North Carolina Press, 1998), 130–34; Victoria E. Bynum, *The Free State of Jones: Mississippi's Longest Civil War* (Chapel Hill: University of North Carolina Press, 1996), 115–21.

convention of the States . . . It would be an appeal on both sides from the sword to reason and justice."[97]

Yet Davis beat back every attempt to unseat his administration. A bill to limit the tenure of cabinet officers to two years died on Davis's desk, and his congressional backers kept turning the trick for him on crucial votes. Despite the desertions and draft resistance, the Confederacy managed to mobilize more than three-quarters of its available military manpower. In fact, far from being intimidated by his administration's losses at the polls, Davis had still more demands to make of Congress in name of Confederate nationhood. When the last session of the First Confederate Congress arrived in Richmond on December 7, 1863, Davis immediately urged new taxes and fresh additions to the conscription laws that allowed the government to reach into the civilian labor pool to reassign and reallocate workers. Two months later, he also obtained a new and expanded suspension of habeas corpus, a supervisory monopoly over all blockade-running enterprises, and on February 17, 1864, a compulsory funding bill that would compel Confederate citizens to pay their taxes either in specie or in government bonds. Once again, the centralizing authority of the Richmond government had overridden the localism and individualism that three years before had been the very cause of southern secession. "Will you please to inform me," demanded North Carolina governor Zebulon Vance, "what remains of the boasted *sovereignty* of the States?"[98]

None of these measures, however, could stanch the ebbing of the Confederacy's territory and armies, and so on November 7, 1864, when the second (and last) session of the Second Congress met, Davis finally decided to trade in the last symbol of the old South in a bid to save the new Confederacy. He asked Congress to allow the Confederate government to purchase 40,000 slaves, enlist them as soldiers in the Confederate army, and emancipate them upon completion of their enlistment as a reward for service. "Should the alternative ever be presented of subjugation or of the employment of the slave as a soldier, there seems no reason to doubt what should then be our decision."[99]

97. "Letter of Alexander Stephens on State Sovereignty," September 22, 1864, in *The Rebellion Record: A Diary of American Events*, ed. Frank Moore (New York: G. P. Putnam, 1868), 11:182–84; Steven E. Woodworth, "The Last Function of Government: Confederate Collapse and Negotiated Peace," in *The Collapse of the Confederacy*, eds. Mark Grimsley and Brooks Simpson (Lincoln: University of Nebraska Press, 2001), 23; Escott, *After Secession*, 155.

98. Davis, "To the Senate and House of Representatives of the Confederate States," December 7, 1863, in *Messages and Papers*, 1:366, 369, 371; "Secret Session," February 1 and February 17, 1864, in *Journal of the Congress of the Confederate States of America, 1861–1865*, 3:648–53, 797; Gary W. Gallagher, *The Confederate War: How Popular Will, Nationalism, and Military Strategy Could Not Stave Off Defeat* (Cambridge, MA: Harvard University Press, 1997), 28–29; Eicher, *Dixie Betrayed*, 142; Vance to Gabriel J. Rains, March 31, 1863, in *Papers of Zebulon Baird Vance*, 2:102.

99. Davis, "To the Senate and House of Representatives of the Confederate States," November 7, 1864, in *Messages and Papers*, 1:495.

Actually, the proposal to arm the slaves and offer them the carrot of emancipation to guarantee good service had not originated with Davis. Richard Ewell, the scapegoat of Gettysburg, had suggested this to Jefferson Davis after First Bull Run in 1861, even volunteering to "command a brigade of Negroes," and Davis continued to get advice from desperate citizens to dismiss "all squeameshness about employing negroes in civilized warfare." The idea was formally introduced on January 24, 1864, by Patrick Cleburne, the Army of Tennessee's Irish-born corps commander. Significantly, Cleburne was not a slave owner himself and had little interest in slavery. His principal rationale was the preservation of Confederate independence: "As between the loss of independence and the loss of slavery, we assume that every patriot will freely give up the latter—give up the negro slave rather than be a slave himself."[100]

This was asking much more of Southerners, in the name of the Confederacy, than Cleburne realized; he was, in fact, asking them to surrender the cornerstone of white racism in order to preserve their nation, and that was more than Davis felt he could safely ask. All copies of Cleburne's written proposal were destroyed, by Davis's order. But ten months later Davis felt he no longer had room for choice, and so in November 1864 Davis introduced his proposal for arming the slaves to the Confederate Congress. This time, even Davis's closest political allies stopped short. Howell Cobb, who thought he was fighting the war to preserve slavery and not some elusive Confederate nationalism, warned Davis, "The day you make soldiers of them is the beginning of the end of the revolution. If slaves will make good soldiers our whole theory of slavery is wrong." North Carolina newspapers bitterly attacked the proposal as "farcical"—"all this was done *for the preservation and perpetuation of slavery*," and if "sober men . . . are ready to enquire if the South is willing to abolish slavery as a condition of carrying on the war, why may it not be done, as a condition of *ending the war?*" North Carolina's soldiers were even more terse in their dismissal of the plan. "I did not volunteer to fight for a free negroes country," J. F. Maides wrote home. "I do not think I love my country well enough to fight with black soldiers." Without slavery, Virginia governor William Smith exclaimed, the South "would no longer have a motive to continue the struggle."[101]

The continuing collapse of the Confederate field armies eventually frightened even the most diehard slaveholders in Congress, and when General Lee added his endorsement to a bill introduced into the Confederate Congress by Mississippian Ethelbert Barksdale in February 1865, the opposition crumbled. On March 8, with a margin of only one vote in the Senate, the Congress voted to authorize

100. Pfanz, *Richard S. Ewell*, 139; Howell and Elizabeth Purdue, *Pat Cleburne: Confederate General* (Hillsboro, TX: Hill Jr. College Press, 1973), 267; O. G. Eiland to Davis, July 20, 1863, in *Freedom's Soldiers: The Black Military Experience in the Civil War*, ed. Ira Berlin et al. (New York: Cambridge University Press, 1998), 103–4.

101. Beringer, *Why the South Lost the Civil War*, 384–85; Michael Fellman, *The Making of Robert E. Lee* (New York: Random House, 2000), 215.

the recruitment of black soldiers. Seventeen days later, the first black Confederate companies began drilling in Richmond.[102]

Would African Americans have fought to save the Confederate nation? They just might have, since southern blacks demonstrated repeatedly throughout the war a healthy skepticism of all white intentions and promises, in blue or in gray, and were prepared to grasp for liberty without regard to who offered it. A skeptical Georgia slave told Union major George Ward Nichols that it was all well and good that the Union armies had come to bring him freedom, "but, massa, you'se'll go way tomorrow, and anudder white man'll come." Nichols could only nod in agreement: "He had never known any thing but persecutions and injury from the white man" and saw no reason to put more trust in one class of white people than another. "Freedom and liberty is the word with the Collered people," wrote a free black Louisianan; if fighting for the Confederacy "makes us free we are happy to hear it."[103] In the event, it was really too late for anyone to find out. Less than a month after the Confederate Congress authorized black enlistment, the war was over and the prospect of black Confederates was left to drift off into the realm of might-have-been.

Yet this is not to say that the idea of creating a Confederate nation was a fore-ordained failure. Southerners may have lost faith in the Confederate government's success in waging war but not in the fundamental notions of Confederate nationalism, and especially not white racial supremacy. The move to recruit black soldiers may have rocked some Southerners, but not all of them, and belated as its appearance was, it testified to the degree to which Davis and like-minded Southerners had managed to move the Confederacy toward thinking of itself as a nation whose collective survival was more important than the preservation of its individual parts. Southerners assured themselves to the very end that God was with the Confederacy, and labored to incorporate Confederate nationalism into novels, plays, music, and even spelling books. And whatever disenchantment Southerners experienced with the Davis administration, they converted Robert E. Lee and the Army of Northern Virginia into near deities in whom they never lost confidence. What the Confederacy demonstrated was this truth, that it was easier to create a nation than it was to create a nation-state.

The Confederate nation-state did not survive the Civil War, but the Southerners who died in its battles, and the four years of fire that it sustained in the teeth of the North's industrial and military might, are a warning not to underestimate how close they came to succeeding. The Confederacy's internal fractures were not more serious

102. "Open Session," March 8, 1865, in *Journal of the Congress of the Confederate States of America, 1861–1865* (Washington, DC: Government Printing Office, 1904), 4:670; Bruce Levine, *Confederate Emancipation: Southern Plans to Free and Arm Slaves During the Civil War* (New York: Oxford University Press, 2006), 118.

103. George Ward Nichols, *The Story of the Great March from the Diary of a Staff Officer* (New York: Harper, 1865), 59; "A Colored Man," September 1863, in *Freedom's Soldiers*, 110; Mohr, *On the Threshold of Freedom*, 288–89.

than the ones other governments have lived with, nor was a nation that glamorized a Romantic aristocracy an impossibility; what made it ultimately unsustainable was the constant military pounding to which it was subjected. The Confederacy might have survived its fractures; culturally speaking, it actually did, as postwar Southerners went about converting the basic elements of Confederate nationalism—race, class, and sectional politics—into the badges of a peculiar people. What the Confederate government could not survive was the defeat of its armies in battle.[104]

What Jefferson Davis needed was time—time bought by military victory, time to persuade slaveholders and nonslaveholders that each served the other's best interests, time to make the kind of mistakes in finance and domestic policy that all politicians must make when they attempt to invent a regime on untried blueprints. But time was not on the side of the Confederacy, and the hands pushing the clock were attached to soldiers in blue.

104. Gallagher, *The Confederate War*, 87, 140, 157, 163, 172; Anne Sarah Rubin, *A Shattered Nation: The Rise and Fall of the Confederacy, 1861–1868* (Chapel Hill: University of North Carolina Press, 2005), 102–11, 138, 141, 153, 163, 246–48.

CHAPTER NINE

WORLD TURNED UPSIDE DOWN

Willard Glazier was a lithe, sharp-witted nineteen-year-old when he enlisted in the 2nd New York Cavalry in 1861. Starting out as an ordinary private, he soon climbed the ladder of promotion, and at the end of August 1863 he was commissioned as a second lieutenant for Company M of the 2nd New York. That was where his promotions ended. In a skirmish at New Baltimore, Virginia, on October 19, 1863, Glazier's horse was shot from under him, and he was captured by Confederate cavalry.[1]

Just as neither North nor South had been prepared to wage war, neither had been prepared to deal with one of the major encumbrances of war, the keeping of enemy prisoners. Both governments quickly constructed elaborate exchange systems to get enemy prisoners off their hands and to retrieve their own soldiers. But the exchange systems were cumbersome, the personnel needed for running the system were sorely needed elsewhere, and more often than not the improvised prisoner camps degenerated into slow-moving pools of maltreatment, humiliation, hunger, and death. Glazier got a taste of this early on, when the Virginia militia who shoved him along the road from New Baltimore to Warrenton neatly stripped him of his watch and his overcoat, then dumped him into Libby Prison, a converted tobacco warehouse that had become Richmond's principal holding pen for Union officers. There Glazier languished until May 1864, when Libby Prison was closed down and the inmates piled onto trains that would take them further South. Glazier then bounced from one prison camp to another in Georgia and South Carolina until he was finally delivered to a camp near

---

1. Willard Glazier, *The Capture, the Prison Pen, and the Escape: Giving a Complete History of Prison Life in the South* (Hartford, CT: H. E. Goodwin, 1867), 38.

Columbia in November. There Glazier and a friend slipped into a column of paroled prisoners who were leaving the camp and made off into the woods.

Then began the most curious part of Glazier's adventures. Without food, weapons, or even decent clothing, Glazier and his friend somehow had to find their way to Union lines from deep within rebel territory, and they had not the faintest idea of how to do it. Nevertheless, Glazier had some unsuspected allies, fashioned for him by the war and emancipation, and he recognized those allies as soon as they came down the road he was standing on. Those allies were, of course, black slaves, for in spite of the conventional wisdom up to 1863, the slaves had known all along that the war and the Yankees meant freedom, and now Willard Glazier was about to have a similar epiphany on that Carolina road. The slaves walked by him, eyeing Glazier and his friend suspiciously. "I reckon deys Yankees," remarked one. "Golly, I hope to God dey is," replied another. Glazier took his chance. "We are Yankees and have just escaped from Columbia," he pleaded. "Can't you do something for us?" The slaves stopped and laughed. "Ob course," they replied eagerly, and one added, "I'll do all I can for you, marster."[2]

So Willard Glazier, Federal officer and prisoner of the Confederacy, became the ward of the most powerless class of people in the American republic. With black slaves as his providers and guides, Glazier and his friend were passed surreptitiously from one plantation to another. Eventually Glazier and his friend met up with two other bands of fugitive Yankee prisoners, and all them were moved by night with slave guides and sheltered by day in huts and barns. One slave family found and repaired a boat to get them across the Savannah River; another slave resoled Glazier's worn-out shoes. Twenty miles north of Savannah, on December 15, Glazier blundered into Confederate pickets and was recaptured. Four days later he slipped away again and found his way once more to "the hut of a negro." Occasionally he was even able to beg a meal from a hard-eyed white farmer's wife who held no love for Confederate conscription agents and tax gatherers. A free black family near Cherokee Hill, Georgia, found him a guide named March Dasher, another free black who at last guided Glazier to Federal lines in northern Georgia on December 23, 1864.[3]

As a white male and an officer, Glazier was the embodiment of a social order in which white men held power and ruled over submissive white women and black slaves. But the chance of war had inverted those relationships: Willard Glazier found himself powerless and completely dependent on the leadership and goodwill of black slaves and farm women. That same chance determined Willard Glazier's story over and over again throughout the war years, for the Civil War imposed on American society as much social disruption as it did physical destruction. Within that disruption, for one brief and bloody historical moment, an entirely new way of ordering race and gender within a republican society became possible.

2. John Algernon Owens, *Sword and Pen: or, Ventures and Adventures of Willard Glazier in War and Literature* (Philadelphia: P. W. Ziegler, 1889), 222.

3. Glazier, *The Capture, the Prison Pen, and the Escape*, 287–306.

BY THEIR OWN STRONG ARMS

After more than a century, nothing disenchants the romantic image of the Civil War as a crusade for freedom and against slavery more than the realization that white Northerners were less than enthusiastic about the Emancipation Proclamation, although emancipation helped fend off the possibility of outside intervention in the war and provided nearly two hundred thousand extra soldiers and sailors to help win it. Even among Northerners who genuinely believed that slavery was an evil, emancipation was celebrated largely for the way it redeemed the reputation of a white republic and not as a down payment on the way to civil equality to African Americans. Emancipation cured the problem of slavery, but emancipated African Americans were a problem to be dealt with in quite another way.

Even Abraham Lincoln appeared to many blacks to have signed the Emancipation Proclamation with one finger crossed behind his back, and it was clear that many Northerners (Lincoln included) believed that the next step for freedmen after emancipation was colonization to Central America or the American Southwest, or repatriation to Africa. "The African race here is a foreign and feeble element," explained Lincoln's secretary of state, William Henry Seward—a view that was echoed by the secretary of the Treasury, Salmon Chase, who reluctantly agreed that "the separation of the races" was unavoidable and that African Americans should seek "happier homes in other lands," and by the Republican Speaker of the House, Schuyler Colfax, who stated the problem of the free black with unbecoming precision: colonization was "the most beneficent yet projected for the amelioration of the African, and at the same time the relief of the people of the country from the evils of a black population in their midst."[4]

This was decidedly not a view shared by free and newly freed black people, as well as being a horribly shortsighted concept of beneficence. But if numbers and influence meant anything, there did not seem at first to be much they could do about it. Out of a total population in the United States of 31,443,000 in 1860, African Americans numbered only about 4,441,000, or about 14 percent of the population, and of that number, less than 500,000 were free. Of those who were free, only a small number enjoyed anything like full participation in the political life of their communities or the republic as a whole. Still, it is one measure of the promise of liberal democracy in America that from the very beginning of the Civil War, African Americans consciously set out to make the conflict both a war against slavery and a struggle for full equality in the life of that democracy. To reach this goal meant that free blacks

---

4. Frederick J. Blue, *Salmon P. Chase: A Life in Politics* (Kent, OH: Kent State University Press, 1987), 83–84; LaWanda Cox, "The Perception of Injustice and Race Policy: James F. McGogy and the Freedmen's Bureau in Alabama," in *Freedom, Racism, and Reconstruction: Collected Writings of LaWanda Cox* (Athens: University of Georgia Press, 1997), 183; Lincoln, "Address on Colonization to a Deputation of Negroes," in *Collected Works*, 5: 371–72.

in the North and newly freed slaves in the South would be forced to make alliances, sometimes willingly and sometimes not, with the unreliable and halfhearted sympathies of Northern whites. William Wilson, a Brooklyn schoolteacher, wickedly asked whether whites were as trustworthy and "*as good by nature* as we are." If there were moments of hesitation and second thought, though, they were exceedingly rare. By adding their numbers to the white volunteers, African Americans could lay claim to "a common cause" that whites and blacks shared equally. If blacks could fight and die alongside whites, they were certainly fit to vote and work alongside them, too. "No nation ever has or ever will be emancipated from slavery," wrote a black schoolteacher in the pages of the newspaper *Anglo-African* in 1861, "but by the sword, wielded too by their own strong arms."[5]

The actual conditions in which black volunteers found themselves turned out to be something less than ideal. Both the state-recruited "colored infantry" of New England and Louisiana and the new federal United States Colored Troops were to be segregated, all-black regiments—all black, that is, except for the officer grades, which were reserved for whites. When Massachusetts governor John Andrew tried to issue a state commission as a second lieutenant to Sergeant Stephen Swails of the 54th Massachusetts, one of the two "colored" infantry regiments raised by the Bay State, the Bureau of Colored Troops obstinately refused to issue Swails a discharge from his sergeant's rank, and Swails's promotion was held up until after the end of the war. "How can we hope for success to our arms or Gods blessing," raged the white colonel of the 54th, Edward Hallowell, "while we as a people are so blind to Justice?"[6]

Black soldiers also had their patience tried to the point of mutiny by the War Department's decision to pay them only $10 a month (the same pay as teamsters and cooks) instead of the $13 paid to white volunteers, and to issue some black regiments inferior equipment and weapons. Medical services for black soldiers were thinner on the ground than for white volunteers, and black soldiers died from camp diseases at three times the rate of their white counterparts. Black soldiers also suffered taunts and humiliation from the white civilians whose nation they were enlisting to save, and from white soldiers whom they were supposed to fight beside. In August 1862 a mob of immigrant workers, fearful of job competition from free blacks, attacked

5. *Historical Statistics of the United States, Colonial Times to 1970* (Washington, DC: Government Printing Office, 1975), 1:8–15; Alfred M. Green, in *The Negro's Civil War: How American Negroes Felt and Acted during the War for the Union*, ed. James M. McPherson (New York: Pantheon, 1965), 32–33; Wilson, in Mia Bay, *The White Image in the Black Mind: African American Ideas About White People* (New York: Oxford University Press, 2000), 76.

6. "Northern Black Sergeant to the Headquarters of the Department of the South," October 15, 1864, in *Freedom, A Documentary History of Emancipation, 1861–1867: Series Two, The Black Military Experience*, Ira Berlin et al., eds. (New York: Cambridge University Press, 1982), 342.

the Lorillard and Watson tobacco warehouses in Brooklyn (Watson's employed only blacks, Lorillard's employed a mix of black and white workers); the following March, an angry mob of whites burned down homes in a black neighborhood in Detroit. Other riots broke out in Troy and Buffalo, and in July 1863 savage anti-draft riots in New York City quickly turned into race riots that resulted in the murder and beatings of dozens of blacks. In November of that year, the 2nd USCT was mobbed in the streets of Philadelphia as it prepared to board a troop train for New York.[7]

The greatest danger posed to the black soldier, however, came from the Confederates, and not just the conventional dangers faced by all Union soldiers in combat. The Confederate government acted as early as August 1862 to frighten off any prospect of black recruitment by issuing a general order threatening that any "commissioned officer employed in drilling, organizing or instructing slaves with a view to their armed service in this war . . . as outlaws" would be "held in close confinement for execution as a felon"; on December 24, Jefferson Davis followed this with a proclamation warning that "all negro slaves captured in arms be at once delivered over to the executive authorities of the respective States to which they belong, to be dealt with according to the laws of said States." What the "authorities of the respective States" had in mind was up to them, but South Carolina took the lead in proposing to put free blacks to work on "the Chesterfield coal pits" and sell any former slaves back into slavery. This required a cumbersome process of hearings and determinations, so impatient Confederates soon found shorter ways of dealing with the problem. Edmund Kirby Smith, who had overall command of Confederate forces west of the Mississippi, simply advised General Richard Taylor to skip the niceties and execute black soldiers and white officers on the spot. "I hope . . . that your subordinates who may have been in command of capturing parties may have recognized the propriety of giving no quarter to armed negroes and their officers. In this way we may be relieved from a disagreeable dilemma."[8]

That attitude, combined with the explosive power of racial hatred and the blood heat of battle, could produce singularly ugly results. On April 12, 1864, the onetime slave trader and now Confederate general Nathan Bedford Forrest overran the small

---

7. Dudley Taylor Cornish, *The Sable Arm: Negro Troops in the Union Army, 1861–1865* (New York: Longmans, Green, 1956), 185; David W. McCullough, *Brooklyn—and How It Got That Way* (New York: Dial Press, 1983), 35–36; Paul A. Gilje, *Rioting in America* (Bloomington: Indiana University Press, 1996), 91; Joseph T. Glatthaar, *Forged in Battle: The Civil War Alliance of Black Soldiers and White Officers* (New York: Free Press, 1990), 191–96.

8. "General Orders No. 60," August 26, 1862, in *The War of the Rebellion*, Series Two, 4:857; "General Orders No. 111," in *Messages and Papers of Jefferson Davis and the Confederacy*, 1:274; Gregory J. W. Urwin, *Black Flag over Dixie: Racial Atrocities and Reprisals in the Civil War* (Carbondale: Southern Illinois University Press, 2004), 41–42, 166; Kirby-Smith to Taylor, June 13, 1863, in *Report on the Treatment of Prisoners of War by the Rebel Authorities During the War of the Rebellion* (Washington, DC: Government Printing Office, 1869), 641; Richard Reid, *Freedom for Themselves: North Carolina's Black Soldiers in the Civil War Era* (Chapel Hill: University of North Carolina Press, 2008), 94–95.

Union garrison of Fort Pillow, on the Mississippi River. Fort Pillow was defended by only 600 Union soldiers, a little more than a third of them black soldiers from the 6th U.S. Colored Heavy Artillery, and after three assaults, the Confederates forced the little outpost to surrender. What happened afterward became the subject of fiercely tangled controversy, but it seems clear in retrospect that at the very least Forrest lost control of his men, who proceeded to massacre 231 Union soldiers, most of them black, after they had surrendered. A white soldier of the 13th West Tennessee (Federal) Cavalry left a graphic description of the rampage:

> We all threw down our arms and gave tokens of surrender, asking for quarter . . . but no quarter was given. Voices were heard upon all sides, crying, "Give them no quarter; kill them; kill them; it is General Forrest's orders." I saw 4 white men and at least 25 negroes shot while begging for mercy, and I saw 1 negro dragged from a hollow log within 10 feet of where I lay, and as 1 rebel held him by the foot another shot him. These were all soldiers. There were also 2 negro women and 3 little children standing within 25 steps from me, when a rebel stepped up to them and said, "Yes, God damn you, you thought you were free, did you?" and shot them all. They all fell but 1 child, when he knocked it in the head with the breech of his gun.[9]

This was, as the commandant of the United States Colored Troops units in Tennessee remarked in a letter to his congressman, a "game . . . at which two can play." In Kansas, an indignant white Federal officer in Jim Lane's Kansas brigade learned that "one of the colored prisoners" from his unit who had been captured by Confederates in your camp "was murdered by your Soldiers." He wanted "the body of the man who committed the dastardly act" or else "I shall hang one of the men who are prisoners in my camp." Ultimately, Lincoln himself took a hand in the matter by promising in July 1863 that "for every soldier of the United States killed in violation of the laws of war, a rebel soldier shall be executed; and for every one enslaved by the enemy or sold into slavery, a rebel soldier shall be placed at hard labor on the public works." In the face of this threat, the Confederates backed down from their plans for execution and reenslavement. Still, they refused to exchange black Federal prisoners for white Confederate ones, and so the entire prisoner exchange cartel that had been established in 1862 broke down, choking prisoner-of-war camps (which had been designed to be mere transit points before exchange) into overcrowded death swamps.[10]

9. "Statement of William J. Mays, Company B, Thirteenth Tennessee Cavalry," April 18, 1864, in *War of the Rebellion*, Series One, 32(I):525; John Cimprich, *Fort Pillow, a Civil War Massacre, and Public Memory* (Baton Rouge: Louisiana State University Press, 2005), 72–85.

10. Brig. Gen. Augustus Chetlain to Washburne, April 14, 1864, in *War of the Rebellion*, Series One, 32(I):364; James M. Williams, May 26, 1863, in *Freedom: A Documentary History of Emancipation 1861–1867: Series Two (Book One): The Black Military Experience*, ed. Ira Berlin et al. (Cambridge: Cambridge University Press, 1993), 574; Lincoln, "Order of Retaliation," July 30, 1863, in *Collected Works*, 6:357; Craig L. Symonds, *Lincoln and His Admirals: Abraham Lincoln, the U.S. Navy, and the Civil War* (New York: Oxford University Press, 2008), 48.

Still, the chance to lend their own hands to the process of freedom made up in some measure for the inequities and harassment visited on African American volunteers. "It really makes one's heart pulsate with pride as he looks upon those stout and brawny men, fully equipped with Uncle Sam's accoutrements upon them," wrote James Henry Gooding, a black corporal in the 54th Massachusetts, "to feel that these noble men are practically refuting the base assertions reiterated by copperheads and traitors that the black race are incapable of patriotism, valor, or ambition."[11] It also helped that the white officers of the USCT regiments were, on the whole, better-trained and better-motivated than their counterparts among the white volunteers. Since the USCT were mustered directly into federal rather than state service, officers' commissions came through the War Department rather than through politicians in the state capitals, and the Bureau of Colored Troops quickly instituted a rigorous application and examination process to screen whites who wanted to become USCT officers. As a result, officers' commissions in the USCT frequently went to experienced former sergeants and officers from white volunteer regiments, many of whom were ardent abolitionists who saw the USCT as the troops themselves saw it, as a lever for self-improvement.[12]

The ultimate proof of their faith would be in combat—although that depended on whether Union generals could actually be persuaded to let the USCT fight, instead of merely doing occupation duty or manual labor. "Can we not fight our own battles, without calling on these humble hewers of wood and drawers of water," complained one of George Meade's staffers. "We do not dare trust them in the line of battle." Nathaniel Banks, however, was one of the rare abolitionists in the Union high command (although a better abolitionist than a general, as it turned out), and in May 1863 he hazarded his three all-black Louisiana Native Guard regiments on a series of attacks on Confederate fortifications at Port Hudson, Louisiana. "They answered every expectation," Banks reported afterward, "In many respects their conduct was heroic. . . . The severe test to which they were subjected, and the determined manner in which they encountered the enemy, leaves upon my mind no doubt of their ultimate success." The Philadelphia poet George Henry Boker exulted in how

Bayonet and sabre stroke
Vainly opposed their rush
Through the wild battle's crush.
With but one thought aflush,
Driving their lords like chaff.
. . . All their eyes forward bent,
Rushed the Black Regiment.

11. James Henry Gooding, *On the Altar of Freedom: A Black Soldier's Civil War Letters from the Front*, ed. Virginia M. Adams (Amherst: University of Massachusetts Press, 1991), 9.

12. Glatthaar, *Forged in Battle*, 107–8.

"Freedom!" their battle cry,
"Freedom! or leave to die!"
Ah! and they meant the word.
. . . Soldiers, be just and true!
Hail them as comrades tried;
Fight with them side by side;
Never in field or tent
Scorn the Black Regiment.[13]

The action at Port Hudson was followed the next month by the hand-to-hand defense of a post at Milliken's Bend, Louisiana, by five Union regiments, four black and one white. Even the commander of the Confederates, Henry E. McCullough, was forced to concede that "this charge was resisted by the negro portion of the enemy's force with considerable obstinacy, while the white or true Yankee portion ran like whipped curs almost as soon as the charge was ordered."[14]

The bloodiest laurels for black soldiers were won by the cream of the black volunteers, the 54th Massachusetts, with a blue-stocking Harvard-educated colonel, Robert Gould Shaw, at its head. On July 18, 1863, Shaw and the 54th Massachusetts spearheaded an infantry attack on Battery Wagner, one of the outlying fortifications covering the land approaches to the harbor of Charleston, South Carolina. A full day's worth of bombardment by Federal gunboats offshore had failed to silence the Confederate artillery in the fort, and when the 54th raced forward to the fort's walls, their ranks were shredded by Confederate fire. Nevertheless, the 54th swept up over the walls and into the fort, with Shaw and one of his black color sergeants dying side by side on the parapet.

> The regiment advanced at quick time, changed to double-quick when at some distance on. The intervening distance between the place where the line was formed and the Fort was run over in a few minutes. When within one or two hundred yards of the Fort, a terrific fire . . . was poured upon them along the entire line, and with deadly results. They rallied again, went through the ditch, in which were some three feet of water, and then up the parapet. They raised the flag on the parapet, where it remained for a few minutes. Here they melted away before the enemy's fire, their bodies falling down the slope and into the ditch.[15]

13. George H. Boker, "The Black Regiment," in *Poems of the War* (Boston: Ticknor and Fields, 1864), 101–3.

14. Theodore Lyman, May 18, 1864, in *Meade's Headquarters, 1863–1865: Letters of Colonel Theodore Lyman from the Wilderness to Appomattox*, ed. G. R. Agassiz (Boston: Massachusetts Historical Society, 1922), 102; "Reports of Maj. Gen. Nathaniel P. Banks, U.S. Army, commanding Department of the Gulf," May 30, 1863, in *War of the Rebellion*, Series One, 26(I):45; Richard Lowe, "Battle on the Levee: The Fight at Milliken's Bend," in *Black Soldiers in Blue: African American Troops in the Civil War Era*, ed. John David Smith (Chapel Hill: University of North Carolina Press, 2002), 117–24; "Report of Brig.-Gen. Henry E. McCullough," June 8, 1863, in *War of the Rebellion*, Series One, 24(II):467.

15. "Letter of Edward L. Pierce," July 22, 1863, in *The Rebellion Record: A Diary of American Events*, ed. Frank Moore (New York: G. P. Putnam, 1864), 7:215.

The 54th gamely hung on to one corner of Battery Wagner, but they were finally pushed off after a stubborn resistance. Sergeant William H. Carney staggered back from the fort with wounds in his chest and right arm, but with the regiment's Stars and Stripes securely in his grasp. "The old flag never touched the ground, boys," Carney gasped as he collapsed at the first field hospital he could find.[16]

The valor of the black troops at Port Hudson, Milliken's Bend, and Battery Wagner sent waves of amazement over the North—bemused and often condescending amazement, but amazement all the same. Abraham Lincoln, who had been as dubious about the fighting qualities of the black soldiers as other whites, now agreed that "the use of colored troops constitute the heaviest blow yet dealt to the rebellion." Ulysses Grant concurred. In a letter to Lincoln one month after the assault on Battery Wagner, Grant noted that "by arming the negro we have added a powerful ally. They will make good soldiers and taking them from the enemy weakens him in the same proportion as they strengthen us."[17] The ordinary Union soldier felt the same way. "The colored troops are very highly valued here & there is no apparent difference in the way they are treated," wrote one USCT officer in Virginia. "White troops and blacks mingle constantly together & I have seen no single Evidence of dislike on the part of the soldiers. The truth is they have fought their way into the respect of all the army." It was time, now that black soldiers had proven themselves under fire, for white Northerners to begin thinking about what was owed to African Americans at home. "The American people, as a nation, knew not what they were fighting for till recently," wrote Corporal Gooding, but now it was clear that "there is but two results possible, one is slavery and poverty and the other is liberty and prosperity."[18]

The achievements of blacks as soldiers forced on Lincoln and the federal government the question how African Americans who fought to defend the Union could any longer be denied full political equality—the right to vote, to be elected to office, to serve on juries, to benefit from publicly funded schools—in that Union. "Once let a black man get upon his person the brass letters U.S.," said Frederick Douglass, "let him get an eagle on his button, and a musket on his shoulder and bullets in his pockets, and there is no power on earth which can deny he has won the right to citizenship in the United States." (For Douglass, that claim had a personal tinge: two of his sons, Claude and Lewis, were with the 54th Massachusetts, and a third, Frederick junior, worked as a recruiter for the black regiments among freed slaves in Mississippi). Lincoln, who in 1858 had only been willing to endorse the *natural*

16. Luis Fenollosa Emilio, *A Brave Black Regiment: The History of the Fifty-fourth Massachusetts, 1863–65* (Boston: Boston Book, 1894), 79–84; Stephen R. Wise, *Gate of Hell: Campaign for Charleston Harbor, 1863* (Columbia: University of South Carolina Press, 1994), 103–5.

17. Grant to Lincoln, August 23, 1863, in *The Papers of Ulysses S. Grant*, 9:196–97; Howard C. Westwood, "Grant's Role in Beginning Black Soldiery," *Illinois Historical Journal* 79 (1986): 197–212.

18. Lincoln, "To James C. Conkling," August 26, 1863, in *Collected Works*, 6:409; Glatthaar, *Forged in Battle*, 168; Gooding, *On the Altar of Freedom*, 19.

equality of whites and blacks, could not reconcile asking blacks for the risk of their lives without also offering them the privileges of *civil* equality as well. "Negroes, like other people, act upon motives," Lincoln argued in a public letter addressed to James Cook Conkling in the fall of 1863 and widely published across the North. "Why should they do any thing for us, if we will do nothing for them? If they stake their lives for us, they must be prompted by the strongest motive, even the promise of freedom. And the promise being made, must be kept."[19]

The principal difficulty lay in determining where an experiment in black civil rights ought to take place. His authority as president ran only as far as the District of Columbia and the wartime zones of the army, and he had no way to unilaterally reverse state actions that denied free blacks the right to vote. That problem, however, was solved for Lincoln by the Federal navy when it seized New Orleans in April 1862 and opened most of southern Louisiana to Federal occupation by the end of the year. In the summer of 1863 Lincoln approved a plan for electing a Unionist state legislature in Louisiana that would rescind the state secession ordinance and adopt a new state constitution. In March 1864, Lincoln urged the new Unionist governor of Louisiana, Michael Hahn, to make some limited provision in the new state constitution for black voting rights. "I barely suggest for your private consideration," Lincoln proposed softly (since he had no more authority as president to require things of a civilian Unionist government than he had of the old slave-state government), "whether some of the colored people may not be let in—as, for instance, the very intelligent, and especially those who have fought gallantly in our ranks. They would probably help, in some trying time to come, to keep the jewel of liberty within the family of freedom."[20]

In the event, Hahn's constitutional convention abolished "slavery and involuntary servitude" and prohibited the legislature from making any law "recognizing the right of property in man." It balked at granting full voting rights to blacks, however, and would only concede that in the future the legislature might consider "extending suffrage to such other persons, citizens of the United States, as by military service, by taxation to support the government, or by intellectual fitness, may be deemed entitled thereto." But the camel's nose was in the tent, and Lincoln had signaled that the federal government would back up any steps taken toward political equality, even if granted grudgingly and of necessity. When Lincoln sent one of his White House staffers, William O. Stoddard, to Arkansas as a federal marshal in 1864 to assist in the organization of a Unionist state government there, he enjoined Stoddard to "do all you can, in any and every way you can, to get the ballot into the hands of the freedmen!"[21]

19. Lincoln, "To James C. Conkling," August 26, 1863, in *Collected Works*, 6:409.

20. Lincoln, "To Michael Hahn," March 13, 1864, in *Collected Works*, 7:243.

21. "Constitution of Louisiana—1864," in *The Federal and State Constitutions, Colonial Charters, and Other Organic Laws*, ed. Francis Newton Thorpe (Washington, DC: Government Printing Office, 1909), 3:1429, 1433; William O. Stoddard, *Inside the White House in War Times: Memoirs and Reports of Lincoln's Secretary*, ed. Michael Burlingame (Lincoln: University of Nebraska Press, 2000), 139.

It proved harder to turn the tide of Northern white opinion at home than it had been among Northern soldiers in the army, and black soldiers were the first to discover this, almost literally in the streets of Northern cities. In the great Northern urban centers of Boston, New York, and Philadelphia, segregated streetcar systems immediately became a flashpoint for conflict, especially when, as in New York City, streetcar operators began throwing black soldiers off the cars and into the streets. When the widow of a black sergeant was pushed off a New York City streetcar by a policeman, a public scandal followed, with Horace Greeley's *New York Tribune* growling, "It is quite time to settle the question whether the wives and children of the men who are laying down their lives for their country . . . are to be treated like dogs."[22]

In Philadelphia, where white and black abolitionists had been demanding an end to segregation on the city rail lines since 1859, a coalition of Republican and black civic organizations appealed to the city's Democratic mayor, and then finally to the state legislature, to end racial discrimination in public accommodations throughout Pennsylvania. In occupied New Orleans, fights broke out between streetcar drivers and black soldiers and were resolved only by a compromise that allowed black officers to ride with whites while relegating black enlisted men to the "star cars" (blacks-only streetcars marked with a black star). In Washington, D.C., the veteran black abolitionist Sojourner Truth deliberately challenged a whites-only rule on the city streetcars by standing at streetcar stops and screeching "I want to ride!" at the top of her lungs. When a conductor on another streetcar tried to throw Truth off the car, he dislocated her shoulder; she promptly hired a lawyer, sued the streetcar company, and forced the company to abandon its racial discrimination policies. "Before the trial was ended," Truth announced sardonically, "the inside of the cars looked like pepper and salt."[23]

Not every battle for equality ended so happily. Free Northern blacks could achieve the victories they won because they operated in a largely urban context, where many of them had already established visible places in Northern society and where white allies were fairly close at hand. Even then, only Massachusetts enacted significant bans on segregation in hotels, restaurants, and theaters. Among the newly emancipated freedpeople of the South, the story was bleaker. Lacking education, property, or even a clear sense of what emancipation might mean, slaves slipped away to the Union armies or celebrated their liberation as the Union forces marched southward past them, even as they had no certainty what the next step might be. A Federal officer marching down toward Murfreesboro wrote that "at every plantation negroes

22. James M. McPherson, *The Struggle for Equality; Abolitionists and the Negro in the Civil War and Reconstruction* (Princeton, NJ: Princeton University Press, 1964), 232; Paludan, *"A People's Contest,"* 220–21.

23. Stephen J. Ochs, *A Black Patriot and a White Priest: Andre Cailloux and Claude Paschal Maistre in Civil War New Orleans* (Baton Rouge: Louisiana State University Press, 2000), 91–92; Larry G. Murphy, *Sojourner Truth: A Biography* (Santa Barbara, CA: ABC-CLIO, 2011), 98–101; Nell Irvin Painter, *Sojourner Truth: A Life, A Symbol* (New York: W. W. Norton, 1996), 210–11.

came flocking to the roadside to see us. . . . They have heard of the abolition army, the music, the banners, the glittering arms . . . [and they] welcome us with extravagant manifestations of joy. They keep time to the music with feet and hands and hurrah 'fur de ole flag and de Union,' sometimes following us for miles." An estimated ten thousand liberated slaves packed up and trailed after William Tecumseh Sherman and his army in 1864, shouting, "Yesterday I was a slave, to day I am free. We are all white now." However, they quickly learned that emancipation was only the beginning of a new and uncharted future, and they did not receive much in the way of direction from either Northern or Southern whites. In December 1864 one of Sherman's corps commanders—the inaptly named Jefferson C. Davis—marched his troops across Ebenezer Creek, just north of Savannah, on a pontoon bridge built by his engineers, then took up the bridge and abandoned some 2,000 "contrabands" to the mercies of pursuing Confederate cavalry. The Federal armies frequently seized newly freed slaves and forced them into service as manual laborers, while embittered Southern whites evicted their former slaves from white-owned property and refused to hire freedpeople to work for them. Another 135,000 freedmen, lacking any particular direction for the future, simply enlisted in the USCT and hoped for the best.[24]

In a few places in the South, conscientious whites attempted to intervene and help the freedpeople toward literacy and economic independence. The Northern "Gideonites" who descended on Port Royal in 1862 set up schools and churches and pressed the Lincoln administration (through their own influential political networks at home) to have the plantations that had been abandoned by Port Royal's white masters before the Union seizure of the Sea Islands divided among the former slaves who had once worked those lands. Even so, as the abolitionist William Kimball protested in 1864, the United States could not simply "unloose the chains that have bound them" and then take no further action; to "set them adrift to contend and compete under our methods of individualism or isolated interests, is to doom them to conditions hardly to be preferred to those from which they are about to escape." In 1865, Congress took its own steps for setting the freedpeople on their feet by organizing the Freedmen's Bureau, which was designed to establish schools, educate blacks in the intricacies of labor contracts, oversee wage and labor relations, and open up public lands to black settlers. But the experiment in land redistribution at Port Royal foundered on the greed of Northern white land speculators (who had the money to outbid the freedpeople at the open auctions of seized Confederate property) and on postwar legal challenges lodged by former plantation owners who successfully disputed the federal government's wartime authority to seize their

---

24. Glatthaar, *The March to the Sea and Beyond*, 60; Nathaniel Cheairs Hughes and Gordon D. Whitney, *Jefferson Davis in Blue: The Life of Sherman's Relentless Warrior* (Baton Rouge: Louisiana State University Press, 2002), 308–14; August Meier and Elliott M. Rudwick, *From Plantation to Ghetto* (New York: Hill and Wang, 1976), 182.

property. And the Freedmen's Bureau was never sufficiently funded or staffed to deal with the multitude of problems arising from the needs of 2 million newly freed slaves. Yet it was the most significant step toward actively engineering some small measure of racial equality taken by the United States before the 1960s.[25]

In the end, the most important agents for change would have to be the freedpeople themselves, since (in the abolitionists' lexicon) self-transformation was the most appropriate form of change in a republic. As the freedpeople soon learned, even the most well-intentioned white assistance (such as Kimball's) reeked of paternalism and was based on condescending perceptions of blacks as "a people in a state of infantile weakness and inexperience; whom, from the irrepressible laws and conditions of the human mind, we must govern and control, either wisely and beneficently or otherwise." Many freedpeople simply hit the road, sometimes in a nameless determination to put the scenes of slavery behind them, sometimes in a pathetic search for family members who had been sold away to other parts of the South years before, sometime in pursuit of land or work they could own and define for themselves. "They had a passion, not for wandering, as for getting together," wrote one white observer in South Carolina, "and every mother's son among them seemed to be in search of his mother; every mother in search of her children. In their eyes the work of emancipation was incomplete until the families which had been dispersed by slavery were reunited." Others sought to strike down roots in the soil they knew the best. In central Tennessee, the number of farms shot up from 19,000 in 1860 to nearly 30,000 in 1870, with more than three-quarters of that increase representing black farmers who either owned or rented their land.[26]

That did not mean, however, that they were eager to assimilate themselves to white society. Blacks withdrew from the white churches where their masters had ruled over faith and practice, and formed their own congregations. In defiance of the most vicious symbol of white dominance under slavery, the freedpeople rushed to county courthouses to legalize slave marriages and adopt surnames of their own choosing. In July 1865 Tennessee's Bedford County courthouse issued marriage licenses to 422 couples, 406 of which were black; in nearby Rutherford County that September, 431 black couples had their marriages legalized in a single week. Never again would a white man with an auctioneer's bill in his hand come between black husband and black wife, and never again would an African American be known simply as so-and-so's Tom or Dick or Cuffee or Caesar. Mr. Carver's George would become George Washington Carver; James Burroughs's child slave Booker would

25. William Kimball, "Our Government and the Blacks," *Continental Monthly* 5 (April 1864): 433–34; Paul Skeels Peirce, *The Freedmen's Bureau: A Chapter in the History of Reconstruction* (Iowa City: University of Iowa, 1904), 34–45; George R. Bentley, *A History of the Freedmen's Bureau* (Philadelphia: University of Pennsylvania Press, 1955), 38–43.

26. Thomas V. Ash, *Middle Tennessee Society Transformed, 1860–1870: War and Peace in the Upper South* (Baton Rouge: Louisiana State University Press, 1988), 187.

borrow his stepfather's first name to create a last name for himself and become Booker Taliaferro Washington.[27]

So many of these steps seem so basic, and others so halting, that it is easy to lose sight of how much ground was really gained by African Americans in their stride toward civil equality. On one hand, it was disappointingly true that, as late as the 1850s, whites in Iowa, Illinois, Indiana, and Oregon had voted to ban any free black settlement in their states. Outside New England, where free black males already had some measure of voting rights, not a single Northern state initiative to extend voting rights to blacks succeeded during the war, and publicly funded schooling remained closed to blacks in most Northern states. On the other hand, the thick carapace of prejudice and legalized discrimination was also showing clear and open cracks under the hammer blows of the black soldier and the black orator. Five New England cities voted to abolish segregated schools; California and Illinois repealed all of their invidious "black laws" (except, in Illinois, the ban on black voting). On the federal level, Congress repealed exclusionary laws on racial hiring and abolished its restraints on black participation in the federal court system, and on February 1, 1865, John S. Rock was presented by Charles Sumner to plead before the bar of the Supreme Court, the first African American to be admitted as counsel before a court that a decade before had declared that he was not even a citizen. "The Dred Scott Decision Buried in the Supreme Court," ran the *New York Tribune*'s headline. The article went on to say, "Senator Charles Sumner and the Negro lawyer John S. Rock [were] the pall-bearers—the room of the Supreme Court of the United States the Potter's Field—the corpse the Dred Scott decision!"[28]

For African Americans, the future seemed without limits: three centuries of bondage had passed away, and even if African Americans had not yet achieved the levels of equality they yearned for, they had still reached levels none had ever dreamed possible before the war. In November 1864, two weeks after Maryland officially abolished slavery, Frederick Douglass returned to Baltimore for the first time since his flight from slavery twenty-six years before. He was "awed into silence" by the changes the war had wrought, and as he spoke to a racially mixed meeting at an African American church, he declared that "the revolution is genuine, full and complete."[29]

Douglass was, for once, being an optimist. It was not an optimism widely shared by other racial minorities who found themselves with less at stake and thus less to

27. Leon Litwack, *Been in the Storm So Long: The Aftermath of Slavery* (New York: Knopf, 1979), 230, 240–51; Ash, *Middle Tennessee Society Transformed*, 210; Janette Thomas Greenwood, *First Fruits of Freedom: The Migration of Former Slaves and Their Search for Equality in Worcester, Massachusetts, 1862–1900* (Chapel Hill: University of North Carolina Press, 2009), 48–87.

28. Neely, *Lincoln and the Triumph of the Nation*, 114–15; George A. Levesque, "Boston's Black Brahmin: Dr. John S. Rock," *Civil War History* 26 (December 1980): 335–36.

29. Blight, *Frederick Douglass' Civil War* 186.

gain by the war. By 1861, many of the most familiar Indian tribes had been driven out of their ancient lands east of the Mississippi and either penned into reservations and "civilized" with white agriculture, education, and churches or else forcibly relocated west of Mississippi with the tribes of the unsettled western plains. Few of these uprooted eastern tribes had much connection with the larger issue of slavery and disunion, except for the "civilized" Cherokees of the federally designated "Indian Territory" south of Kansas, who had been removed from their Alabama and Georgia homelands in the 1830s and who retained black slavery and a rudimentary plantation system.

Like blacks, Indians seized on the war as an opportunity for advancing or protecting political agendas of their own, although in the case of the Indians, those agendas varied from place to place and tribe to tribe. The Iroquois of western New York had been resisting federal pressure to surrender their reservation lands and move west since the 1830s, and during the Civil War many Iroquois stepped forward to volunteer for the Union army on the premise that Iroquois cooperation in winning the war would induce an appreciative federal government to leave them alone on their lands. In southern Minnesota, the failure of the federal government to meet its treaty obligations with the Santee (Eastern Dakota) Sioux of the Minnesota River reservation provoked a bloody uprising in August 1862 that led to the deaths of more than 350 white settlers. In the Indian Territory, intratribal political factions among Cherokee, Creeks, and Seminoles led to a miniature civil war among the tribes, with various factions soliciting Confederate or Union intervention in the Territory to promote their own control. The semi-nomadic tribes on the plains of the unorganized western territories took advantage of the withdrawal of Federal regular units to overrun white settlements and communications routes to the Pacific.[30]

The more Native Americans involved themselves in the Civil War, the more they seemed to lose by it. As many as 2,000 Iroquois may have volunteered for Union service, including the nearly all-Iroquois 132nd New York, but their willingness to fight for the Union was interpreted by the federal government as a willingness to further assimilate themselves into white culture, and it only fed postwar government pressures to dissolve the New York reservations and, as a New York state legislature report recommended, absorb the Iroquois "into the great mass of the American people." The Sioux uprising in Minnesota was brutally suppressed by hastily recalled Union troops, and thirty-eight Sioux and half-Sioux were hanged for their role in the uprising on December 26, 1862. The tribes of the Indian Territory were devastated by fighting between pro-Confederate and pro-Union bands all through the war, and the plains tribes suffered much more in the long run by the withdrawal of the

---

30. Laurence M. Hauptman, *The Iroquois in the Civil War: From Battlefield to Reservation* (Syracuse, NY: Syracuse University Press, 1993), 11–16, 148; Duane Schultz, *Over the Earth I Come: The Great Sioux Uprising of 1862* (New York: St. Martin's Press, 1992), 5–12; Daniel F. Littlefield, *Africans and Seminoles: From Removal to Emancipation* (Westport, CT: Greenwood Press, 1977), 180–91.

regulars than they could have imagined. In the absence of the regulars, untrained and vengeful white western volunteer regiments took up responsibility for dealing with unruly bands of Cheyenne, Mescalero, Navajo, Comanche, and Kiowa, and the volunteers showed little of the discipline and none of the restraint that the regulars had exercised on western outpost duty. On November 29, 1864, 600 peaceful Cheyenne and Arapaho who had camped at Sand Creek, Colorado, under promises of protection by Federal troops at nearby Fort Lyon were surprised by a force of Colorado volunteers determined to avenge Cheyenne raids on white settlements on the Platte River. The Cheyenne chief Black Kettle vainly waved a large Stars and Stripes to prove the peaceful intentions of his village, but the Colorado volunteers cut down 150 Cheyenne and Arapaho, most of them women and children whom the white volunteers afterward mutilated.[31]

Other, less visible ethnic and racial groups saw their fortunes fluctuate during the war as well. Stereotyped images among Anglo-Americans defined Jews as cunning moneylenders and "Shylocks." "What else could be expected from a Jew but money-getting?" asked the *Southern Illustrated News* in an 1863 article titled "Extortioners." Those prejudices guaranteed that American Jews would be regularly targeted in both North and South as aliens and swindlers who fattened themselves, through war contracts and shady dealing, on the sufferings of their presumably Christian neighbors. In December 1862 Ulysses Grant grew so convinced that "the Jews, as a class" were guilty of "violating every regulation of trade established by . . . Department orders," that he ordered the expulsion of "this class of people" from his Mississippi military district—not thinking that this order would include sutlers as well as more than a few Jewish soldiers. The protests that erupted over Grant's order (including a Senate resolution condemning it as "illegal, tyrannical, cruel and unjust") went all the way up to Lincoln, who promptly had the order rescinded. Grant's prejudices notwithstanding, 7,000 Jews (out of an American Jewish population of about 150,000) enlisted to fight for the Union, and six of them won the Congressional Medal of Honor for bravery in action, while another 1,340 Jews joined the Confederate forces.[32]

Hispanic Americans constituted an even smaller piece of the American ethnic pie, especially since the Anglo-Texans who turned Texas into an American republic

31. Alvin M. Josephy, *The Civil War in the American West* (New York: Knopf, 1991), 269–92, 305–16; Jerome A. Greene and Douglas D. Scott, *Finding Sand Creek: History, Archeology, and the 1864 Massacre Site* (Norman: University of Oklahoma Press, 2004), 18; Scott Nelson and Carol Sheriff, *A People at War: Civilians and Soldiers in America's Civil War, 1854–1877* (New York: Oxford University Press, 2007), 252–53.

32. John Y. Simon, "That Obnoxious Order," in *Jews and the Civil War: A Reader*, ed. Jonathan D. Sarna and Adam Mendelsohn (New York: New York University Press, 2010), 353–61; Jean Edward Smith, *Grant* (New York: Simon and Schuster, 2001), 225–27; *Journal of the Senate of the United States, Begun and Held at the City of Washington, December 1, 1862* (Washington, DC: Government Printing Office, 1863), 78; Rosen, *The Jewish Confederates*, 162–63.

and then an American state in the 1840s successfully drove most of Texas's small His-panic population south into Mexico. However, when Confederate Texans mounted a small-scale invasion of the New Mexico territory in early 1862, a combined force of Federal regulars, Colorado militia, and a company of the mostly Hispanic 2nd New Mexico Volunteers under Lt. Col. Manuel Chavez faced the Texans at Glo-rieta Pass, on the Santa Fe Trail. Together, on March 28, 1862, the Anglo-Hispanic Union troops administered a thorough drubbing to the Texans, sinking Confeder-ate hopes of western conquest beneath the sands of the New Mexico desert.[33]

Much to the surprise of those who thought that the Civil War would be "a white man's war," the conflict quickly broadened, by policy and by accident, to include a kaleidoscope of races and ethnic minorities, from Battery Wagner to Glorieta Pass. Each of these groups saw the confusion of civil war as a moment of opportunity, whether they had rights and respect to win or political agendas to build or merely scores to settle. None of them saw their hopes fully realized. What is remarkable is how the issues and battles of the Civil War made those hopes soar. "This is es-sentially a people's contest," Lincoln told Congress in 1861, a war that would justify confidence in what Lincoln's Whig forerunner Daniel Webster had called "a popu-lar government, erected by the people . . . responsible to the people" and "just as truly emanating from the people, as from the State governments." In 1861, neither Lincoln nor his Congress could have dreamed of the ways in which many differ-ent kinds of American people were eager to claim a seat at that democracy's table.

"THE LIVES WHICH WOMEN HAVE LED SINCE TROY"

For Virginia governor Henry Wise, the Union was like a marriage of man and woman. "It is with the Union of the States as it is with the union of matrimony," Wise explained in 1860—in it, the husband must be "a good man, a good citizen, a good moralist," and so long as his honor is not questioned by his wife, all within that marriage would be peace. The moment the wife challenged that authority, however, then "he will burst the bonds of union, as the burning Wythes were bursted by the vigorous limbs of the yet unshorn Nazarite." Abraham Lincoln took precisely the opposite view. It was actually easier for a husband and wife to be divorced, because they could go out of each other's sight, but the North and the South were bound together geographically in ways which made anything less than conjugal union impossible. To secessionists, "the Union, as a family relation, would not be anything like a regular marriage at all, but only as a sort of free-love arrangement."[34]

33. Thomas S. Edrington and John Taylor, *The Battle of Glorieta Pass: A Gettysburg in the West, March 26-28, 1862* (Albuquerque: University of New Mexico Press, 1998), 7-8, 28.

34. Simpson, *A Good Southerner*, 224-25; Lincoln, "Speech from the Balcony of the Bates House at Indianapolis, Indiana," February 11, 1861, and "Annual Message to Congress," December 1, 1862, in *Collected Works*, 4:195, 5:527-28.

If secession was equivalent to the disruption of a marriage, then civil war could hardly be less than the overthrow of gender itself. On Wise's logic, divided Americans could not avoid some uncomfortable reflection on gender roles in American society, not just as symbol but as reality. A house divided was literally a house whose meanings and roles were now being contested, and each individual within this divided American household would feel the impact of that challenge in a different way. For Southern slaveholders such as Wise, authority and fatherhood were the prerogatives of men, and the threat posed first by John Brown, then by Lincoln, and then by the invading Yankee armies was really a threat to strip slaveholders of their "fatherhood" over their slaves and their families. For the black males whom Wise enslaved, it offered the opportunity to assert a manhood and fatherhood that slavery had denied them. And as American men struggled to define themselves in the midst of civil war, American women likewise found a fresh series of opportunities to question what gender roles meant in the ambiguous context of a liberal democracy.[35]

From time out of mind in European societies, adult males had been assigned the primary role of providers and leaders. The combined risks and necessities of biological reproduction limited the mobility of women and restricted them, with few exceptions, to the subordinate role of caring for children, performing gender-based "women's work" (spinning, carding, butter making, sewing, making and mending clothes, storing and preparing food, making soap and candles, household cleaning), and yielding to the direction and authority of men. The twin dictatorship of tradition and biology gave husbands the role of command and women the role of support, and these were taken as verities from which no more appeal could be made than an appeal against the weather. In America, however, re-creating these ancient patterns of subordination, like the re-creation of other patterns of European social organization, had been neither easy nor straightforward. The disorientation and disorganization of migration frequently jumbled the boundaries of gender; on top of this, the turmoil of the Revolution and the Revolution's appeal to an equality of natural rights over traditional hierarchy rendered unquestioned male control over women much less easy to assume and much less legitimate in America.[36]

Yet it would be a grave mistake to overestimate the independence of women in the new republic. "It is needful," warned Catharine Beecher, the sister of Harriet Beecher Stowe, "that certain relations be sustained, which involve the duties of

---

35. LeAnn Whites, "The Civil War as a Crisis in Gender," in *Divided Houses: Gender and the Civil War*, ed. Catherine Clinton and Nina Silber (New York: Oxford University Press, 1992), 7, 11.

36. Rosemarie Zagarri, *Revolutionary Backlash: Women and Politics in the Early American Republic* (Philadelphia: University of Pennsylvania Press, 2007), 166–67.

subordination." That included "the relations of husband and wife, parent and child, teacher and pupil, employer and employed, each involving the relative duties of subordination." Otherwise, "Society could never go forward, harmoniously, nor could any craft or profession be successfully pursued, unless these superior and subordinate relations be instituted and sustained." American law continued to be guided by English common law until well into the nineteenth century, and under English common law, marriage very nearly meant the legal annihilation of a woman. Up to the point that an adult woman married, she suffered no special restrictions and could own property in the same way as men; once a woman was married, however, her property and property rights were automatically transferred to her husband, and she was permitted to own nothing in her own name. Married women could not make contracts, could not sue, could not write a will, and could not buy or sell, except over their husbands' signatures. The United States might be a liberal democracy, but it was a democracy of patriarchs, where adult males controlled public institutions and the organization of their families and spoke as their families' voices in their communities. The vast majority of black women in the republic were chattel slaves for whom the word *patriarch* had a much more ominous meaning. The small number of free black women occupied only the poorest rungs of the economic ladder, and many deliberately stayed unmarried in order to retain what few property rights they were entitled to.[37]

Still, the logic of democracy always agitated restlessly for more and greater liberty, independence, and property, and the intrusion of market capitalism joined hands with that logic. Attaching artificial power, especially in the form of the steam engine, to the manufacture of goods transformed laborers, who lived by raw physical strength, into operatives, who lived by tending machines, and machines could be tended by women as readily as by men. "The whirl and whiz of belts and clogs, all seemed like the greetings of cherished friends," declared the heroine of Charlotte Hillbourne's "factory girl" novel. "I wrote and sang and chatted, fearless of listening critics, and my daily invocations to Heaven's throne were heard only by the great Father, as they arose from my lips, while bending busily over my daily task."[38]

At the same time, men's work was increasingly transferred out of the home-based shop or farm and into commerce; the home ceased to be a productive unit over

37. Catharine Beecher, *A Treatise on Domestic Economy: For the Use of Young Ladies at Home, and at School* (Boston: T. H. Webb, 1843), 26; Toby Ditz, *Property and Kinship: Inheritance in Early Connecticut, 1750–1820* (Princeton, NJ: Princeton University Press, 1986), 119; Catharine Clinton, *The Other Civil War: American Women in the Nineteenth Century* (New York: Hill and Wang, 1984), 12–19; Suzanne Lebsock, *The Free Women of Petersburg: Status and Culture in a Southern Town, 1784–1800* (New York: W. W. Norton, 1984), 100–104.

38. Charlotte S. Hilbourne, *Effie and I: or, Seven Years in a Cotton Mill* (Cambridge, MA: Allen and Farnham, 1863), 67.

which they presided, and instead became a refuge from the cares and weariness of market competition—a refuge that wives erected as a solace for their battered husbands "to smoothe, to comfort and to heal." Men "go forth into the world, amidst the scenes of business" only to "behold every principle of justice and of honor, and even the dictates of common honesty disregarded, and the delicacy of our moral sense is wounded," wrote Sara Josepha Hale, the editor of the *Ladies' Magazine*, in 1830. In "the sanctuary of home," by contrast, women bestow "sympathy, honor, virtue," and "there disinterested love is ready to sacrifice every thing at the altar of affection. To render home happy, is woman's peculiar province."[39]

Two paths, then, opened up for American women in the decades before the Civil War: retreating more deeply into domestic life or demanding competitive personal rights for themselves in a market-oriented society where women's exclusion no longer made any workaday sense. In July 1848, a group of 200 women, led by Elizabeth Cady Stanton and Lucretia Mott, organized a women's rights convention at Seneca Falls, New York. The Declaration of Sentiments that the Seneca Falls convention adopted announced that "the history of mankind is a history of repeated injuries and usurpations on the part of man toward woman, having in direct object the establishment of an absolute tyranny over her," and they concluded by demanding what women in America had possessed in only one place since the Revolution (in New Jersey) and which they had not had at all since 1807—the right to vote. Two years later, they organized a National Women's Rights Convention, at which was denied

> the right of any portion of the species to decide for another portion, or of any individual to decide for another Individual what is and what is not their "proper sphere"; that the proper sphere for all human beings is the largest and highest to which they are able to attain; what this is, can not be ascertained without complete liberty of choice; woman, therefore, ought to choose for herself what sphere she will fill, what education she will seek, and what employment she will follow, and not be held bound to accept, in submission, the rights, the education, and the sphere which man thinks proper to allow her.[40]

Did this include marching to war? The most immediate test of any claim to civil equality would be the equality of the bayonet, since the most ancient and durable "proper sphere" was the one that shielded women from involvement in war and assigned to men the role of combatants. For that reason, the Civil War opened the

39. Sara Josepha Hale, "Home," *Ladies' Magazine and Literary Gazette* 3 (May 1830): 218; E. Anthony Rotundo, *American Manhood: Transformations in Masculinity from the Revolution to the Modern Era* (New York: Basic Books, 1993), 23–25; Louisa Susanna McCord, in O'Brien, *Conjectures of Order*, 1:278.

40. "Declaration of Sentiments" and "Second Worcester Convention, 1851—Resolutions," in Elizabeth Cady Stanton, Susan B. Anthony, and Matilda Joslyn Gage, *History of Woman Suffrage* (New York: Fowler and Wells, 1881), 1:70, 826; Clinton, *The Other Civil War*, 76.

risky question of what women—if they wanted that vote and the other civil rights which went with it—could or would do once the unsettled atmosphere of war settled over them. At the most basic level, the outbreak of the Civil War rallied the sectional patriotism of women fully as much as that of men. "The secession of Virginia is the work of her women," George Fitzhugh proclaimed in 1861. "With a prescience and a zeal surpassing that of men" and reminiscent of the "annals of Sparta," Southern women "urged on the present revolution, and . . . are now devoting all their energies and industry to clothe the soldier, to heal his wounds, to tend on him in sickness, and to relieve the wants of his family." Sarah Morgan of Baton Rouge, who kept one of the war's most interesting diaries, did not believe in secession, "but I do in Liberty. . . . The North cannot subdue us. We are too determined to be free."[41]

Some of that patriotism was mixed with the half-formed expectation that crossing over into the state of war meant entrance to a new social territory. "I've often longed to see a war," wrote Louisa May Alcott in April 1861, "and now I have my wish." For Alcott, war made her "long to be a man" and thus upset the entire hierarchy of gender values. "Felt very martial and Joan-of-Arc-y," Alcott wrote after a visit to Fort Warren in Boston harbor, "as I stood on the walls with the flag flying over me and cannon all about." The nineteen-year-old Morgan loathed "women who lounge through life, between the sofa and rocking chair with dear little dimpled hands that are never raised except to brush away a fly." The war excited Morgan to the point of anger at her confinement, and she wrote angrily, "If I was only a man! I don't know a woman here who does not groan over her misfortune in being clothed in petticoats; why can't we fight as well as the men?" Julia LeGrand, another prolific Confederate diary keeper, also chafed at the bonds of womanhood, and sighed against leading "the lives which women have led since Troy fell . . . while men, more privileged, are abroad and astir, making name and fortune and helping make a nation."[42]

Almost as an answer to that complaint, a number of American women managed to slip into direct roles in combat by donning men's clothing and volunteering for the armies as men (and given the lax medical examination processes, this turned out to be easier than it might seem). Some of these women, such as Lucy Matilda Thompson, were simply following lovers, husbands, or brothers who cooperated in the disguise: Thompson saw her husband enlist in the 18th North Carolina in 1861, and then "cut her thick hair close to her head, took up a few seams in one of her husband's suits, oiled her squirrel musket, and boarded a troop train for Virginia, under the name of 'Private Bill Thompson.'" Not until her husband was killed and she herself wounded in 1862 was Thompson discovered to be a woman and summarily

41. George Fitzhugh, "Women of the South," *DeBow's Review* 31 (August 1861): 147, 150; Sarah Morgan, *The Civil War Diary of Sarah Morgan*, ed. Charles East (Athens: University of Georgia Press, 1991), 74.

42. Louisa May Alcott, *The Journals of Louisa May Alcott*, ed. Joel Myerson and Daniel Shealy (Boston: Little, Brown, 1989), 105; *Civil War Diary of Sarah Morgan*, 77, 85; Marilyn Mayer Culpepper, *Trials and Triumphs: Women of the American Civil War* (Lansing: Michigan State University Press, 1991), 39.

discharged. For other women, the war offered an opportunity not to follow men but to evade them and to escape the restraints of custom imposed by a "proper sphere." Sara Emma Edmonds "was born into this world with some dormant antagonism toward man" and "longed to go forth and do" by killing "one rebel after another." Edmonds managed to serve, with or without male connivance, as a Union nurse, spy, and soldier, and the frontispiece illustration to her 1865 memoirs shows her booted and spurred (and skirted), with a hard-set jaw and a savage grip on her riding crop, ready to ride down any opposition—even from her readers.[43]

All told, between 250 and 400 women disguised as men found their way into either the Federal or Confederate armies. A variety of complications made their enlistments short ones. "There was a corporal taken sick on the picket line close by us the other night," wrote Henry Hunt of the 64th New York.

> . . . the corporal was taken to a house close by and before morning there was a little corporal in bed with her. It appears that she enlisted with her lover last fall and dressed in men[']s clothes and by some means deceived the doctor when examined and has been with the Army all winter and tented with her sweetheart.[44]

Others managed to elude detection and dismissal for considerable periods of time, some until the close of the war and beyond. Elizabeth Compton, a Canadian, enlisted seven different times under different names and with different male disguises, serving in the 125th Michigan for eighteen months in one instance before being detected. Jennie Hodgers was mustered into the 95th Illinois in 1862 as "Albert Cashier," survived forty battles and skirmishes, and continued to live as an honored male Civil War veteran until 1911, when an automobile accident disclosed his/her identity. Some women kept their secrets far longer than anyone expected. In 1934, a farmer near the old Shiloh battlefield unearthed nine human skeletons with bits of uniforms and buttons that identified them as soldiers; one of the skeletons was that of a woman.[45]

Other women managed to find near-military roles that gave them a place in uniform without necessarily putting a rifle in their hands. Zouave regiments, for instance, followed the French model by enlisting *vivandières*, uniformed women auxiliaries such as Mary Tebe of the 114th Pennsylvania, who followed her husband into the Army of the Potomac and kept store, collected the regimental wash, and ventured out under fire to bring water to the wounded. Kady Brownell of the 1st

---

43. John Anderson Richardson, *Richardson's Defense of the South* (Atlanta: A. B. Caldwell, 1914), 604; Sara Edmonds, *Nurse and Spy in the Union Army: The Adventures and Experiences of a Woman in Hospitals, Camps, and Battle-fields* (Philadelphia: W. S. Williams, 1865), 101.

44. Furgurson, *Chancellorsville 1863*, 32.

45. DeAnn Blanton and Lauren Cook, *They Fought Like Demons: Women Soldiers in the American Civil War* (Baton Rouge: Louisiana State University Press, 2002), 7; Richard Hall, *Patriots in Disguise: Women Warriors of the Civil War* (New York: Paragon House, 1993), 20–26, 100–101, 158, 161.

Rhode Island, Bridget Divers of the 1st Michigan Cavalry, and Annie Etheridge of the 3rd Michigan served in similar roles.

Women who could not manage a way into uniform could still find a direct military role as a spy. Precisely because social convention disconnected white women from the waging of war, it was easier for women to obtain and pass along military information without being suspected. Actress Pauline Cushman parlayed her acting talents into a series of elaborate ruses that allowed her to pry information out of admiring and complaisant Confederate officers; Belle Boyd used an equal measure of talent as a northern Virginia coquette to elide the same kinds of information out of Federal officers. At the other social extreme, African American women were also generally dismissed as militarily harmless, a miscalculation that Harriet Tubman and Sara Edmonds used to immense advantage. Tubman, who had escaped from slavery in Maryland twenty years before the war and who had amassed considerable experience venturing south to guide runaways to the North, undertook spying expeditions for the Federal troops on the Carolina Sea Islands. Edmonds colored her white skin with silver nitrate to penetrate the Confederate lines on the Peninsula in 1862. Whether in uniform or not, the war permitted these women to experiment with a series of dramatic and subversive role reversals in gender—and in Edmonds's case a reversal of both gender *and* race.[46]

None of these reversals was permanent, and most of them involved only the occasional acting out of a forbidden role within accepted male definitions of those roles. Despite the prediction of one Confederate commentator that "the beginning of our career as an independent nation . . . ought to be signalized by the beginning of a nobler, loftier career for women," by and large Union and Confederate women stayed within the traditional circle of women's "proper sphere" and turned their energies to the performance of war-related work defined as gender-appropriate. "As I can't fight," resolved Louisa May Alcott, "I will content myself with working for those who can." Doing war work could begin with acting as recruiting cheerleaders, pushing and shaming men into volunteering. Kate Cumming, a Confederate nurse, frankly told a lieutenant from the 24th Alabama that "a man did not deserve the name of a man, if he did not fight for his country; nor a woman, the name of woman, if she did not do all in her power to aid the men. . . . He had the candor to acquiescence in all I said." Sara Edmonds agreed that "the women down South are the best recruiting officers—for they absolutely refuse to tolerate, or admit to their society, any young man who refuses to enlist; and very often send their lovers, who have not enlisted, skirts and crinoline, with a note attached, suggesting the appropriateness

---

46. Edward J. Hagerty, *Collis' Zouaves: The 114th Pennsylvania Volunteers in the Civil War* (Baton Rouge: Louisiana State University Press, 1997), 94; Edward G. Longacre, *Custer and His Wolverines: The Michigan Cavalry Brigade, 1861–1865* (Conshohocken, PA: Combined Publishing, 1997), 23–24; L. C. Sizer, "Acting Her Part: Narratives of Union Women Spies," in *Divided Houses: Gender and the Civil War*, ed. Catherine Clinton and Nina Silber (New York: Oxford University Press, 1992), 127–30.

of such a costume unless they donned the Confederate uniform at once." A soldier in the 23rd North Carolina wrote home in August, 1861, to describe how "the La-dies" in a fellow-soldier's "naborhood had formed themselves in to Companyes and were drilling and said they would guard the young men that would not volunteer." Sometimes the encouragements to enlistment overlapped the boundaries of sexual innuendo: "None but the brave deserve the fair," a Charleston newspaper warned in 1861, and even Jefferson Davis urged Confederate women to prefer the "empty sleeve" of the wounded soldier to the "muscular arm" of the stay-at-home coward.[47]

"War work" also converted women's domestic skills to the national cause, par-ticularly for making clothes. In 1861, neither the North nor the South possessed the kind of large-scale clothing manufacturing that the immense numbers of en-listees required for uniforms, and the slack in uniform production had to be taken up by women at home. The Ladies Springfield Aid Society proudly reported in 1862 that it had sewn cotton shirts, drawers, socks, slippers, handkerchiefs, towels, pillow cases, and bandages, and still found time to pack off "large quantities of cornstarch, barley, tea, crackers, soap, jars, jellies, pickles, fruits. . . ." The Ladies Gunboat Fair in Charleston in 1862 was specifically designed to raise money to fund a building program for Confederate ironclads. Other aid organizations began demanding new and unprecedented levels of organization skill from women. In 1861, 3,000 New Yorkers organized the Women's Central Relief Association, and in a rare but grudg-ing concession, twelve women were elected to serve on the governing board of the association. Overall, as many as 20,000 aid societies, great and small, were set up and operating by the end of 1861; South Carolina and Alabama had a hundred each.[48]

As the war and the casualty lists lengthened, women received little in the way of reward for these sacrifices. Over time, the "war work" of recruitment and support required more and more sacrifice, especially in the South, where the sheer lack of resources drove most of the Southern aid societies out of business before the end of 1862. It made little sense to praise the moral influence of women when it became

---

47. "Education of Southern Women," *DeBow's Review* 31 (October/November 1861): 390; Alcott, *Journals*, 105; Kate Cumming, *Kate: The Journal of a Confederate Nurse*, ed. R. B. Harwell (Baton Rouge: Louisiana State University Press, 1959), 191–92; Edmonds, *Nurse and Spy*, 332; Leonidas Torrence to Sarah Ann Tor-rence, August 2, 1861, in "The Road to Gettysburg: The Diary and Letters of Leonidas Torrence of the Gaston Guards," ed. Haskell Monroe, *North Carolina Historical Review* 36 (October 1959): 481; Drew G. Faust, "Altars of Sacrifice: Confederate Women and the Narratives of War," in *Divided Houses: Gender and the Civil War*, ed. Catherine Clinton and Nina Silber (New York: Oxford University Press, 1992), 175–79.

48. "Christening the Palmetto State" (October 17, 1862), in *The Rebellion Record: A Diary of American Events*, ed. Frank Moore (New York: G. P. Putnam, 1862), 6:15; Julieanna Williams, "For Our Boys—The Ladies' Aid Societies," in *Valor and Lace: The Roles of Confederate Women*, ed. Mauriel P. Joslyn (Gretna, LA: Pelican, 2004), 25–30; Mary Elizabeth Massey, *Bonnet Brigades: American Women and the Civil War* (New York: Knopf, 1966), 34–35; Culpepper, *Trials and Triumphs*, 256, 258, 261; George Rable, *Civil Wars: Women and the Crisis of Southern Nationalism* (Urbana: University of Illinois Press, 1991), 139; Katharine Prescott Wormeley, *The Other Side of War: With the Army of the Potomac—Letters from the Headquarters of the United States Sanitary Commission During the Peninsular Campaign in Virginia in 1862* (Boston: Ticknor, 1889), 6.

increasingly clear that the immense distances covered by Civil War armies unstrung any effective notion of moral control over the men in uniform. Much as Union and Confederate women might try to transport the moral values of home to camp through letters (and the volume of letters to and from the Union army reached the astonishing level of 180,000 a day in 1862) or even to keep their influence more direct by visiting husbands in camp, it was soon apparent that they had little real power to deal with the camp visits of other kinds of women. The *Richmond Examiner* howled in dismay that "shame-faced prostitutes" were "disporting themselves extensively on the sidewalks, and in hacks, open carriages, etc." in the Confederate capital. Around the Army of the Potomac's camps near Washington, the number of prostitutes and camp followers mushroomed from 500 to 5,000 in 450 known brothels by 1862. The domestic "sanctuary" was all well and good, but not when the war transported men to more dubious localities.[49]

It also made little sense to talk about choosing one's "proper sphere" when subsistence itself was becoming the necessity. The simple absence of men from farms and shops forced the wives they had left behind to shift for themselves, whether that was the "sphere" they wanted or not. Although local and state governments made generous promises of support for soldiers' families, little of that support was ever forthcoming in meaningful quantities. Bereft of the men who formed the traditional center of patriarchal authority, women had to improvise new ways of organizing their lives. Women who had defined their lives by domestic work inside the house now found themselves behind the plow in the fields. "Most of the women around here who live on farms have to do all their work alone, their husbands being in the army," wrote a curious soldier in Tennessee. "I got some butter the other day of a woman who has six little children and a place of fifty acres which she has cultivated alone and supported herself and children besides. Don't you think this is doing pretty well for one woman?"[50]

Perhaps it was, but the satisfaction these women derived from "doing pretty well" had to be balanced against the incessant grind of dread and anxiety over the fate of their husbands, brothers, and sons. When those fears culminated at last in the news of death in battle, the results could range from raw stoicism to outright derangement. Mary Chesnut's friend Colonel John Hugh Means was killed at Antietam; Means's wife lay down, covered her face, and a little while after, when "she remained quiet so long, someone removed the light shawl which she had drawn over her head. She was dead." Is it any wonder, Chesnut asked, that "so many women die? Grief and constant anxiety kill nearly as many women as men die on the battlefield."[51]

---

49. E. Susan Barber, "Depraved and Abandoned Women: Prostitution in Richmond, Virginia, Across the Civil War," in *Neither Lady nor Slave: Working Women of the Old South*, ed. Susanna Delfino and Michele Gillespie (Chapel Hill: University of North Carolina Press, 2002), 163–65; Thomas P. Lowry, *The Story the Soldiers Wouldn't Tell: Sex in the Civil War* (Mechanicsburg, PA: Stackpole, 1994), 68.

50. Culpepper, *Trials and Triumphs*, 266.

51. Ibid., 126, 264; diary entries for June 9, 1862 and September 23, 1863, in Mary Chesnut, *Mary Chesnut's Civil War*, ed. C. Vann Woodward (New Haven, CT: Yale University Press, 1981), 371, 426.

The toll that privation, dislocation, and death took on the loyalty of women was especially severe in the South. Unlike Northerners, women in the Confederacy had to deal with invasion and occupation, including everything from vandalism by unruly Federal soldiers to conflicts with restless slaves. As early as the summer of 1861, Kate Stone noticed that "the house servants have been giving a lot of trouble lately—lazy and disobedient." Ada Bacot tried to run her South Carolina plantation after the death of her husband, but she found her slaves "disregarded" her "orders . . . more & more every day"; one teenaged slave was "so impertinent" that Bacot lost all self-control and "slaped him in the mouth before I knew what I did." But the relationships were not always ones of white dominance. In the absence of their menfolk, some Southern white women found comfort in sexual "connection" with their slaves. "I will tell you a fact that I have never seen alluded to publicly," reported Richard J. Hinton, a British-born officer in a Kansas "colored" regiment, "that there is a large amount of intercourse between white women and colored men." Wartime testimony before the American Freedman's Inquiry Commission about amours between male slaves and mistresses was so shocking that the commission eliminated thirty-two pages of it from its printed proceedings.[52]

In some instances, Confederate women put up spirited resistance to the Union occupation forces. Peter Osterhaus, a Prussian-born Federal general in the Army of the Tennessee, was asked by a Mississippi woman if he wouldn't make war on women and children; he replied that as far as he could see, "the women carried on this war. He had intercepted many a letter from the young ladies in which they urged their lovers to fight well and never give up." After Baton Rouge fell to Federal forces in 1862, Sarah Morgan and her sister Antoinette made small Confederate flags for themselves; Morgan "put the stem in my belt, pinned the flag to my shoulder, and walked down town, creating great excitement among women & children" and among the Federal occupation troops. When Confederate cavalry stampeded in panic through Winchester, Virginia, in 1864, "a large number of the most respected ladies joined hands & formed a line across the principal street, telling the cowardly Cavalrymen that they should not go any further unless they ran their horses over their bodies." Beholding the Winchester women from the Union perspective, one Union general sneered that "Hell is not full enough, there must be more of these Secession women of Winchester to full it up."[53]

---

52. Diary entry for June 29, 1861, in Kate Stone, *Brokenburn: The Journal of Kate Stone, 1861–1868*, ed. John Q. Anderson (1955; Baton Rouge: Louisiana State University Press, 1995), 33; Drew G. Faust, *Mothers of Invention: Women of the Slaveholding South in the American Civil War* (Chapel Hill: University of North Carolina Press, 1996), 62; Martha Hodes, *White Women, Black Men: Illicit Sex in the Nineteenth-Century South* (New Haven, CT: Yale University Press, 1997), 126–27, 146.

53. *The Civil War Diary of Sarah Morgan*, 67; *The Civil War Memoirs of Captain William J. Seymour: Reminiscences of a Louisiana Tiger*, 142; Rable, *Civil Wars: Women and the Crisis of Southern Nationalism*, 74, 80, 84, 101, 140, 171; Larry B. Maier, *Gateway to Gettysburg: The Second Battle of Winchester* (Shippensburg, PA: Burd Street Press), 71.

In New Orleans, Confederate women grew so hostile and malevolent in their behavior that the occupation commander, Benjamin Butler, issued a general order that threatened that "when any female shall by word, gesture, or movement, insult or show contempt for any officer or soldier of the United States, she shall be regarded and held liable to be treated as a woman of the town plying her avocation"—in other words, a prostitute. Butler's proclamation was ill-timed and even more ill-worded—it even aroused unfavorable comment in the British Parliament—but it did underscore Butler's frustration with women who refused to behave passively in the face of male conquest. What Butler failed to see behind the contempt the New Orleans women had for Yankee soldiers was the corresponding contempt they nurtured for the Confederate men who had abandoned them to Butler's unkind embrace, and what Butler's proclamation unwittingly underscored for Confederate women was how exposed and undefended the Confederacy had left them in their hour of peril. Poorer women who were not quite on the same social level as the "respected ladies" of Winchester stated their disgust more frankly. "The men of Atlanta have brought an everlasting stain on their name," wrote Julia Davidson, an angry Georgia farm wife. "Instead of remaining to defend their homes, they have run off and left Atlanta to be defended by an army of women and children. . . . God help us for there is no help in man."[54]

For that reason, by 1862, fewer Confederate women were lending their aid to recruitment duties, or sending their men off willingly. Some were refusing to keep up farms, and others were demanding that the Confederate government return their men. In many cases, Southern farm women and planters' wives were forced to rely on male slaves to run their farms and plantations for them, which in most cases dangerously loosened the bonds of slave discipline. The Confederate Congress responded sluggishly with a series of conscription exemptions designed to keep the most critically needed men at the most critical jobs. But many of the exemptions, especially the infamous "twenty-nigger law," only fanned the resentment of the yeoman classes without doing much to improve the South's chances.

As the blockade further pinched Southern resources, even the wealthiest Southern women were besieged with the need to economize, while the yeoman farmers slipped into outright poverty. "We are all in a sadly molting condition," wrote Mary Chesnut in the fall of 1863. "We had come to the end of our good clothes in three

---

54. E. R. McKinley, diary entry for September 9, 1863, in *From the Pen of a She-Rebel: The Civil War Diary of Emilie Riley McKinley*, ed. Gordon Cotton (Columbia: University of South Carolina Press, 2001), 48; "General Orders No. 28," May 13, 1862, in *War of the Rebellion*, Series One, 25:426; Dick Nolan, *Benjamin Franklin Butler: The Damnedest Yankee* (Novato, CA: Presidio, 1991), 177.

years, and now our only resource was to turn them upside down or inside out—mending, darning, patching." George Washington Whitman was amazed at the wretched conditions he found among the once prosperous farms of northern Virginia in 1862: "The villages we have passed through are the most God forsaken places I ever saw, the people seem to have next to nothing to eat as the men have all gone in the Secesh army, and how they are going to get through the winter I dont know."[55]

Southern women were being forced to assume roles of independence for which they had little preparation, and the independence that events foisted on them was not always with the kind of independence they might have welcomed. At the same time, however, Southern men were becoming ever more critically dependent on the women for supplies of food from the fields and clothing from the home. The bargain of "proper" spheres was turning upside down as the Confederacy weakened, and Southern women, far from rallying round the flag, now turned on Confederate men in rage. "I am so sick of trying to do a man's business," complained Elizabeth Neblett to her soldier-husband in 1863. "I have a great mind to get Morphine & take it, see if I will not be happier. . . . If it shortens my life, it will be an end most devoutly wished."[56]

These mutterings of disloyalty came mostly from Confederate women who stayed put; a far darker kind of misery awaited those who tried to turn refugee. As early as 1862, Federal invasions of northern Virginia and Tennessee were dislodging large numbers of Southerners, mostly women whose men had left for the army and who feared the unlovely rule of Yankee occupiers, and mostly those with slaves who feared that their slaves could not be relied upon anywhere near the Northern armies. Over the course of the war, nearly 250,000 Southerners fled from the battle zones to areas deeper within the Confederacy. Taken together with the flight of blacks in the other direction and with the three million men sucked up into the whirlwind of the armies as they crossed state after state and river after river, the Civil War produced a demographic disruption all across the eastern half of North America that had no equal in the American memory.[57]

Nor did the problems stop once Southerners had gotten away to a reasonable distance from the Yankee invaders. Once removed, refugee planters who had dragged

---

55. *Mary Chesnut's Civil War*, 459; *Civil War Letters of George Washington Whitman*, 73.

56. Escott, *After Secession*, 120–21; 150, 151; Elizabeth Neblett, diary-letter for August 28, 1863, in *A Rebel Wife in Texas: The Diary and Letters of Elizabeth Scott Neblett, 1852–1864*, ed. Erika L. Muir (Baton Rouge: Louisiana State University Press, 2001), 150, 151.

57. Rable, *Civil Wars: Women and the Crisis of Southern Nationalism*, 183; Stephen V. Ash, *When the Yankees Came: Conflict and Chaos in the Occupied South, 1861–1865* (Chapel Hill: University of North Carolina Press, 1995), 247.

their slaves along with them had no work for the slaves to do and no income from cotton planting to feed them. In order to earn money from their slaves, refugee planters hired them out in record numbers to public and private war industries, as teamsters, ironworkers, and even "nitre diggers." This, in turn, only further destabilized the slave work regimen. As slaves moved out of the plantation environment and into the wider boundaries of urban employment for cash, the old systems of supervision broke down, while wartime conditions made it impossible to develop a new work system to absorb the sudden influx of industrial slaves.[58]

Even without the excess baggage of slaves, Southern women refugees found the incessant string of moves from one unfamiliar place to another, or from one increasingly reluctant brace of relatives to another, to be a counsel of despair. The longer the war rolled on, the more all trace of Southern civic life disappeared, as individual survival became the paramount concern. Sarah Morgan and her family fled Baton Rouge under a barrage of Union shells to seek refuge on a plantation near Port Hudson; when the war came up to Port Hudson, they fled again to Lake Pontchartrain, and then finally into occupied New Orleans, where Sarah was sheltered under the roof of her Unionist half-brother. "Give me my home, my old home once more," she lamented, in what could have been the words of every Confederate woman tossed in the tornado of destruction and disappointed expectations for their own womanhood. "O my home, my home! I could learn to be a woman there, and a true one, too. Who will teach me now?"[59]

As the war forced women into new and unaccustomed roles, it simultaneously undermined women's notions of their reliance on men, and introduced them to new views of their own capacities. This was particularly true for women who stepped into the void created by the army medical services' miserable unpreparedness for handling the frightful casualties of Civil War battlefields. Women had been assigned to so many domestic roles related to caregiving that it required only the shortfall in male medical personnel before women began to volunteer themselves as nurses, and in a few cases, such as that of Union army surgeon Mary Walker, as doctors. Before the 1850s, army medicine, like the army itself, had been the preserve of male doctors and male nurses, and women could scarcely find opportunity for medical education in the United States, much less an opening for medical practice.[60]

The work of Florence Nightingale during the Crimean War had cracked that particular wall of gender separation down to its foundations, and Nightingale

58. Clarence Mohr, *On the Threshold of Freedom: Masters and Slaves in Civil War Georgia* (Athens: University of Georgia Press, 1985), 113, 118, 153–57; Mary Elizabeth Massey, *Refugee Life in the Confederacy* (Baton Rouge: Louisiana State University Press, 2001 [1964]), 29, 37, 249; Rubin, *A Shattered Nation*, 64–68; Nelson and Sheriff, *A People at War*, 264–67; Drew G. Faust, "Altars of Sacrifice: Confederate Women and the Narratives of War," *Journal of American History* 76 (March 1990): 1213–14.

59. Diary entry for March 10, 1863, *The Civil War Diary of Sarah Morgan*, 435.

60. Nelson and Sheriff, *A People at War*, 116–19.

became the stepping-stone for a small number of American women to open up military nursing to women volunteers. Not surprisingly, female nurses were at first not welcomed by the doddering army medical establishments. "There is scarcely a day passes that I do not hear some derogatory remarks about the ladies who are in hospitals, until I think, if there is any credit due them at all, it is for the moral courage they have in braving public opinion," wrote Kate Cumming in 1863. But the administrative record soon carved out by Dorothea Dix as the superintendent of army nurses in the North, by Captain Sally Tomkins and her Richmond hospital, and by U.S. Sanitary Commission nurses on the Federal hospital ships on the western rivers soon dampened the carping. Tompkins, the sister of a Confederate colonel, opened her own private hospital for 1,330 Confederate soldiers in Richmond and managed to evade bureaucratic efforts to incorporate her hospital into the army hospital system by obtaining a captain's commission from Jefferson Davis. She was "original, old fashioned and tireless in well doing," recalled Thomas De Leon, ". . . as simple as a child and as resolute as a veteran."[61]

What was far more discouraging to women nurses was the appalling slaughter churned up by battle, and the dirt and incompetence that pervaded the army medical services. When Cornelia Hancock and a group of army nurses caught up with the Army of the Potomac at Fredericksburg in 1864, they walked into an abandoned church that the army had converted into a hospital. There "the scene beggared all description." The two male surgeons with them "were paralyzed by what they saw," Hancock wrote home, for "rain had poured in through the bullet-riddled roofs of the churches until our wounded lay in pools of water made bloody by their seriously wounded condition." Louisa May Alcott, who nursed briefly in a military hospital in Georgetown before falling dangerously ill, described her hospital as a "perfect pestilence-box . . . cold, damp, dirty, full of vile odors from wounds, kitchens, wash rooms, & stables." By the end of the war, only 3,200 women had actually served as nurses in the armies, not more than a fifth of the overall number of military nurses.

Rather than take the risks posed by nursing, far more women found their ways to new jobs in Northern and Southern textile mills, hurriedly manufacturing cartridges, clothing, and military equipment under the wide umbrella of government war contracts. The absence of men also created a gap in teaching, another previously all-male profession that now began to admit women, and the explosive growth in government paperwork opened up employment for women in government and Treasury offices. By the end of the war, the U.S. Treasury was employing 447 "treasury girls" as copyists and currency counters.[62]

61. Cumming, *Kate: The Journal of a Confederate Nurse*, 178; David B. Sabine, "Captain Sally Tompkins," *Civil War Times Illustrated* 4 (November 1965): 36–39; Thomas De Leon, *Belles, Beaux and Brains of the 60's* (New York: G. W. Dillingham, 1907), 389.

62. Cornelia Hancock, *South After Gettysburg: Letters of Cornelia Hancock, 1863–1868*, ed. H. S. Jaquette (New York: T. Y. Crowell, 1956), 92; Alcott, *Journals*, 114; Victoria E. Ott, *Confederate Daughters: Coming of Age During the Civil War* (Carbondale: Southern Illinois University Press, 2008), 95–96; Nina Silber, *Daughters of the Union: Northern Women Fight the Civil War* (Cambridge, MA: Harvard University Press, 2005), 79; Nelson and Sheriff, *A People at War*, 242.

What is not clear is whether these new opportunities, however much satisfaction they gave, opened any new windows for redefining political or social power for women. Many of the wartime positions available to women were as replacements for men, and those positions often disappeared as soon as the war was over and the men returned. It was only at incidental moments that a real departure for women and genuine movement toward gender equality took shape. In 1863, a core group of women veterans of the Seneca Falls convention organized a Women's National Loyal League, which took as its primary object the creation of a massive petition drive in support of an amendment to the Constitution that would abolish slavery as a legal institution. That, in turn, became the organizational platform from which Elizabeth Cady Stanton and Susan B. Anthony launched a parallel movement in 1866, the American Equal Rights Association, to ensure a similar constitutional amendment which would grant voting rights to women.

The only real weapons Stanton and Anthony had at their disposal were petitions and persuasion, and they gained little ground against the entrenched legal restraints that deprived women in many states not only of the vote but also of the most basic republican privilege, property ownership. Mary Ashton Livermore, who had already carved out a prominent career as a reformer and editor of a religious magazine in the 1850s, turned her organizing talents to private fund-raising for the United States Sanitary Commission during the war. When she attempted to sign a contract for constructing the fairgrounds for the 1863 Northwestern Sanitary Fair in Chicago, however, she was politely informed that no contract with her signature on it had any legal standing, even if she paid the contractors in cash. Only her husband's signature carried any standing in Illinois law. "By the laws of the state in which we lived, our individual names were not worth the paper on which they were written." In the face of this legal stonewalling and the demand to combine gender and racial civil rights, Stanton and Anthony were unable to hold their equal-rights movement together, and the drive fractured into a radical wing led by Stanton and Anthony (which continued to press for a national constitutional amendment) and a moderate wing led by Mary Livermore and Henry Ward Beecher (which wanted to limit the campaign to what could be accomplished in state legislatures). None of them lived to see American women gain the right to vote in 1920.[63]

The war brought changes to American women, but only some changes and only to some women. In the confusion caused by the war, both the number of women

63. Mary Ashton Livermore, *My Story of the War: A Woman's Narrative of Four Years Personal Experience* (New York: Arno Press, 1972 [1889]), 435–36; Wendy Hamand Venet, *Neither Ballots nor Bullets: Women Abolitionists and the Civil War* (Charlottesville: University of Virginia Press, 1991), 154–55.

who left the domestic sphere to find work in the field, the government office, or the hospital and the number of jobs that women were admitted to be capable of doing increased. But the war that had made this movement possible also doomed its further growth, since so much of this work was the creature of the war itself. The legal structure of restraints on women remained unchanged, and once the war was over, the tide of women's advance into new realms of work and life receded to its prewar boundaries. This retreat was reinforced by a certain measure of class as well as gender expectations. Black women and lower-class white women had never been part of the domestic expectation, and both had always worked outside the domestic boundary; only the national emergency of the war sanctioned the movement of upper- and middle-class white women in the same outward direction. Once that emergency was over, the class bias of women's work reasserted itself, and women's work outside the family circle reclaimed its stigma of being "poor folks' work."

The Civil War represented neither advance nor retreat for American women, but only a moment of unspeakable turbulence when all the customary handholds disappeared and men and women were forced to find new ways through the storm of conflict. For Clara Barton, who made her Civil War nursing career the foundation for organizing the International Red Cross, the war meant a gain of what Barton estimated to be "fifty years in advance of the normal position which continued peace . . . would have assigned her." For Susan B. Anthony, the postwar crusader for women's rights, the war actually stifled most of the progress women had made toward winning the right to vote. It was "the crime of the ages" for the United States to fight "for national supremacy over the states to enslave & disenfranchise—and then refuse to exercise that power on behalf of half the people." Barton and Anthony looked at the war from two very different angles, and perhaps neither were entirely right or, as another generation would demonstrate, entirely wrong.[64]

A "UNION ALWAYS SWARMING WITH BLATHERERS"

By the fall of 1863, the Civil War had taken on new and unexpected shapes for all Americans. The political goals of the war had expanded for both Northerners and Southerners, from simple reunion to emancipation in the Northern case, and from simple secession to the forging of a new Confederate nation in the South. The added turmoil of moving millions of people out of their homes and out of the accustomed tracks of their lives, and the relentlessly-lengthening casualty lists threatened to break up and disorganize an entire generation of American lives. After two years of dislocation, shock, and carnage, Americans were groping in exhaustion for the

64. Stephen B. Oates, *A Woman of Valor: Clara Barton and the Civil War* (New York: Free Press, 1994), 377–79; Anthony to Clara Barton, September 14, 1881, in *The Selected Papers of Elizabeth Cady Stanton and Susan B. Anthony*, vol. IV: *When Clowns Make Laws for Queens, 1880–1887*, ed. Ann D. Gordon (New Brunswick, NJ: Rutgers University Press, 2006), 49.

meaning and purpose of the war that would give them some idea of why the war was being fought. For those answers they turned to the philosophers, moralists, and clergymen who constituted the intellectual elite of the American republic and made it what Walt Whitman cheerfully described as a "Union always swarming with blatherers."[65]

America was the offspring of movements of the mind, and the South was not the only place in American life where the Enlightenment was enmeshed in the challenge of the Romantics. The most formidable reply to the burden of Enlightenment reason came from Immanuel Kant, and it is from Kant's formulations of a "transcendent" realm of knowledge that Northern Romantics formulated a critique of Enlightenment politics. Kant's foremost American admirer was Ralph Waldo Emerson, a former Unitarian clergyman who had abandoned the ministry to take up a life of writing and lecturing across the country. Around Emerson clustered the crown jewels of Boston's Romantic intellect—Henry Hedge, George Putnam, Margaret Fuller, George Ripley, Orestes Brownson, and Bronson Alcott—whom Emerson styled as Transcendentalists, "from the use of that term by Immanuel Kant, of Konigsberg, who replied to the skeptical philosophy of Locke." The Transcendentalists found the "buzz and din" of democratic politics distasteful. They withdrew from an engagement with democratic political culture and celebrated a radical individualism built upon "self-reliance" and "self-culture." That, in turn, gave them little to admire and still less to understand about a civil war in a democracy. Emerson wanted "to insulate the individual—to surround him with barriers of natural respect, so that each man shall feel the world as his, and man shall treat man with as a sovereign state with a sovereign state," and he held himself aloof from even the most pressing reform movements.[66]

Few of the Transcendentalists bothered their heads with abolition; Emerson, in particular, had been notoriously slow to embrace the anti-slavery cause, not so much from indifference to the moral question at stake as from his reluctance to imbrue his hands in politics. "Society gains nothing whilst a man, not himself renovated, attempts to renovate things around him." Slavery he opposed, but largely out of the Kantian conviction that slavery was a denial of human authenticity (or free will). With the firing on Fort Sumter, Emerson was surprised almost in spite of himself with how "a sentiment mightier than logic, wide as light, strong as gravity, reaches into the college, the bank, the farm-house, and the church" and was sweeping up even the most detached and self-reliant minds up in a "whirlwind of patriotism." Still, few New England intellectuals stayed for long within that whirlwind. Rather than seeing the war as the test of liberalism's virtues, the Romantic historian Francis

65. Walt Whitman, "By Blue Ontario's Shore," in *Leaves of Grass* (Philadelphia: Rees, Welsh, 1882), 467.

66. Ralph Waldo Emerson, "The Transcendentalist," in *The Selected Writings of Ralph Waldo Emerson*, ed. Brooks Atkinson (New York: Modern Library, 1950), 93; Emerson, "The American Scholar," in *Representative Men: Nature, Addresses and Lectures* (Boston: Houghton Mifflin, 1883), 112.

Parkman thought that the war had exposed "the fallacies of ultra democracy," and though he supported the war, it was more for the opportunities it gave young New England blue bloods to demonstrate the individual virtues of heroism, fortitude, and manliness.[67] The death of Robert Gould Shaw at Battery Wagner, for instance, was seen less as a blow for racial justice and more as proof that Boston's wealthy mercantile elite had not grown stagnant and effeminate.

> Here is her witness: this, her perfect son,
> This delicate and proud New England soul
> Who leads despisèd men, with just-unshackled feet,
> Up the large ways where death and glory meet,
> To show all peoples that our shame is done,
> That once more we are clean and spirit-whole.[68]

Some Romantic intellectuals even hoped that the Civil War would burst the bubble of Americans' overweened confidence in democracy and lead to the replacement of democratic turbulence with a more orderly and organic notion of society—with themselves as the acknowledged elite. In New York, George Templeton Strong condemned Americans' preoccupation with "democracy and equality and various other phantasms" and hoped that they "will be dispersed and dissipated and will disappear forever" in the face of civil war. America required the discipline of a strong government, and Charles Stillé, a lawyer and later provost of the University of Pennsylvania, blamed much of the North's inability to bring the war to a swift conclusion on the discord of democratic politics, "which seems to be the sad but invariable attendant upon all political discussions in a free government, corrupting the very sources of public life. . . ."[69]

Romanticism, however, was not the only optic of Northern intellectuals, and no one looked less like a Romantic than Abraham Lincoln. Although he was a politician rather than a philosopher, Lincoln was nevertheless very directly the child of the Enlightenment, of the Declaration and the Constitution. Lincoln argued down slavery by an appeal to the "sacred principles of the laws of nature," and hailed "the constitution and the laws" as "hewn from the solid quarry of sober reason." For Lincoln, the

67. James Elliot Cabot, *A Memoir of Ralph Waldo Emerson* (Boston: Houghton Mifflin, 1888), 2:600; Robert D. Richardson, *Emerson: The Mind on Fire* (Berkeley: University of California Press, 1995), 395; George M. Fredrickson, *The Inner Civil War: Northern Intellectuals and the Crisis of the Union* (New York: Harper and Row, 1965), 55–56, 65–66, 141–44; Wilbur R. Jacobs, *Francis Parkman, Historian as Hero: The Formative Years* (Austin: University of Texas Press, 1991), 128–29.

68. William Vaughn Moody, "An Ode in Time of Hesitation," in *The Columbia Book of Civil War Poetry: From Whitman to Walcott*, ed. Richard Marius (New York: Columbia University Press, 1994), 133.

69. Strong, diary entry for November 29, 1860, in *Diary of the Civil War*, 6; Charles J. Stillé, "How a Free People Conduct a Long War: A Chapter from English History," in *Union Pamphlets of the Civil War*, 1:89.

war was a test of the practical worth of liberalism—of whether ordinary people of any race were entitled by nature to govern themselves and create their own governments, and whether that government could be content with allowing those people to pursue their own self-interest and self-improvement. The great offense of slavery was that it forbade self-interest and self-improvement—the interests of the slave counted for nothing, and the improvement of one segment of society would throw the others (starting with the slaveholders) dangerously out of kilter; the great offense of secession was that it was, in reality, nothing but a malevolent attempt to disrupt a constitutional order that encouraged all people, irrespective of race, to pursue that interest and that improvement. "On the side of the Union," Lincoln said,

> it is a struggle for maintaining in the world, that form, and substance of government, whose leading object is, to elevate the condition of men—to lift artificial weights from all shoulders—to clear the paths of laudable pursuit for all—to afford all, an unfettered start, and a fair chance, in the race of life.[70]

The fall of 1863 gave Lincoln a perfect opportunity to articulate that understanding of the war when the commonwealth of Pennsylvania, following the battle at Gettysburg, arranged for the reburial of Gettysburg dead in a new cemetery at the center of the battlefield. Lincoln was invited by the organizers to deliver "a few appropriate remarks" at the dedication ceremonies in Gettysburg on November 19, 1863. He was not the featured speaker—that honor went to the former president of Harvard, Edward Everett, who launched into an oration two and a half hours long—and he needed to do no more in his remarks than is done when a bottle of champagne is cracked over a ship's bow at its launch. He was respectful enough of the scope of that assignment to limit himself to only 272 words. In those words, Lincoln nevertheless managed to justify the ways of democracy more eloquently than anyone, then or now.[71]

Lincoln reached in his first sentence to the Declaration of Independence for authority: "Fourscore and seven years ago, our fathers brought forth on this continent a new nation, conceived in Liberty, and dedicated to the proposition that all men are created equal." By "equal" he meant not a predetermined result but rather an equal starting point in the eyes of law and government, a common point from which any man could make himself. The idea that a nation could be founded on a *proposition* was ludicrous to the Romantic reactionaries of nineteenth-century Europe, and they were not reluctant to point to the Civil War as proof that attempting to build a government around something as bloodless and logical as a proposition was futile.

70. Lincoln, "Address Before the Young Men's Lyceum of Springfield, Illinois," January 27, 1838, "Resolutions in Behalf of Hungarian Freedom," January 9, 1852, "Fragment on Slavery," July 1, 1854, and "Message to Congress in Special Session," July 4, 1861, in *Collected Works*, 1:115, 2:116, 222, 4: 438.

71. Frank L. Klement, "'These Honored Dead': David Wills and the Soldiers' Cemetery at Gettysburg," in *The Soldiers' Cemetery and Lincoln's Address* (Shippensburg, PA: White Mane, 1993), 10.

Lincoln accepted that challenge: the war indeed would be the test of whether "that nation or any nation so conceived and so dedicated can long endure," or whether democracies, wobbling around on the stilts of a proposition about equality, were doomed to self-destruction the moment a sizable minority decided it had no desire to abide by the will of a majority's decision. The sacrifices of Gettysburg, Shiloh, Murfreesboro, Chancellorsville, and a hundred other places demonstrated otherwise, that men would die rather than lose hold of that proposition. Reflecting on that dedication, the living should themselves experience a new birth of freedom, a determination—and he drove his point home with a deliberate evocation of the great Whig orator Daniel Webster—"that government of the people, by the people, for the people, shall not perish from the earth."[72]

The Republican newspapers heartily applauded it: the address was a "brief but immortal speech," editorialized John W. Forney's *Philadelphia Press.* The Democratic papers, predictably, spurned it as "mere trash" and "unworthy of comment."[73]

Southern intellectuals had a very different task: to demonstrate that the South really was a cultural world unto itself. Offering up the proof of a unique Southern cultural identity would make it easier to justify a separate Southern political regime, and that would build consensus behind the battle lines and shore up popular support for the Confederate government, even when that government undertook policy initiatives, from military conscription to economic nationalization, which seemed to contradict the immediate reasons the Southern states had seceded from the Union in the first place. By discovering and revealing the outlines of a distinctively Southern culture, Confederate intellectuals would create the rock around which the changing tides of war would splash in vain.

They certainly had the appetite for this task. Although the South had fewer resources to support them and fewer magazines and quarterlies for platforms, an intellectual network based on James Henry Hammond and William Gilmore Simms of South Carolina, Henry Hughes of Mississippi, Josiah Clark Nott of Alabama, and the Virginians Nathaniel Beverley Tucker, Thomas Roderick Dew, George Fitzhugh, and George Frederick Holmes provided the backbone of Southern intellectual life. It also embraced the novelists Augusta Jane Evans, Caroline Gilman, Augustus Baldwin Longstreet (the uncle of Confederate general James Longstreet), and John Pendleton Kennedy, the poets Edgar Allan Poe and Paul Hamilton Hayne. Their writing crowded into the four principal Southern journals, the *Southern Quarterly Review*, *DeBow's Review*, the *Southern Literary Messenger*, and the *Southern Review.*[74]

72. Lincoln, "Address Delivered at the Dedication of the Cemetery at Gettysburg," November 19, 1863, in *Collected Works*, 7:23.

73. Joseph George, "The World Will Little Note? The Philadelphia Press and the Gettysburg Address," *Pennsylvania Magazine of History and Biography* 114 (July 1990): 394–96.

74. Drew Gilpin Faust, *A Sacred Circle: The Dilemma of the Intellectual in the Old South, 1840–1860* (Baltimore: Johns Hopkins University Press, 1977), 83–84; O'Brien, *Conjectures of Order*, 1:531, 2:747–48.

Southern intellectuals tapped the energy of a long-festering resentment at the condescension shown them in the prewar decades by Northern publishers and editors. "The true gentleman was educated at a Northern college, wore clothing made at the North or imported by the North, employed a Northern teacher, male or female, listened to a Yankee parson, and read Northern books, magazines and newspapers," complained *DeBow's Review* in the heady summer of 1861. "We have been in a state of pupilage, and never learned to walk alone." If only Southerners would shake off this Yankee-induced "pupilage," they would realize that they actually possessed a distinct and self-defining culture of their own. This culture was built upon the fundamental (and Romantic) realization that nations are made not by adherence to propositions but by the cultivation of an ineluctable but palpable national character.[75]

The great error of the Enlightenment was that (as Thomas Dew explained in 1853) in their enthusiasm for reason, "the philosophers and encyclopaedists published their theories and principles without daring to apply them. . . . Their investigations, consequently, became eminently *Utopian*. Every principle was pushed out to its greatest extent,—the speculation of the philosopher was not hampered at each step by the difficulty of practical application. These abstract speculations were like theoretic mechanics, who sit in their closets and contemplate diagrams and figures, representing levers, pulleys, &c, with all the accuracy of mathematic precision." The result, of course, was that when "the French revolution came, and the evils of government were at last to be corrected, unfortunately for France, there was nothing but this Utopian philosophy to shed light on the path of the revolution," and the result was not government of, by or for the people, but the Reign of Terror.[76]

Rather than worship reason, Southerners "accept as true the faith of our fathers, believe in the authority of the Bible, attested by the voice of the civilized world for almost two thousand years; heed and respect the lessons of history, ancient and profane, and pursue no Utopias that promise to change man's nature, his social habitudes, and his inequalities of condition, because we believe in nature and in nature's God." Societies could never be built from the sort of grasping, advantage-calculating individuals who populated the North. "The world has seen many instances of governments devised on theoretical principles, mainly with a view to the security of equal rights," wrote Nathaniel Beverly Tucker of the College of William & Mary, but "how these have succeeded, history and the present abject condition of those countries which were the subjects of those experiments, show but too plainly." The true basis of society was the community, not the individual and the individual's

---

75. "The Future of Our Confederacy," *DeBow's Review* 31 (July 1861): 40.

76. Thomas Dew, *A Digest of the Laws, Customs, Manners, and Institutions of the Ancient and Modern Nations* (New York: D. Appleton, 1853), 587.

rights. "One of the principal ends of the establishment of government is to provide, in the collective responsibility of the whole, a substitute for the responsibility of the individual. . . ."[77]

Still, Southern intellectuals stalled on the same fundamental issue that had dogged Southern society from the start: slavery. Was slavery of the essence of the South, woven into the warp and woof of its cultural fabric so completely that any description of the South must also be a description of the slave system? Or was slavery merely an economic accident, a superficial aspect of a more profound, underlying organism of Southern culture? The intellectuals' answer, surprisingly, was the latter. "The differences between the Northern and Southern portions of the former American Union never involved a moral question," declared *DeBow's Review* in that same midsummer issue of 1861; "these and all former issues are now dead." James Henley Thornwell, the prince among Southern Presbyterian theologians, stood among slavery's most ardent defenders right up to the point of secession, but in 1861, he began to express doubts about slavery that he would never have permitted to see daylight in earlier times. Thornwell told his friend and biographer, Benjamin Palmer, that "he had made up his mind to move . . . for the gradual emancipation of the negro, as the only measure that would give peace to the country."[78]

If slavery was not the South's cultural trademark, what was? Was there really such a thing as Southernness? Oddly, no one seemed more convinced that there was than the soldiers of the Union armies. Much as they had enlisted to preserve a common America, the deeper they marched into the South, the more it really did seem to resemble a foreign country. "It is vain to deny that the slave system of labor is giving shape to the government of the society where it exists, and that that government is not republican either in form or spirit," exclaimed the abolitionist general John W. Phelps. "It was through this system that the leading conspirators sought to fasten upon the people an aristocracy or a despotism; and it is not sufficient that they should be merely defeated in their object and the country be rid of their rebellion." The rank and file felt much the same way. "The papers used to talk a great deal about Union people in Virginia, and their love for their country," wrote one soldier in the 5th Maine, but "it never happened to be our fortune to see any of those exceptions to Southern character. . . . Possibly this may seem a hard statement, but it is not so hard as was the reality." So at just the moment when Southerners wanted to claim culture rather than slavery as the basis of Confederate identity, Northerners were moving

77. O'Brien, *Conjectures of Order*, 2:996, 1012; Nathaniel Beverly Tucker, *A Series of Lectures on the Science of Government Intended to Prepare the Student for the Study of the Constitution of the United States* (Philadelphia: Carey and Hart, 1845), 43, 67.

78. J. Q. Moore, "The Belligerents," *DeBow's Review* 31 (July 1861): 73–74; James Thorwell, *The Life and Letters of James Henley Thornwell*, ed. Benjamin Morgan Palmer (Richmond: Whittet and Shepperson, 1875), 482–83; William W. Freehling, "James Henley Thornwell's Mysterious Antislavery Moment," *Journal of Southern History* 57 (August 1991): 396–406.

in precisely the opposite direction and holding Southerners to their prewar word that the protection of slavery was its guiding star.[79]

In pursuit of a Southern national culture, Confederates invented new national emblems (the Confederate great seal featured an image of George Washington's statue in Richmond and the pious motto *Deo vindice*, "God will vindicate"), a new grammar (through defiantly Confederate school textbooks such as the *Confederate Primer* [1861], the *First* and *Second Confederate Speller* [1861], *Boys and Girls Stories of the War* [1863], and the *Dixie Primer for the Little Folks* [1863]), new popular music ("God Save the South," "The Bonnie Blue Flag," "The Southrons' Chaunt of Defiance," "Stonewall Jackson's Way," "General Lee's Grand March"), art (William D. Washington's *The Burial of Latané*), anthologies of poetry (William Shepperson's *War Songs of the South*), histories (Edward Pollard's *The First Year of the War* and its successive "years" through 1864), and novels (Augusta Jane Evans's *Macaria; or Altars of Sacrifice*).[80]

This represents a remarkable volume of effort, even if Southerners themselves were dubious of its quality. "In this Titanic struggle which is going on, the genial pursuit of letters is at an end, and for nearly three years little has appeared which is worthy either of the genius or attainments of our people," J. D. B. DeBow sighed. "The glorious struggle has scarcely inspired one song which will live beyond the generation that now burns with martial ardor and rushes to the deadly field." But as in the failure of Confederate political nationhood, it was the war that proved the principal block to Confederate cultural nationhood. The grinding demands of the war and the blockade, Northern occupation of the Southern heartland, and the disruptions in supplies of paper, ink, type, pens, and books had all hampered the exercise of a Confederate imagination, and the looming shadow of defeat meant that any hope of delineating a Southern national character in its literature or culture would need to rely on time and experimentation.[81]

Military failure intruded in a more direct way on Southerners' religious confidence. If the Confederate nation really, at its core, was built around the determination to "accept as true the faith of our fathers" and "believe in the authority of the Bible, attested by the voice of the civilized world for almost two thousand years," then it was certainly entitled to expect the protection of Almighty God, especially over against the godless Yankee nation. "Those who defend free society must, for

---

79. J. W. Phelps to R. S. Davis, June 16, 1862, in *War of the Rebellion*, Series One, 15:488; George W. Bicknell, *History of the Fifth Regiment Maine Volunteers, Comprising Brief Descriptions of Its Marches, Engagements, and General Services* (Portland, ME: H. L. Davis, 1871), 69.

80. Michael T. Bernath, *Confederate Minds: The Struggle for Intellectual Independence in the Civil War South* (Chapel Hill: University of North Carolina Press, 2010), 182–204; Drew Gilpin Faust, *The Creation of Confederate Nationalism: Ideology and Identity in the Civil War South* (Baton Rouge: Louisiana State University Press, 1988), 24–26, 69.

81. DeBow, "Editorial," *DeBow's Review* 34 (July 1864): 98; Bernath, *Confederate Minds*, 268.

this reason alone, if consistent, reject the Bible . . . because the institution of slavery accords with the injunctions and morality of the Bible." Hence, "all free society must reject the Bible if it approve its own institutions and disapprove slavery." Southerners should be free to add to whatever catalog of cultural distinctiveness they could assemble a distinctive "morals and religion," and expect a divine blessing "in this great struggle" where (as Benjamin Palmer put it) "we defend the cause of God and religion. . . ." The burden of that cause, Palmer explained, is "to conserve and to perpetuate the institution of domestic slavery as now existing . . . with the right, unchanged by man, to go and root itself wherever Providence and nature may carry it."[82]

In practice, however, the South's self-image as a God-blessed people proved to be surprisingly shallow. In nine Southern states, clergymen were actually forbidden to hold public office; even James Henley Thornwell accepted the drawing of a bright line between religion and public life in the South, commenting, "The business of a preacher, as such, is to expound the Word of God" and not to "expound to senators the Constitution of the State, nor to interpret for judges the laws of the land." As it was, many of slavery's most vigorous defenders displayed little in the way of religiosity. James Henry Hammond scoffed privately at Christianity as the religion of "an infuriated Demon, seeking whom he may destroy. . . . The result of my experience of Life and Him is that I pant for *Annihilation*." And "Stonewall" Jackson, that paragon of martial piety, had a very poor estimate of Southern religion. "I am afraid that our people are looking to the wrong source for help, and ascribing our successes to those whom they are not due," Jackson complained. "If we fail to trust in God & to give him all the glory our cause is ruined. Give to our friends at home due warning on this subject." However much the Southern Confederacy liked to speak of itself as a divine cause, so little provision had been made for chaplains' services in the Army of Northern Virginia that fully half of the regiments in Jackson's corps in the spring of 1863 were without one.[83]

When, by 1864, defeat was looking the Confederacy in the eyes, the arms of the pious dropped nervelessly to their sides, and they concluded that God was deserting them, if not because of his opposition to slavery, then as a consequence of Southern unbelief. "God's dark providence enwraps me like a pall," agonized Moses Drury Hoge, one of the most prominent Presbyterian divines in Virginia, "The idolized expectation of a separate nationality, of a social life and literature and civilization of

82. Palmer, *Thanksgiving Sermon, Delivered at the First Presbyterian Church, New Orleans, November 29, 1860* (New York: G. F. Nesbitt, 1861), 7, 12–13.

83. Hammond, diary entry for October 3, 1854, in *Secret and Sacred: The Diaries of James Henry Hammond, A Southern Slaveholder*, ed. Carol Bleser (New York: Oxford University Press, 1988), 264; O'Brien, *Conjectures of Order*, 2:955; Thornwell, "Sermon on National Sins," in *The Collected Writings of James Henley Thornwell*, ed. John B. Adger (Richmond, VA: Presbyterian Committee of Publication, 1871-1873), 4:511; William White Narrative, R. L. Dabney Papers, Southern Historical Collection; Eaton, *A History of the Southern Confederacy*, 105.

our own, together with a gospel guarded against the contamination of New England infidelity, all this has perished, and I feel like a shipwrecked mariner thrown up like a seaweed on a desert shore." God had judged the Confederacy. He had taken from them the devout "Stonewall" Jackson as a warning, and when the warning went unheeded, he struck the Confederate cause into the dust. It was "their want of faith" that was the "crying sin of the people of God throughout our beleaguered, devastated, and bleeding country," and now they had paid for it. "Can we believe in the justice of Providence," lamented Josiah Gorgas, "or must we conclude we are after all wrong?"[84]

Southern theologians were not the only ones to find disappointment in trying to turn the war into an intellectual struggle. As the war lengthened, the meanings that Northern religious thinkers attached to the war also splintered in frustration. The Transcendentalists were secular thinkers; but they had their religious counterpart in Horace Bushnell, a Congregationalist minister in Hartford, Connecticut, who had carved out a reputation by horrifying more orthodox Congregationalists with his admiration for a Kantian religion of intuition and feelings. He also had a consistently Romantic disdain for the pushing and striving of democracy. Like George Templeton Strong but very much unlike Abraham Lincoln, Bushnell was convinced that the war had only shown how little popular government was to be trusted, and in 1864 he interpreted "the true meaning of the present awful chapter of our history" as proof that "popular governments, or such as draw their magistracies by election from among the people themselves," were inferior to the national character to be found in historic communities based on race, religion, or tradition.[85]

It was among the evangelicals that the meaning of the Civil War took on its most dramatic and apocalyptic colorings. American evangelical Protestants had largely chosen the Whigs as their party of choice, and when the Whigs failed to adopt wholeheartedly the moral crusades of the evangelicals, the withdrawal of Northern evangelicals helped destroy the Whig Party and lay the basis for the rise of the Republicans. With the coming of the war, Northern evangelicals swung enthusiastically behind the causes of the Union and anti-slavery. The great Presbyterian preacher and commentator Albert Barnes (who had opened the 1856 Republican convention with prayer) declared two weeks after Fort Sumter that the war would "render the world the abode of industrious freedom, peace, domestic joy, and virtuous intelligence."[86]

84. Hoge, May 15, 1865, in Peyton Harrison Hoge, *Moses Drury Hoge: Life and Letters* (Richmond: Presbyterian Committee of Publication, 1899), 235; Daniel W. Stowell, *Rebuilding Zion: The Religious Reconstruction of the South, 1863–1877* (New York: Oxford University Press, 2001), 38–40; Gorgas, diary entry for July 17, 1863, in *The Journals of Josiah Gorgas*, 75; Eugene D. Genovese, *A Consuming Fire: The Fall of the Confederacy in the Mind of the White Christian South* (Athens: University of Georgia Press, 1998), 37–38, 54–55, 63–71.

85. Bushnell, "Popular Government by Divine Right," in *God Ordained This War: Sermons on the Sectional Crisis, 1830–1865*, ed. D. B. Cheseborough (Columbia: University of South Carolina Press, 1991), 104, 117.

86. James H. Moorhead, *American Apocalypse: Yankee Protestants and the Civil War, 1860–1869* (New Haven, CT: Yale University Press, 1978), 41, 50, 62, 76; Carwardine, *Evangelicals and Politics in Antebellum America*, 99–103, 286–90, 307.

The American Tract Society's agent Hollis Read went a step further and prophesied in *The Coming Crisis of the World, or the Great Battle and the Golden Age* (1861) that the Civil War would be the prelude to the return of Jesus and the onset of the millennium; it would be "one of the last mighty strides of Providence towards the goal of humanity's final and high destiny."

> A few more such strides, a few more such terrific struggles and travail-pains among the nations; a few more such convulsions and revolutions, that shall break to pieces and destroy what remains of the inveterate and time-honored systems and confederations of sin and Satan, and the friends of freedom may then lift up their heads and rejoice, for their redemption draweth nigh. The Day Of Vengeance Has Always Preceded And Been preparatory to the Year of the Redeemed.[87]

Yet Northern evangelicals could not escape the uneasy sense that slavery—even if not exactly the Southern form of it—was indeed sanctioned by the Bible, and they found themselves driven to the unlikely expedient of arguing, not from the letter of the Bible but from its much more intangible spirit—a tactic that set them uncomfortably close to the Romantics.[88]

No matter what their interpretations of the war, religious as well as secular intellectuals of every stripe set out to institutionalize these meanings. Secular intellectuals, so far as they could be teased out of their studies, and Romantic Protestants banded together to create the United States Sanitary Commission (USSC) in 1861, with the mission of raising and channeling private donations and large-scale giving to the support of the Union army. The USSC was, from the start, an exercise in benevolent elitism. Just as its leaders had no faith in the abstract rationalism of democracy, they had no practical use for unorganized charity, and they struggled throughout the war to redirect clothing, blankets, camp goods, food, and even pen and ink through their own intelligent and efficient hands. "Neither the blind masses, the swinish multitudes, that rule us under our accursed system of universal suffrage, nor the case of typhoid can be expected to exercise self-control," growled George Templeton Strong, the USSC's treasurer; if good was to be done for the soldier, better that it be done by the elite, who really knew how to organize their efforts. Thus, Strong and the USSC's upper-class New York and Boston officers struggled to turn the USSC into the model of what a properly administered nation ought to look like.[89]

Beside the USSC, and often in conflict with it, the evangelicals organized the United States Christian Commission (USCC), which sent 5,000 volunteers into

---

87. Hollis Read, *The Coming Crisis of the World, or, The Great Battle and the Golden Age* (Columbus, OH: Follett, Foster, 1861), 242.

88. Mark A. Noll, *The Civil War as a Theological Crisis* (Chapel Hill: University of North Carolina Press, 2006), 44–45.

89. Strong, diary entry for November 5, 1862, in *Diary of the Civil War*, 272.

the Union armies to distribute tracts, hold religious meetings and in general do for the Northern soldier's soul what the USSC aimed to do for the Northern soldier's body. Evangelical chaplains, with or without the cooperation of their fellow officers, sponsored revival meetings in both armies. As early as 1862, large-scale "conversion seasons" swept through both Union and Confederate troops: the Army of the Cumberland and the Army of Northern Virginia both experienced large-scale revivals of religion during the winter and spring of 1864. Not content with converting soldiers, Northern evangelicals organized the National Reform Association in 1863 to press for the passage of a "Bible Amendment" that would explicitly unite evangelical Protestantism and republicanism by rewriting the preamble to the Constitution to read: "Recognizing Almighty God as the source of all authority and power in civil government, and acknowledging the Lord Jesus Christ as the Governor among the nations, His revealed will as the supreme law of the land, in order to constitute a Christian government. . . ."[90]

None of America's religious leaders was prepared for the depth or the severity of the wounds that Civil War combat and the disruption of civil society inflicted on these attempts to give meaning to the war. Northern evangelicals who had so confidently expected the war to light up the path to the millennium were cruelly disappointed by profiteering and corruption. The uncertain notes on which the war ended looked like anything but a preparation for the return of Jesus Christ to earth. Charles Grandison Finney, who had been smiting slavery with great revivalistic blows for thirty years, warned his Oberlin College students in 1863 that although "the south *must be reformed* or *annihilated*," still "the *north* are not *yet just*. . . . The *colored man* is still *denied* his *equal rights*" and "is *most intensely hated* & *persecuted* by a *majority*." It saddened and angered Finney that after two years of war, "in no *publick proclamation either* north or *south* is *our great national sin recognized*."[91]

No one, however, lost more confidence in religious interpretations of the war than the ordinary soldier. The general disappearance of moral restraint among Civil War soldiers mocked the efforts of chaplains and USCC volunteers, at all but the most exceptional moments, to force the war into Christian shape. "It is hard, very hard for one to retain his religious sentiments and feelings in this Soldier life," admitted one New Jersey surgeon. "Every thing seems to tend in a different direction. There seems to be no thought of God of their souls, etc. among the soldiers." Even more than ordinary camp immorality, it was the shock of Civil War combat

90. Drew G. Faust, "Christian Soldiers: The Meaning of Revivalism in the Confederate Army," *Journal of Southern History* 53 (February 1987): 73–75; Morton Borden, "The Christian Amendment," *Civil War History* 25 (June 1979): 160.

91. Charles Grandison Finney, sermon outline, 1863, in Finney Papers, Oberlin College Archives.

and the apparent randomness of death on the battlefield that wrecked peacetime faith in an all-knowing, all-loving God. An Illinois surgeon named John Hostetter remarked, "There is no God in war. It is merciless, cruel, vindictive, unchristian, savage, relentless. It is all that devils could wish for." The chaplains talked in vain to Edward King Wightman about divine purpose and meaning in the war: "A minister and a soldier are antipodes in sentiment. The one preaches 'election' and the other fatalism." Even the lay preacher and future president James A. Garfield told William Dean Howells after the war that at the sight of "dead men whom other men had killed, something went out of him, the habit of his lifetime, that never came back again: the sense of the sacredness of life and the impossibility of destroying it."[92]

Although American Protestants had been confident at the beginning of the war that they would be able to interpret the war in ways that their secular counterparts could not, the war itself proved otherwise, and American religion instead became one of the Civil War's major cultural casualties. Never again would evangelical Christianity so dominate the public life of the nation or come so close to wedding its religious ethos to American democracy. From the 1860s onward, American Protestantism was increasingly marked by the quiet erosion of faith, and religious experience became plagued more and more by incessant questioning, by decaying faith, and an increasing appeal to feeling and imagination over against confessional reason or evangelical conversion. "Perhaps people always think so in their own day, but it seems to me there never was a time when all things have shaken loose from their foundations," wrote one of Finney's correspondents in 1864. "So many are sceptical, doubtful, so many good people are cutting loose from creeds & forms. . . . I am sometimes tempted to ask whether prayer can make any difference." Evangelicals themselves would unwittingly aid this process by withdrawing in confusion from their public roles to concentrate on ever more personalized forms of religious conversion and exotic attempts to hook current events onto the promise of the coming millennium.[93]

The public discourse of American intellectuals would, by the 1890s, be taken over by the Romantic intellectuals who had risked so little in the war, and who had therefore lost so little in it. They would be immeasurably aided in this process by the postwar impact of Charles Darwin and his shocking but quintessentially Romantic theory of evolution. But the Civil War proved nearly as deadly to the credibility of American Protestant intellectuals as did any Darwinian apes. Taken

---

92. Edward King Wightman, *From Antietam to Fort Fisher: The Civil War Letters of Edward King Wightman, 1862–1865*, ed. E. G. Longacre (Madison, NJ: Fairleigh Dickinson University Press, 1985), 56; Robertson, *Soldiers Blue and Gray*, 227; Linderman, *Embattled Courage*, 128.

93. Anne Rose, *Victorian America and the Civil War* (New York: Cambridge University Press, 1992), 17–66.

together, the Civil War baffled and horrified both secular and Protestant intellectuals, and only in later years, when suffering could be transmuted by memory into moral triumph, and racism effaced by memories of battlefield heroism, could they even begin again to mention the subject. For men of the mind, as well as for men of color and women of all descriptions, America during the Civil War was a world turned upside down.

CHAPTER TEN

STALEMATE AND TRIUMPH

David Howe was an officer, but evidently no gentleman.

Around noon on July 14, 1863, Howe turned the corner at the foot of Prince Street in the mostly Irish North End of Boston. His job was to deliver notices to an unstated number of Prince Street men that their names had been pulled from a drum by draft enrollment officers, and under the terms of the new Federal Enrollment Act, they had ten days to report for induction into the United States Army. Serving these notices was not a popular job, and on an upstairs floor in one Prince Street building Howe was confronted by an Irish woman who refused to accept what was probably a notice for one of the men in her family. She must not have found either Howe's manners or Howe's news all that welcome, because after some time spent arguing, the woman hauled off and slapped Howe across the face.[1]

Enraged at the woman's boldness, Howe announced that as an agent of the United States government, he intended to have the woman arrested, which he may have supposed would shut her up fast. It didn't. She shrieked and howled more loudly, and in short order a curious and not altogether friendly-looking crowd began to drift together around Howe. The nervous officer hurriedly descended to the street with the crowd milling after him, and there a quick-witted policeman bundled him into a store at the corner of Prince and Causeway Streets and persuaded the crowd to disperse. After a while the coast seemed clear, and Howe quietly stepped back out into Prince Street with as much of his dignity as he had left. His timing could not have been worse. The crowd from the Irish woman's building had dispersed only long

1. William F. Hanna, "The Boston Draft Riot," *Civil War History* 36 (September 1990): 262–73.

enough to gather up sticks, stones, and reinforcements, and they came boiling down Prince Street just in time to catch Howe out in the open, where they proceeded to beat the draft officer to within an inch of his life.[2]

Howe's erstwhile police protector now sent off for more policemen. By the time they arrived, the crowd had swollen to more than 300 people, and they nearly stomped the hapless coppers to death. With its blood up, the crowd needed direction, and according to the *Boston Journal*, it got it from "an Irishwoman" who held up "a photograph of her boy who she said was killed in battle," and led them all to Haymarket Square, four blocks away. It was now 2:00 PM, and the crowd was numbering near 500.[3]

Massachusetts governor John Andrew was at that moment across the Charles River listening to the salutatorian at the Harvard College commencement drone out a scrupulously esoteric oration in Latin. Andrew was on the point of nodding off when an aide jabbed him awake with an urgent message about a disturbance in the North End. Andrew had been anticipating trouble in Boston, but not over the draft: the all-black 55th Massachusetts had been due to parade through Boston and Andrew had prudently put the militia and Federal artillerymen from the harbor forts on notice in case race-baiting toughs tried to stir up a little trouble. Andrew's face paled at the whispered news, causing the Harvard salutatorian to forget his Latinate lines, and the governor abruptly walked off the platform and left the commencement audience stewing in whisper and rumor. By 6:00 PM Andrew had mobilized four companies of militia and a battery of artillery and ordered them to rendezvous at the Cooper Street arsenal, only two blocks from Haymarket Square; in another hour, two companies of Federal heavy artillerymen were on their way to the arsenal as well.[4]

The heavy artillerymen were the last to arrive at the Cooper Street arsenal, and they were only just in time. Around seven-thirty, a mob nearly 1,000 strong roared around the corner of Cooper Street, throwing bricks and bottles and shattering the glass in the arsenal windows. The officers in charge of the troops in the arsenal—Federal artillery major Stephen Cabot and Massachusetts militia captain E. J. Jones—stepped outside and ordered the crowd to disperse. Instead, the rocks and bottles now came showering down on the two officers, and some of the militia fired a volley over the heads of the crowd to scare them into flight. The volley only maddened the mob, and now the enraged men and women in the street began an attack on the arsenal in earnest, hurling paving stones, bricks, and anything else they could lay hands on. Like the Richmond bread riot three months before, women angrily took charge of the assault. A Boston reporter saw "one Amazonian woman . . . with

2. William P. Marchione, *Boston Miscellany: An Essential History of the Hub* (Charleston, SC: History Press, 2008), 110–11.

3. Judith Ann Giesberg, "'Lawless and Unprincipled': Women in Boston's Civil War Draft Riot," in *Boston's Histories: Essays in Honor of Thomas H. O'Connor*, ed. James O'Toole and David Quigley (Boston: Northeastern University Press, 2004), 72.

4. Hesseltine, *Lincoln and the War Governors*, 304–6.

hair streaming, arms swinging, and her face the picture of phrenzy . . . rushed again and again to the assault." One neighborhood girl remembered women holding up their infants to the windows of the arsenal and daring the soldiers inside to shoot.[5]

Cabot refused to allow his men to fire. But after forty-five minutes, the crowd began slamming its collective weight against the arsenal doors, and Cabot had no choice but to order one of the 6-pounder howitzers his artillerymen had brought with them loaded with a double charge of canister. At eight-fifteen the door gave way before the mob, and Cabot gave the order to fire. The gun blast blew the mob back into the street, and within a few minutes they had scattered out of sight. Eight people were dead, four of them small children.

The mob was not done, however. Bloodied and desperate, the crowd regrouped around the corner and broke into whatever gun shops they could find for weapons. Robertson James, a second lieutenant in the 54th Massachusetts, barricaded himself with a dozen other soldiers on the upper floor of Read's Gun Shop; below, the mob was "hunting down any man in certain localities . . . wearing the uniform of our army." As James recalled, black soldiers' lives "were not worth five minutes purchase." As they worked their way down the line of shops that led toward old Faneuil Hall, the rioters were headed off by a squad of policemen, two companies of militia, a company of mounted dragoons with drawn sabers, and the mayor of Boston with the Riot Act in his hand. The shiver of sabers in the red summer sunset cowed them, and the mob gradually broke up and faded into the oncoming dusk. By 11:00 PM, Boston was quiet again.[6]

With that, it became apparent even to the most blue-dyed Yankee and the most radical Republican that Richmond was not the only city in 1863 that was beginning to stagger under the weight of the war's burdens. No city in America was more identified with abolitionism than Boston; no governor had pressed more quickly or more tirelessly to move emancipation and abolition to the front of the war agenda than Governor John Andrew. But the people in the streets of Boston had not been prepared for the costs that a war to emancipate African American slaves would impose on them. They had certainly not bargained for the war to turn into a nightmare that requisitioned their sons, brothers, and fathers by force, then sent them off to be slaughtered either to no apparent purpose or in the name of a purpose linked with black freedom. The temper of the war was failing in the North in 1863; emancipation and abolition were all well and good, but they would mean nothing if not secured by Union military victory. And if the war could not be won, and soon, perhaps it might be better to admit that it could never be won at all.

5. Giesberg, "'Lawless and Unprincipled,'" 71–76.

6. William Schouler, *A History of Massachusetts in the Civil War* (Boston: E. P. Dutton, 1868), 1:476–80; Robert D. Richardson, *William James: In the Maelstrom of American Modernism, A Biography* (Boston: Houghton Mifflin, 2007), 55.

IF IT TAKES ALL SUMMER

Grant's victory at Chattanooga in November 1863 brought the Federal armies only one-third of the way between their old base in Kentucky and the Confederacy's Atlantic and Gulf coastlines. Now that Grant had complete power over all the western Federal armies, he might choose to push southward directly to Atlanta and complete the disruption of the Confederacy's western rail links, or he might shift his line of operations to aim at Mobile, Alabama, which would close one of the Confederacy's last remaining ports and, in the process, roll over the Confederacy's vital foundries and arsenals in northern Alabama.

His first inclination was to strike for Mobile. In August Grant wrote to Charles Dana in the War Department, "I am very anxious to take Mobile while I think it can be done," and four months later, he told General in Chief Halleck that he wanted "to move by way of New Orleans and Pascagoula on Mobile. . . ." A move on Atlanta was a logistical impossibility right now, Grant explained to Halleck; instead he proposed to leave only a garrison strong enough to secure Chattanooga, then move the old Army of the Cumberland via steamboat down to New Orleans for the campaign against Mobile "and with the balance of the army make a campaign into the interior of Alabama, and possibly Georgia." This plan might have the additional bonus of forcing "Lee to abandon Virginia and North Carolina" to protect Georgia. In any case, the government should give up looking to capture Richmond and concentrate its attention on the West instead. Grant was now convinced that the campaigns in Virginia were really only so much tactical boxing, and that the only way to strike a truly decisive blow at the Confederacy was to slash away at its strategic intestines in Alabama, Georgia, and the Carolinas.[7]

Halleck replied in January to Grant's Mobile proposal, cautiously authorizing Grant to proceed—but with the crippling requirement that all of Tennessee first be securely in Union hands. What was more, "I have never considered Richmond as the necessary objective point of the Army of the Potomac," Halleck added in February. For him, the real question of the war was how best to defeat Lee's army. If Grant were permitted to concentrate Union forces in the West, then "all the forces which Lee can collect will be moved north, and the popular sentiment will compel the Government to bring back the army . . . to defend Washington, Baltimore, Harrisburg, and Philadelphia."

Halleck's hesitation was not the only wet blanket on Grant's plans. In January, much to Grant's annoyance, Nathaniel P. Banks, the Federal military commander in Louisiana, took a joint army-navy expedition up the Red River into the upcountry

7. Grant to Dana, August 5, 1863, and Grant to Halleck, January 19, 1864, in *The Papers of Ulysses S. Grant*, 9:146–147 and 10:39–40; Grant to Halleck, December 7, 1863, *The War of the Rebellion*, Series One, 31(III):349–50; Stoker, *The Grand Design*, 344–49; Catton, *Grant Takes Command*, 101–2.

of Louisiana and eastern Texas. Banks's expedition was a political move rather than a military one. Both Lincoln and Banks wanted to consolidate the hold of the newly reconstructed government in occupied Louisiana over the rest of the state (and its valuable cotton) and perhaps send a useful message to the French in Mexico about Federal intentions for Texas. "In regard to General Banks' campaign . . . it was undertaken less for military reasons than as a matter of State policy," Halleck explained to Grant. "It was . . . connected with our foreign relations, and especially with France and Mexico, that our troops should occupy and hold at least a portion of Texas." All the same, it drained away men and supplies Grant had been counting on for his Mobile campaign. Just as he had done after Corinth and after Vicksburg, Grant was forced to sit on his triumphs.[8]

Grant did not sit still for long in Tennessee, any more than he had in Mississippi the year before. In December 1863, Congress proposed to reward Grant for the Chattanooga victory by reviving the rank of lieutenant general, a grade filled only once before in the history of the United States Army, by George Washington. The bill passed the Senate on February 24, 1864, and Halleck then wired Grant to come to Washington to receive the commission.[9]

The promotion to lieutenant general did two things for Grant. First, it immediately made him senior in rank to Halleck, who remained only a major general, and effectively booted Grant up to general in chief of the Federal armies. Halleck, with uncommon graciousness, stepped aside as general in chief to make way for Grant and assumed the new post of chief of staff to Secretary of War Stanton (a function he had actually been exercising since July 1862). Second, the promotion brought Grant east to meet with Lincoln and Stanton on March 8, and two days later the new lieutenant general rode out to the headquarters of the Army of the Potomac to meet George Gordon Meade and take the measure of the eastern army.[10]

Grant had heard rumors ever since the preceding summer that Lincoln wanted to drop Meade from command of the Army of the Potomac, chiefly because of Meade's failure to follow and destroy Lee after Gettysburg, and the corollary of these rumors was that Lincoln meant to bring Grant east as Meade's replacement. Knowing what a

8. Halleck to Grant, January 8 and February 16, 1864, and C. H. Dana to Grant, January 10, 1864, in *War of the Rebellion*, Series One, 32(II):40–42, 58, 311, 313; Gary D. Joiner, *Through the Howling Wilderness: The 1864 Red River Campaign and Union Failure in the West* (Knoxville: University of Tennessee Press, 2006), 48–51; Ludwell H. Johnson, *Red River Campaign: Politics and Cotton in the Civil War* (Kent, OH: Kent State University Press, 1993 [1958]), 42–44.

9. Halleck to Grant, March 6, 1864, in *War of the Rebellion*, Series One, 32(III):26. Winfield Scott had enjoyed the *brevet* rank of lieutenant-general, but brevets were little more than honorary designations; Grant was the first to be designated as a *full* lieutenant-general since Washington.

10. "Lieutenant General," February 24, 1864, *Congressional Globe*, 38th Congress, 1st Session, 797–98.

political cockpit the Army of the Potomac was, Grant had no desire whatever to offer himself as the next target for East Coast military intrigue. In the same letter in August 1863 in which he had broached the Mobile plan to Charles Dana, Grant laboriously thanked Dana "for your timely intercession in saving me from going to the Army of the Potomac. Whilst I would disobey no order I should beg very hard to be excused before accepting that command." Even after his appointment as general in chief, Grant seems to have been determined to keep his headquarters in the west, and proceed with his plans to give the Army of the Potomac the shorter end of the strategic stick.[11]

In spite of himself, Grant was impressed with Meade and the army, and the War Department and various Republican congressional nabobs pressed on Grant the fact that Congress had bestowed the grade of lieutenant general on Grant principally in the hopes that he would lead the Army of the Potomac into battle against Lee in a showdown of tactical wits. "Unless this army of foes is defeated and broken, and our Capitol relieved of its fierce frowns," argued Grant's own chief of staff, John A. Rawlins, "we cannot hope that the recognition of the rebel government will be much longer postponed by European governments."[12] By the time Grant returned to Nashville, he had decided to move his headquarters east and take up general tactical command of the eastern theater. He also revised his plans for operations in Virginia to include yet another overland campaign across the Rappahannock for the Army of the Potomac in order to confront Lee and bring the Army of Northern Virginia to battle.

Grant knew that he was taking considerable risks in coming east. For one thing, he was a westerner and a stranger with surprisingly little personal grandeur or charisma about him. "Grant is a man of a good deal of rough dignity; rather taciturn; quick and decided in speech," observed Theodore Lyman as he studied the new commander. "He habitually wears an expression as if he had determined to drive his head through a brick wall, and was about to do it." It took easterners such as Lyman some time to get used to a general who had no interest in fine reviews and hip-hip-hoorah. "Grant . . . paid us a visit yesterday," George Washington Whitman wrote to his mother on April 14, 1864. "There was no grand Review as is generally the case, but the Regiments just fell in line and Grant rode along and looked at them and then went on about his business." A civilian friend of one of Grant's staff officers was amazed that "there is no glitter or parade about him. To me he seems but an earnest business man."[13]

---

11. Grant to Dana, August 5, 1863, in *Papers of Ulysses S. Grant*, 9:147.

12. Jean Edward Smith, *Grant* (New York: Simon and Schuster, 2001), 292; James H. Wilson, *The Life of John A. Rawlins* (New York: Neale, 1916), 407; Hattaway and Jones, *How the North Won*, 517.

13. Theodore Lyman, April 12, 1864, in *Meade's Headquarters*, 81; *Civil War Letters of George Washington Whitman*, 114; William S. McFeely, *Grant: A Biography* (New York: W. W. Norton, 1981), 159.

Grant was also aware that, as a westerner, he was likely to be resented as an inter-loper by the Army of the Potomac. "The enlisted men thoroughly discussed Grant's military capacity," Frank Wilkeson remembered. "Magazines, illustrated papers, and newspapers, which contained accounts of his military achievements, were sent for, and eagerly and attentively read." Most of the veterans were skeptical. "Old sol-diers, who had seen many military reputations—reputations which had been made in subordinate commands or in distant regions occupied by inferior Confederate troops—melt before the battle-fire of the Army of Northern Virginia, and expose the incapacity of our generals, shrugged their shoulders carelessly. . . ." Wilkeson, who would be going into his first campaign under Grant, discovered that "Grant's name aroused no enthusiasm. The Army of the Potomac had passed the enthusiastic stage. . . ."[14]

Grant anticipated that skepticism, and he even toyed with the idea of bringing McClellan back into the Army of the Potomac at some level to rally the jaded army. He also wisely retained Meade as titular commander of the Army of the Potomac (even though Grant himself would travel with the army and give all the orders that mat-tered). In some cases, though, Grant was facing problems that political savvy had no way of addressing. This particular army was largely composed of three-year volunteers, and in the spring and summer of 1864, many of those enlistments were due to expire. The constant defeats the army had suffered had slowly undermined the veterans' en-thusiasm for another term of service, and only about half of the Army of the Potomac's veterans would be persuaded to reenlist. Unless he could win some kind of smashing victory soon, Grant was liable to see a large part of the Army of the Potomac legally desert him.[15]

Staggering as these problems were, Grant managed to stay on his guard about letting the Army of the Potomac eat up all his attention and resources. He still be-lieved that the really decisive blows that would win the war were going to have to land somewhere outside the old battlefields north of Richmond. To that end, Grant also provided for three other simultaneous offensives to begin in the West and below Richmond. Intended to help realize much of the original plan Grant had proposed to Halleck, those three offensives would depend largely on the men designated to lead them. First and foremost, there was William Tecumseh Sherman. Grant pro-posed to combine George Thomas and the Army of the Cumberland with Grant's old Army of the Tennessee from the Vicksburg campaign and put them both under the command of Sherman. At the same time as Grant's overland campaign would

14. Wilkeson, *Recollections of a Private Soldier*, 36–37.

15. Brooks D. Simpson, *Let Us Have Peace: Ulysses S. Grant and the Politics of War and Reconstruction, 1861–1868* (Chapel Hill: University of North Carolina Press, 1991), 63–64; Grimsley, *And Keep Moving On*, 21–22.

open in Virginia, Sherman would advance south toward Atlanta with a view toward taking the city by the end of the summer.

In addition to Sherman, Grant also looked to Nathaniel Banks for help. Banks was supposed to finish his Red River expedition in time to launch a combined army-navy operation against Mobile in tandem with Grant and Sherman's advances. With Sherman occupying the rebel Army of Tennessee, there would be little at hand to defend Mobile, and when the port fell into his hands, Banks could then move his men north through Alabama without serious opposition, wrecking Selma in his path, and then turn east and meet Sherman at Atlanta.

Lastly, Grant was looking for help from Major General Benjamin F. Butler, the Massachusetts politician who had outraged New Orleans and made the "contrabands" the beginning of a new Federal policy on slavery in 1861. Butler was to take command of two Federal army corps (about 33,000 men) and deposit them on the old James River peninsula, below Richmond. While Grant and the Army of the Potomac would clinch Lee in battle along the Rappahannock line, Butler and his men could slip past the thin Confederate defenses on the James and capture Richmond or at least cut Richmond's rail communications with the rest of the South. Lincoln aptly summed up the plan in one phrase: "Those not skinning can hold a leg."[16]

Grant was less forthcoming about his reservations concerning the overland path across the Rapidan and the Rappahannock that Halleck and Lincoln insisted had to be taken en route to the climactic battle they wanted fought with Lee and the Army of Northern Virginia. McClellan's temptation to play at politics had tainted with halfheartedness the idea of using the navy's command of the Chesapeake waterways to outflank the Confederates, push up the James River, and besiege Richmond. Surprisingly, that was exactly what Lee dreaded the most. "I considered the problem in every possible phase," Lee told one of his division commanders in 1863, and unless he could carry the war onto Northern soil and make the North pay the price the South was paying, then taking a defensive stance would only end with him being pushed back into a siege of Richmond, and a siege—as the sieges of Sevastopol and Kars had shown during the Crimean War—had only one end in modern warfare, that of surrender. Nothing about the results of the Gettysburg campaign had changed Lee's mind. "We must destroy this army of Grant's before he gets to the James River," Lee told Jubal Early. "If he gets there it will become a siege, and then it will be a mere question of time." This was also what Grant was convinced would be the inevitable outcome of affairs in the east, for the simple reason that armies had become too big to defeat in a single, cataclysmic battle, and too dependent on railroads and cities as

16. Stoker, *The Grand Design*, 351–54; Edward G. Longacre, *General Ulysses S. Grant: The Soldier and the Man* (Cambridge, MA: Da Capo Press, 2006), 212–16; John Hay, diary entry for April 30, 1864, in *Inside Lincoln's White House*, 194.

supply centers to survive in the field if those cities were locked up and captured. His intention, Grant wrote, was to "beat Lee's army north of Richmond if possible." But no amount of beating was liable to put the Army of Northern Virginia permanently out of commission; at least, none so far had done that. Instead, Grant mused, "after destroying his lines of communication north of the James River," it would be better to "transfer the army to the south side and besiege Lee in Richmond or follow him south if he should retreat."[17]

Almost from the first, things began to go wrong with Grant's big strategic picture. For one thing, Banks's expedition up the Red River turned into an unpleasant little fiasco that tied up those forces (along with 10,000 of Sherman's men who had been sent to reinforce him) until the end of May. By that time, Banks would have been a month late just starting for Mobile, and in fact, he never even got going at all, and spent the rest of the war in New Orleans. Sherman would have to take Atlanta himself, and without any helpful distractions at Mobile by Banks. Meanwhile, Butler and his "Army of the James" made a brave landing below Richmond on the James peninsula on May 5, 1864. Butler actually got within five miles of Richmond on May 11, only to be turned back by a desperate Confederate defense at Drewry's Bluff on May 16. Butler withdrew back to the James River and entrenched himself in the Bermuda Hundred, a small area largely surrounded by a bend in the James. There the Confederates sealed off his small army, like a "bottle tightly corked."

Grant's biggest problem was presented by Robert E. Lee and the Army of Northern Virginia. Grant did not simply propose to throw himself at Lee, and like Hooker a year before, he chose not to try to force a crossing of the Rappahannock at Fredericksburg. Instead, the Army of the Potomac, with Meade and Grant, 3,500 wagons, 29,000 horses, 20,000 mules, and 120,000 men, again turned wide to the west, splashed across the Rapidan River on May 4, and plunged at once into the eerie gloom of the Wilderness. Despite the apparently irresistible juggernaut of his numbers, Grant had only about 65,000–70,000 veterans; the rest were unseasoned troops scraped from hither and yon (conscripts, replacements, the heavy artillery regiments of the Washington defenses; even Ambrose Burnside made a reappearance from Ohio with his old 9th Corps). Grant had to hope that he could move through the Wilderness fast enough to force Lee to fall back upon Richmond. "It was a good day's work in such a country for so large an army with its artillery and fighting trains to march twenty miles, crossing a river on five bridges of its own building, without a single mishap, interruption or delay," wrote Andrew A. Humphreys, Meade's chief of staff. All the same, nightfall found the lead elements of the Army of the Potomac

17. "Report of Lieut. Gen. U.S. Grant, U. S. Army, Commanding, Armies of the United States, of Operations, March, 1864–May, 1865," July 22, 1865, in *War of the Rebellion*, Series One, 34(I):18; "Lee's Offensive Policy," *Southern Historical Society Papers* 9 (March 1881): 137; Nolan, *Lee Considered*, 85.

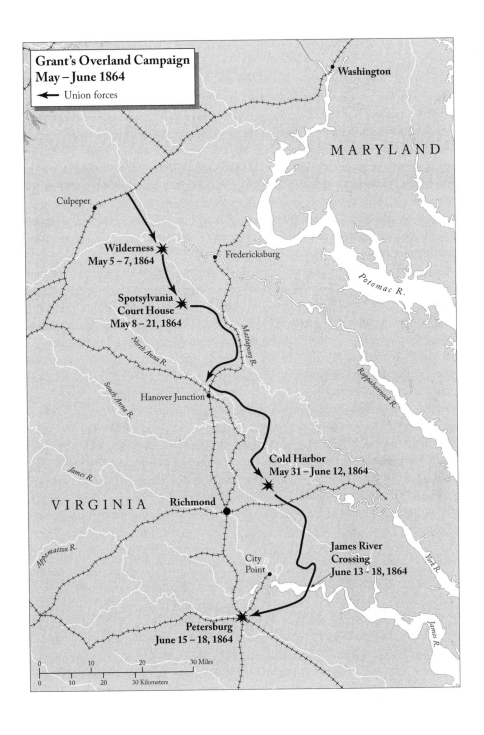

Grant's Overland Campaign
May – June 1864

← Union forces

Washington

MARYLAND

Culpeper

Wilderness
May 5 – 7, 1864

Fredericksburg

Potomac R.

Spotsylvania
Court House
May 8 – 21, 1864

Mattapony R.

North Anna R.

Rappahannock R.

South Anna R.

Hanover Junction

Cold Harbor
May 31 – June 12, 1864

James R.

VIRGINIA

Richmond

City
Point

James River
Crossing
June 13 – 18, 1864

York R.

Appomattox R.

James R.

Petersburg
June 15 – 18, 1864

0   10   20   30 Miles
0 10 20   30 Kilometers

no more than halfway along the narrow rutted roads of the Wilderness, and the army was forced to stop and wait for daylight.[18]

This presented precisely the sort of opportunity Lee prayed for, since the tangled and unfamiliar terrain of the Wilderness would eliminate the Federal advantages in numbers and artillery and allow the Army of Northern Virginia an even chance in a fight. And that spring, Lee needed all the help the Virginia terrain could give. Three weeks before Grant crossed the Rapidan, Lee warned Jefferson Davis, "I cannot see how we can operate with our present supplies. . . . There is nothing to be had in this section for man or animals." (No exaggeration, this: after three years of war, the countryside "seemed almost uninhabited and not even the bark of a dog or sound of a bird broke the dreary silence.") Lee's health was so poor that he admitted to his son Custis in April, "I feel a marked change in my strength . . . and am less competent for duty than ever."[19]

Moreover, Lee's three corps commanders—James Longstreet (who had rejoined the Army of Northern Virginia with his corps after Bragg's debacle at Missionary Ridge), A. P. Hill, and Richard Ewell—were all veteran officers with at least a full year of experience at corps command behind them. But each of them had failed Lee at Gettysburg. Even worse, Longstreet had performed ineffectively in Tennessee after Chickamauga, and quarreled so bitterly with his subordinates that two of them, LaFayette McLaws and Evander Law, resigned. Richard Ewell was "loved and admired" by his men, "but he was not always equal to his opportunities." There would remain some question about how reliable their performance would be in the upcoming battles. Yet the morale of the ordinary soldier of the Army of Northern Virginia remained resilient. "The whole command is in fine health and excellent spirits and ready for the coming struggle confident of whipping Grant, and that badly. We all believe that this is the last year of the war." John L. Runzer, of the 2nd Florida, resolved: "Whereas, we . . . believe, as we did, from the first, that the cause in which we are engaged . . . is just and right . . . Be it resolved, That we are determined never to give that cause up."[20]

18. Hagerman, *The American Civil War and The Origins of Modern Warfare*, 248; Grimsley, *And Keep Moving On*, 21–22; Andrew A. Humphreys, *The Virginia Campaign of '64 and '65: The Army of the Potomac and the Army of the James* (New York: C. Scribner's Sons, 1883), 19; Longacre, *General Ulysses S. Grant*, 220.

19. Gordon C. Rhea, *The Battle of the Wilderness May 5–6, 1864* (Baton Rouge: Louisiana State University Press, 1994), 9; Lee to G. W. C. Lee, April 9, 1864, in *The Wartime Papers of Robert E. Lee*, 695–96.

20. McHenry Howard, *Recollections of a Maryland Confederate Soldier and Staff Officer Under Johnston, Jackson, and Lee* (Baltimore: Williams and Wilkins, 1914), 253; Gary W. Gallagher, "The Army of Northern Virginia in May 1864: A Crisis of High Command," *Civil War History* 36 (July 1990): 101–7; Gallagher, *Lee and His Army in Confederate History* (Chapel Hill: University of North Carolina Press, 2001), 202; E. Porter Alexander, *Military Memoirs of a Confederate: A Critical Narrative* (New York: C. Scribner's Sons, 1907), 360; Rhea, *The Battle of the Wilderness*, 24.

The most immediate problem that Lee had to face, however, was concentrating his forces to meet Grant. In the interest of casting his net for supplies as far as he dared, Lee's three army corps, numbering only about 70,000 men, were widely scattered along the south side of the Rappahannock. When Lee ordered them to rendezvous to face Grant, Richard Ewell's corps, moving eastward on the Orange Turnpike through the Wilderness, collided with the vanguard of the Army of the Potomac's 5th Corps, heading south on the one usable north-south road through the Wilderness, the Germanna Plank Road. A firefight erupted. Meade, anxious to get out of the Wilderness before the main body of Lee's army arrived, tried to shoulder the Confederates aside, only to find the rebels in significantly greater numbers than he had planned for, and with a more aggressive spirit. "These lunatics were sweeping along to that appallingly unequal fight, cracking jokes, laughing," wrote a Virginia artilleryman of his fellow Southerners, "and with not the least idea in the world of anything else but victory."[21]

Meade called up John Sedgwick's 6th Corps to cover the 5th Corps's southward-extended left flank. They, in turn, were overlapped by rebel infantry from Hill's corps, coming up to meet them along the Orange Plank Road (a parallel to the Orange Turnpike) as twilight descended. That night, Meade moved the 9th Corps (Burnside's) and the 2nd Corps (under Winfield Scott Hancock) around behind the firing lines so that, at five o'clock on the morning of May 5, Hancock and the 2nd Corps were in position to attack Hill. With a gigantic lurch forward, they smashed right over Hill's rebels on the Plank Road. "Tell Meade we are driving them most beautifully," Hancock exulted.[22]

The exultation lasted only for an hour. Without any warning, the last of Lee's infantry corps, under James Longstreet, arrived and knocked the overconfident Federals back to their starting point. It was now Lee's turn to exult, and he was so jubilant at the appearance of Longstreet that he almost tried to lead one of Longstreet's brigades personally (until a Texas sergeant grabbed the bridle of Lee's horse and the protective shout went up, "General Lee to the rear!"). This confused melee of attacks and counterattacks through the dense underbrush and burning woods, little of it with any sense, produced a total of 18,000 casualties for the Army of the Potomac and another 10,000 or so for the Army of Northern Virginia. By midnight on the evening of May 6, both armies had lapsed into an uncomfortable quiet, too exhausted and confused to carry the fight on further.[23]

21. William Meade Dame, *From the Rapidan to Richmond and the Spottsylvania Campaign: A Sketch in Personal Narrative of Scenes a Soldier Saw* (Baltimore: Green-Lucas, 1920), 71–72.

22. Judson, *History of the 83rd Pennsylvania Volunteers*, 94; David M. Jordan, *Winfield Scott Hancock: A Soldier's Life* (Bloomington: Indiana University Press, 1988), 119.

23. J. Tracy Power, *Lee's Miserables: Life in the Army of Northern Virginia from the Wilderness to Appomattox* (Chapel Hill: University of North Carolina Press, 1998), 23; Robert K. Krick, "'Lee to the Rear,' the Texans Cried," in *The Wilderness Campaign*, ed. Gary Gallagher (Chapel Hill: University of North Carolina Press, 1997), 182.

Almost exactly one year before, Fighting Joe Hooker had found himself in the same situation and at the same location near the old Chancellorsville House, and he had elected to retreat. Much of the Army of the Potomac must have expected that Grant would make the same move, following the dingy and depressing pattern they had known for three years—attack, stall, withdraw across the Rappahannock. But Grant was not Hooker, and he was not like anything else the Army of the Potomac had ever seen. In the early morning hours of May 7, Grant arose, wrote out his orders, ate breakfast, and then moved out onto the road in the predawn darkness with his headquarters staff, past the burning wreck of the Wilderness and the long lines of Winfield S. Hancock's 2nd Corps standing by the roadside—and headed *south*.

For the first time since his arrival among them, the Army of the Potomac began to cheer Grant. "No doubt it was inspired by the fact that the movement was south," wrote Grant with characteristic detachment. "It indicated to them that they had passed through the 'beginning of the end' in the battle just fought. The cheering was so lusty that the enemy must have taken it for a night attack."[24] Frank Wilkeson recalled that "Grant's military standing with the enlisted men this day hung on the direction we turned at the Chancellorsville House."

> If to the left, he was to be rated with Meade and Hooker and Burnside and Pope—the generals who preceded him. At the Chancellorsville House we turned to the right. Instantly all of us heard a sigh of relief. Our spirits rose. We marched free. The men began to sing. The enlisted men understood the flanking movement. That night we were happy.[25]

Sixty miles away, in Washington, Lincoln and Stanton had heard nothing from Grant after the last of the Army of the Potomac had disappeared into the maw of the Wilderness, and an aide noticed that the tension was so great for Stanton that he could not even reach for a piece of paper without twitching. But on May 8 Grant finally had an official dispatch to send to Lincoln, and John Hay noticed that, despite the punishing losses, for the first time Lincoln was happy with what one of his generals was doing in Virginia. Lincoln remarked to Hay, "How near we have been to this thing before and failed. I believe if any other general had been at the head of that army it would have not been on this side of the Rapidan. It is the dogged pertinacity of Grant that wins." Two days later, Grant sent Halleck a letter that had an ever larger measure of "pertinacity" to it: "I am now sending back . . . all my wagons for a fresh supply of provisions and ammunition, and purpose to fight it out on this line if it takes all summer."[26]

24. Ulysses S. Grant, "Personal Memoirs," 539.

25. Catton, *Grant Takes Command*, 208; Wilkeson, *Recollections*, 80.

26. Benjamin P. Thomas and Harold M. Hyman, *Stanton: The Life and Times of Lincoln's Secretary of War* (New York: Knopf, 1962), 300; Hay, diary entry for May 9, 1864, in *Inside Lincoln's White House*, 195; Grant, "Personal Memoirs," 550–51.

Grant suspected that, as badly hurt as his own army was, Lee's was probably weakened even more. So, shaking off the blow he had received in the Wilderness, Grant began feeling to his left, seeking to move southward around the battered flank of Lee's army and out onto the open ground between the Rappahannock and Richmond. His first objective was Spotsylvania Courthouse, a little country crossroads eleven miles southeast of the Wilderness. If he could get there before Lee, the Army of the Potomac would lie at right angles to Richmond and the Army of Northern Virginia, and Lee would have no choice but to attack him there or abandon the Confederate capital. Once again, the roads were poor and the maps unreliable, and as a result, Lee managed to beat Grant to Spotsylvania Court House by the afternoon of May 8.

The Confederates had only a little time to build up their defenses before Grant's army arrived, but by this point in the war, all but the greenest volunteers knew how to scratch up effective entrenchments by the rule of the minute. By the time Grant was ready to attack on May 10, the Army of Northern Virginia was dug into a five-mile-long line, featuring a prominent horseshoe-shaped bulge that easily fended off repeated headlong Federal attacks. For one moment that evening, a carefully selected division of twelve regiments under Colonel Emory Upton was allowed to try something different—a swift dash in column with bayonets only, no firing, no deploying into line of battle. Upton's column waited under cover of a woodline until 6:35 that evening, then at a signal sprinted 200 yards to strike a point on the western side of the Confederate bulge. The rebels hardly had time to look up. "They came on us with a yell and never made any halt," wrote a Georgian, "We were simply overwhelmed and forced to retire, *every man for himself*." Unhappily, the success of Upton's attack surprised the Army of the Potomac, too, because the orders for supports to come up behind Upton went astray. Upton's men were left dangling and had to withdraw.[27]

Two days later, on May 12, Grant tried Upton's tactic again, only with Winfield Hancock's 2nd Corps and Horatio Wright's 6th Corps, and this time the results were an exercise in military horror. At one point on the Confederate bulge, in a trench known as the "Bloody Angle," attackers and defenders grappled in vicious hand-to-hand, rifle-to-rifle combat, like two crowds of enraged beasts. The commander of the Vermont Brigade remembered that "it was not only a desperate struggle but it was emphatically a hand-to-hand fight."

> Scores were shot down within a few feet of the death-dealing muskets. A breastwork of logs and earth separated the combatants. Our men would reach over the breastworks and discharge their muskets in the very face of the enemy. Some men clubbed

27. Henry Walter Thomas, *History of the Doles-Cook Brigade, Army of Northern Virginia, C.S.A.* (Atlanta: Franklin, 1903), 478–79; Stephen E. Ambrose, *Upton and the Army* (Baton Rouge: Louisiana State University Press, 1992 [1964]), 32.

their muskets, and in some instances used clubs and rails. . . . The slaughter of the enemy was terrible. The sight next day was repulsive and sickening, indeed. Behind their traverses, and in the pits and holes they had dug for protection, the rebel dead were found piled upon each other. Some of the wounded were almost entirely buried by the dead bodies of their companions that had fallen upon them. Many of the dead men were horribly mangled, and the logs, trees, and brush exhibited unmistakeable signs of a fearful conflict.[28]

The 2nd Corps actually tore its way through the Bloody Angle, but a fallback line had already been improvised by the Confederates, and the Federal attack ground to a halt. By the close of day, with another 18,000 casualties to add to those in the Wilderness, the Army of the Potomac was still unable to dislodge Lee from his position around Spotsylvania Court House. But Grant had lost nothing of his pertinacity. On May 14, true to his promise to fight matters out "if it takes all summer," Grant again decided to move around Lee's right.[29]

From that point on, Grant's campaign became a deadly leapfrog with Lee, Grant and the Army of the Potomac always looking to slide quickly and deftly around Lee's right, and Lee always moving just fast enough to get his army in front of them again. In a violent arc of turning movements, over poor roads and through bottomless mud, always dropping closer and closer to Richmond, Grant pushed his army one step ahead of Lee, until finally by the first of June, Grant had fought his way down to another desolate little crossroads called Cold Harbor, only ten miles northeast of Richmond.

At that point he ran out of maneuvering room. In front of Grant was Lee, his men arriving just in the nick of time on June 1 to throw up instant entrenchments and repulse an initial assault by the Army of the Potomac's 6th Corps; on Grant's left was a familiar and fatal stream, the Chickahominy River, trickling into the James; on the right was the road back north, which he had promised not to take. His options gone, Grant ordered a massive frontal assault on June 3, and the results were even worse than Spotsylvania. In less than eight hours, 4,500 Federal soldiers were shot down. The regimental chaplain of the 2nd Connecticut Heavy Artillery, which had been pulled out of its comfortable barracks in the Washington fortifications to fight as infantry in this campaign, noted that his unit lost their colonel and 51 others dead, plus 333 wounded, in one charge on June 1. The traumatized chaplain wrote home despairingly, "You cannot conceive the horror & awfulness of a battle. I never

28. "Reports of Brig. Gen. Lewis A. Grant, U.S. Army, Commanding Second Brigade," August 30, 1864, in *War of the Rebellion*, Series One, 36(I), 704; John Cannan, *Bloody Angle: Hancock's Assault on the Mule Shoe Salient, May 12, 1864* (Cambridge, MA: Da Capo Press, 2002), 153; William D. Matter, *If It Takes All Summer: The Battle of Spotsylvania* (Chapel Hill: University of North Carolina Press, 1988), 248–49.

29. George Walsh, *Damage Them All You Can: Robert E. Lee's Army of Northern Virginia* (New York: Forge Books, 2002), 475.

wish to *hear* another much less *see* it. I went out to see this but found myself in such danger I soon fled. . . . Pray for me. I cannot write—am not in a fit state of mind."[30]

Now was the moment of decision for Grant. He had sustained 55,000 casualties since crossing the Rapidan a month before, and he was losing still more veteran soldiers as regimental enlistments expired. The old story that Grant was a military butcher who simply kept feeding an unlimited supply of Union reinforcements at the Confederates until the Southerners were finally overwhelmed by sheer numbers surfaced for the first time after Cold Harbor, although it is surprising how, even with the horrendous casualty lists, Grant still lost proportionately fewer men than Lee. All through the war, Robert E. Lee lost more men in one offensive gambit after another than any Federal commander; even when facing Grant directly, Lee still lost a higher percentage of his forces in battle than Grant, despite the fact that Grant took the offensive at every point from the Wilderness to Cold Harbor. Nor did Grant always have a bottomless barrel of fresh troops to draw upon. Andrew Humphreys, as Meade's chief of staff, recorded after the war that the Army of the Potomac received only about 12,000 effective reinforcements during the first six weeks of the overland campaign, while it lost not only the names on the bloody casualty lists but also thirty-six infantry regiments that simply chose to go home rather than reenlist. Over the long haul, Grant husbanded the lives of his men far more effectively than Lee; it was Lee, not Grant, who bled armies dry.[31]

One other thing that was evident, too, was that Grant was far from overwhelming Lee or anyone else at Cold Harbor, and all Grant had to show for a month's grinding campaigning was the lesson that the Confederates could not be beaten by an army marching overland at them. The McClellan odor had made anyone else's proposals for sieges and operations along the James guilty by mere association. But Grant had now played all the cards there were to play on the overland route, and the Army of the Potomac was no closer to victory now than when he started.

> From the proximity of the enemy to his defenses around Richmond it was impossible by any flank movement to interpose between him and the city. I was still in a condition to either move by his left flank and invest Richmond from the north side or continue my move by his right flank to the south side of the James. While the former might have been better as a covering for Washington, yet a full survey of all the ground satisfied me that it would be impracticable to hold a line north and east of Richmond that would protect the Fredericksburg railroad—a long, vulnerable line which would exhaust much

30. Gordon C. Rhea, *Cold Harbor: Grant and Lee, May 26–June 3, 1864* (Baton Rouge: Louisiana State University Press, 2002), 362; Ernest B. Furgurson, *Not War but Murder: Cold Harbor 1864* (New York: Knopf, 2000), 102.

31. Humphreys, *The Virginia Campaign of '64 and '65*, 100; Grant, "Personal Memoirs," 598; Catton, *Grant Takes Command*, 240–41; Edward H. Bonekemper, *Ulysses S. Grant: A Victor, Not a Butcher: The Military Genius of the Man Who Won the Civil War* (Lanham, MD: Regnery, 2004), 186, 191.

of our strength to guard, and that would have to be protected to supply the army, and would leave open to the enemy all his lines of communication on the south side of the James.[32]

So Grant imperturbably sat down and informed Halleck that he intended to change his line of operations from the Fredericksburg-Richmond line to the James River, "transfer the army to the south side" of the James, and either barge into Richmond from below or "besiege Lee in Richmond."[33]

This, of course, was what Halleck and Lincoln had always been sure they must prevent their generals from doing. Lincoln's methodology, ever since McClellan, had been to push his generals after Lee, not Richmond. However, Grant merely observed that Lee's men had acquired a considerable knack for entrenching themselves and making head-on attacks a very costly proposition. By June, he and the Army of the Potomac had paid enough for George McClellan's sins, and Grant was ready to do what he had suspected in the first place needed to be done: strike directly at Richmond and the Army of Northern Virginia's vital depots and rail links, then force the Confederates out into the open country, where they would be compelled to fight, starve, or both.

This was, of course, essentially the same thing he had done at Vicksburg. And with the memory of Vicksburg in mind, Grant aimed to pull back secretly from the Cold Harbor lines, steal a march down to the James, cross the river over a 2,100-foot-long pontoon bridge that is still one of the greatest wonders of military engineering, and wind up on the south side of the James below Richmond while Lee was still in his lines above the city. He would then cross the Appomattox River and seize the vital rail junction at Petersburg, twelve miles below Richmond, where all the major rail lines from the rest of the South—Norfolk & Petersburg, Weldon, Southside, Richmond & Danville—came together to form the logistical lifeline of the Army of Northern Virginia. Cut those lines at Petersburg, and both Richmond and the Army of Northern Virginia were doomed to die on a withered vine.[34]

Coming from any other general, not a syllable of this plan would have been even remotely acceptable to Lincoln. But Grant had Lincoln's confidence to a degree that no other general had in this war, and Lincoln was inclined to give Grant his head. Lincoln remarked in the spring of 1864 to one of his White House secretaries, William O. Stoddard, that "Grant is the first general I've had" who "hasn't told me what his plans are. I don't know, and I don't want to know. I'm glad to find

32. "Report of Lieut. Gen. U.S. Grant," July 22, 1865, in *War of the Rebellion*, Series One, 34(I):18.

33. Grant to Halleck, June 5, 1864, in *War of the Rebellion*, Series One, 36(I):11.

34. Smith, *Grant*, 372; Longacre, *General Ulysses S. Grant*, 237.

a man who can go ahead without me." That, of course, was not literally true: Grant had telegraphed all the details to Halleck, Halleck had passed them on to Lincoln, and Lincoln had taken the whole plan in at once. "Have just read your despatch," Lincoln wired Grant while Grant was already on the road. "I begin to see it. You will succeed. God bless you."[35]

On June 12, Grant quietly evacuated his Cold Harbor lines, moving so swiftly and unobtrusively that Lee knew nothing of the withdrawal until the next morning. Lee "was in a furious passion" when he discovered that Grant had slipped away under his nose. It was "one of the few times in the war" when Lee completely lost his temper, and as Eppa Hunton, who commanded a brigade in George Pickett's division, warned, "when he did get mad, he was mad all over." Grant then proceeded to execute the biggest turning movement of the war, quick-marching his men, corps by corps, down to the James and across the marvelous pontoon bridge, and then across the Appomattox, while Lee was still trying to decide where they had gone. The first of Grant's troops to arrive hurled a preliminary attack against the Confederate defenses, capturing one and a half miles' worth of the thinly manned lines (which had only been built as a precaution in 1862). By the sixteenth, three Federal army corps with more than 50,000 men were poised at the gates of Petersburg, with no more than 10,000 Confederates, some of them merely "transient forces" called out for the emergency, to bar the way. "The city is ours. There is not a brigade of the Army of Northern Virginia ahead of us," shouted the jubilant men of Frank Wilkeson's battery. "On all sides I heard men assert that Petersburg and Richmond were ours; that the war would virtually be ended in less than twenty-four hours."

But the Federal assaults were uncoordinated and cautious, as if unable to believe that they faced little more than an unlocked door. By the time Grant and Meade were able to sort matters out and throw their full weight against Petersburg on the seventeenth, Lee had frantically moved enough divisions down to Petersburg to make resistance too stiff. Both armies began digging in, and Grant reluctantly conceded that the opportunity for a quick capture of Petersburg and Richmond had been lost.[36]

35. Stoddard, in *Recollected Words of Abraham Lincoln*, 426; T. Harry Williams, *Lincoln and His Generals* (New York, Knopf, 1952), 307; Catton, *Grant Takes Command*, 176–77; Lincoln, "To Ulysses S. Grant," June 15, 1864, in *Collected Works*, 7:393.

36. P. G. T. Beauregard, "Four Days of Battle at Petersburg," in *Battles and Leaders*, 3:540–43; August V. Kautz, "The Siege of Petersburg: Two Failures to Capture the 'Cockade City,'" in *Battles and Leaders*, ed. Cozzens, 6:401; Wilkeson, *Recollections*, 157–58; Bonekemper, *Ulysses S. Grant*, 190; Eppa Hunton, in Noah Andre Trudeau, *Bloody Roads South: The Wilderness to Cold Harbor, May–June 1864* (Boston: Little, Brown, 1989), 316; A. Wilson Greene, *Civil War Petersburg: Confederate City in the Crucible of War* (Charlottesville: University of Virginia Press, 2006), 185–89.

Grant continued to experiment with ways of breaking the impasse at Petersburg, but none of them really worked. On July 30, with Grant's blessing, a regiment of Pennsylvania coal miners exploded an immense mine under the center of the Confederate entrenchments. The mine blew what a staff officer, William H. Powell, described as "an enormous hole in the ground about 30 feet deep, 60 feet wide and 170 feet long, filled with dust, great blocks of clay, guns, broken carriages, projecting timbers, and men buried in various ways—some to their necks, others to their waists, and some with only their feet and legs protruding from the earth." The plan had been for a division of black Federal soldiers to rush into the crater created by the mine, peel back the twisted ends of the Confederate line, and allow the rest of the Army of the Potomac to pour through the gap toward Petersburg. At the last minute, however, the black division was replaced with a white division that had no training or preparation for the assault, and when the new division rushed into the crater, no one had any clear idea what to do next. The stunned Confederates rallied, sealed off the crater, and, after stubborn but disorganized Federal resistance, managed to recapture the crater and most of the Federal soldiers in it. The battle of the Crater became simply one more in the long string of the Army of the Potomac's missed chances, and Grant admitted to Halleck, "It was the saddest affair I have witnessed in the war. . . . I am constrained to believe that had instructions been promptly obeyed that Petersburg would have been carried with all the artillery and a large number of prisoners without a loss of 300 men."[37]

The lack of a dramatic victory, and the prospect of a long and empty siege, fell painfully short of what the country had expected from Grant, and the price for that disappointment was liable to be severe: 1864 was an election year, and if Lincoln had nothing to show for three years of war but Grant besieging Petersburg and Richmond for who knew how long, then it was entirely possible that the North would turn to another president and another solution. But there was still one other voice to be heard from before that decision would be made, and it would belong to a man who was at that moment almost a thousand miles away.

TO ATLANTA AND THE SEA

The only piece of Grant's overall strategic plan in 1864 that actually worked the way he hoped was the move he had outlined from Chattanooga to Atlanta, and the principal reason this part succeeded when so many others miscarried was the simple fact

---

37. William H. Powell, "The Battle of the Petersburg Crater," in *Battles and Leaders*, 4:551; 40–41; Michael A. Cavanaugh and William Marvel, *The Petersburg Campaign—The Battle of the Crater "The Horrid Pit," June 25–August 6, 1864* (Lynchburg, VA: H. E. Howard, 1989), 40–41; Richard Slotkin, *No Quarter: The Battle of the Crater, 1864* (New York: Random House, 2009), 140–42; Grant to Halleck, August 1, 1864, *War of the Rebellion*, Series One, 40(I):17–18.

that he had entrusted it to William Tecumseh Sherman. The war had turned a nodding acquaintance between the two men into one of the most formidable friendships
in American history. Part of this mutual admiration grew out of the company misery
is supposed to enjoy: the careers of both men before the Civil War had followed
much the same dismal course, for in both cases the army proved a poor employer,
and a West Point education was a poor preparation for anything but army employment. Sherman veered erratically from the army into banking, then into near desti-
tution when his San Francisco bank failed, and after that into real estate speculation.
He arrived at the year 1857 thirty-seven-years old but looking more like a man of
sixty, a nervous, fidgety chain smoker with a thin coating of reddish hair and a perpetually scraggly shadow of beard. "I am doomed to be a vagabond," he wrote. "I look
upon myself as a dead cock in the pit, not worthy of future notice."[38]

However, in 1859 Sherman successfully applied for the superintendency of the
new Louisiana State Military College. There, the transplanted Ohioan spent two of
the happiest years of his life, until he gradually came to think of himself as being as
much a Louisianan as anything else. He did not particularly like slavery, but he also
believed that it was the only condition fit for blacks, and he was perfectly willing to
defend Louisiana slavery if necessary, provided that Louisiana did not put herself
beyond the pale by attempting to secede from the Union: "I am willing to aid Louisiana in defending herself against her enemies so long as she remains a state in the
general confederacy; but should she or any other state act disunion, I am out."

> Disunion and Civil War are synonymous terms. The Mississippi, source and mouth,
> must be controlled by one government. . . . Louisiana occupies the mouth of a river
> whose heads go far north, and does not admit of a "cut off." Therefore a peaceable dis-
> union which men here think possible is absurd. It would be war eternal until one or the
> other were conquered. . . . I always laughed when I heard disunion talked of, but I now
> begin to fear it may be attempted.[39]

Disunion was exactly what Louisiana proposed in 1861, and one week before Louisiana adopted its secession ordinance, Sherman resigned from the military college and
headed north. After a wait of five months, he was summoned to Washington and
commissioned as colonel of the 13th U.S. Infantry.[40]

Sherman's first round of Civil War service nearly finished him. He commanded
a brigade of infantry at First Bull Run, and then was promoted and transferred to

38. John F. Marszalek, *Sherman: A Soldier's Passion for Order* (New York: Free Press, 1993), 119.

39. Sherman to Thomas Ewing, December 23, 1859, in *General W. T. Sherman as College President*, ed.
Walter L. Fleming (Cleveland: Arthur M. Clark, 1912), 89.

40. Mark Wells Johnson, *That Body of Brave Men: The U.S. Regular Infantry and the Civil War in the West*
(Cambridge, MA: Da Capo Press, 2003), 12.

the Department of the Ohio. Unfortunately for Sherman, the department commander resigned, and until the new commander could be appointed and arrive on the scene, Sherman had to assume responsibility for organizing and administering the entire department. The nervous excitement was too great for a man of Sherman's high-strung temperament—he quarreled with the press, declared that it would require 200,000 reinforcements to subdue the Confederates, and insisted on returning runaway slaves to their owners. Finally, on November 15, Don Carlos Buell showed up to take charge of the Department of the Ohio, and Sherman was moved over to Henry Wager Halleck's department in St. Louis. Vengeful newspaper reporters circulated stories that Sherman had actually gone insane, and it looked as though his second military career had gone broke even faster than his bank.[41]

In a rare display of perspicacity, Halleck discounted the newspaper stories, and when Halleck began moving up the Tennessee River in March 1862, he gave Sherman command of a division and sent him to Pittsburg Landing to reinforce Grant. There, on April 6, Sherman's division, posted around the little Shiloh Baptist Church, was the first in the way of the Confederate wave that rolled over the Grant's army. To the surprise of his quondam critics back in Ohio, Sherman displayed an unexpectedly cool head in the midst of the Confederate onslaught. The peculiar geography of battle transformed Sherman: he personally rallied shattered regiments, plugged up holes in the Federal lines, and had four horses shot from under him. Under his direction, the right flank of Grant's army managed to perform the most difficult maneuver in the military textbooks, an orderly retreat under fire. "All around him were excited orderlies and officers," wrote one observer after Shiloh, "but though his face was besmeared with powder and blood, battle seemed to have cooled his usually hot nerves." Halleck obtained Sherman's promotion to major general, and when Grant finally began his great move on Vicksburg at the end of 1862, it was Sherman whom Grant asked Halleck for as a division commander.[42]

Sherman eventually became as indispensable to Grant as "Stonewall" Jackson had been to Robert E. Lee. And Sherman was as unabashed in his admiration for Grant as any Confederate for Marse Robert: "I believe you are as brave, patriotic and just as the great prototype, Washington—as unselfish, kind-hearted, and honest as a man should be—but the chief characteristic is the simple faith in success you have always

41. Sherman to John Sherman, October 26, 1861, in *Sherman's Civil War: Selected Correspondence of William T. Sherman, 1860–1865*, ed. Brooks Simpson and Jean V. Berlin (Chapel Hill: University of North Carolina Press, 1999), 163; Lee Kennett, *Sherman: A Soldier's Life* (New York: HarperCollins, 2001), 144; David J. Eicher, *The Longest Night: A Military History of the Civil War* (New York: Simon and Schuster, 2001), 148.

42. Charles Bracelen Flood, *Grant and Sherman: The Friendship That Won the Civil War* (New York: Farrar, Straus and Giroux, 2005), 109.

manifested, which I can liken to nothing else than the faith a Christian has in the Saviour." Like Grant, Sherman made a deep and favorable impression on Charles Dana. "On the whole, General Sherman has a very small and very efficient staff; but the efficiency comes mainly from him," Dana wrote to his chief, Secretary of War Stanton, in July 1863. "What a splendid soldier he is!"[43]

When Grant went east at the end of 1863 to supervise operations in the Virginia theater, there was no question but that Sherman would take command in the west and conduct the operations Grant had planned against Atlanta. He shared Grant's notion of the primary importance of the western theater. "From the West, when our task is done," Sherman prophesied, "we will make short work of Charleston and Richmond, and the impoverished coast of the Atlantic." Gone was the paranoid behavior Sherman had manifested in Kentucky. Under Grant's tutelage, he had developed into an energetic field commander, capable of quick decisions and even quicker movement. Instead of waging war by the defensive book, carefully preserving Southern property as the armies tiptoed past it, Sherman now began to talk about bringing it all crashing to the earth, about putting the thumbscrews to the South. In September 1863, he urged Halleck and Lincoln to turn the war into a campaign of desolation, since desolation was the only language the Confederates would understand.

> I would banish all minor questions, assert the broad doctrine that a nation has the right, and also the physical power to penetrate to every part of our national domain, and that we will do it—that we will do it in our time and in our own way; that it makes no difference whether it be one year or two, or ten or twenty; that we will remove and destroy every obstacle, if need be, take every life, every acre of land . . . that we will not cease till the end is attained. . . . I would not coax them or even meet them half way but make them so sick of war that generations would pass away before they would again appeal to it. . . . The people of this country have forfeited all right to a voice in the councils of the nation. They know it and feel it and in after-years they will be better citizens from the dear-bought experience. . . .[44]

To a Tennessee woman who objected to manners so cruel, Sherman replied with a shrug: "War is cruelty. There is no use trying to reform it, the crueler it is, the sooner it will be over."[45]

There was one point on which Sherman had not changed his opinions, and that was the future of the black slaves his soldiers encountered in Tennessee and

43. Dana, *Recollections of the Civil War,* 76.

44. Sherman, *Memoirs of General W. T. Sherman,* 365.

45. Sherman to Grant, March 10, 1864, in "General Sherman's Reply," *Littell's Living Age* 87 (October 28, 1865): 189; Lloyd Lewis, *Sherman: Fighting Prophet* (New York: Harcourt, Brace, 1932), 307–8, 330.

Mississippi. "Do you really think we worship Negroes?" Sherman asked sarcastically when a Southerner pressed him about the future of the slaves. He bowed to the Emancipation Proclamation as a military necessity, but he consistently declined to use black Union soldiers in combat (though later he conceded to assigning them garrison duties), and he publicly doubted whether freed slaves could be "manufactured into voters, equal to all others, politically and socially."[46]

Notions such as that had destroyed the career of many an officer in the Army of the Potomac. But the eastern army was Lincoln's and Stanton's, an army so close to the politicians that it could hardly help but endure close political scrutiny. The western armies were something else: their uniforms were sloppier, their drill was slouchier, and their overall opinion of themselves was boundlessly higher. Away over the Appalachians, Sherman's politics were less noticeable, and less of a liability so long as Grant continued to sponsor him and Sherman kept on winning battles. The time would come when politics would catch up with Sherman, and then they would nearly destroy him.[47]

For now, it was the soldiers in Chattanooga who were Sherman's chief concern. The force that Grant left Sherman was something of a hodgepodge. The heart of it was George H. Thomas's 61,000-man Army of the Cumberland (comprising the 14th and 20th Corps). Beside them were two smaller commands Grant had amalgamated for Sherman, the old 24,000-man Army of the Tennessee (comprising the 15th Corps and units of the 16th and 17th Corps) under a marvelous young engineer named James B. McPherson, and the 13,500 men of the Army of the Ohio under John M. Schofield (4th and 23rd Corps). Together with his cavalry, Sherman had more than 98,000 men at his disposal, along with 254 guns in his artillery train, and at the beginning of May (just as Grant was crossing his wagons over the Rapidan and into the Wilderness), he moved out of Chattanooga, pointed like a dagger at Atlanta.[48]

Opposing him was what was left of the beaten and demoralized Confederate Army of Tennessee. The disaster at Missionary Ridge ought to have spelled the end for this luckless army, had not the individual corps commanders taken over and managed to patch the army back together in northern Georgia. At least Braxton Bragg was gone now, and in his place Jefferson Davis appointed the one-time victor of First Bull Run, General Joseph E. Johnston. Douglas Cater of the

46. *Memoirs of General W. T. Sherman*, 1037.

47. James L. Huston, "Putting African-Americans in the Center of American National Discourse: The Strange Fate of Popular Sovereignty," in *Politics and Culture of the Civil War Era: Essays in Honor of Robert W. Johannsen*, ed. Daniel J. McDonough and Kenneth W. Noe (Selinsgrove, PA: Susquehanna University Press, 2006), 113.

48. Jacob Dolson Cox, *Atlanta* (New York: C. Scribner's Sons, 1882), 21; David Conyngham, *Sherman's March Through the South, with Sketches and Incidents of the Campaign* (New York: Sheldon, 1865), 29–30.

19th Louisiana glowingly described Johnston as "possessed of a magnetism which held such sway over his army that there was a feeling of security pervading every part of it." Cater found that "the faith our soldiers had in their commander" was so great that "they feared no surprise nor wrong movement."[49] Unfortunately for Johnston, that admiration was not shared by Jefferson Davis, who appointed Johnston to general command in the West in 1863 and watched Johnston allow Vicksburg to fall into Grant's hands with but little interference. That was not the kind of security the Confederacy could afford, and not until Braxton Bragg had nearly destroyed the Army of Tennessee would Davis relent and put it directly under Johnston's direction.

Johnston arrived at the army's winter encampments around Dalton, Georgia, on December 27, 1863, and what he found there was not encouraging. The Army of Tennessee had 70,000 men on its rolls, but only 36,000 actually present for duty, and a critical shortage of horses hobbled the cavalry, artillery, and wagons. By the end of April, however, Johnston had successfully reorganized the army, called in furloughs, distributed amnesties to deserters, and scraped together enough reinforcements to swell the Army of Tennessee back up to 53,000 men, with calls out for another 14,000 from Georgia's coastal garrisons and local militia. This still gave Sherman a three-to-two edge over Johnston, and so Johnston decided that the best campaign would be a defensive one, using the mountains, ridges, streams, and gaps of northern Georgia to stymie Sherman's advance at every step and forcing him to waste time and thin out his supply line. It escaped Johnston's notice that this was a formula largely designed to lose, even if the loss was a slow one.[50]

Defensive warfare, however, was Joseph Johnston's long suit, and from the moment Sherman's army clanked out of Chattanooga on the roads toward Atlanta until the middle of July, Johnston and the Army of Tennessee tick-tacked across northern Georgia as if it were a gigantic chessboard, holding defensive positions Sherman dared not attack, waiting for Sherman to waste time maneuvering around them, and then slipping back to a new position just as Sherman was about to spring the trap. On June 27, seething with frustration, Sherman risked an all-out frontal attack on Johnston's positions on Kennesaw Mountain. In two hours Johnston's men mowed down 3,000 Federals, and Sherman went back to the chessboard war. It took Sherman until the middle of July to cover the 120 miles that separated Chattanooga from Atlanta, and when at last the Federal army arrived there, it found Johnston securely

49. Cater, *As It Was: Reminiscences of a Soldier of the Third Texas Cavalry and the Nineteenth Louisiana Infantry*, 169, 178–79.

50. Stanley F. Horn, *The Army of Tennessee* (Indianapolis: Bobbs-Merrill, 1944), 311–13; Craig L. Symonds, *Joseph E. Johnston: A Civil War Biography* (New York: W. W. Norton, 1992), 249–50; Winston Groom, *Shrouds of Glory: From Atlanta to Nashville: The Last Great Campaign of the Civil War* (New York: Grove Press, 1995), 17.

entrenched around the city, waiting for Sherman to commence a lengthy and futile siege.[51]

Sherman, with a vulnerable 300-mile-long supply line stretching back through Chattanooga to the Ohio River, could not easily afford such a siege. He "did not fear Johnston with reinforcements of 20,000 if he will take the offensive," but so long as Johnston was safely cooped up inside Atlanta, Nathan Bedford Forrest's cavalry, now based as an independent command in northern Mississippi, could easily slip northward into Tennessee and slice Sherman's jugular in half-a-dozen places. Sherman tried to forestall the threat of such a raid by dispatching Brigadier General Samuel Sturgis and 8,100 cavalry and infantry to find and destroy Forrest. But Forrest, with no more than 3,500 men, found Sturgis first at Brice's Crossroads, and on June 10, 1864, Forrest routed Sturgis's men, capturing most of Sturgis's artillery, 176 wagons full of supplies, and 1,500 prisoners. "The panoplied and militant host of Sturgis consumed nine days in the march from Memphis to Brice's Cross-Roads," smirked one satisfied Confederate, "but, with Forrest on its trail, what was left of that host covered the same distance on the return in two nights and one day." If Forrest could now get loose on Sherman's supply lines while Sherman was bogged down in front of Atlanta, Sherman would have no alternative but to withdraw back into Tennessee, and the last prop of Grant's great offensive would collapse.[52]

At this moment, however, Jefferson Davis stepped in to present Sherman with an unlooked-for gift. However successful Johnston's campaign might have seemed as a defensive operation, it appeared to Davis, who had no incentive to think well of Johnston in the first place, as though Johnston was performing nothing more than a halfhearted retreat when the object of the war in the west was to push the Federals back into Tennessee. So on July 17 Davis abruptly relieved Johnston and turned the Army of Tennessee over to John Bell Hood. No one could have been more the opposite of Johnston, both temperamentally as well as professionally. Hood had spent most of the war in the Army of Northern Virginia, commanding a brigade of Texans whom he happily and recklessly threw at whatever Union position lay before him. Personally brave to a fault, Hood knew nothing of caution, and one of Sherman's scouts (or one of his colonels, depending on the version of the story) recalled seeing Hood bet $2,500 in a poker game "with nary a pair in his hand." In 1863, he had lost the use of his left arm while leading his men at Gettysburg, and three months later, as part of Longstreet's corps at Chickamauga, lost his right leg to a bullet while personally leading his men into the teeth of Federal fire.

51. Steven E. Woodworth, *Nothing but Victory: The Army of the Tennessee, 1861–1865* (New York: Knopf, 2005), 522–26.

52. Sherman to Halleck, July 16, 1864, in *War of the Rebellion*, Series One, 38(V):150; Thomas W. Duncan, *Recollections of Thomas D. Duncan, A Confederate Soldier* (Nashville, TN: McQuiddy, 1922), 150.

Aggressiveness like that was just what Davis wanted for the Army of Tennessee, and since Hood was still on the spot in Georgia, it seemed only natural to give the army to Hood to be sure something would be done with it. Not a little of that conclusion was helped by Hood's own ambitious backstabbing of Johnston. "Here is Gen. Joseph E. Johnston's reward for shielding his soldiers and inflicting losses in Gen. Sherman's army until his own little army could successfully offer battle and turn back the advancing hosts of Sherman's invaders," Douglas Cater complained. "This change of commander . . . had an effect on the army that was hard to overcome," and from that point on Cater was convinced that Hood would simply drown the Army of Tennessee in blood. "This order sounded the death knell of the Confederate States of America," he added. "The mistake that our soldiers then made was in not laying down their arms and stopping further bloodshed."[53]

For Sherman, Hood's appointment was good news: it meant that the Confederates would at last come out and fight in the open, where Sherman was sure he could beat them. Sure enough, only three days after assuming command, Hood took the Army of Tennessee out of its Atlanta defenses and flung them at the heads of Sherman's columns. Between July 20 and 28, Hood launched three major assaults, at Peachtree Creek (north and slightly west of the city), near Decatur (east of the city), and at Ezra Church (west of the city), each of which failed to stop Sherman, and all of which taken together cost Hood 19,000 casualties. Hood now slumped wearily into the defenses Johnston had prepared, and settled down to the siege he had been appointed to avoid.[54]

For Sherman, a siege was still a risky proposition; but with Hood in command, he counted on less vigilance than he would have expected from Johnston. Sherman spent the first half of August using his cavalry to feel around behind Atlanta, looking to cut Hood's rail line south of the city. Sherman's cavalry were no match for the rebel horsemen commanded by General Joseph Wheeler, however, and at the end of August, Sherman finally concluded that he would have to do the job with infantry instead. On August 25, leaving only one corps in front of the Atlanta lines, Sherman stole around below Atlanta to Jonesboro, on the Atlanta & Macon Railroad. There his men tore up the railroad tracks, heated the iron rails over bonfires of crossties, and twisted the rails around tree trunks in what became known as "Sherman neckties." Looking out over the deserted Federal lines around Atlanta, Hood at first

53. Archer Jones, *Civil War Command and Strategy* (New York: Free Press, 1992), 201–2; Lewis, *Sherman: Fighting Prophet*, 383; Brian Craig Miller, *John Bell Hood and the Fight for Civil War Memory* (Knoxville: University of Tennessee Press, 2010), 111–22; Cater, *As It Was*, 183–84, 185.

54. Richard M. McMurry, *John Bell Hood and the War for Southern Independence* (Lexington: University Press of Kentucky, 1982), 127–34; Richard M. McMurry, *Atlanta 1864: Last Chance for the Confederacy* (Lincoln: University of Nebraska Press, 2000), 150–57; Philip L. Secrist, *Sherman's 1864 Trail of Battle to Atlanta* (Macon, GA: Mercer University Press, 2006), 145–48.

thought Sherman had retreated and that he had won a great victory. "Last night the enemy abandoned the Augusta railroad and all the country between that road and the Dalton railroad," he jubilantly reported to Secretary of War Seddon. Too late, he realized where Sherman really was, and by the time Hood got his army down to Jonesboro, Sherman had finished with the railroad and was ready to deal with Hood. After a stiff, two-day fight at Jonesboro on August 31 to September 1, during which Hood ordered his "men to go at the enemy with bayonets fixed, determined to drive everything they may come against," Hood decided to abandon Atlanta and withdraw southward. "Hood . . . blew up his magazines in Atlanta and left in the night-time," Sherman telegraphed Halleck on September 3. "So Atlanta is ours, and fairly won."[55]

With the fall of Atlanta, the first of Grant's strategic objectives was at last in hand. Ironically, the second of these also dropped into Federal hands at nearly the same time. On August 5, David Farragut sailed a combined flotilla of wooden warships and ironclad monitors into Mobile Bay, and hammered the Confederate forts around the Bay into silence. Although a minefield of Confederate "torpedoes" blocked him from penetrating all the way into the Bay, Farragut took his own flagship, *Hartford*, to the head of the line and plunged into the minefield with the memorable order "Damn the torpedoes! Full speed ahead."[56] The mines sank one of Farragut's monitors, the *Tecumseh*, but most of the mines turned out to be ineffective and the rest of the fleet passed safely into the bay. On August 23, 1864, Mobile was effectively sealed off to blockade-runners.[57]

The question now was what to do with Sherman. It was the navy and not Banks's infantry that had locked up Mobile, and so Grant's old idea of Federal infantry linking up with Sherman from Mobile was rendered moot. There was little point in stopping with Atlanta, and Sherman urged Grant not to waste his time and men garrisoning northern Georgia. Instead, Sherman proposed to launch a gigantic raid down through Georgia to Savannah, where he could link up with the Federal forces occupying the Carolina coastline. "The possession of the Savannah River is more than fatal to the possibility of Southern independence," Sherman argued to Grant over the telegraph. "They may stand the fall of Richmond but not all of Georgia."[58]

55. Hood to Seddon, August 26, 1864, F. A. Shoup to William Hardee, August 31, 1864, and Sherman to Halleck, September 3, 1864, in *War of the Rebellion*, Series One, 38(V):777, 990, 1007; Marc Wortman, *The Bonfire: The Siege and Burning of Atlanta* (New York: Public Affairs, 2009), 301–10.

56. Farragut was probably not quite so concise; his response was more likely, "Damn the torpedoes! Four bells, Captain Dayton. Go ahead, Jouett, full speed." See Craig L. Symonds, *The Civil War at Sea* (Santa Barbara, CA: Praeger, 2009), 154.

57. Foxhall A. Parker, *The Battle of Mobile Bay and the Capture of Forts Powell, Gaines and Morgan* (Boston: A. Williams, 1878), 26, 29.

58. Sherman to Grant, September 20, 1864, in *War of the Rebellion*, Series One, 39(II):412.

The reasons Sherman listed behind that argument were threefold. First, he could fan out across the rich Georgia countryside between Atlanta and Savannah and destroy everything of any possible logistical value to the Confederacy. The capture of Atlanta had effectively cut off the northern Confederacy (and with it, Lee and the Army of Northern Virginia) from its communications with the arsenals and foundries of northern Alabama. Now Sherman would put the torch to the fields and farms that fed the Confederate armies. Second, he could demonstrate to foreign nations and to the Confederate people how weak and powerless the Richmond government had become, when it could not stop a Federal army from trampling across its geographical abdomen. "I propose to act in such a manner against the material resources of the South as utterly to negative Davis' boasted . . . promises of protection. If we can march a well-appointed army right through his territory, it is a demonstration to the world, foreign and domestic, that we have a power which Davis cannot resist," Sherman told Grant again on November 6. "This may not be war but rather statesmanship, nevertheless, it is overwhelming to my mind that there are thousands of people abroad and in the South who reason thus: If the North can march an army right through the South, it is proof positive that the North can prevail."[59] Third, Sherman expected that by putting a major Federal army at the mouth of the Savannah River, he would be in a position to swing north and take Charleston, which had resisted Federal land and sea attacks for two years, from behind.

This was, obviously, an outrageously risky proposition, and both Grant and Lincoln objected that such a march would string out Sherman's already lengthy supply lines to even more vulnerable lengths. Also, they pointed out, Sherman made no mention of what might happen if Hood and the Army of Tennessee decided to imitate Bragg's maneuver of 1862 and swing an end run around Sherman back up into Tennessee. Sherman's reply was the essence of military daring: he did not propose to use a supply line. He was going to conduct a large-scale infantry version of one of Forrest's raids. Like Forrest, he would strip his army down to the bare essentials and encourage his men to forage off the Georgia countryside for whatever else they needed until they struck the coast. "I can make this march, and make Georgia howl!" Sherman assured Grant. "We have on hand over 8,000 cattle and 3,000,000 [rations of] bread," and for anything else, "we can forage in the interior of the State." As for Hood, Sherman did not particularly care what the southern general did. Sherman would detach 60,000 men under George Thomas to return and hold Tennessee, but he would keep the rest of his army (nearly 62,000 men) on the road to Savannah come what may. "Damn him," Sherman snarled at the mention of Hood. "If he'll

59. Sherman to Grant, November 6, 1864, in *War of the Rebellion*, Series One, 39(II):660; Marszalek, *Commander of All Lincoln's Armies*, 295; Lewis, *Fighting Prophet*, 431.

go to the Ohio River, I'll give him rations. Let him go north. My business is down south."[60]

Grant mulled the proposition over, and on October 13 persuaded Lincoln to approve it. One month later Sherman marched out of Atlanta, his bands playing "Glory, Glory Hallelujah" and one-third of the city of Atlanta going up in flames behind him. Moving in four immense columns, Sherman swept aside the feeble resistance of the Georgia militia and burned a swath fifty miles wide across the state. He instructed his men to "forage liberally on the country during the march," an order they obeyed with gusto. "This is probably the most gigantic pleasure expedition ever planned," exclaimed one Illinois captain. "We had a gay old campaign," wrote another soldier. "Destroyed all we could not eat . . . burned their cotton & gins spilled their sorghum, burned & twisted their R[ail] roads and raised Hell generally." On December 10 Sherman turned up outside Savannah, and on December 21 the Confederate defenders evacuated the city before Sherman could trap them inside. "I beg to present to you, as a Christmas gift, the city of Savannah," Sherman telegraphed Lincoln, "with 150 heavy guns and plenty of ammunition, and also about 25,000 bales of cotton."[61]

Along the way, Sherman's men confiscated nearly 7,000 mules and horses, 13,000 cattle, 10.4 million pounds of grain, and 10.7 million pounds of animal fodder. All told, Sherman estimated that his march to the sea cost the Confederacy all "the corn and fodder in the region of country thirty miles on either side of a line from Atlanta to Savannah," plus "the sweet potatoes, cattle, hogs, sheep, and poultry, and . . . ten thousand horses and mules, as well as a countless number of their slaves." On a rough estimate, that set "the damage done to the State of Georgia and its military resources at one hundred millions of dollars; at least twenty millions of which has inured to our advantage, and the remainder is simple waste and destruction." Sherman admitted that "this may seem a hard species of warfare." But it would concentrate Southern minds wonderfully, and bring "the sad realities of war home to those who have been directly or indirectly instrumental in involving us in its attendant calamities."[62]

60. Sherman to Grant, October 9, 1864, in *War of the Rebellion*, Series One, 39(II):162; Sherman, *Memoirs*, 627; Lewis, *Fighting Prophet*, 430; Noah Andre Trudeau, *Southern Storm: Sherman's March to the Sea* (New York: Harper, 2008), 42.

61. "Special Field Orders No. 120," November 8, 1864, in *War of the Rebellion*, Series One, 39(II): 713; Mark Grimsley, *The Hard Hand of War: Union Military Policy Toward Southern Civilians, 1861–1865* (Cambridge: Cambridge University Press, 1995), 169; Sherman to Lincoln, December 22, 1864, in *War of the Rebellion*, Series One, 44:783.

62. Burke Davis, *Sherman's March* (New York: Random House, 1980), 12, 24, 31, 118; Glatthaar, *The March to the Sea and Beyond*, 130; Hattaway and Jones, *How the North Won*, 654; "Sherman's Campaign," in *The Rebellion Record: A Diary of American Events*, ed. Frank Moore (New York: G. P. Putnam, 1866), 9:7.

Meanwhile, just as Sherman had expected, Hood took the Army of Tennessee off on a diversionary campaign through northern Mississippi and up into Tennessee, hoping to compel Sherman to break off his march and follow him back out of Georgia. "Unless the Army could be heavily reinforced," Hood reasoned, "there was, in the present emergency, but one plan to be adopted: by manoeuvres to draw Sherman back into the mountains, then beat him in battle, and at least regain our lost territory." Contrary to Sherman's expectations, Hood's opportunities for causing serious damage in Tennessee were far greater than had been expected. For one thing, Hood had Forrest's cavalry with him, and that was danger enough on its own terms; for another, George Thomas, who was supposed to be covering Tennessee on Sherman's behalf, was slow to get the infantry Sherman had left him concentrated in one place. If Hood moved fast enough, it was entirely possible that he could isolate parts of Thomas' command while they were still on the roads back to Nashville, and annihilate them by pieces.[63]

However, Hood's 39,000 men were pitifully unequipped for a November campaign. Hood himself was too much of a physical wreck from his wounds, and the opium and alcohol he took as a cure for pain, to seize the opportunities thrown into his path. On November 30, at Franklin, Tennessee, Hood caught up with part of the force Thomas was supposed to be using to watch him, and attempted to overwhelm it by throwing his men at the Yankees in a daylong frontal assault. All those tactics did was leave Hood with 6,300 casualties, including twelve of his general officers and fifty-five regimental commanders, while the Federals slipped away north to join Thomas at Nashville.[64]

Unwilling to admit defeat, Hood advanced on Nashville, where Thomas had concentrated his 60,000 men, and tried to besiege it. Grant was frantic to see Hood destroyed, and warned Thomas, "If you delay attack longer the mortifying spectacle will be witnessed of a rebel army moving for the Ohio River. . . . I am in hopes of receiving a dispatch from you to-day announcing that you have moved." However, Thomas would not be hurried, even by Ulysses S. Grant. "They treat me as if I were a boy and incapable of planning a campaign," complained the normally unflappable Thomas. "If they will let me alone, I will fight this battle just as soon as it can be done." Only when he was satisfied of the odds, on December 15, 1864, did Thomas move out from Nashville and smash Hood's army in a running two-day battle. Hood fell back into Mississippi, where he found that he could rally only 15,000 men. The ill-starred Army of Tennessee was finished, and so was Hood, who resigned on January 13, 1865. Also finished, for that matter, was the Confederacy. Just as Grant had

63. John Bell Hood, *Advance and Retreat: Personal Experiences in the United States and Confederate States Armies* (New Orleans: Hood Orphan Memorial Fund, 1880), 244.

64. Jacob Dolson Cox, *The Battle of Franklin, Tennessee, November 30, 1864* (New York: C. Scribner's Sons, 1897), 89–91, 211–14.

predicted a year earlier, and Sherman had predicted in October, the real heart of the Confederate war effort lay along the terrible line that stretched from Fort Henry to Savannah, and once that line was in Federal hands, the Virginia theater, along with Lee and his fabled army, was living on borrowed time.[65]

VICTORY BY BALLOT

The summer of 1864 was one of the gloomiest seasons of the war for Lincoln and his administration. Grant was bogged down below Petersburg after a campaign that had cost the Union staggering casualties, Sherman was still struggling slowly toward Atlanta, and the *Alabama* was still burning Northern merchantmen on the high seas. To add insult to injury, Lee detached from the Army of Northern Virginia four infantry divisions and four cavalry brigades under General Jubal Early (about 14,000 men) and sent them on a raid into the Shenandoah Valley. Lee hoped that Early's raid, like "Stonewall" Jackson's in 1862, would draw off Federal troops from the Petersburg siege. In the event, not only did Early chase the Federals out of the Shenandoah, but on July 11 he even dared to cross the Potomac and make a lunge at Washington. Grant was forced to pull an entire infantry corps (Horatio Wright's 6th Corps) out of the Petersburg lines and send it to Washington, where the troops arrived just in time to fend off an attack by Early on the outer ring of Washington's fortifications. Early merely drew off into Maryland, where he extorted immense ransoms from the citizens of Hagerstown and Frederick. When the citizens of Chambersburg, Pennsylvania, refused to pay a ransom of $500,000 for their town, Early unhesitatingly burned the town to the ground. "The entire heart or body of the town is burned," wrote one despairing civilian. "The Courthouse, Bank, Town Hall, German Reformed Printing Establishment, every store and hotel in the town, and every mill and factory in the space indicated, and two churches, were burnt," along with "three and four hundred dwellings . . . leaving at least twenty-five hundred persons without a home or a hearth."[66]

Lincoln faced opposition from other quarters than just Jubal Early in the summer of 1864. Supreme Court interference in his war powers and proclamations remained a vivid possibility until Roger Taney's death in October, and the president continued to endure criticism and harassment from the Democrats, and especially

65. Grant to Thomas, December 11, 1864, in *War of the Rebellion*, Series One, 45(II):143; James Lee McDonough, *Nashville: The Western Confederacy's Final Gamble* (Knoxville: University of Tennessee Press, 2004), 264; Connelly, *Autumn of Glory*, 513.

66. Steven Bernstein, *The Confederacy's Last Northern Offensive: Jubal Early, the Army of the Valley, and the Raid on Washington* (Jefferson, NC: McFarland, 2011), 106; Benjamin Shroder Schneck, *The Burning of Chambersburg, Pennsylvania* (Philadelphia: Lindsay and Blakiston, 1864), 16.

from the Peace Democrats, who seized on Grant's overland campaign as an example of Republican butchery and incompetence. But with the fall of 1864 meaning another presidential election, Lincoln also now had to deal with a rising tide of disgruntlement from within his own Republican party, some of it within his own cabinet.

Salmon P. Chase, Lincoln's secretary of the Treasury, had always considered himself better presidential material than Lincoln, and he had been sorely disappointed in 1860 when he was passed over for the Republican nomination. "He never forgave Lincoln for the crime of having been preferred for President over him," wrote Alexander McClure, the prominent Pennsylvania Republican, "and while he was a pure and conscientious man, his prejudices and disappointments were vastly stronger than himself, and there never was a day during his continuance in the Cabinet when he was able to approach justice to Lincoln."[67] Chase's disappointment had not abated after three years of serving as Treasury secretary, and he was particularly incensed at Lincoln's habit of parceling out tasks to the members of his cabinet as though they were so many errand boys, rather than paying earnest heed to the presumably wiser counsel that Chase longed to unburden himself of. Now, with the 1864 election looming large and the armies conquering little, Lincoln was looking more and more like a liability to the Republican Party, and Chase's moment seemed to have come at last.

In December 1863 Chase's supporters began building a boom for Chase as a dump-Lincoln candidate. The marriage of his daughter, Kate Chase, to Rhode Island governor William Sprague gave Chase a foothold in New England politics and unlocked the Sprague fortune and the blockhouse-like Greek Revival mansion at 6th and E Streets in Washington that Sprague bought for the secretary's political uses. In February 1864 Chase's political manager, Kansas senator Samuel C. Pomeroy, arranged for the publication of a pro-Chase pamphlet, *The Next Presidential Election*, which declared that a second term for Lincoln would be a national calamity, that the next president needed to be a statesman with a record of advanced economic thinking, and that Lincoln was manifestly inferior to Jefferson Davis as an executive. Though the pamphlet did not expressly advocate a Chase presidency as the alternative, it was clear that no more likely person to fill such a need was then living in the Republic than Salmon P. Chase. The pamphlet itself was a cheap, discreditable essay in political character assassination, and it looked all the more cheap for having been distributed to Senator John Sherman's Ohio constituents by means of Sherman's postage-free frank.[68]

67. McClure, *Lincoln and Men of War-Times*, 132.

68. William Frank Zornow, *Lincoln and the Party Divided* (Norman: University of Oklahoma Press, 1954), 49–50.

The impact might not have been nearly so embarrassing for Chase had not Pomeroy also boiled down its essential points into a "strictly private" circular letter to Republican Party backers two weeks later naming Chase—"a statesman of rare ability and an administrator of the highest order" whose "private character furnishes the surest guarantee of economy and purity in the management of public affairs"—as the proper successor to Lincoln. The idea that Chase would sit in Lincoln's cabinet and encourage his political foot soldiers to stab Lincoln in the back made party regulars blanch. Chase rushed to Lincoln to swear that he had known nothing about the Pomeroy circular, and he even offered to resign from the Cabinet. Lincoln pointedly gave Chase's protests a chilly reception, and, knowing that it would be easier to keep a leash on Chase's ambition inside the cabinet rather than outside, refused the resignation. The Chase boomlet had worried Lincoln a good deal, and McClure remembered that it was the only occasion when he had seen Lincoln "unbalanced . . . like one who had got into water far beyond his depth."[69]

Lincoln now had Chase where he wanted him: Chase's chances for the nomination vanished into thin air, and even the Republicans in his native Ohio rejected any notion of his candidacy. "The Pomeroy Circular has helped Lincoln more than all other things together," wrote one of John Sherman's constituents. At the end of June Chase offered again to resign over a minor disagreement about patronage, and this time Lincoln accepted his offer. "You and I have reached a point of mutual embarrassment in our official relation which it seems can not be overcome, or longer sustained," Lincoln wrote coldly. He replaced him with William Pitt Fessenden, the chair of the Senate Finance Committee. That December, Lincoln got rid of Chase once and for all by kicking him upstairs to become chief justice of the Supreme Court, a position that no one had any hope of using as a springboard for the presidency.[70]

The kind of clash Lincoln had with Chase was really little more than a cloakroom dispute, and it paled by comparison with the struggle Lincoln faced when his fellow Republicans openly declared their disagreements with him on substantial questions of war policy. The Thirty-eighth Congress, which had been formed in the painful 1862 elections (and which met for its first session on December 7, 1863), counted 102 Republican Representatives in the House and 36 Republicans in the Senate, which gave them a clear majority over against the 75 Democratic Representatives in the House and 9 Democrats in the Senate.[71] Of the Republican senators,

---

69. Burton J. Hendrick, *Lincoln's War Cabinet* (New York: Little, Brown, 1946), 486–87; Frederick J. Blue, *Salmon P. Chase: A Life in Politics* (Kent, OH: Kent State University Press, 1987), 223–25; McClure, *Lincoln and Men of War-Times*, 134.

70. John Niven, *Salmon P. Chase: A Biography* (New York: Oxford University Press, 1995), 366; David H. Donald, *Lincoln* (New York: Simon and Schuster, 1995), 508; Lincoln, "To Salmon P. Chase," June 30, 1864, in *Collected Works*, 7:419.

71. *Tribune Almanac for 1864* (New York: Tribune Association, 1864), 24.

seventeen of them formed an especially critical core of radical Republican determination. They expressed themselves time and again in pressing for the swiftest and most extreme solutions to the problems of war policy, including emancipation and black civil rights.

The figurehead of the Senate Radicals was Charles Sumner of Massachusetts, and no one could match Sumner's eloquence in pleading for an aggressive prosecution of the war, emancipation, and racial equality. While Sumner was a great talker, he had few skills as a practical politician. Far more talented among the Radicals in wielding the political knife was Benjamin Franklin Wade, crude and competent, and the author of the greatest anti-slavery *bon mot* in the history of the Congress. (In the debates in the 1850s over the extension of the slavery into the territories, one southern senator shed eloquent tears over the Republicans' refusal to allow him to take his old black mammy to Kansas with him; Wade replied that he had no objection to the senator's taking his mammy with him to Kansas, only to selling her once he got there.) Sumner and Wade were joined in radicalism by Zachariah Chandler of Michigan, Henry Wilson of Massachusetts, Lyman Trumbull of Illinois, and the unfortunate Pomeroy of Kansas, and Wilson, Wade, Sumner, Trumbull, and Chandler all sat together as one phalanx on the right side of the aisle on the floor of the Senate.[72]

Most of the Radicals were old veterans of the anti-slavery struggle, and many had even longer ties to the old Whig Party; as a result, they were inclined to regard Lincoln as a political novice. "I begin to despair of ever putting down this rebellion through the instrumentality of this administration," raged Ben Wade; Lincoln's ideas "could only come of one, born of poor white trash, and educated in a slave state." While Lincoln hesitated over colonization, compensated emancipation, and the recruitment of black soldiers, the Radical Republicans used the majority they achieved in the Senate after the withdrawal of the Southern senators to lead the way in expelling Democratic senators of dubious loyalty, in abolishing slavery in the District of Columbia, in amending the Militia Act to open up recruitment to black soldiers, in repealing the Fugitive Slave Law, in barring the issue of charters to District of Columbia streetcar companies that practiced racial discrimination, and in equalizing pay for the USCT regiments.[73] The conventional wisdom about these Radical Republicans sees them as vengeful, ambitious men, eager to use emancipation as a means of subduing the South once and for all to Northern free-labor capitalism. There may be some debate about their lust for vengeance or self-aggrandizement,

72. Ben Perley Poore, *Perley's Reminiscences of Sixty Years in the National Metropolis* (Philadelphia: Hubbard Bros., 1886), 1:538; Allan G. Bogue, *The Earnest Men: Republicans of the Civil War Senate* (Ithaca, NY: Cornell University Press, 1981), 97–98, 109–10, 130.

73. Henry Wilson, *History of the Antislavery Measures of the Thirty-seventh and Thirty-eighth United-States Congresses, 1861–64* (Boston: Walker, Wise, 1864), 65, 222–23, 292, 376.

but it is certainly true enough that they had embraced the protection of Northern industry through high tariffs, the opening of western public lands to homesteaders as a means of avoiding the formation of a propertyless urban proletariat, and the replacement of slavery in the South with free labor. By these means, argued Wade, the Union would "build up a free yeomanry capable of maintaining an independent republican Government forever."[74]

"For nearly two generations, the slaveholding class, into whose power the Government early passed, dictated the policy of the nation," wrote Henry Wilson. It scarcely took the war to convince them that the South was an obstacle to the triumph of Republicanism and needed a root-and-branch re-creation. The Radicals crafted the confiscation bills in 1861 and 1862 and called for the treatment of rebels as traitors whose penalty, "as established by our fathers, was death by the halter." Their no-compromise attitude and determination to grant the Republican Party a lock on the national government frequently made them impatient with Lincoln's administration. In 1862 they tried to unseat Seward as secretary of state, and a few obliquely suggested that even Lincoln should resign.[75]

Lincoln, by contrast, has been portrayed as a moderate and far-seeing statesman, desiring only to end the war without bitterness. Lincoln, after all, had won the Republican nomination in 1860 precisely on the grounds that he was more of a moderate than Seward or Chase and could win more votes, while his slowness in moving toward emancipation has been interpreted as proof of Lincoln's distaste for Radicals. Deep in Lincoln's temperament was a resistance to radical schemes of social change. "In declaring that they would 'do their duty and leave the consequences to God,'" the abolitionists "merely gave an excuse for taking a course that they were not able to maintain by a fair and full argument. To make this declaration did not show what their duty was." Sometimes, Lincoln said to his attorney general, the Missourian Edward Bates, these Radical Republicans were "almost fiendish" in their intensity to bully him into agreement with their agenda. "Stevens, Sumner and Wilson, simply haunt me," Lincoln complained to Missouri senator John B. Henderson. "Wherever I go and whatever way I turn, they are on my trail."[76]

74. Wade to Zachariah Chandler, September 23 and October 8, 1861, in Zachariah Chandler Papers, Library of Congress; Wade, "Property in Territories," March 7, 1860, *Congressional Globe*, 36th Congress, 1st Session (Appendix), 154.

75. Hans L. Trefousse, *The Radical Republicans: Lincoln's Vanguard for Racial Justice* (Baton Rouge: Louisiana State University Press, 1968), 4–16; Wilson, *History of the Anti-Slavery Measures*, 377; Herman Belz, *Abraham Lincoln, Constitutionalism, and Equal Rights in the Civil War* (New York: Fordham University Press, 1998), 101–3; Bogue, *The Earnest Men*, 229.

76. Lincoln, "Speech at Worcester," September 12, 1848, in *Collected Works*, 2:2–3; *The Diary of Edward Bates*, 333; Lincoln to John B. Henderson, in Walter B. Stevens, *A Reporter's Lincoln*, ed. Michael Burlingame (Lincoln: University of Nebraska Press, 1999), 170–73.

But Lincoln shared more ground with Radical thinking on the key issues of abolition and black civil equality than he often admitted, and it is significant that the Radicals also sought and got policy statements from Lincoln for use in directing their legislative campaigns, while he never gave any such to Republican moderates. William Lloyd Garrison broke ranks with Wendell Phillips and other abolitionists and openly supported Lincoln's reelection. "There is no mistake about it in regard to Mr. Lincoln's desire to do all that he can see it right and possible for him to do to uproot slavery," Garrison assured his wife after meeting with Lincoln in the White House in the summer of 1864. Sumner remained a close family friend of the Lincolns all through the war; Lincoln's strongest political ally in the House of Representatives was Owen Lovejoy, brother of the abolitionist martyr Elijah Lovejoy and one of the most Radical Republicans in Congress. Lovejoy had stood loyally behind Lincoln for being "at heart as strong an anti-slavery man as any of them," reminding his fellow radicals that Lincoln had to be the president of the whole Union, not just the Radicals' part of it, and thus was "compelled to *feel* his way." When Lovejoy died in 1864 Lincoln paid tribute to him as "my most generous friend" in Congress, and he told Shelby Cullom "that he was one of the best men in Congress." As much as the Radicals were "bitterly hostile" to him "personally," and "utterly lawless—the unhandiest devils in the world to deal with," Lincoln also admitted that "after all their faces are set Zionwards." As he told John B. Henderson, "Sumner and Wade and Chandler are right about [abolition]. . . . We can't get through this terrible war with slavery existing."[77]

If Lincoln resisted the Radicals, it was not so much because of outright disagreements over ideology, but because he was determined to keep the hands of Congress off his presidential prerogatives (especially as commander in chief) and to prevent the long-term outcomes of the war from backfiring, either through further bankrupting the county through endless conflict or so wrecking the Southern economy that the freed slaves would have nothing to be free for afterward. If the Radicals were impatient with Lincoln, it was not so much because of a difference of principles, but on differences of timing and political tactics, especially where these concerned the military conduct of the war, abolition, and Lincoln's proposals for reconstructing the Union—although that provided more than enough room for antagonism and headaches.

As early as December 1861 the Radicals tried to deal themselves a piece of Lincoln's war powers by creating a seven-member House-Senate committee, known as the Joint Committee on the Conduct of the War, with Wade and Chandler as the unofficial handlers. "I hold it to be our bounden duty . . . to keep an anxious, watchful

77. Garrison to Helen E. Garrison, June 11, 1864, in *Letters of William Lloyd Garrison*, vol. V: *Let the Oppressed Go Free, 1861–1867*, ed. W. M. Merrill (Cambridge, MA: Harvard University Press, 1979), 212; Hans L. Trefousse, "Owen Lovejoy and Abraham Lincoln During the Civil War," *Journal of the Abraham Lincoln Association* 22 (Winter 2001): 31; John Hay, diary entry for October 28, 1863, in *Inside Lincoln's White House*, 101; Allan G. Bogue, *The Congressman's Civil War* (New York: Cambridge University Press, 1989), 43.

eye over all the executive agents who are carrying on the war at the direction of the people, whom we represent and whom we are bound to protect in relation to this matter," declared William Pitt Fessenden. Although it was never actually stated in so many words, the joint committee was understood as the Radicals' lever for pressuring Lincoln and the Union military into waging a more and more Radical version of the war. In February 1862, the committee moved first against Brigadier General Charles P. Stone, a McClellanite general who had botched a small-scale military operation at Ball's Bluff on the Potomac. It was clear that Stone was a surrogate for McClellan, whom the Radicals had already come to hate as a Democrat and halfhearted. As an object lesson, the committee had Stone arrested and imprisoned for six months without so much as a chance to hear the charges—whatever they were—against him. Nothing bound the committee to observe the customary legal safeguards for those it examined, and the hapless generals and politicians who were haled before the committee were unable to respond to their accusers, or even (like Stone) to see a copy of the charges that had led to their investigation in the first place. Over the course of the war, the joint committee held 272 meetings and issued eight fat volumes of proceedings, including condemnations of the massacre at Sand Creek and the slaughter of the black soldiers at Fort Pillow.[78]

Lincoln did not entirely welcome the meddling of the joint committee, and even though Ben Wade offered Lincoln the use of the committee's services to call the House or the Senate into closed-door sessions on war policy, Lincoln ignored what he rightly saw as an attempt to manipulate his prerogatives as president. But much as Lincoln was careful to guard his own constitutional powers from overeager interference by the joint committee, it is significant that Lincoln never actually attacked the committee, and he made no attempt to intervene on behalf of Stone or any of the other hapless generals the committee summoned for questioning. After all, the simple threat of the committee's existence was useful for prodding reluctant generals into action. By the same token, the committee members groused to themselves about Lincoln and occasionally used their hearings to air ill-disguised hints about the direction of war policy, but they never actually challenged Lincoln the way they would challenge and then impeach his successor in future years. The committee, and the Radicals for whom it spoke, recognized in Lincoln an ideological equal but not a practical political one, and their constant agitation for more drastic prosecution of the war amounted to an ongoing criticism not of Lincoln's principles but of what they saw as Lincoln's imperfect application of them.[79]

---

78. "Military Disasters," December 9, 1861, *Congressional Globe*, 37th Congress, 1st session, 31; Tap, *Over Lincoln's Shoulder*, 21–24, 165–66; Sears, *Controversies and Commanders*, 33–46.

79. Bogue, *The Congressman's Civil War*, 101–3.

It was not the war but the shape of the Reconstruction that must follow it that be- came the most serious issue between Lincoln and the Radical Republicans. Acting on his premise that secession was a legal impossibility, Lincoln urged Congress to accept new governments for the Southern states as soon as a Unionist majority among the citizens could make Reconstruction there ready. In March 1862 he appointed Andrew Johnson, a Unionist Democrat and the only Southern senator who had steadfastly refused to resign from the U.S. Senate after his state seceded, as "Military Governor of the State of Tennessee . . . until the loyal inhabitants of that state shall organize a civil government in conformity with the Constitution of the United States." Over the next four months, Lincoln appointed Edward Stanly, an old North Carolina Whig, as military governor of the occupied eastern shore of North Carolina, and John Smith Phelps as military governor for Arkansas, both with a similar mandate to restore their states to the Union. In occupied Louisiana, a provisional military government actually managed to have two elected representatives (from the two occupied con- gressional districts), Benjamin Flanders and Michael Hahn, seated in the House.[80]

Then, on December 8, 1863, Lincoln published "A Proclamation of Amnesty and Reconstruction," which offered occupied Louisiana a Reconstruction scheme de- tailing a process for the formation of a new state government. Any inhabitant of Louisiana could obtain a pardon for participating in the rebellion by taking a loyalty oath to the U.S. Constitution and "all acts of Congress passed during the existing re- bellion with reference to slaves" and "all proclamations of the President made during the existing rebellion having reference to slaves, so long and so far as not modified or declared void by decision of the Supreme Court." In other words, with one eye kept firmly on the chance that his actions might be challenged in the federal courts, Lincoln was offering to trade presidential pardons for submission to the Emancipa- tion Proclamation before the Taney Court got a chance to void the Proclamation. The only exclusions Lincoln kept in place would be for high-ranking Confederate military officers, politicians who had resigned federal offices (and who had therefore violated their oath to support the Constitution), and anyone guilty of abusing Fed- eral prisoners, "colored persons or white persons." Then, when 10 percent of the 1860 voting population had taken the loyalty oath, occupied Louisiana could reestablish its state government, and any provisions in reestablished state governments that would make black freedom permanent and provide for the education of freed slaves "will not be objected to by the national Executive."[81]

80. Edwin M. Stanton to Andrew Johnson, March 3, 1862, in *Report of the Joint Committee on Reconstruc- tion, at the First Session, Thirty-Ninth Congress* (Washington, DC: Government Printing Office, 1866), 5; Edwin M. Stanton to Edward Stanly, May 20, 1862, in *War of the Rebellion*, Series One, 9:397; William C. Harris, *With Charity for All: Lincoln and the Restoration of the Union* (Lexington: University Press of Kentucky, 1997), 40, 59–71, 78–81, 84.

81. "Proclamation of Amnesty," December 8, 1863, in McPherson, ed., *Political History of the Rebellion*, 147–48.

Lincoln, not knowing how the war might turn out, hoped to use this proclamation as a means of wedging emancipation into the constitutions of as many occupied states as soon as possible. The Radicals, however, criticized this plan as too flimsy and too unrealistic a foundation for genuine Reconstruction, in Louisiana or anywhere else. A number of the Radicals, headed by Wade and Sumner, argued that the seceding states had committed "state suicide" and should now be treated as conquered provinces and made to pass again through the entire process of territorialization before being readmitted to the Union. And when Louisianans attempted to follow Lincoln's directives and re-create a Louisiana constitution, they unwittingly lent the Radicals a stick to beat them with by endorsing only emancipation and not black voting rights, even for black Louisiana soldiers. Lincoln delicately pointed out this oversight to Michael Hahn, the new Louisiana governor, and pressed Hahn privately to have black voting rights included in the new state constitution. The damage had been done, however, and when representatives from the newly reconstructed Louisiana government showed up in Congress in 1864, the Radicals, led by Sumner, prevented them from being officially recognized.[82]

Then in July 1864, the Radicals moved to take the initiative on Reconstruction out of Lincoln's hands altogether. Henry Winter Davis in the House and Ben Wade in the Senate sponsored a bill that, although it stopped short of "territorializing" the seceder states, still upped the ante of Reconstruction far above Lincoln's levels. Instead of the 10 percent of the 1860 voting population specified in the Lincoln proclamation as the requisite for Reconstruction, the Wade-Davis bill demanded the "enrollment" of all white male citizens of states where "military resistance . . . shall have been suppressed" and the extraction of a loyalty oath from "a majority of the persons enrolled in the State." Once the loyalty of a white majority had been established (and this time no inclusion of black citizens would be permitted, since that would make the readmission process too quick and painless), the "loyal people" of a state could elect a convention and reestablish their state government. However, no one who had served in the Confederate army or held political office under the Confederacy was eligible to vote for a delegate to this convention or be elected as a delegate. Likewise, no matter what the form of state government eventually drawn up by the convention, no one who had ever served in the Confederate military or civil service could vote for, or be elected to, any office. Moreover, all public debts under the Confederate regime were to be repudiated (which meant that those holding Confederate bonds,

82. LaWanda Cox, *Lincoln and Black Freedom: A Study in Presidential Leadership* (Urbana: University of Illinois Press, 1985), 72–74; Joseph G. Dawson, *Army Generals and Reconstruction: Louisiana, 1862–1877* (Baton Rouge: Louisiana State University Press, 1982), 16–23; Edward L. Pierce, *Memoir and Letters of Charles Sumner* (Boston: Roberts Bros., 1893), 4:214–23.

notes, or currency lost everything they had invested), and "involuntary servitude" was to be "forever prohibited."[83]

What this did, in effect, was to lengthen Reconstruction almost indefinitely, since it was difficult to see how half of the present population of any Confederate state could be persuaded to take a loyalty oath to the United States before a long time had passed. Lincoln, who understood perfectly what a shambles the Wade-Davis bill would make of Reconstruction, simply killed it by means of a pocket veto. He was not unsympathetic to the Radicals' determination that reconstructed governments be genuinely loyal to the Constitution, but he was also convinced that they had forgotten that his administration did not have all the time in the world. Emancipation—the goal both he and the Radicals shared—was as yet only a military action, and dignified only by what he could claim as his war powers. While the war was still on and Union occupation forces clearly held the whip handle, emancipation could be forced down Southern throats relatively easily. But let the war end suddenly, or let his administration lose the upcoming election in November to a Democratic peace candidate, and the military justification for emancipation would evaporate at the same moment that the shooting stopped. The military threat behind emancipation would cease to exist, and civil court challenges to the permanent legality of emancipation would immediately flood into the federal courts.

Better to take an imperfect Reconstruction that got emancipation onto the books now than delay Reconstruction so long that a changed political or military climate might make emancipation impossible. Lincoln, in a document issued after Congress adjourned, insisted that he was not "inflexibly committed to any single plan of restoration," and that he was not going to undo the "free State constitutions and government already adopted" in places such as Louisiana. This did not do much to convince either Davis or Wade. On August 5 the two Radicals published a defiant manifesto reminding Lincoln, in terms that Lincoln himself ironically had to acknowledge, that "if he wishes our support, he must confine himself to his Executive duties—to obey and execute, not to make the laws—to suppress by arms armed rebellion, and leave political re-organization to Congress."[84]

The people whose support Lincoln most dreaded losing, and seemed closest to losing by 1864, were the 21 million citizens of the North and border states. To Lincoln, it seemed that they, too, had lost faith in him. Emancipation, even delayed as long as it had been by Lincoln, was still far in advance of the racial consciousness of

83. "An Act to Guarantee to Certain States Whose Governments Have Been Usurped or Overthrown a Republican Form of Government," in *The Radical Republicans and Reconstruction, 1861–1870*, ed. Harold Hyman (Indianapolis, IN: Bobbs-Merrill, 1967), 128–34; "Rebellious States," May 4, 1864, and "Reconstruction Bill," July 2, 1864, *Congressional Globe*, 38th Congress, 1st Session, 2108, 3491.

84. "Bill for Reconstruction," in McPherson, ed., *Political History*, 316–18; "Protest of Sen. Wade and H. W. Davis, M.C.," in *The American Annual Cyclopaedia and Register of Important Events of the Year 1864* (New York: Appleton, 1865), 307–10.

most Americans, and the Democratic press in particular dwelt heavily upon the economic penalties white workers would have to pay if emancipation unleashed a flood of free blacks who came north and competed for jobs. Worse than emancipation, however, was the backlash stimulated by Congress's decision to institute military conscription in 1862 and then adopt a federal conscription law in March 1863.

No one in Washington in 1861 had really planned to resort to mass conscription to fill the armies, simply because no one had thought it would be necessary. The flood tide of volunteers who enlisted in 1861 seemed to provide all the manpower anyone could possibly want for the war. But the enlistments of the forty regiments that Congress had authorized for two years back in 1861 ran out in mid-1863, and as they did, few of the two-year veterans showed much enthusiasm for reenlistment. At the same time, the tide of volunteers who had enlisted in three-year regiments in 1861 and 1862 had noticeably flattened by 1863. In July 1862, Radical Republican senator Henry Wilson of Massachusetts drew up a new Militia Act to replace the outdated 1795 Federal militia ordinance, and in addition to setting aside the racial color line and permitting black enlistment, the new act mandated the enrollment by each state of all male citizens between the ages of eighteen and forty-five, and authorized the president to set quotas for each state to meet in the event that a draft would be necessary.[85]

In order to avoid resorting to an outright draft of unwilling men, the states tried to stimulate volunteering by offering bounties to recruits. "Most of us were surprised," wrote one Pennsylvania volunteer in 1862, "when, a few days after our arrival in [Camp Curtin], we were told that the County Commissioners had come down for the purpose of paying us each the magnificent sum of fifty dollars. At the same time, also, we learned that the United States Government would pay us each one hundred dollars additional. . . ."[86] By 1863, these bounties were no longer a surprise. Considering that the average workingman's annual wages ranged between $300 and $500 in the 1860s, these bounties were considerable sums of money, and reluctant volunteers could frequently be enticed into service by the prospect of a bounty that could buy enough land for a farm or a homestead.[87]

The prime difficulty with the bounty system—apart from the appearance it gave of bribing Northern males to do what should have been their civic duty—was how liable it was to abuses of various sorts. Communities and states eager to fill up state volunteer quotas found themselves competing with other communities and states

---

85. Wilson, *History of the Anti-Slavery Measures*, 203–17; "An Act to Amend the Act Calling Forth the Militia," July 17, 1862, in *Statutes at Large*, 37th Congress, 2nd Session, 597–600.

86. Miller, *The Training of an Army*, 106.

87. Clarence D. Long, *Wages and Earnings in the United States, 1860–1890* (Princeton, NJ: Princeton University Press, 1960), 14–15.

for volunteers. Presently the politicians began a bidding war for recruits and offered multiple bounties that could total more than $1,000 when added up. That, in turn, invited the appearance of "bounty jumpers," who enlisted in one state or community to receive a bounty, then deserted and reenlisted under another name in another state to pick up another bounty. One bounty jumper, John O'Connor, who was caught in Albany, New York, in March 1865, confessed to having bounty-jumped thirty-two times before being caught.[88]

If the bounties were the carrot for enlistment, then the draft was clearly the stick. It did not take long for a draft to become necessary: little more than two weeks after the passage of the new Militia Act, Lincoln authorized Stanton to initiate a draft that would yield 300,000 men. On August 9, Stanton issued orders describing how the governors of the states were to implement the enrolling and drafting of soldiers. It did not turn out to be that easy. The formula for establishing state quotas was complex and unclear, various categories of exemptions from the draft were fuzzy, and above all, draftees were permitted to hire substitutes, in what amounted to a personalized bounty system. In Chester County, Pennsylvania, where the county quota for draftees was set at 1,800 men, local notables passed the hat to raise a local bounty fund that they hoped would entice volunteers to fill up the county quota; another three hundred draftees, such as Samuel Pennypacker, hired a substitute. "My grandfather . . . paid $300 for a substitute in Norristown who was only too willing to go to the front in my stead. I do not know of his name or his fate."[89]

The need for men in this war was insatiable, and so in March 1863 Congress passed an Enrollment Act that bypassed the state governments entirely and created a series of federal enrollment boards that would take responsibility for satisfying the federally assigned state quotas. Each congressional district was expected to establish an enrollment board of three members, headed by a provost marshal, which would draw up a roll of all eligible males within their district. Despite the anger and anxieties that enrollment touched off, enrollment did not necessarily mean conscription. Although each congressional district was issued a quota of volunteers to recruit for each draft call, men would be drafted only from those districts that otherwise failed to meet that quota through volunteering. Districts that could provide sufficient volunteers, or bounties high enough to lure volunteers, would not need to draft anyone, and in the end only seven Northern states would be subject to all four of the draft calls issued under the Enrollment Act.[90]

88. James W. Geary, *We Need Men: The Union Draft in the Civil War* (DeKalb: Northern Illinois University Press, 1991), 32–48.

89. Douglas R. Harper, *"If Thee Must Fight": A Civil War History of Chester County, Pennsylvania* (West Chester, PA: Chester County Historical Society, 1990), 204.

90. Geary, *We Need Men*, 54–63, 67–70, 83–84.

Even conscription itself did not necessarily translate into war service. Of the 292,000 names that were drawn from the enrollment lists for the first draft call in 1863, less than 10,000 actually wound up in uniform. Most of the rest were released for disability or on claims to exemption, while another 26,000 hired substitutes (among the hirers being a future president of the United States, Grover Cleveland). Over 50,000 Northerners escaped service by another provision in the Enrollment Act known as "commutation," which allowed draftees to pay $300 as an exemption fee to escape the draft. Immigrants proved to be equally adept at avoiding conscription: far more entered the army as substitutes, taking the chance of battles and disease in exchange for the benefits of hiring themselves out as soldiers. Even when subsequent draft calls in 1864 and 1865 are added to these figures, no more than 47,000 men were actually conscripted into the Union armies.[91]

Yet despite the loopholes and commutation provisions, the idea of a compulsory military draft was still a strong dose for Americans to swallow, especially since after 1863 conscription now meant fighting in a war to free black slaves. Moreover, the commutation fee cast the ugly specter of class conflict over the draft: a wealthy man might have no difficulty coming up with the $300 commutation fee or finding and hiring a substitute, but a workingman was looking at what might be an economic wall too high to scale, while the availability of substitutes grew scarcer with each passing month. That, together with the inherently repulsive notion that in a democracy someone could hire a substitute to get shot in his place, was calculated to provoke the bloodiest sort of response among the poor. Anti-draft disturbances erupted within days of the implementation of the Enrollment Act and a new draft call.

The worst incidents of anti-draft violence erupted in New York City in mid-summer 1863, two days after the first draft of names was drawn in the 9th Congressional District. Almost from the beginning of the war, New York City had been a hotbed of labor unrest: as men marched off to war and as war contracts sent manufacturing production soaring, New York workingmen found that labor was suddenly at a premium, and they did not hesitate to use the situation to bargain and strike for higher wages. Rumors that the government would use prisoners of war and even South Carolina "contrabands" to break strikes against war-related business had already inflamed working-class tempers when the Enrollment Act became public in the spring of 1863. The terms of the act looked like nothing so much as an attempt to draw workingmen out of this highly attractive labor market and send them into battle so that more blacks could be free to compete for wages and break up strikes—all the while offering a $300 commutation fee for factory owners and their sons.

---

91. Eugene Converse Murdock, *Patriotism Limited, 1862–1865: The Civil War Draft and the Bounty System* (Kent, OH: Kent State University Press, 1967), 211; Tyler Anbinder, "Which Poor Man's Fight? Immigrants and the Federal Conscription of 1863," *Civil War History* 52 (December 2006): 372.

On July 13, angry crowds of workingmen erupted. For four days, mobs of whites attacked and burned the homes of Republican politicians, tried to demolish Horace Greeley's *New York Tribune*, and lynched any African Americans they happened to lay their hands on, in addition to burning the Colored Orphan Asylum to the ground. Dr. John Thayer, a chemist who worked in the U.S. Assay Office in Wall Street, saw "the whole road way & sidewalks filled with rough fellows (& some equally rough women) who were tearing up rails, cutting down telegraph poles & setting fire to buildings."

> The furious, bareheaded & coatless men assembled under our windows & shouted for Jeff Davis! . . . Towards evening the mob, furious as demons, went yelling over to the Colored-Orphan Asylum in 5th Avenue . . . & rolling a barrel of kerosine in it, the whole structure was soon in a blaze, & is now a smoking ruin. What has become of the 300 innocent orphans I could not learn. . . . Before this fire was extinguished, or rather burnt out, for the wicked wretches who caused it would not permit the engines to be used, the northern sky was brilliantly illuminated, probably by the burning of the Aged Colored-Woman's Home in 65th Street. . . . A friend . . . had seen a poor negro hung an hour or two before. The man had, in a frenzy, shot an Irish fireman, and they immediately strung up the unhappy African. . . . A person who called at our house this afternoon saw three of them hanging together.[92]

Eventually Federal troops fresh from Gettysburg were brought into New York City. They calmly shot the rioters down, and the riots collapsed. But riots popped up elsewhere—in Boston, in Milwaukee, in the marble quarries of Vermont, and across the upper Midwest—and they were often linked, like the New York City riots, to labor disputes. In the Pennsylvania coalfields, bitter labor disputes between the miners and mine owners were dragged into the operation of the draft when appointments as provost marshals and enrollment officers went to mine officials and the families of mine owners, ensuring that the draft would be used, and perceived, as a weapon in labor disputes. "Now is the time for the operators . . . to get rid of the ringleaders engaged in threatenings, beatings, and shooting bosses at the collieries and put better men in their places," argued one Pennsylvania coal mine owner. "It is far better to send them into the army and put them in the front ranks, even if they are killed by the enemy, than that they should live to perpetuate such a cowardly race." Miners took their cues from such lines, evading the draft and waylaying enrollment officers as just one more aspect of their struggle against the mine bosses. Unfortunately for

92. Ernest A. McKay, *The Civil War and New York City* (Syracuse, NY: Syracuse University Press, 1990), 197–212; Iver Bernstein, *The New York City Draft Riots: Their Significance for American Society and Politics in the Age of the Civil War* (New York: Oxford University Press, 1990), 7–14; A. Hunter Dupree and Leslie H. Fishel, "An Eyewitness Account of the New York Draft Riots, July 1863," *Mississippi Valley Historical Review* 47 (December 1960): 476–77.

the miners, the mine owners had the authority of the Federal government behind them: in Luzerne County, a hundred miners were arrested, and seventy of them were imprisoned in the dungeons at old Fort Mifflin in Philadelphia.[93]

Aggravating all of these problems for Lincoln behind the lines was the uniformly bad news from the lines in the summer of 1864. As he feared, that May a Radical Republican splinter group called a convention in Cleveland to dump Lincoln and nominate John Charles Frémont for the presidency instead. In late August, the Democratic National Convention adopted a "peace and union" platform for the 1864 presidential campaign, and it was obvious that they would nominate as their candidate Lincoln's former general, George Brinton McClellan.

The little general had become the darling of Lincoln's Democratic critics, endorsing Democratic candidates for governorships and allowing himself to be discussed for the presidential nomination for more than a year. "I think that the original object of the war . . . the preservation of the Union, its Constitution & its laws, has been lost sight of, or very widely departed from," McClellan wrote in July 1864, when the Republican Francis Blair attempted to elicit from him an assurance for the newspapers that he would not be interested in the Democratic presidential nomination: "I think the war has been permitted to take a course which unnecessarily embitters the inimical feeling between the two sections, & . . . I deprecate a policy which far from tending to that end tends in the contrary direction."[94]

This was as much as begging for the Democratic nomination, and when the Democratic convention met in Chicago a month later, McClellan won the nomination easily. He was also confident that, at least this time, he would easily win a national campaign. In his acceptance letter on September 4, 1864, McClellan declared that "I believe that a vast majority of our people, whether in the Army & Navy or at home, would, with me hail with unbounded joy the permanent restoration of peace on the basis of the Federal Union of the States without the effusion of another drop of blood."[95]

Abraham Lincoln was not sure that McClellan was wrong. On August 22, Henry J. Raymond, the chair of the Republican National Committee, warned Lincoln that "the tide is setting strongly against us." Pennsylvania "is against us"; Indiana "would go 50,000 against us to-morrow. And so of the rest." On the same day, William H. Seward's longtime political manager, Thurlow Weed, warned Lincoln "that his re-election was an impossibility. . . . The People are wild for Peace." Lincoln was not

93. Grace Palladino, *Another Civil War: Labor, Capital, and the State in the Anthracite Regions of Pennsylvania, 1840–1868* (Urbana: University of Illinois Press, 1990), 124–35; Barnet Schecter, *The Devil's Own Work: The Civil War Draft Riots and the Fight to Reconstruct America* (New York: Walker Publishing, 2005), 19.

94. "To Francis P. Blair," July 22, 1864, in *Civil War Papers of George B. McClellan*, 584.

95. "To the Democratic Nomination Committee," September 4, 1864, in *Civil War Papers*, 591.

even sure he could rely on Grant to rally around, and he told Alexander McClure that, as far as he knew, "I have no reason to believe that Grant prefers my election to that of McClellan." Weighed down with grief, a morose Lincoln wrote out a memorandum that he folded and had all the members of his cabinet endorse without reading. Inside its folds, the memorandum read:

> This morning, as for some days past, it seems exceedingly probable that this Administration will not be re-elected. Then it will be my duty to so co-operate with the President elect, as to save the Union between the election and the inauguration; as he will have secured his election on such ground that he can not possibly save it afterwards.[96]

Lincoln later explained the memorandum as a last-ditch war plan, a challenge to McClellan to use the lame-duck period between the election and the next president's inauguration to rally all the nation's energies for a "final trial." Seward poured scorn on any idea that presumed action on the part of George McClellan: "And the General would answer you 'Yes, Yes;' and the next day when you saw him again and pressed these views upon him, he would say, 'Yes, Yes;' & so on forever, and would have done nothing at all." At least in that case, Lincoln said, "I should have done my duty and have stood clear before my own conscience." Looking back, McClure had been certain that "there was no period from January, 1864, until the 3rd of September of the same year when McClellan would not have defeated Lincoln."[97]

In fact, the election was not going to turn out that way. On the day Lincoln drafted his letter, Farragut shot his way into Mobile Bay; a week later, Atlanta fell to Sherman. The *Alabama* went to the bottom of Cherbourg harbor in June, and in October, Grant's cavalry commander, an aggressive knock-down brawler named Philip Sheridan, cleared Virginia's Shenandoah Valley of Jubal Early's Confederates in a spectacular miniature campaign. These triumphs buoyed Northern morale higher than it had been since Vicksburg, and made talk of peace seem like a giveback of victory.

To make matters worse for the Democrats, McClellan alienated the peace faction of the party (including his vice presidential nominee, George Pendleton, who was "an avowed peacemonger," according to George Templeton Strong) by insisting that reunion rather than peace be made the first priority of the platform. While Pendleton announced that he was "in favor of exacting no conditions, and . . . opposed to any course of policy which will defeat the reestablishment of the Government upon its old foundations," McClellan had no intention of espousing any peace platform that simply allowed the Confederacy to go its own way as an independent nation.

96. Lincoln, "Memorandum Concerning His Probable Failure of Re-election," *Collected Works*, 7:514.

97. J. G. Nicolay and John Hay, *Abraham Lincoln: A History* (New York: Century, 1890), 9:218; Charles B. Flood, *1864: Lincoln at the Gates of History* (New York: Simon and Schuster, 2009), 261; "Before My Own Conscience," in Lincoln, *Conversations with Lincoln*, ed. Charles M. Segal (New York: Putnam, 1961), 359; McClure, *Lincoln and Men of War-Times*, 124, 203.

He would make whatever concessions the Confederates asked so long as those concessions led the Confederacy back into the Union, but if the Confederate government was not interested in reunion, then "we must continue the resort to the dread arbitrament of war."[98]

McClellan was aware that this would cost him the support of the hard-core Peace Democrats, but he could not reconcile the battles he had fought and the lives that had been lost with a settlement that permitted the North and South simply to walk away from each other like strangers. "I intend to destroy any and all pretense for any possible association of my name to the Peace Party," McClellan wrote two weeks before the election, "I, for one, could not look in the face of my gallant comrades of the Army & Navy who have survived so many bloody battles, & tell them that their labors and the sacrifices of such numbers of their slain & crippled brethren had been in vain."[99] The result was to divide Democratic loyalties at just the moment when only united effort could hope to upset the incumbent Republicans.

So, almost when it was past expectation, Lincoln was handed hope again for the war—or rather, for both of his wars. On September 22, 1864, Frémont, the Radical splinter candidate, withdrew his competing nomination, and Lincoln was allowed to go on bearing the party banner alone. And not only the banner of the Republicans—in a last appeal to the War Democrats, the Republican nominating convention had chosen as Lincoln's vice presidential candidate the Tennessee Unionist Democrat Andrew Johnson, and announced they would not run under the banner of the Republican Party only, but as the "National Union Ticket." On election day, November 8, 1864, Lincoln and Johnson carried 55.1 percent of the popular vote (2.2 million to McClellan's 1.8 million), and 212 out of 233 electoral votes, while the Republicans/ Unionists in Congress won 145 out of 185 seats in the House and 40 out of 52 in the Senate. Most surprising of all, Lincoln garnered 78 percent of the votes of the soldiers, including the Army of the Potomac, thus destroying forever the mystique of McClellan as the hero of the armies.[100] At last, Lincoln had the political mandate that had eluded him for the four years of his first term. He had, at least for the time being, won his political war. It now remained to be seen how he would win the war that still waited for him down below Petersburg.

98. George Templeton Strong, diary entry for September 8, 1864, in *Diary of the Civil War*, 483; Thomas S. Mach, *"Gentleman George" Hunt Pendleton: Party Politics and Ideological Identity in Nineteenth-Century America* (Kent, OH: Kent State University Press, 2007), 105.

99. McClellan to Allan Pinkerton, October 20, 1864, in *Civil War Papers*, 591, 615.

100. *Tribune Almanac and Political Register for 1865* (New York: Tribune Association, 1865), 67; James M. McPherson, *For Cause and Comrades: Why Men Fought in the Civil War* (New York: Oxford University Press, 1997), 176; Kreiser, *Defeating Lee*, 216–17.

CHAPTER ELEVEN

A DIM SHORE AHEAD

For a man who believed in the "cold, calculating" power of "reason" to order his life, Abraham Lincoln retained a peculiar interest in the folk religion of dreams, portents, and signs. Herndon thought Lincoln was "superstitious," and claimed that Lincoln had consulted a fortune-teller "to give him his history, his end, and his fate," and once tried to cure his son Robert of a dog's bite with "a supposed mad stone." Lincoln once described to John Hay and Francis Carpenter a portent he had seen just after his nomination for the presidency in 1860. Exhausted from the celebrations, Lincoln was resting "on a lounge in my chamber" when he saw a reflection of himself in the "swinging glass" that sat on top of a bureau opposite the couch. "My face, I noticed, had two separate and distinct images. . . . I was a little bothered, perhaps startled, and got up and looked in the glass, but the illusion vanished." He lay down, the "illusion" returned, "and then I noticed that one of the faces was a little paler—say, five shades—than the other." He was troubled by the strange double image, and a few days later he tried to conjure it up before a mirror at his home. He did, and it worried Mary, who was sure he was playing with something occult. "She thought it was a sign that I was to be elected to a second term of office and that the paleness of one of the faces was an omen that I should not see life throughout the last term."[1]

1. Herndon, "Lincoln's Superstition," in *The Hidden Lincoln*, 409–10; Lloyd Lewis, *Myths After Lincoln* (New York: Readers Club, 1941), 289–98; Carpenter, *Six Months at the White House with Abraham Lincoln*, 163–65.

More than omens in mirrors, it was his dreams that haunted Lincoln. Sad-eyed Willie, who died in 1862, often visited his dreams, and in June 1863, when Mary and his youngest son, Tad Lincoln, were visiting in Philadelphia, Lincoln wired her to put the boy's small gift pistol away: "I had an ugly dream about him." But it was the recurring dreams about assassination that increasingly preyed on Lincoln's mind. In more untroubled moments, Lincoln dismissed people's fears about assassins. "I have received quite a number of threatening letters since I have been president, and nobody has killed me yet," he assured a Missouri congressman; "the truth is, I give very little consideration to such things." But the threats paced more and more around the edges of his consciousness. He alarmed both Mary and his self-appointed bodyguard, Ward Hill Lamon, by describing a dream in which he saw himself awakened in the White House by the sound of weeping and sobbing. His dream-self moved from room to room in search of the sound until he came to the East Room of the White House, where he found a "throng of mourners," a guard of soldiers, and a catafalque, where a body was lying in state. Lincoln's dream-self asked one of the soldiers, "Who is dead in the White House?" The answer was chilling: "The President. He was killed by an assassin."[2]

Lamon, whom Lincoln had named United States marshal for the District of Columbia, was already uneasy for Lincoln's safety in Washington, and on election night in 1864 he went to the extreme of curling up like a guard dog outside Lincoln's door in a blanket, armed with a collection of knives and revolvers. Lincoln thought Lamon "insane upon the subject of his safety," but it was a derangement that also possessed the secretary of war, Edwin Stanton, who made sure that Lincoln's carriage had a secure cavalry escort, that a company of infantry guarded the White House grounds, and that a District of Columbia policeman accompanied the president whenever Lincoln went to the theater.[3]

Sometimes, though, the dreams pointed to happier conclusions. The dreams about Willie actually gave Lincoln a comfort that eluded the boy's mother. "Did you ever dream of some lost friend and feel that you were having a sweet communion with him," Lincoln asked an army staffer. "That is the way I dream of my lost boy Willie." And there was a particular dream that came back to him again and again, and always just before the arrival of good tidings. In this dream, his dream-self stood on the deck of "some singular, indescribable vessel," pointed toward a dim shore ahead. He had dreamt this dream just before some of the most important victories of the war, and he had it again in April 1865. As he told his cabinet at a meeting the next morning, he knew that

2. Lincoln, "To Mary Todd Lincoln," June 9, 1863, in *Collected Works*, 6:256; D. T. Lamon, *Recollections of Abraham Lincoln, 1847–1865* (Lincoln: University of Nebraska Press, 1994 [1895]), 115–17; James Rollins, in *Recollected Words of Abraham Lincoln*, 384.

3. Donald, *Lincoln*, 594; Thomas and Hyman, *Stanton: The Life and Times of Lincoln's Secretary of War*, 319, 393–401.

it meant that good news was once again on the way. "I think it must be from Sherman," Lincoln explained. "My thoughts are in that direction, as are most of yours."[4]

But perhaps the dream had a meaning wider than Sherman. There was a dim shore ahead for the whole nation in the spring of 1865, an unmapped future that would involve reintegrating the Confederate states back into the political Union, bringing freed slaves into the full citizenship that their centuries of unrewarded labor had earned them, and manhandling the old Democratic South into the new Republican future of railroads, markets, and free labor. But, as Lincoln told his cabinet that day, he was confident that his dream was proof that the dimness would yield to certainty, and that everything that was now confused, bloodied, and embittered would all be sorted out at last.

General Grant had been sitting in on the cabinet meeting that morning. When it adjourned, Lincoln asked if the general and his wife would be interested in attending Ford's Theatre that night, where the Lincolns had promised to go to see actress Laura Keene's benefit performance of *Our American Cousin*. The general, pleading conflict of schedule, declined. The Lincolns would have to find someone else to join them in the box at the theater that night. Perhaps by that time Lincoln would have heard the good news his dream had promised.[5]

THE PASSING OF THE DEAD

Sherman's march across Georgia delivered a fatal body blow to the Confederacy. The fragile network of southern railroad lines had already been badly shaken by Rosecrans's capture of Chattanooga in 1863, while the fall of Atlanta to Sherman a year later wrecked the single most important rail junction between the lower Confederacy and Virginia. The march to the sea finished off what was left of the shorter regional rail lines in Georgia and made it almost impossible to keep Lee's army in Virginia supplied with food and ammunition from the granaries and factories of the lower South.

The situation for Lee was made even gloomier by the siege of Petersburg. Lee had dreaded the possibility of a siege being clamped around Richmond and Petersburg ever since McClellan's Petersburg campaign, since he knew full well that a siege would destroy both his army and the Confederate capital. Pinned through the winter of 1864–65 into a maze of trenches below Petersburg, the James River throttled by the Federal army, soldiers of the besieged army were under the strain of constant day-in, day-out pressure, with none of the usual opportunities between battles for reorganization and reequipment. "Lee's Miserables" (as they liked to call themselves,

---

4. LeGrand B. Cannon, in *Recollected Words of Abraham Lincoln*, 78; Welles, diary entry for April 14, 1865, in *Diary of Gideon Welles*, 2:282–83.

5. Horace Porter, "Lincoln and Grant," *Century Magazine* 30 (October 1885): 956; *The Personal Memoirs of Julia Dent Grant (Mrs. Ulysses S. Grant)*, ed. John Y. Simon (New York: Putnam, 1975), 155–56.

after Victor Hugo's 1862 best seller, *Les Misérables*) would be shackled to one comparatively small area from which to forage and draw supplies, an area they would quickly eat down to the bare bone. "I have no doubt that there is suffering for want of food," Lee reported sadly. "The ration is too small for men who have to undergo so much exposure and labor as ours."[6]

Only by clinging to the Weldon & Petersburg railroad (which ran south from Petersburg to North Carolina) and the Southside railroad (which ran west to Lynchburg and the Shenandoah Valley) did Lee manage to keep any supplies filtering into the hands of his army. "There is nothing within reach of this army to be impressed," Lee despondently informed the Confederate secretary of war. "The country is swept clear; our only reliance is upon the railroads." But even those lines were unsure and vulnerable to Grant's unceasing pressure. In October, Grant suddenly reached westward from his own lines and cut the Weldon & Petersburg railroad. Later the same month, Philip Sheridan, Grant's fiery chief of cavalry, tracked down and defeated Jubal Early's small Confederate force in the Shenandoah, and proceeded to lay waste to the entire valley.

Yet Lee could not simply walk away from Richmond: too much of the vital munitions that armed his soldiers came from Richmond factories; too much of the food that managed to reach his army's mouths came by the railroads that terminated in Richmond and Petersburg. And so, for the first time in the war, the Army of Northern Virginia began to suffer a crisis in morale. "The common soldier perceived that the cause was lost," wrote Sara Agnes Pryor, the wife of a Confederate officer. He could read collapse in the streets of Petersburg, since (as Pryor acidly remarked) the town had never been "so healthy":

> No garbage was decaying in the streets. Every particle of animal or vegetable food was consumed, and the streets were clean. Flocks of pigeons would follow the children who were eating bread or crackers. Finally the pigeons vanished having been themselves eaten. Rats and mice disappeared. The poor cats staggered about the streets, and began to die of hunger. . . . An ounce of meat daily was considered an abundant ration for each member of the family.[7]

Lee's men could read collapse even more clearly in the letters that filtered through into the hands of the Confederate soldiers below Petersburg. Those letters now began to tell the terrible tale of civilian starvation, the devastation by Yankee raiders, and the relentless impressment of the ever-shrinking fruits of Southern agriculture by the Confederate War Department. "We have been impressing food and all the necessaries of life from women and children, and have been the mean of driving thousands from their homes in destitute condition," Lee admitted sadly to James Longstreet in February 1865. The suffering of Confederate women now reached the breaking point, and their letters

6. Lee to Seddon, January 11, 1865, and January 27, 1865, in *The Wartime Papers of Robert E. Lee*, 881, 886.

7. Mrs. Roger A. Pryor, *Reminiscences of Peace and War* (New York: Macmillan, 1904), 267.

began to teem with encouragements to desert from the Army of Northern Virginia. "The Condition of the country at large was one of almost as great deprivation & suffering as the army itself," wrote Edward Porter Alexander, the chief of artillery in Longstreet's corps. "Naturally, the wives & mothers left at home wrote longingly for the return of the husbands & sons who were in the ranks in Virginia. And naturally, many of them could not resist these appeals, & deserted in order to return & care for their families."[8]

Beginning in early January 1865, men began to desert by the hundreds, and then the thousands. "Since Sherman's victories," exulted a soldier in the 20th Maine, "we see the affect it is having on Lee's Army." They were even deserting in groups, "not only privates but many officers with them." Over a period of ten days in February, the army lost 1,094 men to desertion; between February 15 and March 18, 1865, almost 8 percent of Lee's army disappeared either into the Union lines or into North Carolina. Lee himself turned harsh and punitive in an attempt to stop the flow of desertions. On February 25 he rejected a captured deserter's appeal for mercy without even reading the appeal, and ordered the man shot. "Hundreds are deserting nightly," Lee explained to the Confederate adjutant general, Samuel Cooper, "and I cannot keep the army together unless examples are made of such cases." It did little good. On March 4, George Meade reported to his wife that "deserters still continue to come in, there being 75 yesterday," and more than half of them brought their weapons with them, a sure sign that it was not a shortage of fight that afflicted them. "If we stay here," wrote one Union officer who had passed forty deserters through his lines in forty-eight hours, "the Johnnies will all come over before the 4th of July." Yet Lee and his army remained the one outpost of hope for what remained of the Confederacy. Josiah Gorgas hit emotional bottom in mid-January, feeling the finger of despair on his pulse, until he remembered "the brave army in front of us, sixty thousand strong. As long as Lee's army remains intact there is no cause for despondency."[9]

For Grant, the issue was now to tighten his grip on Petersburg and Richmond, slowly draining away the rebel army's life. On the other side of the siege lines at Petersburg, the resolve of the Confederates, which had seemed so formidable when the siege began the summer before, was visibly weakening, and the real question increasingly seemed to be whether Grant was going to be able to keep Lee from slipping out of Petersburg before Grant could deliver a knockout blow. As for Sherman, he was opposed by little more than 20,000 Confederates. The old Army of Tennessee had been broken up after

8. Edward Porter Alexander, *Fighting for the Confederacy: The Personal Recollections of General Edward Porter Alexander*, ed. Gary W. Gallagher (Chapel Hill: University of North Carolina Press), 508–9; Michael Fellman, *The Making of Robert E. Lee* (New York: Random House, 2000), 172–75; Scott Nelson and Carol Sheriff, *A People at War*, 274–77.

9. William Livermore to "Friend Abbie," February 26, 1865, "20th Maine Infantry," in Gettysburg National Military Park Vertical Files, #6-ME20; Lee to Longstreet, and Lee to Cooper, February 25, 1865, in *The War of the Rebellion*, Series One, 46:1258; Douglas Southall, *Lee's Lieutenants: A Study in Command* (New York: Charles Scribner's Sons, 1942–44), 3:623–24; Bruce Catton, *A Stillness at Appomattox* (Garden City, NY: Doubleday, 1953), 330; George G. Meade to Margaretta Meade, March 4, 1865, in George G. Meade Papers, Box 1/Folder 4, Historical Society of Pennsylvania; Gorgas, diary entry for January 25, 1865, in *The Journals of Josiah Gorgas*, 149.

Hood's resignation, and its last effective pieces shipped over to the Carolinas to join what was left of the forlorn and homeless garrison of Wilmington, North Carolina, to threaten Sherman. At the urging of the Confederate Congress, command of this patchwork army was at last given back to Joseph E. Johnston by a grudging and suspicious Jefferson Davis on February 23, 1865. Sherman was mildly apprehensive at the return of Johnston, but Johnston knew that it was by now too late to do any serious damage to Sherman. "In my opinion these troops form an army too weak to cope with Sherman," Johnston sighed. All that Lee could advise him was to "hope for the best."[10]

With such small Confederate forces left in the Carolinas, Grant's impulse in December 1864 had been to pull Sherman and his army out of Georgia entirely and use the navy to transport them up to the James River, where they could reinforce Grant for a fresh assault on Petersburg in the spring. But Sherman demurred, insisting that he could accomplish much more by setting off on yet another raid, this time up into the Carolinas, where he could wreck the Army of Northern Virginia's last rail lines and supply centers in the Carolinas. Sherman enlisted Halleck as an ally in his cause, and on December 18, Grant once more gave way to Sherman and authorized this new raid. After pausing to rest and refit in Savannah, Sherman and his army were again on the march. In their path was South Carolina, the state whose secession lay at the beginning of the war, and Sherman's men were determined to make South Carolina suffer in retribution. "South Carolina cried out first for war," one of Sherman's Iowans swore, "and she shall have it to her hearts content. She sowed the Wind. She will soon reap the whirlwind." Now Sherman's men pillaged and burned without any regard for the needs of forage or food, leaving "a howling wilderness, an utter desolation," behind them. On February 17 the state capital, Columbia, fell to Sherman, and that evening an immense fire blackened the central part of the city. Sherman was accused of having deliberately set the fire as a gesture of revenge, and though he denied the charge, he felt little sorrow over it. "Though I never ordered it and never wished it, I have never shed many tears over the event, because I believe it hastened what we all fought for, the end of the war."[11]

Lincoln, too, had plans for the spring. One of them concerned emancipation. All of Lincoln's actions to end slavery, including the Emancipation Proclamation itself, had been taken on the basis of his presidential war powers. And that created a problem at the point where the war ended. Strictly speaking, Lincoln had only emancipated slaves; he had not abolished the legal institution of slavery. It was, at least theoretically, possible that slavery could be reinstituted on the other side of the war in some new guise and with a different set of victims. Or it could emerge again from the border states, where the war powers he had used for the Emancipation Proclamation gave him no authority. And since the *Dred Scott* decision, banning the federal

---

10. Symonds, *Joseph E. Johnston*, 344.

11. Glatthaar, *The March to the Sea and Beyond*, 79, 142; James M. Merrill, *William Tecumseh Sherman* (Chicago: Rand McNally, 1971), 283.

government from interfering with slavery as legal property, still stood as the last word of the federal courts on the subject, the courts might lift no finger to prevent this from happening. In fact, a postwar legal challenge to the Emancipation Proclamation might very well undo even what the Proclamation had done. "The emancipation proclamation," Lincoln told General Stephen Hurlbut in July 1863, is "I think . . . valid in law," and he hoped it "will be so held by the courts." But he could not be sure.

Only a constitutional amendment, forever outlawing slavery as an institution across the entire country, could absolutely secure the wartime gains made for emancipation. But amending the Constitution was a long reach. The Constitution had been amended only twelve times, and Lincoln himself, back in 1848, had counseled against "a habit of altering it. . . . New provisions, would introduce new difficulties, and thus create, and increase appetite for still further change." The Radical Republicans in the Senate learned how much instinctive aversion there was to constitutional amendments when they adopted an abolition amendment in April 1864 only to see it fail, by a vote of 93 to 65, to obtain the necessary two-thirds majority needed in the House.[12]

But eventually Lincoln could see no other way to make black freedom tamper-proof, and he insisted on making a thirteenth amendment part of the platform he ran upon in the 1864 election. On December 6, 1864, in his annual message to Congress, Lincoln urged Congress to take his reelection as a good moment for reconsidering the amendment, if only because the incoming Congress in December 1865 would likely do it anyway. "I venture to recommend the reconsideration and passage of the measure at the present session," Lincoln reasoned. "The next Congress will pass the measure if this does not. Hence there is only a question of time as to when the proposed amendment will go to the States for their action. And as it is to so go, at all events, may we not agree that the sooner the better?"[13]

As renewed debate on the amendment began in the House on January 6, Lincoln buttonholed former Whigs and Democrats to bring them into line (among the political horse trading he performed was the promise to New York Democrat of a plum patronage position in exchange for his vote). "You and I were old Whigs, both of us followers of that great statesman, Henry Clay," Lincoln said as he oiled the cooperation of James Rollins, a Missouri congressman. "I have sent for you as an old Whig friend to come and see me, that I might make an appeal to you to vote for this amendment. It is going to be very close; a few votes one way or the other will decide it." He was even more blunt with two other fence-sitters, who were frankly informed that they should "remember that I am President of the United States, clothed with immense power, and I expect you to procure those votes." He was not wrong in his

12. Lincoln, "Speech in United States House of Representatives on Internal Improvements," June 20, 1848, and "To Stephen A. Hurlbut," July 31, 1863, in *Collected Works*, 1:488, 6:358.

13. Lincoln, "Annual Message to Congress," December 6, 1864, in *Collected Works*, 8:149.

anxiety. When the House roll was called on January 31, 1865, the proposed amend-ment squeaked through the House with just three votes to spare, 119 to 56. But it was done. "I wish you could have been here the day that the constitutional amendment was passed forever abolishing slavery in the United States," wrote Charles Douglass from Washington to his father, Frederick Douglass, "Such rejoicing I never before witnessed, cannons firing, people hugging and shaking hands, white people, I mean, flags flying. . . . I tell you things are progressing finely. . . ." Lincoln's own Illinois, appropriately, was the first state to ratify the new amendment, followed by Pennsyl-vania and Massachusetts.[14]

It was less clear-cut who was winning on the subject of Reconstruction. Lincoln was prepared to push forward with his 10 percent plan for Reconstruction in Louisi-ana, but the Radicals remained reluctant to endorse any template that did not clearly overturn the old racial and economic order of the agrarian South. Lincoln was far from blind to the faults of his plan. But he was eager to first bring as many of the former rebel states into Reconstruction as fast as they could be gotten there, and then worry about opening the ears of Southerners to his hints to include emancipa-tion and black civil rights as part of their new constitutions.

Lincoln's admirers, then and now, have been inclined to ascribe this to Lincoln's generosity and desire to end the war on a note of forgiveness. That certainly seemed to be the message Lincoln had for the country when he stood on the Capitol steps on a blustery March 4 to take his second oath of office as president. In the brief address he gave before taking the oath, Lincoln reviewed the fundamental causes of the war—slavery, . . . the demand for slavery's extension westward into the territories, and . . . the idea that the Constitution permitted secession from the Union when those demands were not met. But he also took the opportunity of this review to set these immediate causes of war in the context of a larger metaphysical, almost theo-logical question. Lincoln looked beyond the material causes of the war and urged Northerners and Southerners alike to think of it (as John Brown had prophesied before his execution in 1859) as a judgment by God on a crime that the whole nation, not just one section, had been guilty of.

Perhaps, Lincoln speculated, the war ultimately was not about secession or slav-ery but about the mysteries of divine providence and moral judgment. In this life, the Bible told him that offenses are unavoidable, and slavery had certainly been an offense. Slavery had grown up from the first in America without anyone's particular bidding, and in spite of the best intentions of the Founders. But like sinners in the hands of an angry God, not even those who had merely inherited such offenses have the right to plead inability and innocence. "If we shall suppose that American Slavery

14. Rollins, in Fehrenbacher, ed., *Recollected Words of Abraham Lincoln*, 384; John Alley, in Allen Thorndike Rice, ed., *Reminiscences of Abraham Lincoln by Distinguished Men of His Time* (New York: North American, 1886), 585–86; Trefousse, *The Radical Republicans*, 298–300; Blight, *Frederick Douglass' Civil War*, 186.

is one of those offences which, in the providence of God, must needs come, but which, having continued through His appointed time, He now wills to remove, and that He gives to both North and South, this terrible war, as the woe due to those by whom the offence came," Lincoln asked, "shall we discern therein any departure from those divine attributes which the believers in a Living God always ascribe to him?"[15]

But if the time had now come, at whatever the cost, to rip up slavery by the roots, then human beings could only bow their heads to that cost as the price of a national life in which "offences must needs come." Perhaps it would be only justice, Lincoln said, that "all the wealth piled up by the bond-man's two hundred and fifty years of unrequited toil shall be sunk," and "every drop of blood drawn with the lash" shall now "be paid by another drawn with the sword." These words were bound to surprise and enrage those who thought of themselves as the righteous, who had suffered innocently from the depravity of the "slave power." But they could protest all they liked; their argument would not be with Lincoln. "As it was said three thousand years ago, so still it must be said, 'the judgments of the Lord, are true and righteous altogether.'" Americans must not waste their energies now in judgment—that belonged to the inscrutable God who moved all things in such mysterious ways—but in the one exercise that still was within their grasp, that of mercy.

> With malice toward none; with charity for all; with firmness in the right, as God gives us to see the right, let us strive on to finish the work we are in; to bind up the nation's wounds; to care for him who shall have borne the battle, and for his widow, and his orphan—to do all which may achieve and cherish a just, and a lasting peace, among ourselves, and with all nations.

Eloquent as these words were as religious philosophy, they were also read as a promise of a speedy and painless Reconstruction. Certainly speed was part of Lincoln's Reconstruction agenda. After four years of war, Congress had passed the Thirteenth Amendment by the slimmest of margins, and efforts by the Radicals to promote a Reconstruction bill in Congress guaranteeing the freed slaves the right to vote had died on the floor. Allowing Reconstruction to proceed under the single eye of the executive branch might get better, faster, less ambiguous results than with all the cooks in Congress stirring the pot. A month after the inaugural, Lincoln once again called on Louisianans (whose state was furthest along the road to Reconstruction) to open "the elective franchise" to the "very intelligent" among African Americans and "those who serve our cause as soldiers." His appointment of Salmon Chase as Taney's successor on the Supreme Court was also a direct way of dealing with the threat of postwar legal appeals from the war's military results. "Judge

---

15. Lincoln, "Second Inaugural Address," March 4, 1865, in *Collected Works*, 8:333.

Chase would only be sustaining himself . . . as regarded the emancipation policy of the government," Lincoln remarked to a newspaper correspondent, and added to George Boutwell, "We want a man who will sustain the Legal Tender Act and the Proclamation of Emancipation."[16]

Keeping the cards securely in his own hands was uppermost in his mind when at the end of March 1865 Lincoln came down to the James River to confer with Grant and with Sherman, who had come up from the Carolina coast by steamer for the meeting. There, Lincoln talked to his premier generals about the kind of terms he wanted given to the South and its armies if and when they surrendered. He advised them to offer whatever they thought would induce surrender of the Confederate armies as a whole, since it would be better to let them give up their arms as organized groups rather than pressing the Confederates so hard that they broke up into innumerable guerilla bands. He expressed the hope that Jefferson Davis could be allowed to escape the country, rather than running the risk of a sensational treason trial, and Sherman remembered Lincoln suggesting that the generals might even offer to recognize the existing rebel state governments, especially in North Carolina, as an inducement to surrender "till Congress could provide others." And since Congress had now adjourned (and with the new Congress elected in November not scheduled to assemble until December 1865), Lincoln had a free hand to end the war, resuscitate the Southern state governments, and move them toward black civil rights without Congress encumbering or endangering the process.[17]

This did not mean, however, that Lincoln was willing to grant the Confederates any kind of blank check. Lincoln had been willing, as early as mid-1863, to allow friends and intercessors to open up secret negotiations with Richmond, but only on terms Jefferson Davis at once rejected. As late as February 1865 Lincoln himself came down to Hampton Roads to meet with a Confederate peace commission headed by his old friend Alexander Stephens, the Confederate vice president. Lincoln offered to swap $400 million in United States bonds if the Confederate states would rejoin the Union and adopt the Thirteenth Amendment prospectively, with the understanding that it would be gradually phased in over a period of—as Stephens later claimed Lincoln said—five years. But the negotiations foundered on Lincoln's insistence that the Confederate states abandon all claim to treat with the

16. Lincoln, in *Recollected Words*, 15, 38; Lincoln, "Last Public Address," April 11, 1865, in *Collected Works*, 8:403.

17. William T. Sherman, *Memoirs of General W. T. Sherman*, 810–13. Gideon Welles said that Lincoln accompanied his injunction to "frighten" the Confederate leaders "out of the country, open the gates, let down the bars, scare them off" with a gesture that reminded Welles of someone "shooing sheep out of a lot"; see Welles, "Lincoln and Johnson," in *Civil War and Reconstruction*, 191.

United States as a separate government, and the Hampton Roads conference in particular turned up empty after Jefferson Davis dismissed any form of surrender.[18]

Lincoln even went so far, after his meeting with Grant and Sherman, as to authorize members of the Virginia legislature to assemble as a Union government—but only if they understood that there would be "no receding by the Executive of the United States on the slavery question." And then, after reflecting on the inadequacies of this proposal, Lincoln cancelled it a week later. He wanted peace, and he wanted it done quickly enough that he could supervise it. But he would brook Southern foot-dragging on Reconstruction no more than he would welcome Radical meddling.[19]

Sherman, and possibly Grant as well, mistook Lincoln's desire for the fastest Union solution to peace as a desire for any solution so long as it was fast, and as a result, both Grant and Sherman came away from their meeting with the president in possession of a certainty about Lincoln's easygoing intentions that Lincoln himself did not entirely share. Neither Grant nor Sherman could have realized how quickly they were going to have to deal in hard terms with that uncertainty, since almost all of their generals believed that at least one more major battle in Virginia would probably have to be fought. "The great fight may yet be fought out in this vicinity," George Meade warned in March. That apprehension was not necessarily misplaced, either, since Lee staged a breakout attempt from the Petersburg lines on March 25, lunging toward Fort Stedman, on the far right of Grant's lines.[20]

But the attack was beaten back, and with it, the last of the Army of Northern Virginia's fabled aggressiveness faded. On March 27 Grant once again began sliding the Army of the Potomac around to his left, looking to cut Lee's last supply line into Petersburg, the Southside railroad. On April 1 Philip Sheridan's 12,000 cavalrymen, supported by the infantry of the 5th Corps of the Army of the Potomac, overran the last Confederate outpost on the extreme end of Lee's lines at Five Forks, effectively shutting off the Southside. At four the next morning the entire left of the Federal line went over the top against Lee's trenches, and only the stubborn resistance of two small Confederate forts kept the entire Army of Northern Virginia from collapsing into Federal hands that night.[21]

18. Stephens, *A Constitutional View of the Late War Between the States*, 2:598–616; William C. Harris, *Lincoln's Last Months* (Cambridge, MA: Harvard University Press, 2004), 115–21; Robert M. T. Hunter, "The Peace Commission of 1865" (1877), in *The New Annals of the Civil War*, eds. Peter Cozzens and R. I. Girardi (Mechanicsburg, PA: Stackpole, 2004), 495–98; Reagan, *Memoirs*, 166–79.

19. Lincoln, "To John A. Campbell," April 5, 1865, and "To Godfrey Weitzel," April 12, 1865, in *Collected Works*, 8:386, 406–7.

20. George G. Meade to Margaretta Meade, March 4, 1865, in George G. Meade Papers, Box 1/Folder 4, Historical Society of Pennsylvania.

21. A. Wilson Greene, *The Final Battles of the Petersburg Campaign: Breaking the Backbone of the Rebellion* (Knoxville: University of Tennessee Press, 2008), 112–25, 294–309; Earl J. Hess, *In the Trenches at Petersburg: Field Fortifications and Confederate Defeat* (Chapel Hill: University of North Carolina, 2009), 245–79.

That one night, however, was enough for Lee. He had been anticipating the necessity of "abandoning our position on the James River" since February, when he sketched out a what-if strategy for James Longstreet. After informing Jefferson Davis that the Petersburg lines could no longer be held, Lee skillfully pulled his army out of the Richmond fortifications and crossed what was left in the Petersburg trenches over onto the north side of the Appomattox River. There, he turned west, designating Amelia Court House as the rendezvous point for the whole army. He planned to meet the last supply trains out of Richmond at Amelia Court House and, afterward, pick up a spur line of the Richmond & Danville railroad that would take the Army of Northern Virginia south to join Johnston in the Carolinas. Davis, with a small escort and the official papers and records of the Confederate government, also headed west, staying ahead of Lee and the army and ultimately turning and escaping to the south. Richmond was abandoned, left to its mayor to be surrendered to Grant on April 3, 1865. Fires set by the Confederate provost marshal to destroy the arsenal and magazines roared out of hand and rioters and looters took to the streets until at last Federal soldiers, their bands savagely blaring "Dixie," marched into the humiliated capital and raised the Stars and Stripes over the old Capitol building.[22]

Lee, meanwhile, struggled westward to Amelia Court House. He was dogged by two major problems, one of which was the geographical position of his army. Except for the troops Grant detached to occupy Richmond, Grant and the Army of the Potomac were on the south side of the Appomattox River, and as soon as Lee bolted westward, so did Grant, pacing Lee step for step on his side of the Appomattox, keeping between Lee and the never-never land to the south, never letting Lee get far enough ahead to curl around the head of the Federal columns and break for the Carolinas. Lee's other problem surfaced as soon as he concentrated his men at Amelia Court House on April 5. In the last hours in Richmond, the orders that were to have sent supply trains to meet Lee's men in Amelia Court House were never received, or perhaps were never given in the first place. Either way, Lee found only limited supplies of food waiting for him there. He also found that the last troops out of Richmond, mostly the men of Richard Ewell's corps, were still on their way to Amelia Court House.[23]

Lee was forced to waste an entire day foraging and waiting for Ewell to catch up, and by the time he was ready to move on, he found that Sheridan's cavalry had cut the rail line eight miles below Amelia Court House. With Grant's infantry now breathing down his neck, Lee had no choice but to strike westward again, this

22. Lee to John C. Breckinridge, February 21, 1865, and to James Longstreet, February 22, 1865, in *Wartime Papers of R. E. Lee*, 906, 908; Michael Ballard, *A Long Shadow: Jefferson Davis and the Final Days of the Confederacy* (Athens: University of Georgia Press, 1997), 44, 46; Ernest B. Furgurson, *Ashes of Glory: Richmond at War* (New York: Knopf, 1996), 333, 336–37.

23. William Marvel, *Lee's Last Retreat: The Flight to Appomattox* (Chapel Hill: University of North Carolina Press, 2001), 50–51.

time toward Lynchburg, where there were Confederate reinforcements and more supplies to be had. The problem was getting there. "Hundreds of men dropped from exhaustion; thousands threw away their arms; the demoralization appeared at last to involve the officers; they did nothing to prevent straggling; and many of them seemed to shut their eyes on the hourly reduction of their commands, and rode in advance of their brigades in dogged indifference."[24]

By now, Grant was rapidly closing in on the fleeing Confederates. On April 6, Sheridan's cavalry caught up with Lee's rear guard as it was crossing a little tributary of the Appomattox River called Sayler's Creek, and sliced off 7,000 prisoners with hardly any effort. In a desperate effort to keep Grant from getting any closer, Lee had the bridges over the Appomattox burned, but on the morning of April 7 one Federal corps discovered a neglected wagon bridge over the river and crossed over in hot pursuit. Lee now had one hope, and only one: if he could reach Appomattox Station before the Federal cavalry, he could be supplied there from Lynchburg, and perhaps make a stand that would force Grant to back off and give him maneuvering room. (It might have worked: Grant admitted to John Russell Young that his own logistical tether was so attenuated that "he could not have kept up his pursuit a half day longer.") But it turned out to be impossible. Sheridan's cavalry got to Appomattox Station on the evening of April 8, while Lee was still several miles back up the road. When Lee shook out a battle line to back them away the next morning, the early morning fog burned off to reveal two infantry divisions of the 24th Corps and two brigades of the 25th Corps coming up to relieve the federal cavalry, with the 5th Corps of the Army of the Potomac coming up behind them.[25]

Stopped in front by Sheridan's horsemen, and pressed from behind by Grant's infantry, Lee knew that at last the end had come. It was what he had feared from the beginning: "It will all be over—ended—just as I have expected it would end from the first," Lee lamented. He had gambled on disheartening the North by invading Maryland in 1862 and Pennsylvania in 1863; he had gambled on the siege of Petersburg dragging on long enough to turn Northern voters against Lincoln. None of it had worked, and now his army was trapped. Grant had sent several notes to Lee by courier on April 7 and 8 concerning a possible meeting of the generals, and so Lee sent flags of truce through the lines and asked to see Grant personally. "In ten minutes more," wrote Union brigadier general Thomas C. Devin about that morning,

24. Pollard, *The Lost Cause*, 704.

25. Young, in Thomas Nelson Page, "Robert E. Lee: Man and Soldier," in *The Novels, Stories, Sketches and Poems of Thomas Nelson Page* (New York: Charles Scribner's, 1912), 18:224; Philip H. Sheridan, "The Last Days of the Rebellion," in *Battles and Leaders*, ed. Cozzens, 6:526–35; Greg Eames, *Black Day of the Army: The Battles of Sailor's Creek* (Burkeville, VA: E. & H. Pubs., 2001), 166; Chris Calkins, *The Battles of Appomattox Station and Appomattox Court House, April 8–9, 1865* (Lynchburg, VA: H. E. Howard, 1987), 25–30; Henry E. Tremaine, *Sailors' Creek to Appomattox Court House, 7th, 8th, 9th April, 1865, or, The Last Hours of Sheridan's Cavalry* (New York: C. H. Ludwig, 1885), 34–38.

the charge would have been ordered for the whole line and we would have been on and over them like a whirlwind. Our men were terribly vexed at the truce. It was laughable to see the old troopers come up to the edge of the hill [overlooking the Confederate positions], look down at the position of the Rebs and go back growling and damning the flag of truce.[26]

For the dwindling band of Confederates, however, the surrender could not have come more quickly. "Within range of my eye," wrote a Confederate surgeon, "there were a great number of muskets stuck in the ground by the bayonet, whose owners, heart-sick and fainting of hunger and fatigue, had thrown them away, and gone, none knew whither." The remainder were living on "corn, stolen from the horses' feed, and parched and munched as they marched."[27]

Grant, who had been pounding along at the head of his army, leaving bag and baggage days behind in the dust, was at that moment in the throes of a migraine, "but the instant I saw the contents of the note I was cured." Lee selected as a meeting place the home of Wilmer McLean in the little crossroads village of Appomattox Court House, about four miles above Appomattox Station. Grant arrived with his staff later that morning, painfully conscious of the contrast between Lee, immaculate in a full general's uniform and dress sword, and himself, clad in the only things he owned in the absence of his baggage, a pair of muddy boots and a standard-issue frock coat with his lieutenant general's shoulder straps sewn on. The meeting was formal, and after some polite chitchat between Grant and Lee about old Mexican War times, they got down to business. Grant's terms, bearing in mind his discussions with Lincoln, were surprisingly mild. There was no more talk of unconditional surrender: all Confederate soldiers would surrender their arms and promptly be paroled (no ghastly death march to a prison camp, no imprisonment of Confederate officers pending treason trials), all officers could retain their swords and other sidearms, and paroled soldiers could claim any captured horses and mules they wished to take home with them. "This done," Grant specified, "each officer and man will be allowed to return to his home, not to be disturbed by U.S. authority so long as they observe their paroles and the laws in force where they may reside."[28]

The terms were written out and acknowledged, and then the negotiation was over. Lee walked out onto the porch of the McLean house and (as one of Grant's

---

26. Thomas C. Devin, "Didn't We Fight Splendid," *Civil War Times Illustrated* 17 (December 1978): 38.

27. Marvel, *Lee's Last Retreat*, 167–71; John S. Wise, *The End of an Era* (Boston: Houghton, Mifflin, 1901), 429; J. H. Claiborne, "Last Days of Lee and His Paladins," in *War-Talks of Confederate Veterans*, ed. G. S. Bernard (Dayton, OH: Morningside Press, 2003 [1892]), 256.

28. "Report of Lieut. Gen. U.S. Grant," July 22, 1865, in *War of the Rebellion*, Series One, 34(I):56; Chris Calkins, *The Appomattox Campaign, March 29–April 9, 1865* (Lynchburg, VA: H. E. Howard, 1997), 169–77; Ulysses S. Grant, "Personal Memoirs," 735–41; Charles Marshall, *Appomattox: An Address Delivered Before the Society of the Army and Navy of the Confederate States* (Baltimore: Guggenheimer, Weil, 1894), 19–21, and "Occurrences at Lee's Surrender," *Confederate Veteran*, February 1894, 42.

staff wrote) "signaled to his orderly to bring up his horse . . . and gazed sadly in the direction of the valley beyond, where his army lay . . ."

> He thrice smote the palm of his left hand slowly with his right fist in an absent sort of way, seemed not to see the group of Union officers in the yard, who rose respectfully at his approach, and appeared unaware of everything about him. All appreciated the sadness that overwhelmed him, and he had the personal sympathy of every one who beheld him at this supreme moment of trial. The approach of his horse seemed to recall him from his reverie, and he at once mounted. General Grant now stepped down from the porch, moving toward him, and saluted him by raising his hat. He was followed in this act of courtesy by all our officers present.[29]

George Henry Mills of the 16th North Carolina watched Lee ride slowly back up the road toward his regiment: "As he passed the men all ran down to the road and surrounded him, everyone trying to shake hands with him, many of them in tears." Lee took off his hat and spoke briefly: "Boys, I have done the best I could for you. Go home now, and if you make as good citizens as you have soldiers, you will do well, and I shall always be proud of you. Goodbye, and God bless you all." To Mills, Lee "seemed so full that he could say no more, but with tears in his eyes" he rode off toward his headquarters, "and that was the last we ever saw of him."[30]

The next day was consumed with the administrative paperwork of the surrender—making up parole lists, printing parole forms, Lee issuing his farewell order to the Army of Northern Virginia, and the handover of the rebel cavalry's equipment. The day following, the Confederate artillery surrendered its guns, and on April 12 the infantry of the Army of Northern Virginia marched out of its pitiful little camps for the last time. When Lee abandoned the Petersburg siege lines, he could still count 56,000 men in the ranks; now, the Army of Northern Virginia only had 26,018 names to put on the parole lists.[31]

They tramped defiantly down their last road through the center of Appomattox Court House to where units of the Army of the Potomac were drawn up, on either side, to watch them stack their still-gleaming weapons and furl their shredded star-crossed battle flags. Waiting for them by the roadside was the 1st Brigade, 1st Division, 5th Corps, under the command of Joshua Lawrence Chamberlain. Four years before, Chamberlain had been a professor of rhetoric at Bowdoin College; two years before, at Gettysburg, Chamberlain and his 20th Maine Volunteers had held Little Round Top. Now, commanding his own brigade, Chamberlain impulsively brought his men to attention and ordered a salute to the ragged Confederates. At the head of the Confederate column rode General John B. Gordon, who was startled

29. Horace Porter, *Campaigning with Grant* (New York: Century, 1907), 472–85.

30. Mills, *History of the 16th North Carolina Regiment*, 68.

31. Glatthaar, *General Lee's Army*, 461–71.

and uncertain at what Chamberlain's men were about to do. But then, as it dawned on Gordon what Chamberlain meant, he slowly and deliberately returned it.

> . . . When the head of each division column comes opposite our group, our bugle sounds the signal and instantly our whole line from right to left, regiment by regiment in succession, gives the soldier's salutation, from the "order arms" to the old "carry"— the marching salute. Gordon at the head of the column, riding with heavy spirit and downcast face, catches the sound of shifting arms, looks up, and, taking the meaning, wheels superbly, making himself and his horse one uplifted figure, with profound salutation as he drops the point of his sword to the boot toe; then facing to his own command, gives word for his successive brigades to pass us with the same position of the manual,—honor answering honor. On our part not a sound of trumpet more, nor roll of drum; not a cheer, nor word nor whisper of vain-glorying, nor motion of man standing again at the order, but an awed stillness rather, and breath-holding, as if it were the passing of the dead![32]

Two days later, far away in Raleigh, North Carolina, William Tecumseh Sherman received a note from Joseph E. Johnston asking if he was willing to make "a temporary suspension of active operations." Johnston had never really been able to stop Sherman once he had rolled out of Georgia. Charleston, which had defied everything the Federal navy could throw at it from the sea, dropped tamely into Sherman's bag as his fire-eyed army marched past on land. On March 6, Sherman's men splashed across the Pee Dee River into North Carolina, making a union with Grant a matter of only a few weeks. Johnston made just one serious effort to slow Sherman down, at Bentonville, North Carolina, on March 19, but Sherman merely brushed him aside. "Johnston had the night before marched his whole army . . . and all the troops he had drawn from every quarter, determined, as he told his men, to crush one of our corps and then defeat us in detail," Sherman reported to Grant three days later, but "we pushed him hard, and came very near crushing him," and Sherman was now "satisfied that Johnston's army was so roughly handled . . . that we could march right on to Raleigh."[33]

On April 12, Johnston was summoned to Greensboro, North Carolina, by Jefferson Davis, who had escaped from Virginia and who spoke hopefully of raising new armies to carry on the war. Johnston briefly told him that "to attempt to continue the war" was hopeless. "Having neither money nor credit, nor arms but those in the

---

32. Frank P. Cauble, *The Surrender Proceedings, April 9, 1865, Appomattox Court House* (Lynchburg, VA: H. E. Howard, 1987), 93–100; Chamberlain, *The Passing of the Armies: An Account of the Final Campaign of the Army of the Potomac, Based upon Personal Reminiscences of the Fifth Army Corps* (Dayton, OH: Morningside Press, 1982 [1915]), 261; Chamberlain to Sara Brastow, April 13, 1865, in *Through Blood and Fire: Selected Civil War Papers of Major General Joshua Chamberlain*, ed. Mark Nesbitt (Mechanicsburg, PA: Stackpole, 1996), 178–79.

33. Sherman to Grant, March 22, 1865, in *War of the Rebellion*, Series One, 47(II):950.

hands of our soldiers, nor ammunition but that in their cartridge-boxes, nor shops for repairing arms or fixing ammunition, the effect of our keeping the field would be, not to harm the enemy, but to complete the devastation of our country and ruin of its people." Any further continuation of it would be "the greatest of human crimes." Davis wearily gave him permission to open negotiations with Sherman, and on April 14 Johnston sent his note through the lines, begging to be given the same terms Grant had given Lee.[34]

Another two hundred miles south, in Charleston harbor, an immense crowd of Federal soldiers and New York celebrities had gathered in the ruins of Fort Sumter to watch Major General Robert Anderson once more raise the same flag he had taken down four years before, to the day. Everywhere, the red slashed banners of the Confederacy were coming down, the old flag was going up again, and the war would be over.[35]

But there was one last act in the drama to be played out, and with cunning appropriateness, it would be played out in a theater, almost onstage. On Good Friday, April 14, President Lincoln met his cabinet in a rare mood of relaxation and good humor, and told them of the dream he had had, the dream that always promised good tidings. In the evening he and Mary were joined by the only couple they could persuade to spend Good Friday with them at the theater, Clara Harris (the daughter of New York senator Ira Harris) and her fiancé, Major Henry R. Rathbone. Together they set out in the presidential carriage for Ford's Theatre, only a short distance from the White House, to watch Laura Keene and the lead actors from her New York City theatre company in her 1,000th performance in a popular comedy of manners called *Our American Cousin*. The theatre's owner, John Ford, had beseeched the Lincolns to attend that night in order to boost gate receipts. Sure enough, when the Lincolns arrived shortly after curtain time, the theatre was packed to its capacity, and the little orchestra in the pit struck up a rousing "Hail to the Chief" as the Lincolns made their way to a private box overlooking stage left. The cast cheerfully ad-libbed "many pleasant allusions" to the president into their lines, recalled War Department clerk James Knox, who was sitting in the audience, "to which the audience gave deafening responses, while Mr. Lincoln laughed heartily and bowed frequently to the grateful people."[36]

Somewhere in the confusion of the surrender celebrations and the hectic gaiety of the theatre, the security net Lamon and Stanton had drawn around Lincoln

34. Nathaniel Cheairs Hughes, *Bentonville: The Final Battle of Sherman and Johnston* (Chapel Hill: University of North Carolina Press, 1996), 216; Johnston, *Narrative of Military Operations . . . During the Late War Between the States* (New York: D. Appleton, 1874), 398–400.

35. F. Milton Willis, *Fort Sumter Memorial: The Fall of Fort Sumter, A Contemporary Sketch* (New York: Edwin C. Hill, 1915), 35–45.

36. Julia Adeline Shepherd, April 16, 1865, in *We Saw Lincoln Shot: One Hundred Eyewitness Accounts*, ed. Timothy S. Good (Jackson: University Press of Mississippi, 1995), 55–56; Harold Holzer, "Eyewitnesses Remember the 'Fearful Night,'" *Civil War Times Illustrated* 32 (March/April 1993): 14.

fell down: Lamon was in Richmond on government business, and John Parker, the District of Columbia policeman Stanton had detailed to guard the president, sauntered casually away from the door of the box to get a better view of the play. At approximately 10:00 PM, a twenty-six-year-old actor, John Wilkes Booth, slipped up a stairway to the outer door of the president's box. He was stopped there by someone, possibly by Lincoln's footman, Charles Forbes, but Booth merely showed him his card and assured him that the president, who was known to be fond of actors, had asked to see him.[37]

This was not at all implausible. Lincoln loved the theater, especially Shakespeare, and invited the English Shakespearean James Hackett for a private performance at the White House. And Booth was a member of one of the greatest acting families of the day—his brother Edwin was an outstanding Shakespearean whom Lincoln greatly admired. But John Wilkes Booth was also a rabid Confederate sympathizer. He had gathered around him a weird little coterie of conspirators—a Confederate deserter named Paine, a half-wit named David Herold, and a few others of even lower mental visibility—who were pledged to take personal revenge on Lincoln and his administration. Booth had originally planned, with the help of the Confederate secret service, to kidnap Lincoln and deliver him to Richmond. But the collapse of the Confederate armies convinced Booth that a more dramatic step was needed. Instead of kidnapping Lincoln, he would murder him in public, while his co-conspirators simultaneously assassinated the vice president, the secretary of state, and General Grant. Booth only learned about the special performance of *Our American Cousin* and Lincoln's agreement to attend on the morning of the fourteenth, when he stopped at Ford's Theatre to pick up some mail. But the plan formed at once in his mind, and that night he and his peculiar gaggle of friends were ready to strike. Using his familiarity with the building and staff at Ford's Theatre, Booth was able to walk unnoticed into the theatre, ascend to the packed galleries, pass by the footman, and quietly open the outer door to the passageway leading to the president's box.[38]

Once inside the narrow passageway, Booth wedged the outer door shut to ensure he would not be discovered and waited until the one point in the play when (as he well knew, from his familiarity with the play) all but one of the actors, Harry Hawk (playing Asa Trenchard), had left the stage. Then, drawing a small, single-shot derringer, he opened the inner door of the presidential box, stepped up behind Lincoln, and shot him behind the left ear. For a second no one in the house moved. Major Rathbone sprang up to seize Booth, but Booth had a long-bladed hunting knife in his other hand that he used to slash Rathbone's arm, cutting an artery. Then Booth vaulted over the rail of the box and onto the stage, ran past the dazed stagehands to

37. Edward Steers, *Blood on the Moon: The Assassination of Abraham Lincoln* (Lexington: University of Kentucky Press, 2001), 116; Michael W. Kauffman, *American Brutus: John Wilkes Booth and the Lincoln Conspiracies* (New York: Random House, 2005), 225.

38. William Hanchett, *The Lincoln Murder Conspiracies* (Urbana: University of Illinois Press, 1986), 53–54.

the theater's backstage door, where a horse was tied for him, and galloped off into the dark of the Washington streets. At the same instant, Lincoln slumped forward in the rocking chair provided for him in the box, while Mary, "on her knees uttered shriek after shriek at the feet of the dying president."[39]

Soldiers and civilians began smashing on the door of the box and were finally let in by the bloodied Major Rathbone. An army surgeon, Dr. Charles A. Leale, who had been sitting in the audience only forty feet from the box, was beside Lincoln in minutes and helped to lay him out prostrate on the floor; another surgeon, Charles Sabine Taft, was sitting down with the orchestra and was quickly boosted up to the box from the stage. Leale, whose specialty was gunshot wounds, could see at once that Lincoln's wound was mortal. But he managed to keep Lincoln's uneven breathing going, and the unconscious president was moved across the street to a room in a boardinghouse. There, at 7:22 AM the next morning, with members of his cabinet around his deathbed and his wife sobbing insanely in the front parlor, Abraham Lincoln died. "Now," said Edwin Stanton, as tears streamed freely down his cheeks, "he belongs to the ages."[40]

TREASON MUST BE MADE INFAMOUS

Supreme Court chief justice Salmon P. Chase remembered the night of Lincoln's assassination as "a night of horrors." Or so it seemed to Chase, not only because of the shame and brutality of Lincoln's murder and the possibility that Chase "was one of the destined victims," but also because of what Lincoln's death meant for a peace process that had only just begun. Chase arose early the next morning—"a heavy rain was falling, and the sky was black"—and met with Attorney General James Speed to discuss the procedures earlier chief justices had used for swearing in vice presidents as the new president. But the conversation lingered over "the late president," and Speed mournfully shook his head over the impact Lincoln's murder would have on the plans for Reconstruction. "He never seemed so near our views," Speed remarked. "At the [cabinet] meeting he said he thought [he] had made a mistake at Richmond in sanctioning the assembling of the Virginia Legislature and had perhaps been too fast in his desires for early reconstruction."[41]

39. "Major Rathbone's Affidavit," in John Edward Buckingham, *Reminiscences and Souvenirs of the Assassination of Abraham Lincoln* (Washington, DC: R. H. Darby, 1894), 75–76; Knox, in "Eyewitnesses Remember the 'Fearful Night,'" 14.

40. John Hay and John George Nicolay, "The Fourteenth of April," *Century Magazine* 39 (January 1890): 436; Charles S. Taft, "Abraham Lincoln's Last Hours," *Century Magazine* 45 (February 1893): 635; James Tanner to Henry F. Walch, April 17, 1865, in Howard H. Peck, "James Tanner's Account of Lincoln's Death," *Abraham Lincoln Quarterly* 2 (December 1942): 179; Bryan, *The Great American Myth*, 189.

41. Chase, diary entry for April 15, 1865, in *Inside Lincoln's Cabinet: The Civil War Diaries of Salmon P. Chase*, ed. David H. Donald (New York: Longmans, Green, 1954), 267–68.

Lincoln's uncertainty about the speed of the Reconstruction process as the war came to an end is not surprising. It was still not clear what freedom actually meant for the newly free slaves, or even (until the Thirteenth Amendment was formally ratified in December) whether freedom was a fact for all the slaves. As the Federal armies rolled over large parts of the South, Southern white Unionists sprang up to seize political control of Southern state capitals, but their attentions were mostly preoccupied with evening up political scores with the secessionists who had plunged them into the war rather than with the civil rights of the newly freed slaves. Even in Louisiana, where Lincoln had taken more than a presidential interest in the structure of a new Louisiana government, all the personal pressure in the world had been unable to persuade the new white Unionist government to make any provision for black civil rights.

But already three major questions were beginning to emerge from the thinning battle smoke of the war, and in Lincoln's absence, these would not become the ruling problems of the next dozen years. The first of these questions was a holdover from Lincoln's wartime disagreements with the Radicals: what was the constitutional status of the Confederate states? If Lincoln was right in maintaining that secession was a nullity, then were the Confederate states to be restored at once to their *status quo* of 1860? Or if, as the Radicals insisted, they were "conquered provinces" that had lost their statehood privileges, were they to be reorganized by Congress or by the president and the military? The second question concerned the freed slaves: what was their legal status? True, they were no longer slaves; but did that automatically promote them to the place of citizens, with all the civil rights of citizens? And what was a citizen, exactly? The implication of the Constitution, based on the requirement that the president be a "natural born Citizen, or a Citizen of the United States," was that citizenship was a matter of *jus soli*, of being born on the national land or soil. But *Dred Scott* inserted a different requirement for citizenship, that of *jus sanguinis*— citizenship by specific birthright—which the court then used to deny Scott, as a man of "African descent," any civil standing in the federal courts.[42] Did this mean that emancipated slaves were to be left in legal limbo, while white Confederates returned to all the privileges of citizenship they had repudiated?

That introduced the third and most practical question of Reconstruction: who would now be in power, not only in the old Confederacy, but in Washington itself? The end of slavery meant, practically, an end to the three-fifths clause—there would be no more slaves to count in that fashion. But this only created another nightmare: if the Southern states could now return to Congress, they would be able to demand that their delegations be increased by counting their black populations in full, rather than by the three-fifths rule—yet without actually giving those blacks the right to vote for the increased number of representatives the South would be entitled to. With those added numbers, the result would be the rollback of every initiative

---

42. Fehrenbacher, *The Dred Scott Case*, 69–70; Michael Vorenberg, "Reconstruction as a Constitutional Crisis," in *Reconstructions: New Perspectives on the Postbellum United States*, ed. Thomas J. Brown (New York: Oxford University Press, 2006), 167–68.

the Republicans had achieved in their brief dominance of the wartime Congress—protective tariffs, government assistance to the railroads, the Homestead Act, the national banking system—as well as assumption of the Confederate war debt.

The way for Republicans in Congress to head off this unintended consequence of emancipation would be to seize control of the Reconstruction process as a congressional prerogative so as to prevent a too-hasty return of the Confederate states to the Union, to correct the Constitution's fatal ambiguity over citizenship in order to qualify the freedpeople for it, and to ensure that, as citizens, the freedpeople would be able to exercise all the rights—to vote, to hold public office, to access the court system, to own property—that went with citizenship. The freedman would then (promised Frederick Douglass) "raise up a party in the Southern States among the poor," and establish a long-term Republican political hegemony in the formerly Democratic South.[43]

With political power in hand, the freedpeople would also become the foot soldiers of a re-creation of the defeated South in the image of free-labor liberalism. "In my view, the war has just begun," announced the veteran abolitionist orator Wendell Phillips. Merely subtracting slavery from the Southern social equation was not enough. "You do not annihilate a social system when you decree its death," Phillips explained. "You only annihilate it when you fill its place with another"—another, in this case, meaning a regime based on free labor, universal education, and manufacturing. "The whole fabric of southern society *must* be changed," urged Thaddeus Stevens, "and never can be done if this opportunity is lost. How can republican institutions, free schools, free churches, free social intercourse exist in a mingled community of nabobs and serfs? . . . If the South is ever to be made a safe Republic let her lands be cultivated by the toil of the owners, or the free labor of intelligent citizens." A few even advocated, as "the only certain road to Union-izing the South, to plant in it colonies of Northern men." The South thus would be remade into the image of a New England landscape, with small factories, free enterprise, banks, schools, and wages. "I look to a popular education so advanced that under . . . impartial law all creeds and all tongues and all races shall be gathered with an equal protection," Phillips explained. "The great trouble of the South lies in its ignorance. Awake it to enterprise."[44]

---

43. "Interview with a Colored Delegation respecting Suffrage," February 7, 1866, in *The Political History of the United States of America During the Period of Reconstruction (From April 15, 1865, to July 15, 1870)*, ed. Edward McPherson (Washington, DC: Solomons & Chapman, 1875), 55; Heather Cox Richardson, *Westward from Appomattox: The Reconstruction of America after the Civil War* (New Haven, CT: Yale University Press, 2007), 52; Kenneth Stampp, *The Era of Reconstruction, 1865–1877* (New York: Knopf, 1965), 96; Garrett Epps, *Democracy Reborn: The Fourteenth Amendment and the Fight for Civil Rights in Post–Civil War America* (New York: H. Holt, 2006), 32–33.

44. Phillips, in *The Radical Republicans and Reconstruction, 1861–1870*, ed. Harold Hyman (Indianapolis, IN: Bobbs-Merrill, 1967), 480, 483; Stevens, "Reconstruction," September 6, 1865, in *Selected Papers of Thaddeus Stevens*, 23; Peyton McCrary, "The Party of Revolution: Republican Ideas About Politics and Social Change, 1862–1867," *Civil War History* 30 (December 1984): 330–50; "Desperation and Colonization," *Continental Monthly* 1 (June 1862), 664.

These advocates could not have had more willing recruits than the freedpeople, who at once began to organize Loyal Leagues, Equal Rights Leagues, and Union Leagues in the South to demand full citizenship rights. The slave, wrote Frederick Douglass, had wanted "no war but an Abolition war," and as freedmen, they now wanted "no peace but an Abolition peace; liberty for all, chains for none; the black man a soldier in war; a laborer in peace; a voter at the South as well as the North; America his permanent home, and all Americans his fellow-countrymen." Alongside the freed slave, helping to inch along the progress toward a New Englandized, free-market South, was the Freedmen's Bureau. Created in March 1865, the bureau's mandate was "the supervision and management of all abandoned lands, and the control of all subjects relating to refugees and freedmen" in those "declared to be in insurrection." Although the bureau was originally conceived as a relief agency, "for the immediate and temporary shelter and supply of destitute and suffering refugees and freedmen," it had within it the germ of radicalism, since the bill that created the bureau authorized it to divide up plantation lands that had been seized from Southern whites for nonpayment of taxes or confiscated as retribution for rebel war service, and assign "not more than forty acres" of these lands to black applicants as their own farms.[45]

After six decades of Jacksonian hands-off-slavery policies in Washington, the Freedmen's Bureau was an unprecedented venture into new administrative waters—so unprecedented that the scope of the bureau's enabling legislation was far from clear. Title to the lands that the bureau distributed was only "such title thereto as the United States can convey," which meant that it could easily be challenged in the state courts by former landowners. The freedmen, clearly, had no compunction about taking over their former masters' lands as their own. "We has a right to the land where we are located," explained a freedman named Bayley Wyat. "For why? I tell you."

> Our wives, our children, our husbands has been sold over and over again to purchase the lands we now locates upon; for that reason we have a divine right to the land. . . . And den didn't we clear the land, and raise de crops ob corn, ob cotton, ob rice, ob sugar, ob everything. And den didn't dem large cities in de North grow up on de cotton and de sugars and de rice dat we made . . . ? I say dey has grown rich and my people poor.[46]

But how far were white Northerners willing to go in support of what could easily appear as a cynical strategy to extend civil rights to the freedpeople, and then buy their votes with confiscated Southern property? William Tecumseh Sherman, who

45. William S. McFeely, *Frederick Douglass* (New York: W. W. Norton, 1991), 291; John C. Rodrigue, "Introduction," in H. C. Warmoth, *War, Politics, and Reconstruction: Stormy Days in Louisiana* (Columbia: University of South Carolina Press, 2006), lii; "An Act to Establish a Bureau for the Relief of Freedmen and Refugees," March 3, 1865, in *Statutes at Large*, 38th Congress, 2nd Session, ed. G. P. Sanger (Boston: Little, Brown, 1866), 13:507–9.

46. Ronald E. Butchart, *Northern Schools, Southern Blacks, and Reconstruction: Freedmen's Education, 1862–1875* (Westport, CT: Greenwood Press, 1980), 178.

otherwise lavished no affection on black people, seemed to be willing to go quite a long way when he issued Special Field Orders No. 15, setting aside "the islands from Charleston south, the abandoned rice-fields along the rivers for thirty miles back from the sea, and the country bordering the Saint John's River, Fla. . . . for the settlement of the negroes now made free by the acts of war and the proclamation of the President of the United States . . . so that each family shall have a plot of not more than forty acres of tillable ground . . . in the possession of which land the military authorities will afford them protection until such time as they can protect themselves or until Congress shall regulate their title."[47]

But in reality, this was an agreement Sherman had made only after warnings from Halleck in December 1864 that Sherman was attracting unwanted attention for his "almost criminal dislike to the negro," and only under the eye of Secretary of War Stanton, who had come down to Savannah on January 11 to make some not-so-discreet inquiries about "the negro question." Even then, Special Field Orders No. 15 only granted the freedmen "a possessory title" to their forty acres, subject to "all claims or conflicts that may arise under the same"—which could mean very nearly nothing.[48]

In fact, just how tone-deaf Sherman might really be to "the negro question" became manifest when Sherman met with Joseph Johnston to negotiate the surrender of Johnston's broken-down army of Confederates at Durham Station, North Carolina, on April 18. Sherman offered Johnston the kind of terms he thought Lincoln had authorized: the disbanding of all remaining Confederate armies, which were to "deposit their arms and public property" in their respective state arsenals; a general amnesty; reestablishment of the federal courts; and "the recognition by the Executive of the United States, of the several State governments, on their officers and Legislatures taking the oaths prescribed by the Constitution of the United States. . . ." No judgment, trials, or imprisonment, no mention of slavery, and certainly no allusion to black civil rights.[49]

These arrangements were far beyond Sherman's powers as an army commander to grant, even in the fairest of seasons; and as Sherman was to learn, they were infinitely beyond what Stanton as secretary of war and the Radicals in Congress were willing to tolerate. One of Sherman's staff members hand-carried the surrender terms to Washington, where Stanton read them on the afternoon of April 21. That evening Stanton called in Grant and erupted, and the next day Stanton released a public repudiation of Sherman's agreement and sent Grant down to North Carolina to rein him in. Humiliated, Sherman withdrew the surrender terms and accepted Johnston's surrender on April 26 on terms similar to those Grant had written out

47. "Special Field Orders No. 15," January 16, 1865, in *War of the Rebellion*, Series One, 47(II):61–62.

48. Sherman, *Memoirs of General W. T. Sherman*, Thomas and Hyman, *Stanton*, 357–58.

49. "Memorandum or Basis of Agreement Made This 18th Day of April, A. D. 1865, Near Durham's Station," in *War of the Rebellion*, Series One, 47(III):243–44.

for Lee at Appomattox. Any freed slave who imagined that Northern whites such as Sherman were eager to join in redrawing titles, laws, and property rights, or that the Freedmen's Bureau had some plenary authority to remake the world, might be in for a highly unpleasant surprise.[50]

If it looked as though William Tecumseh Sherman was taking away with one hand what he had just given with the other, he was a model of pristine consistency compared to the new president, Andrew Johnson. The selection of Andrew Johnson as Lincoln's running mate in the 1864 election was a baffling proposition even to people who knew both of them. Johnson was an old-line Tennessee Democrat who worshipped at the political shrine of the man Lincoln loathed, Andrew Jackson. But like Jackson, his saving grace was his fervent Unionism. Appointed military governor of Tennessee in 1862, Johnson had meted out a harsh justice to rebel planters and promised black Tennesseans in 1864 that he would "be your Moses, and lead you through the Red Sea of war and bondage to a fairer future of liberty and peace." It was public commentary of that sort, along with Lincoln's anxiety to demonstrate how Southern yeomen were turning their backs on the Confederacy, that earned Johnson his place on the National Union Ticket. Lincoln overlooked the fact that Johnson's Unionism was really an expression of his yeoman's suspicion of the planter class, not of sympathy for black slaves. "Damn the Negroes," Johnson told one Tennessee correspondent, "I am fighting these traitorous aristocrats, their masters"; even Johnson's private secretary, William G. Moore, admitted that Johnson "exhibited a morbid distress and feeling against the negroes."[51]

Initially, the Radical Republicans made the same mistake about Johnson, largely because a good many of them shared Johnson's animus toward the South's "traitorous aristocrats." On the afternoon of the day Lincoln died, a delegation of Radicals headed by Ben Wade (as the chair of the Joint Committee on the Conduct of the War) called on Johnson to take his political temperature, and Johnson enthusiastically assured them that they could "judge of my policy by my past. . . . *Treason* is a crime; and *crime* must be punished. . . . Treason must be made infamous and traitors must be impoverished." This sounded, to the Radicals, like an endorsement for land redistribution, raising the bar of Reconstruction in the South, and recruiting the freed slaves to fashion a new political order. "Johnson, we have faith in you," boomed Wade. "By the gods, there will be no trouble now in running the government." And Johnson fortified Wade's confidence two days later by suggesting that a

50. Sherman, *Memoirs*, 840–45; Brooks D. Simpson, "Facilitating Defeat: The Union High Command and the Collapse of the Confederacy," in *The Collapse of the Confederacy*, ed. Grimsley and Simpson, 98.

51. Hans L. Trefousse, *Andrew Johnson: A Biography* (New York: W. W. Norton, 1989), 183; McPherson, *The Struggle for Equality*, 317; Howard B. Means, *The Avenger Takes His Place: Andrew Johnson and the 45 Days That Changed the Nation* (Orlando, FL: Harcourt, 2006), 55; Hans L. Trefousse, "Andrew Johnson and the Freedmen's Bureau," in *The Freedmen's Bureau and Reconstruction: Reconsiderations*, ed. Paul A. Cimbala and Randall M. Miller (New York: Fordham University Press, 1999), 42.

good example might be set to traitors by hanging a good baker's dozen of the Confederate leaders. Zebulon Vance and Joseph E. Brown, the Confederate governors of North Carolina and Georgia, were arrested; Jefferson Davis was finally captured by Federal cavalry near Irwinville, Georgia, on May 10, and imprisoned in Fortress Monroe. Although Booth was tracked down by the army and shot to death in a barn in northern Virginia on April 26, scores of suspects were arrested by Stanton and eight were put on trial before a hard-jawed military tribunal. Four of them were hanged on July 7.[52]

And yet, for all the appearances of grim-faced radicalism in Johnson, Wade and his colleagues could not have been more wrong about the new president. Not only was Johnson's support for Reconstruction limited to what it could do for poor whites rather than freed blacks, but Johnson's Democratic political instincts set him against almost every other part of the Republican agenda, including tariffs, the new national banking system, the use of paper money rather than specie by the federal government, and federal investment in internal improvements. "The war of finance is the next war we have to fight," Johnson prophesied, and that included "prohibitory tariffs" and "the manufacturers and men of capital in the Eastern States"—in other words, precisely the people Lincoln and the Republicans had championed. "The aristocracy based on $3,000,000,000 of property in slaves . . . has disappeared," Johnson rejoiced,

> but an aristocracy, based on over $2,500,000,000 of national securities, has arisen in the Northern states, to assume that political control which the consolidation of great financial and political interest formerly gave to the slave oligarchy. . . . We have all read history, and is it not certain, that of all aristocracies mere wealth is the most odious, rapacious, and tyrannical? It goes for the last dollar the poor helpless have got; and with such a vast machine as this government under its control, that dollar will be fetched. It is an aristocracy that can see in the people only a prey for extortion.[53]

If Johnson had a solution to the problems posed by the freedpeople, it was bounded on one side by his refusal to grant former slaves any kind of political equality with white men, and on the other by Johnson's conclusion that the best conclusion to the story of black people in America would be a fast ship to Africa. "There is a great problem before us," Johnson informed a black regiment, drawn up for his review, on October 10, 1865, "whether this race can be incorporated and mixed with the people of the United States . . . If it should be so that the two races cannot agree and live

52. Eric L. McKitrick, *Andrew Johnson and Reconstruction* (Chicago: University of Chicago Press, 1960), 137; Trefousse, *Benjamin Franklin Wade*, 249–50; James L. Swanson, *Bloody Crimes: The Chase for Jefferson Davis and the Death Pageant for Lincoln's Corpse* (New York: William Morrow, 2010), 309–16.

53. Johnson, "Interview with Charles G. Halpine," March 5, 1867, in *Political History of the United States During Reconstruction*, 141; W. E. B. Du Bois, *Black Reconstruction in America, 1860–1880* (1935; New York: Free Press, 1998), 260.

in peace and prosperity," then "they are to be taken to their land of inheritance and promise, for such a one is before them."[54]

Just how deeply the Radicals had misjudged Johnson became apparent when Johnson issued his own plan for a presidential Reconstruction on May 29, 1865. It was, for all intents and purposes, what Sherman had offered Joe Johnston, only in more spacious detail. Pardons, restoration of confiscated property, and restored civil rights were extended to all but the uppermost echelons of the former Confederate leadership, and even they were permitted by "special application" to be pardoned. And to smooth the path to restoration, Johnson added a series of proclamations appointing interim provisional governors and urging the writing of new state constitutions based upon the voter qualifications in force at the time of secession in 1861—which meant, in large but invisible letters, no blacks. The governors would organize state conventions that would repudiate the state's secession ordinance, disallow any obligation to pay off Confederate war debts, and write new voting laws; then regular elections for governor, state legislature, and Congress could be held, and the new state legislatures would ratify the Thirteenth Amendment. And in the process, former Confederate soldiers and officers who retook control of the new state conventions could keep the freedpeople as close to legal peonage as possible.[55] Both Radical and moderate Republicans were stupefied. "My Dear Wade," wrote Charles Sumner to Bluff Ben, "the rebels are all springing into their old life, & the copperheads also. This is the President's work. . . . We must let him know frankly, that we will not follow his fatal lead. . . . We must also let the country know that we will not consent to this sacrifice." The anti-slavery evangelist Charles Grandison Finney denounced Johnson as a "piece of rottenness under the nose of God" and prayed that God would "put him to bed." But Johnson was undaunted; and since Congress would not reconvene until December, there was little (as Lincoln had anticipated) to prevent the president from running the show pretty much on his own until then.[56]

As he passed out pardons on application, Johnson proceeded to appoint provisional governors for North Carolina on May 29, Mississippi on June 13, Georgia and Texas on June 17, Alabama on June 21, South Carolina on June 30, and Florida on July 11 (he also recognized as legitimate the Unionist state governments that had already been erected in Virginia, Louisiana, Arkansas, and his own Tennessee). Instead of being hanged, Confederate leaders were at first surprised by Johnson's

54. Johnson, "Speech to the Negro Soldiers," October 10, 1865, in John Savage, *The Life and Public Services of Andrew Johnson: Including His State Papers, Speeches and Addresses* (New York: Derby and Miller, 1866), 93–94.

55. "By the President of the United States: A Proclamation," in *Messages and Papers of the Presidents*, 6:310–14.

56. Sumner to Wade, August 3, 1865, in *The Selected Letters of Charles Sumner*, ed. B. W. Palmer (Boston: Northeastern University Press, 1990), 2:320–21; James David Essig, "The Lord's Free Man: Charles G. Finney and His Abolitionism," *Civil War History* 24 (March 1978): 25–45.

generosity, then relieved, and then defiant. None of the reconstructed governments extended voting rights to the freedmen; South Carolina even balked at repudiating its share of Confederate debt. Carl Schurz, on a fact-finding tour of the South, believed that the surrenders of the Confederate armies had made public opinion in the Southern states "so despondent that if readmission at some future time under whatever conditions had been promised, it would have been looked upon as a favor." But when "day after day went by without bringing the disasters and inflictions which had been vaguely anticipated," Southerners grew more secure and resistant, "until at last the appearance of [Johnson's amnesty] proclamation substituted new hopes for them." As soon as "they found that the control of everything was to be again put in their hands," wrote one frantic observer to Lyman Trumbull, "they became insolent . . . drunk with power, ruling and abusing every loyal man, white and black." Christopher Memminger put it more simply: Johnson "held up before us the hope of a 'white man's government,' and this led us to set aside negro suffrage. . . . It was natural that we should yield to our old prejudices."[57]

This overreach, however, was the undoing of presidential Reconstruction. Several southern conventions only repealed secession rather than repudiating it, the new state legislature in Mississippi refused to ratify the Thirteenth Amendment, and a few states ratified the amendment but only with the proviso that the states and not the federal government had the right to determine the political future of the freedpeople. In Arkansas, the legislature actually appropriated funds to pay pensions to Confederate veterans. In a series of "Black Codes," Mississippi and South Carolina passed labor laws that bound blacks to employers almost as tightly as slavery once bound them to masters. Other codes established patterns of racial segregation that had been impossible under slavery, barred African Americans from serving on juries or offering testimony in court against whites, made "vagrancy," "insulting gestures," and "mischief" offenses by blacks punishable by fines or imprisonment, forbade black-white intermarriage, and banned ownership by blacks of "fire-arms of any kind, or any ammunition, dirk or bowie-knife."[58]

The most visibly outrageous result of presidential Reconstruction involved the people who found top-level state employment in the Johnson governments, and the representatives they sent to Washington to sit in Congress. Across the lower South, former Confederates moved right back into the places of state power they had held before the war. Alexander Stephens, former Confederate vice president and now pardoned by Johnson, was elected by the Georgia legislature to the Senate; Herschel

---

57. Col. J. W. Shaffer to Trumbull, December 25, 1865, in Horace White, *The Life of Lyman Trumbull* (New York: Houghton Mifflin, 1913), 242; Memminger to Schurz, April 26, 1871, in Carl Schurz, *Speeches, Correspondence and Political Papers of Carl Schurz*, ed. Frederic Bancroft (New York: G. P. Putnam's, 1912), 2:256.

58. "Laws in Relation to Freedmen," Senate Executive Doc. No. 6, 39th Congress, 2nd Session (1867), 192–99; John C. Rodrigue, *Reconstruction in the Cane Fields: From Slavery to Free Labor in Louisiana's Sugar Parishes, 1862–1880* (Baton Rouge: Louisiana State University Press, 2001), 67.

V. Johnson, who had sat in the Confederate Congress, was picked for the other Georgia Senate seat. In the House of Representatives, Cullen Battle, until recently a Confederate general, showed up to represent Alabama; William T. Wofford, who had commanded a Confederate brigade at Gettysburg, was there for Georgia; two of Virginia's eight representatives had been members of the state secession convention in 1861. Along with the restoration of white power came an upsurge of anti-black violence. "You have doubtless heard a great deal of the Reconstructed South, of their acceptance of the results of the war," wrote a Freedmen's Bureau agent in South Carolina. "This may all be true, but if a man . . . had the list of Negroes murdered in a single county in this most loyal and Christian state, he would think it a strange way of demonstrating his kindly feelings toward them."[59]

When Congress finally reassembled in December 1865, the mutterings against presidential Reconstruction had become loud and irritated. The representatives of the new Johnson-approved governments appeared on December 4 to take their seats, but the clerk of the House of Representatives, Edward McPherson (whose property at Gettysburg had been fought over on July 1, 1863), omitted their names from the roll call and refused to recognize them. The House Radicals, with Thaddeus Stevens in the lead, then seized the initiative by referring the entire matter of Reconstruction to a joint House-Senate Committee on Reconstruction (which would be, for all practical purposes, a reincarnation of the Joint Committee on the Conduct of the War), thus grabbing the oversight of Reconstruction out of Johnson's hands, as Ben Wade and Henry Winter Davis had tried to do in 1864. In the Senate, Wade and Sumner were ready with a bill for black voting rights in the District of Columbia and resolutions banning the readmittance to the Union of any state that did not also endorse equal voting rights for all adult males, regardless of color. "I deny the right of these States to pass these laws against men who are citizens of the United States," spluttered Henry Wilson, and he was seconded by Lyman Trumbull of Illinois, who introduced a federal civil rights bill just after the New Year that contained a forthright definition of federal citizenship, based on *jus soli*: "All persons born in the United States . . . are hereby declared to be citizens of the United States," declared the new bill, "and such citizens, of every race and color . . . shall have the same right, in every State and Territory in the United States . . . as is enjoyed by white citizens."[60]

But Wilson and Trumbull were soon to learn that Reconstruction was no easier to accomplish in Congress than in the White House. Wilson was promptly interrupted

59. "Names of Claimants from the Insurrectionary States," in *Political History During Reconstruction*, 107–9; Richard N. Current, *Those Terrible Carpetbaggers* (New York: Oxford University Press, 1988), 45.

60. "Organization of the House," and "Reconstruction," December 4, 1865, *Congressional Globe*, 39th Congress, 1st session, 1, 3–4, 6; Wilson and Sherman, "Protection of Freedmen," December 13, 1865, *Congressional Globe*, December 13, 1865, 39th Congress, 1st Session, 41–42; "An Act to Protect All Persons of the United States in Their Civil Rights, and Furnish Means of Their Vindication," April 9, 1866, in *Statutes at Large*, 39th Congress, 1st session, 14:27–30.

by John Sherman of Ohio, who pointed out that "there is scarcely a State in the Union that does not make distinctions on account of color. . . . Is it the purpose of this bill to wipe out all these distinctions?" And in the House of Representatives, Wisconsin Democrat Charles Eldridge accused the promoters of the civil rights legislation of an "insidious and dangerous" plan to "lay prostrate at the feet of the Federal Government the judiciary of the States." The only citizenship Eldridge knew was the citizenship of the states: "I hold that the rights of the States are the rights of the Union, and that the rights of the States and the liberty of the States are essential to the liberty of the individual citizen." Garret Davis of Kentucky called the bill "a bald, naked attempt to usurp power and to bring all the sovereign and reserved powers of the States to the foot of a tyrannical and despotic faction in Congress," crying that it gave the vote "to a race of men who throughout their whole history, in every country and condition in which they have ever been placed, have demonstrated their utter inability for self-government."[61]

This was deliberately seeing ghosts for bedsheets. The Radicals were driven by neither a demonic thirst for centralized government nor an idealized passion for racial egalitarianism. "This doctrine does not mean that a negro shall sit on the same seat or eat at the same table with a white man," Thaddeus Stevens replied in 1867. "That is a matter of taste which every man must decide for himself. The law has nothing to do with it." But insofar as the black man born in the United States and the white man born in the United States were considered politically, their identity was based not on being black or white but on being citizens. "We will have no permanent settlement of the negro question," warned the New York editor Theodore Tilton, "till our haughtier white blood, looking the negro in the face, shall forget that he is black, and remember only that he is a citizen."[62]

The stage was now set for a direct confrontation between the president and the Radical wing of what was supposed to be his own party. The Radicals began by setting out once again their version of Reconstruction's primary question: that secession was tantamount to state suicide, that the former Southern states were now in the position of territories, and that the Constitution clearly placed territories under the oversight of Congress. "Congress alone is authorized to deal with the subject of reconstruction," wrote one Radical congressman to Charles Sumner, and that grant of authority included an unprecedented level of intervention in local Southern affairs, just as it would in any Federal territory. That included the requirement of black voting rights and land reform: "Our safety and the peace of the country require us to

61. Sherman and Eldridge, "Rights of Citizens," *Congressional Globe*, December 13, 1865 and March 2, 1866, 39th Congress, 1st session, 41–42, 1154–55; Garrett Davis, "Article XV," February 26, 1869, *Congressional Globe*, 41st Congress, 2nd session, 1630–31.

62. Stevens, "Reconstruction," January 3, 1867, *Congressional Globe*, 39th Congress, 2nd session, 252–53; Tilton, "One Blood of All Nations," February 27, 1864, in *Sanctum Sanctorum: or, Proof-Sheets from an Editor's Table* (New York: Sheldon, 1870), 104–5.

disenfranchise the rebels and to enfranchise the colored citizens in the revolted states and thereby confide the political power therein to . . . safe hands." This led the Radicals to push not only for the civil rights bill but also for renewal of the Freedmen's Bureau (since the Bureau would be given much of the responsibility as a federal watchdog for violations of the civil rights bill) and confirmation of Sherman's forty-acre order.[63]

Johnson interpreted these actions as an assault on his presidential authority as well as on his old Democratic deference to state and local power—which is precisely what they were. But unlike Lincoln, who had defused attacks like these by moving softly around them, Johnson hurled the full force of his anger at the Radicals. On February 7 Johnson received a delegation of African American leaders, headed by Frederick Douglass, and proceeded to harangue them on the impossibility of granting political equality to blacks. When Douglass tried to object, Johnson cut him short: "I do not like to be arraigned by some who can get up handsomely-rounded periods and deal in rhetoric, and talk about abstract ideas of liberty, who never periled life, liberty, or property." Douglass took his objections out the door with him and published them in a Washington newspaper. "I know that d——d Douglass," screeched Johnson when he read Douglass's comments; "he's just like any nigger, & he would sooner cut a white man's throat than not."[64]

Having turned from playing Moses to playing Pharaoh, Johnson struck back at Congress. On February 19 he vetoed the Freedmen's Bureau renewal bill, arguing that Congress had no right to fasten federal oversight agencies on states it was determined to bar from their due representation in Washington—and he let people draw their own conclusions from his contention that the Southern states were still *states*. Three days later, in a Washington's Birthday speech at the White House, Johnson linked himself to Andrew Jackson, fighting off a new set of enemies of the Union. "Who has suffered more than I have?" Johnson whined. When a voice in the crowd asked him to name names, Johnson singled out Stevens, Sumner, and Wendell Phillips, as though they were public enemies. And then, as if to crown these gaffes, Johnson vetoed the civil rights bill on March 27, effectively burning whatever bridges he still had to the Republican Party that had nominated him only a year and a half before. Even moderate Republicans were aghast at Johnson's recklessness, especially since the civil rights bill had been written and rewritten by Lyman Trumbull of Illinois specifically to appease Johnson.[65]

63. Edward Belcher Callender, *Thaddeus Stevens: Commoner* (Boston: A. Williams, 1882), 133–40; Hans L. Trefousse, *Thaddeus Stevens: Nineteenth-Century Egalitarian* (Chapel Hill: University of North Carolina Press, 2001), 178–80; Trefousse, *The Radical Republicans*, 316.

64. James Oakes, *The Radical and the Republican: Frederick Douglass, Abraham Lincoln, and the Triumph of Anti-slavery Politics* (New York: W. W. Norton, 2007), 250; McFeely, *Frederick Douglass*, 247; Trefousse, *Andrew Johnson*, 241–42.

65. Epps, *Democracy Reborn*, 135; Johnson, "Speech of the 22d February, 1868," in *Political History During Reconstruction*, 59, 61; White, *The Life of Lyman Trumbull*, 272–74.

Rather than managing Congress in Lincoln's style, Johnson had only succeeded in colliding with it and making himself look the worse for the wear. On April 9, Congress successfully overrode Johnson's veto of the civil rights bill (although the Senate managed the override only by a single vote); a second version of the Freedmen's Bureau bill was passed, and when Johnson vetoed it again, Congress overrode that veto as well. Finally, on April 30, determined to put black civil rights beyond the reach of Johnson's interference and Johnson's vetoes, William Pitt Fessenden in the Senate and Thaddeus Stevens in the House introduced a proposal for a new constitutional amendment, bluntly establishing a *jus soli* baseline for defining United States citizenship, and subordinating state citizenship to it.

> All persons born or naturalized in the United States, and subject to the jurisdiction thereof, are citizens of the United States and of the State wherein they reside. No State shall make or enforce any law which shall abridge the privileges or immunities of citizens of the United States; nor shall any State deprive any person of life, liberty, or property, without due process of law; nor deny to any person within its jurisdiction the equal protection of the laws.

This effectively removed the definition of both citizenship and voter eligibility from state jurisdiction and handed it to the federal government. But this was not all: the amendment went on to expel from Congress any member of the House or Senate, or any civil or military officer of the United States, who had been "engaged in insurrection or rebellion against the same, or given aid or comfort to the enemies thereof," and imposed repudiation of the Confederate debt on the former Confederate states, so that anyone still holding Confederate securities and expecting to get them redeemed was left to use them as wallpaper. Predictably, Johnson gagged on the amendment. But since amendments to the Constitution do not require a presidential signature, both houses of Congress passed this Fourteenth Amendment by the required two-thirds majority in June 13, 1866, and forwarded it to the state legislatures for ratification without even bothering to send Johnson the customary notification resolution.[66]

Johnson attempted to fight back with what powers he still had in hand, but by the summer of 1866 even the small standing he had as president was dwindling. The popular songwriter Henry Clay Work set his contempt for Johnson to music:

> Who shall rule this American nation? Say, boys, say!
> Who shall sit in the loftiest station? Say, boys, say!
> Shall the men who trampled on the banner?
> They who now their country would betray?
> They who murder the innocent freed men? Say, boys, say!
> chorus: No never! no, never! The loyal millions say;
> And 'tis they who rule this American nation, They, boys, they!

66. "Civil Rights Bill—Again," April 9, 1866, "Reconstruction," April 30, 1866, and "Reconstruction Again," June 13, 1866, *Congressional Globe*, 39th Congress, 1st session, 1861, 2286–87, 3145–49.

Who shall rank as the family royal? Say, boys, say!

If not those who are honest and loyal? Say, boys, say!

Then shall one elected as our servant

In his pride, assume a regal way?

Must we bend to the human dictator? Say, boys, say!

Shall we tarnish our national glory? Say, boys, say!

Blot one line from the wonderful story? Say, boys, say!

Did we vainly shed our blood in battle?

Did our troops resultless win the day?

Was our time and our treasure all squander'd? Say, boys, say![67]

With congressional elections looming in the fall of 1866, Johnson embarked on a desperate bid to rally popular support for his collapsing Reconstruction plan, making a whirlwind speaking tour of the North, a "swing round the circle," and dragging a reluctant General Grant with him to provide moral support. A National Union Convention, designed to unite moderate Republicans and Northern Democrats behind Johnson, met in Philadelphia in August, but it was upstaged by a Radical-sponsored Southern Loyalists' Convention, which paraded through the streets of Philadelphia in September to hear Frederick Douglass and Quaker activist Anna Dickinson offer impassioned appeals for black equality. Johnson, for his part, could not seem to open his mouth without offending people, and his rough country mannerisms (in contrast to Lincoln's, which had been smoothed by a lifetime of trying to elude his backwoods origins) dampened support across the North rather than rousing it. "I care not for dignity," Johnson boasted, and promptly provided all the proof necessary. When a heckler in Cleveland on September 3 shouted that Johnson couldn't look a man in the face, Johnson lost all self-control and began shouting,

I wish I could see you; I will bet now, if there could be a light reflected on your face, that cowardice and treachery could be seen in it. Show yourself. Come out here where we can see you. If ever you shoot a man, you will stand in the dark and pull your trigger . . . Those men—such a one as insulted me here tonight—you may say, has ceased to be a man, and in ceasing to be a man shrunk into the denomination of a reptile, and having so shrunken, as an honest man, I tread on him.[68]

In the November elections, the Republicans crushed Johnson's moderate and Democratic friends, and, taking no hint from his "swing round the circle," voters

67. William Bolcom, Joan Morris, and Clifford Jackson, vocal performance of "Who Shall Rule This American Nation?" by Henry Clay Work, recorded 1975, on *Who Shall Rule This American Nation? Songs of the Civil War Era*, Nonesuch Records H 71317.

68. J. Matthew Gallman, *America's Joan of Arc: The Life of Anna Elizabeth Dickinson* (New York: Oxford University Press, 2006), 82–83; Johnson, "In Cleveland, September 3," in *Political History During Reconstruction*, 135–36.

gave the Radicals a veto-proof majority in both houses of Congress—43 to 9 in the Senate, 173 to 53 in the House. Johnson had now lost control not only of his public image but also of his administration. Even Tennessee, to Johnson's embarrassment, gave up on Johnson and ratified the Fourteenth Amendment as part of a deal that would guarantee the readmission of Tennessee's representatives and senators to Congress on Congress's terms. "We have fought the battle and won it," crowed Parson Brownlow, who was now Tennessee's Republican governor and the deadly political enemy of Andrew Johnson. "Give my respects to the dead dog in the White House."[69]

THE GOVERNMENT OF THE UNITED STATES ABANDONS YOU

The results of the congressional in 1866 were an open invitation to the Radicals, with Thaddeus Stevens the dominant Radical of the House and Ben Wade the new president pro tem of the Senate, to take up the reins of Reconstruction from Johnson's faltering hands and substitute a congressional Reconstruction plan. They moved first on January 22, 1867, by passing a bill that called the newly elected 40th Congress to order on March 4, 1867, immediately after the close of the 39th Congress, rather than the following December, so as to give Johnson no opportunities for mischief during a congressional recess. With that foundation securely under foot, the Joint Committee on Reconstruction turned to the scaffolding of congressional Reconstruction, and on March 2, 1867, Congress enacted the first of three major Reconstruction Acts. Declaring that "no legal State governments or adequate protection for life or property now exists in the rebel states," the First Reconstruction Act consolidated most of the old Confederacy into five "military districts": Virginia would constitute the first, the Carolinas the second, Georgia, Alabama, and Florida the third, Mississippi and Arkansas the fourth, and Texas and Louisiana the fifth. Each district would be supervised by an army general appointed by the president, and other army officers and Freedmen's Bureau agents would act as adjuncts to the civilian administrations in properly registering voters.[70]

Despite such martial appearances, the "military districts" really did employ most of the civilian procedures associated with organizing territories. Civil governments would exist, but the army would have overall supervision of the civil process and fine-tune the operation of civil government until the state regimes began to look like what Congress wanted. When "the people of any one of said rebel States"—which included all adult males of "whatever race, color, or previous condition," but not

---

69. Stampp, *Era of Reconstruction*, 114–15; D. M. DeWitt, *The Impeachment and Trial of Andrew Johnson* (New York: Russell and Russell, 1967 [1903]), 100.

70. "An Act to Provide for the More Efficient Government of the Rebel States," March 2, 1867, in *Statutes at Large*, 39th Congress, 2nd session, 14:428–29.

former Confederate civil officials or military officers—were willing to write a new state constitution embracing the Thirteenth and Fourteenth Amendments, Congress would recognize a Southern state and admit its civil representatives as members of Congress rather than mere "delegates."

President Johnson, of course, vetoed the First Reconstruction Act. The Radicals anticipated this, and Congress overrode the veto without hesitation. In fact, they anticipated more than just a veto. On the same day that Congress passed the First Reconstruction Act, a rider was attached to a military appropriations bill to limit Johnson's ability to make military appointments and issue orders to military commanders, and to force the president to pass all of his orders through the general in chief (which in this case was Grant). This would ensure, as much as possible, that the new district commanders would see themselves as answerable more to Grant and Congress than to the president. And to make sure that Johnson would not try to circumvent the operation of the Reconstruction Act through his use of civilian patronage appointments, Congress added the Tenure of Office Act in March 1867. The new statute prevented the president from unilaterally removing civilian government job holders until the Senate approved a successor for that office, a step designed to further clip Johnson's presidential wings. (If the Senate was in recess, the president would be allowed only to "suspend" an officeholder until the Senate reconvened.) Johnson vetoed the act; Congress overrode the veto.[71]

The third stone in the new edifice of Reconstruction was the Second Reconstruction Act, passed on March 23, 1867, which established the procedures for registering eligible white and black voters—and excluding any Southern participants "in any rebellion or civil war against the United States." Johnson vetoed this one, too; Congress just as easily overrode the veto. "We must establish the doctrine of National Jurisdiction over all the States in State matters of the Franchise," warned Thaddeus Stevens, "or we shall finally be ruined."[72]

Andrew Johnson's presidency was by this point so impotent that simply getting rid of him seemed worth considering, especially since Ben Wade, as the president pro tem of the Senate, would be his constitutional successor. Discussions among the Radicals about impeaching Johnson and removing him from the presidency had flickered as early as his veto of the civil rights bill in 1866 (Hannibal Hamlin, whom Johnson had supplanted as vice president in 1864, took up the impeach-Johnson cry that fall, asking, "Did we fight down the rebellion to give the South more power?"). But not until January 1867, when it was clear that the incoming Congress would

71. "An Act Regulating the Tenure of Certain Civil Offices," March 2, 1867, in *Statutes at Large*, 39th Congress, 2nd session, 14:430–32.

72. "An Act Supplementary to an Act Entitled 'An Act to Provide for the More Efficient Government of the Rebel States,'" March 23, 1867, in *Statutes at Large*, 40th Congress, 1st session, ed. G. P. Sanger (Boston: Little, Brown, 1869), 15:2–5; Stevens, "To Edward McPherson," August 16, 1867, in *Selected Papers of Thaddeus Stevens*, 324.

give them almost unstoppable momentum, did the Republican caucus in the House begin seriously considering such a move.[73]

Once considered, however, action quickly followed: on January 7 (the same day as the Senate overrode Johnson's veto of a bill to extend voting rights to blacks in the District of Columbia), James Ashley, the Radical Ohio representative who had been the floor manager for the Thirteenth Amendment, moved for Johnson's impeachment on the grounds that he had "corruptly used" the presidential pardoning, veto, and appointment powers. That effort died in the House Judiciary Committee, which found no specific evidence it could use as the basis for impeachment proceedings beyond Johnson's political truculence. When the 40th Congress began work in March, Ashley tried again, hoping that a new Judiciary Committee would be more favorable to impeaching a conspirator who "came into the presidency by the door of assassination" and who might even have been complicit "in the assassination plot." But the new committee had no more desire to challenge the president than its predecessor had, and in June the impeachment proposal was dropped again, by a 5–4 vote.[74]

Emboldened by these failures, Johnson struggled to regain the initiative—and undercut the Reconstruction Acts—by denying military commanders in the five districts the power to invalidate fraudulent registration and voting procedures. This, in effect, liberated Southern civil authorities to create fanciful voting requirements that would invariably disqualify black voters. This was so transparent a maneuver that even some of the military district commandants balked, and when Philip Sheridan, the commander for Texas and Louisiana, ignored an opinion criticizing military intervention in voter registration from Johnson's compliant attorney general, Henry Stanbery, Johnson dismissed Sheridan on July 31, 1867. This cost Johnson the patience of Ulysses S. Grant, who had regarded Sheridan as a protégé, and who in his role as general in chief advised military commanders that Stanbery's opinion had neither "language or manner entitling it to the force of an order." Sheridan's dismissal set off a new flurry of impeachment demands, this time from Thaddeus Stevens and the Joint Committee on Reconstruction. But once again, no one in Congress could produce any hard evidence that Johnson had broken a law.[75]

73. Charles Eugene Hamlin, *The Life and Times of Hannibal Hamlin* (Cambridge, MA: Riverside Press, 1899), 510.

74. "Impeachment of the President," January 7, 1867, *Congressional Globe*, 39th Congress, 2nd session, 320; David O. Stewart, *Impeached: The Trial of President Andrew Johnson and the Fight for Lincoln's Legacy* (New York: Simon and Schuster, 2009), 74–75, 82–83; "Impeachment of the President," March 7, 1867, *Congressional Globe*, 40th Congress, 1st Session, 18–19.

75. Paul Andrew Hutton, *Phil Sheridan and His Army* (Norman, OK: University of Oklahoma Press, 1999), 24–25; Roy Morris, *Sheridan: The Life and Wars of General Phil Sheridan* (New York: Crown, 1992), 291; Joseph G. Dawson, "General Phil Sheridan and Military Reconstruction in Louisiana," *Civil War History* 24 (January 1978): 133–51; Grant to John Pope, June 28, 1867, in *Papers of Ulysses S. Grant*, 17:204.

On the other hand, the dismissal of Sheridan was not nearly enough of a victory to sustain the longer reach of Johnson's counterattack. In July 1867, the Radicals passed a Third Reconstruction Act that transferred all powers of "suspension, removal, appointment, and detail" of the Southern military district commanders into the hands of "the General of the army of the United States." This was a military counterpart to the Tenure of Office Act, and it made clear that the district military commanders (such as Sheridan) would have all the power they needed to oversee voter registration and "ascertain, upon such facts or information as they can obtain, whether such person is entitled to be registered under said act," without presidential meddling.[76]

If Grant was now to inherit most of the military powers that Johnson thought properly belonged to himself, Johnson was determined to control Grant, and to that end he proposed evicting the current secretary of war, Edwin M. Stanton, and installing Grant in his place. Grant's reaction was evasive, and with good reason, since Stanton was a friend of the Radicals and such a move would bring Johnson into collision with the Tenure of Office Act. But Johnson had decided that by now he had nothing to lose; besides, the Tenure of Office Act did permit him the power to make, and unmake, appointments during a congressional recess. On August 5, just days after Congress adjourned for its 1867 summer recess, Johnson tartly informed Stanton that "public considerations of a high character constrain me to say that your resignation as Secretary of War will be accepted." Stanton (who had been secretly warned by Grant of Johnson's plans) just as tartly refused: "Public considerations of a high character, which alone have induced me to continue at the head of this Department, constrain me *not* to resign the office of Secretary of War before the next meeting of Congress." This Johnson classified as "not merely a disinclination of compliance with the request for his resignation; it was a defiance, and something more."[77]

On August 12 Johnson announced that Stanton was now "suspended" and Grant would function as the interim secretary of war. There matters hung until December, while Johnson hoped that the situation could be diverted into the courts, where he could rely on the Supreme Court to rule the Tenure of Office Act unconstitutional. But Congress moved first, and on January 13 the Senate refused to approve Stanton's removal from office and ordered him back to his post. Grant, who prudently declined an order from Johnson to defy the Senate, obligingly vacated the War Department the next day, allowing Stanton to move back in and barricade himself in his old

---

76. C. H. Pyle and R. M. Pious, *The President, Congress, and the Constitution: Power and Legitimacy in American Politics* (New York: Free Press, 1984), 204–6; "An Act Regulating the Tenure of Certain Civil Offices," March 2, 1867, in *Statutes at Large*, 39th Congress, 2nd Session, 14:430–32; "An Act Supplementary to an Act Entitled 'An Act to Provide for the More Efficient Government of the Rebel States,'" July 19, 1867, in *Statutes at Large*, 40th Congress, 1st Session, 15:14.

77. Johnson, "To the Senate of the United States," December 17, 1867, in *Messages and Papers of the Presidents*, 6:583.

chamber. Johnson frantically began casting around for a more willing replacement for Stanton, considering George McClellan, William Sherman, and even a War Department clerk by turns. He finally prevailed on Adjutant General Lorenzo Thomas to take the job, and on February 21 Johnson officially dismissed Stanton from office.[78]

The uproar in Congress over this fresh assault on its authority was immediate, and two days later the House voted to impeach Johnson by a landslide vote of 126 to 47. On March 5 the Senate convened itself as a court to begin hearing the testimony that would lead to Johnson's conviction. The trial itself turned out to be a wearisome affair—Johnson refused to appear personally and carried out his defense through his lawyers, and most of the arguments turned on the constitutional niceties of the Tenure of Office Act and other congressional legislation. Nearly all of the spectators who daily crowded the Senate galleries knew that the decision would be settled by politics rather than evidence. When the Senate at last voted on Johnson's guilt on May 16, 1868, a critical group of moderate Republicans headed by William Pitt Fessenden pulled shy of condemning the president, and Johnson was saved from conviction by a single vote.[79]

The victory, however, proved an empty one for Andrew Johnson. Two weeks later, the Republican National Convention met in Chicago and nominated Ulysses S. Grant as the Republican candidate for president. Johnson tried to stimulate some interest among his former Democratic friends about getting the Democratic nomination, but the Democrats wanted no more to do with Johnson than did the Republicans. Instead they nominated Horatio Seymour, the wartime governor of New York who had egged on the draft rioters in 1863. Grant won handily, and the South was made safe for Reconstruction.

The sound and the fury in Washington was only one part of the Reconstruction struggle. An equally critical part was being played out in the South, where the congressional Reconstruction governments were already stripping away whatever they could of the economic and political order of the old Confederacy. Much of the new political leadership of Reconstruction came from white Southern Unionists and from Northern activists and soldiers who had settled in the South after the war. For almost a century after Reconstruction, the conventional view of these Northern reconstructors portrayed them as political vultures, a pack of opportunists and adventurers who hurriedly packed their belongings into cheap carpetbags for the trip South (hence the name "carpetbaggers") and proceeded to pick the bones of the defeated South

78. George Congdon Gorham, *Life and Public Services of Edwin M. Stanton* (Boston: Houghton, Mifflin, 1899), 2:426, 428–30; M. S. Gerry, "Andrew Johnson in the White House, Being the Reminiscences of William H. Crook," *Century Magazine* 76 (October 1908): 863–64; Hans L. Trefousse, *Impeachment of a President: Andrew Johnson, the Blacks, and Reconstruction* (Knoxville: University of Tennessee Press, 1975), 132–36.

79. Michael Les Benedict, *The Impeachment and Trial of Andrew Johnson* (New York: W. W. Norton, 1973), 168–80; Stewart, *Impeached*, 149; Cook, *William Pitt Fessenden*, 232.

clean, while Southern white Unionists were dismissed as "scalawags" who betrayed the South in return for the corrupt spoils of Reconstruction government.

But the carpetbaggers were a much more diverse lot than the stereotype allowed: some, such as the Gideonites at Port Royal, South Carolina, were idealists and educators who wanted to improve the lives of the freedpeople and turn them into productive models of small-scale Republican farmers; some, such as Lincoln's secretary John Hay, saw economic opportunities in the South, and for $500 bought a Florida orange grove that was soon producing an annual crop worth more than $2,500; others, like the New Yorker and general George Eliphaz Spencer, were simply following a pattern already established by prewar Northern investors, buying up Southern cotton and brokering its sale to a cotton-starved Europe for a whopping annual profit of $40,000; and still others, such as Captain John Emory Bryant of the 8th Maine, joined the Freedmen's Bureau and moved from there into Georgia politics as one of the founders of the infant Georgia Republican Party.[80]

Many of the carpetbaggers, in fact, were actually welcomed by Southerners for the investment capital they brought into the war-scorched South. They came largely from the ranks of the same middle-class business and professionals who filled the ranks of the Republican Party. The carpetbaggers struck up political alliances with the disgruntled Southern scalawags who, like William Brownlow, blamed the South's destruction on the planters, and were happy to engineer a new Republican political order in the South. Like the carpetbaggers, the scalawags were neither angels nor devils: many of them had been Southern Whigs in the 1840s and '50s, while some had been born in the North but came South before the war to seek their fortunes, and still others had been anti-war dissidents.[81]

The carpetbaggers struck up an even more critical alliance with the freedmen of the South and with the tiny cadre of free Southern blacks who at first formed the core of black political leadership in the South. Once congressional Reconstruction torpedoed the Black Codes and secured the ratification of the Fourteenth Amendment, black voters entered into Southern political life in substantial numbers. More than 2,000 black men held political office, ranging from Hiram Revels, who took over Jefferson Davis's old Mississippi Senate seat in 1870, and P. B. S. Pinchback, the governor pro tem of Louisiana in 1872, all the way down the scale of office to sheriffs, registrars, and justices of the peace. Later critics of Reconstruction would ridicule these black officeholders as barefoot illiterates fresh from the cotton fields. In its "qualities of ignorance, corruption and depravity," complained

80. William Roscoe Thayer, *John Hay* (Boston: Houghton, Mifflin, 1915), 1:271; Current, *Those Terrible Carpetbaggers*, 29–31; Ruth Currie-McDaniel, *Carpetbagger of Conscience: A Biography of John Emory Bryant* (Athens: University of Georgia Press, 1987), 40–41.

81. James Alex Baggett, *The Scalawags: Southern Dissenters in the Civil War and Reconstruction* (Baton Rouge: Louisiana State University Press, 2003), 14–41.

ex-Confederate congressman Ethelbert Barksdale in 1890, Mississippi's Reconstruction constitutional convention "was . . . a fool's paradise for the negroes," and
even the sympathetic New Yorker George Templeton Strong could not suppress a
smirk over reports about "the enfranchised field hand, a phrase or two about the
honorable member from Congo, and the intelligent boot-black who represents the
county of Tackahoosho, and some stories of black voters putting their ballots into
the post office." What neither Barksdale nor Strong noticed, or wanted to notice,
was that almost half of the black officeholders had been born free, and the sprinkling
of college graduates, lawyers, and Union army veterans among the black officeholders holds up at least as well (given the paucity of opportunities for education and
advancement for African Americans in the Confederate South) by comparison with
the prewar patterns of white officeholding. Nor did they constitute some universal
blight on Southern government; in only one state legislature—South Carolina—
were freedmen actually a majority.[82]

The new civil governments that this three-way alliance of carpetbaggers, scalawags,
and freedmen created under the eye of the Federal military district commanders
were far from perfect. True to at least one aspect of the legend of the carpetbaggers,
the new Reconstruction governments spent money on an unprecedented scale, and
raised Southern taxes to extraordinary levels to finance that spending, all of which
later led to accusations that the money had been squandered on shady contracts and
corrupt deals. In South Carolina, the tax rates doubled even though the war had
wiped out property values; and while the state debt jumped from $5 million in 1868
to over $16 million in 1871, legislators voted themselves a free bar, and even a bonus
of $1,000 to the Speaker of the House, Franklin J. Moses, to cover his losses at the
racetrack.[83]

But much of this political vulgarity stemmed from the sheer confusion and dislocation of the postwar years, and from the costs of building the free-labor Jerusalem
in the South's brown and devastated land. The infrastructure of roads, rail lines, and
harbors had been devastated by the war, and transforming the Southern landscape
into a replica of schoolhouses, shops, and whitewashed churches left little alternative

---

82. Richard L. Hume and Jerry B. Gough, *Blacks, Carpetbaggers, and Scalawags: The Constitutional
Conventions of Radical Reconstruction* (Baton Rouge: Louisiana State University Press, 2008), 6; Sarah
Woolfolk Wiggins, *The Scalawag in Alabama Politics, 1865–1881* (Tuscaloosa: University of Alabama Press,
1977), 128–30; Eric Foner, "Introduction," in *Freedom's Lawmakers: A Directory of Black Officeholders During Reconstruction* (New York: Oxford University Press, 1993), xiii–xxxi; Billy W. Libby, "Senator Hiram
Revels of Mississippi Takes His Seat, January–February 1870," *Journal of Mississippi History* 37 (November
1975): 381–94.

83. Benjamin Ginsberg, *Moses of South Carolina: A Jewish Scalawag During Radical Reconstruction* (Baltimore: Johns Hopkins University Press, 2010), 108; John S. Reynolds, *Reconstruction in South Carolina,
1865–1877* (Columbia, SC: State Co., 1905), 258; James Shepherd Pike, *The Prostrate State: South Carolina
Under Negro Government* (New York: D. Appleton, 1874), 197, 199–200; "A Romance of Rascality," *New
York Times* (December 26, 1878).

to vastly increased taxation and spending. Whatever the degree of corruption plaguing the congressional Reconstruction governments, they did bring vast numbers of new voters, both newly free blacks and Southern yeomen, into a more broadly based democratic process than had ever before prevailed in the South.[84] By the end of 1868, this new alliance of Southern blacks and Southern and Northern whites had completely restructured the constitutions of six of the Southern states and incorporated the Fourteenth Amendment into the political heartland of the old Confederacy.

In despair, some of the most ardent old secessionists counseled accommodation or even outright capitulation. Robert E. Lee's old lieutenant James Longstreet accepted the lucrative federal post of customs surveyor in Republican New Orleans and campaigned for Grant in 1868. Former Georgia governor Joseph Brown and former South Carolina representative (and Speaker of the U.S. House) James Lawrence Orr, also joined the Republicans and advocated cooperation with the Radicals. J. D. B. DeBow revived the old *DeBow's Review* and called upon Southerners to encourage the immigration of Northern workers and Northern industry. In 1869, when Congress adopted the Fifteenth Amendment, which specifically prohibited any abridgement of voting rights "on account of race, color, or previous condition of servitude," the new Southern governments ratified the amendment in less than a year. By 1870 all of the former Confederate states had been satisfactorily reconstructed and readmitted to the Union.[85] The Civil War, at least in the sense that secession had made it, now seemed complete.

Yet, despite the apparent successes of congressional Reconstruction, the health of the Reconstruction governments remained critically dependent on two restraints. One was the continued exclusion of the most dangerous ex-Confederates from political power in the South, and the other was continued support and encouragement from Washington, especially in the form of soldiers who would be available to enforce the civil rights statutes. During Ulysses S. Grant's two terms as president, from 1869 until 1877, both of those restraints gradually melted away.

Some of the slow erosion of federal support for Reconstruction occurred simply from attrition. Thaddeus Stevens died in August 1868, asking to be buried in a segregated cemetery for African American paupers so that "I might illustrate in death the principles which I advocated through a long life, Equality of man before his Creator." The next year, Ben Wade lost his powerful Senate seat when the Ohio legislature was captured by Democrats; Edwin Stanton died on Christmas Eve, 1869, only

84. F. B. Simkins and R. H. Woody, *South Carolina During Reconstruction* (Chapel Hill: University of North Carolina Press, 1932), 137–38, 148, 155, 175; Michael Perman, *The Road to Redemption: Southern Politics, 1869–1879* (Chapel Hill: University of North Carolina Press, 1984), 33–34, 81; James S. Allen, *Reconstruction: The Battle for Democracy* (New York: International Publishers, 1937), 140–44.

85. Ottis Clark Skipper, "J. D. B. DeBow, the Man," *Journal of Southern History* 10 (November 1944): 420–21; "Judge James L. Orr," in U. R. Brooks, *South Carolina Bench and Bar* (Columbia, SC: State Co., 1908), 1:186; Piston, *Lee's Tarnished Lieutenant*, 106, 106, 109, 123.

four days after Grant nominated him to sit on the Supreme Court; Henry Wilson left the Senate in 1872 to run as Grant's vice president, and died in 1875; James Ashley accepted the territorial governorship of Montana from Grant and left Congress; Salmon P. Chase drifted back to his old Democratic friends and died in the spring of 1873; Charles Sumner followed him the next year, having pleaded with Congress to pass a newer and more stringent civil rights bill (which it did in 1875).[86]

Also gone was the Republican majority in the House, which was replaced in 1874 by the first Democratic majority since the beginning of the Civil War, and the Republican majority in the Senate, which was lost in the elections of 1878. Without the cutting edge provided by Stevens, Wade, and Sumner, the surviving Radicals lost their taste for bold interventions in state affairs. Not until 1888 would Republicans regain sufficient numbers in Congress to renew their efforts to impose federal supervision of Southern voting with a fresh "Force Bill," drafted by Henry Cabot Lodge. The bill passed the House, only to die a lingering death in the Senate. It had all been, in the memorable title of Judge Albion Tourgee's 1879 memoir, "a fool's errand, by one of the fools."[87]

As it was, they got little enough encouragement from President Grant. Although Grant's administration has frequently been portrayed as a miasma of corruption, presided over by a military genius who turned out to be a political nincompoop, his administration was probably no more spotted than most of the prewar administrations—James Buchanan, for instance, presided over one of the most corrupt cabinets in the nineteenth century—and not much worse, in fact, than the graft and bribery that went on under the table of Lincoln's wartime administration. Grant was also more politically skilled than his critics estimated, as his adroit sidestepping of Andrew Johnson demonstrated. And he demonstrated considerable determination to smash anti-black civil violence from the Ku Klux Klan. On the other hand, it was also true that Grant was not a political risk taker. His slogan—"Let us have peace"—guaranteed that he would take equal offense at the prodding of both Radicals and Democrats, unless it was skillfully handled, and as the Radicals lost the services of Wade, Ashley, Stevens, and Sumner, the prodding became progressively more flaccid. By that time, even the Republican faithful had lost heart in the fight. The cries for help from Southern blacks for government intervention increasingly came to sound in Republican ears like the demands of populist farmers for currency inflation or unionized workers for economic regulation. "Is it not time for the colored race to stop playing the baby," asked the *Chicago Tribune* irritably in 1875.[88]

86. Thomas Frederick Woodley, *Great Leveler: The Life of Thaddeus Stevens* (New York: Stackpole, 1937), 414; Richard N. Current, *Old Thad Stevens: A Story of Ambition* (Madison: University of Wisconsin Press, 1942), 320.

87. Edward L. Ayers, *The Promise of the New South: Life After Reconstruction* (New York: Oxford University Press, 1992), 50–51; Current, *Those Terrible Carpetbaggers*, 368–75.

88. Richardson, *Westward from Appomattox*, 150–53.

In disgust, many of the surviving Radicals staged a back-door rebellion in 1872 in an effort to dump Grant from the party ticket, and they eventually ran Horace Greeley as the joint presidential nominee of what was briefly called the Liberal Republicans, as well as the Democrats. Greeley was crushed in the election (he failed to win even a single electoral vote), but the divisions made in the Republican Party's ranks only further weakened their resolve to enforce the Reconstruction legislation their party had created. In the fall of 1875, when gun-toting whites in Mississippi attacked Republican political rallies in Yazoo City and Jackson, the Republican governor, a former Union army general named Adelbert Ames, appealed to Grant for troops to put down the rioters. So did Daniel H. Chamberlain, the Republican governor of South Carolina, after six blacks were shot to death in Hamburg, South Carolina, as whites attempted to disarm a "colored militia." Officially, Grant promised Reconstruction governors "every aid for which I can find law or constitutional power. Government that cannot give protection to then life, property, and all guaranteed civil rights . . . to the citizen . . . is in so far a failure." Unofficially, Grant and his attorney general informed Adelbert Ames that "the whole public are tired out with these annual autumnal outbreaks in the South and the great majority are now ready to condemn any interference on the part of the government." No troops were sent; the federal forces already stationed in Mississippi remained in their barracks. The following spring Ames resigned.[89]

The failure of Radical Republican nerve after 1870 is linked, as Grant's telegram to Ames indicated, to a larger loss of interest in Reconstruction across the North. As the Civil War and its burning issues receded from memory, as a new generation and a new decade turned its energies westward, as a new flood of immigrants (for whom the Civil War was a topic of only incidental interest, and for whom African Americans represented only an unwelcome source of competition for jobs) poured into the ports of the East Coast and California, Reconstruction became simply an uninteresting holdover from a political era that was rapidly closing. As early as 1867, Illinois Radical Elihu Washburne was warned by former Philadelphia congressman Henry D. Moore that, even though "the Republican Party have done a great work for the Negro . . . we should be satisfied *for the present* with what we *have* done, and protect him in the rights we have given him in those States where he was formerly a Slave and had no rights at all, but here we should stop."[90] It was easy, after five more years of political infighting, to believe that with congressional Reconstruction and the Fifteenth Amendment, everything had been done for the African American that ought to be done.

In fact, some of the most important aspects of a complete Reconstruction remained ominously incomplete. The freedpeople now had citizenship and political

---

89. Andrew L. Slap, *The Doom of Reconstruction: The Liberal Republicans in the Civil War Era* (New York: Fordham University Press, 2006), 199; Stephen Budiansky, *The Bloody Shirt: Terror After Appomattox* (New York: Viking, 2008), 205, 221–40; "To Daniel H. Chamberlain," July 26, 1876, in *Papers of Ulysses Simpson Grant*, 27:199; McFeely, *Grant*, 419–25.

90. Trefousse, *The Radical Republicans*, 373.

rights, but those rights might have a short life span if unaccompanied by economic leverage. The Freedmen's Bureau struggled for the few years of its life to serve as a national employment bureau for black laborers, and even paid to transfer 30,000 freemen to jobs in Texas, Mississippi, Illinois, and Massachusetts. But comparatively few of the freedpeople wanted to work if it meant working in the South, and many of the employers in the North wanted little more than a handy pool of strikebreakers to draw from. Johnson's pardon schemes overturned any possibility of a massive redistribution of land from the hands of Southern whites to those of Southern blacks, and few even of the Radicals were prepared to make much of a point about promoting black land ownership.

Republican ideas of political economy praised the free wage laborer and independent property owner as the foundation of liberty—which, ironically, was the very conviction that restrained the Radicals from the wholesale appropriation of someone else's property (even rebel property) to make property owners out of the freedpeople. In large measure, the Radicals' willingness to use military force and army generals to ensure black voting rights was simply an effort to substitute armed federal force for the more unappetizing alternative of land redistribution. But political rights divorced from economic realities, and from economic clout, can easily turn weightless, and once the political will to enforce black voting rights began to dissipate, the entire structure of African Americans' hard-won civil equality began to come apart.[91]

And then, by the end of Grant's second administration, it started to disappear entirely. In 1873, a massive economic depression, triggered in the United States by the financial collapse of Jay Cooke, turned Northern attention away from the political survival of Reconstruction to the economic survival of the Northern economy. At the same time, the Supreme Court, ever the stronghold of Democratic disgruntlement since *Dred Scott*, handed down a critical civil rights decision on an 1873 appeal by New Orleans butchers against a Louisiana state charter that monopolized meatpacking in New Orleans. In the *Slaughterhouse Cases*, the butchers sued under the equal protection provisions of the Fourteenth Amendment, but the Supreme Court replied that the amendment applied only to equal protection under *federal* law, not state law. "There is a citizenship of the United States, and a citizenship of the State, which are distinct from each other"—hence, the "privileges and immunities" attached to federal citizenship had no application to state governments.[92]

91. William Cohen, "Black Immobility and Free Labor: The Freedmen's Bureau and the Relocation of Black Labor, 1865–1868," *Civil War History* 30 (September 1984): 221–34.

92. "Slaughter-House Cases," in Christian Samito, ed., *Changes in Law and Society During the Civil War and Reconstruction: A Legal History Documentary Reader* (Carbondale: Southern Illinois University Press, 2009), 261–72; Michael A. Ross, *Justice of Shattered Dreams: Samuel Freeman Miller and the Supreme Court During the Civil War* (Baton Rouge: Louisiana State University Press, 2003), 200.

The second blow came in *U.S. v. Cruikshank* in 1875. A disputed election in Colfax, Louisiana, led to the deaths of more than 100 black people and the indictment of 98 white people on federal charges of violating the rights of black citizens. Only nine of the arrested whites were actually brought to trial, and three, including William Cruikshank, were convicted. But on appeal, the Supreme Court declared that the federal government had no jurisdiction over state voting practices, except when the states were acting *as* states. Violations by individuals were matters beyond the reach of the Constitution. "The Constitution of the United States has not conferred the right of suffrage upon any one, and . . . the United States have no voters of their own creation in the States."[93]

In an effort to circumvent *Slaughterhouse Cases* and *Cruikshank*, Congress passed the last of the great Reconstruction legislation in the form of the Civil Rights Act of 1875. The bill, enacted in homage to the recently deceased Charles Sumner, mandated that "all persons within the jurisdiction of the United States shall be entitled to the full and equal enjoyment of the accommodations, advantages, facilities, and privileges of inns, public conveyances on land or water, theaters, and other places of public amusement," regardless of "race and color," and gave jurisdiction over the bill to "the district and circuit courts of the United States," rather than the states.[94]

But the bill survived as a federal statute only until 1883, when the Supreme Court overturned it in the *Civil Rights Cases*. The federal courts had thus slowly removed the federal protections that Reconstruction had placed around black civil rights at every level. "We have been, as a class, grievously wounded, wounded in the house of our friends," declared the aging Frederick Douglass. "I look upon it as one more shocking development of that moral weakness in high places which has attended the conflict between the spirit of liberty and the spirit of slavery from the beginning. The whole essence of the thing is a studied purpose to degrade and stamp out the liberties of a race. It is the old spirit of slavery, and nothing else."[95]

As the determination of federal authority weakened, the failure of the Reconstruction governments to put a solid economic footing under black civil rights slowly allowed the free-spending Republican administrations of the old South

---

93. Heather Cox Richardson, *The Death of Reconstruction: Race, Labor, and Politics in the Post-Civil War North, 1865–1901* (Cambridge, MA: Harvard University Press, 2001), 150; "United States v. Cruikshank," in Samito, ed., *Changes in Law and Society During the Civil War and Reconstruction*, 284.

94. "An Act to Protect All Citizens in the Civil and Legal Rights," March 3, 1875, in *Statutes at Large*, 43rd Congress, 2nd session (Washington, DC: Government Printing Office, 1875), 18(III):335–37.

95. *Civil Rights Cases* was a combination of five civil suits: *United States v. Stanley, United States v. Ryan, United States v. Nichols, United States v. Singleton*, and *Robinson* et ux. *v. Memphis & Charleston R.R. Co.*; Neff, *Justice in Blue and Gray*, 148–49; Archibald Cox, *The Court and the Constitution* (Boston: Houghton Mifflin, 1987), 111; Douglass, "The Supreme Court Decision," October 22, 1883, in *The Life and Writings of Frederick Douglass*, ed. Philip S. Foner (New York: International Publishers, 1955), 4:393, 402.

to sink into political quicksand. Without land, the freedmen were forced into sharecropping arrangements on white-owned land that bound them into new webs of dependency on white landowners. As white economic leverage over the freedpeople increased, their willingness to politically challenge Southern whites shrank. As it was, in none of the Reconstructed states did African Americans ever have control of the Reconstruction government, and only in South Carolina, Mississippi, and Louisiana did blacks ever gain a majority of the registered voters. Now even those majorities began to falter, and African Americans soon learned that there were few whites eager to shore those majorities up. Southern Unionist scalawags had entered into the Reconstruction alliance with misgiving, and over time the enemies of Reconstruction were able to play on the residual loyalty of poor whites to a whites-only democracy at least enough to paralyze Southern white support for black civil rights.

The Northern carpetbaggers were longer in their support of Southern blacks, but the Panic of 1873, with its catastrophic fall in world agricultural prices, ruined the economic base of the carpetbaggers and forced many of them to sell out. The Northerners who worked for the Freedmen's Bureau began leaving the South after 1869, when Congress unwisely closed down the bureau, and in 1876 the federal troops who had been stationed in the South to stiffen the resolve of the Reconstruction governments were gradually cut back by a cost-conscious Congress to only 3,000 (out of a total army enlistment of 17,000).[96]

Southern whites did not wait for the Reconstruction governments to stagger to their end unaided. It would be interesting to speculate what might have happened if Andrew Johnson had obeyed his original impulse in the spring of 1865 to hang a dozen, or even more, of the Confederate leaders, since a punitive action on that scale would have decapitated the potential leadership of any future Southern resistance. Instead, Johnson issued more than 13,000 pardons to former Confederate officers and officials, and as the political resolve of President Grant and the Congress evaporated, many of the former Confederate leaders stepped forward to reassert their old roles. The veteran survivors of the Confederate armies, without jobs, often without land, and frequently without direction, found it all too easy to fall in behind them.[97]

What resulted was little better than a low-level resumption of hostilities, only this time in the form of terrorism against blacks and their white Republican allies.

96. Paul A. Cimbala, *Under the Guardianship of the Nation: The Freedmen's Bureau and the Reconstruction of Georgia, 1865–1870* (Athens: University of Georgia Press, 1997), 209–16; John A. Carpenter, *Sword and Olive Branch: Oliver Otis Howard* (1964; New York: Fordham University Press, 1999), 136–56; James T. King, *War Eagle: A Life of General Eugene A. Carr* (Norman: University of Oklahoma Press, 1964), 293; Bensel, *Yankee Leviathan*, 380.

97. Glenna R. Schroeder-Lein and Richard Zuczek, eds., *Andrew Johnson: A Biographical Companion* (Santa Barbara, CA: ABC-CLIO, 2001), 7.

Quasi-guerilla movements such as the Knights of the White Camellia, the White League, and the Ku Klux Klan became, in effect, the armed struggle of the old Southern white leadership and the Southern Democrats to restore whites-only rule in the South. In a few cases, such as that of Arkansas Unionist governor Powell Clayton, the Reconstruction governments successfully struck back at the Klan's use of assassination, intimidation, and fraud. More often, it was easier to inundate Washington with demands for federal military protection—demands that, under the Grant administration, were treated with mounting annoyance as tokens that the Reconstruction governments were failures, and that it might be better to let political matters in the South take their course with a minimum of federal intervention.[98]

Playing to that concern, other Southern Democrats portrayed themselves as "Redeemers," struggling to free themselves not from blacks but from corrupt and bribe-ridden regimes. To sweeten their image, many of the Redeemers promoted the image of a "New Departure" in which the interests of both blacks and whites for better government would converge in the election of virtuous Southern Democrats who, in public at least, had made their peace with Reconstruction. Once installed, however, "Redeemer" governments turned their attention first to disenfranchising African Americans through literacy tests and poll taxes, fastening the bondage of sharecropping and indebtedness on black farmers, and eventually, between 1890 and 1908, creating elaborate codes of "Jim Crow" laws that rigorously segregated African Americans into the poorest housing, the worst educational opportunities, and political oblivion. As the once formidable Republican voter base paled and faded, the road to white Democratic Redemption lay fearfully open.[99]

The presidential election of 1876, which pitted Republican Rutherford B. Hayes against New York Democrat Samuel J. Tilden, has generally been singled out as the end of Reconstruction. Actually, Southern Redeemers had been picking off isolated Reconstruction governments all through the 1870s, until by 1876, only South Carolina, Florida, and Louisiana were still under some form of Republican rule. In the fall of 1876, the Republican lock on the White House was closely challenged by Tilden and the promise of the Democrats to sweep away the corruptions of the Grant administration. Tilden might have won the election—in fact, should have

---

98. David Mark Chalmers, *Hooded Americanism: The History of the Ku Klux Klan* (Durham, NC: Duke University Press, 1981), 8–21; Wyn Craig Wade, *The Fiery Cross: The Ku Klux Klan in America* (New York: Oxford University Press, 1998), 31–53; Powell Clayton, *The Aftermath of the Civil War in Arkansas* (New York: Neale, 1915), 91–163; Ted Tunnell, *Crucible of Reconstruction: War, Radicalism, and Race in Louisiana, 1862–1877* (Baton Rouge: Louisiana State University Press, 1984), 153; James Dauphine, "The Knights of the White Camelia and the Election of 1868: Louisiana's White Terrorists; a Benighted Legacy," *Louisiana History* 30 (Spring 1989): 173–90; George C. Rable, *But There Was No Peace: The Role of Violence in the Politics of Reconstruction* (Athens: University of Georgia Press, 2007), 74–75.

99. Perman, *Road to Redemption*, 16–17, 58–60, 66; Nelson and Sheriff, *A People At War*, 308.

won it, since he topped Hayes by a quarter of a million popular votes, and ought to have been awarded the 185 electoral votes needed to win the Electoral College—but the Southern and Northern wings of the Democratic Party had fractured over the disposition of lucrative new harbor-clearing projects and a new transcontinental rail line that Southern Democrats wanted built from Memphis and New Orleans westward through Texas. In the five politically volatile months between the election and inauguration day, Hayes and the Southern Democrats patched together an electoral deal that permitted the Republicans to claim favorable recounts in Louisiana, Florida, and South Carolina, in exchange for the proposed "internal improvements" and a promise of non-interference by federal troops in future Southern elections. On March 1, 1877, Hayes was declared president-elect by a margin of exactly one electoral vote. The next day, President Grant informed the Reconstruction governments that he could no longer respond to their requests for federal troops in protecting black voters.[100]

Hayes was inaugurated three days later, and he immediately appointed an ex-Confederate as his postmaster general, one of the most influential patronage-dispensing posts in the federal government. He warned a delegation of South Carolina blacks on March 10 that "the use of the military force in civil affairs was repugnant to the genius of American institutions, and should be dispensed with if possible." (Despite this "repugnance," Hayes had no hesitation four months later in using federal troops to suppress a great national railway strike). So there was no surprise when, on April 10, Hayes refused to intervene in the disputed South Carolina governor's election, and withdrew the federal troops that had been protecting governor Daniel H. Chamberlain in the statehouse in Columbia. Chamberlain, seeing the handwriting on the wall, conceded the election to one of Robert E. Lee's former cavalry chiefs, Wade Hampton. "Today," Chamberlain bitterly informed his disheartened black supporters, "by order of the President whom your votes alone rescued from overwhelming defeat, the Government of the United States abandons you, deliberately withdraws from you its support, with the full knowledge that the lawful government of the State will be speedily overthrown."[101] In Mississippi, Republican ex-governor Adelbert Ames wrote out what may serve as the epitaph of Reconstruction:

100. C. Vann Woodward, *Reunion and Reaction: The Compromise of 1877 and the End of Reconstruction* (Boston: Little, Brown, 1951), 166–69, 191–202, 216.

101. Walter Allen, *Governor Chamberlain's Administration in South Carolina: A Chapter of Reconstruction in the Southern States* (New York: G. P. Putnam's Sons, 1888), 481; Richard Zuczek, *State of Rebellion: Reconstruction in South Carolina* (Columbia: University of South Carolina Press, 1996), 190–201; Current, *Those Terrible Carpetbaggers*, 361.

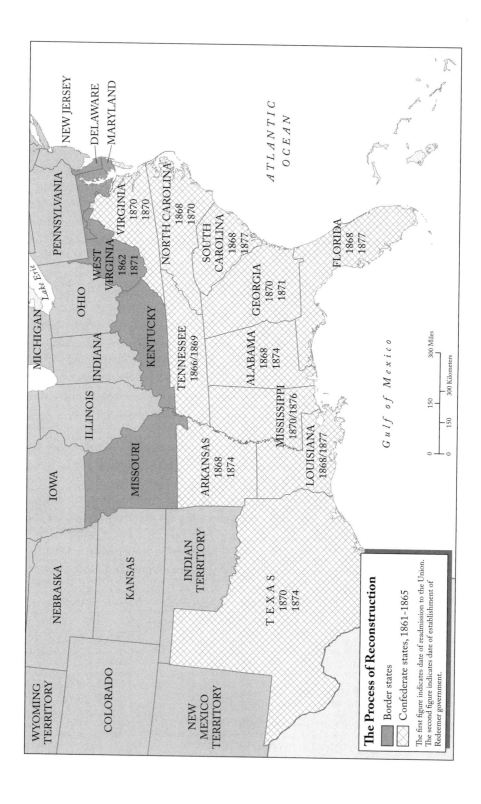

The Process of Reconstruction

■ Border states

▨ Confederate states, 1861–1865

The first figure indicates date of readmission to the Union.
The second figure indicates date of establishment of
Redeemer government.

WYOMING TERRITORY

NEBRASKA

COLORADO

KANSAS

NEW MEXICO TERRITORY

INDIAN TERRITORY

T E X A S
1870
1874

IOWA

MISSOURI

ILLINOIS

INDIANA

MICHIGAN

Lake Erie

OHIO

PENNSYLVANIA

NEW JERSEY

DELAWARE

MARYLAND

WEST VIRGINIA
1862
1871

VIRGINIA
1870
1870

KENTUCKY

NORTH CAROLINA
1868
1870

TENNESSEE
1866/1869

SOUTH CAROLINA
1868
1877

ARKANSAS
1868
1874

MISSISSIPPI
1870/1876

ALABAMA
1868
1874

GEORGIA
1870
1871

FLORIDA
1868
1877

LOUISIANA
1868/1877

ATLANTIC OCEAN

Gulf of Mexico

0   150   300 Miles

0   150   300 Kilometers

Yes, a *revolution* has taken place—by force of arms—and a race are disenfranchised—they are to be returned to a condition of serfdom—an era of second slavery. Now it is too late. The nation should have acted but *it* was *"tired* of the annual autumnal outbreaks in the South.". . . The political death of the Negro will forever release the nation from the weariness from such "political outbreaks."[102]

Well, not forever. But for then, the Civil War and its era were finally over.

---

102. Blanche Ames, *Adelbert Ames, 1835–1933: General, Senator, Governor* (North Easton, MA: Argosy-Antiquarian, 1964), 434; Current, *Those Terrible Carpetbaggers*, 323.

EPILOGUE

I t was not until August 20, 1866, that President Andrew Johnson officially declared that the Civil War was "at an end and that peace, order, tranquility, and civil authority now exist in and throughout the whole of the United States of America." Peace enough certainly existed, at least in the sense that the organized shooting was by then long over, but tranquility was quite another matter. Overall, approximately one out of every ten white males of military age in 1860 was dead by 1865 from some war-related cause. Between 1866 and 1885 the Federal War Department issued three successive enumerations of Union army wartime deaths, finally arriving at a figure of 360,222. Precise as this sounds, it was in fact an approximation; and indeed, based on census reconstructions, the numbers of deaths may have been under-reported, on both sides, by as much as 20 percent. There were no death or grave registration units in the Civil War armies; after-action reports contained reckonings of the number killed in action, but those reports relied on the record keeping of sergeants and adjutants who might have limited time and limited information for their accounts. In battles where key officers were killed, tallies and reports were often never made; in some instances, officers were encouraged to undercount their casualties in order to soften the blow to civilian morale back home. At the Wilderness in 1864, Gouverneur K. Warren, commanding the 5th Corps of the Army of the Potomac, was overheard telling a staffer not to report "data which he had gathered at the hospitals. 'It will never do, Locke, to make a showing of such heavy losses,' quickly observed Warren." After that, wrote Morris Schaff, the officer who overheard Warren,

"I always doubted reports of casualties until officially certified." (Robert E. Lee also appears to have pressured officers to revise their casualty reports downward).[1]

Even with this caveat in mind, it seems safe to say that something like 110,000 Northern men were killed outright in battle, with another 250,000 dying of disease, accidents, and even sunstroke; the number of wounded, which could mean anything from minor punctures to double amputation and blindness, was pegged at another 275,000. Added to the 7,000 or so navy dead and wounded, and the butcher's bill for the preservation of the Union amounted to at least 640,000 dead and wounded. In practical terms, six out of every hundred men of military age in the North died during the war, and one out of every six who actually served perished. Of the soldiers who served, one out of every sixty-five was killed, one out of every fifty-six died of his wounds, one of every thirteen or fourteen died of disease, and one out of every ten was wounded. Every one of these statistics, in turn, generated ripples throughout American society for decades thereafter. As many as 200,000 more Northern soldiers may have died as a result of wounds, disease, and other causes in the single decade after the war. Attached to each of these figures were widening networks of parents or dependent families that saw their breadwinners and children lost or horribly mutilated emotionally and physically by the war. By 1900, the federal government would be paying pensions to nearly a million Union veterans or their dependents, in what amounted to the nation's first Social Security system. By 1879, pension pay-outs amounted to 11.25 percent of the entire federal budget (at a time when the pension costs for the entire British empire stood at less than 3.5 percent). By 1903, there were 970,322 Civil War pensioners (both veterans and widows of veterans) at a total cost of almost $139 million, which had now become 22.5 percent of all federal expenditures.[2]

But these costs paled beside the toll that the war exacted from the Confederacy. Confederate war deaths were, in terms of overall numbers, fewer than the Union's, although the quality of Confederate record keeping (not unaffected by the amount of Confederate destruction in the last year of the war) is even less reliable than its Union counterpart. Estimates of Confederate battle-related deaths range from 74,500 to 94,000, while between

1. Drew G. Faust, *This Republic of Suffering: Death and the American Civil War* (New York: Knopf, 2008), 255; Faust, "'Numbers on Top of Numbers': Counting the Civil War Dead," *Journal of Military History* 70 (October 2006): 1005–6; "By the President of the United States of America. A Proclamation," in *Messages and Papers of the Presidents*, DC: Government Printing Office, 1908), 9:3632–36; Morris Schaff, *The Battle of the Wilderness* (Boston: Houghton Mifflin, 1910), 210; *New York Monuments Commission for the Battlefields of Gettysburg and Chattanooga: Final Report on the Battlefield of Gettysburg* (Albany: J. B. Lyon, 1900), 1:91.

2. William F. Fox, *Regimental Losses in the American Civil War, 1861–1865* (Albany, NY: Albany Publishing Co., 1889), 526; Frederick Dyer, *A Compendium of the War of the Rebellion* (Des Moines, IA: Dyer, 1908), 1:12; Vinovskis, "Have Social Historians Lost the Civil War? Some Preliminary Demographic Speculations," in *Toward a Social History of the American Civil War*, 1–12, 21–28; E. B. Long, "The People of War," in *The Civil War Day-by-Day: An Almanac, 1861–1865* (Garden City, NY: Doubleday, 1971), 700–722; John William Oliver, *History of the Civil War Military Pensions, 1861–1865* (Madison: University of Wisconsin, 1917), 117; Francis Amasa Walker, *Discussions in Economics and Statistics, Volume Two: Finance and Taxation, Money and Bimetallism, Economic Theory* (New York: Henry Holt, 1899), 44; *American*

110,000 to 160,000 Confederate soldiers died of various diseases. But the Confederacy had a far smaller pool of military manpower to draw upon: not only was the military-age population of the South smaller, but it was restricted until the very end of the war to whites, so the war cut a far wider swath through the racial power structure of the South than the numbers may at first suggest. All told, this means that eighteen out of every one hundred Confederate soldiers never came back, three times the death-rate of the Union army. It is almost impossible to estimate how many Southern civilians may have died war-related deaths, due to the disruption of the war and dangers of being a refugee.[3]

Along with these lives, a large portion of the prewar Southern economy vanished into the smoke that hung over the devastated Confederacy. Although embittered Southerners were wont to blame most of their losses on Yankee pyromaniacs, the single biggest item in the bill was caused simply by emancipation. Of the $7.2 billion worth of Southern property listed in the 1860 census, $2.4 billion existed in the form of slaves, as the chief capital investment of cotton agriculture. The Emancipation Proclamation and the Thirteenth Amendment simply erased the slave assets of the South. A second blow was fiscal in nature, as the money that Southerners had converted into Confederate bonds and notes disappeared the moment it became clear that the United States government had no intention of assuming any part of the Confederate government's debt obligations. Only after these losses came the destruction of physical capital: as much as 43 percent of the South's non-slave agricultural assets were destroyed by the war. By 1865, a third of the cattle, horses, and mules of the South were gone, and in the absence of slave labor to till the soil, Southern farm values fell by half. In Alabama, per capita wealth among white farmers fell to one-sixth of what it had been in 1860. In Georgia, one-quarter of the state's rail lines were piles of useless, twisted iron, and the state controller general helplessly estimated that "almost four-fifths of the entire wealth of Georgia had been destroyed or rendered unproductive." Even here, though, the plundering of agricultural property included that done by Confederate impressment officers as well as by Yankee foragers.[4]

By 1870, the accumulated value of all Southern property stood at only $2.05 billion, which means (after wartime inflation is factored in) that the war cost the South

---

Almanac and Treasury of Facts, Statistical, Financial, and Political for the Year 1879, ed. A. R. Spofford (Washington, DC: American News, 1880), 177, 179; *The American Almanac, Year-book, Cyclopaedia and Atlas* (New York: New York American and Journal, 1904), 474, 503.

3. Thomas L. Livermore, *Numbers and Losses in the Civil War in America, 1861–1865* (Boston: Houghton Mifflin, 1900), 5–9; Faust, *This Republic of Suffering*, 149; Mary Elizabeth Massey, *Refugee Life in the Confederacy* (Baton Rouge: Louisiana State University Press, 2001 [1964]), 64–65; J. David Hacker, "A Census-Based Count of the Civil War Dead," *Civil War History* 57 (December 2011): 307–48; "By The Numbers: Civil War Mortality Reconsidered," *Civil War Monitor* 1 (Winter 2011): 16–17.

4. Long, "Economics of War," in *The Civil War Day-by-Day*, 700–722; Claudia D. Goldin and Frank D. Lewis, "The Economic Cost of the American Civil War: Estimates and Implications," *Journal of Economic History* 35 (June 1975): 299–326; Mary A. DeCredico, *Patriotism for Profit: Georgia's Urban Entrepreneurs and the Confederate War Effort* (Chapel Hill: University of North Carolina Press, 1990), 115; Douglas B. Ball, *Financial Failure and Confederate Defeat* (Urbana: University of Illinois Press, 1991), 300–301; Paul F. Paskoff, "Measures of War: A Quantitative Examination of the Civil War's Destructiveness in the Confederacy," *Civil War History* 54 (March 2008): 35–58.

between $5 billion and $8 billion. The irony in these figures is that if Southerners in 1861 had accepted the kind of slave buyout plan Lincoln devised for Delaware that November, then, for the $6.6 billion the Civil War cost the entire nation, every slave could have been freed at market value, with enough to fund the purchase of forty acres and a mule for every slave family, and still have had $3.5 billion in hand as a fund for promoting black economic entrance into a market economy.[5]

It has long been a truism that the Civil War ruined the South but became the maker of the Northern industrial economy; that, in turn, has generated suspicious comment that the war was actually a deliberate mechanism of Yankee capitalists and industrialists to seize control of the republic from its agrarian patriarchs. But the wastage of the Southern economy in the postwar years was not entirely a product of the war, nor was the explosion of Northern industry. Southerners had pegged their prewar economic success to cotton, and believed devoutly that King Cotton would force the European nations to intervene on their behalf. Too many of them had spent too much time in an environment in which the laws of demand—whether of slaves or commodities—allowed them to ignore the complementary laws of supply. And sure enough, even before the War had come to its first major battle, cotton consumers in Europe were busy shifting to other sources of supply. The viceroy of Egypt "with a laugh" assured the Confederate propagandist Edwin De Leon, "If your people stop the cotton supply for Europe, my people will have to grow more and furnish them." And so they did. India doubled its exports of cotton to Britain; Brazil quadrupled its cotton exports; Egypt was shipping more than half a million bales to British cotton mills by 1865. Cotton remained king; it simply transferred its throne.[6]

But war rarely acts as anyone's friend, and if it was no friend to Southern cotton growing, it was also no friend to Northern industry. The rate of commodity growth actually slackened in the four postwar decades, and manufacturing showed a boom only in certain narrow sectors. In a few places, industrial employment rose at giddying speed: in Chicago, it quadrupled between 1860 and 1870, and tacked on another 50 percent of 1870 employment numbers over the next decade. But in Philadelphia, the economic impact of secession and government war contracts was broad rather than deep; some Philadelphia manufacturers made sizable personal profits out of war contracting, but the overall structure of the Philadelphia economy, not to mention its politics, underwent little reorganization during the war. In Pennsylvania's rural Chester County, the war multiplied land values and boosted the Phoenix Iron Works in Phoenixville to a competitive level with British ironmakers. But it also starved to death the cotton and woolen mills that had been the original foundation of Northern industry in the first half of the nineteenth century, and wiped out the small-scale iron mills that once occupied the banks of Chester County's Brandywine Creek. As much as Northern

5. Jeremy Atack and Peter Passell, *A New Economic View of American History*, 2nd ed. (New York: W. W. Norton, 1994), 356–60, 362–63, 373.

6. Edwin De Leon, *Secret History of Confederate Diplomacy Abroad*, ed. William C. Davis (Lawrence: University Press of Kansas, 2005), 1–2; Egerton, "Rethinking Atlantic Historiography," 82–84.

industrial muscle was vital to providing the weight of arms and material that gave the Union armies victory, much of its astounding output was channeled to the production of articles, from siege guns to uniforms, that had no peacetime value or market. Few of the officers and bureaucrats who learned how to manage large-scale production and distribution were ever able to translate those lessons into the peacetime economy.[7]

If there was any segment of Northern industry that enjoyed a boost from the war, it was the railroads. No single technological innovation of the nineteenth century was dearer to the heart of old Whigs and new Republicans than the railroad, and no industry meant more to the support of the armies than the private railroad companies that Stanton harnessed to the Union war effort. All told, the federal government handed rail corporations 158 million acres of public lands and more than $64 million in federal bonds to underwrite construction. By the 1870s, one-third of all the iron being manufactured in the United States went into rails. The same story was repeated on the state level, especially in the South. The Southern rail system staged an astonishing recovery, with much of the rolling stock being provided by demobilization sales of locomotives and cars by the U.S. Army's military railroad system. "Nine-tenths of the railroads in the South are now in operation," announced *Scientific American* at the close of 1866, "consisting of ninety roads with aggregate length of 8,170 miles." That, in turn, created a host of large-scale subsidiary industries in machines and tools that helped make the great ironworks (such as the Phoenix Ironworks) immensely profitable, but that left the small-scale prewar mills dropping ever further behind.[8]

Yet even the boost given to the railroads by the war was tangential rather than direct; it was not so much the war as the free hand a Republican Congress was given in 1862 to fund railroad construction that put new sources of wealth behind the railroad industry. Any other excuse to override Democratic opposition to such "internal improvements" would probably have produced the same result. Northern agriculture and Northern finance benefited far more from the war than did Northern industry and Northern railroads. The outbreak of the war and its demands for foodstuffs neatly coincided with the mass introduction in the late 1840s and 1850s of mechanical seeders, steel plows, and McCormick reapers (250,000 of them were in use by the end of the war), and the potent combination of wartime demand and machine-based productive capacity combined to swell the production of Northern

7. J. Matthew Gallman, *Mastering Wartime: A Social History of Philadelphia During the Civil War* (Cambridge: Cambridge University Press, 1990), 299–328; Robin L. Einhorn, "The Civil War and Municipal Government in Chicago," in *Toward a Social History of the American Civil War*, 132–38; Iver Bernstein, *The New York City Draft Riots: Their Significance for American Society and Politics in the Age of the Civil War* (New York: Oxford University Press, 1990), 195–96; Harper, "If Thee Must Fight," 363–67; Wilson, *The Business of Civil War*, 214–15.

8. Louis M. Hacker, *The Triumph of American Capitalism: The Development of Forces in American History to the End of the Nineteenth Century* (New York: Simon and Schuster, 1947), 370–71; "Quartermaster-General," *Army and Navy Journal* (December 9, 1865): 251; "Interesting Official Statistics," *Scientific American* 15 (December 25, 1866): 402.

wheat and oats by 35 percent, Northern wool by 66 percent, and Northern potatoes by 28 percent; exports of wheat, even during the war, doubled over prewar export levels, as did exports of pork and corn. Moreover, Northern wartime price inflation helped Northern farmers pay off their land indebtedness with cheap greenbacks, and doubled land values in major western states such as Illinois and Iowa. "Creditors were running away from debtors," smirked William McCormick, of the reaper family, "who pursued them in triumph and paid them without mercy."[9]

Northern financiers benefited in even more remarkable ways. The seven Democratic administrations that straddled the first six decades of the nineteenth century gave little if any encouragement to the development of American finance by holding the government's role in the economy strictly to exchanges of specie. A good deal of the capitalization of American industry in the 1820s and 1830s had to be imported from abroad. But the war and the Republicans changed that: first, the threat of the civil war drove foreign investors off the American securities market, drove down demand, and allowed American investors to step into the vacuum; then, the Republicans dismissed the Democrats' abiding suspicion of the financial markets and took the nation off the gold standard; finally, the immense amounts of money needed to carry on the war created a new class of financiers—bankers, insurers, and brokers such as Jay Cooke—who dealt in unprecedented volumes of cash and securities. The creation of the national banking system in 1863, and the subsequent disappearance of state bank currencies from Northern circulation, helped to further shift massive new amounts of financial power in the hands of financiers.[10]

Yet even these entries on the profit side of the war's ledger were mottled with failures and ambiguities. Northern finance quickly outstripped the capacity of the Federal government to oversee and regulate it, and the financial community soon found itself agitating for a return to the gold standard, not to restrain the freewheeling dealings of the financial markets, but to slow down currency inflation and attach the markets to a standard independent of federal control. This meant, in effect, returning the United States to its dependence on the international flow of specie, especially through the hands of British financiers, and when the British financial markets failed in 1873, they carried Jay Cooke and the other American financiers down with them.

The Panic of 1873 hit agriculture the hardest. The farmers who had rashly expanded westward on the balloon of increased wartime production and cost-free

---

9. Paul W. Gates, *Agriculture and the Civil War* (New York: Knopf, 1965), 375–77; Hacker, *The Triumph of American Capitalism: The Development of Forces in American History to the End of the Nineteenth Century* (New York: Simon and Schuster, 1940), 398–99; Louis R. Wells, *Industrial History of the United States* (New York: Macmillan, 1922), 466; R. Douglas Hurt, *American Agriculture: A Brief History* (West Lafayette, IN: Purdue University Press, 2002), 133–47; Harold D. Woodman, "Post-Civil War Southern Agriculture and the Law," *Agricultural History* 53 (January 1979): 319–37; H. W. Brands, *Masters of Enterprise: Giants of American Business from John Jacob Astor and J. P. Morgan to Bill Gates and Oprah Winfrey* (New York: Free Press, 1999), 36.

10. Bensel, *Yankee Leviathan*, 241, 252, 282.

homesteading now suddenly found themselves tied to distant markets where their goods sold for less and less. The dream of easy landownership promised by the Homestead Act in 1862 opened the spigots for emigration westward: Montana, which was organized as a territory in 1864, saw its population balloon from 21,000 in 1870 to 143,000 by 1890; Kansas, which was the source of so much grief before the Civil War, was admitted as a state in 1864 with less than 110,000 inhabitants, but by 1890 it had more than 1.4 million. By 1886 the *North American Review* concluded that "for all practical purposes of bestowing free farms on its growing population, the public domain of the United States is now exhausted."[11]

What the Homestead Act did not tell these hopeful settlers was that the lands of the Great Plains contained some of the most arid, inhospitable, and useless agricultural soils in the world. The weather veered unpredictably from baking hot to freezing cold, and the wind howling across the unforested prairie was enough to drive the isolated mad. "On every hand the treeless plain stretches away to the horizon," wrote one traveler in 1893; "one mile of it is almost exactly like another," and "when the snow covers the ground the prospect is bleak and dispiriting." And the land itself was difficult and intractable to farm: "Some savage quality must be taken from the ground by cultivation." And that was in the best of times. The winter of 1886 was appallingly severe in the West, freezing hundreds of thousands of cattle in enormous snowdrifts, and in the summer of 1887 drought killed off the wheat harvest—as it did for the next ten years. The wheat that did survive brought less and less, as prices on the world markets tumbled from $1.05 a bushel in 1870 to 49 cents in 1894. The farmer who had eagerly seized on the new homesteads opened up in the 1862 found himself, thirty years later, mortgaged, foreclosed, or bankrupt. The territories had been kept safe from slavery, but they had not been kept safe from the fluctuations of the market.[12]

The most important change in the shape of the postwar American economy was organizational rather than industrial or agricultural; but not only did it have nothing to do with the Civil War, it would probably have emerged on its own, war or not. That was the swift rise to dominance of the corporation. Before the Civil War, only about 7 percent of American manufacturing was organized in corporations (which is to say, as business enterprises too large to be successfully owned and managed by an individual or family, but owned indirectly by shareholders through the purchase of stock, managed by a cadre of professional administrators, and overseen by boards of directors who reported to the shareholders). By 1900 corporations accounted for 69 percent of all American manufacturing; between 1897 and 1905 alone, 5,300

11. *Historical Statistics of the United States, Colonial Times to 1970* (Washington, DC: Government Printing Office, 1975), 28, 30; Thomas P. Gill, "Landlordism in America," *North American Review* 142 (January 1886): 60.

12. E. V. Smalley, "The Isolation of Life on Prairie Farms," *Atlantic Monthly* 72 (September 1893): 378–82; Sean Dennis Cashman, *America in the Gilded Age: From the Death of Lincoln to the Rise of Theodore Roosevelt* (New York: New York University Press, 1993), 323.

small-scale firms were consolidated and reorganized into just 318 corporations, and 26 super-corporations (or trusts) controlled 80 percent of major American industrial output. Standard Oil of Ohio, chartered in 1870, was converted into a trust in 1882, by which time it controlled more than 90 percent of American oil refining.[13] "Now," warned James A. Garfield in 1874, "a class of corporations unknown to the early law writers has arisen, and to them have been committed the vast powers of the railroad and the telegraph, the great instruments by which modern communities live, move, and have their being."

> The modern barons, more powerful than their military prototypes, own our greatest highways and levy tribute at will upon all our vast industries. And: as the old feudalism was finally controlled and subordinated only by the combined efforts of the kings and the people of the free cities and towns, so our modern feudalism can be subordinated to the public good only by the great body of the people, acting through the government by wise and just laws.[14]

Not free labor and independent ownership, but "Industrial Feudalism" (in Garfield's phrase) now looked like the future. And along with that feudalism arrived a population of industrial serfs. Large-scale corporate organization made possible large-scale industries, and they in turn drew more inexpensive immigrant labor through America's ports than the territories could easily absorb. Annual immigration, which in 1860 amounted to approximately 150,000 people, had swelled by 1880 to 450,000 per year, and the urban centers of the industrializing North gradually turned into dependent, wage-earning metropolitan anthills. The staggering new scales of labor and production made the prewar slogans about free soil, free labor, and free men sound quaint rather than compelling. After the war, "I found that I had got back to another world," said the title character of William Dean Howells's novel *The Rise of Silas Lapham*, who had survived a wound at Gettysburg, "The day of small things was past, and I don't suppose it will ever come again in this country."[15]

The American generation that inherited this bleak landscape despised itself as no other American generation since. Samuel Clemens and Charles Dudley Warner tagged it the "Gilded Age," meaning that beneath its glittering appearance of

---

13. John Moody, *The Truth About the Trusts: A Description and Analysis of the American Trust Movement* (New York: Moody Publishing Co., 1904), 486–87; Atack and Passell, *New Economic View*, 484, 487; Christian Smith, "Introduction," *The Secular Revolution: Power, Interests, and Conflict in the Secularization of American Public Life* (Berkeley: University of California Press, 2003), 74.

14. Garfield, "The Railway Problem," in John Clark Ridpath, *The Life and Work of James A. Garfield* (Cincinnati: Jones Bros., 1881), 241, 243.

15. Parish, *The American Civil War*, 631–32; Helen Nicolay, *Personal Traits of Abraham Lincoln* (New York: Century, 1912), 381–82; Howells, *The Rise of Silas Lapham* (Boston: Ticknor, 1885), 20; Morton Keller, *Affairs of State: Public Life in Late Nineteenth-Century America* (Cambridge, MA: Harvard University Press, 1977), 185.

success, it had a soul of lead. The novelists and poets cried out first, initially in pain but gradually in disgust. Walt Whitman recalled with desperate fondness the nobility of the wounded soldiers he had met while volunteering in Washington's wartime hospitals. But the vulgarity of the peacetime decades filled him with horror. "Never was there, perhaps, more hollowness at heart than at present, and here in the United States," Whitman complained in *Democratic Vistas* in 1871. The results of the war had made people skeptical of noble causes and wearily tolerant of stupidity, greed, and fraud. "In business (this all-devouring modern word, business), the one sole object is, by any means, pecuniary gain." The up-and-coming novelist Henry James complained archly in 1879 that America was a landscape of cultural desolation:

> No sovereign, no court, no personal loyalty, no aristocracy, no church, no clergy, no army, no diplomatic service, no country gentlemen, no palaces, no castles, nor manors, nor old country-houses, nor parsonages, nor thatched cottages, nor ivied ruins; no cathedrals, nor abbeys, nor little Norman churches; no great Universities, nor public schools—no Oxford, nor Eton, nor Harrow; no literature, no novels, no museums, no pictures, no political society, no sporting class.[16]

Henry Adams, the grandson of John Quincy Adams and great-grandson of John Adams, was enraged at what he saw as the betrayal by government of the public trust his ancestors had handed down. He depicted postwar government as cesspool of selfishness: of government contractors amassing corrupt fortunes, of cynical politicians selling their votes to the highest bidder, of railroad moguls who used federal subsidies to crush out small-scale competition and buy the silence of federal officials. Adams carried his contempt all the way to the desk his grandfather and great-grandfather had occupied, that of the president of the United States, Ulysses S. Grant. "Grant's administration outraged every rule of ordinary decency," Adams complained; it was corrupt, visionless, and helpless. Grant himself was "inarticulate, uncertain, distrustful of himself, still more distrustful of others, and awed by money." He should, Adams raged, "have lived in a cave and worn skins." Mark Twain had more tolerance for Grant, but he was unsparing when it came to the financiers. "In my youth there was nothing resembling a worship of money, or of its possessor, in our region," Twain wrote in his unpublished *Autobiography*; "no well-to-do man was ever charged with having acquired money by shady methods." Once, "people had desired money," but the corporation "taught them to fall down and worship it."[17]

16. James, "Hawthorne" (1879), in John Morley, ed., *English Men of Letters* (New York: Macmillan, 1894), 13:42–43.

17. Whitman, "Democratic Vistas," in *The Portable Walt Whitman*, ed. Mark Van Doren (New York: Viking Press, 1945), 399–400; Adams, *The Education of Henry Adams*, ed. J. T. Adams (New York: Modern Library, 1931), 266, 280, 297; Clemens, "Friday, February 16, 1906," in *Autobiography of Mark Twain: The Complete and Authoritative Edition*, ed. Harriet Elinor Smith (Berkeley: University of California Press, 2010), 1:364.

The instinct of many survivors of the war was to create sanctuaries from this corruption where they could preserve the meanings they thought they had fought for. The veterans of the Union armies quickly melted back into the civilian population with a minimum of tension, separating back into the spectrum of lives and occupations they had temporarily left behind. But the turmoil over Reconstruction sparked the establishment of a wave of veterans' organizations. These included the Boys in Blue, Soldiers and Sailors Leagues, White Boys in Blue, Conservative Army and Navy Union, Colored Soldiers Leagues, National Conventions of Soldiers and Sailors—but the most expansive of them all was the Grand Army of the Republic (GAR). Originally founded in 1866, the GAR became one of the principal refuges for old soldiers who had fought for a very different world than the one they found around them.[18]

In more than 7,000 GAR posts across the United States, former soldiers could immerse themselves in a bath of sentimental memory; there, they reestablished a ritualized camp geography, rekindled their devotion to emancipation, and preached the glories of manly independence. "By this service, without distinction of race or creed," read one of the GAR's service booklets, prescribing the proper procedures for memorializing the war dead, "we renew our pledge to exercise a spirit of fraternity among ourselves, of charity to the destitute wards of the Grand Army, and of loyalty to the authority and union of the United States of America, and to our glorious flag, under whose folds every Union soldier's or sailor's grave is the altar of patriotism." The GAR would be one of the few postwar organizations that, as one black GAR member declared, "ignores the prejudice of race and regards as equally worthy all those who rendered the country service."[19]

Likewise, the Northern Protestant evangelicals, who had so confidently anticipated a free-labor millennium at the end of the war, now retreated before the intellectual onslaught of Darwin and the "Social Darwinism" that so conveniently apologized for the social and economic inequities of American capitalism. Some, such as Dwight L. Moody and John Wanamaker, struggled to harmonize Christ and capitalism; others, such as Walter Rauschenbusch, rejected capitalism and evangelicalism in favor of a "Social Gospel" that would fight for the new urban masses as the abolitionists had once fought for the slaves; many more, such as Jonathan Blanchard of Wheaton, withdrew behind the private ramparts of what became known to twentieth- and twenty-first-century Americans as "fundamentalism" and dreamed of an apocalyptic solution for the complexities of their world. "It is one of the ruling ideas of the century that man is fully capable of self-government," concluded one

18. Robert Burns Beath, *History of the Grand Army of the Republic* (Cincinnati: Jones Bros., 1888), 26; Stuart McConnell, *Glorious Contentment: The Grand Army of the Republic, 1865–1900* (Chapel Hill: University of North Carolina Press, 1992), 85–118.

19. Joseph Foster Lovering, *Services for the Use of the Grand Army of the Republic* (Boston: Headquarters of the Grand Army of the Republic, 1881), 14; Barbara Gannon, *The Won Cause: Black and White Comradeship in the Grand Army of the Republic* (Chapel Hill: University of North Carolina Press, 2011), 25–26.

of the participants in the first important "fundamentalist" convention, the Niagara Bible Conference, in 1875. But "according to Scripture, all these hopes are doomed to disappointment. . . . *Mene, Tekel, Upharsin*, is written concerning modern democracies no less than concerning Babylon of old." Evangelical Protestantism, which had acquired so massive a grip on public culture, now began a Napoleonic retreat to the fringes of that culture, abandoning all hope for transforming a world that had somehow gone beyond hope.[20]

The spectacle of President Johnson's public combat with the Radical Republicans awoke defeated white Southerners to the realization that the Northern war effort was a coalition, not a monolithic anti-Southern movement, and that within the coalition, moderate and Radical Republicans, War Democrats, abolitionists, free blacks, and colonizationists stood together mainly because the South had forced them to an inalterable choice between the Union and slavery. Some parts of this coalition were quite satisfied once the Union had been secured, and cared little or nothing about the future of African Americans.

It was the genius of the Redeemers to realize that the path toward the restoration of white supremacy in the South lay in splitting that coalition. To that end the Redeemer governments advertised themselves as benign representatives of a "New South" who would relieve the North of the burden of Reconstruction and black civil rights, a burden which the Redeemers rightly suspected that most Northerners never really wanted to shoulder in the first place, and shouldered only because the only alternative to Reconstruction any of them knew was the slave regime of the old South. The "New South" mythology, which burst into full flower in the 1880s, worked to allay Northern concern that the abandonment of Reconstruction was tantamount to a reversal of Appomattox. They did so first by asserting that it was Southern concern for its unique sectional identity, and not slavery, that had been the cause of secession. "Slavery was not the ultimate or proximate cause of the war," declared former Confederate general Richard Taylor, "and Abolitionists are not justified in claiming the glory and spoils of the conflict."[21]

New South advocates then reassured Northerners that the South had learned its lesson about playing with secession and was willing to embrace the Northern economic order and judge itself by Northern standards. The first assertion allowed the New South partisans to suggest that race was not, after all, the main concern of the war; the second allowed them to suggest that the North and the Federal government could safely let the South govern its own affairs, political as well as racial. In his famous 1886 speech to the New England Society of New York City, Henry Grady, the thirty-six-year-old editor of the *Atlanta Constitution*, promised that

20. Ernest R. Sandeen, *The Roots of Fundamentalism: British and American Millenarianism, 1800–1930* (Chicago: University of Chicago Press, 1970), 148; Rose, *Victorian American and the Civil War*, 68–78.

21. Taylor, "Reminiscences of the Civil War," *North American Review* 260 (January–February 1878): 78.

when the New South "stands upright, full-statured and equal among the people of the earth," it would understand "that her emancipation came because through the inscrutable wisdom of God her honest purpose was crossed, and her brave armies beaten." As Southerners reflected on the war, declared Grady, they were now "glad that the omniscient God held the balance of battle in His Almighty hand and that . . . the American Union was saved from the wreck of war."[22]

There were two serious problems with the New South image. One was that many Southerners were unwilling to make even this much of a concession for the sake of redemption; the other was that much of what the New South boosters claimed for the South simply wasn't true. Far from bravely admitting that the South was wrong and asking to be trusted again for that honesty, many ex-Confederates insisted that they had been right all along and that they hadn't the faintest interest in asking Northern pardon for any of it. As the ex-Confederate officer John Innes Randolph sang in Baltimore:

Oh, I'm a good old Rebel,
Now that's just what I am;
For this "fair Land of Freedom"
I do not care a dam.
I'm glad I fit against it—
I only wish we'd won,
And I don't want no pardon
For anything I've done.[23]

"Had we been true to our God and country," wrote Kate Cumming, "with all the blessings of this glorious, sunny land, I believe we could have kept the North, with all her power, at bay for twenty years."[24]

This so-called Lost Cause (the term was coined by Edward Pollard in 1866) defended the old order, including slavery (on the grounds of white supremacy), and in Pollard's case even predicted that the superior virtues of the old South would cause it to rise ineluctably from the ashes of its unworthy defeat. "Civil wars, like private quarrels, are likely to repeat themselves, where the unsuccessful party has lost the contest only through accident or inadvertence," Pollard defiantly wrote, "The Confederates have gone out of this war, with the proud, secret, deathless, *dangerous* consciousness that they are the better men, and that there was nothing wanting but a change in a set of circumstances and a firmer resolve to make them the victors."

---

22. Richard M. McMurry, "The War We Never Finished," *Civil War Times Illustrated* 28 (November/December 1989): 62–67; Grady, "The New South," in J. Chandler Harris, *Life of Henry W. Grady, Including His Writings and Speeches* (New York: Cassell, 1890), 82–93.

23. Randolph, "The Good Old Rebel," *Poems* (Baltimore: Williams and Wilkins, 1898), 30.

24. Cumming, *Kate: The Journal of a Confederate Nurse*, 292.

While the New Southers looked, and looked away at the same time, in the hope of appeasing Northern uneasiness, the devotees of the Lost Cause spurned such gestures, instead staging observances of Jefferson Davis's birthday, organizing the United Confederate Veterans and the United Daughters of the Confederacy, and parading the slashed red Confederate battle flag down dusty Southern streets on one Confederate Memorial Day after another. Jubal Early, who may stand as the single most unreconstructed rebel of them all, refused even to contribute funds to a monument to Robert E. Lee in Richmond when he learned that the pedestal would be carved from Maine granite.[25]

A far greater difficulty in making a case for the New South was the persistent and intractable backwardness of the Southern economy. To be sure, not everything about the post-Reconstruction South was necessarily a step backward: Republicans continued to hold on to some Southern counties and districts for decades after the end of Reconstruction, and in a number of places African Americans continued to vote, and (thanks to the patronage appointments of successive Republican presidents) to hold federal offices in the South. In further defense of the New South strategy, it was also true that the Southern states welcomed with undisguised relief the influx of Northern railroaders, miners, and loggers who fanned out across the South in the 1880s and 1890s as the mining and timber reserves of the far West were gradually depleted. Southern women retained a greater number of the social freedoms that the war had put in their path for longer than their Northern counterparts, including a greater freedom to work and to run businesses.

But all the same, not even the most optimistic New South propagandists could deny for long that the South remained an economic backwater—that its experiments in developing domestic steel and iron industries were a failure; that its networks of postwar textile mills were built on the exploitation of uprooted white workers, most of whom were women and children; that its lumbering industry mostly fed the commercial appetites of the North and left Southern hillsides waste and denuded. Southern per capita income in 1900 still stood at only half that of the rest of the nation.[26]

Above all, they could not deny the ugly fact of racial injustice. From the 1880s onward, the post-Reconstruction white governments grew unwilling to rely just on intimidation and violence to keep African Americans away from the ballot box and themselves in power, and turned instead to systematic legal disenfranchisement. Recognizing the close intersection of economic status and political power,

25. Pollard, *The Lost Cause*, 729; Michael Kammen, *Mystic Chords of Memory: The Transformation of Tradition in American Culture* (New York: Knopf, 1991), 102–21.

26. *The Promise of the New South*, 8, 37, 42, 77, 146, 102–4, 110–11, 137–46.

Southern state governments gradually imposed rigorous segregations of black and white, which ensured that blacks would occupy only the second-class railway cars, the scantiest institutes of education, and the bottom rung of the economic ladder. In the broadest sense, segregation apportioned the towns and the cities to whites and the fields to blacks, and bound blacks to an agricultural peonage—whether in the form of sharecropping or debt tenancy—that smothered the resourcefulness and economic potential of one-quarter of the Southern population. In the name of white supremacy, the South marginalized itself.[27]

Behind the facade of reconciliation and racial paternalism that the New Southers erected, there was far more common ground between the New South and the Lost Cause than either was eager to admit. The New South novelist Thomas Dixon freely admitted that "the Old South fought against the stars in their courses—the resistless tide of the rising consciousness of Nationality and World-Mission," whereas "the young South greets the new era and glories in its manhood." Yet Dixon also entertained notions of white supremacy that would have delighted the last Lost Causer: "This is a white man's government, conceived by white men, and maintained by white men through every year of its history,—and by the God of our Fathers it shall be ruled by white men until the Arch-angel shall call the end of time!"[28]

Both New Southers and Lost Causers seized on Robert E. Lee and canonized him after his death in 1870 as a kind of Protestant saint. For the New Southers, Lee's dignified surrender of the Army of Northern Virginia was a model of Christian fortitude in the face of disaster. His willingness in the years following Appomattox to help rebuild Washington College, a war-shattered Virginia educational institution, as the College's first postwar president set yet another example of patience and hope. And in order to add charity to the lengthening list of Lee's virtues, the New South promoters highlighted Lee's repeated exhortations to young Virginian men to put the war behind them and to cultivate the arts of peace. All of these pieces of Lee's character seemed to underscore the determination of the South to face the future as part of the reunited American nation.

Yet as much as Lee "avoided all discussion of political questions" in the years after Appomattox, he was privately unreconciled to black freedom and predicted that the United States was "sure to become aggressive abroad & despotic at home." Lee also gave the Lost Cause an answer to its most besetting question, which was why, if the Southern armies really had contained what Pollard called the better men, God had let the South lose to the grasping, mercenary, and infidel Northerners. In Lee, the Lost Cause found a solution, for Lee's courageous and humble bearing showed them that suffering might be a nobler calling than victory, and that the South could claim

27. Paul Gaston, *The New South Creed: A Study in Southern Mythmaking* (Baton Rouge: Louisiana State University Press, 1976), 202–3.

28. Thomas Dixon, *The Leopard's Spots* (New York: Doubleday, Page, 1902), 439, 446.

through Lee that it had surrendered not to superior political morality but only to superior numbers.[29]

These confusions of meaning and disappointment of intentions help to explain why the Civil War occupies so small a space in American high culture. The American Civil War never gave birth to a national epic, an American *War and Peace*, and with the exception of Stephen Crane's psychological 1895 novella *The Red Badge of Courage* (based on the battle of Chancellorsville) and Ambrose Bierce's frighteningly bitter short stories, America's major prose writers in the postwar period passed the Civil War by on the other side. Although the published output of Civil War–related novels and stories is fairly considerable, their strength lies in their sheer quantity rather than their quality.

The closest one comes in American literature to a frank appreciation of the War occurs, not in the writings of the Northern victors, but in the galaxy of great twentieth-century Southern novelists, from William Faulkner to Walker Percy. These authors succeeded largely because they finally came to terms with the poisonous role that race has played in the construction of a Southern mentality. Race was the great ulcer of the Southern innards, wrote Walker Percy, the South's unending shirt of flame,

> and hasn't it always been that way ever since the first tough God-believing, Christ-haunted, cunning violent rapacious Visigoth-Western-Gentile first set foot here with the first black man, the one willing to risk everything, take all or lose all, the other willing just to wait and outlast because sooner or later the first would wake up and know that he had flunked, been proved a liar where he lived, and no man can live with that. And sooner or later the lordly Visigoth-Western-Gentile- Christian-Americans would have to falter, fall out, turn upon themselves like scorpions in a bottle.[30]

By contrast, the heavier artillerists of Northern literature fled from the war and from race: Clemens, Harte, Henry James, and Sarah Orne Jewett can all be read without much suspicion that they had lived through an immense national crisis, or any inkling at all that it had something to do with race.

American poets, meanwhile, seemed moved by the war only for the production of banality, such as John Greenleaf Whittier's "Barbara Frietchie" in *In War Time* (1864), with its melodramatic confrontation of the old flag-waving widow and the somber "Stonewall" Jackson:

> "Shoot, if you must, this old gray head,
> But spare your country's flag," she said.
> A shade of sadness, a blush of shame,

29. Connelly, *The Marble Man*, 95; Pryor, *Reading the Man*, 449–53; Thomas Connelly and Barbara Bellows, *God and General Longstreet: The Lost Cause and the Southern Mind* (Baton Rouge: Louisiana State University Press, 1982), 73–75, 82–83.

30. Percy, *Love in the Ruins: The Adventures of a Bad Catholic at a Time Near the End of the World* (New York: Farrar, Straus and Giroux, 1971), 49.

Over the face of the leader came;
The nobler nature within him stirred
To life at that woman's deed and word:
"Who touches a hair of yon gray head
Dies like a dog! March on!" he said.[31]

or Thomas Buchanan Read's "Sheridan's Ride":

Up from the South at break of day,
Bringing to Winchester fresh dismay,
The affrighted air with a shudder bore,
Like a herald in haste, to the chieftain's door,
The terrible grumble, and rumble, and roar,
Telling the battle was on once more,
And Sheridan twenty miles away.[32]

Walt Whitman, alone among the American poets of the Civil War era, managed to write wartime verse in *Drum-Taps* (1865) and *Sequel to Drum-Taps* (1865–66) capable of piercing the facade of romance and glory without indulging either a cheap pacifism or a maniacal vengeance. Not until the 1920s did Stephen Vincent Benét come the closest of any American poet to creating, in *John Brown's Body* (which won the Pulitzer Prize in 1929), an *Iliad* for the Civil War. Similarly, Civil War–related art rarely rose above the technical level of newspaper illustration, and only a handful of genuinely extraordinary paintings from Winslow Homer, Xanthus R. Smith, Conrad Wise Chapman, and Gilbert Gaul are available to compete with the far vaster output of American artwork on the urban North and the cowboy West.[33]

The single greatest collection of cultural artifacts tossed up by the war is its popular music and lyrics, and many of the Civil War's tunes—Daniel Emmett's "Dixie," Julia Ward Howe's "The Battle Hymn of the Republic," George Root's "The Battle Cry of Freedom," Patrick Gilmore's "When Johnny Comes Marching Home," and Henry Clay Work's "Marching Through Georgia" and the rollicking "Kingdom Comin'"—are still so sturdy and recognizable that they instantly conjure up associations with the Civil War. But once the war's own music is left behind, very little rises in its track. Charles Ives toyed with Civil War melodic fragments and worked "The Battle Cry of Freedom" into a particularly heart-rending moment in his *Three Places in New England*; Aaron Copland set the words of Lincoln against the heroic background of what has become one of the chestnuts of Fourth of July concerts, *A Lincoln Portrait*

---

31. Whittier, "Barbara Frietchie," in *In War Time and Other Poems* (Boston: Ticknor and Fields, 1864), 58–62.

32. Read, "Sheridan's Ride," in *A Summer Story: Sheridan's Ride, and Other Poems* (Philadelphia: J. B. Lippincott & Co., 1865), 75–77.

33. Kathleen Diffley, *Where My Heart Is Turning Ever: Civil War Stories and Constitutional Reform, 1861–1876* (Athens: University of Georgia Press, 1992), 5, 76; Roger G. Kennedy, "Mourning a National Casualty," *Civil War Times Illustrated* 27 (March 1988): 34–38, 45–46.

(1942). Beyond that, only a handful of occasional pieces—a stray symphony here (Roy Harris's *Gettysburg Symphony*), a choral arrangement there (in that last resort of all high-school music directors, Peter J. Wilhousky's setting of the *Battle Hymn of the Republic*)—even notice the Civil War. No *Eroica*, no *Wozzeck*, no *War Requiem*.

Ironically, the most recurrent artistic shape that the Civil War took was statuary, some of it—like Augustus St. Gaudens's memorial on Boston Common to Robert Gould Shaw and the 54th Massachusetts—work of tremendous emotion and real genius. But by and large, the Civil War monument has been treated more as a joke than a genre. Along the same lines, the dearth of great Civil War fiction has never been overshadowed by the immense production of Civil War regimental histories, a quirky and revealing species of non-fiction with a virtually unique place in American letters, but one which American literary critics have yet to notice. Even Edmund Wilson's *Patriotic Gore* (1962), the most famous study of American Civil War–related literature, makes no allusion to the regimental histories that blossomed in far greater numbers after the 1880s than the novels and memoirs upon which he lavished so much attention.

Balanced off against these losses was at least one victory, and that was over slavery. Lincoln's Emancipation Proclamation of January 1, 1863, followed by the Thirteenth Amendment to the Constitution in 1865, and enforced by the Union armies, nailed down the coffin lid on what had always been the most egregious and shameful self-contradiction in American life. But once the war was over, the soft tidal return of racial mythologies robbed emancipation and abolition of their ambitious meanings. In time, people would disgustedly conclude that these had never had any meaning in the first place—that Lincoln was merely a closet racist, that abolition counted for nothing in the absence of economic equality, and that white Northerners too quickly gave up on an "abolition war" for black freedom in order to embrace a painless reunion with their unrepentant foes.

W. E. B. Du Bois, the greatest black writer after Frederick Douglass, was born free, in Massachusetts, in 1868, so segregation, rather than slavery, was the evil that bulked on the horizons of his experience. And the freedom he experienced seemed so hemmed in by racial humiliation that when he published his history of Reconstruction in 1935, he could only conclude that white Northerners had "never meant to abolish Negro slavery, because its profits were built on it," and only decided to "fight for freedom since this preserved cotton, tobacco, sugar and the Southern market." All the palaver about emancipation was simply cant for seducing African Americans into fighting the Union's battles. "Life, Light and Leading for the slaves" would come only "under a dictatorship of the proletariat."[34]

Du Bois was not the only scoffer at emancipation and the Union. Lurking within the snarky contempt of Henry Adams for Ulysses Grant was a Progressive snob's loathing for the ramshackle inefficiencies of democracy, and the idea that 640,000

---

34. Du Bois, *Black Reconstruction in America: An Essay Toward a History of the Part Which Black Folk Played in the Attempt to Reconstruct Democracy in America, 1860–1880* (New York: Oxford University Press, 2007), 633–34, 635.

Americans had died merely to keep such a democracy from imploding seemed so pointless as to cry out for a more sinister explanation. That was the explanation supplied by the Progressives, by Charles and Mary Beard, by Louis Hacker, and by Du Bois as well. At the end of the war, "neither the hopes of the emancipators nor the fears of their opponents were realized," said the Beards in 1921. And why? Because the true purpose of the war was to make the United States into "an industrial and commercial nation following in the footsteps of Great Britain," where "the power of capital, both absolute and as compared to land, was to increase by leaps and bounds . . . positively sustained by protective tariffs that made the hopes of Alexander Hamilton seem trivial." Beard's single-track economic determinism has long since lost its luster. But it has left a pervasive sense that the actual (and ignoble) outcomes of the war fell far, far short of justifying its costs. If the Civil War was fought for emancipation, then it must have been a failure, because mere emancipation, by itself, accomplished so little; if the Civil War had been fought to save the republic, then it was a success, but a success so vapid as not to be worth having (or at least not at that cost).[35]

But "mere" freedom was not looked upon quite so lightly by the freedpeople themselves. When Lincoln's carriage passed a brigade of black soldiers supporting the siege of Petersburg, Virginia, in 1864, they broke ranks and jubilantly surrounded Lincoln's entourage with shouts of "Hurrah for the Liberator, Hurrah for the President." The black wartime correspondent Thomas Morris Chester watched Lincoln pass through the joyful crowds of Richmond's blacks, and wrote: "The colored population was wild with enthusiasm. Old men thanked God in a very boisterous manner, and old women shouted upon the pavement as high as they ever had done at a religious revival. . . . Even then they thought [freedom] must be a pleasant dream, but when they saw Abraham Lincoln they were satisfied that their freedom was perpetual. One enthusiastic old negro woman exclaimed: 'I know that I am free, for I have seen father Abraham and felt him.'" Lincoln was extolled (in Shakespearean terms he would have appreciated) after his death at a freedmen's memorial tribute in Washington as the "dearest friend, the kindest man, as President, we ever knew," and thirty years later, the Negro Literary and Historical Society of Atlanta held up emancipation as "that day, when the clear and happy light of freedom dawned upon our midnight sky of slavery."[36]

35. Charles A. and Mary Ritter Beard, *History of the United States* (New York: Macmillan, 1921), 398; Charles Beard, "Efficient Democracy," in *Pennsylvania State Educational Association: Report of the Proceedings with Papers Read Before the General Sessions, Department and Round Table Conferences; and with Constitution and By-Laws of the State Educational Association . . . December 27, 28, 29, 1916* (Lancaster, PA: Pennsylvania School Journal, 1917), 279.

36. "Hall of Congress, Richmond, April 6, 1865," in *Thomas Morris Chester, Black Civil War Correspondent*, 294–97; William Howard Day, in *Celebration by the Colored People's Educational Monument Association, in Memory of Abraham Lincoln on the Fourth of July, 1865, in the Presidential Grounds* (Washington, DC: McGill and Witherow, 1865), 18; Mrs. H. R. Butler, "Progress of the Negro Woman of the South," in *Thirty-First Anniversary Celebration of the Emancipation Proclamation Held Under the Auspices of the Negro Literary and Historical Society on January 1, 1894 at Bethel A.M.E. Church* (Atlanta: Chas. P. Boyd, 1894), 10.

There were white Northerners, too, who clung resolutely to the visions they had seen written in burnished rows of steel. The Grand Army of the Republic angrily rejected all the appeals for reconciliation issued by the New Southers and energetically condemned the defiant hostility of the Lost Cause. They harshly criticized public displays of the Confederate flag, resisting any attempt to transform its meaning into a national symbol, and when the GAR began to suspect in the 1890s that schoolbook publishers were toning down their accounts of the Civil War to accommodate Southern views and promote Southern sales, the Union veterans mounted a campaign to bring its gray-haired members into public school classes to tell the story of the war as they had experienced it. Schoolbooks "treat the war as a contest between the sections of our country known as North and South, and not as a war waged by the Government for the suppression of rebellion against National authority and meant to destroy National existence." The casual reader "would not be able to distinguish between the patriotism of those who fought to save the Union and those who fought to destroy it," much less to see in Confederate "patriotism" the protection of "slavery with its multiple of horrors."[37]

Other veterans' groups kept nailing the flag of emancipation to the mast as fast as the Lost Causers could tear it down. The Society of the Army of the Tennessee described the war as a struggle "that involved the life of the Nation, the preservation of the Union, the triumph of liberty and the death of slavery." They had "fought every battle . . . from the firing upon the Union flag at Fort Sumter to the surrender of Lee at Appomattox . . . in the cause of human liberty," burying "treason and slavery in the Potter's Field of nations" and "making all our citizens equal before the law, from the gulf to the lakes, and from ocean to ocean." In 1937, when the United Confederate Veterans extended an invitation to the GAR to join it in what amounted to the last great Blue and Gray Reunion at Gettysburg, the ninety-year-old veterans at the GAR's 71st Encampment in Madison, Wisconsin, were adamant that no displays of the Confederate battle flag be permitted. "No rebel colors," they shouted. "What sort of compromise is that for Union soldiers but hell and damnation."[38]

But there was an even greater victory to remember, although it was a victory so thoroughgoing that it has become easy for subsequent generations to take it for granted, or even to discount it as a poor companion to emancipation, and that was the survival of the Union, and with it, liberal democracy in the nineteenth century.

37. T. S. Clarkson, "Committee on School Histories," in *Journal of the Thirtieth National Encampment of the Grand Army of the Republic, St. Paul, Minn., September 3rd, 4th and 5th, 1896* (Indianapolis, IN: Wm. H. Burford, 1896), 10, 234.

38. *Report of the Proceedings of the Society of the Army of the Tennessee at the Twenty-First Meeting, Held at Toledo, Ohio, September 5th and 6th, 1888* (Cincinnati: Society of the Army of the Tennessee, 1893), 145; Stan Cohen, *Hands Across the Wall: The 50th and 75th Reunions of the Gettysburg Battle* (Charleston, WV: Pictorial Histories Pub. Co., 1982), 40.

Goldwin Smith, on tour in America in 1864, said, "An English liberal comes here, not only to watch the unfolding of your destiny, but to read his own. . . . Your re-generation, when it is achieved, will set forth the regeneration of the European na-tions." If a liberal democratic republic as successful as the American one had been turned on itself and fractured from pressures it had created, the rejoicing from every crowned head, every dictator, and every princeling would be heard around the planet. Certainly those crowned heads saw that this was the ultimate stake in the war. This is why so many of them were rooting for the Confederacy.[39]

It was also the principal reason why Frederick Douglass could never write off the war as casually as Du Bois would. Douglass, who fought virtually to his dying day in 1895 to keep the eyes of Americans fixed firmly on his vision of a war that had been fought for freedom and not just the Union, was just as firm in his insistence that achiev-ing freedom would have had precious little significance unaccompanied by preservation of the Union. The two wars were so intertwined that no war for slavery could have suc-ceeded without the war for the Union, and no war for the Union could have succeeded without becoming a war to end slavery. Like Daniel Webster's "Liberty and Union," the white veterans remembered their war as being for both union and emancipation, one and inseparable. "We are sometimes asked in the name of patriotism to forget the merits of this fearful struggle," Douglass declared in 1871, "and to remember with equal admiration those who struck at the nation's life, and those who struck to save it—those who fought for slavery and those who fought for liberty and justice." He would have nothing of it.

> I am no minister of malice. I would not strike the fallen. I would not repel the repent-ant; but may my "right hand forget her cunning and my tongue cleave to the roof of my mouth" if I forget the difference between the parties to that terrible, protracted, and bloody conflict. If we ought to forget a war which has filled our land with widows and orphans, which has made stumps of men of the very flower of our youth; sent them on the journey of life armless, legless, maimed, and mutilated, which has piled up a debt heavier than a mountain of gold, swept uncounted thousands of men into bloody graves, and planted agony at a million hearthstones—I say, if this war is to be forgotten, I ask, in the name of all things sacred, what shall men remember?[40]

What Douglass wanted from the South was not reconciliation but repentance for the attempted assassination of the republic by the slaveholding aristocrats. "The South has a past not to be contemplated with pleasure, but with a shudder," he wrote in 1870. "She has been selling agony, trading in blood and in the souls of men. If her past has any lesson, it is one of repentance and thorough reformation." More than a decade later, Douglass was still not satisfied: "Whatever else I may forget, I shall never forget the

39. Goldwin Smith, "England and America," *Atlantic Monthly* (December 1864)" 753, 763.

40. Douglass, "Unknown Loyal Dead" (1871), in *Life and Times of Frederick Douglass, Written by Himself* (Hartford, CT: Park, 1882), 506.

difference between those who fought to save the Republic and those who fought to destroy it."[41]

In the case of Du Bois, the Beards, and those who have followed in their path, the Civil War approaches the nadir of total loss precisely because at some point they concluded that since liberal democracy was a dead end, an illusion, and never worth fighting for, intentionally or otherwise, the Civil War could never amount to more than a tragic failure. But because Americans in those same years strayed from the path they might have trod at the end of the war does not mean that the Civil War is merely a tragedy.

In 1886 the survivors of Battery B of the 1st New Jersey Artillery gathered together at Gettysburg with the other survivors of the 3rd Corps of the Army Potomac to stroll over the battlefield and visit the graves of the battery's dead in the National Cemetery Lincoln had dedicated twenty-three years before. One elderly man in Battery B's group, who had lost his son at Gettysburg, listened as the old battery mates stood by the boy's grave and "praised his boy's pleasant ways, genial, kindly disposition, and brave deeds." The man was unconsoled. "My boy, my boy, O God, why did you take my boy? He was all I had," he sobbed. It was one of wives of the ex-artillerymen who at last took the old man by the arm and turned him toward the flag on the cemetery flagstaff: "Your boy died for that flag, and while this nation endures his deeds will never be forgotten. When you and I are dead, patriots, standing where we are now, will remember his name and fame."[42] It was a beautiful and quintessentially Victorian moment of nationalistic melodrama, but it underscores a point often missed in the terrible toll of the Civil War's losses and shortfalls, and that is that the Republic *survived*.

Not only survived, but did so (largely in the North and the West) in the free-labor image that nineteenth-century liberals had hoped would triumph over the Romantic aristocrats. For all of the ravenous economic appetites of the corporations and the "modern barons," large segments of the American economy remained the Elysium of small producers, household-based commercial agriculture, and Protestant moralism far into the twentieth century. Big business arrived after the Civil War, to the horror of veteran Republicans such as Garfield, but small business did not depart. Between 1869 and 1919, the average size of American plants and establishments involved in coal and oil shot up from 12 to 107, in rubber from 404 to 967, in machinery from 14 to 112; but in food services, the average size went only from 6 to 10, in chemicals from 10 to 19, in lumber from 6 to 18. In 1870, there were 22,000 flour milling plants in the United States; in 1900 there were 25,000. In cotton textiles, the increase was only from 819 establishments in 1870 to 1,055 in 1900. Even as the United States moved into first place among the world's industrialized nations, the bulk of its population lived in places

---

41. David W. Blight, "For Something Beyond the Battlefield': Frederick Douglass and the Struggle for the Memory of the Civil War," in *Beyond the Battlefield: Race, Memory and the American Civil War* (Amherst: University of Massachusetts Press, 2002), 105–6, 14; Edward T. Linenthal, *Sacred Ground: Americans and Their Battlefields* (Urbana: University of Illinois Press, 1993), 91.

42. Hanifen, *History of Battery B, First New Jersey Artillery*, 82–83.

with fewer than 2,500 residents. Alongside the great new post–Civil War industrial behemoths—Armour, Swift, Pillsbury, Remington, Standard Oil, Pullman—and the pitched conflicts they generated between labor and capital in Martinsburg, Homestead, and Haymarket Square, the harmonious free-labor economy of Henry Clay, Henry Carey, and Abraham Lincoln, in which every man could still "make himself," hummed complacently across the staggering breadth of the American republic.[43]

The nation possessed that breadth because it was *united*, undivided by sectionalism even if its unity was marred by racism. That unity, eight decades later, would be almost all that stood between civilization and the universal midnight of Nazism. The same unity, a hundred years later, would finally hear the Reverend Martin Luther King Jr. summon a nation back to the unfinished work of justice and equality.

Whatever else the Civil War failed to accomplish, and whatever questions it left unanswered, there was at least this: what America would we live in, and what world would others live in, if the American republic had fragmented into two pieces—or maybe three, or even four and five pieces—in 1865? Or if the institution of slavery had survived, either in an independent Southern Confederacy or as the foundation of the new western states whose future had been Abraham Lincoln's greatest concern? The American Freedmen's Inquiry Commission, reporting to Edwin Stanton in the spring of 1864, thought the alternatives to Union *and* emancipation were already too horrible to contemplate: trade wars, foreign intervention, petty dictatorships.

> In such a state of feeling, under such a state of things, can we doubt the inevitable results? Shall we escape border raids after fleeing fugitives? No sane man will expect it. Are we to suffer these? We are disgraced! Are we to repel them? It is a renewal of hostilities! . . . In case of a foreign war . . . can we suppose that they will refrain from seeking their own advantage by an alliance with the enemy?[44]

Each year on September 17, the anniversary of the battle of Antietam, United States Supreme Court Justice Oliver Wendell Holmes, who had been a lieutenant in the 20th Massachusetts that day, received a red rose from his fellow justice Edward Douglass White, a former Confederate soldier from Louisiana whom Holmes joined on the Court when he was appointed by President Theodore Roosevelt in 1902. It was the kind of sentimental gesture that Holmes appreciated and Frederick Douglass would have deplored.

43. Atack and Passell, *A New Economic View of American History*, 473–81; Mansel G. Blackford, "Small Business in America: A Historiographic Survey," *Business History Review* 65 (Spring 1991), 1–26, and *A History of Small Business in America*, 2nd ed. (Chapel Hill: University of North Carolina Press, 2003), 39–42; Eric Foner, "Why Is There No Socialism in the United States," *History Workshop Journal* 17 (Spring 1984): 69.

44. "Final Report of the American Freedmen's Inquiry Commission to the Secretary of War" (May 15, 1864), in *The War of the Rebellion*, Series Three, 4:356, 358, 359.

But Justice White had a point to make. "My God," the old Confederate would mutter in palpable horror as he reflected on the war he had lost. "My God, if we had succeeded."[45]

L'ENVOI

To thee, old Cause!
Thou peerless, passionate, good cause!
Thou stern, remorseless, sweet Idea!
Deathless throughout the ages, races, lands!
After a strange, sad war—great war for thee,
(I think all war through time was really fought, and ever will be really fought, for thee;)
These chants for thee—the eternal march of thee.
Thou orb of many orbs!
Thou seething principle! Thou well-kept, latent germ! Thou centre!
Around the idea of thee the strange sad war revolving,
With all its angry and vehement play of causes,
(With yet unknown results to come, for thrice a thousand years,)
These recitatives for thee—my Book and the War are one,
Merged in its spirit I and mine—as the contest hinged on thee,
As a wheel on its axis turns, this Book, unwitting to itself,
Around the Idea of thee.

—Walt Whitman[46]

---

45. Baker, *The Justice from Beacon Hill*, 438–39.

46. Walt Whitman, *Leaves of Grass* (Philadelphia: Rees Welsh, 1882), 11.

FURTHER READING

ONE. A NATION ANNOUNCING ITSELF

Two magisterial, but very contradictory, surveys of the history of the early republic have been important for this chapter, Sean Wilentz's *Rise of American Democracy: Jefferson to Lincoln* (New York: W. W. Norton, 2006) and Daniel Walker Howe's *What Hath God Wrought: The Transformation of America, 1815–1848* (New York: Oxford University Press, 2009). My understanding of the world context of the early republic's economy has been shaped by my reading of Eric Hobsbawm's *The Age of Revolution, 1789–1848* (New York: World, 1962) and *The Age of Capital, 1848–1875* (New York: Scribner, 1975), and I have used Thomas Cochran's *Frontiers of Change: Early Industrialism in America* (New York: Oxford University Press, 1981), Charles G. Sellers's *The Market Revolution: Jacksonian America, 1815–1846* (New York: Oxford University Press, 1991), and Marc Egnal, *Clash of Extremes: The Economic Origins of the Civil War* (New York: Hill and Wang, 2009), and, for examples of localized confrontations with the market economy, I have borrowed a number of incidents from Christopher Clark's *The Roots of Rural Capitalism: Western Massachusetts, 1780–1860* (Ithaca, NY: Cornell University Press, 1991). The politics of the Jacksonian era have been richly covered in Robert V. Remini's three-volume biography of Andrew Jackson, *Andrew Jackson and the Course of American Empire*, *Andrew Jackson and Course of American Freedom*, and *Andrew Jackson and the Course of American Democracy* (New York: Harper and Row, 1973, 1981, 1984). Remini has also produced a biography of Jackson's nemesis, Henry Clay, in *Henry Clay: Statesman for the Union* (New York: W. W. Norton, 1991), and this has most recently been joined by David and Jeanne Heidler's *Henry Clay: The Essential American* (New York: Random House, 2010). Whig political thinking has been superbly dissected by Daniel Walker Howe in *The Political Culture of the American Whigs* (Chicago: University of Chicago Press, 1979), while the Democrats have their remembrancers in Jean Baker, *Affairs of Party: The Political Culture of Northern Democrats in the Mid-Nineteenth Century* (Ithaca, NY: Cornell University Press, 1983) and Marvin Meyer, *The Jacksonian Persuasion* (Stanford, CA: Stanford University Press 1957). The great Webster-Hayne debate over nullification can be best surveyed by the documents collected by Herman Belz in *The Webster-Hayne Debate on the Nature of the Union: Selected Documents* (Indianapolis, IN: Liberty Fund, 2000).

Simply listing the available literature on American slavery could easily consume a book on its own. Three exceptionally attractive general surveys of the history of slavery are Robert W. Fogel, *Without Consent or Contract: The Rise and Fall of American Slavery* (New York: W. W. Norton, 1989), Peter Kolchin's *American Slavery, 1619–1877* (New York: Hill and Wang, 1993), and Ira Berlin's *Many Thousands Gone: The First Two Centuries of Slavery in North America* (Cambridge, MA: Harvard University Press, 1998). The best single-volume compilation of first-person accounts by African Americans of the slave experience in *Slave Testimony: Two Centuries of Letters, Speeches, Interviews and Autobiographies*, edited by John W. Blassingame (Baton Rouge: Louisiana State University Press, 1977). For this chapter, I have relied on the insights into Southern slavery offered by Albert Raboteau's *Slave Religion: The "Invisible Institution" in the Antebellum South* (New York: Oxford University Press, 1978), John W. Blassingame's *The Slave Community: Plantation Life in the Antebellum South* (New York: Oxford University Press, 1972), and Herbert Gutman, *The Black*

Family in Slavery and Freedom (New York: Pantheon, 1976). Two historians have proven to be particularly significant for me, Eugene Genovese and James Oakes, and especially in Genovese's *The Political Economy of Slavery* (New York: Pantheon, 1965), *The World the Slaveholders Made* (New York: Pantheon, 1969) and *Roll, Jordan, Roll: The World the Slaves Made* (New York: Pantheon, 1974), and Oakes's *The Ruling Race: A History of American Slaveholders* (New York: Knopf, 1982) and *Slavery and Freedom: An Interpretation of the Old South* (New York: Knopf, 1990)—this, despite the fact that Genovese and Oakes represent two very different ways of interpreting slavery. The arguments of Southern slaveholders in defense of slavery have been collected and analyzed by Eugene Genovese and Elizabeth Fox-Genovese in *The Mind of the Master Class: History and Faith in the Southern Slaveholders' Worldview* (New York: Cambridge University Press, 2005) and by Drew Faust, especially in *A Sacred Circle: The Dilemma of the Intellectual in the Old South, 1840–1860* (Baltimore, MD: Johns Hopkins University Press, 1977) and her biography of a South Carolina governor, *James Henry Hammond and the Old South: A Design for Mastery* (Baton Rouge: Louisiana State University Press, 1982). John Majewski offers a powerful analysis of the paradox of a slave economy and its compatibility with liberal democracy in *Modernizing a Slave Economy: The Economic Vision of the Confederate Nation* (Chapel Hill: University of North Carolina Press, 2009). For the bird's-eye view of the slave South, I have used William W. Freehling's *The Road to Disunion: Secessionists at Bay, 1776–1854* (New York: Oxford University Press, 1990). The abolitionist movement still lacks a single comprehensive narrative history, but it has a great biography of William Lloyd Garrison in Henry Mayer's *All on Fire: William Lloyd Garrison and the Abolition of Slavery* (New York: St. Martin's, 1998).

TWO. THE GAME OF BALANCES

The political history of the United States for the dozen years before the outbreak of the Civil War has enjoyed a remarkably rich crop of histories and biographies. For an overall narrative of the movement of North and South toward confrontation over slavery and its extension into the territories, Allan Nevins's "Ordeal of the Union" volumes, *Ordeal of the Union: The Fruits of Manifest Destiny, 1847–1852* and *Ordeal of the Union: A House Dividing, 1852–1857* (New York: Scribner's, 1947) are still without peer in terms of their scope and excitement. David Potter's *The Impending Crisis: 1848–1861* (New York: Harper and Row, 1976) offers a superb overview of these same events in a much shorter scope.

The politics of the Mexican War obviously deserve their own nod, and from this angle, I have found Charles G. Sellers's two-volume *James K. Polk* (Princeton, NJ: Princeton University Press, 1957, 1966) and Paul Bergeron's *The Presidency of James K. Polk* (Lawrence: University Press of Kansas, 1987) quite helpful. But the other aspects of the war have also been well covered in a number of newer books on this almost forgotten conflict by K. Jack Bauer, *The Mexican-American War, 1846–1848* (New York: Macmillan, 1974), by Robert W. Johannsen, *To the Halls of the Montezumas: The War with Mexico in the American Imagination* (New York: Oxford University Press, 1985), and by John S. D. Eisenhower, *So Far from God: The War with Mexico* (New York: Random House, 1989).

The Compromise of 1850 was the offspring of the Mexican-American War, and the connection of the two events is magisterially handled by Nevins and Potter. But I have also found Holman Hamilton, *Prologue to Conflict: The Crisis and Compromise of 1850* (Lexington: University of Kentucky Press, 1964) to be very helpful. The opposition to the Compromise can be understood through K. Jack Bauer's biography *Zachary Taylor: Soldier, Planter, Statesman of the Old Southwest* (Baton Rouge: Louisiana State University Press, 1986). Calhoun's political papers and the two great Compromise speeches he gave in 1847 and 1850 have been collected and published by Ross E. Lence in *Union and Liberty: The Political Philosophy of John C. Calhoun* (Indianapolis, IN: Liberty Fund, 1992). Stephen A. Douglas, the rescuer of the Compromise, has been capably analyzed in Robert W. Johannsen's *Stephen A. Douglas* (New York: Oxford University Press, 1973). Lincoln's early criticisms of Douglas and Kansas-Nebraska are discussed in Don E. Fehrenbacher, *Prelude to Greatness: Lincoln in the*

1850s (Stanford, CA: Stanford University Press, 1962). I have found David Donald's *Charles Sumner and the Coming of the Civil War* (New York: Knopf, 1961) to be as useful as it is legendary.

For the general shape of American politics in the 1850s, no one can afford to ignore Michael F. Holt's *The Rise and Fall of the American Whig Party* (New York: Oxford University Press, 1999) and Joel Silbey's *The Partisan Imperative: The Dynamics of American Politics Before the Civil War* (New York: Oxford University Press, 1985). In addition to Holt's heavyweight tome on the Whigs, I have turned to Thomas Brown, *Politics and Statesmanship: Essays on the American Whig Party* (New York: Columbia University Press, 1985), Eric Foner's *Free Soil, Free Labor, Free Men: The Ideology of the Republican Party Before the Civil War* (New York: Oxford University Press, 1970), Heather Cox Richardson's *The Greatest Nation of the Earth: Republican Economic Policies During the Civil War* (Cambridge, MA: Harvard University Press, 1997), Michael S. Green's *Freedom, Union and Power: Lincoln and His Party During the Civil War* (New York: Fordham University Press, 2004), William E. Gienapp's *The Origins of the Republican Party, 1852–1856* (New York: Oxford University Press, 1987), and the essays in Robert F. Engs and Randall Miller's *The Birth of the Grand Old Party: The Republicans' First Generation* (Philadelphia: University of Pennsylvania Press, 2002). Among the many political biographies of Republicans available, two of the most thorough are Hans L. Trefousse, *Benjamin Franklin Wade: Radical Republican from Ohio* (New York: Twayne, 1965) and Frederick J. Blue, *Salmon Chase: A Life in Politics* (Kent, OH: Kent State University Press, 1986).

The *Dred Scott* decision was clearly the greatest juridical hot potato of the 1850s, and the single most important book on the case is Don E. Fehrenbacher, *The Dred Scott Case: Its Significance in American Law and Politics* (New York: Oxford University Press, 1978). Resistance to the Fugitive Slave Law has been well described in Thomas P. Slaughter's *Bloody Dawn: The Christiana Riot and Racial Violence in the Antebellum North* (New York: Oxford University Press, 1992) and Nat Brandt, *The Town That Started the Civil War* (Syracuse, NY: Syracuse University Press, 1990).

THREE. YEAR OF METEORS

No other single figure in American history has generated so much biography and analysis as Abraham Lincoln. The most comprehensive modern biography of Lincoln is the two-volume magnum opus of Michael Burlingame, *Abraham Lincoln: A Life* (Baltimore, MD: Johns Hopkins University Press, 2009); the most famous and durable single-volume biography of Abraham Lincoln remains Benjamin P. Thomas's classic *Abraham Lincoln* (New York: Modern Library, 1952), although David Donald's *Lincoln* (New York: Simon and Schuster, 1995) is a very close competitor. For those who thirst after every detail, only Mark E. Neely Jr.'s *The Abraham Lincoln Encyclopedia* (New York: McGraw-Hill, 1982) and Earl Schenck Miers's three-volume *Lincoln Day-by-Day: A Chronology* (Washington, DC: Lincoln Sesquicentennial Commission, 1960) will suffice. Lincoln's *Collected Works* were assembled by Roy P. Basler in a nine-volume set under the auspices of the Abraham Lincoln Association and published by Rutgers University Press in 1953 (two supplement volumes were subsequently issued), but these will be augmented by Don and Virginia Fehrenbacher's *Recollected Words of Abraham Lincoln* (Stanford, CA: Stanford University Press, 1996). Two other critical collections of Lincoln-related documents are Emmanuel Hertz's *The Hidden Lincoln, from the Letters and Papers of William H. Herndon* (New York: Viking, 1938) and *Herndon's Informants: Letters, Statements and Interviews About Abraham Lincoln*, edited by Rodney Davis and Douglas Wilson (Urbana: University of Illinois Press, 1998). The finest study of the Lincoln-Douglas debates remains Harry V. Jaffa's *Crisis of the House Divided: An Interpretation of the Issues in the Lincoln-Douglas Debates* (Garden City, NY: Doubleday, 1959).

The preeminent surveys of the national agony that stretched from Lecompton to Sumter remain Allan Nevins's two volumes, *The Emergence of Lincoln: Douglas, Buchanan, and Party Chaos, 1857–1859* and *The Emergence of Lincoln: Prologue to Civil War, 1859–1861* (New York: Scribner's, 1950), and Potter's *The Impending Crisis*. Potter's *Lincoln and His Party in the Secession Crisis* (New Haven, CT: Yale University Press, 1942) remains a remarkably durable and interesting work, but for a much broader chronological sweep and a direct focus on the South and secession, William W. Freehling's *The Road to Disunion: Secessionists Triumphant, 1854–1861* (New York: Oxford University Press, 2007) must be consulted.

For specific studies of secession in the Southern states, William L. Barney, *The Secessionist Impulse: Alabama and Mississippi in 1860* (Princeton, NJ: Princeton University Press, 1974), Steven A. Channing, *A Crisis of Fear: Secession in South Carolina* (New York: Simon and Schuster, 1970) and Michael P. Johnson, *Toward a Patriarchal Republic: The Secession of Georgia* (Baton Rouge: Louisiana State University Press, 1977) remain important contributions. The literature of secession has been captured handsomely in Jon Wakelyn's *Southern Pamphlets on Secession, November 1860–April 1861* (Chapel Hill: University of North Carolina Press, 1996). The events surrounding the attack on Fort Sumter are gracefully recounted in William A. Swanberg's *First Blood: The Story of Fort Sumter* (New York: Scribner, 1957) and most recently in David Detzer's *Allegiance: Fort Sumter, Charleston, and the Beginning of the Civil War* (New York: Harcourt, 2001).

FOUR. TO WAR UPON SLAVERY

The military history of the American Civil War has been so much the object of the military history buff that it is sometimes difficult to disentangle faddism and hobby writing from the serious history of Civil War combat. First reading for any serious student of Civil War combat must be Paddy Griffith's *Battle Tactics of the Civil War* (New Haven, CT: Yale University Press, 1987), followed by Edward Hagerman's *The American Civil War and the Origins of Modern Warfare: Ideas, Organization, and Field Command* (Bloomington: Indiana University Press, 1988), and Brent Nosworthy's sprawling *The Bloody Crucible of Courage: Fighting Methods and Combat Experience of the Civil War* (New York: Carroll and Graf, 2003). Sharply focused studies of American strategic doctrine include Herman Hattaway and Archer Jones, *How the North Won: A Military History of the Civil War* (Urbana: University of Illinois Press, 1983), Archer Jones, *Civil War Command and Strategy: The Process of Victory and Defeat* (New York: Free Press, 1992), and Donald J. Stoker, *The Grand Design: Strategy and the U.S. Civil War* (New York: Oxford University Press, 2010). One fairly eccentric but highly informative interpretation of Civil War combat is Grady McWhiney and Perry D. Jamieson, *Attack and Die: Civil War Military Tactics and the Southern Heritage* (University: University of Alabama Press, 1982).

The opening campaigns of the war mentioned in this chapter can be traced in greater detail in a plethora of battle histories, beginning with William C. Davis's *Battle at Bull Run: A History of the First Major Campaign of the Civil War* (Garden City, NY: Doubleday, 1977), Joanna McDonald's *"We Shall Meet Again": The First Battle of Manassas, July 18–21, 1861* (Shippensburg, PA: White Mane, 1999), Ethan Rafuse's *A Single Grand Victory: The First Campaign and Battle of Manassas* (Wilmington, DE: Scholarly Resources Books, 2002), and David Detzer's *Donnybrook: The Battle of Bull Run, 1861* (Orlando, FL: Harcourt, 2004). George McClellan is the subject of two highly interesting biographies: Ethan Rafuse's *McClellan's War: The Failure of Moderation in the Struggle for the Union* (Bloomington: Indiana University Press, 2005) and Stephen W. Sears, *George B. McClellan: The Young Napoleon* (New York: Ticknor and Fields, 1987), which should be read in conjunction with Sears's book on the Antietam campaign, *Landscape Turned Red: The Battle of Antietam* (New Haven, CT: Ticknor and Fields, 1983), and his history of the Peninsula, *To the Gates of Richmond: The Peninsula Campaign* (New York: Ticknor and Fields, 1992).

The Peninsula brought Robert E. Lee to the forefront of the Civil War, and the four volumes of Douglas Southall Freeman's *R. E. Lee* (New York: C. Scribner's Sons, 1936) and Emory Thomas's *Robert E. Lee: A Biography* (New York: W. W. Norton, 1995) remain the place to begin with the great Virginia general, although readers with a taste for iconoclasm should not miss Thomas L. Connelly's

The Marble Man: Robert E. Lee and His Image in American Society (New York: Knopf, 1977), Michael Fellman's *The Making of Robert E. Lee* (New York: Random House, 2000) or Alan Nolan's *Lee Considered: General Robert E. Lee and Civil War History* (Chapel Hill: University of North Carolina Press, 1991). A more unusual approach to Lee's life can be found through his letters in Elizabeth Brown Pryor's *Reading the Man: A Portrait of Robert E. Lee Through His Private Letters* (New York: Viking, 2008). John Hennessy's *Return to Bull Run: The Campaign and Battle of Second Manassas* (New York: Simon and Schuster, 1993) offers a particularly good account of this long-neglected battle, while the literature on Antietam is particularly rich in having for its chroniclers James V. Murfin in *The Gleam of Bayonets: The Battle of Antietam and Robert E. Lee's Maryland Campaign, September, 1862* (New York: T. Yoseloff, 1965) and Benjamin F. Cooling in *Counter-Thrust: From the Peninsula to the Antietam* (Lincoln: University of Nebraska Press, 2008), as well as an unusual reference work in Joseph L. Harsh's *Sounding the Shallows: A Confederate Companion for the Maryland Campaign of 1862* (Kent, OH: Kent State University Press, 2000).

The final object of the battles came back to the question of slavery and its future, and for understanding the agonizing position of blacks who wanted the war for the Union to become a war for freedom. The most comprehensive survey undertaken of emancipation and its consequences is that of the Freedom and Southern Society Project at the University of Maryland, and especially in the three volumes of the first series of *Freedom: A Documentary History of Emancipation, 1861–1867—The Destruction of Slavery* (New York: Cambridge University Press, 1985), *The Wartime Genesis of Free Labor: The Lower South* (New York: Cambridge University Press, 1990), and *The Wartime Genesis of Free Labor: The Upper South* (New York: Cambridge University Press, 1993), and in a general anthology, *Free at Last: A Documentary History of Slavery, Freedom, and the Civil War* (New York: New Press, 1992). The controversial question of Lincoln's motives and intentions in issuing the Emancipation Proclamation have been handled from numerous angles by Don D. Fehrenbacher, "Only His Stepchildren: Lincoln and the Negro," in *Civil War History* 20 (December 1974), George M. Fredrickson, "A Man but Not a Brother: Abraham Lincoln and Racial Equality," in the *Journal of Southern History* 61 (February 1975), and Paul Finkelman, "Lincoln and the Preconditions for Emancipation" in *Lincoln's Proclamation: Emancipation Reconsidered*, ed. W. A. Blair and K. F. Younger (Chapel Hill: University of North Carolina Press, 2009). LaWanda Cox's *Lincoln and Black Freedom: A Study in Presidential Leadership* (Urbana: University of Illinois Press, 1985) offers a sympathetic portrayal of Lincoln and race; at entirely the other end is Lerone Bennett's forceful but erratic *Forced into Glory: Abraham Lincoln's White Dream* (Chicago: Johnson, 2000). Burrus Carnahan's *Act of Justice: Lincoln's Emancipation Proclamation and the Law of War* (Lexington: University Press of Kentucky, 2007) unties the legal knots surrounding emancipation and the Proclamation.

FIVE. ELUSIVE VICTORIES

The intricate story of the political compromises that kept Kentucky and Missouri from joining the Confederacy has been told in several venerable but still important studies, E. Merton Coulter's *The Civil War and Readjustment in Kentucky* (Chapel Hill: University of North Carolina Press, 1926), Edward C. Smith, *The Borderland in the Civil War* (New York: Macmillan, 1927), William H. Townsend, *Lincoln and the Bluegrass: Slavery and Civil War in Kentucky* (Lexington: University of Kentucky Press, 1955), William E. Parrish, *Turbulent Partnership: Missouri and the Union, 1861–1865* (Columbia, University of Missouri Press, 1963). More recently, provocative new work on the Border States has emerged in Michael Fellman, *Inside War: The Guerilla Conflict in Missouri During the American Civil War* (New York: Oxford University Press, 1989), Lowell H. Harrison, *Lincoln of Kentucky* (Lexington: University Press of Kentucky, 2000), Louis S. Gerteis, *Civil War St. Louis* (Lawrence: University Press of Kansas, 2001), and William C. Harris's *Lincoln and the Border States in the Civil War* (2011). The most important figure in the subsequent campaigning across Kentucky and Tennessee in early 1862 is Ulysses S. Grant, whose *Personal Memoirs* are among the mainstays of Civil War literature (the edition used here is from the Library of America volume of Grant's *Memoirs and Selected Letters*, but the *Memoirs* have been reprinted numerous times over the century since they first appeared). Almost as fascinating a literary monument to Grant is the three-volume biography of Grant begun by Lloyd Lewis in *Captain Sam Grant* (Boston: Little, Brown, 1950) and finished by Bruce Catton in *Grant Moves South* (Boston: Little, Brown, 1960) and *Grant Takes Command* (Boston: Little, Brown, 1968). Grant's most recent biographers have included the highly critical William S. McFeely, in *Grant: A Biography* (New York: W. W. Norton, 1981), a polar opposite in Brooks Simpson in *Let Us Have Peace: Ulysses S. Grant and the Politics of War and Reconstruction, 1861–1868* (Chapel Hill: University of North Carolina Press, 1991), Simpson's *Ulysses S. Grant: Triumph over Adversity, 1822–1865* (Boston: Houghton Mifflin, 2000), Jean Edward Smith, *Grant* (New York: Simon and Schuster, 2001), Edward H. Bonekemper, *A Victor, Not a Butcher: Ulysses S. Grant's Overlooked Military Genius* (Lanham, MD: Regnery, 2004), Joan Waugh, *U.S. Grant: American Hero, American Myth* (Chapel Hill: University of North Carolina Press, 2009), and Michael Ballard, *U. S. Grant: The Making of a General, 1861–1863* (Lanham, MD: Rowman and Littlefield, 2005). Grant's personal and official papers and letters have been made available through the late John Y. Simon's immense project, *The Papers of Ulysses S. Grant* (Carbondale: Southern Illinois University Press, 1967–).

Among the best books on the early western military campaigns is the first volume to offer a comprehensive account of them, Manning Ferguson Force's *From Fort Henry to Corinth* (New York: Scribner's, 1881), which was written as part of the Scribner's campaigns series in the 1880s. Among the more recent accounts of the operations on the Tennessee and Cumberland rivers are James Hamilton, *The Battle of Fort Donelson* (South Brunswick, NJ: T. Yoseloff, 1968) and Benjamin F. Cooling, *Forts Henry and Donelson* (Knoxville: University of Tennessee Press, 1988). The Confederate commanders who struggled to shore up the crumbling edges of the Confederacy's western lines have enjoyed a surprising number of useful and durable biographies, beginning with William Preston Johnston's biography of his father, *The Life of Albert Sidney Johnston* (New York: D. Appleton, 1879). The most significant of these biographies is Grady McWhiney's *Braxton Bragg and Confederate Defeat*, vol. 1: *Field Command* (New York: Columbia University Press, 1969), although McWhiney eventually left it to another biographer, Judith Hallock, to finish the narrative of Bragg's ill-starred career. The overall shape of Confederate decision making in the western part of the country in 1862–63 is covered in Archer Jones, *Confederate Strategy from Shiloh to Vicksburg* (Baton Rouge: Louisiana State University Press, 1961), while Thomas L. Connelly offered a collective biography of the Confederacy's western army in *Army of the Heartland: The Army of Tennessee, 1861–1862* (Baton Rouge: Louisiana State University Press, 1967), and joined with Archer Jones to write *The Politics of Command: Factions and Ideas in Confederate Strategy* (Baton Rouge: Louisiana State University Press, 1973). The first great western battle that resulted from those decisions has been covered with marvelous narrative skill by Wiley Sword in *Shiloh: Bloody April* (New York: Morrow, 1974) and by James Lee McDonough in *Shiloh—In Hell Before Night* (Knoxville: University of Tennessee Press, 1977). The lengthy and varied operations that finally resulted in the capture of the great Confederate outpost on the Mississippi are narrated in Earl Schenck Miers, *The Web of Victory: Grant at Vicksburg* (New York: Knopf, 1955), in James R. Arnold, *Grant Wins the War: Decision at Vicksburg* (New York: J. Wiley and Sons, 1997), and in Michael Ballard, *Vicksburg: The Campaign that Opened the Mississippi* (Chapel Hill: University of North Carolina Press, 2004).

A number of published papers and diaries of Lincoln's cabinet secretaries offer critical glimpses into the operation of wartime politics at the highest levels in the North, beginning with *The Diary of Gideon Welles*, ed. John T. Morse (Boston: Houghton Mifflin, 1911), *The Diary of Edward Bates 1859– 1866*, ed. Howard K. Beale (Washington, DC: Government Printing Office, 1930), and David Donald's edition of Salmon Chase's wartime diaries, *Inside Lincoln's Cabinet: The Civil War Diaries of Salmon P. Chase* (New York: Longmans, Green, 1954). The diaries and papers of Lincoln's wartime secretaries, John Hay and John G. Nicolay, have been exhaustively edited by Michael Burlingame as *Inside Lincoln's White House: The Complete Civil War Diary of John Hay* (Carbondale: Southern Illinois University Press, 1997), *At Lincoln's Side: John Hay's Civil War Correspondence and Selected Writings* (Carbondale: Southern Illinois University Press, 2000) and *With Lincoln in the White House: Letters, Memoranda, and Other Writings of John G. Nicolay, 1860–1865* (Carbondale: Southern Illinois University Press, 2000). The best surveys of the Republican domestic policy agenda during the war are Heather Cox Richardson's *The Greatest Nation of the Earth: Republican Economic Policies During the Civil War* (Cambridge, MA: Harvard University Press, 1997) and Michael Green's *Freedom, Union and Power: Lincoln and His Party in the Civil War* (New York: Fordham University Press, 2004). Salmon Chase's decision to invite Jay Cooke to act as the Treasury's wartime agent was of greater significance to the long-term Union victory than a number of battles, and is described in detail by Ellis Oberholtzer in *Jay Cooke: Financier of the Civil War*, 2 vols. (Philadelphia: G. W. Jacobs, 1907). The war involved not only economic and political difficulties but also legal and constitutional problems for the Union, most of which are surveyed in J. G. Randall, *Constitutional Problems Under Lincoln* (New York: D. Appleton, 1926), Harold Hyman, *A More Perfect Union: The Impact of the Civil War and Reconstruction on the Constitution* (New York: Knopf, 1973), Brian McGinty, *Lincoln and the Court* (Cambridge, MA: Harvard University Press, 2008), Robert Bruce Murray, *Legal Cases of the Civil War* (Mechanicsburg, PA: Stackpole, 2003) and Stephen C. Neff, *Justice in Blue and Gray: A Legal History of the Civil War* (Cambridge, MA: Harvard University Press, 2010). The particular problems posed by the blockade have been searchingly analyzed by Ludwell H. Johnson, "The Confederacy: What Was It? A View from the Federal Courts," in *Civil War History* 32 (March 1986), and Johnson's article on the *Prize Cases*, "Abraham Lincoln and the Development of Presidential War-Making Powers: Prize Cases (1863) Revisited," in *Civil War History* 35 (September 1989).

The fires set in the rear of the Union cause by Democratic and Copperhead dissent have been the particular object of the late Frank L. Klement's attention in a series of volumes, *The Copperheads in the Middle West* (Chicago: University of Chicago Press, 1960), *The Limits of Dissent: Clement L. Vallandigham and the Civil War* (Lexington: University Press of Kentucky, 1970), and *Dark Lanterns: Secret Political Societies, Conspiracies, and Treason Trials in the Civil War* (Baton Rouge: Louisiana State University Press, 1984). Klement entered a strong skepticism about the legitimacy of Lincoln's concerns; by contrast, Mark Neely's Pulitzer Prize–winning *The Fate of Liberty: Abraham Lincoln and Civil Liberties* (New York: Oxford University Press, 1991) offers a comprehensive rebuttal to wartime charges that Lincoln wantonly disregarded the civil rights of dissenters and Democrats and imposed a quasi-dictatorship on the North, while Jennifer L. Weber's *Copperheads: The Rise and Fall of Lincoln's Opponents in the North* (New York: Oxford University Press, 2006) is a spirited defense of Lincoln's worries about Copperhead dissent.

SIX. THE SOLDIER'S TALE

In 1886, the onetime Federal artilleryman Frank Wilkeson was growing disgusted with the flood of Civil War memoirs flowing from the pens of former generals who sought chiefly "to belittle the work of others, or to falsify or obscure it." He sat down to write his own recollections of service in the Army of the Potomac in 1864 and 1865 to give a voice to "the private soldiers who won the battles, when they were given a fair chance to win them," and who "have scarcely begun to write the history from their point of view." Wilkeson himself may have done some self-embroidery of his service in the 11th New York Artillery, but his preference for writing the Civil War from the bottom up has been pursued in a seemingly unending flood of regimental histories (some of which appeared even before the war was over), published diaries, and collections of private letters edited by descendants and scholars of the Civil War soldier. The richness of these sources is due largely to the conjunction of two events: one is the mass movement of American males into the war, and the other is the rising tide of literacy in the American population in the nineteenth century. Americans were clearly confronted with a public event of crisis proportions in their national life, and for the first time in the history of the republic, an overwhelming number of those Americans were literate enough to record their thoughts and descriptions of it.

The most obvious primary source for the ordinary life of the Civil War soldier is the regimental history, which developed between 1885 and 1910 into what amounts to a major genre of American literature. One of the earliest, and arguably the liveliest, of these "regimentals" is Amos Judson's *History of the Eighty-Third Regiment, Pennsylvania Volunteers* (Dayton, OH: Morningside Press, 1986 [1865]), which was published shortly after the end of the war. Free from many of the conventions which later shackled and then strangled the regimental history, Judson's volume bristles with cracker-barrel wit and a keen reporter's eye for the foibles of the American character. After Judson came a string of regimental histories, running out to nearly 800 published volumes. Until 1910, when the soldiers of the Civil War generation began passing swiftly from the scene, most regimental histories were written by survivors of the regiments themselves. But after the Civil War centennial in the 1960s, the regimental history was reborn as a historical genre. The engine of this rebirth was John J. Pullen's *The Twentieth Maine: A Volunteer Regiment in the Civil War* (Philadelphia: Lippincott, 1957), and it proceeded to blossom into numerous great unit histories, such as James I. Robertson's *The Stonewall Brigade* (Baton Rouge: Louisiana State University Press, 1963) and Alan Nolan's *The Iron Brigade: A Military History* (Madison: Wisconsin State Historical Society, 1975). Another genre closely related to the regimental history is the volume of collected war letters. Oliver W. Norton's *Army Letters, 1861–1865* (Chicago: O. L. Deming, 1903) is one of the best examples of such collections, coming directly from the editorial hand of the soldier who wrote them. Most often, however, these collections have been discovered in archives or among family heirlooms and have been reconstructed and edited by modern scholars or archivists. A model for such a modern collection is the assemblage of letters of Edward King Wightman in *From Antietam to Fort Fisher: The Civil War Letters of Edward King Wightman*, ed. by E. G. Longacre (Madison, NJ: Fairleigh Dickinson University Press, 1985). Sometimes soldiers kept their opinions to themselves, or at least to their diaries, and several memorable soldier diaries have survived to be republished in scholarly editions. The most outstanding examples of this sort are Allan Nevins's edition of the diary of the upper-class New York artillery chief Charles S. Wainwright in *A Diary of Battle: The Personal Journals of Col. Charles S. Wainwright, 1861–1865* (New York: Harcourt, Brace and World, 1962) and K. Jack Bauer's edition of *Soldiering: The Civil War Diary of Rice C. Bull, 123rd New York Volunteer Infantry* (San Rafael, CA: Presidio Press, 1977).

Some veterans of the war chose to pour their experiences into a third genre, the personal memoir. The outstanding example of the Civil War memoir is Ulysses S. Grant's *Personal Memoirs*, but the common soldiers also produced memoirs of their service which match Grant's for interest if not for eloquence. Foremost among these soldier memoirs must be *Hard Tack and Coffee: The Unwritten Story of Army Life* (Boston: G. M. Smith, 1887) by John D. Billings. From the Confederate side, Henry Kyd Douglas's *I Rode with Stonewall* (Chapel Hill: University of North Carolina Press, 1940) is the most famous, but it should not eclipse the edition of E. P. Alexander's memoirs, *Fighting for the Confederacy: The Personal Recollections of General Edward Porter Alexander*, by Gary W. Gallagher (Chapel Hill: University of North Carolina Press, 1989).

Not every memoir or regimental history necessarily took the form of a book. Civil War veterans organizations, such as the Military Order of the Loyal Legion of the United States (MOLLUS), regularly met to hear members read papers related to their wartime experiences, and an almost bottomless well of material on the common soldier can be found in the sixty-five volumes of MOLLUS *Papers*, the fifty-five volumes of *Southern Historical Society Papers*, the forty-three volumes of *Confederate Veteran* magazine, and the nineteen volumes of *Confederate Military History*. In another postwar contribution to the history of the common soldier, the adjutants-general of many of the

Northern states issued comprehensive volumes of rosters and unit histories of their state volunteer regiments, the most striking of which are the five volumes of Samuel P. Bates's *History of Pennsylvania Volunteers, 1861–65* (Harrisburg, PA: B. Singerly, 1869).

A number of important studies of the Civil War soldier have attempted to synthesize the vast array of materials available in the regimental histories, letters, diaries, and memoirs into a comprehensive portrait of Wilkeson's "private soldier." The most famous of these synthetic studies are Bell I. Wiley's famous *The Life of Johnny Reb: The Common Soldier of the Confederacy* (Baton Rouge: Louisiana State University Press, 1982 [1943]) and *The Life of Billy Yank: The Common Soldier of the Union* (Baton Rouge: Louisiana State University Press, 1978 [1952]). These two works have been supplemented by James I. Robertson's *Soldiers Blue and Gray* (Columbia: University of South Carolina Press, 1988). Specific aspects of the soldier's experience in combat have been skillfully analyzed in Gerald Linderman's *Embattled Courage: The Experience of Combat in the Civil War* (New York: Free Press, 1987), Joseph T. Glatthaar's *The March to the Sea and Beyond: Sherman's Troops in the Savannah and Carolinas Campaigns* (New York: New York University Press, 1985), and Reid Mitchell's *Civil War Soldiers: Their Expectations and Their Experiences* (New York: Viking, 1988).

The Civil War field officer has attracted comparatively less notice in the current literature than Wilkeson's "private soldier," although T. Harry Williams's *Hayes of the Twenty-Third: The Civil War Volunteer Officer* (New York: Knopf, 1965) is a reminder that even the officer was a common soldier in the Civil War. James A. Garfield, an Ohio officer who later rose to become president of the United States (along with two other Ohio veterans of the Civil War, Hayes and McKinley) left examples of both diaries and letters, which have been edited and published as *The Wild Life of the Army: Civil War Letters of James A. Garfield*, edited by F. D. Williams (East Lansing: Michigan State University Press, 1964), and *The Diary of James A. Garfield*, edited by H. J. Brown and F. D. Williams, 4 vols. (East Lansing: Michigan State University Press, 1967–81). A particularly useful officer memoir is Jacob Dolson Cox's *Military Reminiscences of the Civil War*, 2 vols. (New York: C. Scribner's Sons, 1900). One grade of officer that has enjoyed an outsize degree of attention has been the Civil War surgeon. George Worthington Adams' *Doctors in Blue: The Medical History of the Union Army in the Civil War* (New York: H. Schuman, 1952), H.H. Cunningham's *Doctors in Gray: The Confederate Medical Service* (Baton Rouge: Louisiana State University Press, 1958) and Ira M. Rutkow's *Bleeding Blue and Gray: Civil War Surgery and the Evolution of American Medicine* (New York: Random House, 2005) make the very best of what could hardly help being an appalling story.

And even the regimental colors have biographies. Richard Sauers' two-volume illustrated history of the flags carried by Pennsylvania's volunteer regiments, *Advance the Colors* (Harrisburg, PA: Capitol Preservation Committee, 1987, 1992) photographs and documents every Pennsylvania regimental color, along with a brief history and bibliography for the units which carried them. Those who fled from the colors also have a remembrancer in Ella Lonn's *Desertion During the Civil War* (New York: Century Co., 1928).

SEVEN. THE MANUFACTURE OF WAR

The romance of the blockade-runners is one of the great fictions of the Civil War, elaborated in large part by the post-war recollections of the blockade-runners and concealing the life-and-death struggle which was going on behind the curtain of foreign policy and military supply. The Confederacy's attempts to draw France and England into the war as mediators or belligerents has received surprisingly good coverage from both English and American sources, although the consensus which has emerged from that literature leans toward the opinion that the Confederacy never really had much serious prospect of being actively protected by either European power. Howard Jones's *Union in Peril: The Crisis over British Intervention in the Civil War* (Chapel Hill: University of North Carolina Press, 1993), *Abraham Lincoln and a New Birth of Freedom: The Union and Slavery in the Diplomacy of the Civil*

War (Lincoln: University of Nebraska Press, 1999), and *Blue and Gray Diplomacy: A History of Union and Confederate Foreign Relations* (Chapel Hill: University of North Carolina Press, 2010) make it clear how limited British enthusiasm for the Confederacy really was, and also how differently the Emancipation Proclamation was read at the various levels of British government and society (some observers actually thought that the Proclamation, by inciting slave revolts in the South, actually made the case for intervention stronger). The other major studies of Civil War diplomacy are Frank Owsley's *King Cotton Diplomacy: Foreign Relations of the Confederate States of America* (Chicago: University of Chicago Press, 1931), Frank J. Merli, *The Alabama, British Neutrality, and the American Civil War* (Indianapolis: Indiana University Press, 2004 [1970]), and Lynn Case and Warren Spencer's *The United States and France: Civil War Diplomacy* (Philadelphia: University of Pennsylvania Press, 1970).

The Civil War navies have been the subject of many books, but a useful survey to begin with is Spencer Tucker, *Blue and Gray Navies: The Civil War Afloat* (Annapolis, MD: Naval Institute Press, 2006). Of course, sooner or later the reader's interest will wander back to the daring and duplicity of the blockade-runners and the dreaded commerce raiders, and at that moment, no better suggestions can be offered than the slippery, Latin-quoting John Wilkinson's *The Narrative of a Blockade-Runner* (New York: Sheldon, 1877) and Raphael Semmes's own memoir of his service on the *Sumter* and the *Alabama* in *Service Afloat: Or, the Remarkable Career of the Confederate Cruisers, Sumter and Alabama, During the War Between the States* (Baltimore: Kelly, Piet, 1887). The Confederate navy received its earliest chronicle from one of its own officers, an artilleryman-turned-sailor, John Thomas Scharf, whose *History of the Confederate States Navy* (New York: Rogers and Sherwood, 1887) is a highly partisan but far-reaching account of the Southern navy. More modern work on the Confederate Navy has been done by Raimondo Luraghi, *A History of the Confederate Navy* (Annapolis: Naval Institute Press, 1996) and Warren Spencer, *The Confederate Navy in Europe* (University: University of Alabama Press, 1983). The entanglement of Confederate diplomacy with the Confederate navy and its plans to build warships and commerce-raiders in Britain has been analyzed by Frank J. Merli in *Great Britain and the Confederate Navy* (Indianapolis: Indiana University Press, 2004 [1970]), while the ingenuity with which the Confederates fashioned a fleet of ironclad warships has been told by William N. Still in *Iron Afloat: The Story of the Confederate Armorclads* (Columbia: University of South Carolina Press, 1985). The Confederate secretary of the navy who was the spark for much of that ingenuity has been the subject of two biographers, Rodman Underwood in *Stephen Russell Mallory: A Biography of the Confederate Navy Secretary and United States Senator* (Jefferson, NC: McFarland, 2005) and Joseph T. Durkin in *Stephen R. Mallory: Confederate Navy Chief* (Chapel Hill: University of North Carolina Press, 1954).

Mallory's opposite number in Lincoln's cabinet has also enjoyed outstanding biographical treatment from John Niven in *Gideon Welles: Lincoln's Secretary of the Navy* (New York: Oxford University Press, 1973) and Richard S. West Jr. in *Gideon Welles: Lincoln's Navy Department* (Indianapolis, IN: Bobbs-Merrill, 1943). Welles's famous diaries have been edited by Howard K. Beale in three volumes as *The Diary of Gideon Welles, Secretary of the Navy Under Lincoln and Johnson* (Boston: Houghton Mifflin, 1911). Welles's squadrons have been well analyzed in Stephen R. Taaffe's *Commanding Lincoln's Navy: Union Naval Leadership During the Civil War* (Annapolis, MD: Naval Institute Press, 2009). The momentous combat of the *Monitor* and *Virginia* has never been better told than in William C. Davis's lively *Duel Between the First Ironclads* (Garden City, NY: Doubleday, 1975). In addition to Welles and his management of the Federal navy, Seward and the State Department have been discussed in Glyndon Van Deusen's *William Henry Seward* (New York: Oxford University Press, 1967), while Seward's diplomatic faux pas in the first year of the war have been dealt with in a more positive fashion by Norman Ferris in his aptly titled *Desperate Diplomacy: William Henry Seward's Foreign Policy, 1861* (Knoxville: University of Tennessee Press, 1976) and in Ferris's *The Trent Affair* (Knoxville: University of Tennessee Press, 1977). Managing the war fell in large measure to Stanton, whose biography by Harold Hyman and Benjamin P. Thomas, *Stanton:*

The Life and Times of Lincoln's Secretary of War (New York: Knopf, 1962) is one of the models of Civil War biographical literature. Supplying the war was the task of Montgomery C. Meigs, who has also benefitted from a superb biography by Russell F. Weigley, *Quartermaster General of the Union Army: A Biography of M. C. Meigs* (New York: Columbia University Press, 1959), although one should not miss a fine survey of wartime logistics in Mark R. Wilson's *The Business of Civil War: Military Mobilization and the State, 1861–1865* (Baltimore, MD: Johns Hopkins University Press, 2006). Coordinating the armies for the North really became the province of Henry Wager Halleck, the subject of a high-level biography from John Marszalek, *Commander of All Lincoln's Armies* (Cambridge, MA: Harvard University Press, 2004). An outstanding general survey of the organization of the North's economic resources during the war is Philip Shaw Paludan's *A People's Contest: The Union and the Civil War* (New York: Harper and Row, 1988).

Under the Confederate flag, supply issues are covered in *Confederate Supply* (Durham, NC: Duke University Press, 1969) by Richard D. Goff and *Confederate Industry* (Jackson: University Press of Mississippi, 2002) by Harold Wilson, while the management of the Confederacy's premier ironworks has received special study from Charles B. Dew in *Ironmaker to the Confederacy: Joseph R. Anderson and the Tredegar Ironworks* (New Haven, CT: Yale University Press, 1966). However, none of the Confederacy's supply managers has received as much praise or attention as Josiah Gorgas. Frank Vandiver provided a biography of Gorgas in *Ploughshares into Swords: Josiah Gorgas and Confederate Ordnance* (Austin: University of Texas Press, 1952) and Sarah Woolfolk Wiggins has edited Gorgas's diary, published as *The Journals of Josiah Gorgas, 1857–1878* (Tuscaloosa: University of Alabama Press, 1995). The Confederate rail system and its eventual breakdown has been chronicled in Robert C. Black, *The Railroads of the Confederacy* (Chapel Hill: University of North Carolina Press, 1952).

The argument that the Confederacy adopted a form of "state socialism" in order to meet the war's industrial needs was first put forward by Louise Hill in *State Socialism in the Confederate States of America* (Charlottesville, VA: Historical Publications, 1936), and received a more recent restatement in Raimondo Luraghi's *The Rise and Fall of the Plantation South* (New York: New Viewpoints, 1978). Richard F. Bensel has presented a similar case for interpreting the Confederacy as an example of state centralization in *Yankee Leviathan: The Origins of Central State Authority in America, 1859–1879* (New York: Cambridge University Press, 1990), although less with a view toward portraying the Confederacy as a precapitalist state than toward seeing the war as an experiment in the centralization of state power for both North and South. The "state socialism" or "war socialism" thesis has some attraction, especially for those who interpret the Civil War as a struggle to impose a capitalist industrial order on America, but it has to be qualified by the ways private Southern industry found for dodging Confederate regulation, which Mary A. DeCredico has shown in *Patriotism for Profit: Georgia's Urban Entrepreneurs and the Confederate War Effort* (Chapel Hill: University of North Carolina Press, 1990).

EIGHT. THE YEAR THAT TREMBLED

The movements of the eastern armies that led to the battles of Fredericksburg and Chancellorsville have always stood in the shadow of the great battle that followed them at Gettysburg in the summer of 1863. Fredericksburg used to be especially neglected as an object of military history, although that has changed dramatically with the publication of George C. Rable, *Fredericksburg! Fredericksburg!* (Chapel Hill: University of North Carolina Press, 2002) and Frank Augustin O'Reilly's *The Fredericksburg Campaign: Winter War on the Rappahannock* (Baton Rouge: Louisiana State University Press, 2003). Among more recent books on Chancellorsville, two stand out as leaders: Ernest Furgurson's *Chancellorsville, 1863: The Souls of the Brave* (New York: Knopf, 1992) and Stephen W. Sears's *Chancellorsville* (New York: Houghton-Mifflin, 1996). An excellent survey of both Fredericksburg and Chancellorsville, conceived as being two parts of a single strategy, is Daniel E.

Sutherland's *Fredericksburg and Chancellorsville: The Dare Mark Campaign* (Lincoln: University of Nebraska Press, 1998). The preeminent survey of Gettysburg is Edwin B. Coddington's *The Gettysburg Campaign: A Study in Command* (New York: Scribner's, 1968), followed by Glenn Tucker's *High Tide at Gettysburg: The Campaign in Pennsylvania* (Indianapolis, IN: Bobbs-Merrill, 1958), Stephen W. Sears's *Gettysburg* (Boston: Houghton Mifflin, 2006), and Noah Andre Trudeau, *Gettysburg: A Testing of Courage* (New York: HarperCollins, 2002) as the best single-volume books on the battle itself. Breaking the campaign down into segments, it is impossible not to begin a detailed reading of Gettysburg without Harry W. Pfanz's *Gettysburg: The First Day* (Chapel Hill: University of North Carolina Press, 2001). Pfanz's meticulous study of the second day, *Gettysburg: The Second Day* (Chapel Hill: University of North Carolina Press, 1987), leads the pack on day two of the Gettysburg battle, although it should be read alongside his *Gettysburg—Culp's Hill and Cemetery Hill* (Chapel Hill: University of North Carolina Press, 1993) for a full picture of July 2. The military action of the third day at Gettysburg is dominated by Pickett's Charge (even though, in strict truth, it was not Pickett who was in command of the charge but his superior James Longstreet), and it has found several vivid and precisely detailed microhistories in George R. Stewart, *Pickett's Charge: A Microhistory of the Final Attack at Gettysburg, July 3, 1863* (Boston, Houghton Mifflin, 1959), and Earl J. Hess, *Pickett's Charge—The Last Attack at Gettysburg* (Chapel Hill: University of North Carolina Press, 2001). Nothing on the subject of Gettysburg quite matches William Frassanito's surveys of battlefield photography there in *Gettysburg: A Journey in Time* (New York: Scribner, 1975) and *Early Photography at Gettysburg* (Gettysburg, PA: Thomas, 1995).

In the west, the finest survey of the Confederacy's desperate campaign in 1863 to hold on to its heartland is the second volume of Thomas Connelly's history of the Army of Tennessee, *Autumn of Glory: The Army of Tennessee, 1862–1865* (Baton Rouge: Louisiana State University Press, 1971). The major battles fought in the west from the end of 1862 till the dismissal of Braxton Bragg were for many years the orphans of Civil War military history. But since the 1970s, a series of outstanding battle histories has rejuvenated interest in such desperate but almost forgotten engagements as Iuka, Corinth, Murfreesboro, Chickamauga, and Chattanooga. James Lee McDonough has borne the burden of this rejuvenation with his *Stones River—Bloody Winter in Tennessee* (Knoxville: University of Tennessee Press, 1980) and *Chattanooga—A Death Grip on the Confederacy* (Knoxville: University of Tennessee Press, 1984). In addition, Peter Cozzens's *No Better Place to Die: The Battle of Stones River* (Urbana: University of Illinois Press, 1990), *This Terrible Sound: The Battle of Chickamauga* (Urbana: University of Illinois Press, 1992), and *The Shipwreck of Their Hopes: The Battles for Chattanooga* (Urbana: University of Illinois Press, 1994) are outstanding Civil War battle histories, as is Glenn Tucker's much older *Chickamauga, Bloody Battle in the West* (Indianapolis, IN: Bobbs Merrill, 1963).

The overall struggle of the Confederacy to establish not only its independence but a sense of itself as a separate nation and culture has been brilliantly surveyed in Emory Thomas's *The Confederacy as a Revolutionary Experience* (Englewood Cliffs, NJ: Prentice-Hall, 1971) and *The Confederate Nation, 1861–1865* (New York: Harper and Row, 1979) and Clement Eaton's *A History of the Southern Confederacy* (New York: Macmillan, 1954). The best place to begin the story of Confederate politics is with Jefferson Davis himself, who provided his own history (and his own interpretation) of Confederate politics in *The Rise and Fall of the Confederate Government* (New York: D. Appleton, 1881). Davis has also been the object of several major biographies, the most recent and the most outstanding being Hudson Strode's three-volume *Jefferson Davis* (New York, Harcourt, Brace, 1955–64), William J. Cooper's *Jefferson Davis, American* (New York: Knopf/Random House, 2000), and William C. Davis, *Jefferson Davis: The Man and His Hour* (New York: HarperCollins, 1991). The fractious politicians Davis dealt with in Richmond have also been analyzed individually and as a group by George Rable in *The Confederate Republic: A Revolution Against Politics* (Chapel Hill: University of North Carolina Press, 1994), W. B. Yearns, *The Confederate Congress* (Athens:

University of Georgia Press, 1960), and Thomas B. Alexander and Richard Beringer, *The Anatomy of the Confederate Congress: A Study of the Influences of Member Characteristics on Voting Behavior, 1861–1865* (Nashville, TN: Vanderbilt University Press, 1972).

The Confederacy's military leadership has generally gotten much higher grades than its political leadership, and more sympathetic biographies along with them. Douglas Southall Freeman, *Lee's Lieutenants: A Study in Command* (New York: C. Scribner's Sons, 1942–1944) offers in three massive volumes a collective biography of the command structure of the Army of Northern Virginia. Close behind Lee as an interesting biographical subject is Thomas Jonathan "Stonewall" Jackson, who was the subject of a biography by his chief of staff, Robert Lewis Dabney, even before the Civil War was over. James I. Robertson's massive *Stonewall Jackson: The Man, the Soldier, the Legend* (New York: Macmillan, 1997) can be supplemented by the essays on Jackson's character and campaigns in *Whatever You Resolve to Be: Essays on Stonewall Jackson*, ed. A. Wilson Greene (Knoxville: University of Tennessee Press, 2005 [1992]) and Robert Krick's *The Smoothbore Volley That Doomed the Confederacy: The Death of Stonewall Jackson and Other Chapters on the Army of Northern Virginia* (Baton Rouge: Louisiana State University Press, 2002). The most frequently studied Confederate officer in the west is Nathan Bedford Forrest, whose colorful and combative career has been described in Brian Wills's *A Battle from the Start: The Life of Nathan Bedford Forrest* (New York: HarperCollins, 1992). Braxton Bragg had only a half a biographical life from Grady McWhiney until Judith Lee Hallock's *Braxton Bragg and Confederate Defeat, Volume Two* (New York: Columbia University Press, 1991) completed the two-volume biography McWhiney began in 1969.

The war was hardly over before its survivors began speculating on why the South lost the Civil War, and among modern attempts to answer that question, the most far-reaching, and also the most eccentric, is Richard E. Beringer, Herman Hattaway, Archer Jones, and William N. Still, *Why the South Lost the Civil War* (Athens: University of Georgia Press, 1986). Beringer et alia are followed in interpreting the Confederacy's defeat as a collapse from within by Paul D. Escott in *After Secession: Jefferson Davis and the Failure of Confederate Nationalism* (Baton Rouge: Louisiana State University Press, 1978), David J. Eicher in *Dixie Betrayed: How the South Really Lost the War* (New York: Little, Brown, 2006), and Armstead Robinson in *Bitter Fruits of Bondage: The Demise of Slavery and the Collapse of the Confederacy, 1861–1865* (Charlottesville: University of Virginia Press, 2005). But Anne Sarah Rubin in *A Shattered Nation: The Rise and Fall of the Confederacy, 1861–1868* (Chapel Hill: University of North Carolina Press, 2005) and Gary Gallagher in *The Confederate War: How Popular Will, Nationalism, and Military Strategy Could Not Stave Off Defeat* (Cambridge, MA: Harvard University Press, 1997) argue that the Confederacy succumbed to simple Union military might. Jefferson Davis's last, desperate bid to save the Confederacy by sacrificing the South's most potent symbol of localism and independence has been chronicled by Robert F. Durden in *The Gray and the Black: The Confederate Debate on Emancipation* (Baton Rouge: Louisiana State University Press, 1972) and Bruce Levine in *Confederate Emancipation: Southern Plans to Free and Arm Slaves During the Civil War* (New York: Oxford University Press, 2006).

NINE. WORLD TURNED UPSIDE DOWN

The opening vignette of Willard Glazier's descent into powerlessness is drawn from Glazier's own postwar descriptions (which were based on a wartime diary he kept) and on John Algernon Owen's sensationalized biography of Glazier, *Sword and Pen: or, Ventures and Adventures of Willard Glazier* (Philadelphia: P. W. Ziegler, 1889). The agitation African Americans raised for civil rights and military enlistment has been ably discussed in George M. Fredrickson, *The Black Image in the White Mind: The Debate on Afro-American Character and Destiny, 1817–1914* (New York: Harper and Row, 1965) and James M. McPherson, *The Struggle for Equality:*

Abolitionists and the Negro in the Civil War and Reconstruction (Princeton, NJ: Princeton University Press, 1964). These books are largely concerned with the record of Northern blacks, and Leon Litwack's *Been in the Storm So Long: The Aftermath of Slavery* (New York: Knopf, 1979) should be read for the attention it lavishes on the experience of freedom for former slaves. The record of the African American soldier, once he was permitted to volunteer, has been chronicled in Dudley Taylor Cornish's *The Sable Arm: Negro Troops in the Union Army, 1861–1865* (New York: Longmans, Green, 1956), Joseph Glatthaar's *Forged in Battle: The Civil War Alliance of Black Soldiers and White Officers* (New York: Free Press, 1990) and Noah Andre Trudeau's *Like Men of War: Black Troops in the Civil War, 1862–1865* (Boston: Little, Brown, 1998). The Civil War in the western territories has usually been told from the viewpoint of military action, without much consideration to the racial and ethnic significance of these small-scale conflicts in the context of a war that was preoccupied with the question of race. Alvin M. Josephy's *The Civil War in the American West* (New York: Knopf, 1991) offers a highly readable survey of the various military actions west of the Mississippi.

Women's history has become its own separate department within Civil War studies, and we may as well date its emergence to the nearly simultaneous publication of George C. Rable's *Civil Wars: Women and the Crisis of Southern Nationalism* (Urbana: University of Illinois Press, 1991), *Divided Houses: Gender and the Civil War* (New York: Oxford University Press, 1992), a collection of essays edited by Catharine Clinton and Nina Silber that offers explorations of childhood, spies, nurses, divorce, and even illicit sex, LeeAnn Whites's *The Civil War as a Crisis in Gender: Augusta, Georgia, 1860–1890* (Athens: University of Georgia Press, 1995), and Drew Gilpin Faust's *Mothers of Invention: Women of the Slaveholding South in the American Civil War* (Chapel Hill: University of North Carolina Press, 1996). Following hard on their heels have been numerous studies of gender—LeeAnn Whites's *Gender Matters: Civil War, Reconstruction and the Making of the New South* (New York: Palgrave Macmillan, 2005), Silber and Clinton's *Battle Scars: Gender and Sexuality in the American Civil War* (New York: Oxford University Press, 2006), Nina Silber's *Daughters of the Union: Northern Women Fight the Civil War* (Cambridge, MA: Harvard University Press, 2005), Tracy J. Revels's *Grander in Her Daughters: Florida's Women During the Civil War* (Columbia: University of South Carolina Press, 2005), Anya Jabour's *Scarlett's Sisters: Young Women of the Old South* (Chapel Hill: University of North Carolina Press, 2007), Victoria Ott's *Confederate Daughters: Coming of Age During the Civil War* (Carbondale: Southern Illinois University Press, 2008), and Nina Silber's *Gender and the Sectional Conflict* (Chapel Hill: University of North Carolina Press, 2008)—as well as editions of women's diaries and letters.

The overall disruption of Southern communities has been the focus of some of the best social histories of the Civil War, beginning with Stephen V. Ash, *Middle Tennessee Society Transformed, 1860–1870: War and Peace in the Upper South* (Baton Rouge: Louisiana State University Press, 1988), Wayne K. Durrill, *War of Another Kind: A Southern Community in the Great Rebellion* (New York: Oxford University Press, 1991) on Washington County, North Carolina, and Daniel Sutherland on Culpeper County, Virginia, in *Seasons of War: The Ordeal of a Confederate Community, 1861–1865* (New York: Free Press, 1995). More recently, Anne Bailey has given us *Invisible Southerners: Ethnicity in the Civil War* (Athens: University of Georgia Press, 2006), a study of ethnic diversity and conflict in a Southern state that was supposed to have neither, while A. Wilson Greene has focused on one city in Virginia in *Civil War Petersburg* (Charlottesville: University of Virginia Press, 2006). For the Appalachians, there is Brian D. McKnight's *Contested Borderland: The Civil War in Appalachian Kentucky and Virginia* (Lexington: University Press of Kentucky, 2006) and Jonathan Dean Sarris's *A Separate Civil War: Conflict and Community in the North Georgia Mountains* (Charlottesville: University of Virginia Press, 2006).

American culture in the Civil War era and afterward has been surveyed in Anne C. Rose, *Victorian America and the Civil War* (New York: Cambridge University Press, 1992) and Louise A. Stevenson, *The Victorian Homefront: American Thought and Cultures, 1860–1880* (Boston: Twayne, 1991), although Stevenson devotes most of her book to the post–Civil War decades. The intellectual life of mid-nineteenth-century America can be best understood through Bruce Kuklick's *Churchmen and Philosophers: From Jonathan Edwards to John Dewey* (New Haven, CT: Yale University Press, 1985). D. H. Meyer's *The Instructed Conscience: The Shaping of the American National Ethic* (Philadelphia: University of Pennsylvania Press, 1972) offers a vital anatomy of the central concern of nineteenth-century American philosophy. George M. Fredrickson's *The Inner Civil War: Northern Intellectuals and the Crisis of the Union* (New York: Harper and Row, 1965) is still the prevailing interpretation of Northern intellectuals in interpreting the Civil War, but because he focuses exclusively on the secular intellectuals and the Romantic religionists, the record that emerges from his book is quite a dismal one, with Northern intellectuals being long on fears for social control and remarkably short on intellectual substance. James Moorhead's *American Apocalypse: Yankee Protestants and the Civil War, 1860–1869* (New Haven, CT: Yale University Press, 1978) helps to correct the sense of imbalance induced by Fredrickson's book, but even so, Moorhead is more concerned with millenialism than with the larger picture of evangelical Protestants in the Civil War. Confederate intellectual life has, by contrast, enjoyed an overflow of outstanding studies, starting with Elizabeth Fox-Genovese and Eugene Genovese's *The Mind of the Master Class: History and Faith in the Southern Slaveholders' Worldview* (New York: Cambridge University Press, 2005), Michael O'Brien's two-volume opus, *Conjectures of Order: Intellectual Life and the American South, 1810–1860* (Chapel Hill: University of North Carolina Press, 2004), Michael Bernath's *Confederate Minds: The Struggle for Intellectual Independence in the Civil War South* (Chapel Hill: University of North Carolina Press, 2010), and three shorter books, by E. Brooks Holifield, *The Gentleman Theologians: American Theology in Southern Culture, 1795–1860* (Durham, NC: Duke University Press, 1978), Drew Gilpin Faust, *The Creation of Confederate Nationalism: Ideology and Identity in the Civil War South* (Baton Rouge: Louisiana State University Press, 1989), and Eugene Genovese, *A Consuming Fire: The Fall of the Confederacy in the Mind of the White Christian South* (Athens: University of Georgia Press, 1998). Two ambitious surveys of religion in the Civil War North and South are Harry S. Stout's *Upon the Altar of the Nation: A Moral History of the Civil War* (New York: Viking, 2006) and George C. Rable's *God's Almost Chosen Peoples: A Religious History of the American Civil War* (Chapel Hill: University of North Carolina Press, 2010). But the most incisive and rewarding analysis of religious thought during and about the war is Mark A. Noll's *The Civil War as a Theological Crisis* (Chapel Hill: University of North Carolina Press, 2006).

Louis A. Warren's *Lincoln's Gettysburg Declaration: "A New Birth of Freedom"* (Fort Wayne, IN: Lincoln National Life Foundation, 1964) offers a conventional but detailed history of the writing of the Address and its subsequent reputation.

TEN. STALEMATE AND TRIUMPH

The arrival of Ulysses S. Grant to assume practical control of the war in Virginia marked a critical turning point in the military history of the Civil War. The long and bloody Overland Campaign that Grant waged against Lee has found its ablest chronicler in Gordon Rhea's four volumes on the Overland Campaign: *The Battle of the Wilderness, May 5–6, 1864* (Baton Rouge: Louisiana State University Press, 1994), *The Battles for Spotsylvania Court House and the Road to Yellow Tavern, May 7–12, 1864* (Baton Rouge: Louisiana State University Press, 1997), *To the North Anna River: Grant and Lee, May 13–25, 1864* (Baton Rouge: Louisiana State University Press, 2000), and *Cold Harbor: Grant and Lee, May 26–June 3, 1864* (Baton Rouge: Louisiana State University Press, 2002). Hard on Rhea's heels, however, are Noah A. Trudeau with *Bloody Roads South: The Wilderness to Cold Harbor,*

May–June 1864 (Boston: Little, Brown, 1989) and Mark Grimsley with *And Keep Moving On: The Virginia Campaign, May–June 1864* (Lincoln: University of Nebraska Press, 2002), plus the individual battle studies by Robert Garth Scott, *Into the Wilderness with the Army of the Potomac* (Bloomington: Indiana University Press, 1985), William Matter, *If It Takes All Summer: The Battle of Spotsylvania* (Chapel Hill: University of North Carolina Press, 1988), and Ernest Furgurson, *Not War but Murder: Cold Harbor, 1864* (New York: Knopf, 2002). The siege that Grant was forced to begin at Petersburg has also picked up a number of new admirers, beginning with Noah Trudeau in *The Last Citadel: Petersburg, Virginia, June 1864–April 1865* (Boston: Little, Brown, 1991); several books concentrate on particular parts of the Petersburg siege, such as Michael Cavanaugh and William Marvel, *"The Horrid Pit": The Battle of the Crater* (Lynchburg, VA: H. E. Howard, 1989) and A. Wilson Greene's *The Final Battles of the Petersburg Campaign: Breaking the Backbone of the Rebellion* (Knoxville: University of Tennessee Press, 2008). A valuable adjunct to these books is William Frassanito's photographic history of the Overland Campaign, *Grant and Lee: The Virginia Campaigns, 1864–1865* (New York: Scribner, 1983), which complements his earlier two photographic "then-and-now" books on Gettysburg and Antietam.

Grant's operations in Virginia were only one part of his overall strategic plan for 1864, and he depended heavily on the successes won in Georgia by William Tecumseh Sherman. Lloyd Lewis' *Sherman: Fighting Prophet* (New York: Harcourt, Brace, 1932) is a rare masterpiece of literary craft and remains an outstanding Sherman biography, although it is marred in discussing Sherman's racial prejudices by Lewis' own disparaging comments on black soldiers. Charles Royster's *The Destructive War: William Tecumseh Sherman, Stonewall Jackson, and the Americans* (New York: Knopf, 1991) is a peculiar and (to quote one reviewer) "paradoxical" essay on Sherman and the military theme of destruction in war most often associated with Sherman. But it has forced biographers of Sherman to deal with the problem of endemic violence in American culture, and especially in Michael Fellman, *Citizen Sherman: A Life of William Tecumseh Sherman* (New York: Random House, 1997) and Stanley P. Hirshson, *The White Tecumseh: A Biography of General William T. Sherman* (New York: J. Wiley, 1997). Johnston's decision to settle into a siege around Atlanta was his undoing, and the siege itself has been marvelously spoken for in Albert Castel's *Decision in the West: The Atlanta Campaign of 1864* (Lawrence: University Press of Kansas, 1992), Richard M. McMurry, *Atlanta 1864: Last Chance for the Confederacy* (Lincoln: University of Nebraska Press, 2001), Marc Wortman's *The Bonfire: The Siege and Burning of Atlanta* (New York: PublicAffairs, 2009), Russell S. Bonds' *War Like the Thunderbolt: The Battle and Burning of Atlanta* (Yardley, PA: Westholme, 2009), and Gary Ecelbarger's *The Day Dixie Died: The Battle of Atlanta* (New York: St. Martin's Press, 2010). Franklin was a particular exercise in tactical folly, and has attracted the notice of Wiley Sword in *Embrace an Angry Wind: The Confederacy's Last Hurrah: Spring Hill, Franklin and Nashville* (New York: Harper Collins, 1992) and James McDonough and Thomas Connelly in *Five Tragic Hours: The Battle of Franklin* (Knoxville: University of Tennessee Press, 1983).

Lincoln's difficulties with the Radicals of his own party have been the subject of ongoing debate since Lincoln's death. On the one hand, Hans L. Trefousse's *The Radical Republicans: Lincoln's Vanguard for Racial Justice* (New York: Knopf, 1968) makes a passionate plea for interpreting the Radicals as Lincoln's secret agents for promoting policies Lincoln could not afford to openly endorse. On the other hand, T. Harry Williams's *Lincoln and the Radicals* (Madison: University of Wisconsin Press, 1941) just as passionately argues that Lincoln was a moderate who struggled in vain to keep the Radicals from turning the war into a political vendetta against the South. Individual biographies of the Radicals are not hard to come by, beginning with Hans L. Trefousse's *Thaddeus Stevens: Nineteenth-Century Egalitarian* (Chapel Hill: University of North Carolina Press, 1997), David Donald's *Charles Sumner and the Rights of Man* (New York: Knopf, 1970), and Richard Sewall's *John P. Hale and the Politics of Abolition* (Cambridge, MA: Harvard University Press, 1965). A clearer view of just who the Radicals were as a group emerges from Allan G. Bogue's *The Earnest Men: Republicans of the Civil War Senate* (Ithaca, NY: Cornell University Press, 1981), which used mathematical analyses of roll call votes to identify the core of Radical leadership in the Senate.

Some of the most controversial legislation written by the Congressional Radicals concerned conscription. James Geary's *We Need Men: The Union Draft in the Civil War* (DeKalb: Northern Illinois University Press, 1991) is a clear, precise, and highly illuminating analysis of conscription in the North, and carefully distinguishes the various drafts and draft calls, who was most likely to be conscripted, and how many draftees actually wound up in the Federal armies. The most notorious response to the draft in the North was the New York City draft riot. Iver C. Bernstein's *The New York City Draft Riots: Their Significance for American Society and Politics in the Age of the Civil War* (New York: Oxford University Press, 1990) skillfully sets the riots against the background of New York labor and racial unrest during the war, while Adrian Cook's *The Armies of the Streets: The New York City Draft Riots of 1863* (Lexington: University Press of Kentucky, 1974) and Barnet Schecter's *The Devil's Own Work: The Civil War Draft Riots and the Fight to Reconstruct America* (New York: Walker, 2005) provide the best overall narratives of the New York rioting. New York, however, can only lay claim to the most terrible outbreak of anti-draft violence: Grace Palladino's *Another Civil War: Labor, Capitol, and the State in the Anthracite Regions of Pennsylvania, 1840–1868* (Chicago: University of Illinois Press, 1990), Robert Sandow's *Deserter Country: Civil War Opposition in the Pennsylvania Appalachians* (New York: Fordham University Press, 2009), and Arnold M. Shankman's *The Pennsylvania Antiwar Movement, 1861–1865* (Madison, NJ: Fairleigh Dickinson University Press, 1980) trace the major outbreaks of anti-draft resistance in Pennsylvania.

ELEVEN. A DIM SHORE AHEAD

Specialized studies of the last six months of the war are rarer than for almost any other period of the Civil War. But certainly noteworthy among these for recounting the death agonies of the Army of Northern Virginia are William Marvel's *A Place Called Appomattox* (Chapel Hill: University of North Carolina Press, 2000) and *Lee's Last Retreat: The Flight to Appomattox* (Chapel Hill: University of North Carolina Press, 2002), along with Chris Calkins's *The Appomattox Campaign, March 29–April 9, 1865* (Lynchburg, VA: H. E. Howard, 1997), *The Battles of Appomattox Station and Appomattox Court House, April 8–9, 1865* (Lynchburg, VA: H. E. Howard, 1987), and *The Final Bivouac: The Surrender Parade at Appomattox and the Disbanding of the Armies* (Lynchburg, VA: H. E. Howard, 1988). The assassination of Lincoln is quite another story, although much of the assassination literature is sensationalized storytelling. The standard account is still George S. Bryan's *The Great American Myth: The True Story of Lincoln's Murder* (Chicago: Americana House, 1990 [1940]), but Bryan has been considerably expanded by William Hanchett in *The Lincoln Murder Conspiracies* (Urbana: University of Illinois Press, 1986) and Edward Steers in *Blood on the Moon: The Assassination of Abraham Lincoln* (Lexington: University of Kentucky Press, 2001). Looking at the assassination from the assassin's point of view requires Michael W. Kauffman's *American Brutus: John Wilkes Booth and the Lincoln Conspiracies* (New York: Random House, 2005).

Reconstruction also enjoys a substantial and surprisingly colorful bibliographical history. William A. Dunning, in *Reconstruction, Political and Economic, 1865–1877* (New York: Harper and Brothers, 1907), portrayed Reconstruction as a fanatical and utopian coup, launched by the Radical Republicans in violation of Lincoln's intentions and carried out by a hungry swarm of political vultures known as carpetbaggers and their incompetent black allies. Dunning never lacked for critics among black historians, especially W. E. B. Du Bois and John Hope Franklin. But it was the publication of Kenneth Stampp's *The Era of Reconstruction, 1865–1877* (New York: Knopf, 1965) that decisively turned the "Dunning School" on its head. Stampp, influenced by the civil rights movement of the 1950s, sharply revised the reputation of Radicals and the carpetbaggers and placed the entire Reconstruction effort on the same high moral ground occupied by Martin Luther King Jr. Thirty years later, Stampp's terse and comparatively short book is still in many ways the best introduction to Reconstruction. Stampp has enjoyed many followers, but none has towered so greatly above the rest as Eric Foner, whose *Reconstruction: America's Unfinished Revolution, 1863–1877* (New York: Harper and Row, 1988) expands Stampp's focus to include wartime Reconstruction and other political and economic national developments. Yet a third departure from both Dunning and Stampp lies in Heather Cox Richardson's treatment of Reconstruction as a conflict in political economy in *The Death of Reconstruction: Race, Labor, and Politics in the Post–Civil War North, 1865–1901* (Cambridge, MA: Harvard University Press, 2001) and in her expansion of the scope of Reconstruction policies, in *West from Appomattox: The Reconstruction of America After the Civil War* (New Haven, CT: Yale University Press, 2007), to the western territories, which were, after all, the flash point of the controversies which provoked the War.

Andrew Johnson has attracted little favorable press, but he has enjoyed a number of able biographies. Albert Castel's *The Presidency of Andrew Johnson* (Lawrence: University Press of Kansas, 1979) and Eric L. McKitrick's highly critical *Andrew Johnson and Reconstruction* (Chicago: University of Chicago Press, 1960) both offer useful surveys of Johnson's presidential policies, while Hans L. Trefousse's *Andrew Johnson: A Biography* (New York: W. W. Norton, 1989) sets him clearly in the ideological world of the Democratic Party. Michael Les Benedict in *The Impeachment and Trial of Andrew Johnson* (New York: W. W. Norton, 1973) and David O. Stewart in *Impeached: The Trial of President Andrew Johnson and the Fight for Lincoln's Legacy* (New York: Simon and Schuster, 2009) offer detailed accounts of the first presidential impeachment. The subsequent fate of Reconstruction in individual states has been treated in a growing list of local studies, including Joe Gray Taylor's *Louisiana Reconstructed, 1863–1877* (Baton Rouge: Louisiana State University Press, 1974), C. Peter Ripley's *Slaves and Freedmen in Civil War Louisiana* (Baton Rouge: Louisiana State University Press, 1976), Joseph G. Dawson's *Army Generals and Reconstruction: Louisiana, 1862–1877* (Baton Rouge: Louisiana State University Press, 1982), Stephen V. Ash's *Middle Tennessee Society Transformed, 1860–1870: War and Peace in the Upper South* (Knoxville: University of Tennessee Press, 1988) and *When the Yankees Came: Conflict and Chaos in the Occupied South, 1861–1865* (Chapel Hill: University of North Carolina Press, 1995), Richard Zuczek's *State of Rebellion: Reconstruction in South Carolina* (Columbia: University of South Carolina Press, 1996), Margaret M. Storey's *Loyalty and Loss: Alabama's Unionists in the Civil War and Reconstruction* (Baton Rouge: Louisiana State University Press, 2004), and Mark L. Bradley's *Bluecoats and Tar Heels: Soldiers and Civilians in Reconstruction North Carolina* (Lexington: University Press of Kentucky, 2009).

A number of the participants in Reconstruction have earned their own biographies. Richard N. Current offers an elegant and determinedly revisionist collective biography of the major Southern Republicans in *Those Terrible Carpetbaggers: A Reinterpretation* (New York: Oxford University Press, 1988); Sarah Woolfolk Wiggins in *The Scalawag in Alabama Politics, 1865–1881* (University: University of Alabama Press, 1977), and James A. Baggett in *The Scalawags: Southern Dissenters in the Civil War and Reconstruction* (Baton Rouge: Louisiana State University Press, 2003) do likewise for the scalawags. The Southern opposition to Reconstruction has also had its students and its books, especially Nicholas Lemann in *Redemption: The Last Battle of the Civil War* (New York: Farrar, Straus and Giroux, 2009) and Michael Perman in *Reunion Without Compromise: The South and Reconstruction, 1865–1868* (Cambridge: Cambridge University Press, 1973) and *The Road to Redemption: Southern Politics, 1869–1879* (Chapel Hill: University of North Carolina Press, 1984), where Perman (as opposed to C. Vann Woodward) stresses the continuities between the prewar planter class and the agrarian-based opposition to Reconstruction. Individual leaders of Southern resistance have earned biographical attention from Edward G. Longacre in *Gentleman and Soldier: A Biography of Wade Hampton III* (Nashville, TN: Rutledge Hill Press, 2009) and Ralph Lowell Eckert in *John Brown Gordon: Soldier, Southerner, American* (Baton Rouge: Louisiana State University

Press, 1989). Racial violence in Southern resistance to Reconstruction is handled in George C. Rable, *But There Was No Peace: The Role of Violence in the Politics of Reconstruction* (Athens: University of Georgia Press, 1984) and LeeAnna Keith, *The Colfax Massacre: The Untold Story of Black Power, White Terror, and the Death of Reconstruction* (New York: Oxford University Press, 2008).

The various roles carved out by the freedpeople in the Reconstruction South are examined in Leon Litwack, *Been in the Storm So Long: The Aftermath of Slavery* (New York: Knopf, 1979), Thomas Holt, *Black over White: Negro Political Leadership in South Carolina During Reconstruction* (Urbana: University of Illinois Press, 1977), and Joel Williamson, *After Slavery: The Negro in South Carolina During Reconstruction, 1861–1877* (Chapel Hill: University of North Carolina Press, 1965).

INDEX